Regional Comparisons in Comparative Policy Analysis Studies

Volume Three

Volume Three of the *Classics of Comparative Policy Analysis* contains chapters concerned with "Regional Comparisons in Comparative Policy Analysis Studies" – one of the most prevailing approaches in comparative public policy. Through the prism of inter-jurisdiction comparisons of similarities and variations, they address comparisons in specific policy sectors, governance or institutional constructs, and political regimes. The foci are, nevertheless, on those comparisons between countries or regions, which help to lesson-draw by identifying and understanding the variation in policy analysis and policy making that exists within or across regions. One benefit of regional comparisons is that it often allows studies to hold constant many variables, ranging from colonial legacy to federal systems or from language to specific traditions, and more effectively isolate dependent variables.

Regional organizations like the Organization for Economic Co-operation and Development (OECD) or European Union are also considered as catalysts for regional policy approaches and harmonization, and occupy a major role in this volume. The chapters address a broad and diverse number of countries and geographical areas: Latin America, North America, East Asia, Southeast Asia, Southern Africa, the Baltic states, the Nordic states, Western Europe, Central Europe, Eastern Europe, and Europe as a whole.

"Regional Comparisons in Comparative Policy Analysis Studies" will be of great interest to scholars and learners of public policy and social sciences, as well as to practitioners considering what can be learned or facilitated through methodologically and theoretically sound approaches.

The chapters were originally published as articles in the *Journal of Comparative Policy Analysis* which in the last two decades has pioneered the development of comparative public policy. The volume is part of a four-volume series, *the Classics of Comparative Policy Analysis* including Theories and Methods, Institutions and Governance, Regional Comparisons, and Policy Sectors.

Each volume showcases a different new chapter comparing domains of study interrelated with comparative public policy: political science, public administration, governance and policy design, authored by the JCPA co-editors Giliberto Capano, Iris Geva-May, Michael Howlett, Leslie A. Pal and B. Guy Peters.

Iris Geva-May has been recognized by Thomson Reuters for having pioneered the field of comparative policy analysis since 1998, when she founded the now high indexed *Journal of Comparative Policy Analysis*. She serves as its Founding Editor and the Founding President of the Scholarly Society for International Comparative Policy Analysis (ICPA-Forum). She has published among others *The Logic and Methodology of Policy Analysis, An Operational Approach to Policy Analysis (with Wildavsky), International Library of Policy Analysis*

Series, Routledge Handbook of Comparative Policy Analysis, and *Policy Analysis as a Clinical Profession*. She is Professor Emerita at Simon Fraser University, Vancouver, Canada and currently an Honorary Visiting Professor at SPPA, Carleton University, Ottawa, Canada, and the Wagner School NYU, USA.

B. Guy Peters is Maurice Falk Professor of Government at the University of Pittsburgh, USA, and an Honorary Editor of the *Journal of Comparative Policy Analysis*. He is also the Founding President of the *International Public Policy Association* and Editor of the *International Review of Public Policy*. Among his seminal publications are as follows: *Comparative Politics Theory and Methods, Institutional Theory in Political Science, The Politics of Bureaucracy: A Comparative Perspective, An Advanced Introduction to Public Policy*, and *The Next Public Administration*.

Joselyn Muhleisen serves as the Awards Coordinator for the International Comparative Policy Analysis Forum and the *Journal of Comparative Policy Analysis*. She is a Doctoral Lecturer at the Marxe School of Public and International Affairs, Baruch College, City University of New York (CUNY), USA. She earned her doctorate in political science from The Graduate Center, CUNY, USA. She is the former Assistant Director of the European Union Studies Center, CUNY, USA. She has published work about the development of comparative policy analysis and its relationship to international studies.

Regional Comparisons in Comparative Policy Analysis Studies
Volume Three

Edited by
Iris Geva-May, B. Guy Peters and
Joselyn Muhleisen

With
Foreword by Laurence E. Lynn, JCPA Founding Co-Editor
Introduction to the Series, Iris Geva-May, JCPA Founding Editor, B. Guy Peters Co-Editor, Joselyn Muhleisen Co-Editor

And
Part 2, New Contribution: Comparative Public Administration and Comparative Public Policy, Leslie A. Pal, JCPA Co-editor

Sponsored by

First published 2020
by Routledge
2 Park Square, Milton Park, Abingdon, Oxon, OX14 4RN

and by Routledge
52 Vanderbilt Avenue, New York, NY 10017

Routledge is an imprint of the Taylor & Francis Group, an informa business

First issued in paperback 2021

© 2020 The Editor, Journal of Comparative Policy Analysis: Research and Practice

All rights reserved. No part of this book may be reprinted or reproduced or utilised in any form or by any electronic, mechanical, or other means, now known or hereafter invented, including photocopying and recording, or in any information storage or retrieval system, without permission in writing from the publishers.

Trademark notice: Product or corporate names may be trademarks or registered trademarks, and are used only for identification and explanation without intent to infringe.

British Library Cataloguing-in-Publication Data
A catalogue record for this book is available from the British Library

ISBN13: 978-1-138-33268-3 (hbk)
ISBN13: 978-1-03-208187-8 (pbk)

Typeset in Times
by codeMantra

Publisher's Note
The publisher accepts responsibility for any inconsistencies that may have arisen during the conversion of this book from journal articles to book chapters, namely the inclusion of journal terminology.

Disclaimer
Every effort has been made to contact copyright holders for their permission to reprint material in this book. The publishers would be grateful to hear from any copyright holder who is not here acknowledged and will undertake to rectify any errors or omissions in future editions of this book.

Contents

Citation Information viii
Notes on Contributors xii
Foreword to the Book Series: *The Classics of Comparative Policy Analysis* xvi
Laurence E. Lynn, Jr.

PART 1
An Introduction to the Classics of Comparative Policy Analysis Book Series 1

Why the Classics of Comparative Policy Analysis Studies? 3
Iris Geva-May, B. Guy Peters and Joselyn Muhleisen

PART 2
Lesson Drawing Relationships: Comparing Associated Disciplines and Comparative Policy Analysis 11

Comparative Public Administration and Comparative Public Policy 13
Leslie A. Pal

PART 3
The Classics: Regional Comparisons in Comparative Policy Analysis Studies 29

1 When do Governments Consolidate? A Quantitative Comparative Analysis of 23 OECD Countries (1980–2005) 31
Uwe Wagschal & Georg Wenzelburger

2 Europeanization, Policy Learning, and New Modes of Governance 58
Claudio M. Radaelli

3 Bottom–Up Policy Convergence: A Sociology of the Reception of Policy Transfer in Public Health Policies in Europe 74
Carole Clavier

4	Can Corruption Be Measured? Comparing Global Versus Local Perceptions of Corruption in East and Southeast Asia *Min-Wei Lin & Chilik Yu*	90
5	Independent Professional Bureaucracies and Street-Level Bribery: Comparing Changes in Civil Service Law and Implementation in Latin America *Laura Langbein & Pablo Sanabria*	108
6	A Comparative Study of Abortion Policymaking in Brazil and South America: The Salience of Issue Networks and Policy Windows *Andrzej Kulczycki*	125
7	Father-Friendly Legislation and Paternal Time across Western Europe *Alison J. Smith and Donald R. Williams*	142
8	Reconciliation of Work and Family Life in Europe: A Case Study of Denmark, France, Germany and the United Kingdom *Peter Abrahamson*	160
9	Fiscal Policy Learning from Crisis: Comparative Analysis of the Baltic Countries *Ringa Raudla, Aleksandrs Cepilovs, Vytautas Kuokštis, & Rainer Kattel*	177
10	Failing Family Policy in Post-Communist Central Europe *Steven Saxonberg and Tomáš Sirovátka*	193
11	Comparative Analysis of Governmental Accounting Diversity in the European Union *Rosa Maria Dasí, Vicente Montesinos, & Santiago Murgui*	211
12	A Comparative Study of Asset-based Policy in Asia: Korea, Singapore, and Taiwan *Chang-Keun Han*	230
13	The Challenges of Implementing Merit-Based Personnel Policies in Latin America: Mexico's Civil Service Reform Experience *Mauricio I. Dussauge Laguna*	244
14	Public Personnel Policies and Problems in the New Democracies of Central and Eastern Europe *Tiina Randma-Liiv and Jane Järvalt*	267
15	The Missing Dimension: A Comparative Analysis of Healthcare Governance in Central and Eastern Europe *Monika Ewa Kaminska*	282
16	Made to Measure? Europeanization, Goodness of Fit and Adaptation Pressures in EU Competition Policy and Regional Aid *Carlos Mendez, Fiona Wishlade and Douglas Yuill*	301

CONTENTS

17 Overfishing in Southern Africa: A Comparative Account of Regime Effectiveness and National Capacities 321
Martin Sjöstedt & Aksel Sundström

18 A Legal Perspective on "Privateness" and "Publicness" in Latin American Higher Education 338
Andrés Bernasconi

19 Watching the Watchers: Transgovernmental Implementation of Data Privacy Policy in Europe 353
Abraham L. Newman

20 Managing Urban Growth in Asia 367
Clay G. Wescott and L. R. Jones

21 Governance for Sustainability in East Asian Global Cities: An Exploratory Study 380
Mee Kam Ng

22 Building Collaborative Emergency Management Systems in Northeast Asia: A Comparative Analysis of the Roles of International Agencies 411
Namkyung Oh, Aya Okada & Louise K. Comfort

23 Crucial Factors in Implementing Radical Policy Change: A Comparative Longitudinal Study of Nordic Central Agency Relocation Programs 429
Harald Sætren

24 Housing Conditions, States, Markets and Households: A Pan-European Analysis 450
Michelle Norris and Henryk Domański

25 Regional Policy Agglomeration: Arctic Policy in Canada and the United States 473
Peter J. May, Bryan D. Jones, Betsi E. Beem, Emily A. Neff-Sharum and Melissa K. Poague

Index 489

Citation Information

The chapters in this book were originally published in the *Journal of Comparative Policy Analysis*. When citing this material, please use the original page numbering for each article, as follows:

Chapter 1
When do Governments Consolidate? A Quantitative Comparative Analysis of 23 OECD Countries (1980–2005)
Uwe Wagschal, Georg Wenzelburger
Journal of Comparative Policy Analysis, volume 14, issue 1 (February 2012) pp. 45–71

Chapter 2
Europeanization, Policy Learning, and New Modes of Governance
Claudio M. Radaelli
Journal of Comparative Policy Analysis, volume 10, issue 3 (September 2008) pp. 239–254

Chapter 3
Bottom–Up Policy Convergence: A Sociology of the Reception of Policy Transfer in Public Health Policies in Europe
Carole Clavier
Journal of Comparative Policy Analysis, volume 12, issue 5 (November 2010) pp. 451–466

Chapter 4
Can Corruption Be Measured? Comparing Global Versus Local Perceptions of Corruption in East and Southeast Asia
Min-Wei Lin, Chilik Yu
Journal of Comparative Policy Analysis, volume 16, issue 2 (2014) pp. 140–157

Chapter 5
Independent Professional Bureaucracies and Street-Level Bribery: Comparing Changes in Civil Service Law and Implementation in Latin America
Laura Langbein, Pablo Sanabria
Journal of Comparative Policy Analysis, volume 19, issue 5 (2017) pp. 435–451

Chapter 6
A Comparative Study of Abortion Policymaking in Brazil and South America: The Salience of Issue Networks and Policy Windows
Andrzej Kulczycki
Journal of Comparative Policy Analysis, volume 16, issue 1 (2014) pp. 62–78

Chapter 7
Father-friendly legislation and paternal time across Western Europe
Alison J. Smith, Donald R. Williams
Journal of Comparative Policy Analysis, volume 9, issue 2 (June 2007) pp. 175–192

Chapter 8
Reconciliation of work and family life in Europe: A case study of Denmark, France, Germany and the United Kingdom
Peter Abrahamson
Journal of Comparative Policy Analysis, volume 9, issue 2 (June 2007) pp. 193–209

Chapter 9
Fiscal Policy Learning from Crisis: Comparative Analysis of the Baltic Countries
Ringa Raudla, Aleksandrs Cepilovs, Vytautas Kuokštis, Rainer Kattel
Journal of Comparative Policy Analysis, volume 20, issue 3 (2018) pp. 288–303

Chapter 10
Failing family policy in post-communist Central Europe
Steven Saxonberg, Tomáš Sirovátka
Journal of Comparative Policy Analysis, volume 8, issue 2 (June 2006) pp. 185–202

Chapter 11
Comparative Analysis of Governmental Accounting Diversity in the European Union
Rosa Ma Dasí, Vicente Montesinos, Santiago Murgui
Journal of Comparative Policy Analysis, volume 15, issue 3 (2013) pp. 255–273

Chapter 12
A Comparative Study of Asset-based Policy in Asia: Korea, Singapore, and Taiwan
Chang-Keun Han
Journal of Comparative Policy Analysis, volume 15, issue 1 (2013) pp. 54–67

Chapter 13
The Challenges of Implementing Merit-Based Personnel Policies in Latin America: Mexico's Civil Service Reform Experience
Mauricio I. Dussauge Laguna
Journal of Comparative Policy Analysis, volume 13, issue 1 (February 2011) pp. 51–73

Chapter 14
Public Personnel Policies and Problems in the New Democracies of Central and Eastern Europe
Tiina Randma-Liiv, Jane Järvalt
Journal of Comparative Policy Analysis, volume 13, issue 1 (February 2011) pp. 35–49

Chapter 15
The Missing Dimension: A Comparative Analysis of Healthcare Governance in Central and Eastern Europe
Monika Ewa Kaminska
Journal of Comparative Policy Analysis, volume 15, issue 1 (2013) pp. 68–86

Chapter 16
Made to Measure? Europeanization, Goodness of Fit and Adaptation Pressures in EU Competition Policy and Regional Aid
Carlos Mendez, Fiona Wishlade, Douglas Yuill
Journal of Comparative Policy Analysis, volume 10, issue 3 (September 2008) pp. 279–298

Chapter 17
Overfishing in Southern Africa: A Comparative Account of Regime Effectiveness and National Capacities
Martin Sjöstedt, Aksel Sundström
Journal of Comparative Policy Analysis, volume 15, issue 5 (2013) pp. 415–431

Chapter 18
A Legal Perspective on "Privateness" and "Publicness" in Latin American Higher Education
Andrés Bernasconi
Journal of Comparative Policy Analysis, volume 13, issue 4 (August 2011) pp. 351–365

Chapter 19
Watching the Watchers: Transgovernmental Implementation of Data Privacy Policy in Europe
Abraham L. Newman
Journal of Comparative Policy Analysis, volume 13, issue 2 (April 2011) pp. 181–194

Chapter 20
Managing urban growth in Asia
Clay G. Wescott, L. R. Jones
Journal of Comparative Policy Analysis, volume 9, issue 4 (December 2007) pp. 337–349

Chapter 21
Governance for sustainability in East Asian Global Cities: An exploratory study
Mee Kam Ng
Journal of Comparative Policy Analysis, volume 9, issue 4 (December 2007) pp. 351–381

Chapter 22
Building Collaborative Emergency Management Systems in Northeast Asia: A Comparative Analysis of the Roles of International Agencies
Namkyung Oh, Aya Okada, Louise K. Comfort
Journal of Comparative Policy Analysis, volume 16, issue 1 (2014) pp. 94–111

Chapter 23
Crucial Factors in Implementing Radical Policy Change: A Comparative Longitudinal Study of Nordic Central Agency Relocation Programs
Harald Sætren
Journal of Comparative Policy Analysis, volume 17, issue 2 (2015) pp. 103–123

Chapter 24
Housing Conditions, States, Markets and Households: A Pan-European Analysis
Michelle Norris, Henryk Domański
Journal of Comparative Policy Analysis, volume 11, issue 3 (September 2009) pp. 385–407

Chapter 25
Regional Policy Agglomeration: Arctic Policy in Canada and the United States
Peter J. May, Bryan D. Jones. Betsi E. Beem, Emily A. Neff-Sharum and Melissa K. Poague
Journal of Comparative Policy Analysis, volume 7, issue 2 (2005) pp. 121–136

For any permission-related enquiries please visit:
http://www.tandfonline.com/page/help/permissions

Contributors

Peter Abrahamson is an Associate Professor of Sociology at the University of Copenhagen, Denmark.

Betsi E. Beem is a Senior Lecturer in the Department of Government and International Relations at the University of Sydney, Australia.

Andrés Bernasconi is a Professor in the School of Education at the Pontifical Catholic University of Chile, Santiago, Chile.

Aleksandrs Cepilovs is a Project Manager in the School of Business and Governance in the Ragnar Nurkse Department of Innovation and Governance at the Tallinn University of Technology, Estonia.

Carole Clavier is a Professor in the Department of Political Science at the University of Montreal, Canada.

Louise K. Comfort is a Professor of Public and International Affairs and the Director of the Center for Disaster Management at the University of Pittsburgh, USA.

Rosa Maria Dasí is the Director of the Department of Accounting and a Professor of Accounting and Finance at the University of Valencia, Spain.

Henryk Domański is a Professor and Director of the Institute of Philosophy and Sociology at the Polish Academy of Sciences, Warsaw, Poland.

Mauricio I. Dussauge Laguna is a Professor-Researcher in the Public Administration Department at the Center for Research and Teaching in Economics (CIDE), Mexico City, Mexico.

Chang-Keun Han is an Associate Professor in the Department of Social Welfare at Sungkyunkwan University, Seoul, South Korea.

Iris Geva-May has been recognized by Thomson Reuters for having pioneered the field of comparative policy analysis since 1998, when she founded the now high indexed *Journal of Comparative Policy Analysis*. She serves as its Founding Editor and the Founding President of the Scholarly Society for International Comparative Policy Analysis (ICPA-Forum). She has published among others *The Logic and Methodology of Policy Analysis, An Operational Approach to Policy Analysis (with Wildavsky), International Library of Policy Analysis Series, Routledge Handbook of Comparative Policy Analysis*, and *Policy Analysis as a Clinical Profession*. She is Professor Emerita at Simon Fraser University, Vancouver, Canada and currently an Honorary Visiting Professor at SPPA, Carleton University, Ottawa, Canada, and the Wagner School NYU, USA.

Jane Järvalt is HR Expert/HR Business Partner at European Central Bank.

Bryan D. Jones is a Professor, J. J. "Jake" Pickle Regents Chair in Congressional Studies in the Department of Government at the University of Texas at Austin, USA.

L. R. Jones is George F. A. Wagner Professor of Public Management in the Graduate School of Business and Public Policy at Naval Postgraduate School, Monterey, USA.

Monika Ewa Kaminska is a Postdoctoral Researcher in the Department of Political Economy of the Welfare State and SOCIUM Research Center on Inequality and Social Policy at the University of Bremen, Germany.

Rainer Kattel is a Professor of innovation and public governance at Institute for Innovation and Public Purpose at UCL, UK, and a Research Professor at Ragnar Nurkse Department of Innovation and Governance at the Tallinn University of Technology, Estonia.

Leslie A. Pal is Founding Dean, College of Public Policy, Hamad Bin Khalifa University, Doha, Qatar

Alison J. Smith is a Professor of Social Policy and Research Methods and the Head of Social Policy at the University of Edinburgh, UK.

Andrzej Kulczycki is an Associate Professor in the Department of Health Care Organization and Policy at the University of Alabama at Birmingham, USA.

Vytautas Kuokštis is an Associate Professor at the Institute of International Relations and Political Science at Vilnius University, Estonia.

Laura Langbein is a Professor of policy analysis in the Department of Public Administration and Policy at American University, Washington, D.C., USA.

Min-Wei Lin is a PhD Student in the Department of Public Administration at National Chengchi University, Taipei, Taiwan.

Laurence E. Lynn, Jr. is the Founding Co-editor of the *Journal of Comparative Policy Analysis*. He is the Sydney Stein, Jr. Professor of Public Management Emeritus at the University of Chicago, USA. He chaired the Masters in Public Policy Program at Harvard's Kennedy School of Government. He has been a Fellow of the National Academy of Public Administration and of the Council on Foreign Relations, as well as APPAM President. He has been honored by Lifetime Academic Achievement Awards by the American Political Science Association, American Society for Public Administration, and the Public Management Research Association. He published, among others, *Public Management as Art, Science, and Profession* from the Academy of Management, *Oxford Handbook of Public Management*, and (with Hill) *Public Management: Thinking and Acting in Three Dimensions*.

Peter J. May is the Donald R. Matthews Distinguished Professor Emeritus of American Politics at the University of Washington, Seattle, USA.

Carlos Mendez is a Research Fellow in the European Policies Research Centre at the University of Strathclyde, Glasgow, UK.

Joselyn Muhleisen serves as the Awards Coordinator for the International Comparative Policy Analysis Forum and the *Journal of Comparative Policy Analysis*. She is a Doctoral Lecturer at the Marxe School of Public and International Affairs, Baruch College, City

University of New York (CUNY), USA. She earned her doctorate in political science from The Graduate Center, CUNY, USA. She is the former Assistant Director of the European Union Studies Center, CUNY, USA. She has published work about the development of comparative policy analysis and its relationship to international studies.

Melissa K. Poague is a Professor of Political Science at the University of Louisville, USA, and a Member of the Graduate Faculty in the Master of Public Administration Program.

Vicente Montesinos is a Full Professor at the Department of Applied Mathematics and the Vice-Director of the Institute of Pure and Applied Mathematics of the Universidad Politécnica de Valencia, Spain.

Santiago Murgui is a Professor in the Department of Applied Economics at the University of Valencia, Spain.

Emily A. Neff-Sharum is a Department Chair and Associate Professor in the Department of Political Science & Public Administration at the University of North Carolina at Pembroke, USA.

Abraham L. Newman is a Professor in the Edmund A. Walsh School of Foreign Service and Government Department at Georgetown University, Washington, D.C., USA.

Mee Kam Ng is a Professor in the Department of Geography and Resource Management and a Department Vice-Chairman at the University of Hong Kong.

Michelle Norris is a Professor and the Head of the School of Social Policy, Social Work and Social Justice at University College Dublin, Ireland.

Namkyung Oh is an Assistant Professor of the Department of Public Administration and Urban Studies at the University of Akron, USA.

Aya Okada is an Associate Professor at the Institute of Liberal Arts and Sciences at Kanazawa University, Japan.

B. Guy Peters is Maurice Falk Professor of Government at the University of Pittsburgh, USA, and an Honorary Editor of the *Journal of Comparative Policy Analysis*. He is also the Founding President of the *International Public Policy Association* and Editor of the *International Review of Public Policy*. Among his seminal publications are as follows: *Comparative Politics Theory and Methods, Institutional Theory in Political Science, The Politics of Bureaucracy: A Comparative Perspective, An Advanced Introduction to Public Policy*, and *The Next Public Administration*.

Claudio M. Radaelli is a Professor of Public Policy at UCL, UK.

Tiina Randma-Liiv is a Professor of Public Management and Policy at Tallinn University of Technology, Estonia, where she also serves as the Vice-Dean for Research of the School of Business and Governance.

Ringa Raudla is a Professor of Public Finance and Governance at Tallinn University of Technology, Estonia.

Harald Sætren is a Professor in the Department of Administration and Organization Theory at the University of Bergen, Norway.

Pablo Sanabria is an Associate Professor and Chair of the Department of Organizational Management at Pontificia Universidad Javeriana, Cali, Colombia.

Steven Saxonberg is a Professor at the Department of European Studies and International Relations at the Comenius University, Bratislava, Slovakia. He is also a Guest Professor at the Center for Social and Economic Strategies at the Charles University in Prague and the Department of Social Policy and Social Work at Masaryk University in Brno (both in the Czech Republic).

Tomáš Sirovátka is the Department Head at the Institute for Public Policy and Social Work, and a Professor of Social Policy and Social Work at the Masaryk University in Brno, Czech Republic.

Martin Sjöstedt is an Associate Professor at the Department of Political Science and Quality of Government Institute at the University of Gothenburg, Sweden.

Aksel Sundström is an Associate Professor at the Department of Political Science and Quality of Government Institute at the University of Gothenburg, Sweden.

Uwe Wagschal is a Professor for Political Science and Comparative Politics at the University of Freiburg, Breisgau, Germany.

Georg Wenzelburger is a Professor at the University of Freiburg, Breisgau, Germany, and the Chair of Comparative Politics.

Clay G. Wescott is the Director of the Asia-Pacific Governance Institute, Japan.

Donald R. Williams is an Associate Dean for Administration in the College of Business Administration at Kent State University, USA. He is also a Senior Research Associate at the Luxembourg Institute of Socio-Economic Research.

Fiona Wishlade is a Professor in and a Director of the European Policies Research Centre at the University of Strathclyde, Glasgow, UK.

Chilik Yu is a Professor of Public Policy and Management, and Vice-President (Academic Affairs) of Shih Hsin University, Taipei, Taiwan.

Douglas Yuill is Emeritus Professor in the European Policies Research Centre at the University of Strathclyde, Glasgow, UK.

Foreword to the Book Series: The Classics of Comparative Policy Analysis

LAURENCE E. LYNN, JR.
Founding co-Editor, *Journal of Comparative Policy Analysis*
Sydney Stein, Jr. Professor of Pubic Management Emeritus
The University of Chicago, USA

The Classics of Comparative Policy Analysis Series is both a record of and a milestone in the development of the theories and methods not only of comparative public policy analysis but, as well, of comparative studies in public affairs-related disciplines and professions, which the *Journal of Comparative Policy Analysis (JCPA)* has advanced. Having been present at the founding of the field of public policy analysis in the 1960s and of comparative policy analysis studies through the *JCPA* in 1998, and having been contributed to a field of research, public governance, which is heavily influenced by comparative perspectives, I am pleased that this series calls attention to the extent to which public affairs research has been influenced by the intellectual ambitions of the kinds of scholarship represented in the four volumes of this series.

Publication of this series of research papers that appeared in volume 20:1 of the *JCPA*, 2018, marks and celebrates the twentieth anniversary of the journal. Selections of classic papers provide not only models for scholars, they are of immense value to teachers in creating reading lists and study assignments. As well, they reinforce awareness of the dimensions and content of a vital field of public affairs research.

Especially welcome are new chapters in each volume authored by the *JCPA* co-editors, highlighting the emerging symbiotic relationships between established disciplines and professions and comparative policy studies. These developments advance the fulfillment of an early intention of the policy analysis movement: promoting the integration of the social sciences in public affairs research. Also important in this regard is the attention in the *Classics of Comparative Policy Analysis* to recent development in research fields, such as policy design and governance, harkening back to the emergence in the original policy analysis movement of implementation studies and program evaluation, with their comparative bent. These newer research studies now appear not only in *JCPA* but in a patulous number of public affairs-oriented academic journals and conference agendas.

It is noteworthy that the *Classics of Comparative Policy Analysis Series* appears in unsettled and unsettling times in national and international affairs. The intellectual developments celebrated in this series have been taking place in a relatively stable and liberal global order. Beginning in the aftermath of World War II, various forms of international cooperation gradually took shape, including regional and the United Nations-sponsored governance and shared sovereignty institutions. This order is now challenged by the seemingly ascendant emergence of nationalism and authoritarianism in many of the world's largest and oldest nations and democracies. These developments threaten the rule of law and the rule of reason, both of which have largely come to be taken for granted in the teaching and research of public affairs-oriented disciplines and professions. Activism and tribalism are competing with analysis and democratic deliberation in the shaping of public policy, and it appears at the expense of fairness and social justice and institutional stability.

But the current political context could also provide opportunities for comparative policy studies. Its scholars have perspectives, models, and methods, as well as the disposition, to study the dynamics of instability, changing institutional and organizational environments and their consequences for policymaking and public administration. For example, researchers on federalism, already informed by comparative studies at subnational levels of governance and international institutions, have the tools to address new questions posed by evolving patterns of governance.

As depicted by Geva-May, Peters, and Muhleisen in their introduction to the series and evident throughout the four volumes, the comparative perspective is producing the kinds of intellectual capital that may be of unique value in policy formulation and design. Lesson drawing is increasingly appropriate in an era of worldwide reinventing of governance. Through the publication of this series, and through papers accepted for publication in future volumes of the *JCPA*, the journal will continue to be a pilot light for imaginative and pathbreaking research that sustains the momentum of the development of comparative policy studies.

Part 1
An Introduction to the Classics of Comparative Policy Analysis Book Series

Why the Classics of Comparative Policy Analysis Studies?

IRIS GEVA-MAY, B. GUY PETERS AND JOSELYN MUHLEISEN

The Classics of Comparative Policy Analysis is a collection of the most representative articles in the *Journal of Comparative Policy Analysis (JCPA)* on its twentieth anniversary. The *JCPA* has "pioneered the domain of comparative policy analysis" studies since 1998[1] and is still the only journal explicitly devoted to promoting comparative policy studies. The articles published in the *JCPA* have become classics in the field of comparative policy analytic studies, and have established it as a distinctive field of study since (Thomson Reuters 2008; Radin 2013; Geva-May, Hoffman and Muhleisen 2018). The papers published over the last two decades in *JCPA* are explicitly comparative and could be viewed as cornerstones of comparative public policy analysis theory, methodology, policy inter-disciplinarity, and inter-regional scholarship. Contributors include founders of the field of policy analysis, comparative politics, and comparative public administration and management from which comparative policy analysis (CPA) has derived: Peter deLeon, Duncan McRae, Laurence E. Lynn, B. Guy Peters, Beryl Radin, David Weimer, Frans Van Nispen, Yukio Adachi, as well as second- and third-generation policy analysis scholars who have set high scholarship bars in advancing the field.

The term "comparative" has normatively been associated with descriptive accounts of national similarities or dissimilarities with respect to content or to features of the public policy process requiring information sharing. At the research level, it has traditionally been concerned with cross-national generalizations or explanations of differences among policies. As the founding editors of the *JCPA* declare in the first volume, "JCPA seeks to go beyond these confines and offer an intellectual arena for analyzing comparative explanatory frameworks and research methods, testing models across spatial structures ... and comparing different instruments for achieving similar ends".[2]

The collections of articles included in the volumes of this series support the aim and scope of the *JCPA* to establish points of reference for aspects of comparative policy analytic studies. The four volumes compile, respectively, those foundation articles which contribute to the four main aspects of CPA scholarship advanced by the *JCPA*: (a) Apply or develop comparative methodologies and theories; (b) Investigate valid and reliable means of performing inter-regional or inter-social units comparisons; (c) Investigate the connection among public policy, institutions, and governance factors that can explicate similarities or differences in policymaking; (d) Finally, they focus on the application or utilization of comparative public policy analysis in a variety of policy sectors such as immigration, technology, healthcare, welfare, education, economics, and many others.

Although the chapters included in each volume are classified according to a specific overarching topic, we do find overlaps between, for instance, regional comparisons and methodology or theories, or linkages to institutions as independent variables and policy sectors as dependent variables – thus transcending the single focus of the research presented in each of the volumes.

There is one more aspect that has been explicitly covered neither in the *JCPA* (except for its anniversary Vol 20:1) nor as a separate volume in the present series: the linkages among comparative public policy and the more established fields of comparative politics (political science) and public administration, as well as the newly emerging (or diverging) domains such as governance – from public administration and policy design – from public policy. To open a window to further comparisons among inter-related public domains we introduce a new chapter in Part II of each volume. Authored by the *JCPA* co-editors, the four chapters embrace the notion that the established political science and comparative politics, as well as public administration and comparative public administration, have much to offer to policy studies and to the developing field of CPA studies. It is also noteworthy that the comparative policy analytic studies domain is seen as a source of lesson drawing for the increasing interest in policy design and in governance. The cross-fertilization between these domains can range anywhere between theoretical, conceptual, methodological, and empirical. Identifying points of similarity or difference in enhancing lesson drawing, adaptation, transfer and borrowing, or missed opportunity thereof.

These fundamentals common to all domains of study are addressed by Guy Peters and Geva-May who note down the prospective gift of (comparative) political science to CPA and reciprocal missed opportunities in Volume One; Capano contributes a new chapter on governance, regimes, and comparative public policy in Volume Two; Leslie Pal writes about comparative public administration and comparative public policy in Volume Three; while Howlett addresses the newly emerging branch of policy design and what can be derived from comparative public policy in Volume Four.

In today's politics and policymaking, the reality of global policy convergence, economic competition, and political fads, the cross-national sources of information have proliferated to the extent that any policy analyst, public policy scholar, or policy decision-maker in any given country is bound to be aware of developments that happen in a different "social unit" as Ragin and Zaret (1983) label units of social analysis. Comparisons between social units may be nations or institutions, or points of reference such as policy goals, actor interference, market failures, or intervention in public policy issues of concern. The main reason is lesson drawing in order to maximize utility of policy solutions, avoid failure, or utilize information to seek advantage. Comparative cross-national policy analysis can extend insights, perspectives, or explanations that otherwise would be difficult or impossible to obtain. Lesson drawing (Rose 1991; Geva-May 2004), transfer, borrowing, adoption or adaptations, or sheer inspiration (DeLeon 1998; Geva-May 2002a) increases effectiveness and efficiency, and avoids fallacies. Notwithstanding this stipulation, there is a word of warning: CPA done badly has an immediate effect on the public, and can be financially wasteful or dangerous to the social units and populum immediately involved. Furthermore, it can be detrimental to the credibility of policymaking, as well as to policy analysis as a practical and scholarly domain.

One more contention is that in the *Classics of Comparative Policy Analysis Studies* the terms policy analysis, policy studies, and policy analytic studies are often used by authors interchangeably for a number of reasons: Foremost, because these domains are often similar in their possible points of linkage to the comparative aspects that they cover. Additionally, in today's third generation of policy analysis studies, the borderlines between policy studies, policy design, and policy analysis have frequently blurred and the terminology used has often been transposable. The terms used contain a wider perception of public policy within which domains and sub-domains complement one another despite their very distinct roles. Except for those actually studying or working in these sub-fields, the scholarly work refers to them frequently interchangeably.

We selected the articles in the series not only by thematic relevance and excellence, but also based on how they serve the aim and scope of the *JCPA* (Geva-May and Lynn 1998) which set clear intellectual avenues towards the development of the field beyond the mere prevalent perception of "comparative" as the comparison of two objects – whether institutions or regions. Proven valid enough to have served as scholarly cornerstones in the development of comparative policy studies for two decades, each respective *JCPA* aim drives the focus of each respective volume in the series. **Volume One** presents selections focused on **comparative theory and methodology** development, and comparative **theory testing**: two central aims of the *JCPA*. **Volume Two** addresses **institutions and questions about modes and types of governance** which speaks about the aim of examining the inter-relations between institutions and policy analysis either as dependent or independent variables. **Volume Three** builds on comparative empirical research, as well as lesson drawing and extrapolation, and evaluates comparative research methods through articles on regional policy differences or similarities. **Volume Four** touches on almost all the aims of *JCPA* through studies of specific policy sectors – healthcare, immigration, education, economics, welfare, technology, etc., – particularly allowing for lesson drawing, extrapolation, and possible avoidance of failures within sectors.

Volume One: Theory and Methodology

CPA depends upon the various theoretical and methodological approaches to public policy. The same theoretical perspectives such as the advocacy-coalition framework, multiple-streams models, and agenda-setting are important for understanding national and international policymaking and public policy comparatively. These are applied through lesson drawing and policy transfer, for instance, among others, by Pal (2014), and Wolf and Baehler (2018).

Of particular interest are the linkages of policy theories with various academic disciplines, including economics, political science, sociology, and law, all of which bring their own theoretical perspectives to bear on public policy. Each of the articles included in the first volume demonstrates the need to make difficult theoretical and methodological choices in the study of CPA.

Perhaps the most important aspect of these articles is that the researcher had to make a conscious choice about theory and method, and had to justify those choices. The articles also indicate how they frame policy problems and how they overcome methodological challenges in CPA (Ira Sherkansky 1998; Hoppe 2002; Green-Pedersen 2004; Peters 2005; Saurugger 2005; Stiller and van Kersbergen 2008; Capano 2009; Howlett and

Cashore 2009; Greer et al. 2015; among others). In doing so, many address another aim of the *JCPA*: the evaluation of comparative research methods. One way to both evaluate the aptness of research methods and to test theory is to conduct empirical studies. For example, Green-Pedersen contends with the dependent variable problem in the context of social welfare research (Green-Pedersen 2004).

Volume Two: Comparative Policy Analysis and Institutions

"Evidence-based policymaking" is more difficult than sometimes assumed, depending, as it does, on understanding both the dynamics of public policy and the institutional contexts. Despite this difficulty, there has been a surge of interest in policy designed on the basis of "scientifically" demonstrated effectiveness and the ability to identify those successful policies within various structures.

Drawing on the larger institutionalism and governance literatures, many selections in the second volume are concerned with distinct forms of governance and types of political institutions. Governance and institutions are treated both as independent and dependent variables (Weimer and Vining 1998; Ng 2007; Radaelli 2008). The latter make an important distinction between first-order and second-order instruments. The first are those known to policy analysts, the second less transparent depend on features of institutions that "facilitate or constrain" the adoption of first-order policies. The authors contend that in order to make meaningful comparisons, it is important to analyze the usefulness of policy analysis against the analysis of the institutional features that condition policy choice. While public policy scholars and politicians have given increasing attention to new, innovative governance apparatuses, empirical work basically intends to document whether these instruments are effective in specific jurisdictions and institutional contexts and what can be extrapolated from one milieu to another.

One of the chief institutional explanations of policy variation is the nature of political and bureaucratic institutions within which the policies are developed or implemented. CPA has also considered the influence of particular governance arrangements, for example, public-private partnerships on policy outcomes (Vining and Boardamn 2018). But governance structures and institutions are also reflective of the societies, cultures, and polities that constitute them (Hoppe 2002; Geva-May 2002b). Other studies focus on the determinants of certain governance mechanisms, such as privatization (Breen and Doyle 2013), and the impact of the participation of certain societal groups in the policymaking process (Heidbreder 2015). Thus, public policy, institutions, and society are in complex and reciprocal relationships that require a great deal of care to properly disentangle and analyze.

Major themes that underscore several contributions in the volume on institutions and governance will be unsurprising to policy scholars; many selections are especially concerned with effectiveness, efficiency, and mechanisms of compliance (Lee and Whitford 2009; Ross and Yan 2015).

Volume Three: Comparative Inter-regional Policy Analysis Studies

The selections included in this volume make policy comparisons within and across regions. In fact, CPA studies are mostly regarded as comparisons across political systems, whether they are countries, provinces, cities, or another jurisdiction. Likewise, much of the policy analytic research focuses on how policies have fared in specific jurisdictions (Laguna 2011; Saetren 2015) and which factors that contribute to a policy's success can potentially be applied in other contexts.

This mode of analysis brings CPA closer to comparative politics and sociology, and focuses on many of the variables used in the other social sciences to explain observed similarities or differences in the policy choices made by different political systems. The policy choices of federalist systems, for example, are compared by Radin and Boase (2000); Boushey and Luedtke (2006); Sheingate (2009); and Capano (2015). The latter, for instance, compare the Canadian and US federal systems in order to identify similarities and differences between them that explicate the divergence in their social and economic policies. The argument is based on two typologies – Lowi's typology refers to different types of policies, and Deil Wright's typology refers to different models of intergovernmental systems. Here, we also glance at how other theories and related typologies can be applied to CPA across units of comparative analysis.

Focusing on regional comparisons can offer a solid methodological basis for comparative studies by eliminating sources of variation and allowing scholars to isolate more clearly the influence of independent variable(s). To the extent that countries in a region share culture, language, history, or institutional design, inter-regional studies can also target alternate explanations for policy differences. Alternatively, where there is a high degree of policy similarity in very different countries, the existence of a regional power or institution may explain policy convergence. Several studies included in this volume take this approach when considering the phenomenon of Europeanization, for instance, which considers both regional and institutional policy determinants (Mendez et al. 2008; Raedelli 2008; Sarugger 2005). Many contributions compare the policies or policymaking process in a domain across jurisdictions (Ng 2007; Smith and Williams 2007). Other scholars rather focus on tendencies towards regional agglomeration (May et al. 2005) or policy convergence (Clavier 2010).

The *JCPA* has contributed substantially to the body of inter-regional comparative public policy literature and has devoted a number of Special Issues to the topic. This is reflected in the diversity of regions addressed by this volume's selections: Latin America, North America, East Asia, Southeast Asia, Southern Africa, the Baltic states, the Nordic states, Western Europe, Central Europe, Eastern Europe, and Europe as a whole. Dedicated to CPA, the wide range of cases published in the *JCPA*, and the attempt to understand policy and policymaking in many contexts, has served as a major object of interest among authors, readers, and researchers of comparative inter-regional studies.

Volume Four: Comparing Policy Sectors

Our volume on comparative policy sectors focuses on the major areas of strength in the *JCPA*: markets, money and economy, healthcare, welfare, education, migration, and biotechnology policy. These articles explicitly compare policies within policy sectors. The reader can readily identify the marked differences between more technical domains such as technology (Allison and Varone 2009), and more politicized domains such as immigration (Scholten and Timmermans 2010; Geddes and Scholten 2015), healthcare (Marmor et al. 2010), and higher education (Levy and Zumeta 2011).

Many of the articles in this volume deal with comparisons of differences and similarities in various policy disciplines and sectors within and among political systems. For example, Gornick and Heron (2006) compare working time policies across eight European countries, the US, and Japan. Sheingate (2009), on the other hand, compares biotechnology policy decision-making in the European Union and the US, which are treated in his analysis as different styles of federalist regimes.

The absence of papers that explicitly compare *across* policy sectors is noteworthy in the *JCPA*. This is why the *JCPA* anniversary Special Issue Vol. 20:1 and Part One of each volume in this series have been devoted to the comparison of policy, politics, and administration studies. Yet, we still do not find comparative papers between healthcare and immigration, or policy analysis and psychology, or medicine, or law (Geva-May 2005).

To some extent, this phenomenon represents the difficulties of scholars to master the details of any other policy domain, much less several that might be appropriate for comparison. This does not come as a surprise. To cite Gary Freeman (1985), indeed, the differences across domains within a single country would, on average, be greater than differences between the same domain across countries. That was a rather bold claim, but there are some reasons to expect policy domains to be significantly different, and therefore more difficult to compare. For example, some policy domains – such as defense or taxation – tend to be dominated by the government itself, while others – education, social policy – tend to have significant direct influence by citizens. Still other policy domains such as health and technology will be dominated by expert professionals who can reduce some of the role of government in policy. We could add to this list of variables, but the fundamental point remains that the nature of the policy does influence the ways in which policy is made and implemented. That said, differences across political systems do continue to show up in these domains, and it remains crucial for the student and the researcher of CPA to be sensitive to several sources of variation in process and outcomes.

In sum, the four volumes in the *Classics of Policy Analysis Studies* seek to present scholars the most salient work that the *JCPA* has covered in the last two decades and illustrate the multiple levels of study on which we can pursue the intellectual dialogue on comparative public policy. First, the series offers a centralized resource of work that furthers the aims of the new discipline of CPA and the inter-related fields of political science, sociology, and economics. Second, it contributes to the database of knowledge by investigating, applying, or developing theories and methodologies that ensure the validity and reliability of the comparative policy studies. Third, it extends case studies that enrich the ongoing discussions about what can be learned through comparative policy analytic studies to increase efficiency, effectiveness, transparency, and equity in public policy.

We wish the readers of the *Classics of Comparative Policy Analysis Studies* an interesting journey, from which they can adopt, adapt, borrow, transfer, extrapolate, or be inspired for their comparative studies.

Notes

1. Thomson Reuters. (2008). *Whos Who*.
2. Geva-May, I., & Lynn, E. L, Jr. (1998). Comparative policy analysis: Introduction to a new journal. *JCPA*, *1*(1), 1.

References

Allison, C. R., & Varone, F. (2009). Direct legislation in North America and Europe: Promoting or restricting biotechnology? *Journal of Comparative Policy Analysis*, *11*(4), 425–449.

Boushey, G., & Luedtke, A. (2006). Fiscal federalism and the politics of immigration: Centralized and decentralized immigration policies in Canada and the United States. *Journal of Comparative Policy Analysis*, *8*(3), 207–224.

Breen, M., & Doyle, D. (2013). The determinants of privatization: A comparative analysis of developing countries. *Journal of Comparative Policy Analysis: Research and Practice*, *15*(1), 1–20.

Boardman, A. E., Greenberg, D.H., Vining, A.R. & Weimer, D.L. *Cost-Benefit Analysis: Concepts & Practices*, 2018, Cambridge University Press: Cambridge, UK.

Capano, G. (2009). Understanding policy change as an epistemological and theoretical problem. *Journal of Comparative Policy Analysis*, *11*(1), 7–31.

Capano, G., Howlett, M., & Ramesh, M. (2015). Bringing governments back in: Governance and governing in comparative policy analysis. *Journal of Comparative Policy Analysis: Research and Practice, 17*(4), 311–321.

Clavier, C. (2010). Bottom–up policy convergence: A sociology of the reception of policy transfer in public health policies in Europe. *Journal of Comparative Policy Analysis*, *12*(5), 451–466.

DeLeon, P., & Resnick-Terry, P. (1998). Comparative policy analysis: Déjà vu all over again?, *Journal of Comparative Policy Analysis: Research and Practice*, 1:1, 9–22.

Dunn, W. N. (2008, 2015). *Public Policy Analysis: An Introduction* (4 ed.). Upper Saddle River, NJ: Pearson Prentice Hall.

Freeman, G. P. (1985). National styles and policy sectors: Explaining structured variation. *Journal of Public Policy*, *5*(4), 467–496.

Geddes, A., & Scholten, P. (2015). Policy analysis and Europeanization: An analysis of EU migrant integration policymaking. *Journal of Comparative Policy Analysis: Research and Practice*, *17*(1), 41–59.

Geva-May, I. (Ed.) (2005). *Thinking Like a Policy Analyst: Policy Analysis as a Clinical Profession*. New York: Palgrave Macmillan.

Geva-May, I. (2002a). Comparative studies in public administration and public policy. *Public Management Review*, *4*(3), 275–290.

Geva-May, I. (2002b). From theory to practice: Policy analysis, cultural bias and organizational arrangements. *Public Management Review*, *4*(4), 581–591.

Geva-May, I. with Wildavsky, A. (1997, 2001, 2011). *An Operational Approach to Policy Analysis: The Craft: Prescriptions for Better Analysis*. Kluwer Academic Publishers.

Geva-May, I., & Lynn, L. E. Jr. (1998). Comparative Policy Analysis: Introduction to a New Journal. *Journal of Comparative Policy Analysis*, *1*(1).

Geva-May, I., Hoffman, D. C., & Muhleisen, J. (2018). Twenty years of comparative policy analysis: A survey of the field and a discussion of topics and methods. *Journal of Comparative Policy Analysis: Research and Practice*, *20*(1), 18–35.

Green-Pedersen, C. (2004). The dependent variable problem within the study of welfare state retrenchment: Defining the problem and looking for solutions. *Journal of Comparative Policy Analysis: Research and Practice*, *6*(1), 3–14.

Greer, S., Elliott, H., & Oliver, R. (2015). Differences that matter: Overcoming methodological nationalism in comparative social policy research. *Journal of Comparative Policy Analysis: Research and Practice*, *17*(4), 408–429.

Heidbreder, E. G. (2015). Governance in the European Union: A policy analysis of the attempts to raise legitimacy through civil society participation. *Journal of Comparative Policy Analysis: Research and Practice*, *17*(4), 359–377.

Hoppe, R. (2002). Cultures of public policy problems. *Journal of Comparative Policy Analysis: Research and Practice*, *4*(3), 305–326.

Howlett, M., & Cashore, B. (2009). The dependent variable problem in the study of policy change: Understanding policy change as a methodological problem. *Journal of Comparative Policy Analysis*, *11*(1), 33–46.

Laguna, M. I. (2011). The challenges of implementing merit-based personnel policies in Latin America: Mexico's civil service reform experience. *Journal of Comparative Policy Analysis*, *13*(1), 51–73.

Lee, S. Y., & Whitford, A. B. (2009). Government effectiveness in comparative perspective. *Journal of Comparative Policy Analysis, 11*(2), 249–281.

Leslie A. Pal (2014). Introduction: The OECD and policy transfer: Comparative case studies. *Journal of Comparative Policy Analysis: Research and Practice, 16*(3), 195–200.

Levy, D. C., & Zumeta, W. (2011). Private higher education and public policy: A global view. *Journal of Comparative Policy Analysis: Research and Practice, 13*(4), 345–349.

Marmor, T. R. (2010). Introduction: Varieties of comparative analysis in the world of medical care policy. *Journal of Comparative Policy Analysis, 12*(1–2), 5–10.

May, Peter, Jones B. D., Beem, B. E., Neff-Sharum, E. A. & Poague, M. K. (2005). Regional Policy Agglomeration: Arctic Policy in Canada and the United States, *Journal of Comparative Policy Analysis: Research and Practice*, 7(2), 121–136.

Mendez, C., Wishlade, F., & Yuill, D. (2008). Made to measure? Europeanization, goodness of fit and adaptation pressures in EU competition policy and regional aid. *Journal of Comparative Policy Analysis, 10*(3), 279–298.

Ng, M. K. (2007). Sustainable development and governance in East Asian world cities. *Journal of Comparative Policy Analysis, 9*(4), 321–335.

Peters, G. B. (2005). The problem of policy problems. *Journal of Comparative Policy Analysis, 7*(4), 349–370.

Radaelli, C. M. (2008). Europeanization, policy learning, and new modes of governance. *Journal of Comparative Policy Analysis, 10*(3), 239–254.

Radin, B. A. (2013). *Beyond Machiavelli: Policy Analysis Reaches Midlife*. Georgetown University Press.

Radin, B., & Boase, A. (2000). Federalism, political structure, and public policy in the United States and Canada, *Journal of Comparative Policy Analysis: Research and Practice, 2*(1), 65–89.

Ragin, C. C. (1994). Introduction to qualitative comparative analysis. *The Comparative Political Economy of the Welfare State, 299*, 300–309.

Ragin, C. and Zaret, D. (1983) Theory and Method in Comparative Research: Two Strategies. *Social Forces, 61* (3), 731–754.

Rose, R. (1991). What is lesson-drawing? *Journal of Public Policy, 11*(1), 3–30.

Ross, T. W., & Yan, J. (2015). Comparing public–private partnerships and traditional public procurement: Efficiency vs. flexibility. *Journal of Comparative Policy Analysis: Research and Practice, 17*(5), 448–466.

Rothmayr Allison, C., & Varone, F. (2009). Direct legislation in North America and Europe: Promoting or restricting biotechnology?. *Journal of Comparative Policy Analysis, 11*(4), 425–449.

Saurugger, S. (2005). Europeanization as a methodological challenge: The case of interest groups. *Journal of Comparative Policy Analysis, 7*(4), 291–312.

Scholten, P., & Timmermans, A. (2010). Setting the immigrant policy agenda: Expertise and politics in the Netherlands, France and the United Kingdom. *Journal of Comparative Policy Analysis, 12*(5), 527–544.

Sheingate, A. D. (2009). Federalism and the regulation of agricultural biotechnology in the United States and European Union. *Journal of Comparative Policy Analysis, 11*(4), 477–497.

Smith, A. J., & Williams, D. R. (2007). Father-friendly legislation and paternal time across Western Europe. *Journal of Comparative Policy Analysis, 9*(2), 175–192.

Stiller, S., & van Kersbergen, K. (2008). The matching problem within comparative welfare state research: How to bridge abstract theory and specific hypotheses. *Journal of Comparative Policy Analysis: Research and Practice, 10*(2), 133–149.

Thomson Reuters (2008). Iris Geva-May, *Who's Who*.

Vining, A. R., & Weimer, D. L. (1998). Informing institutional design: Strategies for comparative cumulation. *Journal of Comparative Policy Analysis, 1*(1), 39–60.

Wolf, A., & Baehler, K. J. (2018). Learning transferable lessons from single cases in comparative policy analysis. *Journal of Comparative Policy Analysis: Research and Practice, 20*(4), 420–434.

Part 2

Lesson Drawing Relationships: Comparing Associated Disciplines and Comparative Policy Analysis

Comparative Public Administration and Comparative Public Policy

LESLIE A. PAL

Introduction

Public policy and public administration are overlapping but distinct disciplines. They overlap most obviously when they focus on the state, though each of them today encompasses more extensive research foci. Public administration is preoccupied with the organizational apparatus of the state, its agencies, and management practices extending from budgets to human resources. Public policy analysis also takes account of the state, but from the perspective of decision-making and agenda-setting, and implementation once policy has been decided. Since governments make policy, it is quite logical that students of public policy would also be interested in government structures and the decision-making processes that go into policy formulation and implementation. It is no accident, for example, that Lindblom's 1959 article on incrementalism was published in *Public Administration Review* (1959), but is an anchor for theories of the policy process (Kingdon, 2011; Béland, 2016; Michael Howlett, McConnell, & Perl, 2016; Zahariadis, 2016). Nor is it an accident that one of the founders of the study of public policy was also a leading student of budgeting (A. Wildavsky, 1975, 2018; A. B. Wildavsky, 1979). This logic of disciplinary contiguity explains the numerous schools and programs that combine "administration" (or management) and "policy" in their titles and in their personnel. While few of us approach the ambidexterity of a Guy Peters (Peters, Rhodes, & Wright, 1999; Peters & Pierre, 2001, 2012; Peters & Zittoun, 2016; Peters, 2018), most students of one field have at least a nodding acquaintance of the other.

While the two disciplines have this *logical* overlap, they have wide and significant differences that have kept them fairly siloed. Public administration is more practitioner focused; public policy strives for theoretical generalizations. Public administration can become obsessed with the minutiae of management, from merit systems in human resources to budgeting and finances; public policy can be seduced by the macro-contours of state-society relations. Public administration became preoccupied with new public management (NPM), and now agonizes over whether there is a coherent "post-NPM" (Reiter & Klenk, 2018); public policy continues to prefer the substance in education and health and welfare policy over administrative machinery. These antinomies get even more complicated when we consider the relationship of *comparative* public administration (CPA) and *comparative* public policy (CPP). Public administration as a discipline can be traced back to Weber (Weber, 1958) if not to Woodrow Wilson (Wilson, 1887), while public policy as a distinct field within the social sciences only goes back to the 1950s (deLeon, 2006; Radin, 2013).

Both CPA and CPP emerged from these respective master disciplines, and so have mirrored the same distinctions and differences, but added their own twists. CPA emerged earlier in the immediate post-WWII period and in the context of administration for development (Van Wart & Cayer, 1990; Waldo, 2006). Heady's first mapping of the field was published in 1966, and it was only by the fifth edition (1996) that he acknowledged the existence of a new field of CPP that had emerged in the mid-1970s (Heady, 1996: 48–50). CPP can be conveniently dated from the publication of the Heidenheimer, Heclo, and Adams book of the same title (Heidenheimer, Heclo, & Adams, 1975). While CPP surged ahead (Geva-May, Hoffman, & Muhleisen, 2018) and staked out claims both in methodological and in theoretical approaches such as the advocacy coalition framework (Sabatier & Jenkins-Smith, 1993; Sabatier & Weible, 2007; Weible & Jenkins-Smith, 2016), CPA seemed to have trouble finding its footing. Peters noted in the mid-1909s that it had failed to fulfill "the expectations many scholars had for it during the 1960s and 1970s" (Peters, 1994: 67). CPA seemed mired in a-theoretical single country case studies (see, for example, Subramaniam, 2000; Chandler, 2014), lacked a rigorous methodology, and sometimes even lacked true comparisons (Fitzpatrick et al., 2011; Pollitt, 2011; Gulrajani & Moloney, 2012; Raadschelders, Vigoda-Gadot, & Kisner, 2015).

The *rapprochement* between the two sub-fields began in the 1990s (though the first green shoots appeared in the 1980s – see (Henderson, 1981)) and has proceeded apace. Heady, as mentioned, noted the rise of CPP in his 1996 edition and the positive implications for CPA. Pierre's 1995 collection on bureaucracy and the modern state referred to "policy makers" within a framework that embraced both administrative machinery and policy-making (Pierre, 1995). The logical interconnections became actualized as scholars began to more frequently combine considerations of public administration with public policy (Rabin, 2003; Rabin, Hildreth, & Miller, 2007; O'Flynn, Blackman, & Halligan, 2014). The master discipline of public administration has become (in its more scholarly expressions) more theory driven (see journals such as *Journal of Public Administration Theory and Research* and the relatively new International Research Society for Public Management) and methodologically robust. The master discipline of public policy has "brought the state back in" in several ways, and thus has a refreshed interest in administration, management, organizational behavior, and internal state structures and how they affect policy development and implementation. CPA has advanced considerably in both data gathering and theoretical frameworks (Brans, 2012). Today, the logical contiguity of CPA and CPP has been matched by active cross-fertilization, most broadly stated as a shared interest in state capacity (Van de Walle & Brans, 2018). This is a wide and broad bridge between the two disciplines, and we can break it down into five more specific and more recent intersecting research agendas that are mutually reinforcing, but also fruitfully challenging: (1) transnational administration, (2) public sector reform as a policy field, (3) the state and international development policy, (4) policy transfer, and (5) policy advisory systems.

Intersecting Research Agendas

Transnational Administration

Comparative analysis of either administration or public policy automatically takes one up from the level of the domestic state. Originally, both the master disciplines were focused on the national administration (usually the US or European states – where most of the scholarship was conducted) and national level policies. One important branch of CPP has been global public policy – by the 1990s, scholars who studied national policies began to realize the impact of globalization and the degree to which those national policies were both shaped by global forces (economic and social), and, more importantly, by global institutions and actors (Coleman, 2012; Kaul, 2013; Mamudu, Cairney, & Studlar, 2015; Stone & Ladi, 2015). Among the most important institutions are international organizations (IOs) like the International Monetary Fund (IMF), the World Bank, and the Organisation for Economic Co-operation and Development (OECD). Realist international relations theory would argue that these organizations are mere ciphers for their members, and particularly the most powerful among them. More constructivist approaches have argued for a degree of organizational autonomy, particularly in the formation of norms and standards (Barnett & Finnemore, 1999, 2004). There has thus been a double movement among both international relations scholars and public policy scholars to start taking IOs seriously, and most obviously to take the full measure of the impact of their administrative structures and personnel (Stone & Moloney, 2019). Labors in this particular vineyard has yielded research on the impact of IOs like the OECD (Mahon & McBride, 2008; Pal, 2012; Mahon, 2015), comparative analysis of different IOs and their structures and activities (De Francesco, 2013, 2016), and their role in generating ideas that drive policy at both the global and the national levels (Broome & Seabrooke, 2012, 2015; Seabrooke & Wigan, 2016; Kentikelenis & Seabrooke, 2017). The key point is that CPP has taken the analysis of policy processes and their respective actors to the global level, and once having scaled that height, look around and see that IOs are among the most important of those actors. To understand them as actors, they need to be understood as organizations, and so researchers naturally reach for work that understands organizations from an administrative perspective.

Coupled with this has been an analogous splicing of disciplines on the public administration side, grafting international relations theory to classic CPA to yield a new sub-field of "international bureaucracy" (Bauer, Knill, & Eckhard, 2017). These bureaucracies are different from typical ones at the national level, for obvious reasons pertaining to their membership and scope of activity. Beneath the canopy of organizations like the UN and Bretton Woods institutions, an eco-system of smaller regulatory bureaucracies has grown to make public policy effective in a host of policy fields from food and agriculture to transportation. There is huge scope and potential for comparative work that encompasses both the administrative organizations themselves and their policy impacts.

Public Sector Reform as a Policy Field

Governments constantly tinker with their administrative systems, and this tinkering is the proper subject of public administration and public management, particularly if viewed from a practitioner's perspective. Before 1945, of course, there were major points of administrative reform and innovation in the stages towards the development of the modern state apparatus (A. S. Roberts, 1996; Fukuyama, 2014), but it was not until the 1980s that public sector reform emerged as a policy field in its own right – as something that all self-respecting democratic governments should embrace as part of an effort to "modernize" (Kettl, 2005). In the immediate post-WWII era, of course, this modernization effort was focused on developing countries, and indeed became the driver for CPA as it girded itself to help western powers renovate the administrative structures of aid recipients.

We address this below, but for the moment will focus on the developed countries. The big wave of course was NPM, which became an obsession in public administration as a discipline at the national level, and gave a boost to CPA since the wave spread across the world and provided ample opportunities to test whether it worked, where and how, and what the variations were (Bovaird & Loeffler, 2016; Pollitt & Bouckaert, 2017). But a crucial point was that suddenly, public sector reform and modernization was considered as a separate policy field, with IOs like the OECD chiming in on its importance in navigating an increasingly complex and threatening world (OECD, 1995, 2005).

In considering public sector reform as a policy field, CPP had a new subject matter to which it could apply its analytical tools and theoretical frameworks. How is the public sector reform agenda set? Who sets it? Who are its supporters and opponents? What policy instruments are used? Are there any paradigms and paradigm shifts (NPM of course being the mother of all public administration paradigms). The coincidence of CPP and CPA perspectives deepened after the 2008 financial crisis, with cutbacks and austerity also becoming matters of policy debate, and folding into the earlier efforts of public sector reform. Policy journals eagerly published articles on the logic and nature of these austerity policies, which almost always had a strong public administration component in terms of budgets and fiscal policy, human resources (layoffs), and broader policy effects on pensions and social expenditures (Peters, Pierre, & Randma-Liiv, 2011; Randma-Liiv & Kickert, 2017; Raudla, Douglas, Savi, & Randma-Liiv, 2017).

The State and International Development Policy

We noted above that early CPA was stimulated by the post-WWII interest in non-US administrative systems, and some impetus to assist them through reform. Reports from that period suggest that this was more of an anthropological effort (learn about the distant tribes), and restricted to some US state agencies and foundations (especially the Ford Foundation). The dominant IOs – principally the World Bank – concentrated on market reforms and economic development projects, and generally considered institutions and the administrative state as impediments that should at best interfere as little as possible in these reforms and projects: in short, the infamous Washington Consensus (Williamson, 1990; Woods, 2006). The consensus did not last long after the collapse of the Soviet Union, coupled with a growing admission that administrative capacity, corruption, and the state more generally were crucial variables in economic development. As with NPM in the developed countries, the new paradigm that emerged in international development policy focused on the state and the state administrative apparatus (Wolfensohn, 1996; World Bank, 1997). This was coupled with democracy promotion in the former Soviet states (Carothers, 1996; Nunberg, 1999). In recent years, the World Bank is an institution transformed – its annual World Development reports have had titles like *Governance and the Law* (World Bank, 2017).

For students of global public policy and of key IOs like the World Bank, it becomes unavoidable to take state administration seriously. Administrative issues and the finer points of administrative reform have become central to international development policies (Andrews, 2008, 2012, 2013; Pritchett, Woolcock, & Andrews, 2012; Grindle, 2013) and consequently to a large part of the agenda of organizations like the World Bank and the OECD (World Bank, 2012; Alawattage & Elshihry, 2017). A good deal of the work here has been on how the IOs conceive of governance and administration, and of the challenges of tackling administrative reform in highly corrupt countries, but this has leached back into the study of the administrative capacities of developed states as they too wrestle with corruption (Mungiu-Pippidi, 2015; Mungiu-Pippidi & Johnston, 2017). As Van de Walle and Brans (2018) point out, this trains attention on state capacity building, and so has drawn students of public policy into some unanticipated fields of inquiry, such as training and education in public administration (Pal & Clark, 2016a, 2016b).

Policy Transfer

Interest in policy transfer has surged recently with roots in Richard Rose's work on lesson drawing (Rose, 1991, 1993), which was then developed into a more elaborate framework by Dolowitz and Marsh (1996) and developed further since (Hadjiisky, Pal, & Walker, 2017; Porto de Oliveira & Pal, 2018). This work is interested in how policies move and migrate, mutate and shape-shift across jurisdictions, sometimes leading to convergences and sometimes to resistance. Among the many interesting questions in this field, central ones are about the actors and the processes that facilitate transfer, and hence about organizations and state agencies, and consequently issues of CPA. We have already mentioned IOs above, and they have been identified as one of the most important conduits of policy transfer. And there is a strong connection with international development as well, principally through the World Bank. By the end of the 1990s, the Bank had "developed an enthusiasm for the improvement of 'institutional capability' in poorer nations" (A. Roberts, 2010: 15). This enthusiasm then required some reflection on what constitutes capability, good institutions, and institutional design in public organizations (Fukuyama, 2004, 2013; Holt & Manning, 2014), as well as ways to measure the various elements of governance systems (Arndt & Oman, 2008; Davis, Fisher, Kingsbury, & Merry, 2012).

As mentioned above in connection with emerging work on transnational administration, by the 1990s students of public policy were going global, realizing that domestic policy was often shaped by international forces and actors. IOs were a logical place to look, and the World Bank (and sister IOs) was a natural focus because of its prominence, influence, and impact on policy transfer. But domestic government agencies themselves, through their global networks, also were revealed as important channels of both policy ideas and international regulation in different policy fields (Biermann & Siebenhüner, 2009; Slaughter, 2004a, 2004b, 2004c). A particularly important sub-field of policy transfer studies in this area, though it constitutes a major discipline in its own right, is Europeanization. The EU constitutes an interesting example of an IO that is, at the same time, a member state-based organization and a quasi-federation. The *process* of Europeanization has been defined as the "(a) construction (b) diffusion and (c) institutionalization of formal and informal rules, procedures, policy paradigms ... first defined and consolidated in the making of EU decisions and then incorporated in the logic of domestic ... public policies" (Radaelli, 2003: 30). This is preeminently a bureaucratic process, and so every student of Europeanization is perforce a student of CPA. How do the labyrinths of the EU bureaucracy generate standards and rules, and how do these cascade through the system into regional, domestic, and even local public policies?

The importance of CPA in the study of policy transfer can be seen through a quick review of the chapters of a recent survey of the field (Hadjiisky et al., 2017). Seven of ten chapters, while they were ostensibly focused on the micro-dynamics of policy transfer, grappled at the same time with state actors, institutions, and aspects of public administration. A study on judicial reform in Bulgaria addressed the institutional trace elements of communism and how they affected the receptivity of the Bulgarian state apparatus. Another chapter examined judicial reform in the French system and the attempt to inject "lean management" practices. A piece tracing the transfer of road transport (trucking) regulation naturally focused on regulators and their comparative structures and behavior. An examination of national tobacco advertising regulations in Switzerland traced the interaction of national authorities with cantonal ones. Two chapters dealing with the internationalization of Brazilian policy models, respectively, analyzed the interaction between Brazilian state agencies and IOs, and the strategic impact of state agents as "policy ambassadors". Two further chapters looked at the competition between the EU and the US in policy transfer activities in Bosnia and Herzegovina and Ukraine, and between the EU and Russia in the cases of Armenia, Georgia, and Ukraine. Each of them had to take careful measure of the organizational differences among state agencies, both at the international level and among the counties being studied.

The study of policy transfer is not exclusively the study of IOs or of domestic public administrations, but as seen from these examples, no serious student of policy transfer can ignore institutions, and many of those institutions are state agencies. A thorough understanding of policy transfer will consequently often require a sound grasp of administrative procedures and organizational behaviour.

Policy Advisory Systems

CPP can focus on outputs and outcomes, or on inputs and policy development. The inputs or development focus can be posed broadly in terms of societal and political agenda-setting, or more narrowly in terms of policy design and decision-making. The design and decision-making focus positions research on "the inside" of state agencies, within bureaucracies, or at least those parts of the administrative apparatus that are devoted to supporting policy development – "policy advisory systems". Work on these systems has grown recently (Hudstedt & Veit, 2017), and the research can generally be divided into two streams. One focuses on the institutional matrix of advice in Westminster systems, particularly the role of cabinet offices and ministries (Halligan, 1995, 2010; Dahlström, Peters, & Pierre, 2011; Craft, 2016; Craft & Daku, 2017; Craft & Halligan, 2017). The other concentrates on analytic capacity and the nature of policy work. Painter and Pierre defined policy capacity as "the ability to marshal the necessary resources to make intelligent collective choices about and set strategic directions for the allocation of scarce resources to public ends" (Painter & Pierre, 2005: 2), highlighting the organizational requirements. Craft and Howlett (2012, 2013) took this further in exploring the "externalization" of policy advice to entities such as think tanks, and this has been supplemented by analysis of expert bodies (Crowley & Head, 2017). Wu, Ramesh, and Howlett (2015) developed a useful ninefold framework for understanding policy capacity, extending the authoritative work of Howlett (2013, 2015, 2014, 2011, 2012). Even the OECD has developed a model to bridge institutional design with analytical policy capacity (OECD, 2017).

Policy work (what individual policy analysts do) is embedded within the wider context of producing, offering, and considering policy advice, and at the aggregate level, every political jurisdiction will have its own configuration of organizations and channels whereby policy knowledge and advice is produced and conveyed (Peters & Barker, 1993). In highly centralized or authoritarian systems, it might be the leader and immediate, trusted colleagues (or even family members!); in highly democratic regimes, it might consist of a free-for-all of outside producers (think tanks, institutes, research, and advocacy groups), as well as internal policy units. As well, every system will have its own history, culture, and constitutional formalities that will structure its advisory system. Policy advice in Denmark is not produced and channeled in the same way as in advice in France or Mexico or Canada. The *International Library of Policy Analysis* (series editors: Iris Geva-May and Michael Howlett) is a multi-country series that shows the unique configurations among different systems.

Once again, it is clear that serious work on the subject of how policy advice is generated and channeled within government will require a serious understanding of CPA. In an interesting case of reality mimicking research, governments themselves have been working to improve their policy capacity, and thereby to improve their policy advisory systems and the competencies of policy professionals. The systems approach is reflected in the OECD's preoccupation with institutional design, and particularly the architecture of central administrative agencies (executive cabinet offices, finance, and national planning). Leading examples of improving competency have come from the governments of New Zealand and the United Kingdom (the chaos of Brexit notwithstanding). New Zealand's version is called the "Policy Project". It was launched through the Policy Advice Initiative in 1991–95, followed by Improving the Quality of Policy Advice in 1997–99. These were followed by an exercise in 2010 entitled the Review of Policy Expenditure and Advice, which inspired a Treasury-led policy measurement initiative that required agencies to report on the costs and efficiency of policy advice (Davison, 2015). Criticized for focusing too much on cost rather than content, it led to the Policy Project in 2013, launched with the creation of the Chief Executive of the DPMC as the "Head of the Profession".

The United Kingdom has had a long-standing project to improve the quality of policy advice, extending back to 1999 (HM Government (UK), 1999). The *Civil Service Reform Plan* of that year aimed to refurbish the three primary roles of the civil service: (1) operational delivery of services (e.g., working at borders, administering pensions, running prisons and courts), (2) advising on policy and supporting ministers ("creating policy solutions and communicating policy"), and (3) implementing programs and projects (HM Government (UK), 2012). By 2012 a Head of the Policy Profession for the entire British civil service was designated, as were Department Heads of Policy Profession for all the major departments. Together, they form the Policy Profession Board. Each department of the UK government was to develop a set of "fundamental policy standards" and work to embed these through training and induction procedures. In 2019 the UK Head of the Policy Profession led a review of progress made to date, and released an updated version of its professional competency framework (HM Government (UK), 2019).

Both these country cases (and there are others) show the practical efforts that governments are taking to improve their policy capacity, efforts that mirror the interest that students of CPP have in how policy ideas are generated within government bureaucracies. Scholars of the subject find themselves in conducting qualitative research on state administrative agencies, particularly cabinet offices, and their work is simultaneously about administrative, as well as policy, capacity. Two roads converge.

Conclusion

This chapter has explored the cross-fertilization and intersections between CPA and CPP, but readers will be alert nonetheless to the differences between the two fields. Some roads will not converge, so it might be helpful to conceptualize where and how the convergences occur, and where not. Figures 1 and 2 offer guides. Figure 1 presents a stylized set of "research zones" within CPA. The inner zone of "core public administration" includes all of the typical administrative practices and considerations in managing state agencies – budgeting, finance, back-office organization, service delivery, and implementation. Think of it as the range of competencies and practices that would have to be mastered by someone going on to a career in the public service. There is some low-level theory on these issues and practices, but the focus is on how things get done, often within a specific government, though some comparison is always helpful. The second zone consists of work on institutions and organizations, and is more general (and more generalizable) than work just on state agencies. It offers some greater opportunities for intersection with policy scholars, since in this case it does draw on broader theories about institutions in general. It is also the "zone" within CPA that is interested in interfaces between the public sector and non-governmental agencies and actors, and so becomes a bridge into work, for example, on advocacy coalitions, NGOs, etc. The broadest zone of research with CPA is about state structures, often linked to an interest in policy capacity and good governance. Fukuyama's work on political order is perhaps the exemplar for this (Fukuyama, 2011, 2014). This type of work goes back at least to Huntington and his interest in the relation between traditional and modern authority (Huntington, 1968). He explored this somewhat abstract and macro-sociological question with pointed and specific analysis of state administrative structures (see, for example, his discussion of the "King's Dilemma" in Chapter 3 of *Political Order in Changing Societies*). This "research zone" bristles with opportunities for intersection among political scientists, public administration scholars, and students of public policy, but it does take them to the high plateaus of policy and administration. The views from this elevation can be simultaneously breathtaking and granular, like seeing

Figure 1. CPA: Research Zones.

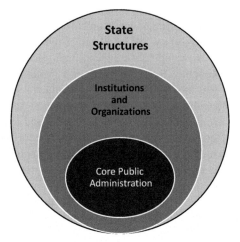

rock fissures on the Himalayas. Work on democracy, authoritarianism, and Islam is of obviously CPP interest, but relies to some extent on informed analysis of administrative cultures and organizational logics (Diamond, Plattner, & Brumber, 2003; Diamond, Fukuyama, Horowitz, & Plattner, 2014; Diamond, Plattner, & Walker, 2016).

Figure 2 is a further stylized presentation of some of the overlaps and divergences among research concentrations around public administration, public policy, and the state. The clearest overlap builds on the point made immediately above – the overlap labeled as "A" is an overlap that simultaneously connects research questions about regimes (state structure), with policy and administration. Overlap "B" is animated by questions that connect the state to public policy, and here we find work on institutional theory and policy processes, without necessarily much attention to administrative minutiae. Overlap "C" is closer to a concern with political institutions and administrative structures, without much connection to the prevailing questions in CPP. Overlap "D" picks up on most of the intersections discussed above, essentially questions about the machinery of state that produces and implements policy. And yet each of these three areas (state, policy, and administration) can be explored within distinctly defined areas of study (political science, administrative studies, and policy studies) with their own preoccupations.

CPA and CPP have had mutually supportive research agendas in the last decade, and this should continue. Policy scholars who focus more on outcomes, on ideas and paradigms, or on non-governmental actors in policy processes will likely not need inspiration or insight from CPA. But any students of CPP who take state institutions seriously, either in policy formulation or in implementation, are likely to turn to research produced by colleagues in CPA. Moreover, CPA researchers increasingly publish on public policy, but from a public administration and institutional perspective. As one example, volume 41 (2018) of the *International Journal of Public Administration* included articles on e-governance, water policy in the EU, tax competition among US counties, social media, governance, migration, environmental policy, and healthcare in France.

More specifically, three broad, related areas hold great promise for continued cross-fertilization between CPA and CPP. Transnational administration and its links to global public policy should continue to be of interest to scholars, even in days when globalization and global public policy are being critiqued and rebuffed. This is in part because of the networks of transnational administrative agencies and actors that are thick on the ground, even if they seem sometimes invisible. Moreover, the critiques and assaults on

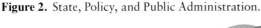
Figure 2. State, Policy, and Public Administration.

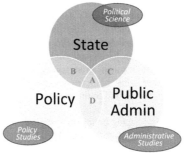

global policymaking are inspiring spirited responses from these same agencies (or at least the peak ones), generating new ideas and policy paradigms. These debates at the global level are perhaps the most important development in public policy in the last decade, and require the skilled analysis by students of both public policy and public administration. The second related area is public sector reform. Design and almost perpetual re-design of public sectors are now bona fide areas of public policy (they often now have their own ministers – euphemistically responsible for "democratic reform"), and so administration has become policy, and there are policies about administration.

Finally, students of CPP will continue to need to revise and re-think institutional theory. Recent work is probing the frontiers and making advances (Rayner, 2015; Araral & Amri, 2016; Peters, 2016; Zahariadis, 2016), but more needs to be done, not least because the very foundations of democratic institutions – the taken-for-granted institutional and governance context for most policy studies – are being challenged (Inglehart, 2016; Deneen, 2018; Mounk, 2018; Sunstein, 2018). As we think about institutional theories and institutional design, and how public policy gets made and implemented in very different types of systems, we will need to draw on the rich traditions and insights of comparative public administration.

References

Alawattage, C., & Elshihry, M. (2017). The managerialism of neoliberal global governance: The case of the OECD. In A. Littoz-Monnet (Ed.), *The Politics of Expertise in International Organizations: How International Bureaucracies Produce and Mobilize Knowledge* (pp. 167–186). London: Routledge.

Andrews, M. (2008). The good governance agenda: Beyond indicators without theory. *Oxford Development Studies*, 36(4), 379–407.

Andrews, M. (2012). The logical limits of best practice administrative solutions in developing countries. *Public Administration and Development*, 32, 137–153. doi:10.1002/pad.622.

Andrews, M. (2013). *The Limits of Institutional Reform in Development: Changing Rules for Realistic Solutions*. Cambridge: Cambridge University Press.

Araral, E., & Amri, M. (2016). Institutions and the policy process 2.0: Implications of the IAD framework. In B. G. Peters & P. Zittoun (Eds.), *Contemporary Approaches to Public Policy: Theories, Controversies and Perspectives* (pp. 73–93). London: Palgrave Macmillan.

Arndt, C., & Oman, C. (2008). *The Politics of Governance Ratings*. Working Paper MGSoG/2008/WP003. Maastricht: Maastricht University, Maastricht Graduate School of Governance.

Barnett, M. N., & Finnemore, M. (1999). The politics, power, and pathologies of international organizations. *International Organization*, 53(4), 699–732.

Barnett, M. N., & Finnemore, M. (2004). *Rules for the World: International Organizations in Global Politics*. Ithaca, NY: Cornell University Press.

Bauer, M. W., Knill, C., & Eckhard, S. (Eds.). (2017). *International Bureaucracy: Challenges and Lessons for Public Administration Research*. London: Palgrave Macmillan.

Béland, D. (2016). Kingdon reconsidered: Ideas, interests and institutions in comparative policy analysis. *Journal of Comparative Policy Analysis*, 18(3), 228–242. doi:10.1080/13876988.2015.1029770.

Biermann, F., & Siebenhüner, B. (Eds.). (2009). *Managers of Global Change: The Influence of International Environmental Bureaucracies*. Cambridge, MA: MIT Press.

Bovaird, T., & Loeffler, E. (Eds.). (2016). *Public Management and Governance* (3rd ed.). London: Routledge.

Brans, M. (2012). Comparative public administration: From general theory to general frameworks. In B. G. Peters & J. Pierre (Eds.), *The Sage Handbook of Public Administration* (pp. 424–438). London: Sage.

Broome, A., & Seabrooke, L. (2012). Seeing like an international organization. *New Political Economy*, 17(1), 1–16.

Broome, A., & Seabrooke, L. (2015). Shaping policy curves: Cognitive authority in transnational capacity-building. *Public Administration*, 93(4), 956–972. doi:10.1111/padm.12179.

Carothers, T. (1996). *Assessing Democracy Assistance: The Case of Romania*. Washington, DC: Carnegie Endowment.
Chandler, J. (Ed.) (2014). *Comparative Public Administration* (2nd ed.). New York: Routledge.
Coleman, W. D. (2012). Governance and global public policy. In D. Levi-Faur (Ed.), *The Oxford Handbook of Governance* (pp. 673–685). Oxford: Oxford University Press.
Craft, J. (2016). *Backrooms and Beyond: Partisan Advisors and the Politics of Policy Work in Canada*. Toronto: University of Toronto Press.
Craft, J., & Daku, M. (2017). A comparative assessment of elite policy recruits in Canada. *Journal of Comparative Policy Analysis, 19*(3), 207–226.
Craft, J., & Halligan, J. (2017). Assessing 30 years of Westminster policy advisory system experience. *Policy Sciences, 50*(1), 47–62. doi:10.1007/s11077-016-9256-y.
Craft, J., & Howlett, M. (2012). Policy formulation, governance shifts and policy influence: Location and content in policy advisory systems. *Journal of Public Policy, 32*(2), 79–98.
Craft, J., & Howlett, M. (2013). The dual dynamics of policy advisory systems: The impact of externalization and politicization on policy advice. *Policy and Society, 32*(3), 187–197. doi:10.1016/j.polsoc.2013.07.001.
Crowley, K., & Head, B. W. (2017). Expert advisory bodies in the policy system. In M. Brans, I. Geva-May, & M. Howlett (Eds.), *Routledge Handbook of Comparative Policy Analysis* (pp. 181–198). London: Routledge.
Dahlström, C., Peters, B. G., & Pierre, J. (Eds.). (2011). *Steering from the Centre: Strengthening Political Control in Western Democracies*. Toronto: University of Toronto Press.
Davis, K. E., Fisher, A., Kingsbury, B., & Merry, S. E. (Eds.). (2012). *Governance by Indicators: Global Power through Classification and Rankings*. Oxford: Oxford University Press and the Institute for International Law and Justice, New York University School of Law.
Davison, N. (2015). *Lifting the Policy Game Across the System: The Case of 'The Policy Project'*. London: Institute for Government.
De Francesco, F. (2013). *Transnational Policy Innovation: The OECD and the Diffusion of Regulatory Impact Analysis*. Colchester, UK: ECPR Press.
De Francesco, F. (2016). Transfer agents, knowledge authority, and indices of regulatory quality: A comparative analysis of the World Bank and the Organisation for Economic Co-operation and Development. *Journal of Comparative Policy Analysis, 18*(4), 350–365. doi:10.1080/13876988.2014.882648.
deLeon, P. (2006). The historical roots of the field. In M. Moran, M. Rein, & R. E. Goodin (Eds.), *The Oxford Handbook of Public Policy* (pp. 39–57). Oxford: Oxford University Press.
Deneen, P. J. (2018). *Why Liberalism Failed*. New Haven, CT: Yale University Press.
Diamond, L., Fukuyama, F., Horowitz, D. L., & Plattner, M. F. (2014). Reconsidering the transition paradigm. *Journal of Democracy, 25*(1), 86–100.
Diamond, L., Plattner, M. F., & Brumber, D. (Eds.). (2003). *Islam and Democracy in the Middle East*. Baltimore, MA: Johns Hopkins University Press.
Diamond, L., Plattner, M. F., & Walker, C. (Eds.). (2016). *Authoritarianism Goes Global: The Challenges to Democracy*. Baltimore, MA: Johns Hopkins University Press.
Dolowitz, D., & Marsh, D. (1996). Who learns what from whom: A review of the policy transfer literature. *Political Studies, 44*(2), 343–357.
Fitzpatrick, J., Goggin, M., Heikkila, T., Klingner, D., Machado, J., & Martell, C. (2011). A new look at comparative public administration: Trends in research and an agenda for the future. *Public Administration Review, 71*(6), 821–830.
Fukuyama, F. (2004). *State-Building: Governance and World Order in the 21st Century*. Ithaca, NY: Cornell University Press.
Fukuyama, F. (2011). *The Origins of Political Order: From Prehuman Times to the French Revolution* (Vol. 1). New York: Farrar, Straus and Giroux.
Fukuyama, F. (2013). Commentary: What is governance? *Governance, 26*(3), 347–368.
Fukuyama, F. (2014). *Political Order and Political Decay: From the Industrial Revolution to the Globalization of Democracy* (Vol. 2). New York: Farrar, Straus and Giroux.
Geva-May, I., Hoffman, D. C., & Muhleisen, J. (2018). Twenty years of comparative policy analysis: A survey of the field and a discussion of topics and methods. *Journal of Comparative Policy Analysis, 20*(1), 18–35. doi:10.1080/13876988.2017.1405618.

Grindle, M. S. (2013). Public sector reform as problem-solving? Comment on the World Bank's Public Sector Management Approach for 2011 to 2020. *International Review of Administrative Sciences, 79*(3), 398–405.

Gulrajani, N., & Moloney, K. (2012). Globalizing public administration: Today's research and tomorrow's agenda. *Public Administration Review, 72*(1), 78–86.

Hadjiisky, M., Pal, L. A., & Walker, C. (Eds.). (2017). *Public Policy Transfer: Micro-Dynamics and Macro-Effects*. Cheltenham, UK: Edward Elgar.

Halligan, J. (1995). Policy advice and the public service. In B. G. Peters & D. J. Savoie (Eds.), *Governance in a Changing Environment*. Montreal and Kingston: Canadian Centre for Management Development and McGill-Queen's University Press.

Halligan, J. (2010). Post-NPM responses to disaggregation through coordinating horizontally and integrating governance. In P. Laegreid & K. Verhoest (Eds.), *Governance of Public Sector Organizations: Proliferation, Autonomy and Performance* (pp. 235–254). Houndmills, Basingstoke: Palgrave Macmillan.

Heady, F. (1996). *Public Administration: A Comparative Perspective* (5th ed.). New York: Marcel Dekker.

Heidenheimer, A. J., Heclo, H., & Adams, C. T. (1975). *Comparative Public Policy: The Politics of Social Choice in Europe and America*. New York: St. Martin's Press.

Henderson, K. M. (1981). From comparative public administration to comparative public policy. *International Review of Administrative Sciences, 47*(4), 356–364.

HM Government (UK). (1999). *Professional Policy Making for the Twenty First Century: Report by Strategic Policy Making Team, Cabinet Office*. Available at: https://ntouk.files.wordpress.com/2015/06/professional-policy-making-for-the-21st-century-1999.pdf.

HM Government (UK). (2012). *The Civil Service Reform Plan*. Available at: https://assets.publishing.service.gov.uk/government/uploads/system/uploads/attachment_data/file/305148/Civil-Service-Reform-Plan-final.pdf.

HM Government (UK). (2019). *Policy Profession Standards: A Framework for Professional Development*. Available at: www.atlas101.ca/pm/wp-content/uploads/2019/03/UK_Policy_Profession_Standards_JAN19.pdf.

Holt, J., & Manning, N. (2014). Fukuyama is right about measuring state quality: Now what? *Governance, 27*(4), 717–728.

Howlett, M. (2013). Conclusion – policy analytic capacity and evidence-based policy-making: Lessons from Canada. In M. Howlett, *Canadian Public Policy: Selected Studies in Process and Style* (pp. 153–169). Toronto: University of Toronto Press.

Howlett, M. (2015). Policy analytical capacity: The supply and demand for policy analysis in government. *Policy and Society, 34*(3–4), 173–182.

Howlett, M., McConnell, A., & Perl, A. (2016). Weaving the fabric of public policies: Comparing and integrating contemporary frameworks for the study of public policy. *Journal of Comparative Policy Analysis, 18*(3), 273–289. doi: 10.1080/13876988.2015.1082261.

Howlett, M., Migone, A., Wellstead, A., & Evans, B. (2014). The distribution of analytical techniques in policy advisory systems: Policy formulation and the tools of policy appraisal. *Public Policy and Administration, 29*(4), 271–291.

Howlett, M., & Wellstead, A. M. (2011). Policy analysts in the bureaucracy revisited: The nature of professional policy work in contemporary government. *Politics & Policy, 49*(4), 613–633.

Howlett, M., & Wellstead, A. M. (2012). Professional policy work in federal states: Institutional autonomy and Canadian policy analysis. *Canadian Public Administration, 55*(1), 53–68.

Hudstedt, T., & Veit, S. (2017). Policy advisory systems: Change dynamics and sources of variation. *Policy Sciences, 50*(1), 41–43. doi:10.1007/s11077-016-9272-y.

Huntington, S. P. (1968). *Political Order in Changing Societies*. New Haven: Yale University Press.

Inglehart, R. F. (2016). How much should we worry? *Journal of Democracy, 27*(3), 18–23.

Kaul, I. (2013). *Global Public Policy: A Policy in the Making*. Paper presented at the 1st International Conference on Public Policy, Grenoble.

Kentikelenis, A. E., & Seabrooke, L. (2017). The politics of world polity: Script-writing in international organizations. *American Sociological Review, 82*(5), 1065–1095. doi:10.1177/0003122417728241.

Kettl, D. F. (2005). *The Global Public Management Revolution* (2nd ed.). Washington, DC: Brookings Institution Press.

Kingdon, J. W. (2011). *Agendas, Alternatives, and Public Policies* (Updated 2nd ed.). Boston: Longman.

Lindblom, C. E. (1959). The science of "muddling through". *Public Administration Review, 19*(2), 79–88.

Mahon, R. (2015). The OECD, gender, and social policy – Parallel stories. In A. Kaasch & K. Martens (Eds.), *Actors and Agency in Global Social Governance* (pp. 82–101). Oxford: Oxford University Press.

Mahon, R., & McBride, S. (Eds.). (2008). *The OECD and Transnational Governance*. Vancouver: UBC Press.

Mamudu, H., Cairney, P., & Studlar, D. (2015). Global public policy: Does the new venue for transnational tobacco control challenge the old way of doing things? *Public Administration, 93*(4), 856–873. doi:10.1111/padm.12143.

Mounk, Y. (2018). *The People vs. Democracy: Why Our Freedom Is in Danger and How to Save It*. Cambridge, MA: Harvard University Press.

Mungiu-Pippidi, A. (2015). *The Quest for Good Governance: How Societies Develop Control of Corruption*. Cambridge: Cambridge University Press.

Mungiu-Pippidi, A., & Johnston, M. (Eds.). (2017). *Transitions to Good Governance: Creating Virtuous Circles of Anti-Corruption*. Cheltenham, UK: Edward Elgar.

Nunberg, B. (1999). *The State After Communism: Administrative Transitions in Central and Eastern Europe*. Washington, DC: World Bank.

O'Flynn, J., Blackman, D., & Halligan, J. (Eds.). (2014). *Crossing Boundaries in Public Management and Policy: The International Experience*. London: Routledge.

OECD. (1995). *Governance in Transition: Public Management Reforms in OECD Countries*. Paris: OECD.

OECD. (2005). *Modernising Government: The Way Forward*. Paris: OECD.

OECD. (2017). *Policy Advisory Systems: Supporting Good Governance and Sound Public Decision Making*. Paris: OECD.

Painter, M., & Pierre, J. (2005). Unpacking state capacity: Issues and themes. In M. Painter & J. Pierre (Eds.), *Challenges to State Policy Capacity: Global Trends and Comparative Perspectives* (pp. 1–18). Houndmills, Basingstoke: Palgrave Macmillan.

Pal, L. A. (2012). *Frontiers of Governance: The OECD and Global Public Management Reform*. Houndmills, Basingstoke: Palgrave Macmillan.

Pal, L. A., & Clark, I. D. (2016a). The MPA/MPP in the Anglo-democracies: Australia, Canada, New Zealand, the United Kingdom, and the United States,. *Policy and Society, 35*(4), 299–313. doi:10.1016/j.polsoc.2016.11.001.

Pal, L. A., & Clark, I. D. (2016b). Teaching public policy: Global convergence of difference? *Policy and Society, 35*(4), 283–297.

Peters, B. G. (1994). Theory and methodology in the study of comparative public administration. In R. Baker (Ed.), *Comparative Public Management: Putting U.S. Public Policy and Implementation in Context* (pp. 67–91). Westport, CT: Praeger.

Peters, B. G. (2016). Institutions and public policy. In B. G. Peters & P. Zittoun (Eds.), *Contemporary Approaches to Public Policy: Theories, Controversies and Perspectives* (pp. 57–72). London: Palgrave Macmillan.

Peters, B. G. (2018). *Policy Problems and Policy Design*. Cheltenham, UK: Edward Elgar.

Peters, B. G., & Barker, A. (1993). *Advising West European Governments: Inquiries, Expertise and Public Policy*. Edinburgh: Edinburgh University Press.

Peters, B. G., & Pierre, J. (2001). *Politicians, Bureaucrats and Administrative Reform*. London; New York: Routledge.

Peters, B. G., & Pierre, J. (Eds.). (2012). *The Sage Handbook of Public Administration* (2nd ed.). London: Sage.

Peters, B. G., Pierre, J., & Randma-Liiv, T. (2011). Global financial crisis, public administration and governance: Do new problems require new solutions? *Public Organization Review, 11*, 13–27. doi:0.1007/s11115-010-0148-x.

Peters, B. G., Rhodes, R. A. W., & Wright, V. (Eds.). (1999). *Administering the Summit: Administration of the Core Executive in Developed Countries*. New York: St. Martin's Press.

Peters, B. G., & Zittoun, P. (Eds.). (2016). *Contemporary Approaches to Public Policy: Theories, Controversies and Perspectives*. London: Palgrave Macmillan.

Pierre, J. (Ed.) (1995). *Bureaucracy in the Modern State: An Introduction to Comparative Public Administration*. Cheltenham: Edward Elgar.

Pollitt, C. (2011). Not odious but onerous: Comparative public administration. *Public Administration, 89*(1), 114–127.

Pollitt, C., & Bouckaert, G. (2017). *Public Management Reform: A Comparative Analysis – Into the Age of Austerity* (4th ed.). Oxford: Oxford University Press.

Porto de Oliveira, O., & Pal, L. A. (2018). Novas fronteiras e direções na pesquisa sobre transferência, difusão e circulação de políticas públicas: Agentes, espaços, resistência e traduções [New frontiers and directions in policy transfer, diffusion and circulation research: Agents, spaces, resistance, and translations]. *Revista de Administração Pública, 52*(2), 199–220. doi:10.1590/0034-761220180078.

Pritchett, L., Woolcock, M., & Andrews, M. (2012). *Looking like a State: Techniques of Persistent Failure in State Capability for Implementation.* Working Paper No. 2012/63: United Nations University – World Institute for Development Economics Research. Available at: www.wider.unu.edu/sites/default/files/wp2012-063.pdf.

Raadschelders, J. C. N., Vigoda-Gadot, E., & Kisner, M. (2015). *Global Dimensions of Public Administration and Governance.* Hoboken, NJ: Jossey-Bass.

Rabin, J. (Ed.) (2003). *Encyclopedia of Public Administration and Public Policy.* New York: Marcel Dekker.

Rabin, J., Hildreth, W. B., & Miller, G. J. (Eds.). (2007). *Handbook of Public Administration* (3rd ed.). Boca Raton, FL: Taylor & Francis.

Radaelli, C. M. (2003). The Europeanization of public policy. In K. Featherstone & C. Radaelli (Eds.), *The Politics of Europeanization* (pp. 27–56). Oxford: Oxford University Press.

Radin, B. A. (2013). *Beyond Machiavelli: Policy Analysis Reaches Midlife* (2nd ed.). Washington, DC: Georgetown University Press.

Randma-Liiv, T., & Kickert, W. (2017). The impact of the fiscal crisis on public administration reforms: Comparison of 14 European countries. *Journal of Comparative Policy Analysis, 19*(2), 155–172. doi:10.1080/13876988.2015.1129737.

Raudla, R., Douglas, J. W., Savi, R., & Randma-Liiv, T. (2017). Fiscal Crisis and Expenditure Cuts: The Influence of Public Management Practices on Cutback Strategies in Europe. *The American Review of Public Administration, 47*(3), 376–394. doi:10.1177/0275074016661029.

Rayner, J. (2015). Is there a fourth institutionalism? Ideas, institutions and the explanation of policy change. In J. Hogan & M. Howlett (Eds.), *Policy Paradigms in Theory and Practice: Discourses, Ideas and Anomalies in Public Policy Dynamics* (pp. 61–80). Houndmills, Basingstoke: Palgrave Macmillan.

Reiter, R., & Klenk, T. (2018). The manifold meanings of 'post-New Public Management' – A systematic literature review. *International Review of Administrative Sciences, On-Line Publication [retrieved June 7, 2018].*

Roberts, A. (2010). *The Logic of Discipline: Global Capitalism and the Architecture of Government.* New York: Oxford University Press.

Roberts, A. S. (1996). *So-Called Experts: How American Consultants Remade the Canadian Civil Service, 1918–1921.* Toronto: Institute of Public Administration of Canada.

Rose, R. (1991). What is lesson-drawing? *Journal of Public Policy, 11*(1), 3–30.

Rose, R. (1993). *Lesson-Drawing in Public Policy: A Guide to Learning across Time and Space.* Chatham, NJ: Chatham House Publishers.

Sabatier, P. A., & Jenkins-Smith, H. C. (Eds.). (1993). *Policy Change and Learning: An Advocacy Coalition Approach.* Boulder, CO: Westview Press.

Sabatier, P. A., & Weible, C. M. (2007). The advocacy coalition framework: Innovations and clarifications. In P. A. Sabatier (Ed.), *Theories of the Policy Process* (pp. 189–222). Boulder, CO: Westview Press.

Seabrooke, L., & Wigan, D. (2016). Powering ideas through expertise: Professionals in global tax battles. *Journal of European Public Policy, 23*(3), 357–374.

Slaughter, A.-M. (2004a). Disaggregated sovereignty: Towards the public accountability of global government networks. *Government and Opposition, 39*(2), 159–190.

Slaughter, A.-M. (2004b). Global government networks, global information agencies, and disaggregated democracy. In K.-H. Ladeur (Ed.), *Public Governance in the Age of Globalization* (pp. 121–155). Aldershot, UK: Ashgate.

Slaughter, A.-M. (2004c). *A New World Order.* Princeton, NJ: Princeton University Press.

Stone, D., & Ladi, S. (2015). Global public policy and transnational administration. *Public Administration, 93*(4), 839–855. doi:10.1111/padm.12207.

Stone, D., & Moloney, K. (Eds.). (2019). *The Oxford Handbook of Global Policy and Transnational Administration.* Oxford: Oxford University Press.

Subramaniam, V. (2000). Comparative public administration: From failed universal theory to raw empiricism. A frank analysis and guidelines towards a realistic perspective. *International Review of Administrative Sciences, 66*(4), 557–572.

Sunstein, C. R. (Ed.) (2018). *Can It Happen Here?: Authoritarianism in America.* New York: Haper Collins.

Van de Walle, S., & Brans, M. (2018). Where comparative public administration and comparative policy studies meet. *Journal of Comparative Policy Analysis, 20*(1), 101–113.

Van Wart, M. R., & Cayer, N. J. (1990). Comparative public administration: Defunct, dispersed, or redefined. *Public Administration Review, 50*(2), 238–248.

Waldo, D. (2006). Comparative public administration: Prologue, performance, problems, and promise. In E. E. Otenyo & N. S. Lind (Eds.), *Comparative Public Administration: The Essential Readings* (pp. 129–170). Amsterdam: Elsevier.

Weber, M. (1958). *From Max Weber: Essays in Sociology*. Translated, edited and with an introduction by H. H. Gerth and C. Wright Mills. New York: Oxford University Press.

Weible, C. M., & Jenkins-Smith, H. C. (2016). The advocacy coalition framework: An approach for the comparative analysis of contentious policy issues. In B. G. Peters & P. Zittoun (Eds.), *Contemporary Approaches to Public Policy: Theories, Controversies and Perspectives* (pp. 15–34). London: Palgrave Macmillan.

Wildavsky, A. (1975). *Budgeting: A Comparative Theory of Budgetary Processes*. Boston: Little, Brown.

Wildavsky, A. (2018). *The Art and Craft of Policy Analysis: Reissued with a New Introduction by B. Guy Peters*. London: Palgrave Macmillan. Originally published 1979.

Wildavsky, A. B. (1979). *Speaking Truth to Power: The Art and Craft of Policy Analysis*. Boston: Little, Brown.

Williamson, J. (1990). What Washington means by policy reform. In J. Williamson (Ed.), *Latin American Adjustment: How Much Has Happened?* Washington, DC: Institute for International Economics.

Wilson, W. (1887). The study of administration. *Political Science Quarterly, 2*(2), 197–222.

Wolfensohn, J. D. (1996). Annual Meeting Address, October 1, 1996. *World Bank Speeches*, Available at: http://web.worldbank.org/WBSITE/EXTERNAL/EXTABOUTUS/ORGANIZATION/EXTPRESIDENT/EXTPASTPRESIDENTS/PRESIDENTEXTERNAL/0,contentMDK:20025269~menuPK:20232083~pagePK:20159837~piPK:20159808~theSitePK:20227585,20025200.html.

Woods, N. (2006). *The Globalizers: The IMF, the World Bank, and their Borrowers*. Ithaca, NY: Cornell University Press.

World Bank. (1997). *World Development Report 1997: The State in a Changing World*. Washington, DC: World Bank.

World Bank. (2012). *Approach to Public Sector Management 2011–2020: Better Results from Public Sector Institutions*. Washington, DC: World Bank. Available at: http://siteresources.worldbank.org/EXTGOVANTICORR/Resources/3035863-1285601351606/PSM-Approach.pdf.

World Bank. (2017). *World Development Report 2017: Governance and the Law*. Washington, DC: World Bank Group. Available at: www.worldbank.org/en/publication/wdr2017.

Wu, X., Ramesh, M., & Howlett, M. (2015). Policy capacity: A conceptual framework for understanding policy competences and capabilities. *Policy and Society, 34*(3–4), 165–171.

Zahariadis, N. (2016). Delphic oracles: Ambiguity, institutions, and multiple streams. *Policy Sciences, 49*(1), 3–12. doi:10.1007/s11077-016-9243-3.

Part 3
The Classics: Regional Comparisons in Comparative Policy Analysis Studies

When do Governments Consolidate? A Quantitative Comparative Analysis of 23 OECD Countries (1980–2005)

UWE WAGSCHAL & GEORG WENZELBURGER

ABSTRACT *Soaring unemployment, various economic stimulus packages, and the financial backlash have left their marks on the public finances of most industrialized countries. Fiscal adjustments are a top priority for the governments of the OECD member states. Against this background, this paper investigates the determinants of fiscal adjustments in the 1990s – a period when many budget consolidations occurred. Through a quantitative analysis, this research shows (1) what variables explain the probability of budget consolidation, (2) what consolidation strategies are most successful, and (3) what factors influence the relative consolidation performance within the group of consolidators.*

1. Introduction

The current debt crisis in countries like Greece, Italy, Spain, Portugal, Japan and even the United States has put the issue of budget consolidation at the top of the political agenda in many countries. Rising interest rates for highly indebted countries and ballooning deficits have increased the political and economic pressure on governments to adjust public finances. However, the consolidation of public finances is a difficult task for governments. Any government that cuts social security benefits, increases taxes, or makes public service employees redundant will trigger protests from the groups concerned and may jeopardize its chances of re-election. Therefore, the question arises: what variables affect the probability of a fiscal adjustment? Or, to be more precise, which factors influence budget consolidations?

The research question of this paper can be analyzed by looking back several decades, to when economic growth in many Western industrialized nations slowed after the first and second oil crises, unemployment levels soared and pressure on public finances increased. In most cases, governments did not respond by introducing severe cuts or tax increases but chose instead to finance the growing monetary demand by increasing budget deficits. As a result, the level of public debt increased. Although public finances did recover temporarily by the end of the 1980s, by the mid-1990s deficits in the OECD countries had increased to a record level. By 1995, the year in which the 23 OECD countries studied here generally recorded their highest levels of debt, the average figure was 73 per cent of GDP.[1] The debt ratio of Belgium, for instance, increased to more than 140 per cent of GDP in 1993, and the Swedish budget deficit reached 11.2 per cent of GDP in the same year (OECD 2009a). Moreover, the currencies of these countries were under tremendous pressure – a situation quite comparable to current circumstances.[2]

In this situation, Belgium and Sweden – and many others – succeeded in balancing their budgets by the end of the 1990s. As a consequence, the average debt ratio was back on more sustainable levels in 2005, amounting to 64 per cent of GDP. Several countries even recorded budget surpluses during subsequent years. Thus, overall, the 1990s can be characterized – on average – as a period of fiscal adjustments in the OECD world. However, these averages conceal the fact that developments were far from uniform. Some countries managed to do much better than others. Countries such as Sweden, Canada, Denmark and Belgium sometimes generated large surpluses, reduced their public debt or built up reserves to cover future contingencies (such as demographic changes). Meanwhile, in other OECD countries such as France and Germany, the level of public debt still continued to rise at the end of the 1990s and the public budgets continued to show a significant deficit each year.

This paper has three aims. First, it seeks to identify the factors which determine how governments respond to budgetary pressures and problems: whether they allow deficits to grow or whether they seek to consolidate. In order to do this, we examine the development of public finances in 23 OECD countries by means of an empirical analysis using panel data. Second, we analyze some specific aspects of budget consolidations in greater detail, focusing in particular on issues of timing and strategy. Finally, we concentrate on the group of budget Consolidators and examine the socio-economic, political and institutional factors influencing the relative extent of these budget consolidations. Methodologically, our approach differs from other studies of budget consolidation (Mink and de Haan 2006; Mulas-Granados 2006; Mierau et al. 2007; Maroto Illera and Mulas-Granados 2008), which analyze annual data.[3] Instead, we focus on consolidation episodes, taking the time perspective of austerity politics more into account. From this comprehensive assessment of fiscal adjustments, we can draw some conclusions with respect to the current situation of public finances in the OECD world.

The remainder of the paper is organized as follows. Section 2 describes the dependent variable, i.e. the budget consolidation, which is a concept used in different operationalizations. Section 3 deals with the theoretical basis and methodological issues. Section 4 analyzes the determinants of budget consolidations by means of a panel logit model, while section 5 discusses the findings of an analysis of some specific aspects of consolidation strategies. In section 6, we examine factors influencing consolidation performance within the group of consolidators. The final section of the paper offers some concluding comments.

2. Budget Consolidations – An Overview

In the existing economics literature, we find numerous studies dealing with budget consolidations and their effects (Alesina and Perotti 1995, 1996, 1997; Zaghini 2001; von Hagen et al. 2002; Brandner 2003; Larch and Salto 2003, Mulas-Granados 2006, Alesina and Ardagna 2010, Lassen 2010). These studies normally use the cyclically-adjusted balance ratios (CAB) or the cyclically-adjusted primary balances (CAPB) as indicators of discretionary fiscal policy. These measures adjust the budget data for changes in the macro-economic environment and/or for the non-discretionary interest payments. Arguably, cyclical adjustment is desirable as it makes it possible to filter out the discretionary effects of fiscal policy. However, the methods of calculation vary so greatly that it is doubtful whether cyclically-adjusted balance ratios are in fact suitable indicators for determining consolidation periods (Wagschal and Wenzelburger 2008). International organizations use different methods for the cyclical adjustment of budget balances and the economics community is still discussing which is most appropriate (see most recently, Girouard and André 2005). Even more problematic is the issue of data quality. For some countries, the adjusted fiscal indicators are only poorly correlated. Looking at different measurements of the CAB for Finland, data from the European Commission and data from the OECD (OECD 2005) for the period 1987–2005 only produce a correlation coefficient of $r = 0.66$. Moreover the data differs to a large extent depending on whether one uses IMF, EU or OECD data. Therefore, the reliability of the CAB and CAPB data can be doubted.[4]

Taking these problems into account, we define consolidation periods by using the (non-cyclically-adjusted) primary balance ratios. Using this indicator avoids discussion of the "correct" method of cyclical adjustment and the associated data problems. In the case of Finland, the correlation for the different data providers and their various calculations of the primary balance ratios is around 0.99. This improved data quality also applies for the other OECD countries.

Two different types of consolidations can be identified. First, a period of consolidation exists when countries reduce a budget deficit and reduce or stabilize the public debt ratio (Type A). Second, instances in which countries that already have a considerable primary surplus significantly reduce their public debt ratio should also be designated as consolidation periods (Type B).

As it is difficult for countries to reduce a deficit and at the same time maintain a public debt ratio at a constant level, the threshold values for Type A consolidations should be set somewhat lower. On the other hand, in the case of a surplus (Type B), stricter criteria must be applied: a consolidation phase only exists if there are high primary surpluses and a significant reduction in debt. For this reason, the following definitions are applied in this study:

(A) A consolidation period exists if a negative primary balance (=primary deficit) improves over a period of least two years by a minimum of 1 percentage point per year and at the same time the public debt ratio during this period remains at least constant (Type A).

(B) A consolidation period exists if there is an average primary surplus of at least 2 per cent of the GDP over a period of at least two years and at the same time the public debt ratio falls by an average of 2 percentage points per year over the course of two years. In total, the reduction in the public debt ratio during the entire consolidation period must be at least 10 percentage points (Type B).

The most difficult decision to make when identifying consolidation phases is to determine threshold values. Previous studies of budget consolidation advanced a variety of criteria for defining consolidation phases. Table 1 gives an overview of the

Table 1. Threshold values used to determine consolidation periods

Study	Indicator	Threshold value
Alesina and Perotti 1995, 1996, 1997	CAPB ("Blanchard Fiscal Impulse")	1) Improvement of 1.5 percentage points in one year 2) Improvement of 1.25 percentage points per year in two successive years
Alesina and Ardagna 1998	CAPB ("Blanchard Fiscal Impulse")	1) Improvement of 2 percentage points in one year 2) Improvement of 1.5 percentage points per year in two successive years
Heylen and Everaert 2000	CAPB	1) Improvement of at least 2 percentage points during the entire period 2) Consolidation begins if the CAPB improves by at least 0.25 percentage points and continues as long as the CAPB improves.
Zaghini 2001; Brandner 2003	CAPB	1) Improvement of more than 1.6 percentage points in one year 2) Improvement of more than 0.8 percentage points per year in two or more successive years
Hagen et al. 2002	CAB	1) Improvement of 1.5 percentage points in one year if the CAB is positive in the previous year and the following year 2) Improvement of 1.25 percentage points per year in two successive years
German Council of Economic Advisers (Sachverständigenrat zur Begutachtung der gesamtwirtschaftlichen Entwicklung 2003)	CAPB	1) Improvement of 2 percentage points in one year 2) Improvement of 1.5 percentage points per year in two successive years
Mulas-Granados 2004	CAPB	Improvement of 1.25 percentage points per year if the CAPB improves in the previous and the following year as well
Guichard et al. 2007	CAPB	• Beginning: Improvement of 1 percentage point per year during two years, if the improvement is more than 0.5 points in the first year • Continuation: If CAPB improves; a deterioration is possible if it does not exceed 0.3 percentage points and if the CAPB improves more than 0.5 points in the subsequent year

most important definitions used in previous research. It is difficult to understand why a certain threshold was used in a specific study. Therefore we fully agree with Brandner's notion that "the question of the numerical threshold values cannot be determined objectively and/or clearly" (Brandner 2003, p. 188). None of the definitions itemized in the table allow any flexibility in terms of fulfilling the criteria. However, it is precisely because of measurement uncertainties that some kind of a "buffer" is appropriate when it comes to determining consolidation phases. Thus, in view of the heterogeneous nature of the data we allow for a "buffer" of 0.2 percentage points.

A further question arises as to whether one-year improvements in the budget balance should really be designated as consolidations. In contrast to most studies displayed in Table 1 we define a consolidation as a process lasting at least two years. The reason for doing so is that a one-year consolidation can be influenced by an austerity packages using creative accounting or one-time measures. Ultimately, one-off improvements in the budget balance can also arise as a result of selling off assets, hiving off loss-making assets, or conducting other transactions within budgets. From a dynamic perspective, it therefore seems highly questionable to designate one-year improvements in budget balances as consolidations. For this reason, we consider it appropriate to deem a consolidation as only properly occurring where public finances have shown an improvement over two successive years. This ensures that a consolidation is based on conscious political choice and substantial consolidation efforts.

A second criterion for assessing budget consolidations is their sustainability (or success). This focuses on the medium-term effect of a consolidation. Once again, the literature differs on the question of how sustainability should be determined. However, most studies argue that the sustainability of a consolidation should be assessed on the basis of the development of the public debt ratio (Alesina and Perotti 1995, 1996, 1997; Zaghini 2001; Brandner 2003). As a decreasing or a stable public debt ratio is already required for the definitions of consolidation phases, it is logical to formulate the sustainability criterion somewhat less rigidly. Consolidations are therefore designated in this research as being successful or sustainable if the public debt ratio in the third year after the consolidation is at least at the same level as in the last year of the consolidation phase. Since our last consolidation episode ends in 2005, our last sustainability criterion ends in 2008.

If we apply the definitions of consolidation to the 23 OECD countries under analysis here, the following picture emerges: the assessment in the period from 1980 to 2005 gives a total of 26 consolidation phases in 17 countries (14 Type A, 12 Type B), of which 16 were successful or sustainable and ten were not sustainable because public debt started to rise again within three years after the consolidation episode (Table 2).

3. Hypotheses and Methods of Analysis

3.1 Hypotheses

The theoretical basis for our analysis is a set of hypotheses derived from different theories of public policy. Schmidt (2000) identifies six different theoretical approaches that can be used to explain policy variance in different policy fields. These approaches

Table 2. Budget consolidations in OECD countries (1980–2005)

Country	Type	Consolidation episode	Sustainability ($t + 3$ after end of episode)
Australia	A	1993–1999	Sustainable
Belgium	B	1993–2005	Sustainable
Denmark 1	B	1984–1989	Not sustainable
Denmark 2	B	1996–2001	Sustainable
Finland	A	1993–2000	Sustainable
UK 1	B	1986–1990	Not sustainable
UK 2	A	1993–2000	Sustainable
Ireland 1	A	1985–1989	Sustainable
Ireland 2	B	1993–2002	Sustainable
Iceland 1	A	1994–2000	Not sustainable
Iceland 2	A	2003–2005	Sustainable
Italy	B	1998–2001	Sustainable
Japan	B	1987–1991	Not sustainable
Canada 1	A	1992–2000	Sustainable
Canada 2	B	2000–2005	Sustainable
New Zealand 1	A	1992–1995	Sustainable
New Zealand 2	B	2000–2005	Sustainable
Netherlands	B	1996–2001	Not sustainable
Norway	A	1992–1997	Not sustainable
Austria	A	1995–1997	Not sustainable
Sweden 1	A	1982–1987	Sustainable
Sweden 2	B	1987–1990	Not sustainable
Sweden 3	A	1993–2000	Sustainable
Spain 1	A	1985–1988	Not sustainable
Spain 2	B	1998–2002	Sustainable
USA	A	1992–2000	Not sustainable

Notes: Based on authors' own calculations. For definitions see text.

have proved remarkably successful in accounting for the development of public expenditure – social expenditure (Siegel 2002), education spending (Wolf 2006), and the determinants of public debt (Wagschal 1996) – and it makes sense to start from the assumption that the factors adduced by these theories may also be relevant to questions of budgetary consolidation. These factors are as follows:

(1) A first set of factors is socio-economic in character. One can argue that the probability of a consolidation period increases with rising pressure on governments from problems such as low economic growth. With a higher level of debt, of interest payments, and of unemployment, there is a greater chance that a budget consolidation will be implemented. Empirical studies of fiscal policy (Mulas-Granados 2006) and budget consolidations (von Hagen and Strauch 2001) have already shown that the initial problem has a significant influence. Moreover, inflation should play a role. With higher inflation, governments face fewer problems when implementing a consolidation (Alesina and Perotti 1995).

(2) A second set of factors are derived from the "parties-do-matter" hypothesis. The basic argument is that left-leaning parties have different political preferences (because of their electorate) from right-wing parties (Hibbs 1977),

e.g. for more public spending. However, with respect to budget consolidation, causal assumptions are ambivalent. On the one hand, some studies of the determinants of public debt and deficits (Wagschal 1996) and the study of deficits (Persson and Svensson 1989) have identified a positive association between left incumbency and budgetary performance, e.g. lower public deficits. Furthermore, a number of authors have argued that left-wing parties are also more likely to be able to reform the welfare state than their opponents (Nixon-goes-to-China logic), just because they are the natural defenders of a big welfare state (Ross 2000; Kitschelt 2001). Include the traditional right-wing aversion to high taxation and the obvious implication is that budget consolidation will be more likely to occur under the auspices of a left-leaning party. On the other hand, the classic hypothesis of partisan influence on public policy strongly implies that left-wing parties prefer big governments (Hibbs 1977) and Keynesian demand policy, which is empirically extremely well documented (Castles 1982; Schmidt 1982, 1996). Therefore, an alternative hypothesis would suggest the strong probability of a negative association between left-leaning parties and consolidation performance.

(3) Power resources theory suggests that a third factor likely to affect policy outcomes is the strength of the trade union movement (Korpi 1980). With regard to consolidation performance, the theory suggests that when trade unions are stronger, the organized struggle against proposed public expenditure cuts will be greater; hence, the greater difficulty in achieving budgetary consolidation.

(4) A fourth factor is the character of political institutions. Several studies in different policy fields have shown that the institutional arrangements of different countries – such as federalism, fiscal decentralization or veto players – have an impact on public policy. It is argued that veto players are responsible for status quo bias in policy and for a failure of policy reforms (Tsebelis 1995, 2002). In addition to the influence of the veto players, the effects of federalism and fiscal decentralization are widely discussed. Again, assumed causal impact is ambivalent. The comparative social policy literature assumes that federalism impedes social expenditure growth, but has a ratchet effect on recent policy settings (see Obinger et al. 2005). Brennan and Buchanan (1980) argue that federalism is likely to curb spending because of tax competition amongst states, while Oates (1972) notes that federalism creates greater efficiency as a consequence of decentralization. However, other political economy approaches assume the logic of higher spending deriving from a "common-pool" problem that leads to a possible "overuse" of the tax subjects by too many state entities (Weingast et al. 1981; Hallerberg and Hagen 1999). Federalism is also criticized because of the absence of scale effects, decision blockades and better access for "rent seekers".

(5) Public expenditure development is highly path dependent, as Wildavsky's theory of budgetary instrumentalism (1964) postulated early on. He argued that budgets are sticky and only very small changes can be observed over time. Rose and Karran (1987) have also stressed the path dependency argument for tax systems. Particularly in countries where the social security system is organized via the insurance principle, social expenditure cannot be greatly changed from

one year to the next as past contributions are seen as establishing social rights of subsequent benefit. Therefore we would expect that budget consolidation would be harder to implement in countries where the insurance principle plays an important role in the social security system.

(6) The sixth theoretical approach takes an international perspective. It posits that the extent of the integration of the economy in the world market is important when it comes to domestic politics. With regard to fiscal policy one would expect that governments in more open economies would have to pay more attention to sound public finances than countries in more closed economies as they must seek to attract foreign investment in a competitive environment – e.g. low taxes, low interest rates, etc. Therefore the likelihood of budget consolidation should be positively related to the degree of the openness of the economy. Moreover, the run-up to European Monetary Union or policy advice in connection with credits from the IMF are international factors that could influence the probability of a fiscal adjustment.

3.2 Methods of Analysis

Budget improvements and deterioration can be analyzed in a variety of ways (Wenzelburger 2009). The first approach is quite simple: it links the definition of budget consolidations to the annual rate of change of a specific indicator. When a certain indicator used to illustrate the budgetary situation of a country improves, a budget consolidation occurs. When it deteriorates, there is no consolidation. As a consequence, one can run a time series cross sectional (TSCS) regression and identify a number of independent variables that influence the development of this specific indicator, i.e. the dependent variable. Carlos Mulas-Granados conducts one such analysis and shows that the explanatory power of the independent variables varies over time and that economic variables (the lagged budget balance, the development of the unemployment rate, or the inflation rate) are the most important determinants for the development of the budget balance (Mulas-Granados 2006: 77). Whereas the empirical analysis is straightforward, the definition of the dependent variable is problematic: Mulas-Granados basically analyzes the determinants of fiscal policy.[5] Therefore, the treatment of budget consolidations as annual changes seems not to be the optimal solution.

A second approach takes into account the characteristics of budget consolidations as time periods. This is in line with our definition of budget consolidation episodes (see section 2): if a certain indicator in a certain country satisfies the criteria during a certain period of time, this period is labeled a consolidation period. Defining budget consolidation in this way has important consequences because it affects the research design. In essence, three designs are possible: First, one can code consolidation countries in a sample with 1 and non-consolidation countries with 0, then compare the means of the different independent variables. Second, one can define consolidation periods as a first step, but then go on to consider the metric data of the indicators in the analysis, e.g. by calculating the differences of the indicators between the first and the last year of the consolidation period (Heylen and Everaert 2000: 115, section 5 and 6 of this paper). Both designs are cross-sectional, which limits the degrees of freedom of the analysis and fails to take into account the dynamics of the situation. A possible remedy is proposed by a third design which splits periods into years coded with 1 (years in a consolidation period) and 0 for the other years (Mierau et al. 2007). Following this strategy, a panel analysis is possible. The disadvantage is that the metric information is lost.

One may conclude that the definition of fiscal adjustments as periods of time is more straightforward than the "annual-rate" solution. Within this approach, three research designs are possible. The most promising solution is to analyze the determinants of budget consolidations by splitting up the consolidation periods into years.

Methodologically, a panel logit regression analysis is an appropriate method for such a research design.[6] In principle, the logistic regression analysis of pooled data faces the same problems as the linear TCSC analysis: heterogeneity, serial correlation, and heteroskedasticity, to name the most important difficulties. The remedies for these problems, however, differ from the ordinary least squares (OLS) case because of the maximum-likelihood estimation and the binary nature of the dependent variable.[7] To correct for serial correlation, Beck et al. (1998) suggest introducing a series of splines and dummy variables. That approach is followed in this analysis. A possible way of dealing with the heterogeneity problem would be to model unit-fixed effects by means of a conditional logistic regression model (Chamberlain 1980; Verbeek 2004: 375). However, a conditional specification has the major drawback that time-invariant units cannot be included in the model. Such a specification would indicate that five of the 23 instances of consolidation identified above would be excluded from the analysis. This does not seem logical as these instances should clearly contribute to our analytical understanding of successful budgetary performance. Thus, even if unit heterogeneity cannot be excluded, the estimation of a conditional logit model is not appropriate.[8] Therefore, in the next section we will estimate a BTSCS analysis without fixed effects.

4. Determinants of Budget Consolidation

The previous sections have briefly discussed a variety of theoretical and empirical approaches that can be used to account for cross-national and over-time variance in public policy. The discussion further identified a series of hypotheses derived from these theories that might assist in explaining variance in budgetary performance and, in particular, the occurrence or non-occurrence of budget consolidation. In this section, these hypotheses will be tested by a binary logistic regression empirical analysis (with 1 = a consolidation period). We use this method, as discussed in the previous section, mainly as it enables us to focus on consolidation episodes while at the same time using the entire sample of 23 OECD countries.[9]

Table 3 displays the findings of the regression estimations. Model 1 is a baseline model including only economic variables. In order to control for serial correlation, a number of splines and a counting dummy are added in all estimations (Beck et al. 1998). In models 2–4 we added three different indicators for partisan ideology (right, left, center), a variable for power resources (strike) and different indicators for the institutional arrangements of the countries (veto-player index and some other institutional features). Some variables could not be included simultaneously due to multicollinearity. In model 5 we tested alternative economic indicators (economic

Table 3. Results of the binary logistic regression analysis

	1		2		3		4		5	
Demand index	−0.610*** (0.116)	0.543	−0.598*** (0.120)	0.550	−0.529*** (0.118)	0.589	−0.605*** (0.120)	0.546		
Economic growth									0.539*** (0.089)	1.714
Misery index, $t-1$	0.299*** (0.077)	1.349	0.284*** (0.083)	1.329	0.327*** (0.081)	1.387	0.273*** (0.087)	1.313		
Debt ratio, t									0.030*** (0.006)	1.031
Inflation	−0.250*** (0.056)	0.779	−0.266*** (0.058)	0.766	0.279*** (0.061)	0.757	−0.272*** (0.061)	0.762	−0.215*** (0.058)	0.807
Cabinet seats right-wing parties			−0.008** (0.003)	0.992					−0.015*** (0.004)	0.986
Left party power in government					0.161* (0.085)	1.174				
Cabinet seats centrist parties							0.003 (0.004)	1.003		
Strike index			0.001 (0.001)	1.001						
Veto-player index (encompassing)			−0.243*** (0.092)	0.784					−0.182*** (0.102)	0.834
Federalism					0.021 (0.091)	1.021				
Form of democracy					0.027 (0.132)	1.028				
Corporatism							−0.119 (0.118)	0.888		
Path-dependency social security system					−0.031*** (0.011)	0.970			−0.047*** (0.013)	0.954

(continued)

Table 3. (*Continued*)

	1		2		3		4		5	
Openness of economy							0.005 (0.004)	1.005		
EMU membership							−0.454 (0.322)	0.635		
Spline 1	0.019*** (0.005)	1.019	0.018*** (0.005)	1.019	0.018*** (0.005)	1.019	0.019*** (0.005)	1.019	0.017*** (0.004)	1.017
Spline 2	0.035*** (0.006)	1.036	0.036*** (0.006)	1.036	0.036*** (0.006)	1.036	0.035*** (0.006)	1.036	0.035*** (0.006)	1.035
Spline 3	−0.061*** (0.013)	0.941	−0.060*** (0.013)	0.942	−0.060*** (0.013)	0.941	−0.061*** (0.013)	0.941	−0.056*** (0.011)	0.945
Counting dummy	0.015 (0.041)	1.015	−0.041 (0.045)	0.960	−0.006 (0.044)	0.994	0.031 (0.048)	1.032	−0.016 (0.043)	0.985
Pseudo R^2	0.3549		0.3609		0.3758		0.3664		0.4378	
Correct classification (%)	84.19		83.13		84.57		85.03		87.46	
Nobs	544		504		538		521		574	

Notes: This table shows the coefficients of the logistic regressions (with 1 = a consolidation period). Standard errors in brackets. Odds ratios in the second column of each model. * = 0.10 Significance level, ** = 0.05 Significance level, *** = 0.01 Significance level (two-tailed tests).

growth instead of the demand index, debt ratio instead of the misery index) and included all the variables that proved to be significant in the other estimations.[10]

The findings in Table 3 are interesting in a variety of ways. First, the socio-economic factors have a significant influence on the consolidation probability. Strong economic growth during the consolidation episode is positively associated, whereas a strong demand for social security expenditures (because of rising unemployment or aging population) is negatively related to the probability of a consolidation episode. The marginal effects displayed in Table 4 show that a marginal increase of the demand index from its mean reduces the probability of a consolidation by 3.5 per cent. On the contrary, a marginal increase of economic growth increases the probability by 1.5 per cent. The indicators for socio-economic problems – the misery index and the level of the lagged (by one year) debt ratio – show that governments are more likely to consolidate public finances when they are confronted with economic pressure (marginal effect: 1.2 per cent).[11] This result confirms the theoretical expectations as well as the empirical results of other studies (von Hagen and Strauch 2001; Mulas-Granados 2006). Moreover, high inflation reduces the pressure and therefore makes budget consolidation less likely – the probability falls by 1.2 per cent for a marginal increase of the inflation.

Do parties matter when it comes to budget consolidation policy? The results of the logit analysis suggest a rather weak connection. The odds ratios for the partisan variables as well as the marginal effects (probability decrease of –0.04 per cent for a marginal increase of the share of right-wing parties in cabinet) show only a very weak connection – even if the negative coefficient for right-wing cabinet seats is significant and the coefficient for the power of left-wing parties is positive (and significant) in model 3.[12] The strike index measuring the influence of organized labor on fiscal policy has no effect on the probability that a budget consolidation will occur. Replacing the indicator by a measure of trade union density does not lead to any significant association either. With respect to the institutional variables, we can observe a significant influence of the veto-player index: the more veto players, the smaller the probability of a budget consolidation. Interpreted substantively, the coefficient indicates that a marginal increase of the veto-player index from its mean (3.5) increases the probability of a budget consolidation by 1.1 per cent. This finding is in line with the theory. It suggests that veto players support the status quo, block

Table 4. Marginal effects for the significant variables

Independent variable	Marginal effect
Demand index	–2.6% (2)
Economic growth	+1.1% (5)
Misery index $t-1$	+1.2% (2)
Debt ratio	+0.1% (5)
Inflation	–1.2% (2)
Cabinet seats right-wing parties	–0.04% (2)
Veto player	–1.1% (2)
Path dependency	–0.6% (3)

Note: Increases of the probability of a consolidation for a marginal increase from the mean of the independent variable based on the estimations of model 2, 3 and 5 (in brackets).

policy reforms and thus hinder budget consolidation. No other institutional variables have any significant effects.[13]

The theoretical expectation for the influence of the path dependency of the social security system on budget consolidations is confirmed. Countries where the social insurance principle plays an important role in the social security system (strong path dependency) have a significantly smaller probability of consolidating their public finances. This can be explained by the rights-conferring nature of social contributions. However, the marginal effects show that the impact is rather weak as the probability of a consolidation is reduced by only 0.6 per cent for a marginal increase. In contrast, the analysis offered here demonstrates absolutely no support for the view that open economies are more successful in consolidating their budgets than closed ones. Moreover, neither the run-up to the Economic and Monetary Union (EMU) nor EMU membership are important in terms of consolidation performance.[14]

To sum up, our analysis suggests that strong pressure from problems, institutional arrangements with few veto players, a tax-financed social security system, a lower share of unemployed and seniors in the population, and high economic growth during the consolidation episode increase the chances that a country will consolidate its public finances. Mixed but generally rather weak evidence is found for partisan influence. Overall, the marginal effects show that the impact of the political and institutional variables is rather weak, whereas the demand index plays a more important role. The goodness of fit with a MacFadden $R\hat{o}$ of approximately between 0.3 and 0.4 is acceptable. The classification result shows that more than 80 per cent of the countries are correctly classified in their original groups by the function. The highly significant influence of the counting dummy and the splines suggest that control for autocorrelation was necessary.

5. Strategies for Sustainable Consolidations

Having examined the main factors in public policy research, which are supposed to have an influence on consolidation performance over time and in different countries, we change our focus on the 26 consolidation periods. Therefore, in a next step, we look more closely at different consolidation strategies – for instance, by investigating the composition and timing of consolidations. Moreover, we compare sustainable with non-sustainable consolidation periods (see Table 2).

The first aspect of budget consolidations we were interested in investigating is their composition. Whether consolidations should be revenue-based or expenditure-based and which strategy is the most sustainable in this respect is a matter of debate (Alesina and Perotti 1997; Zaghini 2001; Alesina and Ardagna 2010; IMF 2010). Daily political discussion generally focuses only on the direct short-term effects and notes that you should not "save to the point of harming the economy". For a sustainable consolidation strategy, however, the dynamic and medium- to long-term aspects are crucial (Giavazzi and Pagano 1990, 1996).

One question is whether or not there is a connection between the sustainability of the consolidation and the change of the expenditure ratio (in percentage of GDP) for the 26 consolidation cases identified in Table 5. The findings are clear-cut. First, all consolidators cut their public expenditures more than the benchmark group of all

OECD countries. Second, expenditures decreased much more in the group of sustainable consolidators than in the group of non-sustainable consolidators. Whereas the former reduced their expenditure by around 6.4 percentage points and therefore cut more than twice as much as the OECD during the same period, there is no difference between the mean values of the non-sustainable consolidators and the OECD average. The latter is measured as the average for all 23 OECD countries.

This finding is consistent with results of several previous studies (von Hagen and Strauch 2001; von Hagen et al. 2002; Guichard et al. 2007). A further and obviously complementary question is whether there is a link between the sustainability of consolidations and the change in government revenues, i.e. either a reduction or increase in taxes, contributions and other non-tax revenues. Table 6 shows the average development for all consolidators as well as for the sustainable and non-sustainable consolidation cases separately. The expectation is that consolidations would be particularly likely to be successful where a state ensured stable or growing revenues. However, on average, the opposite turns out to be the case. On average there is virtually no difference between the change of the revenue ratio (i.e. in

Table 5. Development of expenditure ratios within the consolidation episodes

	Change in the expenditure ratio of the consolidators within the consolidation period (= End − Start)	Change in the expenditure ratio of all OECD countries within the same consolidation periods (= End − Start)
Sustainable consolidations (16 cases)	−6.4	−2.7
Non-sustainable consolidation (10 cases)	−2.6	−2.6
Total	−4.9	−2.7

Note: own calculations based on Table 2 and OECD Economic Outlook Data. Data refers to general government.

Table 6. Development of the revenue ratios within the consolidation episodes

	Change in the revenue ratio of the consolidators within the consolidation period (= End − Start)	Change in the revenue ratio of all OECD countries within the same consolidation period (= End − Start)
Sustainable consolidations (16 cases)	−0.2	0.3
Non-sustainable consolidation (10 cases)	1.4	0.2
Total	0.4	0.3

Note: own calculations based on Table 2 and OECD Economic Outlook Data. Revenue Ratio is measured in percentage of GDP and consists of tax and non-tax revenue. Data refers to general government.

percentage of GDP) and the OECD benchmark. In addition, successful consolidations were on average associated with a slight reduction in revenues. However, examining the findings in greater detail shows that this anomalous result is heavily influenced by Irish consolidation from 1993 to 2002. Excluding the outlier Ireland 2 from the analysis suggests that sustainable consolidation is associated with a very modest increase in taxes and contributions of 0.4 percentage points. A similar result is reported in a study by von Hagen and Strauch, who find that total revenues were increased in consolidation episodes, but the increase was lower in successful consolidations than in unsuccessful ones (von Hagen and Strauch 2001: 330).

Thus, the findings displayed in Tables 5 and 6 confirm the results of the existing studies concerning the connection between macro-economic effects and the composition of fiscal adjustments. This is an important finding for robustness as we based our analysis on a very different approach in terms of the definition of a consolidation episode. A third – and more detailed – perspective takes the changes in the composition of public expenditure over time into account. This is possible with the COFOG data (classification of functions of government) that summarizes public expenditure in ten expenditure categories: general public services; defense; public order and safety; economic affairs; environmental protection; housing and community amenities; health; recreation/culture/religion; education; and social protection (see Castles 2007 for a detailed analysis of the COFOG data). While previous studies have usually focused on the economic categorization of spending (transfers, investment, etc.) (e.g. Alesina and Ardagna 1998), using the COFOG data enables us to look at the changes from a different angle. This perspective shows some similarities but also large differences between the consolidators and the non-consolidators. First, expenditure cuts have been larger in the group of consolidators than in the group of non-consolidators except for defense. Second, whereas both groups have made significant expenditure cuts in the areas of general public services, economic affairs (notably subsidies, investment slightly less so) and defense, huge differences in the expenditure profile during the consolidation episodes can be observed, particularly in social spending: the non-consolidators increased their social expenditures by over 20 per cent, while the consolidators have reduced their social spending on average by 1.4 per cent (see also Wagschal and Wenzelburger 2008).

A fourth aspect of consolidation strategies relates to the timing of the consolidations. Are they initiated after major changes in the party complexion of government or are they just as likely to occur at any stage in the life of a government? In response to this question, we examined the starting point for each consolidation government (i.e. the governments in office during the course of the 26 consolidation periods identified in Table 2 – 48 governments in all) and identified how long after a change in the partisan complexion of government a consolidation commenced and how long that consolidation lasted (see Table 7).[15]

The findings are clear: in 22 of the 35 consolidation governments (63 per cent), the consolidations were started at the latest one year after the change of power. Consolidations obviously have a good chance of success if they are carried out soon after a substantial change in the party complexion of government. In this case the period of consolidation is also longer. This finding, which is referred to in the literature as the "honeymoon" effect (Williamson and Haggard 1994), shows that as a consequence of the enhanced legitimacy conferred by election victory, reforms can be implemented more easily and with a higher level of credibility when the parties in government just have changed. For parties in power for a longer period of time, however, the probability of being able to implement radical reforms is drastically reduced. In the final stages of a first legislative period, only a very few reforms are initiated (there are only seven such cases between 1980 and 2005). When the same party is in office for five years or longer, very few consolidations are pursued (six cases). Thus, it seems to be crucial that budget consolidations are carried out soon after a change of government. This frontloading of reforms is important for two reasons. First, the opportunities for policy implementation are increased. Second, the reform governments have a better chance of deriving positive effects from a reform and not getting punished at the ballot box. These results, obtained by means of simple cross-tabulating, confirm the findings of Guichard et al. (2007: 13), who run probit regressions showing that the probability of a start of a consolidation period is increased in election years.

Finally, the political-economic literature links different institutional arrangements to the budget consolidation performance. Generally speaking, the key point of the argument is that strong and stable governments, especially single-party governments, consolidate significantly better than minimal winning coalitions, surplus or minority governments. The reason is that they are less hampered by coalition negotiations and do not have to satisfy as many special interests. Moreover, it is argued that stable governments have more room to maneuver when they are reforming the budget (Persson and Svensson 1989; Roubini and Sachs 1989).

Table 7. Change in the party complexion of government and duration of the consolidation

Time when the consolidation started after the last change in the party complexion of government	Average consolidation period in years	Cases
At the latest 1 year after the change	3.7	22
Between 2 and 4 years after the change	2.7	7
More than 5 years after the change	3.0	6
Average	3.4	35
Total (not including row 1)	(2.8)	(13)

Sources: Authors' calculations and data collection.

Table 8. Success of consolidation and type of government

	Single party government	Minimal winning coalition government	Surplus government	Minority government
Sustainable consolidations (16 cases)	5	2	3	6
Non-sustainable consolidation (10 cases)	3	3	1	3
Total (26 cases)	8	5	4	9

Note: own calculations. Governments are classified by the mode prevailing during a consolidation episode.

In Table 8 we link the different types of governments (measured as the mode during each consolidation episode) to consolidation success. The type of government does not appear to have a significant influence on the consolidation performance. Countries with minority governments like Sweden, Denmark, Norway and New Zealand managed their public finances quite well. This finding is consistent with the analysis of Mierau et al. (2007), who do not find an important influence of political institutions on the adjustment probability, but runs contrary to numerous findings from the analysis of public deficit and debt. All in all, the picture seems to be rather fuzzy when it comes to the influence of political institutions on fiscal policy.[16]

6. What Determines Consolidation Performance Within the Group of Consolidators?

After having investigated general factors influencing consolidation performance in all the OECD countries (section 4) and having displayed descriptive aspects and some more specific features of the consolidation strategies (section 5), the final stage of our analysis seeks to identify the factors influencing consolidation performance within the group of consolidators. As the regressions are based on the 26 consolidation episodes, these findings tell us something about the determinants of "relative" success within this group. In the analysis two dependent variables are used: first, the reduction of public debt within the consolidation episode and, second, the time span of each consolidation episode. Table 9 shows the results.

In regressions 1 and 2, the impact of five independent variables is estimated for the first dependent variable, e.g. the reduction of public debt during the consolidation period. These two models serve as the economic baseline models and consist of mainly economic and budgetary factors. In equations 3 and 4, we added political and institutional variables.[17]

The findings show that the reduction in aggregate public spending measured relatively to the change of aggregate spending of all OECD countries during the same time-span as the consolidation episode has the strongest impact, according to the beta weights (not shown in Table 9). With this kind of measurement we are able to capture the relative effort of the consolidator in comparison to the OECD benchmark, controlling thereby – at least to a certain extent – for global economic fluctuations and the problem of endogeneity. It also turns out that the developments of government revenues are less important. Again, for the reasons mentioned above, government revenues are measured in relation to the development of all OECD countries. Regressions 1 to 3 therefore reveal that increasing government income is not as effective as a retrenchment of government spending, supporting the descriptive findings of Tables 5 and 6. The controversy over whether tax increases or spending cuts are most effective can be answered on the basis of these results: both measures are of assistance – however spending cuts are more beneficial (see above).

Furthermore, the duration of a consolidation period is a strong predictor of the success of a consolidation. Long perseverance is the second key factor for consolidators. In conjunction with the descriptive finding of a "honeymoon effect", the lesson is that governments should start their consolidation immediately after taking office and should keep it up as long as possible.

The pressure arising from high public debt (in percentage of GDP) displays a (rather weak) small significant impact. When problems are not pressing enough,

Table 9. Determinants of consolidation performance in 26 consolidation episodes

	(1) Δ gross public debt during consolidation period	(2)[c] Δ gross public debt during consolidation period	(3) Δ gross public debt during consolidation period	(4)[c] Δ gross public debt during consolidation period	(5) Duration of consolidation (years)	(6)[d] Duration of consolidation (years)
Constant	-4.93 (4.71)	-4.94 (4.81)	-8.08 (6.06)	-6.71 (6.45)	0.62 (1.94)	0.72 (1.63)
Difference of general government expenditures to the average of OECD countries[e]	-1.55*** (0.27)	-1.40*** (0.49)	-1.46*** (0.25)	-1.05*** (0.38)		
Difference of general government revenues to the average of OECD countries[e]	1.17** (0.53)	0.85 (0.99)	1.15** (0.49)	—[f]		
Gross public debt at the beginning of consolidation	0.11* (0.06)	0.12* (0.06)	0.07 (0.06)	0.09 (0.06)	0.04 (0.02)**	0.03 (0.01)**
Duration of consolidation (years)	2.17*** (0.64)	2.01** (0.77)	2.64*** (0.58)	2.20*** (0.63)		
Partisan complexion of government (1 to 5)[a]			1.21 (0.83)	1.37 (0.87)	0.30 (0.29)	0.32 (0.25)
Strength of government (1 to 4, 1 = single party gov.)			-0.26 (1.31)	-0.97 (1.32)	0.51 (0.41)	0.34 (0.35)
Federalism–unitarism score according to Lijphart (1999)			-3.43** (1.43)	-3.30** (1.52)	0.42 (0.43)	0.26 (0.37)
Fiscal rules (additive Index based on OECD 2009b)			0.38 (1.04)	0.56 (1.08)	-0.26 (0.32)	-0.16 (0.27)

(continued)

Table 9. (*Continued*)

	(1) Δ gross public debt during consolidation period	(2)[c] Δ gross public debt during consolidation period	(3) Δ gross public debt during consolidation period	(4)[c] Δ gross public debt during consolidation period	(5) Duration of consolidation (years)	(6)[d] Duration of consolidation (years)
Misery index[b] at start of consolidation			−1.07 (0.71)	−1.38 (0.77)		
Change of misery index in the OECD during consolidation episodes[e]					0.69*** (0.20)	1.19*** (0.24)
Adj. R^2	0.758	0.487	0.814	0.586	0.344	0.551
F-statistics	20.53	6.69	13.17	5.25	3.18	4.93
N	26	25	26	25	26	25

Notes: This table shows the coefficients of the OLS-regressions. Standard errors in brackets. * = 0.10 Significance level, ** = 0.05 Significance level, *** = 0.01 Significance level (two-tailed tests). a: 1 = Bourgeois hegemony, 2 = Bourgeois dominance, 3 = Balance, 4 = Left-wing party dominance, 5 = Left-wing party hegemony (see Schmidt 1992). Hegemony means the share of cabinet seats equals 100% per cent. Dominance means the share of cabinet seats ranges from greater than 66.6% to less than 100%. Balance means that both tendencies have cabinet shares greater than 33.3% and equal to or less than 66.6%. The calculations are based on yearly data. b = unemployment rate + inflation rate − growth rate; c = without Ireland 2; d = without United Kingdom 2; e = measured for each consolidation period separately; f = this variable is skipped due to very high multicollinearity (VIF > 4.0).

governments seem not to have too much interest in starting a consolidation. Alternatively (not displayed in Table 9 due to multicollinearity), it turned out that the magnitude of the public deficit just before the consolidation is also a relevant explanatory factor. These results are in line with the finding for the entire OECD sample in section 3 (influence of pressure from problems).

Robustness checks revealed a strong impact, especially in one case: Ireland 2. Because of high leverage values we skipped this case in regressions 2 and 4. The effects in regression 2 are considerable: the adjusted Rô dropped substantially and one of the independent variables, the change of revenues during the consolidation period (in relation to the OECD benchmark), became insignificant.

Supplementing what is at this point an essentially economistic model with political and institutional variables (see regressions 3 and 4), we are only able to improve the explanatory power of the model slightly. Within the group of consolidators, the partisan complexion of government – the core variable for partisan theory (Castles 1982) – is irrelevant. It should be noted that the strength of government (in other words, the fragmentation of the government) is also insignificant in all models, though this variable is prominent in theories dealing with the accumulation of public debt (Roubini and Sachs 1989; Perotti and Kontopoluos 2002; Ricciuti 2004).

Lijphart's (1999) federalism–unitarism score, which correlates highly with a dummy for federal states, is used as a proxy for the impact of federalism. In line with the reasoning of the regional fragmentation argument, federal consolidators performed comparatively worse, although qualitative evidence has also suggested that some federal states were able to shift consolidation costs to the sub-national level (for instance in Belgium and Canada). In general, it seems that federal states have problems with fixing all levels of a state to one common consolidation strategy.[18]

Budget institutions are currently among the most prominent variables discussed in the literature on public finances (von Hagen 1992; Hallerberg and von Hagen 1999; Hallerberg 2003; Wehner 2006; Hallerberg et al. 2009). Therefore we included an indicator measuring the use of debt and deficit rules in the regression analyses. We used data from the OECD budget database (except the fiscal revenue rules) and constructed an index ranging from 1 to 4 (membership euro area, existence of an expenditure, balanced budget and public debt rule) (OECD 2009b: 87). We hypothesize that such rules will favor budget consolidation. Other indicators such as the delegation index of Hallerberg et al. (2009)[19] and Wehner's (2006) index of legislative budget institutions were used as well. While the three indices measure budgetary institutions and fiscal rules from different perspectives, their influence still remains insignificant.

Additionally, the IMF (2007, 2011; Kopits and Symansky 1998) and the European Union (European Commission 2009) use their own fiscal rules indices. The fiscal rule strength index (FRSI) from the EU measures several characteristics within the institutional framework of budgetary policy. It captures five different areas of budgetary politics: (i) the statutory base of the rule; (ii) room for setting or revising its objectives; (iii) the body in charge of monitoring respect and enforcement of the rule; (iv) the enforcement mechanisms relating to the rule; and (v) the media visibility of the rule. For comparative reasons the EU is calculating a standardized fiscal rules index (FRI; see Figure 1), with low values indicating a weak institutional barrier.

Figure 1. Consolidation efforts and fiscal rules (2001–2009)

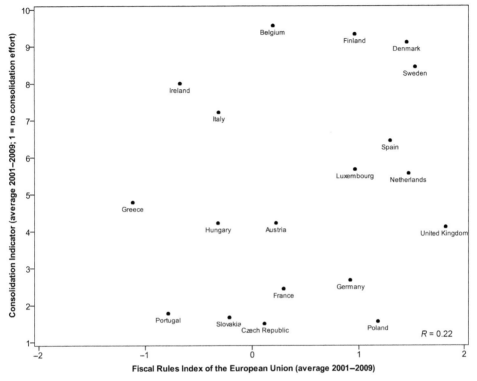

Source: Authors' own calculations and data collection. For a detailed definition of the consolidation indicator see Wagschal et al. (2009: 55). Data for the fiscal rules index is from the European Union (European Commission 2009).

Obviously the number and spread of fiscal rules has increased over the past 20 years. However, the association of this fiscal rules index with consolidation efforts is also weak when looking at bivariate correlations. For this purpose we constructed a 10-point scale indicator going from 1 (no consolidation) to 10 (high level of consolidation), on the basis of the development of the primary deficit and the public debt (Wagschal et al. 2009: 55). We also included the above definition for sustainable (i.e. successful) consolidations. As there is only data for the fiscal rules index for 19 European countries, we are restricted to this smaller sample. Looking at the averages for both variables for the overall period 2001–2009, it is shown that fiscal rules are not particularly important for consolidation efforts, which supports our multivariate findings. The correlation coefficient is only $r = 0.22$, indicating a very weak association.

Finally, the economic pressure for reforms, measured by a so-called "misery index" at the beginning of a consolidation episode, is not a significant predictor of debt reduction. This is somewhat surprising as the debt ratio as well as the initial budget deficit did have an impact and because pressure from problems was one of the major explanatory variables in the analysis of the entire OECD sample (section 3). The second dependent variable is the duration of consolidation measured in years. Regressions 5 and 6 in Table 9 display the results of a multivariate model with socio-economic, political and institutional explanatory factors. Again, partisan complexion, the strength of government, federalism and fiscal rules exhibit no influence. Only two variables turned out to be significant: (1) the level of the public debt at the beginning of the consolidation process and, more importantly, (2) the change in the misery index during the consolidation episode within the entire OECD. In Table 9, it appears that the key factor for the duration of reforms is the improvement of macro-economic conditions. However, due to endogeneity, the causality (and the estimation) remains to be discussed. First, the consolidation might be carried forward because governments harvest the success of their reforms in terms of lower unemployment and higher economic growth, due to the so-called "non-Keynesian" effects of consolidation. Second, the improvement of the fiscal stance could be interpreted as a result of the exogenous reduction of the misery index, which enables governments to consolidate further. Again, one case shows high leverage values in regression 5: United Kingdom 2. The effects of a re-estimation are displayed in regression 6, with a higher adjusted $R\hat{o}$, but no real difference for the significant variables (except the higher significance level) appears.

7. Conclusions

This study has analyzed budget consolidations quantitatively from a variety of perspectives. It included (1) a binary logistic regression analysis of the consolidation probability for 23 OECD countries, (2) a descriptive analysis of specific features of successful consolidations and (3) an analysis of the factors explaining the consolidation performance within the groups of consolidators.

After having discussed some measurement issues, it was shown for the first approach that "demand factors", such as the development of the unemployment rate and the share of elderly in the population, are of particular influence in accounting for consolidation performance. A higher demand for social expenditure from the unemployed and the elderly makes budget consolidation more difficult. The opposite is true for economic growth: high economic growth facilitates budget consolidation considerably. A second important factor is the problems with which governments must cope. The higher the initial debt burden, the interest rate and the unemployment rate in the year before the start of a consolidation period, the more probable a budget consolidation becomes. This result is very much in line with previous studies – which is interesting as our definition of consolidation episodes differs considerably from the "traditional" approach in the literature. Moreover, high inflation reduces the problem load and therefore decreases the probability of a consolidation. When it comes to party effects, the evidence is weak. Although we find a small negative influence of right-wing parties on consolidation performance, the result is not robust and the influence rather small. The same finding applies to the strength of government and the strength of organized labor. In contrast, the number of veto players in a country does affect the probability of a consolidation. A marginal increase of institutional constraints makes consolidations less likely (1.1 per cent). Interpreted in the light of the existing body of empirical studies, this result is promising as it shows that it is not only the economic variables that matter. As other institutional variables, such as federalism or corporatism, do not show any significant influence it seems safe to say that the operationalization of the institutional setting plays an important role. The veto player approach, which summarizes different institutional arrangements, captures the status quo bias of many constraints better than the inclusion of each institutional feature by means of a specific indicator. Finally, the path dependency of the social security system does make a difference when it comes to budget consolidations. Where the insurance principle has a strong role within the social security system, this serves as a constraint on budget consolidation. This is to be explained by the fact that in an insurance-based social security system, cuts are harder to implement as the social contributions can be considered to be "social rights".

The second step of the empirical analysis focused on some particular aspects of what may be described as "consolidation strategies". The analysis demonstrated a number of successful strategies. Expenditure reductions seem to lead to more sustainable consolidations whereas revenue increases are not essential. As this result is obtained based on a very different definition than in the existing literature, the hotly debated hypothesis of Alesina and Ardgana (2010) seems to be robust. Going into more detail, the analysis of the COFOG data revealed that successful consolidators cut expenditure relatively more strongly – especially on social security and health. Furthermore, the analysis showed that reforms should be implemented as early as possible at the start of a legislative period in order to take advantage of the "honey-moon" effect and to allow the reforms to produce positive effects during the legislative period. This supports the empirical results obtained by Guichard et al. (2007).

Which variables explain the different consolidation performance for countries that have carried out budget consolidations? This question is examined in the third step of the quantitative analysis. The dependent variables are the development of the debt ratio and the duration of the consolidation episodes. The results of the analysis show that most of the political and institutional variables do not play a role, and that the economic factors which proved to be influential in the first step of the analysis are considerably more important in accounting for relative performance. The only exception is federalism, which seems to impede consolidations. Surprisingly, fiscal rules seem to have virtually no impact on consolidation efforts.

Some caveats are to be mentioned. First, the findings are influenced by research design. If one examines all OECD countries, veto players make a difference when it comes to budget consolidations, but within the group of the consolidators, the effect vanishes. Second, the results suggest that the politics of budget consolidation are quite complex. Causal factors can be identified when one looks at the evidence from one perspective, but changing the point of view affects the results. Moreover, qualitative evidence indicates that different countries follow very different roads in order to balance their budgets. Third, the conclusions drawn in this paper cannot necessarily serve as a blueprint for the current situation of ballooning deficits. The actual budgetary crisis in many countries is deeper than it was in the 1980s and 1990s. Moreover, the recession and the financial crisis have a much bigger global reach than the recessions in the beginning of the 1980s and 1990s. However, we think that at least the political logic is comparable. Cutting deficits is, at any rate, politically difficult. In the light of the results of this study, one could even argue that governments are currently in a better position for bringing their fiscal houses back in order than in the

1990s. As the problem load is higher than throughout the 1980s and 1990s, the awareness of governments and citizens that fiscal adjustments are necessary should facilitate the implementation of consolidation measures. This brings us to a last point: during the 1990s, successful budget consolidation was in many countries connected to political personalities and a certain leadership quality. Such consolidators were either heads of government or ministers of finance. Names like Göran Persson, Paavo Lipponen, Wim Kok, Margaret Thatcher, Roger Douglas or Paul Martin have become synonymous with successful consolidations. In order to overcome the actual budgetary crisis in many developed countries, leadership, political strategy and communication skills will again be of prime importance.

Notes

1. The following OECD countries were analyzed in this study: Australia, Belgium, Denmark, Germany, Finland, France, Greece, UK, Ireland, Iceland, Italy, Japan, Canada, Luxembourg, New Zealand, the Netherlands, Norway, Austria, Portugal, Sweden, Switzerland, Spain and the USA. As a result of missing data, the number of cases may be lower for partial assessments. All statements in this article refer to the time period prior to 2006, usually the period from 1980 to 2005. This time frame is due to availability of comparable data. Extending the observation period to 1970 would have resulted in a smaller sample. As cross-national variance is more important here than temporal variance, we opted for a larger sample and a somewhat shorter observation period. For all OECD countries the average public debt reached its maximum in 1998 with 74.2 per cent of GDP. The highest public debt level ever can be observed in 2011 with an average debt level of 102.4 per cent of GDP for all OECD countries.
2. Evidently, the actual situation after the financial crisis is different from the state of affairs in the 1990s in many other respects – e.g. the monetary policy stance, the level of international interdependence of economies and financial markets. However, it seems plausible that the political logic that lies behind the politics of fiscal consolidation is quite comparable. Two examples: Fiscal adjustments were a difficult task for governments in the 1990s – and they are still difficult today. The necessity to consolidate was high in the 1990s – and remains so today.
3. So far there has only been a very limited number of comparative studies focusing on consolidation episodes (Heylen and Everaert 2000; Guichard et al. 2007).
4. In a recent study, the IMF criticizes the existing literature – and more specifically the last contribution of Alesina and Ardagna (2010) – for the use of cyclically adjusted deficits (IMF 2010: 96): "The change in the CAPB-to-GDP ratio is an unreliable guide regarding the presence of fiscal consolidation. The standard approach tends to select periods associated with favorable outcomes but during which no austerity measures were actually taken. It also tends to omit cases of fiscal austerity with unfavorable outcomes."
5. In his book on fiscal adjustment, the TSCS analysis of Mulas-Granados is just one of several methods of investigation (hazard models, probit regressions, etc.).
6. A common abbreviation is BTSCS analysis (binary time series cross-sectional analysis) (Beck et al. 1998).
7. Even in the linear case, the methodological debate concerning the correct "remedy" for the different problems linked to the analysis of panel data still continues (e.g. on fixed effects models) (Maddala 1998; Plümper and Troeger 2007).
8. That is the reason why Beck and Katz categorically reject the use of fixed effects (or conditional regression) in a BTSCS analysis: "We show that the use of fixed effects is clearly a bad idea for the binary dependent variable case" (Beck and Katz 2001: 488).
9. For technical details, see the methods section above. For a formal statement of the model, see the paper by Beck et al. (1998).
10. Again, the alternative specification was necessary in order to avoid multicollinearity.
11. Deconstructing the misery index into its components yields the following result (estimation on the basis of model 2): a high lagged unemployment level and a high debt ratio increase the probability of a consolidation significantly, whereas a high short-term interest rate reduces the probability of a consolidation. Thus, while the results for unemployment and debt show the expected direction, the level of interest rates does not. This can be due to an endogeneity problem (consolidation measures might reduce

the level of interest rates), although the time lag was introduced to control for these problems. However, and most importantly, the interpretation of all the other variables does not change when replacing the misery index by its components. We thank the anonymous reviewer for pointing out this problem.
12. In addition, a jackknife analysis of model 2 shows that the result is not robust when excluding the US (the coefficient is no longer significant). The results of the jackknife analysis can be made available upon request.
13. The same result is found when replacing some of the institutional variables with alternative indicators (e.g. including fiscal decentralization instead of federalism).
14. The EMU variable takes the value 1 for EMU members and 0 for non-EMU members. The coding starts in 1992 when the run-up to the EMU started. Alternatively, a dummy only for the run-up was included – without significant influence. The same applies for a third version of the EMU indicator simulating the increased pressure of the EMU run-up taking yearly increasing values starting with 1 in 1992 and ending at 6 in 1997.
15. Excluding from the assessment those successor governments that merely continued a consolidation reduces the number of cases from 48 to 35.
16. However, institutions do matter for effective consolidation strategies. Consolidators often shifted their budget process from a "bottom-up" to a "top-down" model. The pioneering work by Jürgen von Hagen (1992) and subsequently by Hallerberg and von Hagen (1999), Hallerberg (2003) and Hallerberg et al. (2009) focused on the importance of budget institutions in the individual countries. In the consolidation process it is important whether a country follows a so-called "delegations" or a "commitment" approach. Typically, majority systems concentrate more on the delegations approach, which includes a strengthening of the position of the minister of finance, than countries that are organized on the basis of a consensus democracy. Successful consolidators, according to data from von Hagen (1992), von Hagen and Strauch (2001) and Hallerberg (2003), reformed their budget institutions substantially. Especially countries like Canada and Italy strengthened the "delegations institutions", while Belgium and the Netherlands went for a commitment strategy, and some countries such as Sweden choose a mixed strategy (Wagschal and Wenzelburger 2008).
17. We also tested EU membership and a dummy variable for the Maastricht effect. Both variables turned out to be insignificant.
18. Obviously, this result can also be explained with a veto-player argument.
19. The authors collected data for only 16 countries.

References

Alesina, A. and Ardagna, S., 1998, Tales of fiscal adjustment. Why they can be expansionary. *Economic Policy*, **13**, pp. 488–545.
Alesina, A. and Ardagna, S., 2010, Large changes in fiscal policy: Taxes versus spending. *Tax Policy and the Economy*, **24**, pp. 35–68.
Alesina, A. and Perotti, R., 1995, The political economy of budget deficits. *IMF Staff Papers*, **42**, pp. 1–31.
Alesina, A. and Perotti, R., 1996, Reducing budget deficits. *Swedish Economic Policy Review*, **3**, pp. 113–134.
Alesina, A. and Perotti, R., 1997, Fiscal adjustments in OECD countries: Composition and macroeconomic effects. *IMF Staff Papers*, **44**, pp. 210–248.
Beck, N. and Katz, J., 2001, Throwing out the baby with the bath water: A comment on Green, Kim, and Yoon. *International Organization*, **55**, pp. 487–495.
Beck, N., Katz, J. and Tucker, R., 1998, Taking time seriously: Time-series-cross-section analysis with a binary dependent variable. *American Journal of Political Science*, **42**, pp. 1260–1288.
Brandner, P., 2003, Budgetpolitik der Niederlande, Finnlands und Schwedens – Lehre für nachhaltige Konsolidierungen? *Wirtschaftspolitische Blätter*, **50**, pp. 183–204.
Brennan, G. and Buchanan, J., 1980, *The Power to Tax: Analytical Foundations of a Fiscal Constitution* (Cambridge: Cambridge University Press).
Castles, F. G., 1982, The impact of parties on public expenditure, in: F. G. Castles (Ed.) *The Impact of Parties: Politics and Policies in Democratic Capitalist States* (London: Sage), pp. 21–96.
Castles, F. G., 2007, *The Disappearing State? Retrenchment Realities in an Age of Globalisation* (Cheltenham: Edward Elgar).

Chamberlain, G., 1980, Analysis of covariance with qualitative data. *Review of Economic Studies*, **47**, pp. 225–238.
European Commission, 2009, Public finances in EMU 2009, Directorate-General for Economic and Financial Affairs, European Economy 5/2009, Brussels.
Giavazzi, F. and Pagano, M., 1990 Can severe fiscal contractions be expansionary? Tales of two small European countries, in: O. J. Blanchard and S. Fischer (Eds) *National Bureau of Economic Research. Macroeconomics Annual 1990* (Cambridge, MA: MIT Press), pp. 75–122.
Giavazzi, F. and Pagano, M., 1996, Non-Keynesian effects of fiscal policy changes. International evidence and the Swedish experience. *Swedish Economic Policy Review*, 3, pp. 67–103.
Girouard, N. and André, C., 2005, Measuring cyclically-adjusted budget balances for OECD countries. OECD Economics Department Working Papers No. 434, OECD Publishing.
Guichard, S., Kennedy, M., Wurzel, E. and André, C., 2007, What promotes fiscal consolidation: OECD country experiences. OECD Economic Department Working Papers, 553 (OECD Publishing).
Hallerberg, M., 2003, Budgeting in Europe: Did the domestic budget process change after Maastricht? Paper prepared for the 2003 EUSA Conference, Nashville, TN.
Hallerberg, M. and von Hagen, J., 1999, Electoral institutions, cabinet negotiations, and budget deficits within the European Union, in: J. Poterba and J. von Hagen (Eds) *Fiscal Institutions and Fiscal Performance* (Chicago: University of Chicago Press), pp. 209–232.
Hallerberg, M., Strauch, R. and von Hagen, J., 2009, *Fiscal Governance in Europe* (Cambridge: Cambridge University Press).
Heylen, F. and Everaert, G., 2000, Success and failure of fiscal consolidation in the OECD: A multivariate analysis. *Public Choice*, **105**, pp. 103–124.
Hibbs, D. A., 1977, Political parties and macroeconomic policy. *The American Political Science Review*, **71**, pp. 1467–1487.
International Monetary Fund (IMF), 2007, Manual on Fiscal Transparency (Washington, DC: IMF).
International Monetary Fund (IMF), 2010, Recovery, Risk, and Rebalancing, IMF World Economic Outlook October 2010 (Washington, DC: IMF).
International Monetary Fund (IMF), 2011, Fiscal Monitor September 2011. Addressing Fiscal Challenges to Reduce Economic Risk (Washington, DC: IMF).
Kitschelt, H., 2001, Partisan competition and welfare state retrenchment. When do politicians choose unpopular politics?, in: P. Pierson (Ed.) *The New Politics of the Welfare State* (Oxford and New York: Oxford University Press), pp. 265–302.
Kopits, G. and Symansky, S., 1998, Fiscal rules. IMF Occasional Paper 162, Washington, DC.
Korpi, W., 1980, Social policy and distributional conflict in the capitalist democracies. *West European Politics*, 3, pp. 296–316.
Larch, M. and Salto, M., 2003, Fiscal rules, inertia and discretionary fiscal policy. European Economy – Economic Papers No. 194.
Lassen, D. D., 2010, *Fiscal Consolidation in Advanced Industrialized Democracies: Economics, Politics, and Governance. Rapport till finanspolitiska rådet* (Stockholm: Finanspolitiska rådet).
Lijphart, A., 1999, *Patterns of Democracy* (New Haven, CT and London: Yale University Press).
Maddala, G. S., 1998, Recent developments in dynamic econometric modelling: A personal viewpoint. *Political Analysis*, 7, pp. 59–87.
Maroto Illera, R. and Mulas-Granados, C., 2008, What makes fiscal consolidations last? A survival analysis of budget cuts in Europe (1960–2004). *Public Choice*, **134**, pp. 147–161.
Mierau, J. O., Jong-A-Pin, R. and de Haan, J., 2007, Do political variables affect fiscal policy adjustment decisions? New empirical evidence. *Public Choice*, **133**, pp. 297–319.
Mink, M. and de Haan, J., 2006, Are there political budget cycles in the euro area? *European Union Politics*, 7, pp. 191–211.
Mulas-Granados, C. 2004, Voting against spending cuts: The electoral cost of fiscal adjustments in Europe. *European Union Politics*, 5, pp. 467–493.
Mulas-Granados, C., 2006, *Economics, Politics and Budgets. The Political Economy of Fiscal Consolidations in Europe* (Basingstoke and New York: Palgrave-MacMillan).
Oates, W. E., 1972, *Fiscal Federalism* (New York: Harcourt Brace Jovanovich).
Obinger, H., Leibfried, S. and Castles, F. (Eds), 2005, *Federalism and the Welfare State: New World and European Experiences* (Cambridge: Cambridge University Press).
OECD, 2005, *Central Government Debt: Statistical Yearbook 1994–2003* (Paris: OECD).

OECD, 2009a, *OECD Economic Outlook 85* (Paris: OECD).
OECD, 2009b, *Government at a Glance* (Paris: OECD).
Perotti, R. and Kontopoulos, Y., 2002, Fragmented fiscal policy. *Journal of Public Economics*, **86**, pp. 191–202.
Persson, T. and Svensson, L. E. O., 1989, Why a stubborn conservative would run a deficit: Policy with time-inconsistent preferences. *Quarterly Journal of Economics*, **104**, pp. 325–346.
Plümper, T. and Troeger, V., 2007, Efficient estimation of time-invariant and rarely changing variables in finite sample panel analyses with unit fixed effects. *Political Analysis*, **15**, pp. 124–139.
Ricciuti, R., 2004, Political fragmentation and fiscal outcomes. *Public Choice*, **118**, pp. 365–388.
Rose, R. and Karran, T., 1987, *Taxation by Political Inertia. Financing the Growth of Government in Britain* (London: Allen & Unwin).
Ross, F. A., 2000, "Beyond left and right": The new partisan politics of welfare. *Governance*, **13**, pp. 155–184.
Roubini, N. and Sachs, J. D., 1989, Political and economic determinants of budget deficits in the industrial democracies. *European Economic Review*, **33**, pp. 903–938.
Sachverständigenrat zur Begutachtung der gesamtwirtschaftlichen Entwicklung (SVR), 2003, Staatsfinanzen konsolidieren – Steuersystem reformieren. Jahresgutachten 2003/04, Sachverständigenrat zur Begutachtung der Gesamtwirtschaftlichen Entwicklung, Wiesbaden: Statistisches Bundesamt.
Schmidt, M. G., 1982, *Wohlfahrtsstaatliche Politik unter bürgerlichen und sozialdemokratischen Regierungen. Ein internationaler Vergleich* (Frankfurt a.M. and New York: Campus).
Schmidt, M. G., 1992, Regierungen: parteipolitische Zusammensetzung, in: M. G. Schmidt (Ed.) *Lexikon der Politik, Band 3, Die westlichen Länder* (München: Beck), pp. 393–400.
Schmidt, M. G., 1996, When parties matter: A Review of the possibilities and limits of partisan influence on public policy. *European Journal of Political Research*, **30**, pp. 155–183.
Schmidt, M. G., 2000, Die sozialpolitischen Nachzüglerstaaten und die Theorien der vergleichenden Staatstätigkeitsforschung, in: H. Obinger and U. Wagschal (Eds) *Der gezügelte Wohlfahrtsstaat* (Frankfurt a.M. and New York: Campus), pp. 22–36.
Siegel, N. A., 2002, *Baustelle Sozialpolitik. Konsolidierung und Rückbau im internationalen Vergleich* (Frankfurt a.M. and New York: Campus).
Tsebelis, G., 1995, Decision making in political systems: Veto players in presidentialism, parliamentarism, multicameralism and multipartyism. *British Journal of Political Science*, **25**, pp. 289–325.
Tsebelis, G., 2002, *Veto Players: How Political Institutions Work* (Princeton, NJ: Princeton University Press).
Verbeek, M., 2004, *A Guide to Modern Econometrics* (Baffins Lane: John Wiley).
Von Hagen, J., 1992, *Budgeting Procedures and Fiscal Performance in the European Communities*, DG II Economic Papers 96 (Brussels: European Commission).
Von Hagen, J. and Strauch, R., 2001, Fiscal consolidations: Quality, economic conditions, and success. *Public Choice*, **109**, pp. 327–346.
Von Hagen, J., Hallett, A. H. and Strauch, R., 2002, Budgetary consolidation in Europe: Quality, economic conditions, and persistence. *Journal of the Japanese and International Economies*, **16**, pp. 512–535.
Wagschal, U., 1996, *Staatsverschuldung. Ursachen im internationalen Vergleich* (Opladen: Leske and Budrich).
Wagschal, U. and Wenzelburger, G., 2008, *Successful Budget Consolidation. An International Comparison* (Gütersloh: Bertelsmann Foundation).
Wagschal, U., Wenzelburger, G., Metz, T. and Jäckel, T., 2009, *Konsolidierungsstrategien der Bundesländer* (Gütersloh: Bertelsmann Foundation).
Wenzelburger, G., 2009, The analysis of budget consolidations: Concepts, research designs and measurement. *Journal for Economic and Social Measurement*, **34** (4), pp. 269–291.
Weingast, B. R., Shepsle, K. A. and Johnson, C., 1981, The political economy of benefits and costs: A neoclassical approach to distributive politics. *Journal of Political Economy*, **89**, pp. 642–664.
Wehner, J., 2006, Assessing the power of the purse: An index of legislative budget institutions. *Political Studies*, **54**, pp. 767–785.
Wildavsky, A., 1964, *The Politics of the Budgetary Process* (Boston: Brown).
Williamson, J. and Haggard, S., 1994, The political conditions for economic reform, in: J. Williamson (Ed.) *The Political Economy of Policy Reform* (Washington, DC: Institute for International Economics), pp. 527–596.
Wolf, F., 2006, *Die Bildungsausgaben der Bundesländer im Vergleich. Welche Faktoren erklären ihre beträchtliche Variation?* (Münster: LIT-Verlag).
Zaghini, A., 2001, Fiscal adjustments and economic performance: A comparative study. *Applied Economics*, **33**, pp. 613–624.

Europeanization, Policy Learning, and New Modes of Governance

CLAUDIO M. RADAELLI

ABSTRACT *Can a learning-based mode of governance, specifically the Open Method of Coordination (OMC), facilitate Europeanization? The argument is that, in policy areas where the Treaty base for European Union policy is thin or non-existent or where diverging political views hinder the development of law, modes of governance based on Council's guidelines, the co-ordination of national action plans, peer review of reforms, systematic benchmarking, performance indicators, and governance processes open to the regional-local level and the civil society produce convergence towards the EU goals and ultimately Europeanization without the need to create new EU legislation. By comparing evidence from the most mature OMC processes, this article finds that the relationship between learning, policy change, and Europeanization can break down at several points, and that evidence of learning is limited. This is due to deficiencies in the design of the OMC, the lack of participation, and the political/institutional complexities of learning in the EU context.*

Introduction

One of the most important dimensions of Europeanization (Olsen 2002) is the domestic impact of the European Union. From a comparative public policy perspective, this dimension lends itself quite naturally to the appraisal of the impact of the EU on different policies in different countries (Börzel and Risse 2003; Radaelli 2003a; see also the Introduction to this special issue). One classic way to examine Europeanization "as domestic impact of the EU" is to analyze compliance and implementation – for example by looking at the transposition of directives and compliance with EU rules.

The EU, however, is also experimenting with modes of governance that are not based on law and hierarchy. The rationale for these new modes of governance is the following. In policies where the Treaty base for EU competence is thin or non-existent (e.g., higher education and the fight against poverty) or where diverging interests of the member states make agreement on proposed EU legislation impossible (e.g., some labor market reforms), modes of governance based on Council guidelines, peer pressure, benchmarking sensitive to the institutional context, iterative processes of monitoring and indicators can lead the member states to an efficient co-ordination of reforms and thus produce Europeanization.

The mechanism that is supposed to bring about Europeanization is learning. If learning is actually produced via new governance – the argument goes on – this can result in deep Europeanization in terms of convergence with the "growth and jobs" objectives of the so-called Lisbon strategy for competitiveness. Additionally, learning-based governance can avoid the limitations of excessive judicialization, formality, and adversarial legalism.

Of course, these are abstract arguments, arguably more idealistic than ideal-typical (Idema and Kelemen 2006). But, at least at a high level of abstraction, how can the case for learning-based Europeanization be made? The answer lies in Europeanization processes fuelled by a creative combination of "learning by socialization", "learning by monitoring", and "learning by arguing and persuasion". Socialization processes make policy makers more aware of their interdependence, and can inspire more commitment towards EU-level goals. Monitoring enables the EU institutions to keep track of progress and to compare what has been achieved by the 27 member states, individually and as a whole. Although the literature has shown that monitoring can also hinder learning (Sabel 1994), the assumption is that open co-ordination can encourage learning by discussions of indicators, national plans, and peer review. Finally, arguing and persuasion contribute to the refinement of guidelines, timetables, and goals. Most importantly, they are the preconditions for changes of policy preferences. Democratic experimentalism (Cohen and Sabel 1997, Eberlein and Kerwer 2004, Sabel and Zeitlin 2006) – the argument concludes – fosters a re-orientation of policy paradigms.

As mentioned, this learning-based mode of governance has been identified with the Open Method of Coordination (OMC) launched by the Lisbon European Council of March 2000. Five years down the road to the 2010 target, the EU carried out a major mid-term review of Lisbon, prepared by a report collated by a group of experts chaired by the former Dutch Prime Minister Wim Kok. In the aftermath of the Kok report and the mid-term review, the disillusionment with the open method of co-ordination has been at least as great as the disenchantment with the Lisbon vision. The Kok Report (2004: 42) noted that "the open method of coordination has fallen short of expectations. If member states do not enter the spirit of mutual benchmarking, little or nothing happens". Thus, the report has an explanation of why the method has not delivered: member states are not committed to its "spirit" (whatever that may mean). The suggestion has been to encourage more ownership of the method at the level of the member states, by streamlining reporting, indicators, and by focusing on a limited number of politically important targets.

This has led the Commission and the Council to a redefinition of the Lisbon strategy (Commission 2005a, Council 2005) based on "a new cycle of governance" (Commission 2005b: 2) in which "the open method of coordination can be a powerful instrument to assist member states in their effort to adopt a more strategic and horizontal approach and to deliver more efficient policies, as well as involve and mobilize stakeholders and to promote exchange of good practice" (Commission 2005b: 5).

So, notwithstanding the negative findings of the mid-term review of the Lisbon strategy, the EU is still committed to open co-ordination, albeit in a "re-launched", "simplified", and "streamlined" form. One of the principles of the new governance cycle announced by the Commission is a stronger partnership between the EU and the member states in the context of mutual learning (across the member states, and between governments and EU institutions). Learning is therefore presented in official documents as an essential component of EU governance.

Empirically, it is difficult to trace the causal link between learning and policy change – considering that it is often impossible "to observe the learning activity in isolation from the change requiring explanation" (Bennett and Howlett 1992: 290) and that there are different types of change (Hall 1993, Rose 1993). Bearing these challenges in mind, this article looks at learning in the Open Method of Coordination. By comparing policy areas in which the OMC is being used systematically, this article sheds light on the internal contradictions of open co-ordination. By reviewing empirical studies, it finds that there is some evidence of learning at the top (or "EU-level learning"), embryonic evidence of cognitive convergence driven by the top (or "hierarchical learning"), and almost no evidence of learning from below ("bottom-up learning" or "social learning").

Of course, there are also limitations in the analysis presented here. The article does not engage with different definitions and approaches to Europeanization – as mentioned, we take the "domestic impact of the EU" approach off the shelf and do not discuss the others. Neither do we compare the OMC to other modes of governance (see Bulmer and Padgett 2005), partly because we focus on variation within one single mode rather than across modes, and partly because it is very problematic to juxtapose a supposedly "coercive power-based" Community method to persuasion and learning in open co-ordination (Armstrong 2006: 87). Further, there is no claim that learning is a sufficient condition for policy change – it is necessary in some processes of change but not in others (Hall 1993). Finally, the article is an analysis of learning based on a generic template of open co-ordination – but the template varies by policy area and, as mentioned, across time (the re-definition of the Lisbon strategy has provided an opportunity to re-define open co-ordination).

The article is organized as follows. The next section introduces open co-ordination. We then discuss learning in policy processes. Next, we look at how the architecture of the OMC is supposed to produce learning. The subsequent two sections report on empirical evidence, first by looking at how the instruments of learning contained in the OMC perform, and then by making a distinction between learning at the top, learning from the top, and bottom-up learning. The final section concludes.

What is Open Co-ordination?

Although policy processes embodying several features of the OMC emerged throughout the 1990s, the method was established by the Lisbon European Council (23–24 March 2000). The Lisbon summit presented the "new open method of coordination" as a means of spreading best practice and "achieving greater convergence towards the main EU goals". The method – the European Council added – is "designed to help member states to progressively develop their own policies". It is therefore presented as an instrument for policy learning. The OMC is supposed to foster learning processes by drawing on a range of instruments, specified in the Lisbon Conclusions, such as:

- fixing guidelines for the Union combined with specific timetables for achieving the goals ... in the short, medium and long terms;
- establishing, where appropriate, quantitative and qualitative indicators and benchmarks against the best in the world and tailored to the needs of different member states and sectors as a means of comparing best practice;
- translating these European guidelines into national and regional policies by setting specific targets;
- periodic monitoring, evaluation and peer review organized as *mutual learning processes*. (Presidency Conclusions, point 37, emphasis added).

This is the most complete form of the method. Although some of its elements, such as indicators, should be included only "when appropriate", the "method" in its most sophisticated form includes the following components: guidelines, benchmarking, multilateral surveillance, indicators, implementation via domestic policy (this means that no EU legislation is needed), and iterative processes.

The list of OMC policy areas is rather long, and varies from one official document to another. One can group policies in three categories. The first group includes policies where there is a deliberate attempt to use the OMC as the main working method either on the basis of Treaty articles or on the basis of Council Conclusions. Specifically, the first group includes the broad Economic Policy Guidelines (BEPG, Treaty based), the European Employment Strategy (EES, Treaty based), social inclusion (supported by specific Council Conclusions), pensions (Council Conclusions), research and innovation (Council Conclusions), and the information society (Council Conclusions).

The second group includes areas where EU policy makers have manifested their intention to use the OMC, but – so far at least – only a limited amount of the instruments and practice at work in these policies correspond to the "method". To illustrate, national action plans and indicators are often absent in this group, which includes education, environmental policy, better regulation, health care, and migration and asylum policy. Finally, direct taxation is the only case wherein policy makers have used an innovative combination of OMC instruments and practices, but without any deliberative intention to use the method. Accordingly, one can label this group "open coordination in disguise" (Radaelli 2003b).

Learning in Public Policy

At the outset, it is useful to explain different types of learning, why policy makers are interested in learning, who learns, how, and what are the outcomes of learning (Bennett and Howlett 1992). May (1992) has introduced a typology that distinguishes among instrumental policy learning (that is, learning about how to redesign instruments for carrying out the policy), social learning (that is, the redefinition of policy problems via new policy discourses), and political learning (how political actors learn about more sophisticated ways of pushing for their favorite solutions). We will come back to these three types of learning in the empirical sections and in the conclusions.

Regarding the "who" question, domestic politicians and civil servants are the main actors. Why are they interested in learning then? From the point of view of the member states, the OMC is attractive not because it produces learning, but because it enables co-ordination whilst limiting delegation of regulatory power to the Commission and is not subject to review by the European Court of Justice. If – as shown by the literature on the political business cycle (Lewis-Beck and Paldman 2000) – the incumbent's success in bidding for re-election is a function of past policy performance, politicians have an incentive to learn about how to improve competitiveness, employment levels, and so on.

For civil servants, the logic of dense communication implicit in the OMC induces legitimacy-driven adaptation (Knill and Lenschow 2005). Domestic bureaucracies observe and learn, but they are also observed by others and have to survive within the discourse, ideas, and policy models hegemonic within transnational networks (Knill and Lenschow 2005: 590).

On how, the answer comes in three parts. Firstly, policies are collections of hypotheses: if government X does Y, it will obtain Z. Now, all hypotheses contain errors. Bayesian learning (Parmigiani 2002) is the typical way to reduce errors. One can usefully learn by looking at one's own institutional and organizational past, innovation and success in public policy, and evaluation studies – assuming that evaluations address the right questions and that there is a process in which indicators and policy reviews lead to knowledge utilization (see Radaelli and De Francesco 2007).

Secondly, policy makers can look at the experience of others. Indeed, learning from our own experience can be less efficient than learning from others – a point made inter alia by Hemerijck and Visser (2001). More often than not, policy makers have to experience major policy fiascos before they start experimenting with new approaches. Learning from the experience of others is efficient because one does not have to wait for catastrophes at home before lessons are learned.

Thirdly, policy makers can activate learning processes via organizational networks. The idea is that there are solutions to policy problems somewhere in the network, but no one knows where they are. For example, ministers sitting at the Council's table in Brussels may not know how to handle a specific problem of employability, but they may rightly believe that there is an industrial district, or a region, where a solution is working and, perhaps, can be diffused to the rest of the EU, or to some selected member states or regions. These policy makers can seek to foster learning by using a dense OMC organizational network as "radar" (Scott and Trubek 2002). In this approach, learning via organizational networks is all about tapping the benefits of local knowledge – a point made on several occasions by David Trubek.

This introduces an important distinction between hierarchical and bottom-up learning. Obviously, the two forms of learning differ. Co-ordination from above, peer pressure, benchmarking exercises, references to EU indicators – in short, all the paraphernalia of open co-ordination – may well trigger learning dynamics. But one has to admit that this looks like a form of hierarchical learning in disguise or, more appropriately perhaps, a form of "learning from the top" (Smismans 2004 calls it "open method of centralization"). Of course, this is not the same form of learning from the top that one encounters in classic EU directives containing sanctions. All in all, however, domestic policy makers learn how to cope with "instructions" coming from above – that is, from the EU level, specifically from the Council formations in charge of different OMC processes.

This is different from another possible use of open co-ordination, one in which the EU level encourages participation, actively listens to the lessons coming from civil society and local experimentation, and employs organizational networks to diffuse policy-relevant knowledge horizontally (for example, Dutch policy makers learning from the Belgians via EU co-ordination) and bottom-up (for example, EU policy makers redefining their guidelines on employment on the basis of evidence coming from local experiments of job creation). A major issue, therefore, is whether real-world practice of open co-ordination is more similar to learning "from the top" or "bottom-up learning" – this will be discussed below.

Further, we can distinguish between thin and thick learning, following Checkel (1998). Thin learning occurs when an actor learns how to cope with a problem without changing preferences. For example, a member state can devise a new strategy to meet a EU target for social inclusion. By contrast, thick learning implies a change in preferences. For example, a member state may change its paradigm of labor market regulation as a consequence of its involvement in the European Employment Strategy.

Convergence is one of the possible outcomes of learning. But it is a complex concept (Pollitt 2001). There are different levels of convergence. The simplest is convergence at the level of discourse. People speak the same language, but their preferences do not change as a result of a new vocabulary. More problematic is convergence at the level of ideas. This already implies some limited forms of thick learning, *if* one or more member states alter their preferences. For more substantial convergence one has to look at convergence of decisions taken at the domestic level, actions following decisions, and implementation results.

It is useful to conclude this section bearing in mind the limitations of learning in political systems. Under conditions of uncertainty, individuals interpret the same evidence differently (Kahneman and Tversky 1979). Actors involved in policy controversies may not learn because their interpretative frames are somewhat impermeable to empirical evidence (Schön and Rein 1994). Under conditions of ambiguity, the definition of success (and how it was achieved) is problematic and Bayesian learning may be hindered. The self-serving bias of politicians in the attribution of causality, the production of organizational myths, and superstitious learning (Levitt and March 1988: 325–326) change the simple straight line of Bayesian learning, that is,

$$\text{Uncertainty} \rightarrow \text{hypotheses} \rightarrow \text{evidence} \rightarrow \text{learning} \rightarrow \text{change}$$

into the sequence:

$$\text{Uncertainty} \rightarrow \text{hypotheses} \rightarrow \text{experience} \rightarrow \text{ambiguity} \rightarrow \text{bias} \rightarrow \text{political learning}$$

When policy makers learn in a "political mode" (as opposed to Bayesian learning), they are interested in maintaining or expanding their power. Their aim is to learn about the strategies of other actors, how to preserve consensus at home and at the same time tell a convincing story in Brussels, make sure that their favorite policy options are incorporated in EU-level guidelines, and reduce the pressure for adaptation (that is, political learning according to May 1992). In consequence, political learning can make a policy maker smarter in the power game with the EU colleagues, but it does not necessarily produce change and convergence towards common goals.

Governance Mechanisms and their Limitations

One key mechanism of the OMC revolves around tapping local knowledge, exploring and exploiting successful experiences, and diffusing innovation from one system to another. This micro-orientation breaks down political complexities into smaller compounds that are more manageable.

By doing this, the OMC tries to avoid the conflict of preferences about economic governance. All member states want a more competitive Europe, but the question arises what is the model of economic governance that can deliver on competitiveness, given the presence of radically different models of capitalism in Europe (Hall and Soskice 2001)? Convergence on this – the OMC template argues – may well be a product, but it is not a necessary condition for open co-ordination processes to start working efficiently.

Another important mechanism of OMC governance is participation. Participation at different levels of governance (EU, domestic, regional) and across a vast spectrum of actors (including the civil society) is essential for two reasons. One is obvious, that is, legitimacy. The other is less obvious: effectiveness. The method can work like a radar and find solutions only if it involves different actors at different levels. According to Zeitlin, the OMC radar must tap the benefits of local knowledge and experimentation (Zeitlin 2002). Consequently, participation should not be limited to those who operate in EU-level committees, but it should be extended to local-level actors.

The third important learning-enhancing mechanism of the OMC is, as mentioned, the network properties of open co-ordination processes, embodied in specific committees, benchmarking, peer review, multilateral surveillance, scoreboards, trend-charts and other mechanisms for transnational policy diffusion. A common claim (Rodrigues 2003) is that by generating transnational diffusion, policy makers can improve and learn at their own pace.

Are these claims internally coherent? Policy interdependency and the need to co-ordinate the Lisbon strategy across policies push towards a "political space" wherein it may be difficult not to clash over the hard questions of economic governance and models of capitalism. The spring summits of the EU, indeed, have become the focus of broad discussions on competitiveness in which the hard questions surface regularly.

There is another contradiction – between the emphasis on the method as an instrument used by member states to develop "at their own pace" (with greater diversity as the most likely outcome) and the objective need to steer the process of policy change in the direction of "convergence towards the EU goals" (both appear in the Lisbon conclusions).

And there is tension between competitive and co-operative learning. Some of the elements of the OMC, notably benchmarking, are used by companies in the private sector to become more competitive. With competitive learning, a member state obtains new knowledge from other countries, deciphers the lessons to be drawn, adapts innovation to the domestic context, and ultimately becomes more competitive. At the same time, the OMC as "network" suggests more co-operative forms of learning and convergence as final result. A case study of Denmark and Sweden (Jacobsson 2005) has found plenty of evidence that these kinds of tensions are unresolved within the OMC.

As mentioned, the important mechanisms at work in the OMC are socialization, monitoring, and arguing/persuasion. Monitoring encourages predictability, reporting, tasks well specified in advance, whereas learning is essentially disruptive of regularity and may lead to the breakdown of "monitorability" (Sabel 1994). Even if we assume that member states are willing to take the commitment to measure progress towards common goals, there is no structural incentive to produce the indicators that can be used to name and shame them (Idema and Kelemen 2006). Monitoring can also clash with persuasion and deliberative policy making. A policy maker operating in the context of league tables, peer reviews, and tight questioning may not have the right predisposition towards dispassionate argumentation. To conclude, socialization processes and deliberative policy making may be hindered by too much monitoring from above. Yet without monitoring there is no sense of common progress – a key aim of the Lisbon strategy.

OMC Instruments Hit the Road

Empirical evidence on real-world practice of open co-ordination is still limited. With this caveat in mind, this section will review empirical evidence[1] with particular emphasis on the relationship between OMC instruments and learning. In terms of case selection, we will draw on evidence from the first type of OMC processes (see the first substantive section), looking at variation within the most mature type. Learning is most likely to occur where the OMC has been formally established. If there is no trace of learning in type 1 processes, learning in the other two less formalized types is less likely to appear.

The potential for learning processes hinges on several instruments, such as "the systematic diffusion of knowledge and experiences; persuasion supported by practices of peer review and dialogue; knowledge work including the development of a common policy discourse; comparable statistics, and common indicators, repetition, and strategic use of policy linkages" (Borras and Jacobsson 2004: 195).

These instruments nominally exist in most OMCs, but with different degrees of institutionalization. In social inclusion, up until 2001 the member states could use any set of data, but starting with the national plans for 2003 they were requested to use the primary and secondary indicators agreed by the Social Protection Committee. A third range of indicators (optional tertiary indicators) can be used flexibly to accommodate the peculiarities of each member state (Ferrera et al. 2002: 233).

There has been progress with indicators in the pensions OMC, but here the process has been subverted. National pensions "strategy reports" have been presented by member states without previous agreement on indicators. Accordingly, these plans do nothing more than describing the trajectories of domestic policies. Indeed, they are not called national action plans – arguably an acknowledgement of the fact that they do not contain a list of actions that are supposed to meet the guidelines agreed in Brussels. The term "strategy report" is more elusive than "action plan". However, 11 "broad common objectives" for pensions were agreed by the Social Protection Committee and the Economic Policy Committee. So far the main function of the pensions OMC has been to feed information into the formulation of the BEPG.

The main instruments used in innovation policy are the European innovation scoreboard, the European trend-chart, surveys of policy measures, reviews, and workshops on transnational policy learning. The scoreboard contains indicators on knowledge creation, technology transfer, innovation finance, and innovation outputs. The Commission has made the suggestion that member states use the results of the scoreboard "to define, where appropriate, national targets or policy priorities".[2] This is a light use of indicators.

Turning to peer review, the potential for learning is clear. It can socialize actors – socialization effects are important in thick learning (Checkel 1998). It can also provide the preconditions for ideational convergence, that is, convergence of policy makers around a set of criteria that define good policy. Finally, the review process provides policy makers with definitions of success and shared beliefs about countries that learn and countries that do not learn (that is, "heroes" and "villains").

The reality is that peer review means different things in different policies. National Action Plans for employment are not reviewed in depth. Each National Plan is peer reviewed in an hour or so (including the presentation of the member state under review). Mosher and Trubek (2003: 78) conclude that "It is hard to imagine that so truncated a session could produce an in-depth assessment or offer very much useful feedback".

Peer review in pension policy has been quite light so far, with short presentations of descriptive national plans followed by some questions prepared in advance (de la Porte and Nanz 2004). Peer review in innovation policy is more oriented towards the review of successful policies than towards the evaluation of national plans. Casey and Gold (2005) look at reviews of active labor market policies – a component of the EES. They find that "the peer review programme, as it operated in the first round was, at best, a learning process for a limited community of labor market technicians and experts ... Our analysis demonstrates that the peer review element of the OMC ... is likely to have had little impact" (Casey and Gold 2005: 37).

Benchmarking is another instrument used by the OMC to foster learning. It is widely diffused, but in this case again one has to be aware of the different context and political goals in which this technique is used. Mosher and Trubek (2003: 78) report on the limited use of good practice in employment policy. For some member states, good practice is a 2–3 page section to paste at the end of the National Action Plan. Faced with these poor results, the Commission has sought to focus the process on good practice by promoting specific conferences (Mosher and Trubek 2003).

Participation is yet another important component of the OMC as a learning-based mode of governance. It is striking to observe how little the OMC has delivered on its promises, with the exception of social inclusion. Participation is minimal in the BEPG. In employment, participation of trade unions, business organizations, and social movements reflects national styles of participation. Put differently, social actors participate in the OMC when domestic policy styles are already tuned towards participation. The implication is that (at least up until now) the open method has not changed participatory patterns in member states.

In innovation, participation is at the level of civil servants from national ministries, the business community and "innovation enterprises", innovation centers, and so on. In pension policy, the business community has been provided with an opportunity to enter a wider European market for pension funds and other products. Social partners have not been the primary actors, although they are increasingly involved. Finally, in the case of social inclusion, both NGOs (one example is the European Anti-Poverty Network) and more traditional social partners have found a favorable structure of opportunities for participation. This is an area where open co-ordination has partially matched the ambition of the Lisbon architects to provide mechanisms of learning via participatory governance (for evidence see Zeitlin 2005).

However, the European Parliament, national parliaments, regions, and local governments have played a marginal role in *all OMC processes* (Zeitlin 2002, Idema and Kelemen 2006). As Borras and Jacobsson (2004: 199) put it: "empirical research shows that the OMC's openness to various types of actors has not been fully exploited, especially not within the member states".

Learning at the Top, from the Top, and Bottom-up?

In its ideal-typical and most abstract form, the OMC has potential for learning in at least three directions:

- EU-level learning within communities of policy makers engaged in EU policy processes (or "learning at the top");
- hierarchical learning from the EU level down to the domestic and local level (or "learning from the top"); and
- learning from below (i.e., social actors, regions, local governments) to the top (or "bottom-up" learning).

The question, however, is whether the abstract argument stands up to empirical evidence. This section carries on with the examination of empirical evidence by changing the angle of observation to the three types of learning.

Let us start with learning at the top (that is, EU level). There is evidence of learning within political and technical communities involved in the OMC in Brussels. Guidelines and political priorities have been able to change – thus reflecting learning from experience – although impact evaluation studies have not generated much reflexive learning (Zeitlin 2005: 473). In the EES, the recommendations issued to member states have shifted in line with new EES policy priorities.[3] In social inclusion, initially vague goals have been clarified by the publication of indicators. The development of a common set of indicators is a component of EU-level capacity building, having produced "cross-national debate and deliberation about the comparability, appropriateness, and significance of these indicators" (Zeitlin 2005: 471). More importantly, the mid-term assessment of the Lisbon strategy has enabled EU leaders to streamline reporting and indicators. Overall, there is preliminary evidence of learning "at the top".

Let us now turn to learning from the top. One (limited) result is convergence at the level of discourse. OMC-generated vocabulary sells well, often in association with excessive expectations about new governance, and often ignoring the tenacity of national interests (Idema and Kelemen 2006). Armstrong has found preliminary evidence of Europeanization of domestic policy discourses in the analysis of social inclusion in the UK (Armstrong 2006).

Beyond discourse, there is non-negligible cognitive convergence. Cognitive convergence refers to the identification of a common set of beliefs about the main problems and the causal mechanisms at work in a policy area. Zeitlin (2005: 451) mentions how "policy thinking" has changed by looking at the emergence in domestic policy agendas of concepts such as gender mainstreaming, lifelong learning, flexicurity, inclusive labor market policies, activation services, and so on. Bertozzi and Bonoli (2002) show that employment policy has been re-oriented in Germany to reflect dominant OMC policy ideas. Of course, for some member states the OMC has provided an opportunity to upload policy thinking that was already quite popular at home. But in others old policy ideas have been reconsidered (Mosher and Trubek 2003).

Following Brunsson (1989), one should not assume that people or organizations belonging to the same community of discourse take the same decisions. Convergence in "talk" may not produce convergence in decisions. Neither does it produce the same actions: even if a decision is taken, implementation may differ. There is not much evidence that problem redefinition has led to policy change – for example via a mechanism of learning about what works and what does not work (Zeitlin 2005: 472). In some cases, such as Italy, the domestic policy makers have initially reacted negatively to the ESS, by arguing that it did not really fit their own national context (Italian evaluation of the EES, quoted by Mosher and Trubek 2003: 74). In Knill and Lenschow's terms (2005), this is a surprising case of domestic policy makers that, instead of following legitimacy-driven rationality, have followed persistence-driven rationality. However, there is nothing surprising if one enters interests and party politics in the analysis of Europeanization. Quaglia and Radaelli (2007) show that party political considerations trumped any possible legitimacy-driven rationality in the Italian posture towards the EES under the Berlusconi government of 2001–2006.

On Germany, Buchs and Friedrich (2005: 278) observe that "the acceptance of the OMC processes by domestic actors as national policy instruments is limited since the NAPs are regarded as mere reports to the European level rather than policy planning tools". Armstrong (2005: 308) notes that it "is hard to escape the conclusion" that the national plan on social inclusion produced by the UK is "a report, not a plan". Visser observes that the connection between the EU and Dutch employment policies "is weak". He clarifies: "there are phases in which the Netherlands actively used the 'lessons for Europe' in order to change things at home, but this was always on the basis of existing *national* political priorities" (Visser 2005: 199, emphasis original).

Given the problematic relationship between learning and policy change (Bennett and Howlett 1992) and the fact that it is almost impossible to ascribe a case of policy change to the presence of the OMC, one should look at the institutional impact (as opposed to the impact on policies). Ferrera and Sacchi (2005) follow this approach and show that the EES has increased the co-ordination capability of the Italian state. However, the impact of the social inclusion OMC on the same variables is hardly visible, thus suggesting that OMC processes have a differential impact.

What about bottom-up learning then? The scant empirical information on learning in OMC processes directs us towards a problem acknowledged by the Commission itself: up until now, the amount of learning "from the bottom" and across countries has been limited. One explanation for this is that participation falls short of the ideal type of participatory governance designed at Lisbon (Zeitlin 2005, de la Porte and Nanz 2004). If the OMC is all about tapping the benefits of local knowledge, poor participatory governance is a serious hindrance to learning. One key mechanism envisaged by the Lisbon architects is simply not working. Participation is limited in another sense: all too often, the domestic policy makers involved in OMC processes are few and not pivotal in the development of domestic policy. This has something to do with the natural division of labor inside government departments: someone is in charge of the OECD processes, some others attend OMC meetings, and many others deal with more important domestic issues. This is not the best way to embed open co-ordination in national policy development (Shäfer 2006).

The second explanation suggested here is that policy makers are not seeking truth, but power. They may be open to reasoned argumentation, but not to the point of overcoming the basic fact that they are dealing with interests. Governments do not activate voluntary procedures to advance common goals, but to secure their own interests (Shäfer 2006). Let us give some examples. To choose a set of indicators, to designate an innovation as "good practice", to undertake a benchmarking exercise, and to write guidelines are all political processes. They establish hierarchies of domestic solutions. They affect national interests, put pressure on some versions of the "European social model" but not on others, and alter the comparative advantage of member states.

Interestingly, one peculiar way in which policy makers have learned bottom-up is entirely consistent with political learning – in the sense of Peter May (1992). OMC architecture, norms and values are still quite malleable. Skillful policy makers have learned how to use the OMC to upload their preferred interpretation of EU common values (in a given policy area) and to amplify the political space for domestic reforms. As Armstrong concludes in his analysis of the UK engagement with social inclusion: "OMC creates the opportunity for projection and evangelizing, perhaps more so than for learning and adaptation" (Armstrong 2006: 98).

The third reason is the institutional context. Given very different institutional settings across the EU, how can a country learn via benchmarking? One cannot start from the assumption that there are no political problems in defining successful experience, in coding it into narratives and lessons, and in activating memories of success to solve similar problems in different contexts. Although Visser (2005) shows that the OMC is more context-sensitive than OECD benchmarking, the heterogeneity of a union of 27 countries is a barrier to the transfer of lessons. In all processes of policy innovation there are elements that cannot be transferred from one country to another without taking into account institutional legacies, state traditions, and the dominant legal culture.

To conclude on learning, open co-ordination has potential for learning, but it has not delivered, especially in terms of bottom-up learning, due to limited participation, the political aspects of learning, and the still insufficiently critical discussion of benchmarking. So far the OMC has not been very "open". The core of the OMC is a network of civil servants and experts. This may increase the technocratic nature of the EU policy process, rather than opening up pathways for more democratic decisions.

Conclusions

The OMC potential hinges on the fact that learning can be more powerful than hierarchy in changing the beliefs, assumptions, and paradigms upon which policy is built. Changes in the direction of the common EU goals are a manifestation of Europeanization. This article has shown that the link between learning, policy change, and, eventually, Europeanization is interrupted at several points and does not operate with the classic Bayesian features. Going back to May's typology (1992), the OMC provides more evidence of redefinition of policy discourses (social learning, according to May) and political learning than instances of policy learning.

Open co-ordination processes have not generated considerable amounts of horizontal and bottom-up learning. Poor results in terms of bottom-up learning reflect the lack of participation from below, the underestimation of the peculiarities of learning in a political context, and the problems of producing usable knowledge via appropriate instruments. There is evidence of top-down learning in the sense of limited cognitive convergence. This may become important in the future – for example, by creating convergence of beliefs on what "the European social model" should be. More research is needed on scope conditions for different types of learning – to illustrate, do sanctions-based open co-ordination processes create more top-down learning? What are the conditions under which more participation leads to more bottom-up learning? How do the logic of choice and the logic of appropriateness impact on learning mechanisms?

In the meantime, the high-level group chaired by Wim Kok balanced the pessimistic remarks on the open method with the realistic observation that the Community method too "has not delivered what was expected" (Kok Report 2004: 42) – thus raising the important point that we should compare the relative inefficiency of the classic Community method and new modes rather than making bold claims about the potential of open co-ordination in terms of Europeanization.

Acknowledgements

This article draws on research funded by Integrated Project "New Modes of Governance" (www.eu-newgov.org), financially supported by the European Union under the 6th Framework programme (Contract No CIT1-CT-2004-506392). I wish to thank Sabine Saurugger who organized the workshop at the University of Grenoble where I presented a draft (9–10 March 2006), the workshop participants, and the anonymous reviewers of this article. The usual disclaimer applies.

Notes

1. For comprehensive overviews see Zeitlin and Pochet (2005), Borras and Jacobsson (2004), and Zeitlin and Trubek (2003). Sometimes primary documentation makes references to learning, for example the material produced by the EU on the European Employment Strategy (specifically the impact evaluation studies of the Commission). The large majority of studies have been carried out prior to the re-definition of the Lisbon agenda in 2005.
2. See http://trendchart.cordis.lu/AboutUs/pg_04.htm (accessed 8 March 2006).
3. I am grateful to Caroline de la Porte for drawing my attention to this.

References

Armstrong, K., 2005, How open is the UK to the OMC process on social inclusion?, in: J. Zeitlin and P. Pochet (Eds) *The Open Method of Coordination in Action* (Brussels: PIE – Peter Lang), pp. 287–310.

Armstrong, K., 2006, The Europeanization of social exclusion: British adaptation to EU co-ordination. *British Journal of Politics and International Relations*, **8**, 79–100.

Bennett, C. J. and Howlett, M., 1992, The lessons of learning: reconciling theories of policy learning and policy change. *Policy Sciences*, **25**, 275–294.

Bertozzi, F. and Bonoli, G., 2002, Europeanisation and the convergence of national social and employment policies: What can the open method of coordination achieve? Paper prepared for the ECPR joint sessions of workshops, Turin, 22–27 March.

Borras, S. and Jacobsson, K., 2004, The open method of coordination and new governance patterns in the EU. *Journal of European Public Policy*, **11**(2), 185–208.

Börzel, T. and Risse, T., 2003, Conceptualising the domestic impact of Europe, in: K. Featherstone and C. M. Radaelli (Eds) *The Politics of Europeanization* (Oxford: Oxford University Press), pp. 55–78.

Brunsson, N., 1989, *The Organization of Hypocrisy. Talk, Decisions and Actions in Organizations* (Chichester and New York: John Wiley and Sons).

Buchs, M. and Friedrich, D., 2005, Surface integration: The National Action Plans for employment and social inclusion in Germany, in: J. Zeitlin and P. Pochet (Eds) *The Open Method of Coordination in Action* (Brussels: PIE – Peter Lang), pp. 249–285.

Bulmer, S. and Padgett, S., 2005, Policy transfer in the European Union: an institutionalist perspective. *British Journal of Political Science*, **35**(1), 103–126.

Casey, B. and Gold, M., 2005, Peer review of labor market policies in the European Union: what can countries really learn from one another? *Journal of European Public Policy*, **12**(1), 23–43.

Checkel, J., 1998, The constructivist turn in international relations theory. *World Politics*, **50**(2), 324–348.

Cohen, J. and Sabel, C. F., 1997, Directly-deliberative polyarchy. *European Law Journal*, **3**(4), 313–342.

Commission, 2005a, Working together for growth and jobs. A new start for the Lisbon strategy. Communication from president Barroso to the Spring European Council. COM(2005) 24 Final.

Commission, 2005b, Working together for growth and jobs. Next steps in implementing the revised Lisbon strategy. Commission staff working paper, SEC(2005) 622/2.

Council, 2005, Presidency Conclusions, European Council 22 and 23 March 2005, 7619/1/05 CONCL 1.

De la Porte, C. and Nanz, P., 2004, The OMC – a deliberative and democratic mode of governance? The cases of employment and pensions. *Journal of European Public Policy*, **11**(2), 267–288.

Eberlein, B. and Kerwer, D., 2004, New governance in the European Union: a theoretical perspective. *Journal of Common Market Studies*, **42**(1), 121–142.

Ferrera, M. and Sacchi, S., 2005, The open method of coordination and national institutional capabilities: the Italian experience, in: J. Zeitlin and P. Pochet (Eds) *The Open Method of Coordination in Action* (Brussels: PIE – Peter Lang), pp. 137–172.

Ferrera, M., Matsaganis, M. and Sacchi, S., 2002, Open coordination against poverty: the new EU "social inclusion process". *Journal of European Social Policy*, **12**(3), 227–239.

Hall, P., 1993, Policy paradigms, social learning and the state. The case of economic policy-making in Britain. *Comparative Politics*, **25**(3), 275–296.

Hall, P. and Soskice, D. (Eds.), 2001, *Varieties of Capitalism. The Institutional Foundations of Comparative Advantage* (Oxford: Oxford University Press).

Hemerijck, A. and Visser, J., 2001, Learning and mimicking: How European welfare states reform. Unpublished manuscript.

Idema, T. and Kelemen, D., 2006, New modes of governance, the open method of coordination and other fashionable red herring, *Perspectives on European Politics and Society*, **7**(1), 108–123.

Jacobsson, K., 2005, Trying to reform the "best pupils in the class"? The OMC in Sweden and Denmark, in: J. Zeitlin and P. Pochet (Eds) *The Open Method of Coordination in Action* (Brussels: PIE – Peter Lang), pp. 107–136.

Kahneman, D. and Tversky, A., 1979, Prospect theory: an analysis of decision under risk. *Econometrica*, **47**, 263–291.

Knill, C. and Lenschow, A., 2005, Compliance, competition, and communication: different approaches of European governance and their impact on national institutions, *Journal of Common Market Studies*, **43**(3), 583–606.

Kok Report, 2004, Facing the challenge. The Lisbon strategy for growth and employment, Report from the high level group chaired by Wim Kok, Luxembourg, Office for Official Publications of the EC.

Levitt, A. and March, J. G., 1988, Organizational learning. *Annual Review of Sociology*, **14**, 319–340.

Lewis-Beck, M. and Paldman, M., 2000, Economic voting: an introduction. *Electoral Studies*, **19**(2–3), 113–121.

May, P. J., 1992, Policy learning and failure. *Journal of Public Policy*, **12**(4), 331–354.

Mosher, J. and Trubek, D., 2003, Alternative approaches to governance in the EU: EU social policy and the European employment strategy. *Journal of Common Market Studies*, **41**(1), 63–88.

Olsen, J. P., 2002, The many faces of Europeanization. *Journal of Common Market Studies*, **40**(5), 921–952.

Parmigiani, G., 2002, Decision theory: Bayesian, in: N. Smelser and P. B. Baltes (Eds) *International Encyclopaedia of Social Sciences* (Amsterdam: Elsevier), pp. 3327–3334.

Pollitt, C., 2001, Convergence: the useful myth? *Public Administration*, **79**(4), 933–947.

Quaglia, L. and Radaelli, C. M., 2007, Italian politics and the European Union. *West European Politics*, **30**, 924–943.

Radaelli, C. M., 2003a, The Europeanization of public policy, in: K. Featherstone and C. M. Radaelli (Eds) *The Politics of Europeanization* (Oxford, Oxford University Press), pp. 27–56.

Radaelli, C. M., 2003b, The code of conduct in business taxation. *Public Administration*, **81**(3), 513–531.

Radaelli, C. M. and De Francesco, F., 2007, *Regulatory Quality in Europe: Concepts, Measures, and Policy Processes* (Manchester: Manchester University Press).

Radulova, E., 2006, On the emergence of light and heavy soft governance in the EU – the open method(s) of coordination, in: D. De Bievre and C. Neuhold (Eds) *Dynamics and Obstacles of EU Governance* (Cheltenham: Edward Elgar).

Rodrigues, M. J. (Ed.), 2003, *European Policies for a Knowledge Economy* (Cheltenham: Edward Elgar).

Rose, R., 1993, *Lesson-Drawing in Public Policy: A Guide to Learning Across Time and Space* (Chatham, NJ: Chatham House).

Sabel, C., 1994, Learning by monitoring: the Institutions of Economic Development, in: N. Smelser and R. Swedberg (Eds) *Handbook of Economic Sociology* (Princeton, NJ: Princeton University Press and Russell Sage Foundation), pp. 137–165.

Sabel, C. and Zeitlin, J., 2006, Learning from difference: the new architecture of experimentalist governance in the European Union. Paper prepared for presentation at Arena, University of Oslo, 13 June.

Schön, D. A. and Rein, M., 1994, *Frame Reflection* (New York: Basic Books).

Scott, J. and Trubek, D. M., 2002, Mind the gap: law and new approaches to governance in the European Union. *European Law Journal*, **8**(1), 1–18.

Shäfer, A., 2006, A new form of governance? Comparing the open method of coordination to multilateral surveillance by the IMF and the OECD. *Journal of European Public Policy*, **13**(1), 70–88.

Smismans, S., 2004, EU employment policy: decentralization or centralization through the open method of coordination? EUI Working Paper Law no. 2004/1, European University Institute, Florence.

Visser, J., 2005, The OMC as selective amplifier for national strategies of reform, in: J. Zeitlin and P. Pochet (Eds) *The Open Method of Coordination in Action* (Brussels: PIE – Peter Lang), pp. 173–215.
Zeitlin, J., 2002, The open method of coordination and the future of the European Employment Strategy. *Hearing of the European Parliament*, Employment and Social Affairs Committee, 8 July.
Zeitlin, J., 2005, Conclusion, in: J. Zeitlin and P. Pochet (Eds) *The Open Method of Coordination in Action* (Brussels: PIE – Peter Lang), pp. 447–503.
Zeitlin, J. and Pochet, P. (Eds), 2005, *The Open Method of Co-ordinating in Action: The European Employment and Social Inclusion Strategies* (Brussels: Peter Lang Publishing).
Zeitlin, J. and Trubek, D. (Eds), 2003, *Governing Work and Welfare in a New Economy* (Oxford: Oxford University Press).

Recipient of the *JCPA* and ICPA-Forum Award for Best Comparative Paper, The International Francophone Political Science Conference, Grenoble, 2009

Bottom–Up Policy Convergence: A Sociology of the Reception of Policy Transfer in Public Health Policies in Europe

CAROLE CLAVIER

ABSTRACT *Policy convergence is generally studied from the point of view of the state and explained in terms of policy transfer. However, policy convergence also takes place between countries. The sociology of reception of policy transfer argues for the need to consider convergence from the point of view of the local actors involved in the transfer. Based on a case study of public health policy in France and Denmark, this paper shows that while the local embeddedness of public policy does indeed limit convergence, it also allows for policy transfer and therefore convergence.*

This paper is a case study of local policy convergence across national borders – that is, how local policies in different countries become more alike. For local public health policies in France and Denmark, convergence occurs primarily at the level of objectives and content, whereas instruments and policymaking processes remain specific (Bennett 1991). Objectives and content are both based on a conception of health as not simply the absence of disease, but rather "a state of total physical, mental and social well-being" (WHO 1948) and, therefore, influenced by factors such as income, nutrition and social relationships. The impact of these factors, known as the social determinants of health (SDOH), has been widely studied since the 1970s, and the results of this work disseminated through various academic and institutional channels, primarily by the World Health Organization (WHO) (Kickbusch 2003). But how has this knowledge influenced local public health policies like the ones studied in this case study? In the existing literature, the concept of transfer – that is, how institutions in a given time or place use ideas or policies developed by institutions in other times or places (Dolowitz and Marsh 1996) – is often used to explain convergence. In our case study, however, identifying voluntary or compulsory transfer is difficult because there is no direct contact between French and Danish local authorities, nor any constraining policies from central governments, the European Union or the WHO (Bennett 1991).

I have therefore opted for a bottom-up approach in my study of convergence and policy transfer. I examine the reception of policy transfer – that is, how external ideas are integrated into domestic policies and how these ideas circulate locally. Studying the reception of transfer focuses attention away from the initiation of policy transfer and toward the receiving end of transfer. Rather than analyzing how the WHO circulates public health practices based on SDOH, this approach looks at how local health policy actors discover and adopt public health concepts and related practices.

My approach departs significantly from classical policy studies, which place the emphasis on government initiatives. It embraces a political sociology approach to the policy process, considering public policy to be a collective construction that involves a plurality of public and private actors from all levels of government (Hassenteufel 2008). It means that when observing actors at the receiving end of transfer, not only are local policymaking elites (politicians and civil servants) considered, but also public health practitioners who have an input into the content of local public health policies. This paper therefore proposes a sociology of the reception of transfer, examining how new ideas based on SDOH are integrated into local public health policies and how local public health professionals contribute to the transfer and integration of these ideas.

I will first present my theoretical framework, which is based on a review of the literature on policy transfer and its reception. I then describe my empirical research method. The third and fourth sections present my results: how SDOH concepts were integrated into newly emerging policies in the four regions studied, and how the background and career paths of public health professionals contributed to the introduction of SDOH concepts into these policies. The conclusion discusses what this study adds to our understanding of policy transfer and convergence.

The Reception of Policy Transfer

In general, the study of policy transfer aims to understand how public action is inspired by policies from other jurisdictions or from policies adopted in the past. Transfer can explain convergence, although transfer does not necessarily result in convergence and, conversely, convergence can occur without transfer (Evans 2009). Distinguishing different types of transfer (voluntary versus compulsory) and the mechanisms that lead to policy transfer (for example, learning, imitation and diffusion) are major topics in policy transfer studies (Dolowitz and Marsh 1996,

Evans and Davies 1999, Stone 1999, Radaelli 2000, Holzinger and Knill 2005, Evans 2009). In such studies, the reception of policy transfer itself is rarely examined (Hassenteufel 2005); at best, it is seen as an aspect of the transfer process. Nevertheless, we can draw three conclusions from these studies that are useful to an analysis of the reception of policy transfer.

First, a growing body of research examines policy transfer through analyzing the career paths and relationships between policy transfer actors. Certain authors characterize the role of actors according to whether they initiate, facilitate or receive policy transfer (Wolman and Page 2002). Others map the circulation of ideas by collecting biographical data on the careers and networks of transfer actors; examples are studies of economic and policy reform actors in Latin America and studies of healthcare policy elites in France (Dezalay and Garth 2002, Genieys and Smyrl 2008). Studying the actors involved in transfer can also be a gateway to an analysis of the Europeanization process; an example is the influence of the French judicial model in Eastern Europe (Piana 2007). Examining policy actors' career paths is thus an indicator of how ideas circulate among different countries and/or policy sectors. Yet the most studied actors of transfer are the political and administrative elites of governments and international organizations who initiate transfer, along with the material resources and legitimacy they use to impose their opinions (True and Mintrom 2001, Greener 2002, Ogden et al. 2003, Nakano 2004, Stone 2004, Busch and Jörgens 2005, Bomberg 2007, Delpeuch 2008). In contrast, less attention has been paid to transfer between local actors and to the role of local actors in the reception of transfer initiated by national governments (Evans and Davies 1999, Wolman and Page 2002).

Second, proximity is a factor that facilitates policy transfer: ideas are more likely to be transferred if they fit with domestic institutions, representations of policy and political issues and if they provide (partial) solutions to these domestic issues. The importance of proximity has been demonstrated both at the macro level – for example, between a country's institutional, cultural and economic preferences (Lenschow et al. 2005) – and at the micro level – for example, between actors' preferences and the characteristics of the institutions in which these actors operate. This explains, for instance, why the UK and US have adopted the same model of scientific (evidence-based), bureaucratic (complying with rules set by external authorities) medicine. Proximity between the principles of the scientific-bureaucratic model of medicine, the financing systems for the healthcare system, and the preferences of actors in a position to influence health policy in each country has led to policy convergence in the UK and US (Harrison et al. 2002). Macro-level factors satisfactorily explain policy transfer between two countries that share institutional and cultural characteristics, but they do not explain policy transfer between countries like France and Denmark, which have different cultures and institutions. However, transfer between such different contexts may be explained by micro-level proximity between ideas, the preferences of policy actors and domestic institutions. In terms of the reception of policy transfer, it implies that local actors are more likely to take up (or transfer) an idea that corresponds to their preferences and fits with local policymakers' representations of the problem at hand and existing opportunities for intervention.

Finally, research has shown that the ideas and practices exchanged during transfer are selected and adapted to a particular context (Pedersen 2007, Delpeuch 2008, Massey 2009). Whether a country is compelled to import European standards or is inspired to do so of its own accord by foreign policy models, the transferred elements are transformed to blend with the new context, namely with local policy issues, embedded configurations of actors and institutions with their respective responsibilities and interests. This has implications for policy convergence: it is generally thought that these transformations limit convergence because they reinforce the specificities of the particular context into which the idea is transferred (Radaelli 2005). This would suggest that when comparing the reception of an idea in different policies and/or contexts, we would observe differences in how the idea is conceptualized in the different cases.

The literature suggests that policy actors are vectors for the circulation of ideas and that transfer is facilitated by the proximity of the ideas transferred to the context and local policymakers' representation of the issue. It is also known that the original policy or idea transforms during transfer. This means that when comparing the reception of ideas transferred to different policies, we need to focus on how the transfer is conceptualized, on how well the transfer corresponds to the context and policymakers' representations of policy issues, and on how particular policy actors contribute to its circulation. My hypothesis is that the reception of transfer is a cause of convergence because the integration of SDOH into local policies leads to convergence between these local policies. And because the literature suggests that proximity between SDOH and the context of reception facilitates transfer, I also examine whether the context of reception is a secondary cause of convergence, rather than simply a factor that leads to the transformation of transfer and hence a factor that limits policy convergence.

As mentioned above, studying the reception of transfer reveals how ideas being transferred are integrated into local policies and circulated locally. The first results section therefore examines the integration of SDOH into local public health policies; it focuses on the conceptualization of SDOH, on the arguments put forward to legitimize the development of public health policies based on SDOH, and on the actors who circulated SDOH concepts locally. The following section maps the circulation of SDOH concepts from public health spheres to local policies by retracing the career paths of some key public health actors who were in a position to influence the content of local policies.

Case Study and Method

I analyzed the process of transfer reception in local public health policies for two regions in France, Nord-Pas-de-Calais and Alsace, and for two counties in Denmark, North Jutland and Ringkjøbing. Comparison is central to this research as the study of convergence requires comparing the reception of policy transfer between regions/counties. The use of case studies and comparisons is particularly useful in understanding the processes of reception of transfer because it allows for the testing of research hypotheses (Sartori 1991). Whereas strong similarities between local public health policies indicate convergence, significant differences between health systems exclude the argument that convergence is solely the result of functional requirements or similar problems.

Denmark is a universal welfare state where responsibility for health policy, including the provision of healthcare services, is decentralized to counties (Vallgårda 2003).

Counties and towns sometimes also include prevention and health promotion in their four-year health policy programs. By contrast, France is a conservative welfare state in which the central government retains control over both healthcare and public health policies (Rochaix and Wilsford 2005). Local authorities (regions, departments or towns) sometimes develop their own public health policies and can contribute to the central government's policies for the region (called regional health programs).

In this context, the actual development of local public health policies in both countries depends largely on the involvement of local health policy actors and there is great variation between regions within the same country. As the objective was to examine the processes leading to convergence, the four regions were chosen based on the involvement of local authorities, local politicians and other stakeholders (medical professionals, non-profit associations and health insurers). This case study does not provide a representative overview of the development of local public health policies in the two countries and downplays resistance to such policy development, including resistance to the integration of SDOH. However, comparing territories with different levels of policy development would have shifted the focus to differences between the regional cases, whereas the objective was to analyze convergence through an examination of exemplary cases.

The study covers a 15-year time span, from the emergence of local policies in the early 1990s to 2005, when major reforms that had a significant impact on public health were being prepared or implemented.[1] I opted for a qualitative field survey in each of the four regions studied, including long visits to Denmark. I studied the gray literature (health programs) in order to characterize the public health policies and to identify policy transfer and the actors involved in public health policy. Data was collected on the reception of transfer though 49 semi-structured interviews with actors in charge of public health policy within regional and municipal authorities, with co-ordinators involved in the local implementation of these policies, and with heads of national public health organizations supporting local policies. I also established the local context and collected data on the integration of transfer into local policies through another series of interviews with the representatives of partner institutions and non-governmental organizations at the local, regional and national levels, as well as with local politicians.

The Integration of Policy Transfer within Local Public Health Policies

It has been fairly convincingly demonstrated in the public health literature that a population's health status is influenced not only by healthcare, but also by social, environmental and economic factors such as income, housing, transport, social support networks and physical activity (Marmot and Wilkinson 2006). Based on these SDOH, the "new public health" movement promotes policies that: a) emphasize the link between lifestyle and living conditions, and how these affect the population's health, and b) grant public policy a role in supporting lifestyle choices deemed to be healthy and in creating supportive environments for health (Petersen and Lupton 1996). In general, policies are based on two strategies: disease prevention (for example, screening or vaccination) and health promotion (creating supportive conditions for health, such as facilitating access to services, as outlined in the Ottawa Charter for Health Promotion, drawn up in 1986 under the auspices of the WHO). In this section, I recount the emergence of public health policies in the Danish and French regions, placing particular emphasis on the actors who brought knowledge on SDOH to the local level.

Denmark

The two counties studied both launched public health policies informed by SDOH in the early 1990s. The national context was very favorable at this point in time due to evidence that life expectancy was rising at a lower-than-expected rate and to economic and financial pressures on the healthcare system. These factors sparked the government's interest in public health and led to the drawing up of the country's first national public health program in 1989 (Kamper-Jørgensen 1998, Vallgårda 2003). The underlying rationale was that preventing disease and creating better living conditions could help improve not only the population's health but also the country's finances by curbing healthcare expenditure.

In North Jutland, the county had been subsidizing accident prevention programs in the workplace since 1985. But what really triggered the development of public health policy was a large public event in 1990 called the "Health Market". Two nurses obtained the county's support to organize this major three-day event, which advertised existing health promotion interventions, initiated new programs and opened a dialogue between professionals, decision makers and the population on issues like the environment, addiction, traffic accidents, nutrition and health in the workplace. The event resulted in 22 policy recommendations and the county hired the two nurses to integrate these recommendations into the institution's first health program. One of the county's councilors, who later became head of the Health Commission in the county's assembly, supported the policy starting in the early 1990s, seeing it as a political opportunity consistent with his socialist values – a means to tackle social inequalities in health. Consistent with the counties being responsible for healthcare service provision (70 per cent of their budget), the economic argument was also a powerful motivation. This aspect was mentioned in the county's program (Nordjyllands Amt 2000: 17–18) and confirmed by a nurse involved in the implementation of the program in the early days: "It was a very good motivation in the first place because [if you could] keep people out of hospital, it would be cheaper. So I think that's why they started this [policy] in the county" (Interview, 12 May 2004). In 2004, North Jutland county spent DKK 30 million in public health (one per cent of its healthcare budget), which was more than any other county.

The main achievement of the county's health program was a health contract with municipalities based on the Healthy Cities movement initiated by the WHO. This was actually a recommendation from the 1990 Health Market and is still a cornerstone of the county's policy 15 years later. The objective of this initiative was to make cities more supportive environments for health – for example, by improving public and active transportation, creating green spaces and improving access to public spaces for the elderly. Twenty municipalities formally signed contracts with the county to set up Healthy City offices in their municipality, and to co-finance a local health co-ordinator and health interventions within priority areas, thus increasing the number of small-scale health projects implemented across the region. These contracts reflected in spirit the concept of health as a state of well-being that is influenced by a wide range of social determinants. One of the nurses who helped organize the 1990 Health Market was the architect of these contracts, while other health professionals who worked as co-ordinators for the Healthy City offices contributed to their implementation. A nurse, the first co-ordinator of the Healthy City office in Brønderslev (1992–1994), explained how health promotion guided her practice:

> "Health for All by the Year 2000" was the main [strategy]. ... We wanted to make it at the local level, and we believed [that] the closer we were to the citizens, the more healthcare we could provide. ... Healthcare is more than no sickness: it is to make choices, to be strong, and many other things. That was the challenge. (Interview, 12 May 2004)

This nurse's successor, a dental hygienist, explained how the same philosophy still prevailed in 2004 (Interview, 3 May 2004). For instance, at the request of the population and/or professionals, she organized activities like Nordic Walking; a club for overweight boys to practice physical activity and gain confidence; and talks about topics such as nutrition for diabetics.

The county's policy was grounded in the SDOH and health promotion in that it aimed to create conditions that would enable people to improve their health. This is evident in the objectives of policies which addressed issues related to inequalities in health, children, smoking, nutrition and obesity. And in the actions taken, including the creation of bicycle paths, subsidizing a center for healthy workplaces that offers nutrition, physical activity and smoking cessation services, and making the main city's hospital smoke-free in 2007. As one of the nurses explained, the Health Market had been informed by the concepts of disease prevention and health promotion (Interview, 18 June 2004). A booklet describing the Health Market further underlined that health is created outside the healthcare system, through lifestyle and living conditions. It referred to the WHO's program *Health For All by the Year 2000* (Nordjyllands Amt 1990). This commitment was later "strengthen[ed]" (Interview, county health consultant, 15 April 2004) through formal references to the WHO's definition of health and to the WHO's *Health for All by the Year 2000* program in the county's third public health program (Nordjyllands Amt 2000), and with the county's joining the Danish Healthy City network. The latter network has structured and linked the health policies of different local authorities across the country since the early 1990s.

The policy of Ringkjøbing county was also a prevention and health promotion policy. Among its priorities were to improve the health of disadvantaged children, the elderly and people living with chronic diseases; to prevent cancer by supporting workers in their workplaces and hospital patients to change their smoking, nutrition and physical activity habits. Two nurses who worked as health promotion consultants for the county's health department explained that their practice was grounded in the Ottawa Charter on Health Promotion and on the work of Aaron Antonovsky, a sociologist who claimed that specific personal dispositions and appropriate social conditions contribute to create health (Antonovsky 1996). In his theory on the sense of coherence, health is to have a feeling that daily life is understandable, manageable and meaningful. In policy terms, this approach aims to develop individuals' coping strengths by examining what they want and how they experience life, and by creating supportive environments. Antonovsky's work was also explicitly cited by a health policy co-ordinator in Holstebro, a city in Ringkjøbing county, especially in relation to policies on improving the health of children from disadvantaged and/or ethnic backgrounds. It is also implicitly mentioned in North Jutland's third public health program (Nordjyllands Amt 2000: 17).

France

The incorporation of SDOH in France coincided with the emergence of local public health policies in the early 1990s. In France, local public health policies are the result of a double process: implementation of the state's regional health programs and implementation of the policies of local governments (regions, municipalities and departments).

A 1992 report from the High Committee on Public Health (a public body whose mandate is to reflect on and propose health policy) was the first policy document to introduce the idea that health is a social and mental process, not just the absence of disease (HCSP 1992). Two years later, the same institution published another report on the health of the population that featured a presentation of SDOH (HCSP 1994). These reports served as references for regional health policymakers in the following years. At around the same time, the subject of SDOH was raised during the regional healthcare services planning process in Alsace. A public health physician inspector, a medical doctor with special public health training and who works for the state's administration, took part in the planning process and had this to say:

> Talking about health care needs and hospital planning, we told them what determined a population's health and what made people ill. It was news for them [clinicians and hospital directors] when we said that 80% of what makes people ill is not related to healthcare. ... So we organized a regional health conference with over 1000 participants. People fought – like they had never done before – but that was really interesting. They resisted when we presented them with the [consultation process] because it was qualitative and sociological, not at all epidemiological. (Interview, 30 April 2003)

Following the first discussion, the same public health physician inspector followed the advice of a colleague at the Ministry of Health on how to formally introduce SDOH into regional health policy. At the time, this colleague was experimenting with both regional health programs (focusing on aspects other than healthcare) and with a method to determine regional health priorities. They teamed up and organized a meeting with various health and other professionals in the region in order to collect their perceptions on the health of the population. They then went on to organize a conference to present the results of this consultation as well as epidemiological data to regional health policymakers. This inspector noted that this consultative process led to a clash between different epistemic communities. Epidemiologists, clinicians and public health academics (medical doctors with a specialty in public health) were especially averse to this social conception of health because it opened up the field of public health to non-medical actors. Despite opposition, six priorities emerged from the process, including cancer, cardiovascular disease, nutrition and vulnerability, and these priorities gave rise to regional health programs.

And so the ideas of one public health physician inspector working at the Ministry of Health gave rise to programs based on broad regional consultations that led to priority-setting and a rigorous planning process to define objectives and intervention strategies. Integrated into the state's health reform in 1996 (which also aimed to curb health expenditure), the regional health programs were then implemented in every region under the responsibility of the state's administration and in partnership with the Health Insurance and, on a voluntary basis, local governments. Calls for proposals for projects targeting local institutions, professionals and non-profit organizations then allowed for the selection of actions to be funded by the programs.

Implementation of this policy contributed to the introduction of SDOH in the Nord-Pas-de-Calais region in two different ways. First, the consultation process involved a wide variety of actors with an interest in health, whether from a medical, social, judicial or educational perspective. The chosen priorities in the region testify to the broad range of determinants covered: cardiovascular disease, cancer, addiction, vulnerability and social exclusion, children and young people, health and the environment. Second, the planning of the different programs included non-medical actors in the policymaking process and further spread the concept of SDOH. For instance, the public health physician inspector responsible for the children and young people's health program brought together a team of medical doctors, social workers, psychologists and youth workers from several state administrative units (sports, education, justice), local governments and non-profit organizations. Together, they wrote a program that spanned many determinants of health and relied on a number of different inspirations:

We couldn't follow the same planning process as for cancer or heart diseases, which are centered around illness, because young people are not ill. So we had to find a model that accounted for all the influences on health. ... As a group, we read the Ottawa Charter and different [ecological] models and made our own interpretation. (Interview, 22 April 2002)

Additionally, smaller-scale programs were created in order to complement the regional programs in this region and meet the specific health priorities of each district. More co-ordinators and professionals were therefore exposed to SDOH concepts.

Parallel to the state's programs, the regional government in Nord-Pas-de-Calais developed its own policy with a strong emphasis on SDOH. The region's concern for public health stems from its responsibility for local development and dates back to the 1980s, when crises in the traditional mining and textile industries brought attention to the prevalence of social problems with a health dimension, such as alcoholism. A regional politician encouraged initiatives to combat alcoholism, and these were progressively consolidated into a regional public health policy (Cépré 1999). Among the achievements of this policy were the creation of a Regional Office for Health Promotion, which supports professionals and organizations in the development of health interventions, and the creation of "health" mandates within the regional executive assembly, meaning that starting in the early 1980s, one politician was always specifically responsible for health policy. Later, the regional government also contributed to the state's regional health program; its contribution represented 21 per cent of the program's cost between 2000 and 2003.

Similarly, some cities developed their own public health policy. Local policy-makers were often alerted to health as a political issue during a time of crisis (for example, an epidemic or the closing of an industry or hospital), or when epidemiological data for their region revealed a specific health problem in their population. As they did not have any formal responsibility for public health, many of these policymakers built on SDOH concepts to make health intervention part of policies for urban revitalization and social exclusion, as in Lille (Nord-Pas-de-Calais) or Mulhouse (Alsace) (Clavier 2009).

This account of the emergence and main features of county and regional health policies shows how the idea that health is influenced by social factors has shaped local health policies in France and Denmark. Consistent with the literature, it suggests that the reception of transfer is facilitated inasmuch as the ideas transferred provide a solution to local policy and political issues, such as pressures to contain healthcare costs and evidence of social and health problems. Finally, in terms of the reception of policy transfer, it appears that a number of health professionals in key co-ordinating positions, namely nurses in Denmark and public health physician inspectors in France, provided theoretical arguments to ground local health policies (for instance, the Ottawa Charter and data on the SDOH). The next section focuses on how these key actors discovered these sources during their training and professional careers.

Mapping the Circulation of Policy Transfer through Actors' Backgrounds

This section maps the circulation of SDOH concepts and their integration into local policies by key local public health professionals. In addition to the nurses and public health physician inspectors identified in the previous section, I broadened the scope to include co-ordinators of health programs at the regional, county, city and departmental levels, as well as co-ordinators of national networks supporting local policies who were in a position to influence the content of public health policies or spread its principles to other actors by co-ordinating their implementation. Analyzing the characteristics of the background of these individuals provides information about the reception of policy transfer because it shows how these individuals were socialized to different versions of SDOH concepts through their training and career paths. Table 1 summarizes the profiles of these actors in the two countries.

Table 1. Profiles of the actors receiving policy transfer in local public health policies in France and Denmark

	France	Denmark
Profession	Medical doctors	Nurses
	Other	Other
Position	Civil servants	Employees from county and city departments of health
	Local government employees (regions, departments, cities)	
Career	International and domestic careers	Domestic careers
		Continuing education in public health or health promotion
	Community health training	
Sources for SDOH principles	National reports on SDOH and on community health	Declarations and programs from the WHO

In Denmark, nurses accounted for one-third of the 21 respondents (Table 2),[2] or one in eight medical professionals interviewed. It is not atypical that nurses were key actors in the reception and integration of SDOH into local policies in Denmark as public health training is available to nurses through the public health nursing institution. Founded in the 1930s to help reduce infant mortality by providing assistance to the mothers, the institution filled the state's broader ambition to "introduce a comprehensive program of health promotion, e.g. breastfeeding, tranquility, order, cleanliness and regularity" (Buus 2001: 490). The institution has been the bedrock of health promotion in Denmark ever since, attracting nurses who want to re-orient their practice toward more comprehensive interventions that tackle the root causes of ill health and create environments more supportive of health. For instance, the chief public health nurse in Holstebro, a municipality in Ringkjøbing county, had previously worked as a hospital nurse. She had noticed the high return rates for patients with certain pathologies, which led her to question why patients were being sent home with no prevention advice. She wanted to help improve the situation and so trained to become a public health nurse. The same dissatisfaction motivated the nurse who co-ordinated health promotion at Aalborg hospital (North Jutland); although not a public health nurse, she had previously discovered the WHO *Health for All* program while in nursing school and decided to obtain a degree in education because health promotion places an emphasis on education and empowerment.

The ongoing public health training given in Danish universities and in the Nordic School of Public Health in Sweden has contributed to the circulation of knowledge on SDOH and, in particular, on the work of Antonovsky. The later research has received a large audience in the Scandinavian countries because Antonovsky was for a time professor at the Nordic School of Health Promotion. His works have also been taught in nursing courses (as mentioned by the Holstebro public health nurse) and disseminated through a practical book on health promotion based on a study of health promotion practices in Ringkjøbing county (Jensen and Johnsen 2000). One-third of the 18 interviewees whose careers I was able to analyze supplemented their initial training – either in nursing, anthropology, social work, administration, education or journalism – with public health nurse training or public health university degrees. The others discovered SDOH concepts through colleagues who had received public health training or through participating in existing public health interventions.

In Denmark, references to SDOH were grounded in WHO statements or programs: this is representative of the national context as WHO publications have traditionally influenced Danish health policy (Kamper-Jørgensen 1998). Despite cognitive and geographical proximity with WHO-Europe, whose head office is in Copenhagen, only one of the interviewees in this study had actually worked there during her career. A pharmacist who had developed a smoking cessation concept to

Table 2. Initial training of the public health program co-ordinators interviewed in France and Denmark

	Healthcare professionals	Other initial training	Unknown initial training	Total
France	11	14	3	28
Denmark	8	10	3	21

be implemented at pharmacies, she then worked for the WHO to broaden her concept. Afterwards, she obtained a master's degree in public health to "learn more about the theory behind health promotion and disease prevention" and became co-ordinator of the Health Promoting Hospitals network (similar to the Healthy Cities network) (Interview, 16 June 2004).

In France, public health physician inspectors have been influential actors in the reception of SDOH because they have been in a position to implement the regional health programs, which really introduced the idea that health is socially influenced into local health policies. As public health physician inspectors are public health experts within the state's administrations, they are often responsible for writing and implementing regional health programs in the regions – five of the seven co-ordinators of regional health programs in Nord Pas-de-Calais and Alsace that I interviewed were medical doctors with such a public health inspector position (Table 2). In addition, some of them had previously experienced public health practice during research visits to Quebec (a French-speaking province in Canada that is known for its strong public health policy) or through overseas co-operation or international voluntary work in former African colonies and other developing countries. The most striking example is the founder of the regional health programs: he practiced community health[3] as a medical doctor in Africa and, upon his return, became a public health physician inspector. Working in the civil service, he then discovered the principles of Planning, Programming, and Budgeting systems (Benamouzig 2005) and trained in health planning with public health academics who had learned the methods in Quebec. All of these influences then later shaped the regional health programs.

While other professionals such as nurses and social workers also had international careers, most of our respondents discovered SDOH during training organized as part of the implementation of the regional health programs or through contacts with public health mentors. This, for instance, is how one regional health program co-ordinator in Nord-Pas-de-Calais switched from having a clinical practice to being a public health physician inspector. Others experienced the influence of social factors on health while working for non-profit organizations devoted to tackling poverty and exclusion via programs not based on the traditional clinical care model, such as *Association Abbé Pierre* or *ATD-Quart Monde*. These organizations help people in their daily lives (for example, with domestic chores such as meal preparation or laundry), and in so doing provide advice on family planning and help people access healthcare services. One public health inspector interviewed, having worked with ATD, promoted an official policy involving ATD, the state and municipalities so as to take into account the specific issues of deprived populations in the design of clinical practice and access to healthcare.

Half of my respondents (14 out of 28) were non-medical professionals, with 11 being in charge of local, smaller-scale programs such as municipal public health programs or local development programs with a health section. Trained in project management and co-ordination of partnerships encompassing several levels of public action, they were not public health experts but contributed to the integration of SDOH within local policies by spreading the methods of public health tried out within the regional health programs. Indeed, the planning process was based on consultations between the local institutions and professionals from various policy sectors with an interest in health, including healthcare, social work, employment, justice and sports. The ability to listen to the various actors with an interest in health (local government, health professionals, education or cultural non-profit organizations) and balance their respective interests was a highly valued competency.

As key actors in the reception of policy transfer, local program co-ordinators discovered SDOH concepts in various public health practices or documents emanating from the WHO, academics or national reports. French medical doctors trained in Africa and Quebec introduced community health and strategic programming into their health policies, while Danish nurses contributed to the diffusion of health promotion discourses and practices. A comparison of the two countries therefore shows that the reception of transfer in each country is influenced by actors who are in a position to shape local public health policies. The data also confirm the importance of context for the reception of policy transfer as this shaped opportunities for public health training and the public health traditions influent in each country (community health versus WHO-based programs).

Conclusion

The convergence of local public health policies in France and Denmark proceeds from the integration of one idea, namely the social determinants of health (SDOH), in emerging health policies in the regions. By comparing the reception of transfer in each regional case, I was able to identify the processes and conditions that facilitate the reception of SDOH into emerging local public health policies, namely proximity of SDOH to local context and the contribution of local public health professionals in circulating knowledge on SDOH. This study adds to our understanding of policy transfer and convergence in two ways.

First, and contrary to what the term suggests, reception is an active part of transfer that requires the contribution of local public health professionals: due to their training, experience and the positions they hold, they stand at the interface between institutions receiving transfer (in this case, local authorities) and institutions initiating transfer, such as the WHO and public health academics. Retracing their career paths is therefore a way to map the circulation of transfer between the different social spheres involved, and thus study the transfer process in a backward direction. In this case study, public health nurses in Denmark and public health physician inspectors in France acquired knowledge of SDOH concepts and related prevention and health promotion practices through different experiences, including public health nursing and clinical practice in developing countries or with deprived populations. Being in a position to influence local policies, they could facilitate the circulation of SDOH concepts among local policymakers.

This comparison of the reception of transfer in the two countries underlines the influence of the local embeddedness of public health policies on policy transfer and convergence. In each country, proximity between policy transfer and the local context facilitated and shaped the reception of policy transfer. Indeed, public health training and employment opportunities influenced the background of local public health professionals and how they discovered SDOH. The reception of transfer was also facilitated because SDOH offered local authorities opportunities for intervention on policy issues that arose from local governments' other responsibilities, such as pressure towards healthcare cost containment or evidence of social exclusion and sanitary problems.

These results confirm a conclusion from the literature: that policy transfer is transformed by its integration into new institutions and new configurations of actors (Radaelli 2005). But these results also have implications for the understanding of convergence. Context, or the policies' embeddedness, becomes not only a factor that limits convergence, but also one that facilitates the reception of transfer and, hence, convergence.

To arrive at a complete view of the integration of policy transfer within local policies, however, also requires that the practices that local public health professionals deploy to interest policymakers and other local health policy actors in these new ideas be taken into account (Clavier 2007). Besides, other studies need to investigate whether the absence of one or both of the factors identified here (proximity between contextual policy issues and transfer, and actors circulating transfer locally) influence or even impede the reception of policy transfer and explain policy divergence (Holzinger and Knill 2005). Some of my interviewees encountered difficulties in promoting policies based on SDOH when local policymakers did not perceive health as a priority area, which seems to indicate that a lack of proximity was impeding the reception of transfer.

Such a political sociology approach to the reception of transfer clearly furthers our understanding of policy transfer and convergence. By retracing the processes of transfer that have led to convergence in a backward direction, this study brings attention to converging processes in unrelated cases, thus departing from studies questioning how one case converged with another. It also focuses attention on elements of the local context that facilitate the reception of transfer. In this respect, local context becomes a secondary cause of convergence. Convergence therefore is explained "from the bottom up" insofar as it stems as much from the circulation of an idea or public policy model, as from its appropriation by the actors involved in local health policy.

Acknowledgements

This article won best article at the Francophone Political Science Association, in Grenoble, 2009. The award was underwritten by the *Journal of Comparative Policy Analysis* (JCPA), the International Comparative Policy Analysis Forum (ICPA) and Routledge. The English translation of this paper was financed by the CNRS Research Unit "PACTE" (UMR 5194, Institute of Political Studies, University of Grenoble, France), the French Political Science Association (AFSP) and the JCPA. The funding was granted as an Award for the Best Young Scholar's Comparative Paper delivered at the 10th Congress of the AFSP in Grenoble, 7–9 September 2009. The initiative was organized in collaboration with the *Journal of Comparative Policy Analysis*. The author also wishes to thank the Research Centre for Political Action in Europe (CRAPE) (Rennes, France) and Centre Léa-Roback (University of Montreal) for their support and Susan Lempriere for final revisions.

Notes

1. The empirical research in Denmark was carried out before the implementation of territorial organization reforms on 1 January 2007. This reform transformed the existing municipalities and

counties into larger units and split responsibility for health – to the new regions for healthcare, and to municipalities for public health. Likewise, in France the fieldwork was carried out before state regional health policies were affected by the public health law passed in 2004.
2. These data are not exhaustive insofar as they concern only those actors that I interviewed in the four areas studied.
3. Community health is a neighborhood practice which aims to help people take charge of their health and local social development.

References

Antonovsky, Aaron, 1996, The salutogenic model as a theory to guide health promotion. *Health Promotion International*, **11**, 11–18.
Benamouzig, Daniel, 2005, *La santé au miroir de l'économie, une histoire de l'économie de la santé en France* (Paris: PUF).
Bennett, Colin J., 1991, What is policy convergence and what causes it? *British Journal of Political Science*, **21**, 215–233.
Bomberg, Elizabeth, 2007, Policy learning in an enlarged European Union: environmental NGOs and new policy instruments. *Journal of European Public Policy*, **14**, 248–268.
Busch, Per-Olof and Jörgens, Helge, 2005, The international sources of policy convergence: explaining the spread of environmental policy innovations. *Journal of European Public Policy*, **12**, 860–884.
Buus, Henriette, 2001, *Sundhedsplejerskeinsitutionens dannelse: en kulturteorisk og kulturhistorisk analyse af velfærdstatens embedsvaerk* [The Institutionalization of Public Health Nursing] (København: Museum Tusculanum).
Cépré, Ludovic, 1999, L'alcoolisme: un enjeu politique régional de santé publique. *Hérodote*, **92**, 144–160.
Clavier, Carole, 2007, Le politique et la santé publique. Une comparaison transnationale de la territorialisation des politiques de santé publique (France, Danemark). Doctoral dissertation, Université de Rennes 1, Rennes.
Clavier, Carole, 2009, Les élus locaux et la santé: des enjeux politiques territoriaux. *Sciences Sociales et Santé*, **27**, 47–74.
Delpeuch, Thierry, 2008, L'analyse des transferts internationaux de politique publique: un état de l'art.Questions de recherche/Research in question, Centre d'études et de recherches internationales, Sciences Po, Paris.
Dezalay, Yves and Garth, Briant, 2002, *The Internationalization of Palace Wars. Lawyers, Economists, and the Contest to Transform Latin American States* (Chicago: The University of Chicago Press).
Dolowitz, David and Marsh, David, 1996, Who learns what from whom? A review of the policy transfer literature. *Political Studies*, **44**, 343–357.
Evans, Mark, 2009, Policy transfer in critical perspective. *Policy Studies*, **30**, 243–268.
Evans, Mark and Davies, Jonathan, 1999, Understanding policy transfer: a multi-level, multi-disciplinary perspective. *Public Administration*, **77**, 361–385.
Genieys, Wiliam and Smyrl, Marc, 2008, Inside the Autonomous State: Programmatic Elites in the Reform of French Health Policy. *Governance*, **21**, 75–93.
Greener, Ian, 2002, Understanding NHS reform: the policy-transfer, social learning, and path-dependency perspectives. *Governance*, **15**, 161–183.
Harrison, Stephen, Moran, Michael and Wood, Bruce, 2002, Policy emergence and policy convergence: the case of "scientific-bureaucratic medicine" in the United States and United Kingdom. *British Journal of Politics and International Relations*, **4**, 1–24.
Hassenteufel, Patrick, 2005, De la comparaison internationale à la comparaison transnationale. Les déplacements de la construction d'objets comparatifs en matière de politiques publiques. *Revue Française de Science Politique*, **55**, 113–132.
Hassenteufel, Patrick, 2008, *Sociologie politique: l'action publique* (Paris: Armand Colin).
HCSP, 1992, *Stratégie pour une politique de santé* (Paris: La Documentation française).
HCSP, 1994, *La santé en France. Rapport général* (Paris: La Documentation française).
Holzinger, Katharina and Knill, Christoph, 2005, Causes and conditions of cross-national policy convergence. *Journal of European Public Policy*, **12**, 775–796.
Jensen, Torben K. and Johnsen, Tommy J., 2000, *Sundhedsfremme i teori og praksis. En lære-, debat- og brugsbog på grundlag af teori og praksisbeskrivelsen* [Health Promotion in Theory and Practice] (Ringkøbing: Forfatterne og Ringkjøbing Amt).

Kamper-Jørgensen, Finn, 1998, Det forebyggende sundhedsarbejde. Forebyggelsesbegreber [Health-related prevention. Concepts of prevention], in: Finn Kamper-Jørgensen and Gert Almind (Eds.) *Forebyggende sundhedsarbejde* (København: Munksgaard), pp. 17–35.

Kickbusch, Ilona, 2003, The contribution of the World Health Organization to a new public health and health promotion. *American Journal of Public Health*, **93**, 383–388.

Lenschow, Andrea, Liefferink, Duncan and Veenman, Sietske, 2005, When the birds sing. A framework for analysing domestic factors behind policy convergence. *Journal of European Public Policy*, **12**, 797–816.

Marmot, Michael and Wilkinson, Richard (Eds.), 2006, *Social Determinants of Health 2nd Edition* (Oxford: Oxford University Press).

Massey, Andrew, 2009, Policy mimesis in the context of global governance. *Policy Studies*, **30**, 383–395.

Nakano, Koichi, 2004, Cross-national transfer of policy ideas: agencification in Britain and Japan. *Governance*, **17**, 169–188.

Nordjyllands Amt, 1990, *Sundhedsmarked 1990* [The Health Market]. Aalborg: Nordjyllands Amt.

Nordjyllands Amt, 2000, *Det 3. sundhedspolitiske handlings program 2000–2008. En plan for forebyggelse og sundhedsfremme* [The Third Action Plan for Health Policy 2000–2008. A Plan for Prevention and Health Promotion] (Aalborg: Aalborg County Council).

Ogden, Jessica, Walt, Gill and Lush, Louisiana, 2003, The politics of "branding" in policy transfer: the case of DOTS for tuberculosis control. *Social Science and Medicine*, **57**, 179–188.

Pedersen, Lene Holm, 2007, Ideas are transformed as they transfer: a comparative study of eco-taxation in Scandinavia. *Journal of European Public Policy*, **14**, 59–77.

Petersen, Alan and Lupton, Deborah, 1996, *The New Public Health. Health and Self in the Age of Risk* (London: Sage).

Piana, Daniela, 2007, Unpacking policy transfer, discovering actors: the French model of judicial education between enlargement and judicial cooperation in the EU. *French Politics*, **5**, 33–65.

Radaelli, Claudio M., 2000, Policy transfer in the European Union: institutional isomorphism as a source of legitimacy. *Governance*, **13**, 25–43.

Radaelli, Claudio M., 2005, Diffusion without convergence: how political context shapes the adoption of regulatory impact assessment. *Journal of European Public Policy*, **12**, 924–943.

Rochaix, Lise and Wilsford, David, 2005, State autonomy, policy paralysis: paradoxes of institutions and culture in the French health care system. *Journal of Health Politics, Policy and Law*, **30**, 97–119.

Sartori, Giovanni, 1991, Comparing and miscomparing. *Journal of Theoretical Politics*, **3**, 243–257.

Stone, Diane, 1999, Learning lessons and transferring policy across time, space and disciplines. *Politics*, **19**, 51–59.

Stone, Diane, 2004, Transfer agents and global networks in the "transnationalization" of policy. *Journal of European Public Policy*, **11**, 545–566.

True, Jacqui and Mintrom, Michael, 2001, Transnational networks and policy diffusion: the case of gender mainstreaming. *International Studies Quarterly*, **45**, 27–57.

Vallgårda, Signild, 2003, *Folkesundhed som politik. Danmark og Sverige fra 1930 til i dag* [Public Health as Policy. Denmark and Sweden since 1930] (Århus: Århus Universitetsforlag).

WHO, 1948, *Preamble to the Constitution of the World Health Organization as adopted by the International Health Conference, New York, 19 June–22 July 1946; signed on 22 July 1946 by the representatives of 61 States (Official Records of the World Health Organization, no. 2, p. 100) and entered into force on 7 April 1948*.

Wolman, Harold and Page, Ed, 2002, Policy transfer among local governments: an information-theory approach. *Governance*, **15**, 477–501.

Can Corruption Be Measured? Comparing Global Versus Local Perceptions of Corruption in East and Southeast Asia

MIN-WEI LIN & CHILIK YU

ABSTRACT *Since Transparency International first released its annual Corruption Perceptions Index (CPI) in 1995, the CPI has quickly become the best known corruption indicator worldwide. The CPI has been widely credited with making comparative and large-N studies of corruption possible, as well as putting the issue of corruption squarely in the international policy agenda. Despite its enormous influence on both academic and policy fronts, the CPI is not without critics. One often noted critique is that the CPI relies solely on surveys of foreign business people and the expert assessments of cross-national analysts; as such, the CPI mainly reflects international experts' perceptions, not the perceptions of each country's citizens. This study examines the above critique in closer detail. Data from the Asian Barometer Survey is employed to analyze whether international experts' corruption perceptions were similar to those of domestic citizens. The Asian Barometer Survey is a public opinion survey on issues related to political values, democracy, and public reform in 13 different areas around East and Southeast Asia (Cambodia, China, Hong Kong, Indonesia, Japan, South Korea, Malaysia, Mongolia, the Philippines, Singapore, Taiwan, Thailand, and Vietnam). Data analysis indicates that global and local perspectives are only moderately aligned in the 13 areas studied. International experts and domestic citizens differ, to varying degrees, in their evaluation of the extent of public sector corruption in several areas, suggesting the presence of a corruption perception gap. Four implications about the existence of this gap can be drawn for future corruption measurement.*

Introduction

Corruption is increasingly regarded as a major challenge for many countries in Asia (and indeed much of the developing world) and is one of the foremost obstacles to Asia's political, economic, and social development (Diamond 1999; Bhargava and Bolongaita 2004). Despite Asian economies having rebounded from the late 1990s financial crisis,

Quah (2006) argues that the problem of corruption remains symptomatic throughout the region, "significantly cramping the extent and potential of Asia's 'rise'".

One widely used measure of the severity of corruption is provided by Transparency International's (TI) Corruption Perception Index (CPI). The CPI ranks countries and territories around the world based on international experts' and business people's perceptions of the level of public sector corruption. Table 1 depicts the 2005–2011 CPI scores for 17 countries/territories located in East and Southeast Asia. CPI scores range from 0 (highly corrupt) to 10 (very clean). As seen in Table 1, Asia is home to countries perceived to be highly corrupt (e.g. North Korea and Myanmar), and countries that are seen as very clean (e.g. Singapore). The CPI scores from 2005–2011 reveal that a given country/territory's scores typically do not vary much year to year. Generally, TI considers a CPI score of 5 to be the transition point differentiating countries that do and do not have a serious corruption problem. In the 2011 CPI, 11 of the 17 countries/territories listed fail to score above 5.

The CPI data reported in Table 1 indicates that the perceived level of public sector corruption is relatively high for a majority of East and Southeast Asian countries/territories. A fundamental, but seldom addressed, question is whether the domestic population of these countries/territories hold views corresponding with the CPI scores. As often noted by critics, because the CPI is an aggregate index constructed predominantly from international expert assessments and opinion surveys of business executives, it represents only a very narrow range of perceptions.

Table 1. Performance of East and Southeast Asian areas on the CPI, 2005–2011

Country/territory	2005 score (rank)	2006 score (rank)	2007 score (rank)	2008 score (rank)	2009 score (rank)	2010 score (rank)	2011 score (rank)
Cambodia	2.3 (130)	2.1 (151)	2.0 (162)	1.8 (166)	2.0 (158)	2.1 (154)	2.1 (164)
China	3.2 (78)	3.3 (70)	3.5 (72)	3.6 (72)	3.6 (79)	3.5 (78)	3.6 (75)
Hong Kong	8.3 (15)	8.3 (15)	8.3 (14)	8.1 (12)	8.2 (12)	8.4 (13)	8.4 (12)
Indonesia	2.2 (137)	2.4 (130)	2.3 (143)	2.6 (126)	2.8 (111)	2.8 (110)	3.0 (100)
Japan	7.3 (21)	7.6 (17)	7.5 (17)	7.3 (18)	7.7 (17)	7.8 (17)	8.0 (14)
Korea (North)	NA	NA	NA	NA	NA	NA	1.0 (182)
Korea (South)	5.0 (40)	5.1 (42)	5.1 (43)	5.6 (40)	5.5 (39)	5.4 (39)	5.4 (43)
Laos	3.3 (77)	2.6 (111)	1.9 (168)	2.0 (151)	2.0 (158)	2.1 (154)	2.2 (154)
Macau	NA	6.6 (26)	5.7 (34)	5.4 (43)	5.3 (43)	5.0 (46)	5.1 (46)
Malaysia	5.1 (39)	5.0 (44)	5.1 (43)	5.1 (47)	4.5 (56)	4.4 (56)	4.3 (60)
Mongolia	3.0 (85)	2.8 (99)	3.0 (99)	3.0 (102)	2.7 (120)	2.7 (116)	2.7 (120)
Myanmar	1.8 (155)	1.9 (160)	1.4 (179)	1.3 (178)	1.4 (178)	1.4 (176)	1.5 (180)
Philippines	2.5 (117)	2.5 (121)	2.5 (131)	2.3 (141)	2.4 (139)	2.4 (134)	2.6 (129)
Singapore	9.4 (5)	9.4 (5)	9.3 (4)	9.2 (4)	9.2 (3)	9.3 (1)	9.2 (5)
Taiwan	5.9 (32)	5.9 (34)	5.7 (34)	5.7 (39)	5.6 (37)	5.8 (33)	6.1 (32)
Thailand	3.8 (59)	3.6 (63)	3.3 (84)	3.5 (80)	3.4 (84)	3.5 (78)	3.4 (80)
Vietnam	2.6 (107)	2.6 (111)	2.6 (123)	2.7 (121)	2.7 (120)	2.7 (116)	2.9 (112)
Regional average	4.38	4.48	4.33	4.33	4.31	4.33	4.21
Number of countries and territories surveyed	159	163	180	180	180	178	183

Source: Transparency International's Corruption Perception Index, 2005–2011. CPI scores are scaled from 0 (highly corrupt) to 10 (very clean). A country or territory's rank indicates its position relative to the other countries and territories included in the index. A useful heuristic is that an index score below five indicates the presence of a serious corruption problem.

To shed light on the above question, this study examines domestic citizens' and international experts' perceptions of corruption in East and Southeast Asia. For local perspectives on corruption, data from the 2005–2008 Asian Barometer Survey (ABS) was utilized. The ABS was a regional, applied research program based at National Taiwan University that investigated the politically relevant attitudes and behaviors of Asian citizens. For the current study, public opinion data was extracted from ABS results for 13 different areas in East and Southeast Asia: Cambodia, China, Hong Kong, Indonesia, Japan, South Korea, Malaysia, Mongolia, the Philippines, Singapore, Taiwan, Thailand, and Vietnam. Data on global perspectives of corruption in these 13 areas, on the other hand, was taken from TI's Corruption Perception Index. Before presenting data analysis results, an overview of the relevant literature on corruption measurement is provided in the next section.

Measuring Corruption

Developing Indicators/Indices of Corruption

While there is general consensus about the threat corruption poses to the effectiveness of national governance, understanding corruption's true patterns, causes, and consequences has been hampered by the twin fundamental problems of definition (Johnston 1996, 2001, 2005; Brown 2006; Philp 2006) and measurement (Jain 2001; Kurer 2005; Miller 2006; Sampford et al. 2006; UNDP 2008). The process of either defining or measuring corruption is notoriously difficult, largely because (a) corruption is usually illicit and concealed, and (b) what constitutes corrupt or unethical behavior varies according to cultural, legal, and other factors (Svensson 2005). Caiden (2001), for instance, has attempted to identify the 19 "most commonly recognized forms of corruption", but these efforts have not closed the definitions debate since there is simply no universal consensus on the meaning of corruption (UNDP 2008). In fact, the United Nations Convention against Corruption (UNCAC) has deliberately steered clear of defining corruption explicitly or comprehensively, relying instead on enumerated acts to characterize the different types of corruption.

Even if substantial issues over the definition of corruption remain unsettled, scholars and practitioners interested in the multi-faceted and complex phenomenon of corruption have not been deterred from attempting to measure it. Early efforts were based on obtaining objective (or hard) measurements such as number of arrests and convictions for corruption, counts of newspaper stories on corruption, and other official records and statistics. The main difficulty with this approach is that such hard empirical evidence is often a sign of an effective criminal justice system (i.e. anti-corruption agencies, prosecutors, and judges) or the presence of a free and independent press to investigate and expose corruption, rather than a reflection of the actual corruption levels. In highly corrupt countries, there may be virtually no arrests for or media reports on serious corruption, whereas in very clean countries, there may be frequent arrests and convictions for relatively minor offenses.

As a result of these inherent deficiencies in using objective indicators, much research over the past 20 years has focused on utilizing subjective measures of corruption as a substitute. Two main types of subjective measures have been developed – perception-based and experience-based measures. Broadly speaking, perception-based measures are indicators based on the subjective opinions of experts and/or citizens about the extent of corruption in a country, whereas experience-based indicators attempt to measure the citizens' and firms' actual experiences with corruption (such as whether they have paid or been solicited for a bribe in exchange for a public service).[1]

The most widely used perception-based measure of corruption is the Corruption Perception Index, produced annually by Transparency International, a non-governmental organization based in Berlin dedicated to raising public awareness about the severity of the worldwide corruption problem. First released in 1995, the CPI has quickly become the best known of TI's corruption measurement tools. The CPI is a composite index (a survey of surveys) that draws on existing global expert evaluations and business opinion surveys from a variety of third party sources, including commercial risk rating agencies, think tanks, NGOs, and international organizations. Under the working definition of corruption being "the abuse of entrusted power for private gain", the CPI ranks countries and territories around the world yearly according to the perceived level of public sector corruption as determined by experts, business people, and analysts (Heinrich and Hodess 2011). The main rationale for combining and aggregating measures from several data sources is to attenuate concerns about potential measurement errors and biases arising from a single source (Lambsdorff 2007).

After TI's introduction of the CPI, researchers at the World Bank also began publishing an international index of corruption as part of its Worldwide Governance Indicators (WGI) project, which was an elaborate effort to measure, compare, and rank the governance of countries/territories around the world. This indicator, known as Control of Corruption (CC), is one of the six dimensions of governance, defined broadly as "the traditions and institutions by which authority in a country is exercised" (Kaufmann et al. 1999). The CC governance indicator shares some of the same primary sources as the CPI, although it uses slightly different estimation and aggregation procedures (Kaufmann et al. 2010). However, unlike the CPI, the World Bank's CC governance indicator employs a more heterogeneous set of questions about the different types of corruption and incorporates a few data sources that survey ordinary citizens' perceptions of corruption.[2]

The wide accessibility of these two perception-based corruption indices have thus stimulated a substantial amount of academic research on corruption and advanced its study over the past two decades (for excellent reviews, see Svensson 2005; Lambsdorff 2006, 2007; Treisman 2007). Since both the CPI and World Bank's CC governance indicator cover a large number of countries and territories, they have not only made large-N studies of the causes and consequences of corruption possible, but have also placed the issues of combating corruption and improving governance squarely on the international policy agenda of governments and private enterprises. Nevertheless, while these composite indices represent a major step forward in understanding and measuring corruption, strong concerns about the adequacy, validity, reliability, and ultimate usefulness of these perceptual measures persist (for a partial list of critiques, see Lancaster and Montinola 2001; Sik 2002; Arndt and Oman 2006; Galtung 2006; Soreide 2006; Knack 2007; Andersson and Heywood 2009; Langbein and Knack 2010; Pollitt 2010; Razafindrakoto and Roubaud 2010; Hawken and Munck 2011). It is not the intention of the present paper to defend the use of global perception-based corruption indices, or to provide yet another critique on their numerous inherent conceptual and methodological shortcomings. Rather, the purpose of the paper is to address a more mundane, but critical question: Do citizens' perceptions of corruption differ from the experts' perceptions, and, if so, to what extent are they different?

Whose Perceptions Count: Experts or Citizens?

As noted earlier, one often-cited weakness of aggregate indicators of corruption such as the CPI or the Control of Corruption governance indicator is that they give greater weight to the opinions of international business executives and the expert assessment of cross-national analysts. As such, both indices primarily reflect the opinions of mostly foreign experts and business elites, which may be disconnected from the views of the general public in each country under evaluation.

To address such shortcomings, beginning in 2003 TI supplemented the CPI with the Global Corruption Barometer (GCB), a large worldwide survey across dozens of countries that investigates and tracks ordinary people's views toward, and experience of, corruption. TI's own analysis of the GCB and CPI data indicates that, contrary to the above criticism, there is indeed a statistically significant correlation between citizens' and international experts' assessments of the extent of public sector corruption across all countries (Transparency International 2010).[3] Moreover, international experts' general opinions on corruption were also found to align strongly with the local public's specific experiences with bribery – in countries or territories where the experts perceive corruption to be rampant, a higher proportion of citizens reported paying bribes in the past year (Transparency International 2010).[4] The message from TI thus seems clear; since the CPI and the GCB correlate, expert perceptions of corruption were arguably not too dissimilar from average citizens' perceptions, thereby establishing the validity for each of these indicators.

In the literature, a number of studies using other international public opinion surveys have corroborated TI's findings, although none focused on East or Southeast Asia specifically. In a review of major international corruption indices, Ko and Samajdar (2010) compared the CPI with public opinion data taken from two multi-region surveys: the World Values Survey (WVS) and the International Crime Victimization Survey (ICVS). Their analyses show that CPI scores are highly correlated with local people's responses to the bribery questions respectively found in the WVS ($r = -0.86$) and in the ICVS ($r = -0.75$). The authors thereby concluded that, as far as petty bribery is concerned, international corruption indices "can reflect [a] significant variation of domestic perceptions". Also, in a study of the level of government corruption in seven Latin American countries, Canache and Allison (2005) found that there was a similar high degree of correspondence between expert and local judgments.

A recent innovative study conducted by Razafindrakoto and Roubaud (2010) in eight African countries, however, has produced findings that directly challenge the above studies. Surveying both the general public and the so-called experts of those countries, they found that the expert perceptions did not correlate with the ordinary citizens' views at all, but instead were more closely associated with international corruption indicators such as the CPI and the CC governance indicator.[5] More importantly, the authors found that experts – whether domestic or foreign – systematically overestimated the actual extent of, and the local population's tolerance for, corrupt practices. Based on these results, Razafindrakoto and Roubaud posit that most experts were basing their assessments on an erroneous cultural model of "how Africa operates" and/or acting on their personal ideological inclinations.

Moreover, in an analysis of evaluator characteristics within the various data sources of the Worldwide Governance Indicators, Hawken and Munck (2011) discovered that different classes of evaluators systematically generate higher or lower estimates of the level of corruption in countries around the world. For example, they found that experts from commercial risk assessment agencies generally provide stricter assessments of the extent of corruption in a country than those from non-governmental organizations and that only expert ratings from the multilateral development banks can be considered indistinguishable from general public opinion. Hawken and Munck also detected important evaluator differences in regional comparisons as well. For instance, Southeast Asia as a whole received relatively unfavorable assessments from experts in commercial risk rating agencies and in surveys of business executives, but more favorable assessments from surveys of the public. East Asian countries, on the other hand, were favored by experts from multilateral development banks, but disfavored by other business executives and by the citizens at large. The main reason for differences in expert ratings within or between regions is unclear, but the implication is that in most geographical areas, expert and common citizen's perceptions differ, and noticeable variations exist among different classes of experts.

That a discrepancy may exist between expert and the general public's judgments is neither new nor exclusive to studies of corruption. For some time now, it has been well known in environmental policy and the sociology of risk literature that, for whatever reason, experts and lay people frequently disagree on risk perceptions and risk assessments (Bostrom 1997; Sjoberg 1999). The most illustrative example is the case of nuclear power in the 1960s. Scientific opinion at the time declared the risks of nuclear energy to be low, but the general public was alarmed about the safety of this new technology, perceiving the risks of a nuclear disaster to be high. Risk managers and theorists have since been preoccupied with explaining this gap between expert and lay perceptions, and also finding avenues to bridge it. In the policy arena, citizens also frequently disagree with policy experts on important public issues quite frequently, even though the latter is presumed to have the best-informed opinion (Darmofal 2005).

There are common-sense reasons to trust expert assessments. By definition, experts are individuals who, through education, training, and experience, possess extensive specialized knowledge or skills in a particular subject, and thus can act as a reliable information source or adviser. Kaufmann and Kraay (2008) provide three advantages that expert assessments offer over public opinion when measuring multifaceted concepts such as governance or corruption: (1) lower costs (i.e. no need to carry out surveys of individuals or firms across 100 or more countries and territories); (2) the ability to tailor assessments for cross-national comparability; and (3), given the complexity of the concept in question, experts can be more readily called upon to provide technical or specialized information.

Still, expert assessments do have their fair share of important limitations. One is that expert assessments (and the experts themselves) are subject to ideological, cultural, institutional, and other biases. The CPI, for instance, has been severely criticized for relying on data sources whose samples were disproportionally pro-business and male, thereby overlooking the perspectives of most women, the poor, and the disenfranchised (Galtung 2006). Donchev and Ujhelyi (2013) found evidence that, for a given level of corruption, corruption indices based on expert perceptions were not only systematically biased in favor of more economically developed and traditional Protestant countries, but they also tended to penalize larger countries. The second concern is that experts, being a small and relatively homogeneous group, may lack familiarity with the local customs and language, or worse, may only have a superficial knowledge of them (Sik 2002), particularly for smaller countries (Knack 2007). The third issue with expert assessments (and to a lesser extent with citizens' subjective evaluations) is a danger of the echo chamber problem. Individuals assessing corruption levels end up simply repeating conventional wisdom, thus reinforcing a vicious cycle of prior (mis)conceptions (Johnston 2002). Knack (2007) also claimed that, rather than being independent evaluations, expert judgments are often based on experts from different institutions consulting with one another, reading each other's reports, and possibly being influenced by each other's ratings.

By contrast, there are three main reasons local citizen surveys may provide superior indications of corruption levels. One is that citizen opinions are extremely valuable because they represent internal stakeholders who may choose to act upon those views (Kaufmann and Kraay 2008), and governments are less likely to dismiss the views of their citizens (as opposed to external expert assessments, which are often ignored). Second, the views of randomly chosen members of the general public – unlike expert opinions – are more likely to be independent from, and uncontaminated by, other types of judgments (Knack 2007). Third, household surveys of citizens are extremely helpful for assessing the prevalence of petty or low-level corruption (UNDP 2008).

Yet cross-national surveys of citizens face several potential problems that threaten their validity and reliability. First, since most forms of corruption are illegal, some respondents may not answer questions truthfully, especially those in authoritarian countries or in societies where the public acceptance of corruption is low (Mishler and Rose 2008). Second, the general public is also more prone than experts to be influenced by the media and the country's overall political and economic climate (Galtung 2006). The possibility of a home country bias is one of the justifications for using international experts, on the premise that outside reviewers can be expected to act in a more neutral and competent way when evaluating many different countries according to a set of universal standards (Lambsdorff 2007). Third, like all empirical social science research based on subjective data, surveys of citizens are subject to three forms of systematic measurement error: respondents' cognitive problems in understanding/answering questions, respondents' inclination to give socially desirable responses to sensitive questions, and respondents' lack of an informed opinion on a particular issue (Bertrand and Mullainathan 2001).

Nevertheless, scholars and practitioners alike will continue debating over whose perceptions, the global experts or the local citizens, better capture the actual level of corruption in a country. Each has its own strengths and weaknesses for certain purposes. Moving forward, more restraint will be needed when using these two forms of perceptions in academic or policy contexts. In the next section, the central question of the present study is considered: do East and Southeast Asian citizens' perceived levels of corruption mirror those of the global experts?

Perceptions of Corruption in East and Southeast Asia

To gauge individual citizens' perceptions of corruption in society, the Asian Barometer Survey[6] asked respondents the following two questions:

1. How widespread do you think corruption and bribe-taking are in the national government [in the capital city]?
2. How widespread do you think corruption and bribe-taking are in your local/municipal government?

For both questions, respondents were presented with four choices: "hardly anyone is involved", "not a lot of officials are corrupt", "most officials are corrupt", and "almost everyone is corrupt". The original coding scheme was retained, so that higher values would indicate higher levels of perceived corruption. Table 2 presents the data on the

Table 2. Citizens' perceptions of corruption and bribe-taking in the national government

Country/territory	How widespread is corruption and bribe-taking in the national government? (1 to 4 scale)				Valid respondents Total
	Hardly anyone is involved	Not a lot of officials are corrupt	Most officials are corrupt	Almost everyone is corrupt	
Cambodia (Year: 2008; n = 1000; percentage missing = 22.4%)	11 (1.4%)	251 (32.3%)	**348 (44.9%)**	166 (21.4%)	776
China (Year: 2007–2008; n = 5098; percentage missing = 60.8%)	816 (40.9%)	**893 (44.7%)**	229 (11.5%)	58 (2.9%)	1996
Indonesia (Year: 2006; n = 1598; percentage missing = 12.5%)	94 (6.7%)	**616 (44.0%)**	489 (35.0%)	200 (14.3%)	1399
Japan (Year: 2007; n = 1067; percentage missing = 10.3%)	11 (1.1%)	**529 (55.3%)**	367 (38.3%)	50 (5.2%)	957
South Korea (Year: 2006; n = 1212; percentage missing = 5.3%)	15 (1.3%)	**585 (51.0%)**	410 (35.7%)	138 (12.0%)	1148
Malaysia (Year: 2007; n = 1218; percentage missing = 10.0%)	47 (4.3%)	**561 (51.2%)**	356 (32.5%)	132 (12.0%)	1096
Mongolia (Year: 2006; n = 1211; percentage missing = 7.3%)	31 (2.8%)	251 (22.4%)	**482 (42.9%)**	359 (32.0%)	1123
Philippines (Year: 2005; n = 1200; percentage missing = 6.2%)	103 (9.1%)	276 (24.5%)	**457 (40.6%)**	290 (25.8%)	1126
Singapore (Year: 2006; n = 1012; percentage missing = 13.6%)	**443 (50.7%)**	416 (47.6%)	11 (1.3%)	4 (0.5%)	874
Taiwan (Year: 2006; n = 1587; percentage missing = 13.3%)	43 (3.1%)	411 (29.9%)	**763 (55.5%)**	159 (11.6%)	1376
Thailand (Year: 2006; n = 1546; percentage missing = 15.8%)	193 (14.8%)	**725 (55.7%)**	280 (21.5%)	103 (7.9%)	1301
Vietnam (Year: 2005; n = 1200; percentage missing = 19.3%)	115 (11.9%)	**688 (71.0%)**	143 (14.8%)	23 (2.4%)	969

Source: Asian Barometer Survey, 2005–2008.
Note: Cell entries are frequencies, and numbers in parenthesis are percentages. The largest group of responses for each country is highlighted in **bold**. Because of rounding, percentages may not add up to 100. Data was not available for Hong Kong. n = country/territory sample size.

distribution of individual responses to the question about corruption in the national government, disaggregated by country, with the largest share of responses highlighted in bold.

Most local citizens surveyed in the ABS did not think that corruption was widespread in their respective national governments. As depicted in Table 2, a majority of respondents in China, Indonesia, Japan, South Korea, Malaysia, Singapore, Thailand, and Vietnam believed that few national government officials were involved in corruption. Expectedly, Singapore was the only country where more than half of respondents felt that hardly any government official was engaged in corrupt behavior. Conversely, over 66 per cent of the respondents in Cambodia, Mongolia, the Philippines, and Taiwan believe that most or almost all government officials are corrupt. Although no country had the "almost everyone is corrupt" as the most popular response, Mongolia came closest with 32 per cent, followed by the Philippines at 26 per cent). Indonesia was interesting because its citizens were the most evenly split between those who perceived corruption in the national government to be high and those who deemed it to be low (49 per cent versus 51 per cent).

The distribution of individual responses for each country on this corruption perception question nevertheless produced some interesting and unexpected results, especially when compared to the CPI scores (from Table 1) or conventional wisdom. For instance, the percentage of Chinese, Thai, and Vietnamese respondents who believed that corruption is *not* pervasive in their national governments were all above 70 per cent. Additionally, a large majority of Taiwanese citizens (approximately 67 per cent) perceived that most or almost all national government officials *are* corrupt. These two sets of findings certainly defy these countries' performance and placements in the CPI. In the ensuing discussion, these four countries will be used as illustrative cases in the current study's attempt to explore why experts' and citizens' perceptions differ.

What factors explain the perplexing percentages above? While ensuring that underlying data met the necessary research requirements, the problem of missing data as triggered by nonresponses to questionnaire items was noticed. An inspection showed that only 39 per cent (n = 1996) of China's respondents provided useful answers to the question regarding corruption in the national government. Assuming that data collection was conducted properly and data entry errors were kept at a minimum, this means that as much as 61 per cent of Chinese respondents – the highest percentage of abstainers in the ABS – did not answer the question. Those that responded provided mostly favorable assessments of their national government officials. Missing information makes Chinese responses on corruption problematic, and any analysis using this questionnaire item must be treated with caution.[7] Item nonresponse because of respondent error or reticence to answer was less of an issue for Taiwan, Thailand, and Vietnam. Missing values accounted for less than 20 per cent in these countries' surveys.[8]

One explanation that may have impacted the overall pattern of responses was the time period during which the ABS was implemented in each country. This factor partly explains why in the 2006 ABS Survey, two out of three Taiwanese respondents felt their national government was overrun by corrupt officials. There was severe political turmoil in Taiwan during 2006, with a series of corruption scandals involving then President Chen Shui-bian and his close associates being uncovered. As a result, people's indignation toward the Chen administration lingered for months (for more information, see Chu 2007; Yu et al. 2008).

In Thailand, the ABS was conducted a few months before the Thai military staged a successful coup to overthrow Prime Minister Thaksin Sinawatra, a lightning-rod politician who, despite enormous popularity in rural areas, was intensely distrusted by opposition leaders, academics, journalists, and middle-class Bangkok residents. They saw Thaksin as gradually undermining Thailand's democratic institutions, weakening media independence, and establishing a regime extensively fueled by corruption (Ockey 2007). However, without additional context, the events of 2006 do not fully explain why Thai respondents believed that corruption was not a serious public concern and yet ousted Thaksin's administration in 2006, at least partly over corruption. According to a Thai author, this was precisely the source of the problem: it was not the acts of corruption themselves, but the fact that tolerance of corruption was "too deeply ingrained" in Thailand, permeating all sectors of Thai society, as citizens were "easily bored and indifferent toward corruption by politicians and bureaucrats" (Hengkietisak 2010). People's greater acceptance of corruption may constitute another explanation for the difference in perceptions between experts and average citizens.

As for Vietnamese perceptions that corruption was not widespread in the national government, the timing of the survey appears to have been a critical factor. For most of 2005, Vietnam continued its push toward greater economic growth, improved its governance, and intensified the dialogue between the state and society concerning global integration (Luong 2006). In that particular year, there was extensive coverage of major corruption cases by the media, and the Vietnamese authoritarian state toughened its anti-corruption and anti-waste stance by passing the country's first comprehensive anti-corruption legislation (Fritzen 2006). These developments, arguably, provided the Vietnamese ABS respondents with reason to perceive their government leaders as committed to cracking down on graft. Under this scenario, Vietnamese citizens are perhaps more trusting of their government's anti-corruption efforts than the external experts.

Table 2 contains a mixture of both anticipated and unanticipated results. Being cautious, it remains unclear whether the unexpected results should be labeled as citizens' perceptual errors, or as indications of something else, such as wider tolerance of corruption or greater faith in government. In Table 3, the distribution of citizen responses about the existence of widespread corruption in local or municipal governments is reported. Here the data from Hong Kong is included but not Singapore's (the question was omitted from the Singaporean survey due to the country's small size). The percentages in Table 3 closely resemble those in Table 2. First, contrary to perceptions of government corruption at the national level, most Cambodian and Mongolian citizens believed corruption was less rampant at the local level. Second, there were considerably more Chinese respondents believing corruption and bribery to be prevalent in local governments (although item nonresponse was still a problem). On the other hand, citizens of Taiwan and the Philippines carried over their perceptions that corruption and bribe-taking behavior by public officials was just as prevalent in local as in national government.

Citizens' perceptions of corruption in both national and local governments can be aggregated and then averaged to form a measure that captures the citizen's overall evaluation of the severity of public sector corruption in a particular country/territory. This mean perceived corruption from the ABS data can then be compared with expert-based indices of corruption such as the CPI (Table 4). Because countries were surveyed at different times, this study calculates their CPI value as the average of their CPI scores for the two years immediately following their ABS implementation year.[9] The correlation

Table 3. Citizens' perceptions of corruption and bribe-taking in the local/municipal government

Country/territory	How widespread is corruption and bribe-taking in your local/municipal government? (1 to 4 scale)					Valid respondents Total
	Hardly anyone is involved	Not a lot of officials are corrupt	Most officials are corrupt	Almost everyone is corrupt	
Cambodia (Year: 2008; n = 1000; percentage missing = 6.0%)	65 (6.9%)	**420 (44.7%)**	320 (34.0%)	135 (14.4%)	940
China (Year: 2007–2008; n = 5098; percentage missing = 39.5%)	372 (12.1%)	1226 (39.7%)	1143 (37.1%)	344 (11.2%)	3085
Hong Kong (Year: 2007; n = 849; percentage missing = 16.0%)	139 (19.5%)	**486 (68.2%)**	83 (11.6%)	5 (0.7%)	713
Indonesia (Year: 2006; n = 1598; percentage missing = 12.4%)	228 (16.3%)	**620 (44.3%)**	388 (27.7%)	164 (11.7%)	1400
Japan (Year: 2007; n = 1067; percentage missing = 8.2%)	20 (2.0%)	**554 (56.5%)**	366 (37.3%)	40 (4.1%)	980
South Korea (Year: 2006; n = 1212; percentage missing = 5.1%)	35 (3.0%)	**626 (54.4%)**	377 (32.8%)	112 (9.7%)	1150
Malaysia (Year: 2007; n = 1218; percentage missing = 10.0%)	63 (5.7%)	**567 (51.1%)**	342 (30.8%)	137 (12.4%)	1096
Mongolia (Year: 2006; n = 1211; percentage missing = 8.4%)	161 (14.3%)	**438 (39.0%)**	351 (31.3%)	173 (15.4%)	1109
Philippines (Year: 2005; n = 1200; percentage missing = 6.4%)	161 (14.2%)	294 (26.0%)	**451 (39.9%)**	224 (19.8%)	1123
Taiwan (Year: 2006; n = 1587; percentage missing = 10.6%)	56 (3.9%)	423 (29.8%)	**822 (57.9%)**	118 (8.3%)	1419
Thailand (Year: 2006; n = 1546; percentage missing = 15.7%)	358 (27.5%)	**684 (52.5%)**	199 (15.3%)	63 (4.8%)	1304
Vietnam (Year: 2005; n = 1200; percentage missing = 17.8%)	385 (39.0%)	**539 (54.6%)**	54 (5.5%)	9 (0.9%)	987

Notes: Cell entries are frequencies, and numbers in parenthesis are percentages. The largest group of responses for each country or territory highlighted in **bold**. Because of rounding, percentages may not add up to 100. Data was not available for Singapore. n = country/territory sample size.
Source: Asian Barometer Survey, 2005–2008.

Table 4. Analysis of perception differences in the ABS and CPI data using z-scores

Country/territory	Mean perceived corruption (ABS)	ABSZ	CPI score (2-year average)	CPIZ	CPIZ' = −1 × CPIZ	ABSZ − CPIZ'	Absolute value of (ABSZ − CPIZ')
Philippines	2.74	1.05	2.50	−0.93	0.93	0.12	0.12
Singapore	1.51	−2.25	9.25	2.00	−2.00	−0.25	0.25
Cambodia	2.66	0.85	2.05	−1.12	1.12	−0.28	0.28
Mongolia	2.76	1.10	3.00	−0.71	0.71	0.38	0.38
Hong Kong	1.94	−1.11	8.15	1.52	−1.52	0.41	0.41
Malaysia	2.51	0.42	4.80	0.07	−0.07	0.49	0.49
China	2.28	−0.19	3.55	−0.47	0.47	−0.66	0.66
Indonesia	2.45	0.28	2.45	−0.95	0.95	−0.67	0.67
South Korea	2.54	0.52	5.35	0.31	−0.31	0.82	0.82
Thailand	2.10	−0.66	3.40	−0.54	0.54	−1.19	1.19
Taiwan	2.72	1.00	5.70	0.46	−0.46	1.46	1.46
Japan	2.45	0.28	7.50	1.24	−1.24	1.52	1.52
Vietnam	1.87	−1.28	2.60	−0.88	0.88	−2.17	2.17
Regional mean (μ)	2.35		4.64				
Standard deviation (σ)	0.37		2.30				

Notes: ABSZ and CPIZ are the respective z-scores calculated from the ABS and CPI values. The CPIZ was then reversed to produce CPIZ' so that higher values indicate more corruption. In the table, countries are ordered from low to high according to the absolute value of the difference between their ABS and CPI z-scores. The closer the absolute value of the difference in z-scores is to zero (= more congruence), the smaller the perception gap between citizens and experts.

Source: Transparency International; Asian Barometer Survey, 2005–2008.

coefficient between ABS's mean perceived corruption and the CPI values equaled −0.507, suggesting a medium level of perceptual correspondence between the two. However, ABS/CPI correlation was not statistically significant at the usual 0.05 level ($p < 0.077$).

To understand how each country compares to others in the region, standard z-scores were computed for all countries (labeled ABSZ and CPIZ in Table 4).[10] After a few elementary math operations to get the correct signs, the two z-scores were subtracted from one another to obtain an estimate of the corruption perception gap between citizens and experts. For easier interpretation, the absolute value of the differences in z-scores was taken. These results are listed in the rightmost column of Table 4.

As can be seen from the table, the Philippines, Singapore, and Cambodia have the smallest values when the two z-scores were subtracted from one another, indicating a greater congruence in corruption perception between the citizens and experts. The countries where experts and citizens most diverged were Thailand, Taiwan, Japan, and Vietnam – they all had z-score differences greater than one standard deviation.

Results show that only *some* commonality between local people's aggregate perceptions of corruption and global experts' views as provided by the CPI. The lack of a direct, strong correspondence between the two is displayed in Figure 1, where countries' ABS z-scores are plotted against their CPI z-scores. The 45 degree diagonal in the figure is used to indicate perfect congruence between ABS and CPI.

As can be seen from the figure, four types of combinations between (global) expert and (local) citizen perceptions can be identified: (1) both groups perceived corruption in the country to be high (quadrant I); (2) both groups perceived corruption to be low (quadrant II); (3) experts, but not the citizens, perceived corruption to be high (quadrant III), and (4) citizens, but not the experts, perceived corruption in the country to be high (quadrant IV). The distribution of Asian countries across the four quadrants is telling.

Figure 1. A typology of perception differences.

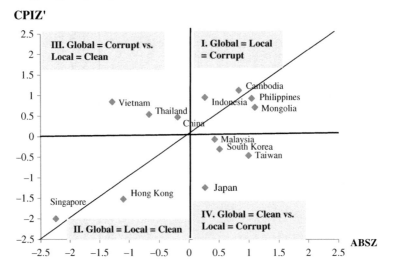

Source: Transparency International; Asian Barometer Survey, 2005–2008.
Note: ABSZ and CPIZ are the respective z-scores calculated from the ABS and CPI values. The CPIZ was then reversed to produce the CPIZ' so that higher values indicate greater corruption.

Asian citizens' aggregate perceived corruption aligned with the expert (CPI) view in only half of the countries (quadrants I and II). Among the countries that performed more poorly in the CPI rankings, only citizens from four countries (the Philippines, Cambodia, Mongolia, and Indonesia) agreed with the experts that corruption was rampant in their governments. Among places that score high on the CPI (lower perceived corruption), citizens from Singapore and Hong Kong also collectively perceived the level of public corruption to be low. For quadrants III and IV, on the other hand, global and local perspectives disagreed, sometimes sharply. In quadrant III are the countries that performed poorly in the CPI rankings (Vietnam, Thailand, and China), while citizens perceived their government to be relatively clean. In quadrant IV, citizens in Japan, Taiwan, South Korea, and Malaysia viewed their government to be relatively corrupt, but the experts believe otherwise. This typology of perception differences between global experts and local citizens should be useful for future research, and the reasons for the existence of or lack of perception gaps for these countries deserves further investigation.

Conclusions

Increasing worldwide concerns about reducing corruption in the public sector give considerable impetus to the search for a reliable measurement of, normally hidden, corruption. So far, aggregate indices based primarily on international expert assessments are the best known and most widely used measurement tools, but validity concerns persist. Critics charge that global corruption indices do not necessarily reflect local views. Although aware of the problem, academic literature has only recently paid attention to the existence, causes, and consequences of a perception gap between international experts and the local citizens concerning corruption in a country (Roca 2010).

This study's objective is to compare international experts' and domestic citizens' perceptions of corruption in East and Southeast Asia and develop a typology of perception differences for future research. Using Asian Barometer Survey data for 13 countries/territories in the region, local citizens' responses to questions about the prevalence of corruption in their national and local government were examined. The study found the correlation between citizens' perceptions and experts' assessments in these selected Asian countries/territories to be only moderately strong. The result is consistent with previous studies using the Latinobarometro or Afrobarometer to test the congruity between expert ratings and mass perceptions of government effectiveness in Latin American and African countries (Kurtz and Schrank 2007). The observed perceptual disparity between the two perspectives did not always have the same direction: in some countries the international experts reported higher levels of corruption, while in others local citizens rated corruption higher. Given these results, a different question naturally emerged: why don't global experts and local citizens agree (more often) in their corruption perceptions?

ABS data limitations do not allow a more in-depth investigation of the factors causing the incongruity between global and local perceptions of corruption; thus, there are more questions than answers. It is fair to say that just as global expert assessments have their particular predispositions and idiosyncrasies, local perceptions have their own dynamics as well. A few possible reasons for the divergence were derived from the extant literature: personal ideology, cultural bias, and the echo chamber problem on the international experts' side; respondent reticence (to give truthful answers to sensitive questions), the effect of media or government influence, and greater tolerance for corruption on the domestic citizens' side. Clearly, this list of explanations is neither definitive nor exhaustive. A more immediate challenge would be finding ways to disentangle and later test these various factors. The result would be a better understanding about the perceptions of corruption itself, and a narrowing of the chasm between international expert and domestic citizen corruption assessments.

In conclusion, four implications can be drawn regarding the future of corruption measurement. First, a multi-measure of corruption that incorporates both global (expert-based) and local (citizen-based) perspectives is necessary. A measure that includes the views of different groups and stakeholders would better approximate the actual levels and trends of corruption in a country. Second, future corruption measures need to be ongoing, not one-shot studies. By having time-series data, scholars and officials can be more confident in measuring corruption and in suggesting anti-corruption initiatives. Time-series data would also allow one to test for the presence of time period-related variables. Third, to the extent that local perspectives are valuable in and of themselves, these perspectives cannot simply be added onto existing corruption indices such as CPI for cross-national comparisons without reasonable adjustments, because (a) practices and behaviors that are acceptable in one country may be viewed as corrupt in another (problem of definition), and (b) the quality and validity of local surveys may be difficult to control over a large number of countries and territories (problem of data collection). Finally, if local perspectives of corruption are to be taken into account for global comparison, they should be entered as *relative changes* to enhance cross-national comparability, in order to reduce potential confounding factors.[11] Although no measure of corruption currently features all of the above requirements, the creation of a more inclusive measure of corruption is a goal that should be supported and encouraged by both academic and practitioner communities.

Notes

1. In all fairness, just as corruption perception indices became popular and near-permanent fixtures in cross-national studies of corruption in the late 1990s and early 2000s, researchers began to argue about the need to go beyond perception-based measures and people's impressions. One approach is to examine the actual experience of people exposed to bribery and corruption, as mentioned in the text. However, some scholars contend that even these experience-based measures of corruption may not be accurate enough (see Johnston 2010; Hawken and Munck 2011). They suggest taking steps to develop more sophisticated objective measures of corruption, such as the time required to obtain permits and licenses, the amount of funds leakage in public works projects, and whether prices paid to suppliers and charged to the public for basic services are reasonable (Johnston 2010). Viewed in this manner, corruption measurement research has indeed nearly come full circle.
2. In the most recent update (2011) of World Bank's CC governance indicator, five out of its 30 sources were surveys of individual citizens: Afrobarometer, Latinobarometro, Vanderbilt University's AmericasBarometer, Gallup World Poll, and TI's Global Corruption Barometer.
3. To be specific, the Pearson's correlation coefficient (r) between global expert evaluations in the 2009 CPI and the local people's perception scores in the 2010 GCB was 0.54 ($p < 0.01$).
4. The Pearson's correlation coefficient between the 2009 CPI scores and the percentage of local citizens who report paying bribes was –0.66 ($p < 0.01$). The coefficient has a negative sign because CPI scores are scaled from 10 (very clean) to 0 (highly corrupt).
5. These experts include, "researchers, development workers, decision-makers, high-ranking public officials, politicians, etc." (Razafindrakoto and Roubaud 2010: 1062).
6. The ABS is a collaborative effort encompassing research teams from 13 political systems in East and Southeast Asia. Each administering team was responsible for survey sampling and implementation in its

area. Most individual national surveys used a variation of multi-stage cluster sampling design (sometimes in combination with probability-proportional-to-size sampling) to select the primary geographic sampling units, households, and respondents, except for four areas which used multi-stage random sampling (Japan, Hong Kong, Mongolia, and Singapore), and mainland China, which used multi-stage stratified area sampling methods. In all countries, target respondents represented a cross-section of voting-age adult citizens, and all interviews were conducted face-to-face by trained fieldworkers in the language of the respondent's choice. The ABS uses a standard questionnaire with identical or functionally equivalent questions, which made comparison of results possible across different areas.
7. While there exist several modern remedies for missing data problems (such as multiple imputation techniques), these approaches were ultimately not considered here because a key assumption of those models – that the data was missing completely at random – was probably not met in the China ABS survey.
8. Although there is no consensus in the literature regarding at what point the amount of missing information becomes problematic for inference and estimation, researchers have suggested that a cutoff point between 5 and 20 per cent is acceptable (see Schlomer et al. 2010).
9. The CPI used data from the previous two years to calculate a country's or territory's annual corruption perception score. As such, the CPI is a lagged index, which may not reflect the most recent developments or situations in a country/territory. To correct for this lag, the subsequent two-year average CPI score was compared with the ABS scores.
10. The formula for computing z-scores is $z = \frac{X_i - \mu}{\sigma}$, where μ is the mean and σ is the standard deviation.
11. The formula for computing relative change is: $\frac{this\ year's\ score - last\ year's\ score}{last\ year's\ score}$.

Acknowledgements

Data analyzed in this article were collected by the Asian Barometer Project (2005-2008), which was co-directed by Professors Fu Hu and Yun-han Chu and received major funding support from Taiwan's Ministry of Education, Academia Sinica, and National Taiwan University. The Asian Barometer Project Office (www.asianbarometer.org) is solely responsible for the data distribution. The authors appreciate the assistance by the institutes and individuals aforementioned. They are also grateful to Transparency International (TI) and TI's chapter in Taiwan for providing additional data used in the article. Lastly, they thank the editor and three anonymous reviewers for their constructive comments and suggestions. The views expressed herein are solely the authors' responsibility.

References

Andersson, S. and Heywood, P., 2009, The politics of perception: Use and abuse of Transparency International's approach to measuring corruption. *Political Studies*, **57**(4), pp. 746–767.
Arndt, C. and Oman, C., 2006, *Uses and Abuses of Governance Indicators* (Paris: OECD Development Centre).
Bertrand, M. and Mullainathan, S., 2001, Do people mean what they say? Implications for subjective survey data. *American Economic Review*, **91**(2), pp. 67–72.
Bhargava, V. and Bolongaita, E., 2004, *Challenging Corruption in Asia* (Washington, DC: The World Bank).
Bostrom, A., 1997, Risk perceptions: 'Experts' vs. 'lay people'. *Duke Environmental Law & Policy Forum*, **8**, pp. 101–113.
Brown, A. J., 2006, What are we trying to measure? Reviewing the basics of corruption definition, in: C. Sampford, A. Shacklock, C. Connors and F. Galtung (Eds) *Measuring Corruption* (Burlington, VT: Ashgate Publishers), pp. 57–79.
Caiden, G., 2001, Corruption and governance, in: G. Caiden, O. P. Dwivedi, and J. Jabbra (Eds) *Where Corruption Lives* (Bloomfield, CT: Kumarian Press), pp. 15–37.
Canache, D. and Allison, M., 2005, Perceptions of political corruption in latin american democracies. *Latin American Politics and Society*, **47**(3), pp. 91–111.
Chu, Y.-H., 2007, Taiwan in 2006: A year of political turmoil. *Asian Survey*, **47**(1), pp. 44–51.
Darmofal, D., 2005, Elite cues and citizen disagreement with expert opinion. *Political Research Quarterly*, **58**(3), pp. 381–395.

Diamond, L., 1999, *Developing Democracy* (Baltimore: Johns Hopkins University Press).
Donchev, D. and Ujhelyi, G. 2013, *What Do Corruption Indices Measure?* Working Paper. University of Houston.
Fritzen, S., 2006, Beyond "political will": How institutional context shapes the implementation of anti-corruption policies. *Policy and Society*, **24**(3), pp. 79–96.
Galtung, F., 2006, Measuring the immeasurable: Boundaries and functions of (Macro) corruption indices, in: C. Sampford, A. Shacklock, C. Connors and F. Galtung (Eds) *Measuring Corruption* (Burlington, VT: Ashgate Publishers), pp. 101–130.
Hawken, A. and Munck, G. 2011, *Does the Evaluator Make a Difference? Measurement Validity in Corruption Research*. Working Paper. The Committee on Concepts and Methods, International Political Science Association (IPSA).
Heinrich, F. and Hodess, R., 2011, Measuring Corruption, in: A. Graycar and R. G. Smith (Eds) *Handbook of Global Research and Practice in Corruption* (Cheltenham: Edward Elgar), pp. 18–33.
Hengkietisak, K. 2010, Tolerance of corruption is too ceeply ingrained. *Bangkok Post*, 20 November. Available at http://www.bangkokpost.com/learning/learning-from-news/208707/tolerance-of-corruption.
Jain, A., 2001, Corruption: A review. *Journal of Economic Surveys*, **15**(1), pp. 71–121.
Johnston, M., 1996, The search for definitions: The vitality of politics and the issue of corruption. *International Social Science Journal*, **149**, pp. 321–335.
Johnston, M., 2001, The definitions debate: Old conflicts in new guises, in: A. Jain (Ed.) *The Political Economy of Corruption* (New York: Routledge), pp. 11–31.
Johnston, M., 2002, Measuring the new corruption rankings: Implications for analysis and reform, in: A. Heidenheimer and M. Johnston (Eds) *Political Corruption: Concepts & Contexts* (New Brunswick, NJ: Transaction Publishers), pp. 865–884.
Johnston, M., 2005, *Syndromes of Corruption: Wealth, Power, and Democracy* (Cambridge: Cambridge University Press).
Johnston, M., 2010, Assessing vulnerabilities to corruption: Indicators and benchmarks of government performance. *Public Integrity*, **12**(2), pp. 125–142.
Kaufmann, D. and Kraay, A., 2008, Governance indicators: Where are we, where should we be going?. *The World Bank Research Observer*, **23**(1), pp. 1–30.
Kaufmann, D., Kraay, A. and Mastruzzi, M. 2010, *The Worldwide Governance Indicators: A Summary of Methodology, Data and Analytical Issues*. World Bank Policy Research Working Paper No. 5430.
Kaufmann, D., Kraay, A. and Zoido, P. 1999, *Governance Matters*. World Bank Policy Research Working Paper No. 2196.
Knack, S., 2007, Measuring corruption: A critique of indicators in Eastern Europe and Central Asia. *Journal of Public Policy*, **27**(3), pp. 255–291.
Ko, K. and Samajdar, A., 2010, Evaluation of international corruption indexes: Should we believe them or not. *The Social Science Journal*, **47**(3), pp. 508–540.
Kurer, O., 2005, Corruption: An alternative approach to its definition and measurement. *Political Studies*, **53**, pp. 222–239.
Kurtz, M. and Schrank, A., 2007, Growth and governance: A defense. *The Journal of Politics*, **69**(2), pp. 563–569.
Lambsdorff, J., 2006, Causes and consequences of corruption: What do we know from a cross-section of countries?, in: S. Rose-Ackerman (Ed.) *International Handbook on the Economics of Corruption* (Cheltenham: Edward Elgar), pp. 3–51.
Lambsdorff, J., 2007, *The New Institutional Economics of Corruption and Reform: Theory, Evidence and Policy* (Cambridge: Cambridge University Press).
Lancaster, T. and Montinola, G., 2001, Comparative political corruption: Issues of operationalization and measurement. *Studies in Comparative International Development*, **36**(3), pp. 3–28.
Langbein, L. and Knack, S., 2010, The world wide governance indicators: Six, one, or none?. *Journal of Development Studies*, **46**(2), pp. 350–370.
Luong, H., 2006, Vietnam in 2005: Economic momentum and stronger state-society dialogue. *Asian Survey*, **46**(1), pp. 148–154.
Miller, W., 2006, Perceptions, experience and lies: What measures corruption and what do corruption measures measure?, in: C. Sampford, A. Shacklock, C. Connors and F. Galtung (Eds) *Measuring Corruption* (Burlington, VT: Ashgate Publishers), pp. 163–185.

Mishler, W. and Rose, R. 2008, Seeing Is Not Always Believing: Measuring Corruption Perceptions and Experiences. Paper prepared for the Elections, Public Opinion and Parties 2008 Annual Conference, University of Manchester, UK, September.

Ockey, J., 2007, Thailand in 2006: Retreat to military rule. *Asian Survey*, **47**(1), pp. 133–140.

Philip, M., 2006, Corruption definition and measurement, in: C. Sampford, A. Shacklock, C. Connors and F. Galtung (Eds) *Measuring Corruption* (Burlington, VT: Ashgate Publishers), pp. 45–56.

Pollitt, C., 2010, Simply the best? The international benchmarking of reform and good governance, in: J. Pierre and P. Ingraham (Eds) *Comparative Administrative Change and Reform: Lessons Learned* (Montreal & Kingston: McGill-Queen's University Press), pp. 91–113.

Quah, J., 2006, Curbing Asian corruption: An impossible dream?. *Current History*, **105**, pp. 176–179.

Razafindrakoto, M. and Roubaud, F., 2010, Are international databases on corruption reliable? A comparison of expert opinion surveys and household surveys in sub-Saharan Africa. *World Development*, **38**(8), pp. 1057–1069.

Roca, T. 2010, *Assessing Corruption: Expert Surveys versus Household Surveys, Filling the Gap*. Working Paper, Universite Montesquieu-Bordeaux IV.

Sampford, C.Shacklock, A.Connors, C. and Galtung, F. (Eds), 2006, *Measuring Corruption* (Burlington, VT: Ashgate Publishers).

Schlomer, G., Bauman, S. and Card, N., 2010, Best practices for missing data management in counseling psychology. *Journal of Counseling Psychology*, **57**(1), pp. 1–10.

Sik, E., 2002, The bad, the worse and the worst: Guesstimating the level of corruption, in: S. Kotkin and A. Sajo (Eds) *Political Corruption in Transition: A Skeptic's Handbook* (Budapest: Central European University Press), pp. 91–113.

Sjoberg, L., 1999, Risk perception by the public and by experts: A dilemma in risk management. *Human Ecology Review*, **6**(2), pp. 1–9.

Soreide, T. 2006, *Is It Wrong to Rank? A Critical Assessment of Corruption Indices*. Working Paper, Chr. Michelsen Institute, Norway.

Svensson, J., 2005, Eight questions about corruption. *Journal of Economic Perspectives*, **19**(3), pp. 19–42.

Transparency International (TI), 2010, *Global Corruption Barometer 2010*. Available at http://www.transparency.org. (Accessed 29 August 2013).

Treisman, D., 2007, What have we learned about the causes of corruption from ten years of cross-national empirical research? *Annual Review of Political Science*, **10**, pp. 211–244.

United Nations Development Programme (UNDP), 2008, *A User's Guide to Measuring Corruption* (Oslo: Olso Governance Center).

Yu, C., Chen, C.-M., Juang, W.-J. and Hu, L.-T., 2008, Does democracy breed integrity? Corruption in Taiwan during the democratic transformation period. *Crime, Law and Social Change*, **49**, pp. 167–184.

Independent Professional Bureaucracies and Street-Level Bribery: Comparing Changes in Civil Service Law and Implementation in Latin America

LAURA LANGBEIN & PABLO SANABRIA

ABSTRACT *Using cross-sectional data, studies of the relation between merit-based bureaucracies and corruption usually find that nations with more professional and politically independent bureaucracies have lower corruption. However, cross-section designs cannot test this policy claim. This study adopts a pre-test–post-test design using lagged data comparing changes in civil service laws and implementation in eight Latin American countries from 2004 to 2012 and data reporting subsequent change in bribe requests by the bureaucrats that the laws are intended to affect. Raising questions about the validity of previous results, it is found that improved laws and implementation were associated with no or increased bribe requests.*

Introduction

The United Nations Convention Against Corruption (2004, p. 10) lists improving the quality of bureaucracies by adopting merit practices and increasing professionalization as a first strategy to prevent corruption, and previous studies find a link between independent professional bureaucracies and less corruption (Evans and Rauch 1999; Rauch and Evans 2000; Kaufmann et al. 2003; Olsen 2005; Lapuente 2008; Dahlström et al. 2009; Cortazar et al. 2014). Yet it is difficult to infer policy-relevant causal evidence from cross-national comparisons (Bardhan and Mookherjee 2007; Lambsdorff 2007; Dahlström 2015; Triesman 2015), particularly when the relevant policy changes and expected consequences happen within countries. For example, in

2002 Mexican President Vicente Fox (Jornada 2002) issued a new civil service law, claiming that it would reduce corruption among Mexican public officials. However, even though today the Mexican federal bureaucracy is regarded as being more developed than most other Latin American bureaucracies, Mexico is still a Latin American country with higher street-level corruption. Mendez (2010) provides evidence of poor implementation of the Mexican career system. Eigen (2014) notes that despite "major reforms to combat corruption", Mexican citizens often must still pay a bribe at the local water commission, the traffic police, the local medical clinic, or the driver's license issuer, to get the desired service. More recently, in 2015, the government announced a new comprehensive reform of the civil service to reduce corruption (Jornada 2015). Even with the passage of time, laws on the books are not necessarily implemented, especially in developing countries, as Sanabria (2015) illustrates for the case of Colombia's civil service career officials, and as BBC (2011) shows for the case of Brazil.

We examine changes in both bureaucracies and subsequent street-level corruption, measured as bribe requests, within a small set of Latin American countries where corruption in public service delivery is widely regarded as a problem. Our findings raise questions regarding the prevailing conclusion that making bureaucracies more professional (i.e. merit-based and independent from political influence) reduces the incentive of street-level government employees to seek bribes from citizens who use the public service they provide.

Our study adds to scholarship on corruption and bureaucratic characteristics in multiple respects:

(a) Our corruption variable is narrowly targeted at bribes requested by different types of street-level bureaucrats, so that the type of corruption we study is clear (Johnston 2005; Knack 2006; Knack and Langbein 2010);
(b) We use a measure of reported (not perceived) corruption (i.e. bribe requests) from the Latin American Public Opinion Project (LAPOP) of Vanderbilt University;
(c) Compared to large-N cross-sectional studies of differences between very diverse countries, we use data at multiple time points within a set of countries in Latin America that share many common traits regarding the adoption and implementation of civil service laws (Grindle 2012);
(d) Our measures of change in laws and practices in a country precede our measure of change in bribes within the same country, reducing the threat of endogeneity (Triesman 2015);
(e) Our data on quality of civil service from Global Integrity (GI) uses experts' assessments and separates de jure from de facto characteristics of bureaucratic quality.

We use both a cross-sectional time series design with country fixed effects and a differences-in-differences design to test policy-relevant hypotheses about changes in laws and subsequent changes in bribes within a country. Compared to cross-sectional observation, designs like these strengthen the validity of tests of causal claims that merit-based, professional bureaucracy can reduce street-level corruption in developing countries, at least in Latin America.

Theoretical Framework

Corruption is commonly defined as "the use of public office for private gains" (Bardhan 1997; Swaleheen 2011, p. 23).[1] We focus on the propensity for providers of many typical public services to request bribes from citizens who seek to use these public services. Bribe requests such as these are more common in some nations, and, within nations, in some places and in some services, than others (Mocan 2004; Johnston 2005). Cross-nationally, corruption and ineffective governance have been found to be associated (Shleifer and Vishny 1993; World Bank 1993; Knack and Keefer 1995; Mauro 1997; Rose-Ackerman 1989, 1997; Rauch and Evans 2000; Van Rijckeghem and Weder 2001; Aidt 2003; Hyden et al. 2003; Mauro 2004; Kristiansen and Ramli 2006; Lambsdorff 2007; Leeson and Sobel 2008; Uslaner 2008; Dahlström et al. 2009; Cortazar et al. 2014; Anderson 2015). Yet corruption is costly, persistent, and begs for causal understanding.

Klitgaard (1988, p. 75) regards corruption as "monopoly plus discretion minus accountability". Because they are often monopoly providers, public officials often choose to ration public benefits (Rose-Ackerman 2007). As a result, officials have discretion to assign the service or benefit to some applicants but not others; they may charge a "special" fee to ration access, or the speed of access, to the service. Independence from political oversight may actually facilitate this transaction. As Uslaner (2008) points out, street-level professional groups can withhold services provided by government at low or zero cost unless they get a gift. The local government official may collect a fee from a squatter rather than issue a notice of violation of property rights. The doctor may give speedier service to a "paying" patient; teachers may be more likely to report for duty when parents offer "extra" pay. A customs official may refuse or delay the release of a firm's goods without an extra payment.

In addition, often there is a significant disparity between stated law and policy implementation, so that implementation may vary from one case to another (Hallward-Driemeier and Pritchett 2015). As recently as 2015, despite "Civil Service Reforms in Guatemala", Ramírez (2015) reports that "a lot of discretion" still "accommodates ... embezzlement, trafficking, ... and corruption". Thus, in some settings, making civil service legally more independent and professional could actually facilitate rather than reduce opportunities for corrupt exchanges, at least for some types of citizens.

However, the more common expectation is that, independent of political interference, and resembling the Weberian ideal (Tanzi 1998), merit-based bureaucracies will foster less corrupt behavior among public officials. Accordingly, Laguna (2010) discusses numerous laws in Mexico designed to reduce corruption by increasing the professionalism, transparency, and accountability of public servants in Mexico. More generally, Finan et al. (2015, p. 3) note that, in order to separate public employment from political interest, in many developing countries "civil service systems are typically much more rigid than their private sector counterparts, with strict formulas defining the hiring criteria, promotion patterns, and wage levels".

Making public organizations more independent and professional by using merit-based rather than political criteria in the recruitment, selection and dismissal of public employees is expected to reduce corruption. This is true especially if it is in the self-interest of an organized group of professionals, and if there are competing suppliers (e.g. Tanzi 1998; Rauch and Evans 2000). Professionals who identify with their profession rather than the political establishment may find that soliciting and accepting bribes would hurt rather than help their career. On the other side of the transaction, citizen-consumers will prefer suppliers who are professional and do not seek a bribe fee.

Thus, two different causal hypotheses are theoretically plausible:

H_1: In the context of the Latin American countries we study, where there is a tradition of disparity between law and practice (Riggs 1964; Inter-American Development Bank

(IADB) 2006; Grindle 2012), public employees whose appointment is increasingly based on professional merit, independent of political control, will be more susceptible to soliciting bribes; or,

H_2: Professional self-interest makes soliciting bribery an irrational choice for a public employee whose promotion is based on professional merit that is independent of political persuasion or control; thus, public employees whose appointment is based on professional merit independent of political control will be less susceptible to soliciting bribes.

Since previous cross-sectional research supports the second hypothesis, we formally test only that conjecture. Following Triesman (2015), we examine changes in both laws and their implementation within eight Latin American countries, and the association of both with subsequent bribe-seeking behavior by public employees who provide services. If we consistently fail to reject the null of no association, or reject it with evidence from a one-sided test that does not favor the second hypothesis, it would raise questions about previous conclusions regarding the efficacy of merit-based bureaucracies to reduce bribe seeking, at least in the contexts that we study.

Context of the Study, Data, and Methods

We use data on both the level and change in merit-based civil service law and implementation, and the level and change in subsequent bribe requests in a subset of Latin American countries. Each country is a presidential system with an imperfect democratic regime scoring between six and eight on the Polity IV index of democracy, where the top score is ten (Societal-Systems Research Inc. 2010). Specifically, we study Brazil, Mexico, Argentina, Colombia, Peru, Venezuela, Ecuador, Guatemala, and Nicaragua.[2] While they differ in population and GDP, all of them increased their GDP per capita at high rates during the period 2004–2012. These countries also share many historical, economic, and political features that ensure greater comparability than global cross-sections. In terms of civil service development, although there are small differences according to the adoption of merit practices, all of them are still characterized by varying efforts to implement what is stated in law (Cortazar et al. 2014).

To measure bribe-based corruption, we use individual-level survey responses in various years from 2004 to 2012 provided by the Americas Barometer of the Latin American Public Opinion Project of Vanderbilt University. The survey asked respondents how many times they have been requested to pay a bribe in the last 12 months in their interactions with the municipal government, the courts, hospitals, and schools, or in the context of their own work.[3] The specific questions are:

- In order to process something in the municipality, a permit for instance, during the last year, has someone asked you to pay a bribe?
- Have you had to pay a bribe at the courts during the past year?
- During the last 12 months, have you had to pay a bribe in order to be assisted in a hospital?
- During the last 12 months, have you had to pay a bribe in a school?
- At work, have you been requested to pay a bribe during the last 12 months?

We focus our analysis of bribe requests on those who have actually used the service.[4] We count the number of (survey-weighted) respondents who respond "yes" to each type of bribe request in each of the countries in our analysis, relative to the total number who report using the service. Because those who do not use a particular service (e.g. a hospital, a court) will not be asked for a bribe, we then divide the number who used the service (regardless of whether they are asked for a bribe) by the number who did not use the service. We expect that professional, independent bureaucracies will both increase the number of service users and reduce the number of bribe requests among the total number of service users. Thus, we adjust for two ratios: number of bribe requests among service users, and number of service users relative to non-service users. The expectation is that the first ratio (the numerator) will decrease, while the second (the denominator) will increase. The formula for calculating this use-adjusted ratio for each public service is:

$$\left(\frac{\left(\frac{BribeRequested}{BribeRequested\ +\ NoBribeRequested}\right)}{\left(\frac{BribeRequested\ +\ NoBribeRequested}{DidNotUseService}\right)}\right) * 100$$

Our analysis examines both levels of and differences in this percentage ratio. For the first analysis, we use percentage ratios for each country for each type of bribe for years that follow the report of the laws. For the second analysis, we use changes in country-level percentage use-adjusted ratios for each type of bribe request from 2008 to 2012, subsequent to the changes in the laws. In addition to examining bribes for specific services, we also examine both within-country yearly levels and differences using a summative use-adjusted bribe index that averages the five bribe ratios for each country.

To compare the quality of civil services in Latin American countries at different points in time, we rely on Global Integrity data.[5] GI hires in-country expert social scientists, journalists, and researchers to produce each country's assessment; a group of peer reviewers then assesses the validity of the responses. Each score is an ordinal "grade" ranging from 0 to 100 for each item. The grades that we record are averages of both de jure and de facto questions in each country. The *in law* (de jure) items record the existence of regulations in each country regarding independence of bureaucracies, forbiddance of patronage, and punishment of corrupt behaviors. We focus on laws that specifically apply to civil servants, including civil servants who deliver services. They are:

- In law, there are regulations requiring an impartial, independent, and fairly managed civil service.
- In law, there are regulations to prevent nepotism, cronyism, and patronage within the civil service.
- In law, there is an independent redress mechanism for the civil service.
- In law, civil servants convicted of corruption are prohibited from future government employment.

The *in practice* questions (de facto) report respondents' beliefs about the effectiveness of those regulations in terms of protection from political interference; merit in selection, recruitment, and dismissal; clear job descriptions; and absence of patronage. The specific items that we use are those that apply to civil servants at all levels:

- In practice, civil servants are protected from political interference.
- In practice, civil servants are appointed and evaluated according to professional criteria.
- In practice, civil service management actions (e.g. hiring, firing, promotions) are not based on nepotism, cronyism, or patronage.
- In practice, civil servants have clear job descriptions.
- In practice, in the past year, the government has paid civil servants on time.
- In practice, civil servants convicted of corruption are prohibited from future government employment.

Consistent with the observation that the adoption of laws requiring merit in recruitment, hiring, and firing of public employees in the Latin American countries we study is common (Zuvanic and Iacovello 2010, p. 152), the summative index for the de jure GI items is high (87 out of 100) and shows too little variation to produce either an eigenvalue or a large Cronbach's alpha (= 0.29).[6] This invariance indicates that the countries in our analysis are institutionally comparable. By contrast, the summative index of the de facto variables averages 50.8; Cronbach's alpha is 0.76 with an eigenvalue of 3.20 (55 per cent of the total factor space of 6) in a principal factor analysis, implying variation in the de facto scores that reflects a common, underlying component.[7] We use both summative indexes (de jure and de facto) in the analyses that follow.[8]

Results

Comparison of Our Sample to Previous Cross-Sectional Studies

We reproduce the positive correlation between standard measures of lower corruption and higher institutional quality even with our sample of comparable countries. Using nine countries in Latin America for which cross-sectional data for 2010 is available (Brazil, México, Argentina, Colombia, Peru, Venezuela, Ecuador, Guatemala, and Nicaragua), a regression of the World Bank's Control of Corruption percentile ranking on the Polity Index of Democracy (reflecting methods of executive recruitment and constraints on executive authority, ranging from −10 to +10) yields a slope of 3.1 ($p < 0.03$). Thus, using the standard methodology, even our small sample finds a significant, positive cross-sectional association between less corruption and a measure of good governance, which includes merit recruitment of constrained executives.

Descriptive Statistics

Table 1 shows the LAPOP survey-weighted average percentage of service users who reported bribes (relative to total number of service users among the total number of respondents). Courts appear to be the dominant source of bribe requests among those who use the service; local governments appear to be another common source of bribe requests. The level of bribe requests among service users appears "low", ranging from 3 in 100 to nearly 2 in 100. While the level of reported bribe requests undoubtedly understates the actual level, our focus is on the considerable variation in bribe requests: 1.8 is 60 times greater than 0.03.

Table 1. Survey-weighted average reported corruption as percentage of respondents who reported service use (relative to total N respondents): Latin America, 2004–2012

Country	Local Government Bribe	Work Bribe	Courts Bribe	Hospital Bribe	School Bribe
Argentina	0.203	0.060	0.223	0.067	0.081
Brazil	0.358	0.084	0.265	0.065	0.089
Colombia	0.186	0.029	0.250	0.039	0.035
Ecuador	0.688	0.055	1.821	0.092	0.161
Guatemala	0.200	0.048	1.415	0.091	0.097
México	0.445	0.115	1.350	0.127	0.161
Nicaragua	0.255	0.087	1.353	0.096	0.091
Peru	0.331	0.073	0.580	0.048	0.105
Venezuela	1.065	0.038	1.373	0.025	0.052

Source: The Americas Barometer by the Latin American Opinion Project (LAPOP) – Authors' calculations. Available data may vary between countries. Survey weights are extracted from the LAPOP dataset. The formula for obtaining the bribe request ratio for each public service is: Bribe = [(BribeRequested)/ (BribeRequested + NoBribeRequested)/(BribeRequested + NoBribeRequested)/(DidNotUse)]*100.

Table 2 reports the changes in bribes from 2004 to 2012 in each country, for each type of bribe. In slightly over half the cases, bribes are decreasing. Mexico stands out in that bribe requests increased in every category in that country, while they decreased in every category in Brazil. The variation in change is also considerable: there is a 4 per cent increase in bribes at work in Guatemala, and a 0.7 per cent drop in bribes from local government officials in Brazil. Table 3 shows the averages for the measures of civil service quality using the 1–100 ordinal scale mentioned previously. According to the GI evaluators, most Latin American countries have relatively well-developed regulatory systems (with the exception of Venezuela), but low levels of practice. This reflects the "prismatic" historical characterization of Latin America (Riggs 1964; Pritchett et al. 2010; Grindle 2012). Recent evidence suggests that laws requiring independent, merit-based, accountable executives in many developing counties create a legal environment with complex and costly regulatory procedures, but weak governance in those countries

Table 2. Differences in reported corruption Latin America 2004–2012

Country	Local Government Bribe	Work Bribe	Courts Bribe	Hospital Bribe	School Bribe	Difference Period
Argentina	−0.025	−0.064	0.010	−0.002	0.011	2008–2012
Brazil	−0.736	−0.645	−0.018	−0.020	−0.029	2006–2012
Colombia	0.024	0.144	−0.036	−0.016	−0.012	2004–2012
Ecuador	−0.193	−0.519	−0.040	−0.069	0.037	2004–2012
Guatemala	0.255	4.034	−0.003	−0.052	−0.044	2004–2012
México	0.203	0.846	0.069	0.103	0.044	2004–2012
Nicaragua	−0.159	−0.827	−0.119	−0.097	−0.142	2004–2012
Peru	0.246	−0.018	0.004	0.023	0.023	2006–2012
Venezuela	−0.231	−0.590	0.015	−0.013	0.008	2006–2008

Source of data and Formula for bribe request ratio: see Table 1.

Table 3. Average quality of civil services, Latin America 2004–2012

Country	Average GI civil service in law index (de jure)	Average GI civil service in practice index (de facto)
Argentina	100,000	66,250
Brazil	91,667	64,236
Colombia	93,750	60,417
Ecuador	87,500	47,222
Guatemala	83,333	38,657
Mexico	88,333	48,611
Nicaragua	79,167	41,059
Peru	100,000	62,500
Venezuela	58,333	28,125

Source: Global Integrity GI – Authors' calculations. Available data may vary between countries.

encourages efforts to avoid implementation (Hallward-Driemeier and Pritchett 2015). Even though de jure quality is highly correlated with de facto quality ($r = 0.91$), we also consistently observe that de jure exceeds de facto quality in the nine-country Latin American cross-section. Weak implementation often accompanies good law.

Table 4 reports the changes from 2004 to 2012 in civil service laws and practice. With respect to laws, Argentina and Peru did not regress from their perfect score, and Venezuela did not change from its average, which is the lowest among the nine countries in our sample. Colombia's score also did not change, while Guatemala reported the largest improvement. The remaining countries showed a slight improvement.

With respect to changes in civil service practice, four nations show substantial declines during the 4–8 years of measurement. Two show small improvements, while three nations show substantial improvements.

The conventional expectation is that improvements in both law and practice will simultaneously reduce bribe requests and increase service use, resulting in a drop in the

Table 4. Differences in quality of civil services, Latin America 2004–2012

Country	Diff. Period	Average GI civil service in law index (de jure)	Average GI civil service in practice index (de facto)
Argentina	2004–2010	0.00	18.75
Brazil	2004–2006	16.67	15.97
Colombia	2007–2011	0.00	2.78
Ecuador	2007–2008	25.00	−22.22
Guatemala	2004–2010	50.00	20.14
Mexico	2004–2011	8.33	−15.28
Nicaragua	2004–2011	8.33	−30.90
Peru	2007–2010	0.00	8.33
Venezuela	2009–2011	0.00	−14.93

percentage ratio. Yet, comparing the changes in bribe requests reported in Table 2 with changes in law reported in Table 4, Guatemala shows substantial improvement in both quality of laws and implementation, but the percentage ratio of bribes at work increases by 4 percentage points; local government bribes increase by 0.3 per cent. Other bribes decrease by a tiny amount (less than 0.06 per cent). In Brazil, consistent with expectation, laws and implementation improve while bribes decrease in every category. In Mexico, Nicaragua, and Venezuela, the laws either do not change or improve only a little (by 8.3 points). However, implementation drops by 15–30 points. In these three nations, where laws do not change and implementation quality drops, if hypothesis 2 is correct, it follows that bribes should consistently increase. Yet bribes increase in Mexico, decrease in Nicaragua, and sometimes decrease in Venezuela. These observations do not consistently support the expectation that poorer merit-based civil service practice will increase bribe requests by government employees.

Differences in Levels, and Differences in Differences

In this section, we consider the eight Latin American countries with lagged GI data (Argentina, Brazil, Colombia, Ecuador, Guatemala, Mexico, Nicaragua, and Peru). We compare LAPOP data on bribes between 2010 and 2012 with the (lagged) civil service index of laws and practice. We first regress yearly data on the bribe request ratio percentage for each country on lagged GI measures of civil service law and practice, with controls for each country as a fixed effect. We next examine differences by regressing *changes* in the average bribe scores for each of the countries on *lagged changes* in the GI indexes of laws and practice. To measure change, we subtract the last available data point from the next available data point. The GI data range from 2004 to 2011, depending on the country; the LAPOP data range from 2004 to 2012 for most of the countries. We make sure that all levels (Y) and changes (ΔY) in the percentage ratio of reported bribes come after the levels (X), or changes (ΔX), in the civil service indexes.[9]

Table 5 (column 1) reports the results of regressing the score for the average percentage ratio of all the types of bribes on the scores for civil service law, civil service practice, and fixed effects for each nation with two time-based observations. The results clearly show no correlation within the average nation. Examining the percentage ratio for each bribe type, we see no association between the quality of civil service law and practice and subsequent bribe requests from local government and court officials (Table 5, columns 2 and 4).[10] Further, because the small N favors finding no significant effects, if we ignore the significance test results in columns 2 and 4, the signs are not consistently in the expected negative direction, and the magnitude of the parameter estimates is small, suggesting that a 10-point increase in the quality of laws or implementation is associated with change in the relative bribe rate among service users of 0.05 per cent or less. With respect to bribes at work, at the hospital, or at school, we see the hoped-for negative association between the quality of civil service laws and fewer subsequent bribes, but that association is counteracted by a positive and higher association between quality of civil service practice and subsequent bribe requests (Table 5, columns 3, 5 and 6).[11] These results show that the association of better laws with lower bribe requests appears to be offset by the association of better implementation with higher bribe requests. This finding is consistent with the expectation that, in developing countries, improved laws increase regulatory costs, making

Table 5. Fixed effects regression of bribe percentage average, local government bribes, work bribes, courts bribe, hospital bribe and school bribe on civil service in law and in practice indexes

Dependent Variable	(1) Bribe Percentage Average	(2) Local Bribe	(3) Work Bribe	(4) Courts Bribe	(5) Hospital Bribe	(6) School Bribe
Civil Service in Law	0.00131	−0.00123	−0.00276***	0.0146	−0.00198***	−0.00206***
	(0.00482)	(0.00319)	(0.000309)	(0.0205)	(0.000277)	(0.000118)
Civil Service in Practice	0.00169	0.00211	0.00381***	−0.00465	0.00403***	0.00316***
	(0.00684)	(0.00474)	(0.000336)	(0.0293)	(0.000298)	(0.000470)
Constant	0.116	0.387***	0.137***	−0.140	0.0705*	0.127***
	(0.125)	(0.0862)	(0.0233)	(0.465)	(0.0347)	(0.0236)
Observations	14	14	14	14	14	14
R-squared	0.117	0.052	0.740	0.202	0.468	0.652
Number of countries	8	8	8	8	8	8

Clustered, robust standard errors in parentheses.
*** $p < 0.01$, * $p < 0.1$.
Source of data and Formula for bribe request ratio: see Table 1. Sample consists of the eight countries for which differences in LAPOP and lagged GI data could be calculated, as presented in the summary statistics.

evasion by bribery a rational response (Hallward-Driemeier and Pritchett 2015). It would also be possible to argue that these results are not substantively significant, since the magnitude of the estimators is small, implying that a 10-unit improvement in quality within each nation is associated with a 0.04 per cent difference (or less) in bribe requests.

Overall, based on levels, the evidence does not support the argument that improving civil service laws and practice is associated with a reduction in the propensity of civil servants on the street to seek bribes. When the results are significant, the association of better laws with fewer bribe requests accompanies a greater association of better implementation with more bribe requests. Further, even the statistically significant results that we report are not clearly substantively important.

Table 6 reports the findings when we look at changes in bribe requests and (lagged) changes in civil service quality within each nation. Table 6 (column 1) suggests that improvement in laws within the average nation in our sample is associated with more bribe requests. While the association is statistically significant, it is not clearly substantively significant. Improvement in practice is not significant. Neither result in column 1 of Table 6 suggests that improvements in civil service law and practice are associated with reductions in average bribe requests from civil servants.

The subsequent results in Table 6 (columns 2–6) report the association between change in civil service laws and practice for each type of bribe request. With two exceptions (schools and courts), the results show no significant correlation between improvement in laws and practice and change in type of bribe request (regardless of direction) in the

Table 6. OLS regression of the difference of bribe percentage average, local government bribes, work bribes, courts bribe, hospital bribe and school bribe on the differences of civil service in law and practice indexes

Dependent Variable: Differenced Variable	(1) Bribe Percentage Average	(2) Local Bribe	(3) Work Bribe	(4) Courts Bribe	(5) Hospital Bribe	(6) School Bribe
Civil Service in Law	0.012*	0.0005	−0.0006	0.0620**	−0.0002	−0.0015**
	(0.005)	(0.0066)	(0.0009)	(0.021)	(0.0003)	(0.0004)
Civil Service Practice	0.006	0.0003	0.0008	0.026	0.001	0.0008
	(0.005)	(0.0062)	(0.0018)	(0.019)	(0.001)	(0.0013)
Constant	−0.106	−0.055	−0.005	−0.462	−0.013	0.0044
	(0.111)	(0.150)	(0.023)	(0.386)	(0.023)	(0.0268)
Observations	8	8	8	8	8	8
R-squared	0.482	0.001	0.082	0.640	0.196	0.212

** $p < 0.05$, * $p < 0.1$.
Source of data and Formula for bribe request ratio: see Table 1. Sample consists of the eight countries for which differences in LAPOP and lagged GI data could be calculated, as presented in the summary statistics.

average country. Further, even if we abandon the standard of statistical significance due to the small *N*, the signs are either in the wrong direction, or, with one exception, an arguably larger positive sign for de jure law counteracts the hoped-for negative sign that is reported for de facto practice. Among the two bribe types with statistically significant results in Table 6 (columns 4 and 6), only one result (column 6) actually shows the hoped-for statistically negative association: a 10-point improvement in the quality of civil service laws in the average nation in our sample is associated with a 0.01 per cent reduction in bribe requests from school officials. However, this magnitude is not likely to be substantively important.

In the final table (Table 7), we regard each bribe request within each country as a set of multiple responses, or repeated measures, from each "respondent" country. Thus we treat each type of bribe request as a separate, but not independent, response from each country-respondent. We then adjust for the nested responses by including a dummy variable for each country and for each bribe type. Using this estimator, the results change from the results in Tables 5 and 6. We now find (Table 7, column 3, which includes controls for all sources of fixed effects) that improvements in the quality of civil service implementation appear significantly to reduce bribe requests, but the practical significance is questionable. Improvements in the quality of civil service law have the expected, but not significant, negative sign.

The evidence from Tables 5–7 does not consistently or even mostly support the expectation that, alone, improving civil service laws and practice will reduce corruption in local service provision. Our predominant findings are that improvement in the quality of laws and practice has no significant effect in reducing subsequent bribe requests. There is some evidence that improving the quality of laws reduces bribes, but that that estimate is offset by the companion result that improving implementation increases bribe requests. There is some evidence in one set of estimates that better laws and implementation slightly reduce

Table 7. Fixed effects regression of difference of type of bribe on the differences of civil service in law and in practice indexes

Dependent Variable: Difference of Type of Bribe	(1)	(2)	(3)
Civil Service in Law	−0.0188*	0.0120	−0.0188
	(0.0104)	(0.0122)	(0.0154)
Civil Service in Practice	−0.0124**	0.00588	−0.0124**
	(0.00528)	(0.00530)	(0.00457)
Constant	0.219**	−0.209	0.117
	(0.0994)	(0.221)	(0.171)
Country FE	YES	NO	YES
Bribe Type FE	NO	YES	YES
Observations	40	40	40
R-squared	0.243	0.169	0.294

Clustered, robust standard errors in parentheses.
** $p < 0.05$, * $p < 0.1$.
Source of data and Formula for bribe request ratio: see Table 1. Sample consists of the eight countries for which differences in LAPOP and lagged GI data could be calculated, as presented in the summary statistics. Multiplied by the five types of public services studied, yielding 40 observations. Fixed effects were estimated using country and bribe type dummies. All country fixed effects are relative to Mexico, the baseline country. All bribe type fixed effects are relative to local government, the baseline bribe type.

bribe requests. The inconsistent empirical evidence in our study, which looks at changes within nations, raises questions about previous evidence from large-*N* cross-sectional research designs. That evidences usually finds that independent, professional, merit-based bureaucracies, are correlated with reduced incidence of bribe requests by public employees, but, unlike evidence from designs that examine changes within nations, cross-section observational evidence is subject to many more sources of systematic error.

While our study raises questions about conclusions from previous research, it has significant limits. In addition to a relatively small *N*, another reason for the absence of consistently significant findings is that our dependent variable is an imperfect measure of street-level corruption, since both service use and bribes are most likely underreported.

It is also possible that the time lag that we use between changes in law and practice and subsequent changes in bribe requests, ranging from two to four years depending on the data for each country, may be too short for changes to appear. No theory tells us what time lag to expect, but it is unlikely that causal changes expected in this example would be delayed by more than four years. We further refrain from claiming that our findings apply to all forms of corruption or to other countries (Yang 2007).

Discussion

In contrast to previous studies of the relation between civil service quality and corruption, we examine levels and changes in actual bribes, laws, and implementation within nations time. We fail to show a consistent association between improvement in civil service law and implementation with reductions in the specific type of corruption targeted by changes in civil service quality – bribe requests made to those who use public services by government officials who control access to the services. Our results raise questions about previous conclusions, based on data from a cross-section of nations and, often, a measure of perceived corruption, that nations with an independent civil service have less corruption.

It is likely that there is probably more variation in bribe requests within each nation than between nations (Seligson 2006; Rodrik 2010; Langbein and Sanabria 2013). Social norms and the behavior of citizens who live near each other are likely to account for the willingness to ask for and pay a bribe: where bribes are common behavior, there is little cost to asking for a bribe, and little reason for those with no alternative service provider to refuse to pay it (Botero et al. 2012; Acemoglu and Jackson 2014). Future research on the efficacy of anti-corruption laws for deterring bribes should focus on within- as well as between-nation variation, and on the role of social norms.

Our results are also consistent with complaints such as those voiced by Ramírez (2015), who observes that, at least in Mexico, the "great expectations" of a modern civil service represented by laws passed from 1991 to 2010 have been dashed by the continuing common practice of politically motivated appointments approved by political bosses. It does not follow that this is a simple "implementation" problem. When common practice and the law conflict, it is likely that social norms often completely replace the law (Tsuneki and Zasu 2015). While governments can lead by changing social norms, it likely that these effects may not be observable in the relatively short time frame that we examine in this research. Future examination of the role of changes in laws in reinforcing or replacing bribe-seeking behavior also requires examination of changes in social norms in different places within nations over time.

Acknowledgement

The authors thank Nicolas Acevedo, research assistant at the Alberto Lleras Camargo School of Government, Universidad de los Andes, for his help with this project.

Notes

1. Corruption and illegal rent seeking are widely regarded as costly transfers because they almost always lead to lower economic growth (Hillman 2009, p. 99; Bentzen 2012). Mauro (1995) provided early empirical evidence that corruption is costly, and a theoretical explanation (2004) of why corruption persists, despite its adverse effects on growth.
2. We include Venezuela in our descriptive results. We drop it from the statistical analysis because the post-test bribe request data for Venezuela are not available for any of the time periods that succeed the pre-test data on the quality and implementation of laws in Venezuela.
3. LAPOP is a public opinion survey carried out every two years by the University of Vanderbilt. Covering numerous topics of governance, its survey design incorporates a weighting scheme to accurately reflect each country's sample size relative to the population. The survey in each country is a stratified, random sample, with different weights in each sample. Our analysis reflects the population weights in each country.
4. The LAPOP survey also asked respondents about bribe requests from policemen, but in that case it did not first ask whether the respondent "used" (i.e. had contact with) the police. In the case of police, the distinction between service "users" and non-users is particularly likely to represent a source of selection bias that needs adjustment in some way. In the absence of information about respondents who did or did not have personal contact with the police, we omit the information in LAPOP on bribe requests from policemen.
5. Global Integrity publishes a yearly assessment of governance for selected countries in selected years, comprising sub-categories of six dimensions, including public administration. The dataset extends from

2004 to 2012, with (different) gaps for the selected countries. We use responses to the questions on public administration.
6. Alpha measures reliability (absence of random error) in a measurement index. It ranges from 0 to 1, where 1 is absence of random error; 0.7 is regarded as sufficiently reliable for practical use. An eigenvalue measures validity (high correlation between measured indicators and an unmeasured underlying common concept). In this study, there are six de facto indicators. If they were perfectly correlated with the single common factor they are assumed to measure, the eigenvalue would be 100. In this study, they are correlated with than half of that space, which is regarded as acceptable for practical use.
7. The Merit Index of the Inter-American Development Bank (IADB), developed by Zuvanic and Iacovello (2010), and the GI index that we use are highly correlated, with a Cronbach's Alpha of 0.74.
8. National laws and practice regarding the hiring, firing, promotion, and pay of independent and professional civil servants are clearly intended to affect public officials at all levels of government, yet this expectation is more likely to be fulfilled in centralized than in decentralized administrative systems. The degree of administrative centralization varies among Latin American countries, and is often weak, making it incapable of reducing interference by regional politicians. Recent empirical evidence tends to find either that centralization has no clear systematic effect on governance in Latin American countries (Tanzi 1996; Faletti 2005; Treisman 2007), or that administratively centralized government appears to have *more* (perceived) corruption (Treisman 2000). Our measures of how laws operate in practice should capture these variations in the implementation of national laws at the local level.
9. Because the GI and LAPOP data cover different countries in each year, the lag varies for each country, and no country in our sample has continuous data for every year. Consequently, the number of observations in our statistical analysis varies by year, making the panels unbalanced and small.
10. Despite the high correlation between country averages of de jure and de facto quality scores, collinearity is unlikely to account for these null results. Of the six regressions reported in Table 5, while three show insignificant estimates, the other three report significant coefficients for the de jure and de facto quality scores, with opposite signs.
11. Civil service quality and practice are both rated on ordinal scales from 0 to 100 by the same raters. Thus we assume that the two variables are measured on the same scale, making it possible to compare the magnitude of the two regression parameter estimates within the same model.

References

Acemoglu, D. and Jackson, M. O., 2014, *Social Norms and the Enforcement of Laws*, M.I.T. Dept. of Economics Working Paper Series. Working Paper 14-16. Available at http://ssrn.com/abstract=2475920 (accessed 13 October 2014).

Aidt, T., 2003, Economic analysis of corruption: A survey. *The Economic Journal*, **113**, pp. F632–F652. doi:10.1046/j.0013-0133.2003.00171.x

Anderson, J. E., 2015, Economic reforms and their impacts on informal payments for government services in transition countries. *International Public Management Journal*, pp. 1–27. doi:10.1080/10967494.2015.1037033

Bardhan, P., 1997, Corruption and development: A review of issues. *Journal of Economic Literature*, **35**:3, pp. 1320–1346.

Bardhan, P. and Mookherjee, D., 2007, Decentralization, corruption, and government accountability, in: S. Rose-Ackerman (Ed) *International Handbook on the Economics of Corruption* (Northhampton, MA: Elgar Publishing), pp. 161–188.

BBC, 2011, Brazil's transport minister quits in corruption scandal. Available at http://www.bbc.co.uk/news/world-latin-america-14055768 (accessed 7 July 2011).

Bentzen, J. S., 2012, How bad is corruption? Cross-country evidence of the impact of corruption on economic prosperity. *Review of Development Economics*, **16**(1), pp. 167–184. doi:10.1111/j.1467-9361.2011.00653.x

Botero, J., Ponce, A. and Shleifer, A., 2012, *Education and the Quality of Government*, Working Paper 18119, Cambridge, MA: National Bureau of Economic Research. Available at http://www.nber.org/papers/w18119 (accessed 9 June 2012).

Cortazar, J. C. C., Lafuente, M. and Sangines, M., 2014, *A Decade of Civil Service Reforms in Latin America (2004–2013)* (Washington, DC: Inter-American Development Bank).

Dahlström, C., 2015, Bureaucracy and corruption. Ch. 8, in: P. M. Heywood (Ed) *Routledge Handbook of Political Corruption* (New York: Routledge), pp. 110–120.

Dahlström, C., Lapuente, V. and Teorell, J., 2009, *Bureaucracy, Politics and Corruption, The Quality of Government Institute Paper Series* (Gothenburg: University of Gothenburg), pp. 21.

Eigen, P., 2014, Reforms against corruption in Mexico. Available at http://unpan1.un.org/intradoc/groups/public/documents/UN/UNPAN012635.pdf (accessed 30 May 2016).

Evans, P. and Rauch, J., 1999, Bureaucracy and growth: A cross-national analysis of the effects of "Weberian" state structures on economic growth. *American Sociological Review*, **64**, pp. 748–765. doi:10.2307/2657374

Faletti, T. G., 2005, A sequential theory of decentralization: Latin American cases in comparative perspective. *American Political Science Review*, **99**(3), pp. 327–346. doi:10.1017/S0003055405051695

Finan, F., Olken, B. A. and Pande, R., 2015, *The Personnel Economics of the State*, Handbook of Field Experiments. National Bureau of Economic Research. NBER Working Paper No. 21825. doi:10.3386/w21825

Grindle, M. S., 2012, *Jobs for the Boys: Patronage and the State in Comparative Perspective* (Cambridge, MA: Harvard University Press).

Hallward-Driemeier, M. and Pritchett, L., 2015, How business is done in the developing world: Deals versus rules. *Journal of Economic Perspectives*, **29**(3), pp. 121–140. doi:10.1257/jep.29.3.121

Hillman, A., 2009, *Public Finance and Public Policy: Responsibilities and Limitations of Government* (New York: Cambridge University Press).

Hyden, G., Court, J. and Mease, K., 2003, *The Bureaucracy and Governance in 16 Developing Countries*, World Governance Survey Discussion Paper 7 (London: United Nations University).

Inter-American Development Bank (IADB), 2006, *The Politics of Policies: Economic and Social Progress in Latin America* (Washington, DC: Inter-American Development Bank – David Rockefeller Center for Latin American Studies).

Johnston, M., 2005, *Syndromes of Corruption* (Cambridge: Cambridge University Press).

Jornada, L., 2002, Apoya Fox establecer el servicio civil de carrera. Available at http://www.jornada.unam.mx/2002/05/26/012n1pol.php (accessed November 2015).

Jornada, L., 2015, Promulgará Peña Nieto reforma que crea Sistema Nacional Anticorrupción. Available at http://www.jornada.unam.mx/ultimas/2015/05/26/promulgara-pena-nieto-reforma-que-crea-el-sistema-nacional-anticorrupcion-3329.html (accessed November 2015).

Kaufmann, D., Kraay, A. and Mastruzzi, M., 2003, *Governance Matter III: Governance Indicators for 1996–2003* (Washington, DC: The World Bank).

Klitgaard, R., 1988, *Controlling Corruption* (Berkeley: University of California Press).

Knack, S., 2006, *Measuring Corruption in Eastern Europe and Central Asia: A Critique of the Cross-Country Indicators*, World Bank Policy Research Working Paper 3968 (Washington, DC: World Bank).

Knack, S. and Keefer, P., 1995, Institutions and economic performance: Cross-country tests using alternative institutional measures. Reprint No. 65 from *Economics and Politics*, **7**(3), pp. 207–227. Center for Institutional Reform and the Informal Sector. University of Maryland at College Park. doi:10.1111/j.1468-0343.1995.tb00111.x

Knack, S. and Langbein, L., 2010, The world governance indicators: Six, one, or none? *Journal of Development Studies*, **46**(2), pp. 350–370. doi:10.1080/00220380902952399

Kristiansen, S. and Ramli, M., 2006, Buying an income: The market for civil service positions in Indonesia. *Contemporary South East Asia*, **28**, pp. 207–233.

Laguna, M. I. D., 2010, Combate a la Corrupción y. Ch. 6, in: J. L. Mendez (Ed) *Políticas Públicas. Los Grandes Problemas de Mexico V. XIII* (Ciudad de Mexico: El Colegio de Mexico).

Lambsdorff, J. G., 2007, Causes and consequences of corruption: What do we know from a cross-section of countries? in: S. Rose-Ackerman (Ed) *International Handbook on the Economics of Corruption* (Northhampton, MA: Elgar Publishing), pp. 1–51.

Langbein, L. and Sanabria, P., 2013, The shape of corruption: Colombia as a case study. *Journal of Development Studies*, **49**(11), pp. 1500–1513. doi:10.1080/00220388.2013.800858

Lapuente, V., 2008, *Why Bureaucracy? Political Power and the Emergence of Autonomous Bureaucracies, The Quality of Government Institute Paper Series* (Gothenburg: University of Gothenburg), p. 23.

Leeson, P. and Sobel, R., 2008, Weathering corruption. *The Journal of Law and Economics*, **51**, pp. 667–681. doi:10.1086/590129

Mauro, P., 1995, Corruption and growth. *The Quarterly Journal of Economics*, **110**, pp. 681–712. doi:10.2307/2946696

Mauro, P., 1997, The effects of corruption in growth, investment, and government expenditure: A cross-country analysis, in: K. Elliot (Ed) *Corruption and the Global Economy* (Washington, DC: Institute for International Economics).

Mauro, P., 2004, *The Persistence of Corruption and Slow Economic Growth* (Washington, DC: International Monetary Fund). IMF Staff Papers 51 (1).

Mendez, J., 2010, El Servicio Profesional de Carrera en la Administración Pública Federal. Ch. 5, in: J. Mendez (Ed) *Políticas Públicas. Los Grandes Problemas de Mexico V.13* (Mexico: El Colegio de Mexico), pp. 179–207.

Mocan, N., 2004, *What Determines Corruption? International Evidence from Micro Data*, NBER Working Paper. No. 10460 (Cambridge, MA: National Bureau of Economic Research).

Olsen, J., 2005, Maybe it is time to rediscover bureaucracy. *Journal of Public Administration Research and Theory*, 16, pp. 1–24. doi:10.1093/jopart/mui027

Pritchett, L., Woolcock, M. and Andrews, M., 2010, *Capability Traps? The Mechanisms of Persistent Implementation Failure*, Center for Global Development Working Paper 234 (December) (Washington, DC: Center for Global Development).

Ramírez, G. I., 2015, Plantean cambios en servicio civil 30 de Julio, Prensa Libre. Available at http://www.prensalibre.com/economia/plantean-cambios-en-servicio-civil (accessed November 2015).

Rauch, J. and Evans, P., 2000, Bureaucratic structure and bureaucratic performance in less developed countries. *Journal of Public Economics*, 75, pp. 49–71. doi:10.1016/S0047-2727(99)00044-4

Riggs, F., 1964, *Administration in Developing Countries: The Theory of Prismatic Society* (Boston, MA: Houghton-Mifflin).

Rodrik, D., 2010, Diagnostics before prescription. *Journal of Economic Perspectives*, 24(3), pp. 33–44. doi:10.1257/jep.24.3.33

Rose-Ackerman, S., 1989, Which bureaucracies are less corruptible? in: A. Heidenheimer, M. Johnston, and V. T. LeVine (Eds) *Political Corruption: A Handbook* (New Brunswick: Transaction Publishers).

Rose-Ackerman, S., 1997, The political economy of corruption, in: K. Elliot (Ed) *Corruption and the Global Economy* (Washington, DC: Institute for International Economics).

Rose-Ackerman, S., 2007, Introduction and overview, in: S. Rose-Ackerman (Ed) *International Handbook on the Economics of Corruption* (Northhampton, MA: Elgar Publishing).

Sanabria, P. (Comp.), 2015, *Gestión del Talento Humano en el Sector Público: Estado del Arte, Diagnóstico y Recomendaciones para el Caso Colombiano* (Bogota D.C.: Ediciones Uniandes).

Sanabria, P., 2010, Dos Pasos Adelante, Uno Hacia Atrás: Colombia y la Configuración de un Servicio Civil Profesional y Meritocrático, in *Boletín Política Pública Hoy*. Bogotá D.C.: Departamento Nacional de Planeación.

Seligson, M. A., 2006, The measurement and impact of corruption victimization: Survey evidence from Latin America. *World Development*, 34(2), pp. 381–404. doi:10.1016/j.worlddev.2005.03.012

Shleifer, A. and Vishny, R., 1993, Corruption. *The Quarterly Journal of Economics*, 108(3), pp. 599–617. doi:10.2307/2118402

Societal-Systems Research Inc., 2010, Polity IV Country Reports, 2008. Available at www.sytemicpeace.org/polity/polity06.htm (accessed 7 December 2011).

Swaleheen, M., 2011, Economic growth with endogenous corruption: An empirical study. *Public Choice*, 146, pp. 23–41. doi:10.1007/s11127-009-9581-1

Tanzi, V., 1996, Fiscal federalism and decentralization: A review of some efficiency and macroeconomic aspects, in: M. Bruno and B. Pleskovic (Eds) *Annual World Bank Conference on Development Economics* (Washington, DC: The World Bank).

Tanzi, V., 1998, Corruption around the world: Causes, consequences, scope and cures. *IMF Staff Papers*, 45, pp. 4.

Treisman, D., 2000, Decentralization and the quality of government, Manuscript UCLA. Available at sscnet.ucla.edu (accessed 22 January 2015).

Treisman, D., 2007, *The Architecture of Government: Rethinking Political Decentralization* (Cambridge: Cambridge University Press).

Triesman, D., 2015, What does cross-national empirical research reveal about the causes of corruption? Ch. 7, in: P. M. Heywood (Ed) *Routledge Handbook of Political Corruption* (New York: Routledge), pp. 95–109.

Tsuneki, A. and Zasu, Y., 2015, On the complementarity between law and social norms. *Review of Law & Economics*, 11(3), pp. 503–512. doi:10.1515/rle-2013-0002

United Nations, 2004, *The United Nations Convention Against Corruption* (Vienna: Office on Drugs and Crime).

Uslaner, E., 2008, *Corruption, Inequality, and the Rule of Law* (New York: Cambridge University Press).

Van Rijckeghem, C. and Weder, B., 2001, Bureaucratic corruption and the rate of temptation: Do wages in the civil service affect corruption, and by how much?. *Journal of Development Economics*, **65**, pp. 307–331. doi:10.1016/S0304-3878(01)00139-0

World Bank, 1993, *The East Asian Miracle: Economic Growth and Public Policy* (New York: Oxford University Press).

Yang, D., 2007, The economics of anti-corruption: Lessons from a widespread customs reform, in: S. Rose-Ackerman (Ed) *International Handbook on the Economics of Corruption* (Northhampton, MA: Elgar Publishing), pp. 512–545.

Zuvanic, L. and Iacovello, M., 2010, The weakest link: The bureaucracy and civil service systems in Latin America, in: C. Scartascini, E. Stein, and M. Tommasi (Eds) *How Democracy Works: Political Institutions, Actors, and Arenas in Latin American Policy Making* (Washington, DC: IADB-David Rockefeller Center for Latin American Studies).

A Comparative Study of Abortion Policymaking in Brazil and South America: The Salience of Issue Networks and Policy Windows

ANDRZEJ KULCZYCKI

ABSTRACT *In Brazil and South America, religion, custom, and law have long made abortion taboo and forced it underground. Major changes sweeping the region are now making abortion increasingly discussed and contested. This article uses conceptual heuristics, theoretical insights, and comparisons across contexts to understand this situation. It explains why legal reforms have occurred in some settings (Colombia, Mexico City) but not in others (Brazil, Chile, Peru), and how incremental policy changes are making abortion safer and less common. It stresses the importance of building issue networks to mobilize capacity and exploit policy windows for securing further bolder reforms in this deeply controversial health care field.*

Introduction

Brazil and South America have experienced major health, demographic, socio-economic, and political changes over the past few decades. Notwithstanding these changes and a worldwide trend toward liberalization of abortion laws (Kulczycki 1999), a restrictive legal and social framework continues to push abortion practice underground across nearly all the region. An estimated 3 million abortions occur in South America annually, nearly all clandestine and often in hazardous circumstances, causing about 700 maternal deaths (WHO 2011). This state of affairs has been shrouded in secrecy until recently, with the attendant problems only tacitly recognized and partially addressed. Abortion is still viewed primarily through a religious and moralistic lens and only occasionally in terms of reproductive rights and social justice.

Nevertheless, abortion has figured increasingly in public discourse and numerous countries are adopting new technologies and policy options to reduce hospitalization rates and procedures unsafe to women. These steps include measures to extend access to emergency contraception,[1] improve post-abortion care, and revise the legal context of abortion. Colombia partly relaxed restrictions on the procedure in 2006, and a year later Mexico City granted women uncomplicated access to first trimester abortion. However, this precedent set by one of the world's largest metropolitan areas was not replicated in

Mexico, or elsewhere in the wider region. Despite much acrimonious debate and many attempts to change existing policies in Brazil and elsewhere in South America, governments typically lack the political will to act on far-reaching policy changes, for which societal consensus remains elusive.

This article analyzes the abortion policy context and the processes at work in Brazil and South America. In particular, it seeks to explain why attempts to reform abortion policy in a way that would lead to a resolution more likely to improve women's health have only succeeded partially in a few settings. The study adopts an interpretative approach that employs concepts and insights from several political science literatures to investigate how abortion has emerged as an issue requiring policy attention, the barriers to implementing policy reform, and the strategies of different groups seeking to overcome them. To better understand the context and processes at work, I first review the legal framework that stipulates the reasons for which abortion is permitted in countries of the region and that helps shape many of the demographic, social, and health consequences. The concept of agenda setting is used to show how abortion has risen in prominence as an issue and how different social and political agents have attempted to construct and influence debate about it. Next, the diverse cases of Brazil, Chile, Colombia, Mexico City, and Peru are compared, each illustrating different stages and dimensions of policy reform. The paper thereby makes sense of the circumstances under which reform advocates seek to influence abortion policy, the constraints they face, and the strategies that they have employed to further their goals. The analysis highlights, in particular, the importance of issue networks and policy windows for determining changes in abortion policymaking.

The comparative analysis focuses more on Brazil along with three medium-sized countries, Chile, Colombia, and Peru. Brazil is South America's demographic and economic powerhouse, accounting for almost half its population, territory, and gross domestic product (GDP). Brazil is now seen as more influential across South America than the USA and has made major gains in maternal and child health (Barros et al. 2010). It was first to realize the widespread diffusion of pharmaceutically induced (medication) abortion, which has improved the safety of many illegal abortion procedures across much of South America. The study additionally considers the situation in Mexico, where the author has for long conducted fieldwork and where the Federal District (the inner core of Mexico City) recently enacted one of the most liberal abortion laws in Latin America, although numerous implementation challenges remain. Together, Mexico and Brazil account for every second person in Latin America and have the world's largest Catholic populations; over 70 per cent of the region's population is Catholic (Holy See 2010), with Church officials staunchly opposed to abortion under nearly all circumstances. Mexico and Brazil also have stronger research capacity and reflect the geographic priorities of international donors interested in abortion research. Furthermore, the article reflects on how these national experiences and theoretical insights from the policymaking literature shed light on the determinants of abortion policymaking elsewhere in South America.

The study is based on multiple sources of evidence including interviews conducted with high-level policymakers, activists, health workers, academics, lawyers, and other key informants; a critical review of information from published literature and data, as well as unofficial documents, media reports, and interest group material. It is argued that without more fundamental social and political change, particularly the development of stronger issue networks and the exploitation of policy windows, only minor efforts will likely occur to confront the reality that abortion is a greater problem than it need be.

Presently, abortion policy reform continues to be channeled away from the legislative agenda by a system of bias. However, recent incremental steps to improve the safety of abortions and to reduce their incidence point the way forward from the existing policy impasse throughout the continent and may have significant political effects.

The Legal Framework of Abortion

South America is home to some of the world's most restrictive abortion laws. The procedure is permitted only under certain circumstances, such as when the mother's life is at risk, the fetus will not live, or the pregnancy results from rape (Table 1). However, rape victims are often denied services by physicians, prohibitive procedure costs, and unnecessarily stringent requirements (Human Rights Watch 2006). Several countries do not permit even therapeutic procedures to preserve a woman's health or to end pregnancies that cannot be continued due to problems with the fetus. In 2011, Guyana and French Guiana, each with under 1 million inhabitants, were the only two South American states to allow abortion on broad grounds.[2]

Since the late 1990s, a number of governments have begun to re-evaluate their abortion laws and policies. At the region's periphery, El Salvador (1998) and Nicaragua (2006) amended their penal codes to eliminate all the legal grounds under which they had previously allowed abortion, and the Dominican Republic (2008) amended its constitution to enshrine the right to life from the moment of conception. Conversely, Colombia (2006) expanded the scope of legal abortion and Mexico City's legislative assembly permitted abortion without restriction and free of charge during the first three months of pregnancy. Women from outside Mexico City receive services on a sliding scale. Several Mexican

Table 1. Abortion laws in South America, 2012

Prohibited under all circumstances	Prohibited except when life of woman endangered	Prohibited except to preserve physical health of woman	Permitted without restriction
Chile	Brazil[a]	Argentina[a]	French Guiana[b]
	Paraguay	Bolivia[a,c]	Guyana[b]
	Venezuela	Ecuador[d]	Uruguay[e]
	Suriname	Peru	
		Columbia[a,c,f]	

[a]Permitted in case of rape.
[b]Permitted in Guyana only up to 8 weeks of gestation (and later in the event of severe health risks) and in French Guiana up to 14 weeks of gestation.
[c]Permitted in case of incest.
[d]Permitted in case of rape when mother is considered mentally incompetent.
[e]Permitted in Uruguay up to 12 weeks of gestation (14 weeks for rape victims and later in cases of severe health risk to the woman or a non-viable fetus).
[f]Permitted in case of fetal impairment.
Note: The data presented in this table are the most recent available as of late 2012, when Uruguay permitted abortion on broad grounds during the first 12 weeks of pregnancy, although certain procedural requirements may inhibit access to the procedure.
Sources: Kulczycki (2011), UN (2002, 2011), and updated from government websites to determine changes.

states added some minor health indications for abortion, but most adopted even tighter restrictions including constitutional amendments banning the procedure. However, women in the Federal District still face many barriers to accessing services related to cost, distance, social stigma, and the low number of facilities offering abortions.[3] Attempts to change abortion laws also occurred in Argentina,[4] Brazil, and elsewhere. In late 2012, Uruguay allowed women limited access to abortion under various conditions for pregnancies up to 12 weeks, but access to services is undermined by various procedural barriers and opt-out clauses.[5] The law is a key determinant of women's access to services and their safety, but also important is the implementation and interpretation of the law, as well as the attitudes of medical providers toward abortion. Nevertheless, from a situation of near uniformity in restrictive statutes across much of the region some 15 years ago, abortion policy has since become increasingly contested and has entered a state of flux.

The Health and Social Context of Abortion

There are scant representative data available on the procedure in the region due to its clandestine nature, the inability to collect reliable data from abortion seekers or providers, the absence of surveillance systems, and the failure to distinguish between spontaneous and induced abortions. However, the most plausible estimates made by the World Health Organization (WHO 2011) show that approximately 3 million abortions are performed annually across South America, equivalent to a ratio of nearly one abortion for every three live births (Table 2). Abortion has exercised a significant role in reducing birth rates across the region over the past five decades. Recent gains in contraceptive use have helped many couples realize their family size preferences; contraceptive prevalence rose from 60 per cent to 73 per cent over 1990–2009 and reached almost 80 per cent in Brazil, Colombia, Paraguay and Uruguay (Kulczycki 2011). This increase is primarily responsible for the estimated decline in the regional abortion rate from 45 to 31 per 1,000 women of childbearing age (WHO 2011). However, this is still higher than rates in the USA or Canada, which permit abortion and have a broader contraceptive mix.

Table 2. Key indicators of abortion in South America, c. 2010

	Demography	Safety
Annual number	2.99 million	More than 99% of abortions are performed clandestinely, many unsafely or under unsafe conditions
Abortion rate	32 abortions per 1,000 women aged 15–44	700 maternal deaths occur annually due to complications related to unsafe abortion (safe abortion services and access to quality medical care could easily prevent the majority of these deaths)
Abortion ratio	1 in 4 recognized pregnancies ends in abortion	About 500,000 women are hospitalized annually for treatment of complications from unsafe abortions. Increasing use of medication abortion has increased the safety of clandestine procedures

Source: Estimates derived from WHO (2011).

South America has a higher proportion of unintended pregnancies (64 per cent) than any other major world region (Singh et al. 2010). This indicates that contraceptives may not be readily accessible to all and may be ineffectively used. Such pregnancies may also result from poor couple communication, nonconsensual sex, economic constraints on women's lives, and cultural expectations, such as for young women to remain virginal and uneducated about sex. Reducing unintended pregnancies requires socio-cultural changes, including adjusting traditional gender roles and family laws, in addition to the provision of accessible, affordable, and quality family planning services.

The adverse impact of strict prohibitions on abortion causes serious problems of public health and social justice. Unsafe abortions may have long-term effects on women's health or their fertility and account for about 13 per cent (the fourth leading cause) of maternal deaths in South America (WHO 2011). Beyond gender, the existing situation reveals numerous social, economic, ethnic, and generational inequalities. For example, poor and young women are more likely to self-induce abortion, to rely on unqualified providers operating in unsanitary conditions, and to delay seeking medical care for fear of legal repercussions or social stigma, with the black market increasing the economic and psychosocial costs for all women.

Hospitalization rates from unsafe abortion have declined throughout South America, but almost half a million women are hospitalized annually due to complications of incomplete abortion, hemorrhage, and infection. This situation severely strains scarce health care resources (Vlassof et al. 2009), although the attendant costs can be considerably reduced by improving post-abortion care and promoting subsequent contraceptive use (Billings and Benson 2005). Since the turn of the century, many countries have promoted emergency contraceptive pills to reduce unintended pregnancies and the consequent need for abortion, but many service providers and groups opposed to their distribution have resisted their implementation (Faúndes et al. 2007). The spread of medication abortion using misoprostol (marketed under the trade name Cytotec) has also improved the safety of clandestine procedures. Acceptance of this proven medication has increased alongside awareness of its other obstetric and gynecologic uses, which include labor induction and the prevention of post-partum hemorrhage, the major cause of maternal mortality.

The Social Construction of the Abortion Debate and the Role of Different Groups

Across South America, abortion generates intense debate among politicians, feminist and religious groups, health professionals, and other members of civil society. Most people surveyed to date tend to favor legalizing therapeutic abortion, but not all forms of elective abortion. Published abortion opinion studies in the region are very limited in number, scope, and quality; a recent review could only identify 26 articles, with all but four surveys conducted in Mexico and Brazil (Yam et al. 2006). These suggest that abortion does not seem to be perceived primarily in terms of public health or social inequalities, perhaps due to its moralistic treatment by the media, limited awareness about different aspects of the issue, patriarchal influences, and the concerted opposition of Catholic bishops and other groups opposed to abortion. At the same time, the pervasiveness of abortion indicates that even those opposed to it act against their stated beliefs when faced with their own unwanted pregnancies.

The relative strengths and weaknesses of national and regional movements for abortion reform can be measured in terms of their ability to secure such changes and in public awareness of the issue. Feminists groups have long campaigned to decriminalize abortion and improve women's sexual and reproductive rights, framing debate in terms of women's autonomy and as a question of social justice and gender equality. South America's transition to democracy in the 1980s and 1990s saw the growth of a dynamic women's rights movement. However, even when socialist movements for reform have included commitments to address women's rights, their promises often went unfulfilled. For example, Sandinista Nicaragua and Allende's socialist government in Chile dismantled some of the progress made on women's rights and proved uninterested in expanding access to abortion (Lagos Lira 2001; Pieper Mooney 2009; Kampwirth 2011). By the 1990s, as women continued to increase their participation in the workforce, many in South America's women's movements were demanding equal rights and insisted that addressing women's interests was fundamental to establishing a truly representative democracy. Nevertheless, women's activists have often felt they had to respond to initiatives by political and social conservatives, such as attempts to increase the penalties for abortion. Legal arguments supporting criminalization of abortion are often framed within the context of the rights of the unborn. In Nicaragua, Sandinista leader Daniel Ortega even found it politically expedient to push through a ban on therapeutic abortions as he campaigned for a third presidential term.

The opposition of Catholic Church leaders and other conservative groups to abortion law reform efforts cannot be underestimated. In Chile, Colombia, Peru, and elsewhere, powerful bishops and conservative politicians are members of the ultra-conservative Opus Dei, guardians of sexual morality. Existing patriarchal structures have made it easier to deny various reproductive rights and to maintain firm gender frameworks in terms of sexual behavior and double standards of sexual morality. Many stakeholders with influence on the practice of abortion hold ambiguous and passive positions. Some are confronted with the conservative stances of their institutions or associations. For example, although an unknown proportion of health professionals support legalization of abortion on public health grounds, many oppose more permissive laws for reasons of professional ethics, moral or religious principles, or because of prevailing gender norms. Further, abortion has become to some extent a bargaining chip between government leaders and conservative sectors (Kulczycki 2007).

Large international reproductive health agencies like the International Planned Parenthood Federation (IPPF), the International Women's Health Coalition, the Population Council, and Ipas, are active in providing programmatic and technical assistance to family planning and related reproductive health programs in South America. Groups hostile to their agenda dismiss them as being "pro-abortion". Nevertheless, they have benefited from international agreements and human rights treaties signed under the auspices of the UN, which have assisted adoption of sexual and reproductive health policies in Brazil, Colombia, and other South American countries. Several well-publicized test cases in 2005–2006 included rulings by the UN Human Rights Committee against the Peruvian government for denying a legal abortion to a woman who had an anencephalic fetus and who was forced to continue the pregnancy to delivery; and by the Inter-American Commission on Human Rights against the Mexican government in favor of the petition by a 13-year-old girl who had been raped and subsequently denied access to a legally permitted abortion by state health and law enforcement officials. The Mexican government was instructed to issue guidance for access to abortion for rape victims and agreed to compensate the young woman and her son for health care, education, and professional development (Walsh 2005).

The Case of Brazil

Following the restoration of democracy in the mid-1980s, Brazil has moved to become a middle-income country and an emerging power with a unified health system (SUS). It has built the world's largest and perhaps most successful HIV/AIDS prevention and treatment programs, supported by successive governments and reducing HIV/AIDS prevalence rates to below 1 per cent (Nunn 2009). Brazil currently allows abortion only in cases of rape or if a woman's life is endangered. Activism on behalf of legalized abortion has increased, but there is very strong organized opposition to any such move in the world's most populous Catholic nation, even if its bishops are regarded as the most theologically diverse on the continent.

Abortion and sterilization were the main methods of birth control in the 1980s and 1990s (Martine 1996). In 2008, health ministry statistics recorded only 3,050 legal abortions and 215,000 hospital admissions for treatment of abortion-related complications within the SUS system (where three-quarters of all births occur). Abortion-related deaths are known to be more common among black and low-income women, whose use of contraception is relatively low. Assuming one in five illegal abortions leads to hospital admissions, over 1 million abortions are estimated to be performed annually (Monteiro and Adesse 2006). Unsafe abortion is the fourth-leading cause of maternal death and is the top cause in cities in the impoverished northeastern states of Bahía and Pernambuco (Barros et al. 2010; Soares et al. 2011). The heavy stigma around abortion and sexual violence create barriers for victims who are trying to access care and support. Misoprostol is now used to perform over one in three abortions, although there are still severe limitations to its access and use (Ipas 2010).

Since the turn of the century, an increasingly heated battle has emerged over abortion. In 2005, the government of Luiz Inácio Lula da Silva advanced its first bill to relax restrictions on abortion, but failed to win strong support from its own governing Workers' Party (PT) or allied parties. In 2007, the President described abortion as a public health issue, not a moral one. Pope Benedict XVI criticized this position and that of Mexico City's recent legalization of abortion when he visited Brazil several months later, stressing the need to respect life "from the moment of conception until natural death". The President pledged that his government would never present a bill in Congress to legalize abortion.

The issue resurfaced with the proposed decriminalization of abortion as part of the inclusion of sexual and reproductive rights in the 2010 draft of the government's third National Programme on Human Rights. The move was applauded by the Brazilian women's movement, but proved controversial and was dropped four months later from the government's human rights plan after a campaign headed up by the Catholic Church. This even referred to the popular former President as "Herod" – a biblical allusion to the king of Judea who ordered the killing of baby boys in and around Bethlehem after the birth of Jesus Christ. In the meantime, the case of a nine-year-old rape victim revived debate on sexual violence, the need for abortion law reform, and the shortcomings of the health system in dealing with the few cases in which abortion is legal. Both the President and his Health Minister vehemently condemned the position taken by the Church for having excommunicated the girl's mother and doctors, but not the stepfather who had impregnated her (Correa 2010).

Political candidates in the 2010 presidential campaign carefully avoided the issue of abortion. Despite her past support for its limited legalization, Dilma Rousseff, the country's first female elected President, expressed hostility to the idea in the run-off contest after the issue was brought against her by the Catholic Church and other religious groups. José Serra, the candidate for the opposition Social Democratic Party, allied himself with religious conservatives in a bid to help his campaign. As a Health Minister a decade earlier, however, he had helped secure the approval of guidelines for health care professionals regarding the termination of pregnancies resulting from sexual violence (De Souza 2011).

Building Issue Networks and Exploiting Political Opportunities

Notwithstanding substantial gains in women's rights, health care, education, and employment, persistent stereotypes about women's sexuality and double standards of sexual morality dominate family, civil and penal laws, and gendered patterns of behavior. Abortion is virtually the only gender issue area where major policy change has not recently occurred in South American countries, many of which have overcome resistance from the Catholic Church and social conservatives to negotiate other controversial topics such as the legalization of divorce. An earlier analysis argued that Argentina, Brazil, and Chile did not de-penalize abortion due to pervasive anti-abortion activism, insufficient public support for substantial law reform, and because issue networks coordinated better with regard to the gender issues of family policy and divorce. Further, conflict between governments (be they authoritarian or democratic) and hegemonic religious institutions was posited to facilitate gender policy reform, whereas cooperation may thwart such change (Htun 2003).

In Argentina, however, the 2001–2002 political-economic meltdown heightened problems of poverty, teenage pregnancy, and child malnutrition, increasing societal support for the new government's reproductive health initiatives. This created political space for considering abortion policy reform, but, as in Brazil, politicians stopped short of tackling the issue further (Kulczycki 2007). In Bolivia, the Church helped convince the Movement Toward Socialism party to trade away abortion rights proposals for concessions in areas such as economic reform. In Mexico, successive authoritarian governments suppressed the Catholic Church's voice for decades and did not exploit opportunities to reform abortion laws. Politicians placed abortion on the legislative agenda, but opted against reform because they did not see it as a political priority (Kulczycki 2007). Clearly, windows of opportunity to pursue policy reform may arise from different sources, and authoritarian and democratic governments alike may be reluctant to pursue such moves if there is no obvious political gain.

The Absence of Policy Reform in Chile

Chile has enjoyed one of the highest economic growth rates in South America and leads the region in human capital development, income per capita, press freedom, and low perception of corruption. It is also characterized by persistent social conservatism, being one of the last countries in the world to legalize divorce, which occurred only in 2004.

Abortion was criminalized in the 1874 penal code, with therapeutic procedures authorized under the 1931 health code. In the 1960s, Chilean physicians and researchers first highlighted the rise in self-induced abortions that required treatment in Santiago hospitals; although they were unwilling to provoke major controversy, their evidence and unease helped ensure Chile was an early adopter of family planning in the region (Faúndes and Barzelatto 2006). Women of all socio-economic strata increasingly and silently procured abortions, with poor women more likely to suffer the consequences of unsafe procedures, a problem worsened when the Pinochet military regime (1973–1989) banned even therapeutic procedures. Improved contraceptive practice has since reduced clandestine abortions, which now tend to be performed by less dangerous methods, lowering the number of abortion-related deaths.

Proponents of decriminalization remain somewhat ambivalent about pushing for desired legal changes, reflecting societal ambivalence on the matter. Chilean feminists have played important roles in networking, lobbying, and activism for the "gender" interests of women. They helped challenge the Pinochet regime's pronatalist agenda in the 1980s, but although feminists have claimed to speak for women of all classes, they have not managed to alter national discourse on motherhood in ways that could increase reproductive agency, particularly for poor women (Pieper Mooney 2009). Their sense of urgency arguably declined since the return to democracy in 1990. Likewise, Chilean physicians have been influential in international medical networks and alliances, but the technical medical elite have clearly had broader goals than women's health, driving maternal health policies in terms of public health and national development, not women's rights. The election of Michelle Bachelet (2006–2010), the country's first female president, signified both the progress made by Chilean women since the democratic transition began and limits to the societal transformation of their status. Women made gains in educational opportunities, labor and marriage laws, and political representation, but reproductive rights, including access to emergency contraception, proved contentious (Haas 2011). Her successor, a billionaire businessman heading a center-right coalition, is an outspoken opponent of abortion. The Catholic Church also remains resolutely opposed to abortion.

Limited Reform in Colombia

Colombia has the second largest population and third largest economy in South America, as well as perhaps its most uneven distribution of wealth that has fueled decades of conflict and has only recently abated. The legal system recognizes social and cultural rights rarely found in Latin America and the constitution promulgated in 1991 included key provisions on political, ethnic, human, and gender rights. Five parliamentary attempts were made over 1975–2006 to decriminalize abortion, each defeated as discourse remained grounded on religious considerations and away from those of health, gender, and rights. The status quo also benefited parliamentarians unwilling to advance reforms. In 2006, the Constitutional Court legalized abortion in the limited cases of threats to a mother's life, pregnancy as a result of rape, or if the fetus is severely malformed (Ceaser 2006; Kulczycki 2011). The court ruled in response to a lawsuit filed by the local affiliate of an international women's rights group (Women's Link Worldwide) which argued that a total ban on abortion unjustly discriminated against women, especially the poor, and violated Colombia's international treaty obligations.

The litigation succeeded for several reasons. Firstly, it took for granted that Colombia is a secular state and used international human rights arguments to argue that a ban on abortion violated women's constitutional rights and threatened their rights to life and health. Secondly, the lawsuit took advantage of a favorable legal and social climate, with the appointment of the first female judge to the bench as well as others known to have argued against penalizing abortion. Thirdly, the Constitutional Court enabled the lawsuit challenging the constitutionality of the abortion ban to be filed directly through the Court rather than through the politicized and potentially hostile National Assembly where previous attempts had been unsuccessful. Colombia has a relatively strong and independent judiciary which could bypass the Church's influence on the public and on politicians regarding such a sensitive issue, further facilitating the agenda of the issue network. Lastly, the litigation successfully built on the advocacy work of the Colombian women's movement, which had for several decades mobilized for the legalization of abortion. The lawyer who filed the lawsuit saw her work as part of a larger strategy to generate change nationally and regionally. However, the court's ruling sparked uproar and continues to be strongly resisted by many health care providers and administrators, as well as by Church leaders and anti-abortion groups. The first legal abortion did not occur for four months, when the Constitutional Court had to authorize the procedure, upon appeal, in the case of an 11-year-old rape victim.

Bold Reform in Mexico City

The 2007 legalization of first trimester abortion in Mexico City resulted from a sustained process of abortion advocacy and awareness-building. Mexican women's groups began to advocate for easier access to abortion and respect for women's reproductive rights in the 1970s, beginning a long struggle with the Catholic Church and social and political conservatives who sought to keep abortion outlawed in nearly all cases except when a pregnant woman's health was threatened. The reform would not have succeeded, however, without the willingness of the center-left PRD (Party of the Democratic Revolution, which controlled the Federal District's legislature) to take up the issue.

Activists and politicians adopted several strategies to build public support for their cause. In 2000, five non-governmental organizations promoting women's sexual and reproductive rights formed a National Pro-Choice Alliance, though this was essentially focused on Mexico City. We can identify four bridge-building activities. First, contacts were developed with hospitals, health officials, and civil society to build the case for legalizing abortion. Second, the Alliance worked closely with favorably disposed health care providers to facilitate the introduction of services. Activists initially focused on strengthening access to abortion in circumstances where it was already legal and on expanding access to medication abortion. Third, the Alliance galvanized activists from various sectors of society (women's and human rights groups, youth groups, Catholics who dissented from their Church's official view, health experts, and academics) when issues related to women's rights came before the public or the legislature, creating openings for reform that could be exploited. Lastly, as the Alliance gained influence, it became a contact point for the media, which expanded its coverage of the issue and increasingly included public health, human rights, social justice, health, as well as diverse theological arguments in support of abortion.

Moreover, the Alliance capitalized on shrewd messaging and a favorable political context. Reformers made use of Mexico's anti-clerical tradition and more recent trend toward secularization, both especially strong in the capital city, to enable more effective messaging about abortion. They stressed longstanding laws mandating separation of church and state, and church teaching that lets Catholics follow their own consciences on moral issues rather than religious doctrine and authority. In this way, reform advocates re-framed abortion as a basic human right related to the improvement of public health and social justice. They emphasized the high human costs of criminalizing abortion, particularly for poor women, thereby shifting debate toward the reduction of maternal mortality. They also juxtaposed the "interruption of pregnancy" in the first trimester with the termination of a pregnancy after 12 weeks of gestation, an effective linguistic sleight of hand which made early abortion seem more acceptable and allowed "abortion" to remain illegal within the letter of the law.

Reformers realized several political opportunities, facilitated by the willingness of the local legislature to exploit the issue. For example, public outrage followed well-publicized cases of young rape victims who were denied access to abortion, opening up debate further. Reform efforts allowed for conscientious objection among providers while mandating institutions to make abortion services available. Determined champions willing to push the abortion issue were found in a legislature dominated by the PRD, whose conflict with the conservative National Action Party was exacerbated by the marginal loss of the PRD's aggrieved candidate in the bitterly contested 2006 presidential election. The Supreme Court narrowly overruled challenges to the new law's constitutionality filed by the Ombudsman of the National Human Rights Commission and the federal government. Reform advocates anticipated that this ruling would move Latin America further toward recognition of a woman's legal right to abortion. However, any such momentum appears to have been arrested and the move provoked a backlash elsewhere in Mexico.

Transforming Attitudes and Re-aligning Reform Efforts in Brazil and Peru

The reforms in Colombia and Mexico showed regional advocates the feasibility of changing attitudes and policies in a socially and politically conservative environment. In October 2011, a meeting for researchers, health practitioners, and advocates was held in Mexico City to capitalize on momentum generated by the Federal District's 2007 decision to eliminate many abortion restrictions. Some of the reflections below derive from the author's discussions held at this meeting and pertain particularly to Brazil and Peru, where abortion reform movements, political will, and favorable public opinion are weaker than in Mexico City. Brazil has an increasingly articulate women's movement, though it is not yet as strategic as in the Mexican capital. Peru permits only therapeutic procedures, but even these cannot always be obtained. Health professionals lack clear protocols and fear prosecution or malpractice lawsuits (Human Rights Watch 2008). Proposals to decriminalize abortion in rape cases have been defeated by conservative political and religious leaders.

In both Brazil and Peru, advocates are using four strategies to promote incremental policy changes which could slowly chip away at abortion restrictions. First, they are promoting expanded access to abortion in circumstances for which it is already legal. Second, they are seeking to increase accessibility to medication abortion, with medical groups calling for the revision of abortion protocols to minimize limits on access to misoprostol, as well as to train more providers in safe abortion care. Third, feminist and human rights organizations have testified before congressional committees on expanding availability of misoprostol for efficient and safe abortion within the public health system. Along with groups such as Catholics for the Right to Decide that dissent from their Church's official position on abortion, they have also distributed materials and sought to educate policymakers, health care providers, and the public about the high human costs of unsafe abortion and the obligation to ensure safe abortion within the full boundaries of the law. Fourth, reproductive health agencies, medical and women's groups have sought to develop clinical standards of practice and protocols for the institutional implementation of therapeutic abortion. These efforts are still not well coordinated and have been rebuffed by stiff opposition, highlighting that issue networks have not yet reached critical mass or influence.

Changing the Discourse and Terms of Debate

The Mexico City experience is inspiring for many reform-minded groups because it offers a broader framework within which to advocate for change and to find language that can more effectively carry abortion arguments to a broader audience. Reformers in Colombia and Mexico successfully argued for the separation of church and state and attempted to align their efforts with the needs of civil society and away from religious dogma. In another lesson taken from Mexico, reform-minded advocates in Brazil, Peru, and elsewhere have sought to stimulate debate through emblematic cases.

In early 2009, a nine-year-old Brazilian rape victim obtained a legal abortion in a case that ignited national outrage and debate. A Catholic cardinal excommunicated the girl's medical team and her mother, yet permitted her rapist to remain in good standing with the church. Health Minister José Temporão said doctors must put law before religion:

> The question posed is very simple. There is a Brazilian law which states that a pregnancy can be interrupted in case of rape. It is legitimate for the church to have its dogmas, but these dogmas must not be imposed on society as a whole.

President Luiz Inácio Lula da Silva added: "In this case, the medical profession was more right than the church" (Correa 2010). The episode led to some re-casting of the way abortion was presented in the media and how it figured in public discussion. Such junctures may shift attitudes and generate the space needed for pushing subsequent attempts at policy reform.

Peruvian advocates have since focused on shifting discussion of abortion away from religious doctrine to issues of women's health and human rights, and re-framing it in terms of pregnancy interruption. In contrast to the reasonably coordinated and cohesive social justice movements in Brazil and Mexico, however, the controversial rule of Peruvian President Fujimori in the 1990s did much to silence opposition. His government also oversaw a major expansion of a family planning initiative marred by coerced sterilizations and abusive treatment of mostly indigenous women in public sector health facilities (Cáceres et al. 2008). The level of grassroots organizing has remained diminished since and women's groups have lost influence. In 2008, however, a prominent women's organization, Promsex (the Center for the Promotion and Defense of the Sexual and Reproductive Rights), launched a lawsuit against the government demanding women's legal rights to therapeutic abortion be upheld and the national protocol for such procedures be implemented. A lawyer with the Human Rights National Coordinator led an effort with the National Lawyer's Association and the Medical Congress to challenge the law requiring health professionals to report women who undergo an abortion. Ahead of the 2011 elections, attempts were made to build public support to amend the penal code to allow abortion in cases of rape and fetal anomaly. These efforts did not advance in Congress, but they have helped legitimize such arguments and created space for future reform efforts.

Discussion

In a number of South American countries, abortion policy has entered a state of flux as longstanding legal and social sanctions against the procedure have been challenged. Activists are increasingly seeking to change discourse on abortion, interjecting public health and social justice arguments to shift debate away from religious considerations. However, their efforts to build more powerful issue networks and to exploit policy windows have met with only partial success to date.

Regarding future prospects for abortion policy reform, a long-term unknown concerns the potential significance of future demographic pressures to maintain restrictive abortion laws. Although fertility rates have now fallen to below replacement level in Brazil, Chile, and Uruguay (closely followed by Argentina and Colombia), the growing acceptance of low fertility and of measures to implement lower family size preferences has not yet translated to widespread acceptance of abortion. Growing concerns about the future implications of falling birth rates will inevitably arise alongside the significant aging that will manifest in the first half of this century. The resultant pressures may motivate policymakers to keep restrictive policies as they contemplate various pronatalist measures (Hodgson, forthcoming).

Another unknown concerns the spread of Protestant evangelical and pentecostalist churches in Brazil and elsewhere in South America at the expense of Catholicism. Protestant evangelical leaders in the Central American states of El Salvador and Nicaragua have been as forceful as conservative Catholic prelates in opposing any relaxation of abortion laws and have not objected to the prohibition of even life-saving therapeutic abortions. On the other hand, as democracy and secularization become further entrenched in South America, and as the demands of the growing middle class expand, it will probably be more difficult for religious leaders to exercise as much influence over abortion policy as they have to date. Although public opinion evinces much ambivalence as to how abortion policy should be defined and formulated, it is equally apparent that many Catholics do not share the hostility of their bishops to abortion and do not necessarily accept that this issue should be reduced to a philosophical or moral plane alone.

There are no simplistic associations between certain types of political regime and the corresponding range of women's rights. Policy change depends not only on ideology and the status of church–state relations, but also on current socio-economic demands, issue advocacy and networking, and political priorities. For example, authoritarian and democratic governments in Chile and elsewhere criticized family planning as part of the US hegemonic project, as well as accepted earlier Cold War paranoia that impacted on family planning policy and subsequent international discourse that advanced health and rights-based arguments in this realm. Even as the proportion of women who used birth control increased, the Pinochet dictatorship promoted pronatalism and banned abortion under all circumstances. Chile has since made rapid political and economic progress, but remains a society where conservative gendered expectations restrict reproductive rights and medical and political elites reinforce traditional concepts of "proper" motherhood and womanhood, with the agency of poor women questioned in particular.

In Chile, as throughout much of South America, there remains a double discourse on morals and ethics, with public intolerance but tacit tolerance of private acts (Shepard 2006). This widely noted norm accepts hidden transgressions of sexual or religious–moral expectations, and prevents frank dialogue on sexual and reproductive issues, especially abortion. It thereby avoids the political challenges of pushing ahead with institutional changes in norms, treats fertility regulation largely as a private matter, and means that widespread abortion is only addressed silently and piecemeal. Perhaps more than elsewhere on the continent, the Catholic Church in Chile earlier adopted a pragmatic approach to contraception as a lesser evil, but it has remained implacably opposed to abortion and reinforced the prevailing social conservatism.

Women's movements contributed to the democratic transitions in South America during the 1980s and in Central America during the 1990s. These movements later appeared to lose momentum in the region, with agendas and strategies altered by recent political, economic, and social changes (Jaquette 2009, Lebon and Maier, 2010). Constitutional reforms and new laws in many new South American democracies had helped overhaul discriminatory family and labor laws, criminalized violence against women, and institutionalized women's issues in government ministries. There is a trend toward more pluralist and more fragmented politics, as is characteristic of the movement towards democracy. However, persistent patriarchal influences and conservative opposition have made it difficult to change laws and social mores regarding women's reproductive rights, as highlighted by the varied experiences of Chile, Colombia, Mexico, Peru, and Brazil.

In the name of modern democratic representation, virtually every Latin American state has instituted far-reaching reforms such as gender quotas for national legislatures and government women's bureaus. These have led to increased equality for women in public life and provide standards and comparative judgments that place states in hierarchical social orders (Towns 2010). Policymakers often look abroad for promising solutions to domestic problems that include health care reforms, although there are many limits to realizing such gains (Marmor et al. 2005). Abortion activists have similarly touted the decriminalization measures in Colombia and Mexico City as examples for the rest of South America to follow. This study argues that the ability to replicate such policy precedents across settings depends heavily on the effective activism of issue networks and the exploitation of political opportunities. Uruguay may still emerge as a reference point in parts of South America, but it has a small population with a relatively liberal stance on various sensitive moral issues and abortion remains illegal in most circumstances in Brazil, by far the largest country in a Catholic region. With growing entrenchment of democracy, policy transfer is unlikely to occur without a more consensual nature of decision-making and the transformation of attitudes further in the direction of more liberal abortion regimes.

Policy reform is contingent in part on the opportunities available to issue networks to gain access to state institutions. In Colombia and Mexico, reform efforts based in major metropolitan centers have succeeded in easing restrictions on abortion, but they have not secured acceptance elsewhere. In Colombia, women's groups and other reform advocates advanced secular arguments, built on international human rights laws, and exploited policy windows. Activists filed a lawsuit successfully challenging the constitutionality of an abortion ban. This was heard by the politically neutral and independent Constitutional Court, severely limiting the ability of the country's powerful bishops and conservative politicians to defeat the reform process, although they have since impeded its implementation. In Mexico City, activists worked with health administrators and politicians favorably disposed to the reform effort who also saw it as part of their battle with the national government. In both countries, reform movements successfully capitalized on a policy window and built on a well-developed issue network that had helped create the groundwork for reform over a number of years.

Attempts at bold policy reform have been contained elsewhere in South America. Kingdon (1984) earlier deduced three elements needed for bold policymaking: the right political leaders should be in place; they should have the right plan; and they should agree on a plan that needs fixing. For now, the question of what to do about abortion is not judged sufficiently pressing to warrant major policy change. However, improved contraceptive use, increased emergency contraception, the institutionalization of post-abortion care and new technologies, particularly medication abortion, continue to help make abortion safer and rarer across the region. These incremental changes represent important advances in women's health and welfare. Additionally, South America is witnessing increasing political pluralism and growing awareness of the existing problems surrounding abortion. Political opportunities may arise unexpectedly and social actors need to be ready to take advantage, a process facilitated by issue networks. It remains to be seen whether more reform-minded political leaders and activists will manage to exploit such opportunities.

Notes

1. Emergency contraception can be used by women when other contraceptive measures have failed, making it a useful tool for preventing unintended pregnancy and abortion. The most common form comprises two high-dose birth control pills, which are effective if taken within five days of unprotected intercourse.
2. Guyana has permitted abortion without restriction as to reason since 1995, but it was not until 2008 that public hospitals would complete abortions that pregnant women had already started earlier. Elsewhere in Latin America, Puerto Rico (which follows US law), several Caribbean states, Cuba, and Mexico City (though not the rest of Mexico) allow first trimester abortion on broad grounds, with Uruguay following suit as this article went to press.
3. Three years after the law was passed, records showed that the 15 hospitals affiliated with the public sector abortion services program had attended to 20,053 women. This is relatively few in relation to the Federal District's population of 8.8 million people. The law has also resulted in a trend toward earlier and safer medical abortion and an increase in post-procedure contraceptive uptake among previous users (Mondragón y Kalb et al. 2011).
4. In 2012, the Argentine Supreme Court ruled that women who have an abortion after being raped would no longer be prosecuted, clarifying a murky legal clause. However, women impregnated as a result of rape still have to undergo a medical evaluation.
5. The final compromise measure passed in Uruguay requires a woman seeking an abortion to meet with an interdisciplinary panel of at least three pertinent professionals (including at least one psychiatrist, one social worker, and one gynecologist) to justify her request, and then reflect for five days before undergoing the procedure. The law also permits physicians and private health centers to cite conscientious objections to avoid carrying out abortions (see "Uruguay Senate Approves First-Trimester Abortions," *New York Times*, October 17, 2012).

References

Barros, F. C., Matijasevich, A., Requejo, J. H., Giugliani, E., Goretti Maranhão, A., Monteiro, C. A., Barros, J. D., Bustero, F., Merialdi, M. and Victora, C. G., 2010, Recent trends in maternal, newborn, and child health in Brazil: Progress toward millennium development goals 4 and 5. *American Journal of Public Health*, **100**, pp. 1877–1889.

Billings, D. L. and Benson, J., 2005, Post-abortion care in Latin America: Policy and service recommendations from a decade of operations research. *Health Policy and Planning*, **20**(3), pp. 158–166.

Cáceres, C., Cueto, M. and Palomino, N., 2008, Policies around sexual and reproductive health and rights in Peru: Conflict, biases and silence. *Global Public Health*, **3**(S2), pp. 39–57.

Ceaser, M., 2006, Court ends Colombia's abortion ban. *Lancet*, **367**, 1645–1646.

Correa, S., 2010, Brazil: one of the abortion front lines. *Reproductive Health Matters*, **18**(36), pp. 111–117.

De Souza, A., 2011, The politics of personality in Brazil. *Journal of Democracy*, **22**(2), pp. 75–88.

Faúndes, A. and Barzelatto, J., 2006, *The Human Drama of Abortion: A Global Search for Consensus* (Nashville, TN: Vanderbilt University Press).

Faúndes, A., Tavara, L., Brache, V. and Alvarez, F., 2007, Emergency contraception under attack in Latin America: Response of the medical establishment and civil society. *Reproductive Health Matters*, **15**, pp. 130–138.

Haas, L., 2011, *Feminist Policymaking in Chile* (University Park, PA: Pennsylvania State University Press).

Hodgson, D., 2013, How problematic will liberal abortion policies be for pronatalist countries?, in: A. Kulczycki (Ed) *Critical Issues in Reproductive Health* (New York: Springer Books).

Holy See, 2010, *Statistical Yearbook of the Church 2008* (Vatican City: Vatican Publishing House).

Htun, M., 2003, *Sex and the State: Abortion, Divorce, and the Family Under Latin American Dictatorships and Democracies* (Cambridge: Cambridge University Press).

Human Rights Watch, 2006, The Second Assault: Obstructing Access to Legal Abortion after Rape in Mexico. *Human Rights Watch*, **18**(1,B), available at http://www.hrw.org/sites/default/files/reports/mexico0306webwcover.pdf (accessed 16 February 2012).

Human Rights Watch, 2008, My Rights, and My Right to Know: Lack of Access to Therapeutic Abortion in Peru. Available at: http://www.hrw.org/en/reports/2008/07/08/my-rights-and-my-right-know-0 (accessed 15 February 2012).

Human Rights Watch, 2010, Illusions of Care: Lack of Accountability for Reproductive Rights in Argentina. Available at: http://www.hrw.org/node/92124 (accessed 2 March 2012).

Ipas, 2010, *Misoprostol and Medical Abortion in Latin America and the Caribbean* (Chapel Hill, NC: Ipas and Lima, Peru: Consorcio Latinoamericano Contra el Aborto Inseguro (CLACAI)). Available at: http://www.ipas.org/Publications/Misoprostol_medical_abortion_in_Latin_America_the_Caribbean.aspx (accessed 15 February 2012).

Jaquette, J. S. (Ed.), 2009, *Feminist Agendas and Democracy in Latin America* (Durham, NC: Duke University Press).

Kampwirth, K., 2011, *Latin America's New Left and the Politics of Gender: Lessons From Nicaragua* (New York: Springer).

Kingdon, J. W., 1984, *Agendas, Alternatives, and Public Policies* (Boston: Little, Brown and Company).

Kulczycki, A., 1999, *The Abortion Debate in the World Arena* (London: Macmillan; and New York: Routledge).

Kulczycki, A., 2007, The abortion debate in Mexico: Realities and stalled policy reform. *Bulletin of Latin American Research*, **26**(1), pp. 50–68.

Kulczycki, A., 2011, Abortion in Latin America: Changes in practice, growing conflict, and recent policy developments. *Studies in Family Planning*, **42**(3), pp. 199–220.

Lagos Lira, C., 2001, *Aborto En Chile: El Deber De Parir* (Santiago: Lom Ediciones).

Lebon, N., Maier, E., eds, 2010, *Women's Activism in Latin America and the Caribbean: Engendering Social Justice, Democratizing Citizenship* (New Brunswick, NJ: Rutgers University Press).

Marmor, T., Freeman, R. and Okma, K., 2005, Comparative perspectives and policy learning in the world of health care. *Journal of Comparative Policy Analysis*, **7**(4), pp. 331–348.

Martine, G., 1996, Brazil's fertility decline, 1965–95. *Population and Development Review*, **22**(1), pp. 47–75.

Mondragón y Kalb, M., Ortega, A. A., Velazquez, J. M., Díaz Olavarrieta, C., Rodríguez, J. V., Becker, D. and García, S. G., 2011, Patient characteristics and service trends following abortion legalization in Mexico City, 2007–10. *Studies in Family Planning*, **42**(3), pp. 159–166.

Monteiro, M. F. G. and Adesse, L., 2006, Estimativas de aborto induzido no Brasil e grandes regiões (1992–2005). Paper presented at the 15th Meeting of the Brazilian Population Studies Association (ABEP), Caxambú, Brazil; 18–22 September 2006. Available at: http://www.ipas.org.br/arquivos/ml2006.pdf (accessed 25 February 2012).

Nunn, A., 2009, *The Politics and History of AIDS Treatment in Brazil* (New York: Springer).

Pieper Mooney, J. E., 2009, *The Politics of Motherhood: Maternity and Women's Rights in Twentieth-Century Chile* (Pittsburgh, PA: Pittsburgh University Press).

Shepard, B., 2006, *Running the Obstacle Course to Sexual and Reproductive Health: Lessons From Latin America* (Westport, CT: Praeger).

Singh, S., Sedgh, G. and Hussain, R., 2010, Unintended pregnancy: Worldwide levels, trends, and outcomes. *Studies in Family Planning*, **41**(4), pp. 241–250.

Soares, G. S., Galli, M. B. and Viana de A.L, P., 2011, *Advocacy for Access to Safe Legal Abortion: Similarities in the Impact of Abortion's Illegality on Women's Health and Health Care in Pernambuco, Bahia, Mato Grosso Do Sul, Paraiba, and Rio De Janeiro* (Rio de Janeiro: Curumim and Ipas).

Towns, A. E., 2010, *Women and States: Norms and Hierarchies in International Society* (Cambridge: Cambridge University Press).

UN, 2002, *Abortion Policies: A Global Review*, Vols. 1–3 (New York: United Nations). Available at: http://www.un.org/esa/population/publications/abortion/ (accessed 25 February 2012).

UN, 2011, *World Abortion Policies 2011* (wallchart) (New York: United Nations, Department of Economic and Social Affairs, Population Division).

Vlassoff, M., Walker, D., Shearer, J., Newlands, D. and Singh, S., 2009, Estimates of health care system costs of unsafe abortion in Africa and Latin America. *International Perspectives on Sexual and Reproductive Health*, **35**(3), pp. 114–121.

Walsh, J., 2005, *International Human Rights Law and Abortion in Latin America* (New York: Human Right Watch). Available at http://www.hrw.org/legacy/backgrounder/wrd/wrd0106/wrd0106.pdf (accessed 2 March 2012).

World Health Organization (WHO), 2011, *Unsafe Abortion: Global and Regional Estimates of the Incidence of Unsafe Abortion and Associated Mortality in 2008*, sixth edition (Geneva: World Health Organization)).

Yam, E. A., Dries-Daffner, I. and Garcia, S. G., 2006, Abortion opinion research in Latin America and the Caribbean: A review of the literature. *Studies in Family Planning*, **37**(4), pp. 225–240.

Father-Friendly Legislation and Paternal Time across Western Europe

ALISON J. SMITH and DONALD R. WILLIAMS

ABSTRACT *Throughout the 1990s fathers across Western Europe were increasingly enabled to spend paternal time, following changes to national legislation regarding access to leave. We create a father-friendly policy index to construct a typology of governmental leave provisions specifically available to fathers by 1996–1997. We then analyze the time spent caring for children by fathers in Western Europe in 1996 and 2001, using the European Community Household Panel survey. We find that the time fathers spend caring for children, and gender inequalities in time caring for children, vary considerably by country. The policy index is correlated with both absolute and relative levels of fathers' time spent caring for children.*

Introduction

Can father-friendly legislation promote equal sharing by men and women of both paid employment and childcare, and if so, which types of legislation? These are the broad questions examined in this paper. We look at the governmental leave provisions that were available to fathers in 16[1] Western European countries for the period 1996–1997 and compare them with the amount of time that fathers spent looking after children in 1996 and 2001.

Many women now participate in the labor market (Crouch 1999) and fathers increasingly participate in household work and childcare (Gershuny 2000). Women, however, are still responsible for the majority of childcare across Europe (Eurostat 2004). It can be said that these social changes, observed in Western European households, have been asymmetric: women have in general become earners to a greater extent than men have become carers. Nonetheless, "father-friendly" legislation has been enacted in many countries, with an eye toward increasing the role that fathers play in childrearing.

Father-friendly legislation is defined as that which, in particular, enables fathers to combine their caring rights and responsibilities with earning. Government-regulated childcare provisions can be classified into three distinct categories: cash transfers, provision of services, and leave (Ditch et al. 1996). We focus on the third category, namely statutory leave provisions, as theoretically we would expect these to be associated with the time fathers spend looking after children. Across the European Union member states, there are various terms for the different variations of leave provision available to fathers, including: paternity leave, parental leave, childcare leave, career breaks, family leave, sick child leave, calamity leave, and so on. For the purposes of this paper, *paternal leave* is used as a broad umbrella term for all types of leave to which fathers have access.[2]

We look at the access that European fathers had to statutory leave to care for young children by 1996–1997. Throughout the 1990s, across Western Europe, fathers were increasingly enabled to spend more time caring for small children following changes in legislation regarding access to paternal leave. A particular example of change in legislation was the European Union directive on parental leave (96/34/EC), which came into force in June 1996 (although parental leave arrangements were already in place in some member states). There were several aims behind the directive, but a primary consideration was to achieve a balanced participation of women and men in family and working life (European Network 1998, EU Council 2000/C 218/02). The question of whether the directive is realizing this aim remains unanswered. There has been little policy impact analysis into the practical significance of this legislation with respect to its increasing the amount of time that men spend with their children (Moss and Deven 1999, Haas 2003).

We explore in this paper the correlations between *paternal time* (time spent caring by fathers) and paternal leave legislation at the national level. National legislation might not be relevant in some employment situations, for example where collective agreements play an important role in social protection. In this case, there can be much variation in the scope of extra-statutory provisions as well as the implementation and uptake of provisions (both statutory and extra-statutory) across companies and occupations, the public and the private sector (Bruning and Plantenga 1999, OECD 2001: 147, Haas et al. 2002). It is not possible to consider all these factors for 16 countries in a short paper, however, so we concentrate on national-level legislation alone.[3] Based on this legislation, we construct an index of the extent of provision for paternal care in each country studied. Using data for most of the countries in Western Europe regarding the time parents spend caring for children from the European Community Household Panel survey (ECHP),[4] we also construct measures of paternal time within each country. We then examine correlations between these measures and the indices of father-friendly legislation.

The paper is organized as follows: first, we review the literature and present the theory regarding the roles that policy can have in affecting paternal child-caring time. We then describe the data and methods used including the construction of the father-friendly policy indices, before presenting the results for the relationships between these indices and paternal time. The paper concludes with discussion of the results and topics for further research.

Literature Review

There has been much research into the role that state arrangements can play to help mothers combine domestic and employment responsibilities (for example, Gornick *et al.* 1997, Dex and Joshi 1999). There is little systematic knowledge of the practical significance of the paternal leave arrangements in Europe, however, with respect to them increasing the amount of time that fathers spend with their children. In fact, the two concepts of paternal leave and paternal time rarely appear in the same paper. Given this, our review is divided into two sections, the first of which considers the literature regarding paternal leave; the second regarding the literature on paternal time.

The European Parental Leave Directive implemented in 1996 (Council Directive 96/34/EC) requires EU member states to ensure the legal entitlement of fathers (and mothers) to a minimum of three months' unpaid leave after the birth of a child. The Directive provides minimum requirements for national statutory (governmental) parental leave legislation, although many member states already had parental leave schemes in place by 1996, most of which exceeded the minimum provisions set out in the directive (NFPI 2000). There is not, at the time of writing, a European directive concerning other types of paternal leave.

The details of the entitlements and the substance of governmental leave provisions have been widely and variously compiled, analysed and commented upon in documents published by the European Commission (EC 1998, European Network 1998; see also Deven and Moss 2002, Haas 2003). A valuable paper in this area comes from Bruning and Plantenga (1999), looking at parental leave uptake in eight European countries. Despite finding considerable variance in parental leave legislation, their conclusions are that parental leave in its current format has had very little impact on equal opportunities. The data show that fathers' take-up rates in all countries remain low (EC 1998, Bruning and Plantenga 1999).

One factor affecting the take-up rates of fathers is whether the leave is, as a rule, defined for the individual or the family. Individual rights refer to each parent having his or her own claim for his or her own period of leave. Sometimes a hybrid strategy is used which entails creating an individual rights period within a broader family-based entitlement. This hybrid strategy creates a "use or lose" situation which increases the likelihood that fathers will make use of leave options as compared to an entirely family-based entitlement (Brandth and Kvande 2001). Wholly transferable parental leave is taken up by men at very low rates, varying from 2.5 per cent in Germany to less than 5 per cent in Italy (Brandth and Kvande 1998, EC 1998, Bruning and Plantenga 1999). The rise of the hybrid strategy witnessed in the Nordic countries appears to be an effective strategy with regard to improving fathers' take-up rates of leave (Ellingsaeter 1999).[5]

Another dimension of leave policy is the amount of leave weeks paid in full, which is an indicator of the degree to which a country is willing to share the burden of forgone earnings with the parents. An alternative most consistent with achieving gender equality is to grant both women and men in all jobs the option of working reduced hours or flexible hours on a temporary basis during the years of childrearing (Bettio *et al.* 1998).

There is a growing body of literature dealing with trends in parental time. Despite frequent reports of the "time squeeze", it would appear that both men and women are in fact spending more time with their children (Fisher *et al.* 1999, Gauthier *et al.* 2004, Sayer *et al.* 2004, Smith 2004, Sandberg and Hofferth 2005). Despite differences and difficulties inherent in the measurement of *paternal time* (time spent caring for children by fathers) across studies and national contexts, a certain degree of consistency exists. Estimates of *primary* paternal time (in which the father reports care as the sole activity, not undertaken simultaneously with other tasks) are, for example, just under two hours per day for the UK in the late 1990s among married employed fathers (Fisher *et al.* 1999). Using primary measures, paternal time across Europe has been found to be between a quarter and a third of maternal time (Eurostat 2004).

Theory

There are a series of rival theories concerning the dynamics and division of labor between couples. These can be usefully divided between economic and cultural considerations (Brines 1994). The economic perspective pays particular attention to the relative amount of income and other resources that spouses may exchange or bargain for unpaid work, most often focusing at the micro-level (e.g. Breen and Cooke 2005). On the other hand, the macro-cultural perspective considers the normative context of childcare, and focuses in particular on the relationship between unpaid work and the social construction of gender, finding that structural effects exist in addition to individual-level processes (McFarlane *et al.* 2000, Geist 2005).

Influences on paternal time can also be divided between those at the micro (household or individual) level and those at the macro-institutional (national legislation or company culture) level (e.g. Hook 2006). In this paper, we concentrate specifically on theories relating to the influence that the state can have on paternal time.[6]

A child can be viewed as a social or a private good, a public or private responsibility. If viewed as a public good, time spent with children is an investment that society in general benefits from and so it is not efficient to expect individuals to cover the costs of a benefit that everyone enjoys (Budig and England 2001). If viewed as a private responsibility, then it is efficient to leave individuals to make their own arrangements. To the extent that children are a public good, the state can greatly ease the difficulties associated with combining parenthood and work. How it does so can affect paternal time.

We define father-friendly legislation as that which could potentially enable fathers to spend more time looking after their children. Sweden was the first country to implement a parental leave scheme in 1974 and this legislation did embody the ideology of shared roles in parenting (Klinth 2002). Not all legislation has historically had this rationale, however, with some parental leave programs instead reinforcing traditional gender roles (Bruning and Plantenga 1999). A third group may be cast in gender-neutral language but still be inaccessible to fathers in practice.

Examining the correlation between father-friendly provision and the amount of paternal time spent across countries is our approach to answering the question: does policy matter? Our hypothesis is that national legislation is positively correlated with paternal time, though the direction of this causal relationship is impossible to determine with cross-sectional data. Legislation can shape behavior, but policy packages also reflect what people desire.

Because we use a multi-country comparison, it is necessary to frame the hypotheses around a theoretical approach that will help to explain the potential differences between countries in the extent of their father-friendliness. Different welfare states inevitably lead to variation in the manner and extent that the parental leave directive and other measures are implemented. The welfare state typology proposed by Esping-Andersen (1990, 1999) provides a useful set of theoretical groupings into which we expect countries to fall.

Esping-Andersen proposed a threefold typology based, in part, around the concept of "decommodification", which is the extent to which individuals are freed from dependence on the labour market. The first category is the "liberal" model, where state intervention is typified by the regulation of markets rather than the provision of social welfare. Combining work and family life is likely to remain a private responsibility and childcare provision is not likely to be organized, paid for (or even regulated) by the state. European countries clustered in this category are typically the UK and Ireland. The second category is the "social-democratic" model, where the role of the state is central and dedicated to universalism, direct state provision or finance, (generous) benefit levels and egalitarianism. Women are expected to be part of the labour market; childcare is viewed as a social responsibility and there is a strong commitment to gender equality. This regime is virtually synonymous with Denmark, Finland, Norway and Sweden. The third category is the "conservative" model. Features of conservative regimes are familialism (dependence on the family for welfare) and heavy stratification by both income and social status. The emphasis is on the family's (almost always the mother's) centrality as care provider, the standard male breadwinner model being assumed, which makes it harder for fathers to spend time looking after children. Continental European countries are situated within this category. There have been persuasive arguments in favour of a fourth "Mediterranean" or Southern European category (Leibfried 1992, Ferrera 1996), based on the extremely residual nature of Southern European social assistance and on strong familialism, although Esping-Andersen (1999) still makes the case for these Southern European countries to be considered in the context of the conservative regime type. Geist (2005) has found that conservative regimes, compared to liberal and social-democratic regimes, inhibit gender equality in the domestic division of labour (controlling for compositional differences). We expect, therefore, that the measures of father-friendly policy will be correlated with these welfare regimes. Given our hypothesis that the policy index will be correlated with the level of paternal caring, we further expect that men will care most in the social-democratic regime type, where father-friendly legislation is most comprehensive, and least in the liberal regime types, where there is the least father-friendly legislation.

Data and Methods

Paternal leave provisions differ across countries. There are various dimensions of variation between them. Our aim is to categorize countries in terms of the content of their paternal leave provisions with respect to these variations. This is done, firstly, by creating an index of how father-friendly minimum national paternal leave provisions were across Western European countries by 1996–1997 and, secondly, by assigning values to each element for every country, using data from a variety of sources (namely Wilkinson 1997, European Commission 1998, European Network 1998).[7] The index is constructed from values measuring each dimension of variation on a scale between "1" and "10". Higher values are assigned when the policy in the country facilitates male parenting. A description of the different elements of the index and the scoring rationale for each element follows. For a summary, see Table 1.[8]

Parental Leave: Individual or Family Right

With the exception of Ireland, Luxembourg and the UK,[9] parental leave was an implemented right of workers in all EU countries by 1997. Parental leave can be organized on a family or individual basis. Whether or not leave is a family right or an individual right is considered highly influential for male parenting. A lowest score of

Table 1. Summary of father-friendly index elements (by 1997)

Element	Score
Family right or individual right	
Individual	10
Combination/hybrid	7
Family	5
No leave	1
Paid or unpaid leave	
High-level wage compensation	10
Low-level wage compensation	5
Unpaid	2
No leave	1
Part time leave allowed	
Leave unconditional	10
Employer's consent	6
Rest allowed	2
No provision	1
Universality of leave	
No conditions	10
Minimal conditions	8
6 months minimum employment	6
12 months minimum employment	4
>12 months minimum employment	2
No leave	1
Paternity leave	
High paternity provision	10
Low paternity provision	5
No paternity provision	1
Emergency leave	
Paid special leave – more than a week	10
Paid special leave – less than a week	6
Unpaid special leave – less than a week	3
No known special leave	1
Government encouragement through awareness programmes?	
Yes	10
No	1

"1" is given to those countries with no leave at all. A score of "5" is given to those countries with only a family right, and a score of "10" to those countries with all of the leave being an individual right. Those countries with a combination of individual and family schemes are awarded "7" points.

Level of Paid Parental Leave

Whether or not parental leave is paid, and by how much, are very important factors in whether men take leave. Where wage compensation is 60 per cent of wages or higher, a score of "10" is awarded.[10] Where a percentage figure is not available but wage compensation was known to have been low, a score of "5" is awarded. France is assigned a score of "3" as paid parental leave was only provided for the second child. A score of "2" is given to those countries with unpaid leave and "1" to those countries with no leave at all.

Part- versus Full-Time Parental Leave

In some programs, parental leave can be taken part-time or full-time. We assume that the more flexible leave is, the more likely is fathers' take-up of the leave. A score of "10" is awarded if part-time leave was an unconditional legal right, a score of "6" if it was only allowed on the employer's consent, a score of "2" if fathers were permitted "rest" periods to feed their child during the working day and a score of "1" if there was no provision for a reduction of working hours for fathers of young children. Rather than part-time parental leave, parents in Spain and Portugal had the right to reduced hours at work (unpaid), and this is scored as part-time leave. In the Netherlands, parental leave could only be taken on a part-time basis.

Universality of Parental Leave

Where there are eligibility conditions, they are generally attached to the period of service in employment.[11] We assume that the more universal is eligibility, the higher will be fathers' usage of leave. Countries are awarded a "10" if there were no conditions attached to leave, "8" if there were minimal conditions (such as the four weeks of service required in Germany), "6" if a period of 6–11 months' employment was required, "4" if 12 months' employment was required, and "2" if the period required was greater than 12 months. Where there was no leave at all a score of "1" is given. Two points are deducted if fathers' eligibility was conditional on the mother being in employment.

Paternity Leave Provision

Paternity leave is defined as leave running at the same time as maternity leave after the birth of a child.[12] Those countries where paternity leave was available for a period of two weeks or more with high wage compensation are awarded "10". Those countries with minimal paternity leave provision (in terms of duration and wage compensation) are awarded "5". In many countries, short leave for personal reasons or holiday leave serves as a kind of short (paid or unpaid) leave provision. This is not included here as paternity leave, but included later in the index under the separate entry of emergency leave. These countries are awarded "1" for paternity leave provision along with all other countries without any provision for paternity leave.

Emergency/Sick Child Leave

In many countries, there is the possibility for employees to take short-term leave of absence to care for sick children. This can either be paid or unpaid. This emergency or family leave is often used where paternity provision is not available and so is not necessarily father-friendly. In other cases, the legal provision for employees to have extra time for visits to school or to care for sick children can greatly reduce work-family conflict and enable fathers to be more involved: "10" points are awarded to countries with paid special leave available for more than a week per year; "6" points are awarded to countries with paid special leave available for less than a week per year; "3" points are awarded to countries with unpaid special leave; "1" point is awarded to those countries without special leave.

Degree of Awareness

There is much variation between countries with respect to whether men are aware of any father-friendly legislation available to them (Eurobarometer 2004). In the Nordic countries there have been public awareness programmes to encourage men to spend time at home on parental leave (Haas 1992, Wilkinson 1997, European Network 1998). It may be that the only way to realize an increase in male parenting is to have it as one of the central motivations behind a leave program. The maximum score of "10" is awarded to countries that had run publicity campaigns, and the minimum score of "1" to those countries that had not.

Having thus described the construction of the father-friendly index, we turn to the European Community Household Panel survey as the source of data for our estimates of paternal time.[13] The key advantage to the ECHP over other data sets is that the same questionnaire is used in all countries, with consistent definitions of variables. Although the ECHP data are longitudinal, we use them as a cross-sectional data set. Our data are taken from the 1996 and 2001 survey years. We focus on 1996 partly because it was the year of the European Parental Leave Directive, and partly as there are the maximum number of countries available for analysis in 1996.[14] Also, problems associated with attrition are fewer earlier in the panel. Data from 2001 are used for comparison purposes. Data are available for 1996 for 14 EU countries.[15] We have limited our analysis to a sample of 9,746 households comprised of (heterosexual) couples living together with young children (under the age of six). We limit the analysis to such couples because the majority of father-friendly legislation applies to fathers with children in this age group.

The ECHP collects information on time spent looking after children through the retrospective survey questions:

"Do your present daily activities include, without pay, looking after children or other persons who need special help because of old age, illness or disability?"

If they answer yes to looking after children, then they are also asked the weekly number of hours spent doing so. The ECHP does not detail this time further, for example, by distinguishing between primary and secondary caring activities. We total the hours reported by the couple and refer to this time as paternal or maternal time respectively (regardless of whether the child is the biological or non-biological child of the parent).

It must be noted that the measure used here has some weaknesses. First, it is a self-reported measure, which might be subject to some gender-based bias (Hiller and Philliber 1986), as well as recall error. In particular, males may overstate the amount of time spent caring. Furthermore, there could be cross-national differences in the extent of the gender bias. Secondly, the definition of "caring" is not precise and might also vary across countries (or cultures). As previously noted, it does not differentiate between primary and secondary caring. Nevertheless, the results of the analysis appear to be consistent with results found in other studies.

One approach for conducting the analysis of interest in this paper would be to compare the average reported hours spent caring across countries, and examine the relationship between the average hours and the policy indices. Following Smith (2006), we instead measure the proportion of fathers spending "substantial" parental time (defined as more than 28 hours of childcare per week). The choice of this cut-off point is based on an examination of the distribution of hours of caring among fathers, which shows a considerable break at 28 hours.[16] One advantage of this approach is that it takes account of different distributions around a given mean. About one-fifth (18 per cent) of the sample of co-resident fathers spends substantial paternal time by this definition. Differences in substantial paternal time between countries are examined by looking at the different percentages of the national samples spending substantial paternal time.[17] We also consider a variable which measures the percentage of the parents spending substantial time in a nation that are fathers. This is measured by aggregating the observations for only those mothers and fathers spending substantial time, and calculating the share of these observations that are fathers.[18] While the first variable provides an absolute measure of fathers' involvement in caring behavior, the second measures their contribution relative to that of mothers.

Results

We construct several composite father-friendly indices for each country (see Table 2).[19] The simplest of these measures is the additive scale, in which we simply sum the values of the elements. A second method is multiplicative (taking the product of the scores and then taking the *nth* root) to allow for non-linear effects. We also conducted a principal components analysis (PCA). This method computes weights for the various components of the index, which can be used to compute a value of the father-friendly index for each country. The PCA indices are constructed so as to have a mean of 0 and standard deviation of 1. We also constructed the indices with only five elements (instead of seven) for comparison purposes, excluding elements 3 and 6. We found that there were negative correlations between these elements of the index and others. In particular, element 6 is negatively correlated with two of the other elements, and element 3 is negatively correlated with one of the

Table 2. Indices of father-friendliness (by 1997), by country

	Sum score		Product score		PCA based on	
	7 elements	5 elements	7th root	5th root	7 elements	5 elements
Finland (Fi)	58	47	6.8	9.3	2.23	2.20
Denmark (Dk)	54	47	6.4	9.3	2.05	2.20
Netherlands (Nt)	34	22	3.9	3.3	0.15	0.11
Belgium (B)	30	21	3.2	2.9	0.04	0.13
Austria (A)	32	16	3.5	2.5	0.05	0.00
Germany (Ge)	32	20	3.6	2.9	−0.06	−0.17
Portugal (P)	33	17	2.8	2.9	−0.27	−0.22
France (Fr)	30	19	2.8	2.6	−0.15	−0.22
Greece (Gr)	29	18	2.6	2.4	−0.30	−0.28
Italy (It)	21	16	2.5	2.5	−0.16	−0.24
Spain (Sp)	24	13	2.4	2.1	−0.40	−0.52
Ireland (Ir)	9	5	1.2	1.0	−1.06	−0.96
Luxembourg (L)	7	5	1.0	1.0	−1.06	−0.96
UK (UK)	7	5	1.0	1.0	−1.06	−0.96

others. Both sets of indices are reported, by country, in Table 2.[20] The values for each element of the index are presented in Appendix Table A1.

As can be seen in Table 2, the values of the father-friendliness indices vary considerably across the countries studied. Interestingly, Table 2 also shows that there are three categories of father-friendliness that cluster regionally according to Esping-Andersen's three categories. Using the product score with five elements, for example, the average index values are 1.00 in the liberal, 9.30 in the social democratic, and 2.68 in the conservative regimes. The welfare state principles underpinning his typology would appear to be highly correlated with those shaping family policies.

Some words of caution are in order. Such clustering as we have obtained may not be highly "robust" because it is based on a limited, if important set of indicators.[21] Nevertheless it helps to focus on some important aspects. It should also be noted that in many countries employees rely heavily on collective agreements to supplement statutory provisions (particularly the Netherlands, Spain, and the UK). Indeed, this is true to some extent for most countries, since provisions are generally increased by collective agreements for public service employees, and differences between the public and private sector are often important. We do not know whether these non-statutory provisions are correlated with our index or with the Esping-Andersen typology. Unfortunately, these collective agreements are difficult to incorporate in cross-national comparisons and consequently are ignored here.

The measures of substantial paternal time are reported in Table 3, by country, and for both 1996 and 2001. The Nordic countries stand out, with men being most likely to spend substantial paternal time (43 per cent in Denmark in 1996) and also taking on the most egalitarian share of substantial parental time. In Denmark in 1996, for example, fathers represented 33 per cent of parents with substantial parental time. Greece and Portugal, on the other hand, exhibit very low values for both the percentage of fathers spending substantial parental time (from 5 to 9 per cent), and the percentage of total substantial parental time that is provided by fathers

Table 3. Paternal time across Western Europe: 1996 and 2001

Country	Percentage of fathers spending substantial paternal time 1996	2001	Percentage of substantial parental time by fathers (as opposed to mothers) 1996	2001
Denmark	43	47	33	37
Finland	29	27	30	36
UK	24	–	21	–
Germany	22	–	20	–
Ireland	19	20	17	19
Spain	18	14	17	15
Belgium	16	12	24	18
Italy	14	12	16	15
Austria	13	9	13	12
Netherlands	12	13	12	16
Luxembourg	12	–	16	–
France	11	11	15	17
Greece	9	5	11	6
Portugal	8	8	12	13

Note: Parents spending more than 28 hours per week are classified as spending substantial time.

(6 to 13 per cent). These cross-national differences appear to be consistent over the time period observed.

Previous analyses have shown a trend of increasing paternal time (Smith 2004). From Table 3 we see that the trends are not consistent across nations. The percentage of fathers spending substantial paternal time has increased between 1996 and 2001 in Denmark, the Netherlands and Ireland. It has stayed the same in France and Portugal, and has decreased in Finland, Belgium, Austria, Greece, Italy and Spain. When looking at the share of substantial parental time, men contribute proportionally more by 2001 in Finland, Denmark, the Netherlands, Portugal, France, Ireland, and less in Belgium, Austria, Greece, Italy and Spain.

The correlation coefficients between the different "father-friendliness" indices and the two measures of paternal time are presented in Table 4. Referring first to the percentage of fathers spending substantial time caring, we find fairly high and significant cross-national correlations for all indices. The correlations are higher when the five element indices are used for all the sources. The correlation coefficient for the five-element product index with the percentage of fathers spending substantial paternal time is 0.73. For the PCA score based on five elements, the correlation coefficient and the percentage of fathers spending paternal time measure is 0.65. Similar correlations are found between the father-friendliness indices and the proportion of parents spending substantial parental time who are fathers. We conclude, therefore, that fathers in the countries with higher values on the father-friendliness index are more likely to spend substantial time caring for children, and engage in a greater share of substantial childcaring, than those in countries with lower indices.

The relationships between the father-friendliness index and the caring measures can be seen in Figures 1 and 2 (using the five-element additive index). It is apparent

Table 4. Correlation coefficients for substantial paternal time measures (1996) with the different indices (by 1997)

Variable	Sum score 7 elements	Sum score 5 elements	Product score/ 7th root	Product score/ 5th root	PCA 7 elements	PCA 5 elements
Percentage of fathers spending substantial paternal time (1996)	0.47 (0.09)	0.64 (0.01)	0.60 (0.02)	0.73 (0.00)	0.61 (0.02)	0.65 (0.02)
Percentage of substantial care carried out by fathers (1996)	0.53 (0.05)	0.70 (0.01)	0.64 (0.01)	0.76 (0.00)	0.58 (0.04)	0.63 (0.02)

Note: Pearson correlation coefficients: p-values (two-tailed) presented in parentheses.

Figure 1. Levels of substantial paternal time (1996) and father-friendly legislation (by 1997) across Europe

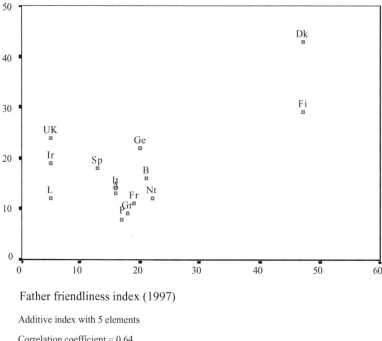

Father friendliness index (1997)

Additive index with 5 elements

Correlation coefficient = 0.64

that the relationships are non-linear, with strong positive effects of Denmark and Finland contributing greatly to the overall positive correlation. Indeed, when these two countries are excluded from the analysis, the estimated relationships become negative (although not significant).

We have noted previously that the cross-sectional approach can tell us nothing about the causal effect of father-friendly policy on paternal time. It is plausible that countries in which considerable numbers of fathers are spending substantial paternal time, are more likely to enact father-friendly legislation. Underlying cross-national cultural differences serve to affect both caring behaviour and policy. There is evidence in the literature, however, to suggest that father-friendly policy is a forerunner to increased paternal time (Brandth and Kvande 2001). As a simple attempt to examine the causal relationships, we have examined the correlation between changes in paternal caring behaviour over the 1996–2001 period and the father-friendliness indices for 1996/1997. Unfortunately data for Luxembourg, Germany and the UK are not available for both years. The analysis on the smaller sample suggests weak positive, but insignificant ($p > .10$) correlations between the indices and changes in both of the paternal care measures.[22]

Discussion

We began the paper by asking whether father-friendly legislation could promote equal sharing by men and women of both paid employment and childcare, and if so,

Figure 2. Share of substantial parental time attributed to fathers (1996) and father-friendly legislation (by 1997) across Europe

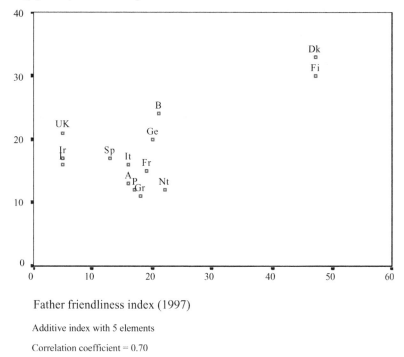

Father friendliness index (1997)

Additive index with 5 elements

Correlation coefficient = 0.70

which types of legislation. We have found a positive association between the father-friendliness of national legislation and paternal time. This result is sensitive to the inclusion of certain countries in the analysis, however.

One unambiguous finding is that national legislation in Western Europe falls clearly into three categories of father-friendliness that cluster regionally according to Esping-Andersen's typology. The relationship between paternal time spent caring for children and welfare regime is less clear, however. While the expected result is found for the social democratic countries, paternal time is also relatively high in the liberal category (the UK and Ireland), where there was virtually no father-friendly provision. Note that our findings for paternal time lend support to the consideration of a fourth Southern European regional cluster.

Does policy matter? Yes, but it obviously is not the only factor. According to the policy index, for example, Portugal is on a par with Belgium and Germany, but this is not reflected in parenting hours or the paternal share of the parenting hours. Perhaps, in the complete absence of policy, families are coming up with their own "work-family" reconciliation strategies.

In conclusion, our findings suggest that an index based on five elements of national legislation is correlated with fathers' caring for children. We suggest that public policy aimed at increasing male parenting should focus on these five elements.

Drawing on them, if governments strive to increase fathers' time with children, then they should adopt public policies with these characteristics:

- Leave should be an individual right;
- There must be high wage compensation;
- Flexibility should be possible in the way leave can be taken, with universal eligibility; and
- Leave should be targeted at men through government awareness programmes.

We expect that policy combining these elements will have the greatest impact on paternal time.

There are many directions for further research. Father-friendly legislation is not the only factor that will affect time spent caring for children by fathers. Variations in the patterns of mothers' and fathers' working hours are likely important factors. The effect that father-friendly legislation has on work hours should be explored in further research. Another topic for future work is to estimate the impact that the father-friendly indices have on estimates at the individual level; for example, to estimate logistic regressions for whether the father spends substantial parental time with a set of common explanatory variables and also the index. Further, it would be interesting to construct more recent values of the index to see whether there has been an improvement across time and to consider the effect this has had on paternal time. Finally, research is needed into the impact of collective bargaining agreements on father-friendly provisions and time spent caring for children.

Acknowledgements

The ECHP is used with the permission of Eurostat, who bear no responsibility for the analysis or interpretations presented here. This project has benefited from the financial support of the ESRC. We are grateful to Janet C. Gornick for her useful comments, as well as for her useful comments, as well as for comments from three anonymous referees.

Notes

1. The 15 European Union member states as of 1996/97 and Norway.
2. Paternal leave is the generic term; specific terms (for example, paternity or parental leave) are also used in our paper in discussions of particular legislation.
3. The exclusion of non-state provisions from the index allows the comparative analysis of the baseline leave provision in Western Europe. Thus the total amount of leave available to fathers in Europe will be underestimated. This should not affect the results of the correlation analysis, unless the presence of such agreements is related to the presence (or absence) of statutory provisions. If there is a positive (negative) relationship, then our correlation analysis may overstate (understate) the effect of statutory provisions.
4. Except for Sweden and Norway as the data are not available.
5. In Norway after the introduction of the father quota, the take-up rates of men increased from 4 per cent in 1993 to close to 80 per cent in 1996 and this percentage seems to be rather stable (Ellingsaeter 1999: 52).
6. Micro-level factors that affect parental time include wage rates of both spouses, educational levels, occupation, the prices of market-provided care, the number of children in the home, and levels of non-labor income. See, for example, Presser (1989), Bryant and Zick (1996), Bianchi (2000), Hallberg and

Klevmarken (2003), Hildebrand and Williams (2003) and Sandberg and Hofferth (2005) for discussions of these variables and trends.
7. The information used to construct the indices refers mostly to the legislation in place as of 1997. As previously noted, most countries with such legislation had it in place prior to that time. Some (such as the UK), did not enact legislation in response to the EU directive until much later. The information is collected for the then 15 member states of the EU, plus Norway.
8. The commentary that follows neglects certain aspects, chiefly differential provisions for single parents and parents of disabled children.
9. The EU parental leave directive was to take effect at a later date in Ireland, Luxembourg and the UK.
10. The choice of 60 per cent is an arbitrary one, somewhat in the mid-range of countries with paid leave. The highest values are found in the Nordic countries at about 80 per cent.
11. Certain groups are also sometimes excluded from leave. For example, small companies in Greece could object to the leave in the case that 8 per cent or more of the workers in the company took parental leave within a year.
12. Parental leave is additional to any paternity leave entitlement. Paternity leave is primarily designed to allow fathers time away from work in the immediate period following the birth of a child.
13. See Peracchi (2002) for a description of the ECHP data.
14. The "time spent caring" variable is not available for the UK, Germany, or Luxembourg after 1996.
15. Sweden is excluded from the analysis due to data limitations. Norway is not a member of the EU and so is not included in the ECHP.
16. For a fuller discussion of the substantial childcare time variable see Smith (2006).
17. Weights are not used, but estimates derived using a weighting procedure only vary by a few percentage points. Results available from the authors on request.
18. Thus, observations for the majority of fathers and the minority of mothers not spending substantial time are excluded.
19. We have not attempted to check the sensitivity of the results to changes in the assignment of these values.
20. The index values for Norway and Sweden have been excluded from Table 2, since these countries are excluded from the subsequent analyses. It should be noted, however, that Norway and Sweden have the highest values for all indices.
21. It is relatively rare to find family policy indices (as opposed to typologies) in the literature. Other family policy indices developed in the literature include a six-point index of gender equality in family leave policy design (Gornick and Meyers 2003: 138). Their index reflects only three features of policy design: paid paternity leave, non-transferable parental leave rights and wage-replacement provisions and has the slightly later baseline date of 2000. For those countries common to the two indices, the highest scoring countries in this index correlate with those in our index, but there is some disagreement with regard to the continental European countries primarily as a function of the introduction of paid paternity leave by 2000. Another set of indices developed by Gornick *et al.* (1997) regarding policies for mothers with preschool children correlates highly with our index, with the exception of the placing of France.
22. These results are available from the authors on request.

References

Bettio, F., Del Bono, E. and Smith, M., 1998, Working time patterns in the European Union: policies and innovations. Report of the group of experts on gender and employment, Employment and Social Affairs, European Commission (DGV), Brussels.

Bianchi, S. M., 2000, Maternal employment and time with children; dramatic change or surprising continuity? *Demography*, **37**(4), 401–414.

Brandth, B. and Kvande, E., 1998, Masculinity and childcare: the reconstruction of fathering. *Sociological Review*, **46**(2), 293–313.

Brandth, B. and Kvande, E., 2001, Flexible work and flexible fathers. *Work, Employment and Society*, **15**(2), 251–267.

Breen, R. and Cooke, L. P., 2005, The persistence of the gendered division of domestic labour. *European Sociological Review*, **21**(1), 43–57.

Brines, J., 1994, Economic dependency, gender and the division of labour in the home. *American Journal of Sociology*, **100**(3): 652–688.

Bruning, G. and Plantenga, J., 1999, Parental leave and equal opportunities: experiences in eight European countries. *Journal of European Social Policy*, **9**(3), 195–210.

Budig, J. M. and England, P., 2001, The wage penalty for motherhood. *American Sociological Review*, **66**, 204–225.
Bryant, W. K. and Zick, C. D., 1996, An examination of parent-child shared time. *Journal of Marriage and the Family*, **58**, 227–237.
Crouch, C., 1999, *Social Change in Western Europe* (Oxford: Oxford University Press).
Deven, F. and Moss, P., 2002, Leave arrangements for parents: overview and future outlook. *Community, Work and Family*, **5**(3), 237–255.
Dex, S. and Joshi, H., 1999, Careers and motherhood: policies for compatibility. *Cambridge Journal of Economics*, **23**, 641–659.
Ditch, J., Bradshaw, J. and Eardley, T., 1996, *Developments in National Family Policies in 1994* (York: Social Policy Research Unit).
Ellingsaeter, A. L., 1999, Dual breadwinners between state and market, in: R. Crompton (Ed.) *Restructuring Gender Relations and Employment: The Decline of the Male Breadwinner* (Oxford: Oxford University Press), pp. 40–59.
Esping-Andersen, G., 1990, *The Three Worlds of Welfare Capitalism* (Cambridge: Polity Press).
Esping-Andersen, G., 1999, *Social Foundations of Post-Industrial Economies* (Oxford: Oxford University Press).
Eurobarometer, 2004, Europeans' attitudes to parental leave. Special Eurobarometer 189/Wave 59.1, European Opinion Research Group EEIG, European Commission, Brussels.
European Commission, 1998, Care in Europe. Joint report of the gender and employment and the gender and law groups of experts, European Commission, Brussels.
European Network Family and Work, 1998, *Men within Family and Work* (Brussels: European Commission DGV).
Eurostat, 2004, *How Europeans Spend their Time: Everyday Life of Women and Men: Data 1998–2002* (Luxembourg: Office for Official Publications of the European Commission).
Ferrera, M., 1996, The 'southern model' of welfare in social Europe. *Journal of European Social Policy*, **6**(1), 17–37.
Fisher, K., McCulloch, A. and Gershuny, J., 1999, British fathers and children. A report for Channel 4 "Dispatches". Institute of Social and Economic Research, University of Essex.
Gauthier, A., Smeeding, T. and Furstenberg, F., 2004, Are parents investing less time in children? Trends in selected industrialized countries. *Population and Development Review*, **30**(4), 647–671.
Geist, C., 2005, The welfare state and the home: regime differences in the domestic division of labour. *European Sociological Review*, **21**(1), 23–41.
Gershuny, J., 2000, *Changing Times: Work and Society* (Oxford, Oxford University Press).
Gornick, J. and Meyers, M., 2003, *Families that Work: Policies for Reconciling Parenthood and Employment* (New York: Russell Sage Foundation).
Gornick, J., Meyers, M. and Ross, K., 1997, Supporting the employment of mothers: policy variation across fourteen welfare states. *Journal of European Social Policy*, **7**(1), 45–70.
Haas, L., 1992, *Equal Parenthood and Social Policy: A Study of Parental Leave in Sweden* (New York: State University of New York).
Haas, L., 2003, Parental leave and gender equality: lessons from the European Union. *Review of Policy Research*, **20**(1), 89–105.
Haas, L., Allard, K. and Hwang, P., 2002, The impact of organizational culture on use of parental leave in Sweden. *Community, Work and Family*, **5**, 319–342.
Hallberg, D. and Klevmarken, A., 2003, Time for children: a study of parent's time allocation. *Journal of Population Economics*, **16**, 205–226.
Hildebrand, V. and Williams, D., 2003, Self-employment and caring for children: evidence from Europe. IRISS/C-I Working Paper 2003–06, CEPS/INSTEAD, Differdange, Luxembourg.
Hiller, D. and Philliber, W., 1986, The division of labour in contemporary marriage: expectations, perceptions and performance. *Social Problems*, **33**, 191–201.
Hook, J., 2006, Care in context: men's unpaid work in 20 countries, 1965–2003. *American Sociological Review*, **71**(4): 639–660.
Klinth, R., 2002, *Göra Pappa Med Barn. Den Svenska Pappapolitiken 1960–1995* (Boréa: Umeå).
Liebfried, S., 1992, Towards a European welfare state: On integrating poverty regimes in the European Community, in: Z. Ferge and J. E. Kolberg (Eds) *Social Policy in a Changing Europe* (Frankfurt: Campus Verlag), pp. 245–280.

McFarlane, S., Beaujot, R. and Haddad, T., 2000, Time constraints and relative resources as determinants of the sexual division of domestic work. *Canadian Journal of Sociology*, 25(1), 61–82.
Moss, P. and Deven, F., 1999, *Parental Leave: Progress or Pitfall? Research and Policy Issues in Europe* (Brussels: CBGS Publications).
NFPI, 2000, *NFPI Briefings 1: Parental Leave* (London: National Family and Parenting Institute).
OECD, 2001, Balancing work and family life: Helping parents into paid employment, in: OECD, *Employment Outlook: 2001* (Paris: Organization for Economic Co-operation and Development), Chapter 4.
Peracchi, F., 2002, The European community household panel: a review. *Empirical Economics*, 27, 63–90.
Presser, H., 1989, Can we make time for children? The economy, work schedules, and childcare. *Demography*, 26(4), 523–543.
Sandberg, J. and Hofferth, S., 2005, Changes in children's time with parents: a correction. *Demography*, 42(2), 391–395.
Sayer, L. C., Bianchi, S. M. and Robinson, J. P., 2004, Are parents investing less in children? Trends in mothers' and fathers' time with children. *American Journal of Sociology*, 110, 1–43.
Smith, A. J., 2004, Who cares? European fathers and the time they spend looking after children. Sociology Working Papers, No. 2004–05, University of Oxford.
Smith, A. J., 2006, Who cares? European fathers and the time they spend looking after their children. Doctoral dissertation, Nuffield College, University of Oxford.
Wilkinson, H., 1997, *Time Out: the Costs and Benefits of Paid Parental Leave* (London: Demos).

Appendix

Table A1. Indices of father-friendliness, by country (by 1997)

Country	1. Family/ individual right[a]	2. Paid/ unpaid leave[a]	3. Part-time leave[a]	4. Eligibility[a]	5. Paternity leave[b]	6. Emergency leave[b]	7. Government encouragement[c]	Sum score
Denmark	7	10	1	10	10	6	10	54
Finland	7	10	10	10	10	1	10	58
Norway	7	10	10	10	10	10	10	67
Sweden	7	10	10	10	10	10	10	67
Austria	5	5	6	4	1	10	1	32
Belgium	10	5	6	4	1	3	1	30
France	10	3*	10	4	1	1	1	30
Germany	5	5	6	8	1	6	1	32
Greece	10	2	1	4	1	10	1	29
Italy	5	5	2	4	1	3	1	21
Netherlands	10	2	6	4	5	6	1	34
Portugal	5	2	6	4	5	10	1	33
Spain	5	2	10	4	1	1	1	24
Ireland	1	1	1	1	1	3	1	9
Luxembourg	1	1	1	1	1	1	1	7
UK	1	1	1	1	1	1	1	7

*Only for second child and thereafter.
Sources: [a]Wilkinson (1997: 67, 74, 78); European Commission (1998); [b]European Commission (1998); [c]European Network 1998 (Not all questions were answered by all participants, for those countries research is authors' own).

Reconciliation of Work and Family Life in Europe: A Case Study of Denmark, France, Germany and the United Kingdom

PETER ABRAHAMSON

ABSTRACT *European Union institutions as well as member states are embracing welfare policies that support reconciliation of work and family life as a means of solving problems of low fertility and gender inequality, and they do so unanimously within a welfare mix approach. Hence, viewing the social policy rhetoric, everything points to a convergence of European welfare models towards a mixed economy of welfare. However, analysing the everyday experiences of families with young children in four European cities leaves the impression of a continuation of past differences. In 1998/1999 no deviation from the traditional welfare and family policy models could be traced in Roskilde (Denmark), Nantes (France), Mannheim (Germany) and York (the United Kingdom).*

Introduction

Are the European welfare states radically changing or are they path-dependent? That has been one of the more debated issues in contemporary social science (Ferrera and Rhodes 2000, Kuhnle and Alestalo 2000, Leibfried and Obinger 2000, Pierson 2001, Castles 2004). The expression "after the golden years" indicates that the welfare state is but a parenthesis of modern history, late 1950s to early 1980s, and it points to changes. The changes are seen to be set off by the so-called crisis of the welfare state expressed by the Organization for Economic Cooperation and Development (OECD) in 1981 and announcing a neoliberal turn. Later on, during the 1990s, the pendulum swung back: instead of being regarded as a burden, welfare measures were viewed as a precondition for an effective business environment (Esping-Andersen *et al.* 2002). Part of the change was accompanied by an emphasis on facilitating women's labour market involvement through collectively organized care for children, the handicapped and the frail elderly. The recent demographic changes, low fertility and longer life-expectancy, has led to a "greying" of society, and has put more pressure on trying to reconcile work and family life in order to liberate female labour from the home (Esping-Andersen *et al.* 2002).

Simultaneously, governments across Europe have changed the ideological wrapping of welfare provisions. No longer are strong liberal, conservative, or socialist views expressed; rather the vocabulary of welfare pluralism emerged as the adequate framework for understanding contemporary welfare policies. This approach sees policies as a negotiated division of labour among the three social orders of modern society: state, market and community, or – in a more elaborate form – social partnerships are envisaged as a collaboration involving two or more of the different social order institutions. Claus Offe (2000: 79) has expressed this thus: "The state, the market and the community represent ideal-typical modes in which people live and act together, the mode of coordination of individuals and their action." Welfare policies in general and policies to try and reconcile work and family life in particular always involve some mixture of intervention from market, state and community actors. What is new is a more flexible approach as to where to put the emphasis and what to recognize as legitimate forms of intervention. Part of the social science literature views this approach as a cover for neoliberal welfare state intervention: more emphasis on market and civil societal institutions and actors and less public involvement (for instance Johnson 1990, 1999); others have – to the contrary – seen it as an opportunity to enhance empowerment of citizens through self-reliance and self-determination, and as such as a way to further less dependency on state support (for instance Evers 1995, Evers and Olk 1997). These are two opposing judgements. The third approach uses the terms welfare pluralism and welfare mix as descriptive, yet equally normative: for instance Robert Pinker (1992) views mixed welfare as "damage control", as a middle way between conservative privatization and socialist socialization.

The thesis guiding the investigation reported here is that a welfare mix approach is dominant in all recent welfare legislation in Europe and most of the other OECD countries, but its particular set-up is heavily influenced by the historically dominant welfare, labour market, and family policy regime prevailing within each nation state. Thus, in Scandinavia traditionally public provisions have dominated, in parts of continental Europe civil societal institutions such as NGOs and the family have dominated, and in the liberal regimes market solutions have dominated.

The social science literature is to a large extent in agreement when it comes to clustering states with respect to welfare regime, labour market regime and family policy regime. However, there is some disagreement about to what extent these regimes overlap. When the focus is on reconciliation of work and family life all three perspectives are important. The general assumption has been that welfare and labour market regimes go hand in hand. This is the now classic position of Gøsta Esping-Andersen (1990: 142): "Our principal hypothesis is that peculiarities of welfare states are reflected in the ways in which labour markets are organized. We will suggest that each of our welfare state regimes goes hand in hand with a peculiar 'labour market regime'." This is confirmed by Colin Crouch (2001: 106–108) in his comparison of welfare and industrial relations regimes.

With respect to the fit between welfare regime and family policy regime not everyone suggests a perfect match. A typical example is Linda Hantrais' (1999) analysis of the regulation of the family/work relationship among the 15 EU member states. Here, her results are presented as a cross-tabulation of national policies with patterns of employment for women with children: she identified a south European cluster, which many have also done with respect to welfare regimes (Leibfried 1992, Abrahamson 1999a); but she also differentiated the continental cluster into a France/Belgium cluster and the other north-west European countries as also recognized by Anneli Anttonen and Jorma Sipilä in their discussion of welfare and care regimes from 1996, and in the analyses by Janet Gornick *et al.* published in 1997.

Other typologies have been developed where Europe is viewed as clustering within four different groups. Ann Gauthier (1996) found the following major models: a pro-family/pro-birth model (for instance France); a pro-traditional model (for instance Germany); a pro-egalitarian model (for instance Scandinavia); a pro-family but not interventionist model (for instance the UK). Similarly Mary Daly and Jane Lewis (2000: 289) confirm this distinction when they point to Scandinavian states, Germany, France and the "welfare states of a Beveridgean provenance (within Europe – Britain and Ireland)":

> [The Scandinavian cluster is]... one of abundant, locally-organized services that are available on a universal basis and funded from taxes;... [While] in Germany there is a relatively large voluntary quasi-statutory sector which, through public funding, provides a range of services related to caring for the elderly as well as for children. Then there is the case of France, which makes a strong distinction between care for children and that for the elderly. Only the former is collectivized and the voluntary sectors play a minimal role... [In the UK childcare] tends to be constructed as a "state-free zone".

What is to be expected, hence, are different combinations of welfare mixes within the various regimes whether they are primarily viewed as labour market regimes, welfare state regimes, or family policy regimes. By selecting Denmark, France, Germany and the UK distinctly different regimes types are represented in the sample. Admittedly, this is not an exhaustive selection to cover all of Europe; southern and eastern European experiences are excluded from our sample.

Methodology and Data

This study situates itself within comparative qualitative methodology utilizing large semi-structured interview samples (see, for instance Windebank 1996, 1999). It is a mainstream approach with respect to the use of interview guide, transcription, and coding (Kvale 1996, Gubrium and Holstein 1997), but it is unusual because the number of interviewees goes far beyond the usual 10 to 20 respondents. In our case we interviewed 160 families (mothers) with preschool children in four cities. In her study of different childcare strategies among French and British mothers Windebank interviewed 112 mothers in two countries. The applied methodology is in this sense a hybrid between the traditional small-scale (anthropological) interview and the traditional large-scale (sociological) survey. This innovative approach has been made possible by software that allows for coding and sorting huge datasets.

Based on the literature on the differentiation of family/work relations and family policy, and not in conflict with a welfare regime approach including the issue of care, the selection of Denmark, France, Germany and the UK are demonstrable cases for illuminating the variation within north-western Europe, as shown in Table 1. In order to narrow the perspective spatially a middle-size city was chosen for investigation within each country. We deliberately avoided the capitals because they in general are atypical being overrepresented with regard to infrastructure and institutions. We chose Roskilde, Nantes, Mannheim and York. Other cities could have been chosen, but we did a thorough job comparing the regions and cities to the nation state and found them to reflect the national averages very well. Space prevents giving a detailed account of this, but the information is freely available.[1] A number of examples should suffice. For instance in York we found a practically perfect match of York to the UK when measured against deprivation: on 15 variables nearly the exact same values were recorded both in the UK generally, and specifically in York. Likewise, when we compared the number of recipients of social benefits in La Loire Atlantique where Nantes is located to all of France we found a very close fit. We also compared net family income for various family types in Baden-Württemberg – where Mannheim is located – and found a very good match on all four family types given when compared with all of Germany. Also in Mannheim we found the same composition of the population with regard to religious affiliation as in all of Germany (45 per cent Catholics, 45 per cent Protestants, 5 per cent Muslims, 5 per cent other). Comparing age distribution and employment ratios revealed similar results. Yet, admittedly, Germany is a tricky case because there is not one Germany, but – at least – three Germanies: north, south and east. In this sense we maintain that Mannheim is average for Germany.

Being convinced we had located typical cities a further process of narrowing the spatial perspective began. We located a typical low-income neighbourhood and an equally typical middle-class neighbourhood by obtaining a thorough overview of the social geography of the cities. In a study by Garreau and Marchais (1994) in Nantes a number of fragile neighbourhoods were located based on three

Table 1. Arrangements of work/family policy relationships within the EU-15

	Pattern of women's labour market participation	
	Strong	Weak
National policies towards women and work		
Strong	a) Denmark, Finland, Sweden b) Belgium, France	Austria, Germany, Netherlands, Luxembourg
Weak	Portugal, United Kingdom	Greece, Ireland, Italy, Spain

Source: Inspired by Hantrais (2004: 73–104).

indicators. In another study Danielle Rapetti (1997) was able to identify what she labelled disassociated and least privileged neighbourhoods. Comparing the hence constructed two sets of maps made the selection of neighbourhoods straightforward. In York we undertook an even more detailed deconstruction of municipal data based on the unit of a ward to derive data at the small unit of enumeration districts, which were then recomposed to geographical areas the size of wards. This was done by examining eight variables including: number of pupils receiving free school meals, percentage of households receiving housing benefits, percentage of population on Income Support or Job Seekers Allowance. In Mannheim we had data on demographic composition (including the share of foreigners), education, employment and receipt of various social services. As an example, the two selected neighbourhoods found themselves at the ends of a continuum plotting the degree of receiving *Jugendhilfe*, social assistance and rent benefits. The final selection of neighbourhoods was made after repeated observation visits had been conducted. The same procedure was followed in Roskilde. In Mannheim and in Nantes the share of young children using various childcare facilities were compared to the whole nation and revealed similar values for the three-to-six-year-olds, namely around 85 and 99 per cent respectively. Regarding the youngest children, our cities had relatively more children in crèches than in the countries as a whole, which is attributable to the urban setting (Abrahamson 1999b: 123, 1999c: 101).

Having suitable country, city and neighbourhood cases, we finally needed relevant respondents. The only initial criterion for being eligible for interviewing was that one had at least one child younger than compulsory primary school. In all eight neighbourhoods we started approaching potential respondents through the local childcare institutions. Through the intermediary help of the staff we reached about half of our respondents. We sought a variety of family and work combinations and forms, so the second half of the respondents were selected strategically through snowballing. After having selected families who agreed to be interviewed, we asked them to fill out a financial form indicating their incomes and outlays. That is, we knew their exact, self-reported, incomes and were able to check whether they were in fact low or middle income as expected from their spatial location. In Table 2 the sample is distributed across social and marital status and number of children:

Table 2. 160 respondent families distributed across social and marital status and number of children

	Social status		Marital status of mother		Number of children in household		
	Low income	Middle income	Married/ cohabiting	Lone parent	1	2	>2
Roskilde	16	24	35	5	20	14	6
Nantes	22	18	34	6	12	19	9
Mannheim	22	18	31	9	11	15	14
York	18	22	35	5	21	9	10

In three of the cities two families in each neighbourhood were "wrongly" located and traded places in the analyses. This was the case for four families in Roskilde. Hence, the method revealed not a perfect but a close match between spatial location and general income characteristics of the respective neighbourhoods.

Changing Family Policies in Europe?

"Kinder haben die Leute immer"[2] (Konrad Adenauer 1957)

Developments have apparently disproved the words of former German chancellor Konrad Adenauer that people always will have children, meaning there is no need for intervention. On the contrary, urgent calls are being made to reconcile work and family life much better. To take one example, the European Commission wrote in 1998: "Better reconciliation between work and family life is of key importance in supporting women's and men's entry and continued participation in the labour market and in achieving equality between women and men" (European Commission 1998: 1).

Changes in the Liberal Regime? (UK)

After a period of conservative rule in the UK, the Labour victory in 1997 signalled a new chapter in welfare policy. The changes can broadly be summarized as an emphasis on activation and an emphasis on social partnerships within the framework of the mixed economy of welfare. This is well documented (Daly and Lewis 2000, Daly 2003, Dean 2003, Driver and Martell 2002). To illustrate this particularly with a view to family policy a government green paper will be discussed briefly: *New Ambitions for Our Country – A New Welfare Contract*. It stated: "A fundamental principle of the welfare state is that it supports families and children" (Department of Social Security 1998: 57). Although the family has changed fundamentally in recent decades, it said, it remains nevertheless one of society's most critical cornerstones. The government's objectives for children and families were set out as follows:

- Support for all families with children, especially poor families;
- Help for unemployed parents to find work by lowering the barriers to work, especially the lack of affordable day care facilities;
- Support for working parents;
- Continued support for parents of an economic and emotional nature even after separating.

This commitment to families and children was given a very precise wording: "Combining parenthood and work is a never-ending juggling act. Being a parent and an employee is far from easy, and working parents need as much support as possible. Our proposal to improve the quality of child care is pivotal" (Department of Social Security 1998: 59). From a rhetorical point of view, there is no doubt that a new era as regards family welfare was being heralded: families were going to be helped so that mothers to an increasing extent could participate in the labour market.

Changes in the Family-Oriented Regime? (France)

Recent changes to the French welfare state were spelt out in the Juppé Plan, and supported further under Lionel Jospin. According to Bruno Palier (1997: 103), the new welfare state was based on three ideas: justice, responsibility and immediate action. He assumed that "the welfare reforms, proposed by former Prime Minister Juppé in 1996, will form the framework for the development of the welfare system in the coming years". His colleague Denis Bouget went as far as to say that "the Juppé plan is the most important reform within the French social security system since its creation" (Bouget, 1998: 161). As far as family welfare is concerned, the provisional target group was low-income families. For example, the universal family allowance (given to families with two or more children) was linked to income. This proved so massively unpopular, however, that it had to be withdrawn. From 1 January 1999, the *allocation familiale* was once again being paid to all parents of two or more children.

Changes in the Male Breadwinner Model? (Germany)

There is a long-time commitment to pluralist welfare strategies and new signs of a different rhetoric when it comes to "recalibration" of the German welfare state (Bahle and Rothenbacher 1998, Offe 1998, Schulz 2000, Leibfried and Obinger 2003). To illustrate this with a particular view to families, a brief introduction of the coalition agreement which outlined the policies of the then new SPD and Green Party government is given below (Sozialdemokratischen Partei Deutschlands und Bündnis 90/Die Grünen, 1998). To enhance conditions for families in the future, "once more to make Germany a child- and family-friendly country", a number of initiatives were put forward. The most important thing to invest in for the future, the document stressed, is the family, and a liberal definition was given as "families are where there are children". In the future it should be easier to reconcile family and work both for men and women. The agreement foresaw an increase in the family allowance and the government envisaged changing childcare payment and leave to parental leave.

The commitment to enhance women's chances to work was put quite poetically: "Only when women's intellectual potential and creativity thrive in the workplace and in society, will our country overcome the challenges of the future!" The government, according to the programme, will endeavour to:

- Put in place effective equality legislation, applicable also to the private sector;
- Develop jobs that square with having children;
- Amend laws that currently discriminate between men and women;
- Boost activation measures to enable more women to escape unemployment;
- Make working hours more flexible and promote improved standards for part-time workers;
- Improve the provision of childcare facilities.

The wording of the agreement demonstrated the commitment to help families in their efforts to reconcile work and domestic duties, thus effectively dispatching the male breadwinner model and adopting instead the dual carer model. However, the actual implementation is left to the local states and municipalities.

Changes in the Dual Carer Regime? (Denmark)

Also within Danish welfare society new trends towards an active orientation of policies can be traced together with an emphasis on welfare mix understandings (Abrahamson 2002, Van Oorshot and Abrahamson 2003, Torfing 2004). This is being illustrated by an official government paper: *Sociale tendenser* (Social Trends, 1999). There the Ministry of Social Affairs said, "we are currently in the process of quietly and without any fuss establishing a vital and necessary change of direction in Danish social policies". The change referred to was related to the understanding that social policy could no longer be seen simply as a question of ensuring that people's basic material and economic needs are satisfied and that the state could no longer be looked to for the solution of problems of a social nature that might arise. This should not be taken to mean a retrenchment of the role of the state, but that its role must change. "In recent years, voluntary social work has become more evident...but what actually counts as well is what we all do separately for our families, friends, neighbours, colleagues, fellow students and so on." In the area of children and families, the report said that the great majority of families with small children value paid work very highly, which is why they generally and increasingly are asking for more public day care facilities. The Ministry of Social Affairs (1999) found that such measures must be adapted more vigorously to the needs of children "so that they can function as places where children can learn and develop".

European Social Policy Rhetoric Points towards Strong Support for Families

On the policy level everything indicates decisive changes in welfare mixes for families with small children and a substantial commitment to supporting these families. The governments in all four countries emphasize a pluralistic approach to welfare provision; it is obvious that a common vocabulary has been developed across Europe, that of the welfare mix, and that this new rhetoric sits uneasily with "old" demarcations of the various welfare regimes. Thus, on an ideological level, judging from formulated intentions, it must be concluded that the capacity of the traditional welfare regime to guide the interplay between citizens and the state with regard to reconciliation of work and family life has been weakened substantially. Instead a convergence towards a common understanding of a European Social Model in the shape of negotiated welfare mixes is evident. Within the traditional welfare regimes there existed very big differences regarding facilitating or hindering women's labour market participation. Now, the emphasis is unilaterally on facilitating women's paid employment through supporting care for children and the elderly and granting leave opportunities; and there is much talk about equal treatment and equal opportunities between men and women.

Coping with Work and Childcare in Four European Cities

However, when the everyday life of families with small children in four cities in Europe were analysed the opposite conclusion was reached, namely that the welfare and family policy regimes were very much alive and determining how and to what extent families could reconcile work and family life. In the following, only the middle-class experiences are discussed. The experiences of the low-income families are reported elsewhere (Abrahamson 2005). The situation in York was exactly as stipulated with Titmuss' (1987 [1972], 1974) residual social policy model where the family and the market are the two dominant institutions when it comes to welfare provision. In Nantes the *école maternelle* was clearly dominating childcare supplemented by social and fiscal welfare provisions. In Mannheim the NGOs in the form of *die freie Träger*, especially the two Christian organizations of *Caritas Verband* and *Evangeliche Kirsche*, dominated together with strong existence of the male breadwinner model. In Roskilde the effects of leave schemes could be traced, but also the rather skewed gender balance, with women working part-time and the only ones to utilize the leave opportunities. Our analyses of the lived daily life of citizens in these middle size cities support the path dependency thesis. Because of the relatively advantageous financial situation the families were rather free to establish the care package they saw as best fitting their specific situation. Thus, in both York and in Mannheim it was quite common to use market solutions for childcare. The existence of part-time kindergartens in both places gave public provision a middle priority, while the main priority was either on market or civil societal solutions. In Nantes and in Roskilde the welfare mixes were such that the main priority was with public provision.

In the following sections this will be illustrated with typical examples by giving voice to some of the middle-class families we have interviewed. This methodology is strongly influenced by the work of Pierre Bourdieu and his colleagues as it was demonstrated in *La Misère du Monde* (1993).

Work and Family Life in the Middle-Class Neighbourhood of Heworth in York, UK

In York the middle-class families prioritized either paid employment by the mothers supported by market solutions to childcare in the form of nannies or child minders, or the mothers adjusted their labour market participation according to the help they could get from civil societal institutions. In any case it involved a lot of "juggling". This can be illustrated with the case of the family Oakes.[3] The family consists of Gregg, 38 years old, who works as an inspector, and Evie, 37 years old, who works part-time as a receptionist. They have three sons, Joshua, eight years old, Jacob, five years old, and Zak, three years old. When we talked to Evie she said the sole reason she took this job was because it "revolves around the children"; otherwise she would not be able to work. She relied heavily on the flexibility of the workplace to match her childcare needs. As she explained:

> I would drop the oldest one off at school, drop him (the middle child) at Nursery, drop the little one off at my Mum's, got to work for an hour and half, come out work at quarter past eleven and pick the middle one up from Nursery, take him to my Mum's, then go back to work at quarter to twelve and cover the dinner time period for when they (other receptionists) changed over, then I would leave – you know do another hour and a half (of work) – and leave at half past one, then do it all in reverse, you know, pick up the youngest two from

my Mum's then go home for an hour and then pick up the oldest one from school.

All this was only possible because her parents lived close by to her place of work, the schools and her home.

Another solution was to buy childcare on the market in the form of a nanny or a child minder. One family we interviewed used the first option in a rather creative way. This family consists of Matt, 31 years old, and Sophie, 30 years old. Their daughter, Charlotte, is three years old. Matt works as a drama theatre production manager about 40 to 60 hours a week, while Sophie works as a coordinator on a flexitime basis for 35 hours per week. The father drops the daughter off at Tang Hall Nursery every morning; she is then picked up by the nanny who looks after her until the mother finishes work. The arrangement with the nanny is that they share her with another family with whom they have been friends for many years – so the time the nanny spends in this mother's house is split with the other family. Thus Sophie said there were "four adults who could juggle their care". She explained that the arrangement reduced the costs of childcare but it did not reduce the "stress of childcare" as the times were so rigid and so short.

Work and Family Life in the Middle-Class Neighbourhood of Doulon in Nantes, France

In Nantes private solutions played an important role in the cases where the mothers prioritized labour market participation, supported by public provisions, or in the cases where the women worked less, the public provisions dominated the childcare situation. We generally found a considerable difference in working time outside the home between mothers and fathers, as was the case with a family where the father was 38 years old and worked as head of research. He worked about 50 hours per week and was usually away from home from eight in the morning to eight in the evening. His wife, 34 years of age, worked about one-third full time teaching in a training centre for unemployed. They both have one hour of commuting time to work. "I give my working hours early enough, that is to say six months before, because I have my timetable about six months before, and it allows me to pay daycare only three days per week, and to have my children with me the rest of the time, or with a baby-sitter or in an outdoor centre."

Another family consists of a father, 39 years of age, trained as an engineer, and currently unemployed. The mother, 37 years old, is a biologist. They have three daughters, ages eight, five and two. We asked whether she had experienced problems matching work and family obligations:

> Yes, of course! That is to say, you always have troubles when you have several children, when you arrive in the evening whereas you have to run to pick up your child, because it's always the same, when you have a child in a nursery, you always have to run to pick it up, whatever the prep school or the day-care. And afterward, you've just arrived from work and you have to take care of the children, to prepare the meal, to go shopping... It's a race, of course! But I don't know what the remedy is?

So, even if the long school hours and the relative availability of crèches make it possible for women in Nantes to reconcile work and care it takes a considerable amount of "juggling".

Work and Family Life in the Middle-Class Neighbourhood of Wallstadt in Mannheim, Germany

In Mannheim, if the mothers prioritized wage work, they had to rely on market solutions for childcare, but it was much more common that women withdrew from the labour market when they became mothers; hence civil societal institutions such as the extended family became the prime sources of childcare. We can give one illustration of the rather unusual situation of a mother with paid employment. She said: "The problem is not the school or the kindergarten, but my working hours." To our question as to whether she was satisfied with the division: kindergarten in the morning and childminder in the afternoon, Mrs. Ngyuen said: "It nearly fits wonderfully. But, of course, it is stressful. Pick up and bring quickly to the childminder. Then I have to hurry to the music school. Then you have to pick up the children in time, or you will have to pay. It is paid by the hour, and in the evenings I have to cook, since our main meal is in the evening." It is obviously quite stressful as a mother to maintain a working career in this context, and relatively few people in our sample did so.

What is much more common is for the mothers to stay at home while the children are small, which we will illustrate with conversations with the Schneiders: "We are three family members", the mother said. "My husband is 33 years old. I am 34 and our son, Thomas, is now nearly four years old." We asked if it would it be easier for her if the kindergarten were open in the afternoon as well, and the following exchange occurred:

"At the moment it's not important for me. I don't work and so I can take care of our son in the afternoon."
"Did you go with your son to a playgroup when he was very young?"
"Yes. We went once a week to a playgroup in Feudenheim. It was important for me to meet other mothers and talk about problems with our children."
"Would you have put your child in a crèche if there were one in Wallstadt?"
"No. I wanted to be at home to have time for my son."

The importance of informal help and the difficulties in reconciling work and family life meant that many mothers reasoned that it was best to stay at home while the children were small. This is illustrated in the case of Mrs. Galinsky. She explained her situation in Wallstadt: "I am 37 and I live together with my son Michael. He is 3½ years old. My husband and I are separated. I moved to Wallstadt because my parents and my brother live here. I needed help after the separation and in Wallstadt I have a good social network. I have good friends in Wallstadt as well." Later she said: "I had to stay at home until he [her son Michael] went to kindergarten. I think that it's not good for children to be in a crèche when they are younger than three years."

Rather than letting family life revolve around work, we concluded that this is a case of the opposite:

> We wanted to have a child and for me it is natural that my child would be much more important than my work in the following years. I adapted my working life to my family life but I have always known that I would have more time for a job when my son is older. The part-time job I will start in January is a first step; for me it is very important that my son doesn't suffer from my career. I will never be of the opinion that I have to work in any case and my son is only of second importance. But I want to have my independence, so it's important for me to have my own income.

To a large extent we experienced that *hausfrau* (homemaker) is still very much a lived experience in Mannheim suburbia, with many women staying at home for several years caring for their children.

Work and Family Life in the Middle-Class Neighbourhood of Svogerslev in Roskilde, Denmark

In Roskilde the mothers utilized the various forms of public provision to a very high degree – including both childcare institutions and leave opportunities – which enabled them to stay affiliated with the labour market at the same time as they managed to work less while the children were small. The optimal situations were those where additional support could be expected from civil society. This is illustrated by the situation of Ulla. She is a 31-year-old bank assistant. Ulla is married to Ulrik, aged 32, who is also a bank assistant and works full time. Ida is five years of age and is in kindergarten; Kit is 16 months old and is at home with Ulla. Ulla works full time for a bank, but took maternity leave to care for Kit, and after that parental leave for a year, also for Kit. At the end of the parental leave in May, Ulla is going to take another three months' leave with Ida, because she wants to be there when Ida starts a preschool class. Ulrik works from 8/8.30 am, to around 4.00 or 5.00 pm, mostly 5.00 pm. He is usually home at 5.45 pm. Ulla explained her situation with work and childcare over the last six years after we had asked whether she had stayed home with Ida when she was born:

> Only for maternity leave, because there weren't any possibility for getting leave at the time. I started working again at the first of December. You could get leave if the employer accepted it, and there weren't many that did. I remember not having the possibility and then the scheme was changed in January, and childcare leave became a legal right for everybody. When Ida was almost two, I took half a year's childcare leave for her.

We also enquired whether she received benefits, and she answered:

> Yes! At the time it was 80 percent. It didn't cost me more than about 1000 kroner a month [€134]. In 1996 I got a boy [Kalle] who was stillborn, because of that I stayed at home for half a year on maternity leave. I was working for half a

year when I got pregnant again and was going to have Kit. I was reported sick. So I haven't been that much at work...

I've worked a little more than a year, before I took my first childcare leave. Then I was working for half a year, when I had maternity leave with Kalle. Which means that I've been working a little less than two years, from the time when I got Ida, and that is almost six years ago. That's not much. When I've been working, it has been full time, because I couldn't get any reduction in my working hours.

By adding up maternity leave, parental leave, childcare leave and sickness benefits Ulla has been able to receive a (modest) income, stay affiliated with the labour market and not working for six years. Here is an example of a middle-class family that can afford to take advantage of the various provisions offered within the local welfare state and labour market agreements. Such arrangements would not be open to lower income families because of the modest compensation

The relatively easy situation of juggling work and care in Svogerslev can be illustrated with the case of Nina and Niels: Nina is 34 years old and has been a childminder for two years. She works full time. Niels, aged 36, works as accounting controller. He also works full time. Brian, age 13, is in school. Ria, age seven, is in a preschool class and after-school care. Magnus, age five, is in kindergarten. Their working life is revealed through the following conversation:

"And you are a childminder..."
"Yes, I have only been that for two years. And before that I was in a kindergarten for 1½ years as 'support' for a boy. And before that I was a home on maternity leave and parental leave and...(laughs)."
"How are your working hours?"
"As a childminder I have to be available 48 hours a week but I don't work that much. Niels works flexitime. He takes our girl to school and the boy in kindergarten and he leaves at a quarter to eight in the morning and is home half past 5–6 o'clock."
"Do you pick them up?"
"No, that's unusual."

Although men do take part in caring for their children in Roskilde, it is still the mothers who usually adjust their labour market involvement so that it fits what they still conceive as their family obligations.

Conclusion

What we found when analysing the ways in which families in four European cities tried to juggle work and childcare in 1998/1999 was the "traditional" picture as would have been expected if people behaved according to their respective family policy, labour market, and welfare regime. The identified new policy orientations towards a "path-guided" welfare mix were nowhere to be found. It can be speculated that our results reflect a time-lag situation. Perhaps the policies identified were so new that they had not been implemented properly yet. Yet, at the time of writing (autumn 2006) nothing indicates that the discrepancies between rhetoric and practice are due to time lag. If we take the case of the UK, Christine Skinner, four years after our initial interview in York, showed that indeed the city had increased some forms of childcare, but at the same time it had reduced other forms, at the end of the day making it even more difficult to juggle care and work (Skinner 2003: 3–4). Other sources cited in this paper commenting four years after our data collection indicate the discrepancy between New Labour rhetoric and everyday practices (Driver and Martell 2002, Daly 2003, Dean 2003). Regarding Germany, Stephan Leibfried and Herbert Obinger (2003: 199) concluded five years after we had finished interviewing in Mannheim that "No comprehensive short or medium term recalibration of the German welfare state has taken place...". Another possible issue is the relationship between central government policies and local policies. The countries involved in this study have various degrees of local governance structures in place. So, the identified discrepancies could be due to local policy orientations that diverged from the central ones. But that was not the case. We interviewed relevant public officials responsible for family policy in each of the cities, and there was nothing in the local administrations that indicated that "our" cities were radically opposed to, or opposite to, the then existing national governments in their priorities (Abrahamson 1999b, 1999c, 1999d).

Concluding from the general policy formulations made by governments in Denmark, France, Germany and the UK, the tendency was towards convergence when it comes to labour market, family and welfare policies to help reconcile work and family life. And there are signs of convergence. Female participation and employment rates are increasing in Germany, France and the UK, while stagnating or dropping slightly in Denmark (European Commission 2005). Expenditure levels on welfare transfers and services are also converging in Europe. The states that spend the least are increasing their budgets, while the big spenders are spending relatively the same or less.

But, the dominant finding from this study was that of traditional difference among the European regimes with respect to reconciliation of work and family life. Families in both York and Mannheim to a large extent created similar care packages, and the welfare mixes developed in Nantes and Roskilde looked quite alike. This indicates the influence of the welfare regime, because a male breadwinner model dominated the two former cities while, in the two latter, a public service model dominated.

The middle-class mothers in the study had rather different opportunities for labour market affiliation. In Roskilde they had the opportunity both to maintain labour market affiliation and at the same time they could spend time together with their small children due to the existence of leave schemes. In Nantes, the families could also enjoy a number of public provisions, but leave was financially insufficient. So, here the mothers had to choose between labour market participation or providing childcare themselves. In York and Mannheim the middle-class mothers chose either to stay within the labour market supported by market solutions for childcare, or they chose to withdraw from the labour market, at least as long as the children were small.

In all four neighbourhoods the father mainly worked full time or more, while the mothers had to juggle childcare and work according to the prevailing welfare mixes available to them; and everywhere it was obvious that civil societal solutions were important for successful juggling.

Finally it can be concluded that the unanimous and positive rhetoric about improving the conditions for working mothers had not reached the daily life of citizens as it unfolded in the four cities at the turn of the millennium. There existed, hence, an enormous discrepancy between what governments said they would do and what they actually did. This finding is parallel to the one given by Prue Chamberlayne (1999) in a study on the role of the informal sector in Germany and the UK. She also found that there was a striking difference between formal ideologies and everyday practices. They all promised a relativization of the family policy regime; but in real life regime dependency prevailed.

Acknowledgements

Generous help with this study was received from Denis Bouget, Université de Nantes, Thomas Bahle, Universität Mannheim and Jonathan Bradshaw, University of York. the work of our research assistants, Isabelle Kaufmann, Claus Wendt, Christine Skinner and Gritt Bykilde, was also invaluable. The whole study, which also included Umeå in Sweden, is reported in Abrahamson *et al.* (2005). Detailed studies of parts of the data are reported in Skinner (2003), Wendt and Maucher (2000, 2004), Almqvist (2005).

Notes

1. Research Reports are available at http://www.ruc.dk/ssc/forskning/projekter/welfare_and_solidarity/.
2. "People will always have children" (quoted in Kaufmann 1996: 15).
3. None of the names used here are the real names of the respondents.

References

Abrahamson, Peter, 1999a, The welfare modelling business. *Social Policy and Administration*, 33, 394–415.
Abrahamson, Peter, 1999b, *The Male Bread-Winner Model Under Change: The Case of Germany Towards the 21st Century* (Roskilde: Roskilde University).
Abrahamson, Peter, 1999c, *The Residual Poverty Oriented Model Under Change: The Case of the United Kingdom Towards the 21st Century* (Roskilde: Roskilde University).
Abrahamson, Peter, 1999d, *The Parental Model Under Change: The Case of France Towards the 21st Century* (Roskilde: Roskilde University).
Abrahamson, Peter, 2002, The Danish welfare state: a social rights perspective. *Journal of Societal and Social Policy*, 1, 57–80.
Abrahamson, Peter, 2005, Coping with urban poverty: changing citizenship in Europe? *International Journal of Urban and Regional Research*, 29, 608–621.
Abrahamson, Peter, Boje, Thomas and Greve, Bent, 2005, *Welfare and Families in Europe* (Aldershot: Ashgate).
Almqvist, Anna-Lena, 2005, *The Care of Children: A Cross-National Comparison of Parents Expectations and Experiences* (Umeå: University of Umeå, Department of Sociology).
Anttonen, Anneli and Sipilä, Jorma, 1996, European social care services: is it possible to identify models? *Journal of European Social Policy*, 6, 87–100.
Bahle, Thomas and Rothenbacher, Franz, 1998, Family policies in Germany: After re-unification the shock of globalization, in: John Ditch, Helen Barnes and Jonathan Bradshaw (Eds) *Developments in national family policies in 1996* (Brussels: European Commission), pp. 37–62.

Bouget, Denis, 1998, The Juppé plan and the future of the French social welfare system. *Journal of European Social Policy*, **8**, 155–172.
Bourdieu, Pierre et al., 1993, *La Misère du Monde* (Paris: Editions du Seuil), English translation 1999: *The Weight of the World: Social Suffering in Contemporary Society* (Stanford: Stanford University Press).
Castles, Francis, 2004, *The Future of the Welfare State: Crisis Myths and Crisis Realities* (Oxford: Oxford University Press).
Chamberlayne, Prue 1999, Cultural analysis of informal care, in: Prue Chanberlayne, Andrew Cooper, Richard Freeman and Michael Rustin (Eds) *Welfare and Culture in Europe: Towards a New Paradigm in Europe* (London: Jessica Kingsley Publishers), pp. 151–171.
Crouch, Colin, 2001, Welfare state regimes and industrial relations systems, in: Bernhard Ebbinghaus and Philip Manow (Eds) *Comparing Welfare Capitalism – Social Policy and Political Economy in Europe, Japan and the USA* (London and New York: Routledge), pp. 105–125.
Daly, Mary, 2003, Governance and social policy. *Journal of Social Policy*, **32**, 113–128.
Daly, Mary and Lewis, Jane, 2000, The concept of social care and the analysis of contemporary welfare states. *British Journal of Sociology*, **51**, 281–298.
Dean, Hartley, 2003, The third way and social welfare: the myth of post-emotionalism. *Social Policy and Administration*, **37**, 695–708.
Department of Social Security, 1998, *New Ambitions for Our Country: A New Contract for Welfare* (London: The Stationary Office).
Driver, Stephen and Martell, Luke, 2002, New Labour, work and the family. *Social Policy and Administration*, **36**, 46–61.
Esping-Andersen, Gøsta, 1990, *The Three Worlds of Welfare Capitalism* (Cambridge: Polity Press).
Esping-Andersen, Gøsta, Gallie, Duncan, Hemerijck, Anton and Myles, John, 2002, *Why we Need a New Welfare State* (Oxford: Oxford University Press).
European Commission, 1998, *Reconciliation between Work and Family Life in Europe* (Brussels: Directorate General V).
European Commission, 2005, *Employment in Europe 2005* (Brussels: DG for Employment, Social Affairs and Equal Treatment).
Evers, Adalbert, 1995, Part of the welfare mix: the third sector as an intermediate area. *Voluntas*, **6**, 159–182.
Evers, Adalbert and Olk, Thomas (Eds), 1996, *Wohlfahrtspluralismus: vom Wohlfahrtsstaat zur Wohlfahrtsgesellschaft* (Opladen: Westdeutscher Verlag).
Ferrera, Maurizio and Rhodes, Martin, 2000, Recasting European welfare states: an introduction. *West European Politics*, **23**, 1–10.
Garreau, Brigitte and Marchais, Pierrick, 1994, Villes et banlieues – fractures urbaines. *Réference. Pays de la Loire*, **6**, 28–31.
Gauthier, Anne, 1996, *The State and the Family: A Comparative Analysis of Family Policies in Industrialized Countries* (Oxford: Oxford University Press).
Gornick, Janet C., Meyers, Marcia K. and Ross, Katherin E., 1997, Supporting the employment of mothers: policy variation across fourteen welfare states. *Journal of European Social Policy*, **7**, 43–70.
Gubrium, Jaber F. and Holstein, James A., 1997, *The New Language of Qualitative Method* (Oxford: Oxford University Press).
Hantrais, Linda, 2004, *Family Policy Matters: Responding to Family Change in Europe* (Bristol: The Policy Press).
Johnson, Norman, 1990, Problems for the mixed economy of welfare, in: Alan Ware and Robert E. Goodin (Eds) *Need and Welfare* (London: Sage), pp. 145–164.
Johnson, Norman, 1999, *Mixed Economies of Welfare: a Comparative Perspective* (London: Prentice Hall Europe).
Kaufmann, Franz-Xaver, 1996, Zur Lage der Familie und der Familienpolitik in Deutschland, in: Friedrich W. Busch and Rosemarie Nave-Herz (Eds) *Ehe und Familien in Krisensituationen* (Oldenburg: Isensee), pp. 13–33.
Kuhnle, Stein and Alestalo, Matti, 2000, Introduction: growth, adjustments and survival of European welfare states, in: Stein Kuhnle (Ed.) *Survival of the European Welfare State* (London and New York: Routledge), pp. 3–18.
Kvale, Steiner, 1996, *InterViews: An Introduction to Qualitative Research Interviewing* (London: Sage).

Leibfried, Stephan, 1992, Towards an European welfare state?, in: Zuza Ferge and Jon E. Kolberg (Eds) *Social Policy in a Changing Europe* (Frankfurt am Main: Campus Verlag), pp. 245–280.

Leibfried, Stephan and Obinger, Herbert, 2000, Welfare state futures: an introduction. *European Review*, **8**, 277–290.

Leibfried, Stephan and Obinger, Herbert, 2003, The state of the welfare state: German social policy between macroeconomic retrenchment and microeconomic recalibration. *West European Politics*, **26**, 199–219.

Ministry of Social Affairs, 1999, *Sociale tendenser 1999* (Copenhagen: Socialministeriet, Den sociale Ankestyrelse).

Offe, Claus, 1998, Der deutsche Wohlfahrtsstaat: Prinzipien, Leistungen, Zukunftsaussichten. *Berliner Journal für Soziologie*, **8**, 359–380.

Offe, Claus, 2000, Civil society and social order: demarcating and combining market, state and community. *Archieve Europeen de Sociologies*, **41**, 71–94.

Palier, Bruno, 1997, A "liberal" dynamic in the transformation of the French social welfare system, in: Jochen Clasen (Ed.) *Social Insurance in Europe* (Bristol: The Policy Press), pp. 84–106.

Pierson, Paul, 2001, Coping with permanent austerity: welfare state restructuring in affluent democracies, in: Paul Pierson (Ed.) *The New Politics of the Welfare State* (Oxford: Oxford UP), pp. 410–456.

Pinker, Robert, 1992, Making sense of the mixed economy of welfare. *Social Policy and Administration*, **26**, 273–284.

Rapetti, Danielle, 1997, Richesse et pauvreté dans la ville: exemple nantais. *Reference. Pays de la Loire*, **18**, 10–15.

Schulz, Brigitte H., 2000, Globalisation, unification, and the German welfare state. *International Social Science Journal*, **52**, 39–50.

Skinner, Christine, 2003, *Running Around in Circles: Coordinating Childcare, Education and Work* (Bristol: Policy Press).

Sozialdemokratischen Partei Deutschlands und Bündnis 90/Die Grünen, 1998, *Koalitionsvertrag: Aufbruch und Erneuerung – Deutschlands Weg ins 21. Jahrhundert* available at http://www.bundesregierung.de.

Titmuss, Richard, 1987 [1972], Developing social policy in conditions of rapid change: the role of social welfare, in Richard Titmus, *The Philosophy of Welfare. Selected Writings* (London: Allen & Unwin), pp. 254–268.

Titmuss, Richard, 1974, *Social Policy* (London: George Allen and Unwin).

Torfing, Jakob, 2004, *Det stille sporskifte i velfærdsstaten* (Århus: Århus Universitetsforlag).

Van Oorshot, Wim and Abrahamson, Peter, 2003, The Dutch and Danish miracles revisited: a critical discussion of activation policies in two small welfare states. *Social Policy and Administration*, **37**, 288–304.

Wendt, Claus and Maucher, Mathias, 2000, *Mütter zwischen Kinderbetreuung und Erwerbstätigkeit. Institutionelle Hilfen und Hürden bei einem beruflichen Wiedereinstieg nach einer Kinderpause* (Mannheim, MZES).

Wendt, Claus and Maucher, Mathias, 2004, Wege des Wiedereinsteigs: Strategien der Vereinbarkeit von Familie und Berufstätigkeit in Dänemark, Deutschland und Frankreich. *Zeitschrift für Familienforschung*, **16**, 5–37.

Windebank, Jan, 1996, To what extent can social policy challenge the dominant ideology of mothering? A cross-national comparison of Sweden, France and Britain. *Journal of European Social Policy*, **6**, 147–161.

Windebank, Jan, 1999, Political motherhood and the everyday experience of mothering: a comparison of the child care strategies of French and British working mothers. *Journal of Social Policy*, **28**, 1–25.

Fiscal Policy Learning from Crisis: Comparative Analysis of the Baltic Countries

RINGA RAUDLA, ALEKSANDRS CEPILOVS, VYTAUTAS KUOKŠTIS, & RAINER KATTEL

ABSTRACT *The experience of a major crisis is often expected to lead to policy learning but the empirical evidence about this is limited. The goal of the paper is to explore comparatively whether the crisis of 2008–2010 has led to fiscal policy learning by civil servants in the three Baltic countries. Despite some differences in the crisis experience, the finance ministry officials in all three countries have identified the same lesson from the crisis: fiscal policy should be counter-cyclical and help to stabilize the economy. The paper also discusses how various factors have influenced policy learning, including the acknowledgment of failure, blame shifting, and analytical tractability.*

1. Introduction

Although the "crisis" in a broad sense is far from being over in Europe, it is worth taking a look back and asking: what have policy-makers learnt from the crisis experience (if anything) so far? While it is often argued that a crisis should lead to policy learning, we still have limited knowledge about whether and how it actually happens. Several authors writing on the topic of policy learning have lamented the underdeveloped state of the literature (Radaelli 2009; Howlett 2012; Dunlop and Radaelli 2016). The same complaint could be voiced even more loudly about the more specific question of whether and how crisis influences policy learning by civil servants. Exploring policy learning by *civil servants* is warranted since they are considered to be among the most important learning actors in the policy learning literature (e.g. Heclo 1974; Bennett and Howlett 1992; Hall 1993; Radaelli 2008). As Heclo (1974, p. 303) has put it, "To officials has fallen the task of gathering, storing and interpreting policy experience". Given that the bureaucrats can influence the policy agenda and shape policy decisions (Hall 1993; Page and Jenkins 2005; Christensen 2013), inquiring into the kinds of lessons they have identified from a crisis can provide valuable insights about the dynamics of policy learning.

With our study, we seek to open up the "black box" of policy learning by civil servants at least a little bit. "Policy learning" refers to the updating of beliefs about key components of policy, based on experiences, analysis, or social interaction (Radaelli 2009, p. 1146; Dunlop and Radaelli 2013, p. 599; Zahariadis 2014). While policy learning may often lead to policy change and the occurrence of change is often viewed as evidence of learning (Bennett and Howlett 1992; May 1992; Hall 1993), it is useful – for the sake of conceptual accuracy – to keep policy *learning* and policy *change* analytically separate (Fenger and Quaglia 2015; van Nispen and Scholten 2015).[1] In this paper we focus on *policy learning* rather than on policy change. In other words, we seek to contribute to the scholarly discussion on whether and how a crisis can lead to the modification of policy beliefs that individual public officials have.[2]

We focus on the field of *fiscal policy* and the lessons that the officials of finance ministries have learnt from the recent crisis experience. Specifically, we look at the three Baltic countries to answer the following research questions: Have the fiscal policy officials learnt anything from the crisis of 2008–2010, and if yes, what? Have the civil servants in the Baltic countries drawn similar or different lessons from the crisis?

We concentrate on *fiscal policy* because the recent crisis in Europe has often been construed as a "fiscal" crisis (Schmidt 2014). Furthermore, given that the issues of fiscal policy have generated a lot of debate in the academic and policy communities since the Great Recession (see e.g. Ban 2015; Vail 2014), it would be insightful to explore how fiscal policy beliefs have evolved among the civil servants after the crisis. While the policy learning framework has been used to examine fiscal policy learning at the EU level (Dunlop and Radaelli 2016) and at the member state level *during* the crisis (Zahariadis 2014), there are no studies that would explore fiscal policy learning in the EU *member states after the crisis*.

Bennett and Howlett (1992, p. 290) have suggested that advancing our knowledge of policy learning would be fruitful via "intensive examination of a few comparable cases". Such an approach allows us to explore qualitatively, first, whether and how policy officials have modified their policy beliefs, and, second, identify factors that have influenced their learning. The three Baltic countries were hit harder by the global financial crisis in 2008–2009 than other European countries (as witnessed by the largest output losses on record) but have also become regarded as "successful" examples of exiting from it via austerity measures (Staehr 2013). Thus, they can provide useful insights about policy learning from crisis.

The three Baltic countries can also be viewed as "most similar" cases, because of their similar historical legacies and development trajectories. Despite their similarities, some small differences regarding the crisis experiences in the Baltic countries did occur (Kattel and Raudla 2013). The cumulative output losses in 2008–2010 were greater in Estonia (20.1 per cent) and Latvia (21.7 per cent) than in Lithuania (14.8 per cent) (Eurostat). While the Estonian government managed to keep the deficit below 3 per cent of gross domestic product (GDP), Lithuania and Latvia recorded significant budget deficits in those years. Whereas Lithuania was able to borrow funds from international markets, Latvia had to turn to the International Monetary Fund (IMF) and the EU for financial support (Bakker and Klingen 2012; Kattel and Raudla 2013). Thus, it would be interesting to explore whether the differences in crisis experience influenced the lessons identified by the civil servants. While a number of studies have examined how the crisis was *managed* in the three Baltic countries (Kattel and Raudla 2013; Kuokštis 2013, 2015; Staehr 2013), so far there have not been any studies that explicitly adopt a *policy learning* perspective and seek to identify what kind of lessons the public officials in these countries draw from the experience of the crisis. Our data come from semi-structured elite interviews with civil servants from the finance ministries in the three Baltic countries.

The paper is structured as follows. Section 2 outlines the theoretical predictions, followed by the empirical analysis in Section 3. Section 4 provides a concluding discussion.

2. Policy Learning from Crisis: Theoretical Discussion

In the existing literature, it is often argued that crises provide opportunities for learning (Hall 1993; Brandstrom et al. 2004; Hogan and Doyle 2007). Indeed, although learning *during* a crisis may be limited, due to the sense of urgency or analytical resource constraints (e.g. Boin et al. 2005; Zahariadis 2014; van Nispen and Scholten 2015), learning *from* the crisis, *after* the crisis, should be more likely, given the possibilities to reflect on what led to it and to evaluate crisis-time actions. Since a crisis is expected to "profoundly shake" those who are exposed to it first hand and hence to motivate them to prevent its recurrence (Brandstrom et al. 2004, p. 192), we would expect policy actors to take stock of the crisis experience. Crises can have a focusing effect by calling into question the existing policies and forcing policy actors to reconsider those policies (Brandstrom et al. 2004; Hogan and Hara 2011; Hogan and Feeney 2012), which should facilitate policy learning. Thus, our first theoretical expectation is:

E1: The experience of a crisis will lead to policy learning among civil servants.

While many studies do indeed argue that crises are conducive to policy learning, there are other studies that point to the necessity of adopting a more nuanced view, in the sense that crises *may* facilitate learning but it is not necessarily guaranteed (Heikkila and Gerlak 2013; Fenger and Quaglia 2015). Based on the existing literature, we can outline a number of theoretical expectations about factors that can influence whether the experience of a crisis leads to policy learning by civil servants.

First, the *nature of the policy area* is likely to influence whether and to what extent the experience of a crisis leads civil servants to draw lessons from it. In particular, the level of analytical tractability is likely to influence policy learning. The more "tractable" the policy problem, the easier it is to (quantitatively) measure performance indicators and to identify causal relationships between policy actions and their effects, and, as a result, the easier it is for the policy bureaucracy to draw lessons from previous experiences (Jenkins-Smith 1985, 1988; Sabatier 1987; Dunlop and Radaelli 2016). Conversely, the more complex the causal relationships, the more ambiguous the policy experience and the more challenging it is to draw causal lessons (Sabatier 1987; Radaelli 2008). Thus, even if the experience of a crisis induces the civil servants to analyse more closely the causal relationships in their policy area – e.g. the factors leading to the crisis, the effects of policy actions undertaken in the midst of the crisis – the intensity of the crisis and the uncertainties surrounding it may make the attribution of causality, and hence policy learning, more challenging than would be the case in "times of normalcy". Thus, the second theoretical expectation we will examine is:

E2: Policy learning is less likely to take place if the policy area is characterized by low tractability of problems.

Second, a crisis is more likely to lead to policy learning if the policy actors identify policy *failure*, meaning that they consider the policy in their area as being (at least partially) responsible for the crisis (Bovens and t'Hart 1995). Without the perception and identification of policy failure, there would be fewer incentives and pressures (if any) to challenge the existing policies and to identify lessons. Conversely, the perception of policy failure is likely to trigger the reconsideration of existing policies and a search for new ideas (May 1992; Zahariadis 2014). Thus, our third theoretical expectation is:

E3: A crisis is likely to lead to policy learning if the policy actors consider the crisis to have resulted from policy failure.

Although the acknowledgement of failure should foster learning, the former may be hindered by several factors. In order to maintain organizational stability, the officials may avoid evaluative efforts, in the fear that the findings might implicate them (May 1992). As Hood (2002, 2010) has emphasized, policy actors are often motivated to avoid blame. If civil servants engage in blame-games and seek to shift the burden of blame to others, the opportunities for learning from the crisis are likely to be more limited. Thus, our fourth theoretical expectation is:

E4: In order to avoid blame, officials would seek to avoid the identification of failure, which limits the opportunities to learn from crisis.

Another issue related to the perception of policy failure is whether the policy actors feel that they (or their organizations) could have done anything to *avoid* the failure. Here again, existing theoretical discussions point to somewhat diverging predictions. On the one hand, based on the rationalistic approaches, we would expect that if the policy officials perceive that they could have contributed to preventing the occurrence of the crisis, they would be more motivated to draw lessons that would help them prevent similar crises in the future (May 1992; Howlett 2012). Hence, our fifth theoretical expectation is:

E5: Policy learning from crisis is more likely if civil servants feel that they could have taken steps to prevent the crisis.

On the other hand, if the civil servants concede that they could have done something to prevent or alleviate the crisis, they would assume a considerable burden of blame (Brandstrom and Kuipers 2003; Hood 2010; Howlett 2012) – and attempts to avoid such attribution of blame would undermine their efforts to draw lessons from the crisis.

Finally, policy learning from crisis by civil servants is likely to be influenced by external actors (especially organizations like the European Union, the IMF, the World Bank, and the Organization for Economic Co-operation and Development (OECD)). Such actors can *facilitate policy learning* by providing new information, an outside view, or a more neutral analysis of the problems, and point to lessons that can be learnt from others who have experienced a similar crisis (Hogan and Hara 2011). Also, through interactions with the officials from external organizations, the "domestic" civil servants can be exposed to new interpretations of the crisis and participate in the discussions that assess different policy alternatives (Radaelli 2008). Thus, our sixth theoretical expectation is that:

E6: Policy learning from crisis by civil servants is facilitated by external actors.

In the following, we will examine the plausibility of the theoretical expectations E1–E6 with an empirical analysis of the Baltic countries.

3. The Empirical Study

3.1. Background Information about the Crisis in the Baltic Countries

Since regaining independence in the early 1990s, the Baltic republics have stood out among the European transition countries as radical pro-market reformers. In the early 1990s, all three countries adopted a mix of policies advocated by the Washington consensus, including fixed exchange rates, liberalization of prices and trade, and wide-ranging privatization. The economic environments created as a result of such neo-liberal policy choices appeared to have put the Baltic republics on an impressive growth track, only interrupted by the Russian crisis at the end of the 1990s. After accession to the EU, all three economies witnessed an unprecedented boom. Between 2004 and 2007 the Baltic republics stood out among the EU countries for their high growth rates: the average annual growth rates for this period were 10.3 per cent in Latvia, 8.5 per cent in Estonia, and 8.2 per cent in Lithuania. These remarkable figures were, however, accompanied by signs of overheating, including double-digit inflation, a housing boom, appreciating real exchange rates, accelerating wage growth (that exceeded productivity growth), and a fast accumulation of net foreign liabilities and soaring current account deficits. One of the key features of the Baltic economies has also been an overwhelming foreign ownership of banking assets. By the time the crisis hit, Estonia and Lithuania had over 90 per cent of banking assets in foreign ownership, Latvia just above 60 per cent (Kattel and Raudla 2013).

The crisis hit all Baltic countries quickly and painfully. The domestic bubbles burst in early 2008, when the credit supply decelerated and banks started tightening credit conditions. The downturn was further exacerbated by negative developments in the external economic environment after the Lehman Brothers' bankruptcy. The cumulative GDP declines in 2008–2010 in the Baltics were among the largest in the world (Bakker and Klingen 2012; Staehr 2013) (see Table 1). In order to bail out the Parex bank, the Latvian

Table 1. Fiscal and economic indicators for Estonia and Latvia 2000–2015.

Year	Budget deficit in Estonia (% of GDP)*	Budget deficit in Latvia (% of GDP)	Budget deficit in Lithuania (% of GDP)	Public debt in Estonia (% of GDP)	Public debt in Latvia (% of GDP)	Public debt in Lithuania (% of GDP)	Real GDP growth in Estonia	Real GDP growth in Latvia	Real GDP growth in Lithuania
2004	2.4	−1.0	−1.4	5.1	14.2	18.7	6.3	8.9	6.6
2005	1.1	−0.4	−0.3	4.5	11.7	17.6	9.4	10.7	7.7
2006	2.9	−0.6	−0.3	4.4	9.9	17.2	10.3	11.9	7.4
2007	2.5	−0.6	−0.8	3.7	8.4	15.9	7.7	10.0	11.1
2008	−2.7	−4.0	−3.1	4.5	18.6	14.6	−5.4	−3.6	2.6
2009	−2.2	−9.0	−9.1	7.0	36.4	29.0	−14.7	−14.3	−14.8
2010	0.2	−8.1	−6.9	6.5	46.8	36.2	2.5	−3.8	1.6
2011	1.2	−3.3	−8.9	6.0	42.7	37.2	7.6	6.2	6.0
2012	−0.2	−0.8	−3.1	9.7	40.9	39.8	5.2	4.0	3.8
2013	−0.2	−0.7	−2.6	10.0	38.2	38.8	1.6	3.0	3.5
2014	0.6	−1.4	−0.7	10.6	40.0	40.7	2.9	2.4	3.0

*Net lending (+) /net borrowing (−)
Source: Eurostat.

government had to ask for international support from the IMF, the EU and Nordic countries in November 2008. In response to the crisis, all three Baltic republics implemented sizable fiscal consolidations in 2008–2010. The fiscal adjustment in Latvia was the largest, adding up to around 16.3 per cent of GDP between 2008 and 2011, followed by Estonia (13.9 per cent) and Lithuania (13.1 per cent). (Kattel and Raudla 2013, 2013) In all three countries, austerity measures were deemed necessary for maintaining their fixed exchange rate, achieving *internal* devaluation (rather than external) and restoring investor confidence (Bakker and Klingen 2012; Kattel and Raudla 2013; Staehr 2013). In addition, in Estonia, fiscal consolidation was also driven by the goal to join the Eurozone as fast as possible; in Latvia by the requirements of the bailout package; and in Lithuania by the need to limit expensive borrowing to cover the budget deficit and to avoid sovereign default (Raudla and Kattel 2011; Bakker and Klingen 2012). Fiscal consolidation in all three countries entailed both expenditure cuts and tax increases, while greater weight was accorded to the expenditure side. The greatest focus on expenditure measures could be observed in Lithuania (with 85 per cent of the total consolidation between 2008 and 2011 made up on the expenditure side), followed by 70 per cent in Estonia, and 60 per cent in Latvia (Raudla and Kattel 2011). In 2010–2011, all three countries returned to a growth path. Estonia joined the Eurozone in 2011, Latvia in 2014, and Lithuania in 2015.

3.2. The Crisis Experience and Policy Learning by Civil Servants

In this paper, we focus on the subjective understandings and interpretations of the civil servants in the three countries. In each country, we conducted interviews with five Ministry of Finance (MoF) officials. In selecting interviewees, we used purposive sampling: we identified officials who have been most closely involved in fiscal policy-making and also made sure that we interviewed civil servants from different levels of the organizational hierarchy in order to capture the potential diversity of viewpoints. The total number of MoF officials closely involved in fiscal policy-making in the Baltic countries is relatively small; hence, we felt that five interviews in each country should be sufficient to provide exploratory insights. The interviews were conducted between August 2014 and September 2015, and each lasted between 1.5 and 3 hours. The interviews were recorded, transcribed and also translated into English (in order to increase inter-coder validity by allowing all authors from the three different countries to read the transcripts). The authors read through all the interview transcripts independently, used open coding to identify the main themes, and then discussed the interpretations jointly in order to increase the validity of the findings. Given that we have defined "policy learning" as "the updating of beliefs about policy" by policy actors, we are primarily interested in their *subjective interpretations* rather than already implemented policy change. In order to capture the shifts in policy beliefs, the interviewees in all three countries were, on the one hand, asked directly what policy lessons could be drawn about the crisis for fiscal policy, whether the crisis has triggered changes in fiscal policy and influenced their normative views on fiscal policy-making. These questions were worded as openly as possible, in order to allow the interviewees to focus on themes that they considered the most relevant. However, in order to identify the subtler changes that the interviewees might not have been able explicitly to word as "lessons" from the crisis, they were also asked about the main causes of the crisis, whether the MoF could have done anything to prevent it, how they assess the actions undertaken during the crisis, and what role has been played by external actors in fiscal policy-making. These questions were also used for exploring the impacts of the various factors outlined in Section 2.

3.2.1.Perceptions of the finance ministry officials about the causes of the crisis of 2008–2010 and its prevention. On the question about the causes of the recent crisis and whether external or internal factors were more important in contributing to the emergence of the crisis, most of the interviewees in the three countries pointed to a *combination* of internal and external factors, with greater weight attributed to *external* causes (global optimism, underestimation of risks, low interest rates) in Estonia and Latvia, and more weight to *internal* causes in Lithuania.

While several Lithuanian officials felt that the government could have, in principle, prevented the *real estate bubble* (e.g. by adopting macro-prudential regulation), the Estonian and Latvian officials felt that not much could have been done to prevent it. As one of the Estonian officials put it, "We did not have domestic banks we could regulate and tell them how many loans to give.... We were in the EU and couldn't use capital restrictions" (Interview Est1). In the words of a Latvian official: "The main objective cause of the overheating was us joining the European Union.... It led to an increase in optimism and cheap interest rates and that, in turn, gave rise to the real estate bubble" (Interview Lat1).

When asked more specifically about whether the *Ministry of Finance* could and should have done something in the realm of *fiscal* policy to *prevent* the crisis, the overall assessment of the Estonian civil servants was that the MoF could *not* have done much (beyond what it actually did). The overall narrative that came through in the interviews was that while the MoF had underestimated the size of the bubble and hence also the positive output gap – which resulted in pro-cyclical fiscal policy – "everyone else", including the European Commission (EC) and the IMF, had done the same. All the officials noted that during the boom the Estonian government was already running surpluses (see also Table 1) and it would have been difficult to gain political support for having an even larger surplus. One of the officials also emphasized that lowering taxes, as the government had done, during the boom was clearly "bad timing" since it fuelled the boom, but this decision was "in the hands of the politicians" (Interview Est3).

Several Latvian interviewees conceded that running the deficits and stimulating the economy during the boom had magnified the bubble. They also argued that if the government had accumulated reserves, the bailout procedure could have been avoided and it would have been easier to "get through the crisis" (e.g. by using the reserves to save the Parex bank). At the same time, the MoF officials felt that their ministry could not have done much to prevent the crisis because fiscal policy decisions tend to be "in the hands of politicians" who can ignore the expert advice of the civil servants.

Most of the interviewees from Lithuania also argued that the government's fiscal policy had been too loose during the boom and that this had resulted from politicians' decisions. As one of the officials emphasized, "Increasing expenditures at a much faster rate than the GDP growth during the boom clearly was a complete nonsense" (Interview Lit5). Another interviewee noted, "The parliament still made those decisions despite experts saying that it would be bad" (Interview Lit4). Similar to the Latvian officials, the Lithuanian interviewees felt that accumulating reserves during the boom would have made it easier to go through the crisis by using reserves to cover the deficits instead of having to borrow at high interest rates. Furthermore, the Lithuanian officials pointed to a range of specific measures that the MoF had proposed during the boom – including the adoption of a fiscal discipline law (requiring a surplus or balanced budget over the medium term), which had been suggested by the IMF mission in Lithuania, the enactment of a comprehensive real estate tax, and a complete elimination of mortgage interest deductions for income tax – but these were not supported by the parliament in their entirety.

3.2.2.The evaluation of crisis-time fiscal policy actions. When asked to evaluate the crisis-time fiscal policy actions undertaken in 2008–2010, the Estonian officials' opinions were rather divided. One of the officials argued unequivocally that by opting for quick consolidation, the government did the "right thing" (Interview Est4). In contrast, another stated that "The austerity measures deepened the crisis" (Interview Est2). The others subscribed to more qualified assessments. They argued that, all in all, while the austerity policy may have been "a little bit harsh", the measures adopted "gave a positive push" by allowing Estonia to "exit the crisis" via joining the Eurozone. In their view, restoring credibility to the economy via entering the Eurozone had a more positive effect on the Estonian economy than expansionary fiscal policy would have done. Curiously, while the official rhetoric of the Estonian government during the crisis period of 2008–2010 did not support a Keynesian approach (Raudla and Kattel 2011), the *ex post* interpretations of crisis-time actions by the officials refer to Keynesian arguments and most of the interviewees felt the need to justify the crisis-time actions with reference to a Keynesian prism. The interviewees argued, for example, "In reality, it cannot be said that we did not follow the Keynesian ideas in our fiscal policy" (Interview Est3) or "We have been criticized for not being Keynesian during the crisis, but in some ways we were. ... During the boom we collected reserves and then at the outset of the recession loosened the fiscal policy in a Keynesian way by running deficits" (Interview Est1). It was also noted that while some of the expenditure cuts (i.e. cuts to salaries, transfers and investments) may have deepened the crisis, the government also tried to stimulate the economy by accelerating the use of the EU structural funds and trying to find consolidation measures that would not negatively affect aggregate demand (like taking out additional dividends from state-owned enterprises).

In Latvia, only one of the interviewed civil servants argued that the consolidation *cooled* the economy – but added that the government "had no choice" since the austerity measures were required by the IMF and the EC (Interview Lat3). The others argued that the fiscal consolidation had been *positive* for the economy. For example,

> The crisis conditions have proven that cutting expenditures during an economic downturn does not always have a negative impact. Therefore, if we compare the theory that is taught in the university with what is going on in real life, the case of Latvia proves that we can restore growth with expenditure cuts. (Interview Lat1)

In Lithuania, all the interviewed officials argued that the government had acted correctly during the crisis. One of the officials did note, though, that the cutting of expenditures had been pro-cyclical ("we were cutting at an inappropriate time"), but this was necessary given the circumstances (Interview Lit5). Another official even argued that it would have been inappropriate to pursue a Keynesian stimulus during the crisis since the economy was imbalanced and it was expensive to borrow (Interview Lit1). Furthermore,

The conditions for Keynesian policy were not present – the economy had to correct itself.... One needs to take guidance from Keynes creatively and not follow the literal textbook approach. Keynes talked about the case of a large closed economy without a fixed exchange rate.... But we were defending a currency board and had to restore investors' confidence. (Interview Lit1)

Another official summed it up as follows: "If you have to borrow at 10 per cent, you do everything you can to cut expenditures" (Interview Lit2).

In sum, the overall opinion of the interviewed MoF officials in *all* countries was that the government in their country had acted *correctly* during the crisis, although there were some dissenting opinions among the interviewees in Estonia and Latvia. Interestingly, the use of Keynesian ideas in assessing the austerity measures undertaken during the crisis varied between the officials in the three countries. In Estonia, some of the officials even tried to argue that the government had tried to follow Keynesian principles in deciding on the austerity measures. In Latvia, the officials viewed the Latvian case as providing evidence of non-Keynesian effects of fiscal consolidation, whereas in Lithuania it was argued that the conditions for Keynesian stimulus during the crisis were not present because of macroeconomic imbalances and lack of financing, while non-Keynesian effects of consolidation were also mentioned.

3.2.3.What has been learnt from the crisis regarding fiscal policy?. When asked about what they learned from the crisis, the MoF officials from all three countries pointed out that as a result of the crisis, fiscal policy has become much more important. As an Estonian official put it: "As a result of the crisis, the importance of fiscal policy is more clearly acknowledged and it is at the centre of attention" (Interview Est3). Also, several interviewees from Estonia and Latvia pointed out that the macroeconomic analytical capacities of the MoF officials improved as a result of the crisis. This seemed to be particularly pronounced in Latvia, where – because of the bailout package – the IMF officials were more closely involved in consulting the MoF. In the words of one of the Latvian officials,

We learnt a lot from the IMF experts. I can really say that the entire crisis period was a good training – in terms of how to work, how to analyse, how to forecast.... Now we go much deeper into details and analyse much more.... Before the crisis, our models were relatively simple but during the crisis, in cooperation with the IMF officials, we improved our models. (Interview Lat4)

Despite the fact that the crisis experience itself had been somewhat different in the three countries, the most important lesson in the eyes of the interviewed MoF officials is essentially the same. The interviewed officials from all countries *concurred* that the main lesson from the crisis is that "fiscal policy should be counter-cyclical and not pro-cyclical" and that "the budget should play a role in macro-economic balancing". The emergence of this "lesson" sounds somewhat paradoxical at first sight: all three countries implemented austerity measures during a major economic downturn in 2008–2010 – actions which could be viewed as *pro*-cyclical – and, in all countries, most of the officials viewed the adoption of austerity measures as having been the "correct" course of action.

There appear to be two main reasons behind the emergence of this – at first sight counter-intuitive – lesson in the countries that have come to be regarded as the champions and positive examples of implementing austerity measures during a major recession. First, as mentioned in the previous subsection, with the benefit of hindsight, the officials in Latvia and Lithuania, but to some degree also in Estonia, view the pro-cyclical fiscal policy preceding the crisis as having contributed to the bubble. Running surpluses during a boom is also viewed as important for building up reserves – which, according to the interviewees from all three countries, helped Estonia to weather the crisis of 2008–2010 better, could have helped Latvia avoid the bailout programme, and allowed Lithuania to avoid expensive borrowing. Thus, in the eyes of most of the officials of all three countries, an important lesson of the crisis is that adopting a counter-cyclical fiscal policy during a boom should help avoid future crises, and, if they do occur, the accumulated reserves should help to overcome them. As the officials observed:

We did tighten the budget during the boom, but not enough.... Accumulating reserves is important. Other countries now also say that this was the right thing to do. Those who had no reserves didn't manage the crisis so well. (Interview Est1)

The crisis has clearly proven that during the good years, if the government spends all the revenues and observes the nominal 3 per cent [of GDP] deficit target, then during a downturn it objectively can't maintain it. (Interview Lat1)

The main lesson is that we should have had a more cautious fiscal policy before the crisis.... We should have run a small surplus, like Estonia, not deficits. (Interview Lat4)

We cannot avoid crises, especially since we are a small country, but we can prepare for them – the bigger the buffer the better. As the Estonian experience shows, if you have a reserve, the landing during the crisis is softer and you don't have to borrow at such high interest rates. (Interview Lit3)

Second, a counter-cyclical role for fiscal policy is prescribed by the Fiscal Compact, which requires the members of the Eurozone to incorporate a structural deficit rule into domestic legislation.[3] All three countries adopted a structural deficit (or balance) rule in 2013–2014, which now guides fiscal policy-making and forces the MoF to pay attention to the cyclical stance of the economy when preparing the budget.

Thus, our interviews indicate that, as a result of the combination of the evaluation of pre-crisis fiscal policies and the implementation of the Fiscal Compact, officials from all three countries have adjusted their views on fiscal policy and have come to endorse the focus on structural balance in fiscal policy-making. This shift has been particularly pronounced in Estonia and Latvia. For example, the Estonian officials noted:

In fiscal policy, we used to focus on the nominal balance but now we strive to focus on the structural balance.... At the moment, in our decisions, the structural balance has more weight than the nominal one.... In order to ensure that fiscal policy is counter-cyclical, the structural balance indicator should be preferred over the nominal one. (Interview Est2)

Before the crisis, the focus of fiscal policy was on the nominal budget balance.... Even if we had surpluses, these were often not planned. Now we take the economic cycle into account in planning the budget. (Interview Est1)

The Latvian officials stated, for example: "Before the crisis, we didn't really have an objective in fiscal policy-making but the structural deficit rule now provides us with a target" (Interview Lat4). "Without the structural rule we wouldn't know how much we can actually afford to spend during the good years" (Interview Lat1). In Lithuania, the interviewees mentioned there had already been discussions about adopting a more counter-cyclical fiscal policy among the MoF officials before the crisis – but the crisis experience and the Fiscal Compact helped to drive home the need for analysing the cyclical stance in fiscal policy-making. "After the crisis, it was clear that nominal indicators are not enough: thus, structural indicators were introduced.... These rules certainly contain more logic and rationality" (Lit 3).

At the same time, most of the interviewees from all three countries conceded that the calculation of the structural position is uncertain; thus it is challenging to use the structural balance/deficit rule as a quantitative yardstick in fiscal policy in *real time* because the *ex ante* and *ex post* evaluations of the cyclical position of the economy can differ significantly. The interviewees also pointed to the fact that the domestic assessments of the structural position tend to diverge from the evaluations of the European Commission, which, in turn, increases uncertainty in fiscal policy-making.

Most of the interviewed officials stated that the new framework laws for budgeting, spurred by the Fiscal Compact, institutionalize the main lessons learnt from the crisis and constitute an important step forward in fiscal governance, but their assessment of the efficacy of the new rules varies somewhat from country to country. In Estonia, the overall opinion of the interviewees is that the new rules were not strictly necessary for Estonia, given its commitment to fiscal discipline, but the new law might provide some additional insurance for the future. The Latvian officials noted that while the MoF supports the new rules and acts as a watchdog, there is still a willingness among politicians to violate them, and that the *politicians* have not really learnt from the crisis. The Lithuanian officials noted that the institutionalization of fiscal policy by creating sounder laws has been an important lesson from the crisis. Thus, while some manipulation might still be possible under the new rules – "implementing completely crazy fiscal policy, like increasing expenditure by 30 per cent when the revenues grow 10 per cent" (Interview Lit5) – is now precluded. At the same time, it was also noted by Lithuanian officials that there might still be willingness among politicians to violate these rules: "The politicians still have the thinking that, ok, there are stricter rules now but other countries don't abide by them, so maybe we shouldn't either" (Interview Lit3).

4. Concluding Discussion

As the interviews indicate, fiscal policy learning from crisis has indeed taken place in all three countries, thus confirming our theoretical expectation E1. The main lesson identified by the finance ministry officials in all three countries is that fiscal policy should strive to be more counter-cyclical and avoid being pro-cyclical – which can be viewed as amounting to a change in policy goals.

As pointed out in the theoretical section, policy learning from crisis is more likely to take place if the policy actors acknowledge policy failure and consider their policy area as having contributed to the emergence of the crisis (e.g. Bovens and t'Hart 1995). Our empirical study indicates, however, that the links between the acknowledgement of failure and policy learning can be more complicated as no unambiguous support could be found for the theoretical expectation E3. In the Latvian and Lithuanian cases, indeed, the interviewed officials conceded that the MoF could have taken preventive steps in fiscal policy before the crisis, that the too loose fiscal policy during the boom had added fuel to the bubble, and hence the lesson for the future is that during a boom governments should run surpluses in order to stabilize the economy. In Estonia, however, in the officials' view, for the most part fiscal policy did *not* contribute to the emergence of the crisis. Still, the main lesson they identified from the crisis is *the same* as in the two other countries: during a boom fiscal policy should be more counter-cyclical. Thus, based on the Estonian case, it appears that policy learning is still feasible even if no clear policy failure is identified.

Our interviews also indicate that the links between the evaluations of *crisis-time actions* and policy learning are not necessarily straightforward – thus, our theoretical prediction E5 was not supported. In Estonia, at least some of the officials viewed the austerity policies as having cooled down the economy even further during the crisis, which, in turn, has driven home the principle that fiscal policy should be counter-cyclical. However, in the other two countries, the officials, for the most part, view the austerity measures as having been justified (despite their pro-cyclicality) but, still, for the future, consider it necessary for fiscal policy to be more *counter*-cyclical. While the interviews with the Estonian officials indicate that they even try to construe the crisis-time actions as having followed (at least some) Keynesian principles, the officials in the other two countries have subscribed more clearly to the notion of non-Keynesian effects of fiscal consolidation. It is also noteworthy that although Estonia did not make extensive use of the accumulated reserves in 2008–2010 (and opted for austerity measures instead), the officials in the other two countries have come to view having a fiscal reserve as an important instrument for being prepared for the next crisis.

How can we explain such non-linear linkages between the officials' evaluation of pre-crisis policies and crisis-time measures (described above) and the policy lessons they drew? On the one hand, it is plausible that the complexity of fiscal policy in general and the increasing intractability of the causal relations during a crisis in particular have played a role here. Given the difficulties involved in estimating the effects of fiscal policy on the economy (and also decreasing consensus in fiscal policy discussions internationally), drawing straightforward lessons from the pre- and crisis-time policies is challenging. Thus, we could see that the level of analytical tractability of the specific field we looked at *did* play a role in policy learning among the civil servants but it did *not* undermine it – implying that our theoretical expectation E2 could not be fully supported. On the other hand, all three countries have been subjected to similar policy pressures from the European Union – which has led to the emergence of the same policy lessons in all three countries, despite somewhat diverging crisis experiences and also different assessments of how fiscal policies contributed to the crisis and their effects during the crisis. Indeed, making fiscal policy more counter-cyclical via adopting structural balance as the main yardstick has been mandated by the European Union through the Fiscal Compact.

It was also argued in the theoretical discussion that the acknowledgment of mistakes and failure may be prevented by attempts to avoid blame (e.g. Hood 2010), which, in turn, would hinder policy learning. As our interviews indicate, however, the ability of the policy bureaucrats to *shift* blame – to other policy-makers (like politicians) – can in fact be conducive to policy learning, which goes against the theoretical expectation E4. Indeed, we can observe that most of the civil servants in these countries blamed the elected officials for undertaking faulty policies. The ability to *shift* the responsibility for problematic decisions to politicians (adopted before the crisis) appears to have allowed the civil servants in the finance ministries to engage in evaluative efforts and policy learning without having to cast themselves in a bad light.

Largely in line with our theoretical prediction E6, we can observe that external actors facilitated policy learning from crisis among the civil servants of the three Baltic countries. In all three cases, developments at the EU level provided a major impetus for policy learning among the MoF officials. The requirements of the Fiscal Compact provided a clear focal point to the officials for modifying their policy beliefs. Although the provisions of the Fiscal Compact were *mandatory* for the members of the Eurozone – and imposed top-down by the EU – our interviews indicate that their adoption has *not* been merely formal and symbolic (i.e. without a corresponding shift in policy beliefs of the local policy actors) but actual normative changes have taken place in the policy beliefs of the civil servants. Still, we can also conjecture that the EU-mandated rules may have, potentially, prevented more *country-specific* fiscal policy discussions and hence also more nuanced policy learning from taking place. In addition to the EU, the IMF contributed significantly to policy learning among the Latvian officials – especially by providing technical knowledge for fiscal policy modelling and forecasting.

In sum, we can see that the theoretical predictions outlined in the analytical framework of our paper do provide a useful starting point for exploring policy learning from crisis among civil servants. As our empirical analysis shows, however, not all of them are supported. This indicates that further theoretical (and also empirical) work is necessary to advance our understanding of whether and how policy learning from crisis takes place.

An important limitation of our study is that we focused only on policy learning by civil servants and not by elected officials, social partners and think tanks. Given the increasing role of the MoF officials in fiscal policy-making – resulting from the crisis and the increasing technicality of fiscal policy owing to the structural deficit rule – providing insights about the shifts in their policy beliefs is valuable. Future studies could systematically compare policy learning from crisis among these different groups of policy actors. Further limitations of our study are that we have zoomed in on individual rather than on institutional (or collective) policy learning and have not examined to what extent the shifts in the policy beliefs of civil servants have been translated into actual policy change. Further studies would hence be needed to order to map the effects of the crisis on policy change over time.

Funding

The research leading to these results has received funding from the Estonian Research Council Grant PUT-1142 and the Norwegian Financial Mechanism 2009–2014 under project No EMP264.

Notes

1. Indeed, even if policy actors have engaged in policy learning, the modified beliefs themselves do not necessarily guarantee that policy change will ensue (Elliott and Macpherson 2010; Fenger and Quaglia 2015). Also, even if policy change occurs, it may take place for other reasons than learning (e.g. electoral considerations, external pressures, resource constraints) (May 1992; Fenger and Quaglia 2015).

2. While several streams of literature related to policy learning (e.g. policy transfer, policy diffusion or lesson-drawing in public policy) focus on *actual* policy change, the focus of our paper is on ideational shifts rather than on whether the lessons are eventually translated into policy.
3. The structural position of the budget is calculated on the basis of a cyclically adjusted position, which is adjusted for one-off and temporary transactions. The cyclically adjusted budget position, in turn, is found by subtracting the cyclical component (or the output gap) from the nominal budget position (for a more detailed discussion, see, for example, Mourre et al. 2014).

References

Bakker, B. B. and Klingen, C., 2012, *How Emerging Europe Came Through the 2008/09 Crisis* (Washington, DC: The IMF).

Ban, C., 2015, Austerity versus stimulus? Understanding fiscal policy change at the international monetary fund since the great recession. *Governance*, **28**(2), pp. 167–183. doi:10.1111/gove.12099

Bennett, C. J. and Howlett, M., 1992, The lessons of learning: Reconciling theories of policy learning and policy change. *Policy Sciences*, **25**, pp. 275–294. doi:10.1007/BF00138786

Boin, A., t'Hart, P., Stern, E. and Sundelius, B., 2005, *The Politics of Crisis Management: Public Leadership Under Pressure* (Cambridge: Cambridge University Press).

Bovens, M. and t'Hart, P., 1995, Frame multiplicity and policy fiascoes: Limits to explanation. *Knowledge and Policy*, **8**(4), pp. 61–82. doi:10.1007/BF02832230

Brandstrom, A., Bynander, F. and t'Hart, P., 2004, Governing by looking back: Historical analogies and crisis management. *Public Administration*, **82**(1), pp. 191–210. doi:10.1111/padm.2004.82.issue-1

Brandstrom, A. and Kuipers, S., 2003, From 'normal incidents' to political crises: Understanding the selective politicization of policy failures. *Government and Opposition*, **38**(3), pp. 279–305. doi:10.1111/goop.2003.38.issue-3

Christensen, J., 2013, Bureaucracies, neoliberal ideas, and tax reform in New Zealand and Ireland. *Governance*, **26**(4), pp. 563–584. doi:10.1111/gove.2013.26.issue-4

Dunlop, C. A. and Radaelli, C. M., 2013, Systematising policy learning: From monolith to dimensions. *Political Studies*, **61**, pp. 599–619. doi:10.1111/post.2013.61.issue-3

Dunlop, C. A. and Radaelli, C. M., 2016, Policy learning in the Eurozone crisis: Modes, power and functionality. *Policy Sciences*, **49**(2), pp. 107–124.

Elliott, D. and Macpherson, A., 2010, Policy and Practice: Recursive Learning from Crisis. *Group & Organization Management*, **35**(5), pp. 572–605. doi:10.1177/1059601110383406

Fenger, M. and Quaglia, L., 2015, The global financial crisis in comparative perspective: Have policy makers "Learnt Their Lessons"? *Journal of Comparative Policy Analysis: Research and Practice*, pp. 1–16. doi:10.1080/13876988.2015.1044808

Hall, P. A., 1993, Policy paradigms, social learning and the state: The case of economic policy-making in Britain. *Comparative Politics*, **25**(3), pp. 275–296.

Heclo, H., 1974, *Modern Social Politics in Britain and Sweden* (New Haven: Yale University Press).

Heikkila, T. and Gerlak, A. K., 2013, Building a conceptual approach to collective learning: Lessons for public policy scholars. *Policy Studies Journal*, **41**(3), pp. 484–512. doi:10.1111/psj.2013.41.issue-3

Hogan, J. and Doyle, D., 2007, The importance of ideas: An a priori critical juncture framework. *Canadian Journal of Political Science/Revue Canadienne de Science Politique*, **40**(4), pp. 883–910. doi:10.1017/S0008423907071144

Hogan, J. and Feeney, S., 2012, Crisis and policy change: The role of the political entrepreneur. *Risk, Hazards & Crisis in Public Policy*, **3**(2), pp. 1–24. doi:10.1515/1944-4079.1108

Hogan, J. W. and Hara, A., 2011, Country at a crossroads: An insight into how an economic crisis led to dramatic policy change. *Risk, Hazards & Crisis in Public Policy*, **2**(3), pp. 1–23. doi:10.2202/1944-4079.1082

Hood, C., 2002, The risk game and the blame game. *Government and Opposition*, **37**(1), pp. 15–37. doi:10.1111/goop.2002.37.issue-1

Hood, C., 2010, *The Blame Game: Spin, Bureaucracy, and Self-Preservation in Government* (Princeton, NJ: Princeton University Press).

Howlett, M., 2012, The lessons of failure: Learning and blame avoidance in public policy-making. *International Political Science Review*, **33**(5), pp. 539–555. doi:10.1177/0192512112453603

Jenkins-Smith, H. C., 1985, Adversarial analysis in the bureaucratic context, in: P. Brown (ed) *Advocacy Analysis* (Baltimore: University of Maryland Press).

Jenkins-Smith, H. C., 1988, Analytical debates and policy learning: Analysis and change in the federal bureaucracy. *Policy Sciences*, **21**, pp. 169–211. doi:10.1007/BF00136407

Kattel, R. and Raudla, R., 2013, The Baltic republics and the crisis of 2008–2011. *Europe-Asia Studies*, **65**(3), pp. 426–449. doi:10.1080/09668136.2013.779456

Kuokštis, V., 2013, The political economy of internal adjustment in the Baltic States: Explaining responses to the crisis, Doctoral dissertation, Vilnius University, 2013.

Kuokštis, V., 2015, Cooperating Estonians and 'Exiting' Lithuanians: Trust in times of crisis. *Post-Soviet Affairs*, **31**(6), pp. 557–575. doi:10.1080/1060586X.2015.1008733

May, P. J., 1992, Policy learning and failure. *Journal of Public Policy*, **12**(4), pp. 331–354. doi:10.1017/S0143814X00005602

Mourre, G., Astarita, C. and Princen, S. 2014. *Adjusting the budget balance for the business cycle: The EU methodology*. European Economy: Economic Papers, no. 536, European Commission.

Page, E. C. and Jenkins, B., 2005, *Policy Bureaucracy: Government with a Cast of Thousands* (Oxford: Oxford University Press).

Radaelli, C. M., 2008, Europeanization, policy learning, and new modes of governance. *Journal of Comparative Policy Analysis: Research and Practice*, **10**(3), pp. 239–254. doi:10.1080/13876980802231008

Radaelli, C. M., 2009, Measuring policy learning: Regulatory impact assessment in Europe. *Journal of European Public Policy*, **16**(8), pp. 1145–1164. doi:10.1080/13501760903332647

Raudla, R. and Kattel, R., 2011, Why did Estonia choose fiscal retrenchment after the 2008 crisis? *Journal of Public Policy*, **31**(2), pp. 163–186. doi:10.1017/S0143814X11000067

Sabatier, P. A., 1987, Knowledge, policy-oriented learning, and policy change: An advocacy coalition framework. *Knowledge: Creation, Diffusion, Utilization*, **8**(4), pp. 649–692.

Schmidt, V. A., 2014, Speaking to the markets or to the people? A discursive institutionalist analysis of the EU's Sovereign debt crisis. *The British Journal of Politics & International Relations*, **16**(1), pp. 188–209. doi:10.1111/1467-856X.12023

Staehr, K., 2013, Austerity in the Baltic states during the global financial crisis. *Intereconomics*, **48**(5), pp. 293–302. doi:10.1007/s10272-013-0472-9

Vail, M. I., 2014, Varieties of liberalism: Keynesian responses to the great recession in France and Germany. *Governance*, **27**(1), pp. 63–85. doi:10.1111/gove.2014.27.issue-1

Van Nispen, F. K. M. and Scholten, P. W. A., 2015, Policy analysis in times of austerity: Puzzling in the shadow of powering? *Journal of Comparative Policy Analysis: Research and Practice*, pp. 1–9. doi:10.1080/13876988.2015.1095430

Zahariadis, N., 2014, Powering over Puzzling? Downsizing the Public Sector during the Greek Sovereign Debt Crisis. *Journal of Comparative Policy Analysis: Research and Practice*. doi:10.1007/s11077-015-9236-7

Failing Family Policy in Post-Communist Central Europe

STEVEN SAXONBERG and TOMÁŠ SIROVÁTKA

ABSTRACT *This article examines the developments of family policies in four post-communist countries (the Czech Republic, Poland, Slovakia and Hungary). A general tendency has emerged of implementing familist, gendered policies that encourage women to leave the labor market to raise children. The interplay of the ideological, economic and institutional legacy of the communist past with new economic, social and political conditions coupled with shifts in values have greatly influenced these policies.*

Introduction

When the communist walls came tumbling down, Central European women found themselves in a historically unique situation. On the one hand, they experienced the highest employment levels in the entire world, with only the Scandinavian social democratic countries coming close. On the other hand, in contrast to the Scandinavian countries, little discussion arose about the need for men to share in the household and child-rearing chores. As a result, the household remained strictly the domain of the woman (Gucwa-Leśny 1995: 128, Heinen 1997: 179). Under such conditions the double burden of paid and unpaid work became particularly onerous.

Since virtually all women worked during the communist era and since a well-developed system of childcare existed, one could imagine that the post-communist regimes would follow the Swedish path of taking measures to encourage men to share in raising children, which would make it much easier for women to pursue careers and balance family and work. Rather than continuing down the path of de-familization (Esping-Andersen 1999), by supporting gender equality in work as well as the home (Saxonberg 2003) and considering both men and women simultaneously as earners and carers (Sainsbury 1999), we show that the post-communist regimes have all tried to reintroduce the traditional familization regime by inducing women to return to the home as they move back toward the path of re-familization.[1] Some countries have *explicitly* supported re-familization (Hantrais 2003) by supporting conservative family policies (Esping-Andersen 1990, Saxonberg 2003) that encourage women to leave the labor market to raise children. Such policies approach Sainsbury's (1999) model of *separate* gender roles. Other countries have rather *implicitly* supported re-familization by backing market-liberal policies based on means-tested family benefits and reliance on market solutions for daycare. Although such policies are usually coded in general neutral terms, given the existing division of household labor and the structural conditions on the labor market, these policies still encourage women to take sole responsibility for raising children and come close to Sainsbury's (1999) model of the *male breadwinner*.

The Re-familization of Family Policies

This section examines family policies by looking at three key areas that influence the ability for women and men to balance work and family: childcare leave schemes, access to daycare and labor market policies. We also compare the Central European countries to Sweden and western Germany, as these two countries are usually considered prototypes respectively for the social-democratic, de-familized, gender equality, earner/carer model and the conservative, familized, separate gender role models.

Paid Family Leave

The Central European countries have two basic types of paid family leave: one is maternity leave, which is insurance based, rather generous and reserved for the first months of the infant's life. Then each country has various types of parental leave, which are not insurance based, less generous, but available for much longer periods of time and open for fathers.

Maternity leave benefits have not changed much during the transformation. They are available for 24–28 weeks except in Poland, where they are limited to 16 weeks (see Table 1). The replacement rates are extremely generous and used to be 90 per cent (Czech Republic and Slovakia) or 100 per cent (Poland and Hungary). However, in the ensuing years the post-communist regimes have lowered the rates in every country but Poland. In addition, all four countries have rather low ceilings, which guarantee that the majority of mothers will receive even lower rates of replacement for lost earnings.

While maternity leave has remained relatively stable, the crucial change occurred during the very first years of the transformation (1990–1992), when the new post-communist governments extended the periods of parental leave, so that parents

Table 1. Paid family leave (2002)

	Maternity leave			Parental leave		Level in % of average wage (and absolute in EUR and national currency)	Main changes during 1990s
	Length (weeks)	Replacement rate	Length	Type of benefit and benefit formula			
Czech Republic	28 (37 multiple births)	69% of daily assessment base, low ceiling	4 years		Universal 1.1 × MSL of adult person (1.54 MSL since 2004)	14.9% €82.6 (2,552 CZK) since 2004 increased to €115.7 (3,573 CZK)	parental leave: benefit level an length increased
Hungary	24	70% low ceiling	a) 2 years (if fulfilling social insurance condition -*child care fee*), b) 3 years, c) 8 years (third children)		Universal a) 70% of wage, ceiling 2 × min wage, b), c) min old age pension	22.8% €82.6 (20,100 HUF)	maternity leave: benefit level decreased
Poland	16 (18 second child, 20 multiple births), 2 (4 weeks) may be used by father	100% low ceiling	4 years		Income – tested Explicit (low level)	15% €83.3 (318.1 PLN) 23.9% = €132.4 (505.8 PLN) in case of lone parent	parental leave: extended to men, benefit level increased for families with 3 (or more) children
Slovakia	28 (37 multiple births)	90% of daily assessment base low ceiling (since 2004 55%)	3 years		Universal 0.913 MSL of adult person	29.6% €88.8 (3,790 SK)	parental leave: benefit level an length increased
Germany	14 (18 multiple births)	100%	3 years		Income-tested Choice: €307 24 months/ €460 12 months	11.1%	parental leave implemented

(*continued*)

Table 1. (*Continued*)

	Maternity leave		Parental leave			
	Length (weeks)	Replacement rate	Length	Type of benefit and benefit formula	Level in % of average wage (and absolute in EUR and national currency)	Main changes during 1990s
Sweden	maternity leave included in statutory parental leave		1.5 year (60 days for each parent, sharing the rest)	Universal (insurance based) 80% of salary first 390 days (up to 7.5 times the basic income level), €6.6 (60 SEK) next 90 days	(80%) min. €16.4 (150 SEK) per day, this is €500 per month	"papa month" implemented

Note: MSL = minimum subsistence level.
Sources: MISSCEEC and MISSOC (2004), available at http://europa.eu.int/comm./employment_social/missceec/missoc; wages by OECD 2002 (Taxing Wages. Special Feature: Taxing Families); COM 2003 (358) final: EIRO 2003, own calculations.

can remain at home with their children another 3–4 years. The post-communist governments extended parental leave to men; however, it was clear that they did not expect any men to actually utilize this right (Castle-Kanerova 1992: 113). In Poland, men did not even gain the right to take parental leave until 1996, when it succumbed to EU pressure (Wiktorow 1996: 28, Nowakowska and Swedrowska 2000: 49). Moreover, the benefit level for extended leave is so low in all four countries that, given the fact that fathers usually have higher incomes than mothers, few men can afford to take advantage of their right to parental leave. As Table 1 shows, parental benefit has remained at the low level of 15 per cent to 30 per cent of gross average wage.

In the Czech Republic and Slovakia, these benefits are universal, but paid in a lump sum regardless of income. This combination of a long leave period with low benefit rates constitutes an explicit re-familization policy, which promotes separate gender roles for men and women, since few men will be willing to utilize their right to parental leave under these conditions (Gornick and Meyers 2003: 112, 145, 242 discuss this for Western Europe).

In Poland parental leave benefits are means tested and restricted to those earning less than the social subsistence minimum. The neutral manner and liberal method of means testing constitutes a more implicit re-familization policy.

Hungary provides a slight exception to the general trend. The conservative first post-communist government (1990–1994) kept a relatively generous two-year parental leave, which the government strangely calls a *childcare fee*. It pays 70 per cent of the recipient's wage, although it is limited to a level of twice the minimum wage. In addition, parents can also receive a flat-rate benefit for up to three years. This ceiling on parental benefits called childcare fees gives the model an explicit familization character that promotes separate gender roles. However, since it gives the greatest encouragement among the Central European countries for men to take parental leave, it also contains some elements of the gender equality, earner/carer model. Although the socialist government cancelled the childcare fee, the next conservative government reinstated it.

Daycare

At the same time that the post-communist regimes have extended parental leave, they have also radically reduced state aid to nursery schools for 0–3 year olds. In addition, they have transferred responsibility for running them to the local authorities. The local authorities in turn have increased the enrolment fees and closed down most of the nurseries.

From 1989, the number of nursery schools dropped dramatically in Slovakia and in the Czech Republic, while in Poland their number was already low (see Table 2). Once again, Hungary provides the exception, as the percentage of children in nursery schools decreased by little more than one per cent.

In the communist countries children could attend nursery schools until they reached three years, after which they could attend kindergarten until they reached six or seven (depending when they were enrolled in primary school). As Table 2 shows, in the absence of nursery schools after 1989, Czech and Slovaks have increasingly turned to kindergartens. However, although kindergartens are allowed to accept children under three, they are not obligated to take them and their decision depends

Table 2. Enrollment rates of children in public pre-school facilities

	1989		2002	
	birth to age two (0–1–2)	age three to five (3–4–5)	birth to age two (0–1–2)	age three to five (3–4–5)
Czech Republic	20.3 (13.2% in nurseries)	78.9%	10.3% (0.7% in nurseries)	94.7%
Hungary	11.7% (11.2% in nurseries)	85.7%	10.1% (9.6% in nurseries)	87.8%
Poland	9.1% (8.7% in nurseries)	48.2%	5.1% (4.2% in nurseries)	49.9%
Slovakia	17.7% (15% in nurseries)	88.6%	5.6% (0% in nurseries)	80.1%
Germany (in 2000)			5%	82%
Sweden (in 2000)			37%	77%
EU-15 (in 2000)			25%	81%

Notes:
1) In post-communist countries, children in pre-school facilities, who do not attend nursery schools attend kindergarten as kindergartens are allowed to accept children 2–3 years old if there is capacity and there is adequate staffing. There is a guaranteed right to attend kindergarten for children one year before entering primary school. In Hungary the guarantee includes all children over 5 years.
2) When computing enrolment rates for children in post-communist countries we only include children over 5 months, because maternity leave covers approximately this period so no children are in nurseries.
3) We have created an estimate of enrolment rates for children 0–1–2 based on data by Gornick and Meyers (2003: 204–205) for Germany, Sweden and EU-15 (average for 9 countries where data available – AUT, BE, DK, FI, FR, GER, LUX, NE, SWE). This estimate is computed from data for children 1–2 which are provided by Gornick and Meyers and our own rough estimate of 5% for children 3–12 months or other information available in some cases. If lower enrolment rates for children 0–1–2 are reported for specific cases compared to our estimate we accept these reported enrolment rates.
Sources: Own calculations based on MONEE database 2004, Gornick and Meyers (2003) own calculations, and for the Czech Republic, *Vývojová ročenka školství v ČR 2003, ÚZIS 2003.*

on the particular school's economic situation and capacity. This tendency to seek places in kindergarten for younger children indicates that a demand still exists for daycare for children under three.

While enrollment rates have radically declined for nursery schools, they have remained high for 3–6 year olds attending kindergarten, except for in Poland. This combination of long parental leave and lack of access to daycare for children under three makes it difficult for women to combine work and careers.

Thus, all four countries have encouraged the re-familization of society. The Czech Republic and Slovakia have done so explicitly, by incorporating the conservative, separate gender role model, based on a combination of low level lump-sum benefits for parental leave and inadequate support for daycare. Meanwhile, Poland has followed a more liberal, implicitly familization model, in which most families cannot receive parental leave benefits, the state does not support access to nursery schools and gives low levels of support to kindergartens. This rather free-market policy supports the male-breadwinner model by inducing women to return to the home, since fathers cannot afford to take parental leave and mothers cannot easily find daycare for their children.

Although Hungary basically follows the conservative, explicitly re-familization path, it does not support separate gender roles as strongly as in the Czech Republic and Slovakia, since it gives fathers greater incentives to stay at home and it provides greater access to nursery schools.

Labor Market Policies

Labor market policies can improve the possibilities of balancing work and family by making it easier to work part-time, so that parents – especially mothers – can choose to spend more time with their children rather than send them to daycare for extended periods. In Western Europe, where labor markets are more flexible, many married women work part-time (Sainsbury 1996: 108, Vleminckx 2002). Moreover, since daycare is *not* readily available in Central European countries for children under three, mothers are even more likely to want to work part-time until their children begin kindergarten, in order to keep a foot in the labor market and to supplement their family incomes.

So far, the Central Europe governments have not followed the Council Directive 98/23/EC and passed legislation giving parents of young children the ability to enforce their right to work part-time. Nor have they introduced tax incentives or other measure to make part-time work easier. Thus, except for Poland, where young mothers can often count on the help of their parents in taking care of the children (Siemienska 1994, Dabrowska-Caban 1997), women work part-time much less than in Western Europe (see Table 3).

Post-communist labor market policies also make it difficult for women to return to work after having been on parental leave for several years. Although one has a legal

Table 3. Employment impact of parenthood and part-time work (2002) in percentages

	Part-time work (% of total employment) Men	Part-time work (% of total employment) Women	Employment impact of parenthood Men	Employment impact of parenthood Women	Women's employment share (% of total employment)	Women's unemployment share (% of total employment)	Employment rate – women aged 15–64 1994–2002 in two points of time
Czech Republic	1.4	4.9	8.7	−41.8	43.6	54.8	66.2–57.1
Hungary	1.7	4.3	7.1	−35.1	45.1	41.0	41.9–49.8
Poland	7.1	16.7	12.8	−12.5	45.4	48.3	51.9–46.4
Slovakia	1.0	2.3	7.6	−29.7	45.7	46.4	52.4–51.4
Germany	5.5	35.3	7.9	−21.4	44.6	43.3	55.0–58.8
Sweden	7.5	20.6	–	–	48.0	44.3	70.6–73.4
EU-15	6.1	30.0	9.5	−12.6	43.1	49.1	49.1–55.8

Note: employment impact of parenthood = absolute difference in employment rates of men and women without children and with a child aged 0–6 in age group 20–50. Part-time employment refers to persons who usually work less than 30 hours per week in their main job.
Sources: Employment impact of parenthood – EC 2004; part-time work – OECD 2003; women's employment share – EC 2003 (and own calculations); women's employment rate – OECD 1999 and 2003 and OECD LFS database for SK in 1994, available at http://www1.oecd.org/scripts/cde/members/lfsdataauthenticate.asp.

guarantee to return to one's job after parental leave, the post-communist governments have not enforced it. This contributes to a widespread feeling of insecurity among women, as employers often lay off mothers returning from their parental leave (Steinhilber 2003: 321). Like other vulnerable groups in the labor market, mothers also suffer because positive labor market policies are much less widespread in post-communist countries than in the EU. Expenditure on measures like training or job subsidies are about 0.5 per cent of GDP in Hungary and Slovakia and less than 0.2 per cent of GDP in the Czech Republic and Poland while in EU countries the average is above 1 per cent (OECD 2003).

The Ideological Legacy and Reform

Many observers have claimed that the anti-feminist ideological legacy from the communist era has strongly influenced post-communist family policies. However, this legacy is similar for all four countries, and thus cannot explain the differences in policies. Rather, we see the ideological legacy as providing a certain atmosphere in which policy decisions were made, but the differences in the policies pursued among the four countries come from the differences in their economic and institutional legacies. The ideological legacy influences both the ideological climate and the ability for women to organize around their interests.

The Ideological Climate

Under communist rule, the term "feminism" became blemished, because the former regime claimed to support gender equality (see, for example, Fuszara 1991, 1994, Robinson, 1995, Siemenska 1994). However, in reality, the communist regimes continued to support traditional gender roles, although almost all women had to work. Thus, it was extremely rare for women to reach influential positions in political or economic organizations. Meanwhile, women continued to have full responsibility for the household chores and childrearing. Consequently, the Czech sociologist, Čermáková (1997: 391), observes that a *gender contract* emerged during the communist era, in which virtually all women worked, but only men had careers. Instead, women accepted lower positions and lower salaries than men, so that they could balance work and family.

Moreover, in contrast to Western Europe, where women fought for the right to work, the communist regimes forced women to work whether they wanted to or not. Consequently, some women experienced work as state exploitation rather than a move toward liberalization. Thus, many women's organizations in the early 1990s made the right for women to stay at home and be housewives one of their main demands (Wolchik 1995, Saxonberg 2001a, 2003).

Inability to Organize

The communist regimes only allowed one official, state-controlled women's organization to exist, which prevented women from organizing around their interests. Consequently, no women's organizations could pressure the communist regimes into adapting de-familization policies. The absence of a women's movement meant that no organizations could induce women themselves to support gender equality. During the first half of the 1990s, feminism remained a *dirty word* (Šiklová 1998, Saxonberg 2003). Women's organizations in Central Europe have continued to be rather weak, although some evidence indicates that they are beginning to grow stronger (the articles in Flam 2001, Saxonberg 2003).

Thus, the anti-feminist ideological legacy continues to influence policies in a familist direction, as policymakers themselves tend to hold anti-feminist values and support policies that encourage women to stay at home. Meanwhile, this anti-feminist legacy also inhibits the emergence of a women's movement that could challenge these moves and gain public support for gender equality.

The Economic Legacy of the Communist Past

Although the anti-feminist ideological legacy provides a backdrop in which policymakers considered strategies over family and gender issues, the economic legacy had the immediate effect of forcing these policymakers to make some quick decisions. In 1989, all four countries originally faced some type of economic crisis after over a decade of decline and stagnation (for example Saxonberg 2001b). Budgetary pressures coming from economic crisis convinced the governments that it was necessary to cut social spending (for example Pestoff 1995, Standing 1996). Under these circumstances it was easy to conclude that re-familization policies would be cheaper than de-familization policies, which tend to require rather generous state support. Thus, for example, in all four countries the governments made cutbacks in funding for nursery schools, but increased the length of extended parental leave, partially because they thought that they would save money (for example Potůček 1999: 108). This is obviously especially true in the Polish case where extended parental leave was income-tested.

The economic legacy also helps explain differences in family policies. For example, the two countries that went the farthest with introducing income-testing (Poland and Hungary) were also the two countries that inherited the greatest foreign debts and budget deficits from the communist era. At the time of the transformation, inflation rates were also extremely high in both countries and in the Polish case even approaching hyperinflation (Saxonberg 2001b). Thus, these two countries faced the greatest pressure to cut costs. This difference in economic pressures can help explain why the socialist government in Hungary felt forced to introduce income-testing for further parental leaves and the social governments in Poland (1993–1997, 2001–present) have kept income-testing intact, while the market-liberal Klaus government in the Czech Republic (1993–1997) kept the extended parental leave benefits universal. Nevertheless, the legacy of communist economics is losing its influence over time as economic development becomes less dependent on communist era developments. Thus, when the conservative Young Democratic government came to power in Hungary in 1998 they reinstated the previous more generous system with income related benefits.

The Institutional Legacy

The post-communist countries share a peculiar institutional arrangement inherited from the communist era, in which two different institutions under the control of two different ministries have provided day care. While the ministry of education has responsibility for the kindergartens (for 3–6 year olds), the ministry of health has responsibility for nursery schools (for 0–3 year olds). Reforms in the 1990s officially gave responsibility to the local municipalities for running nursery schools, but the ministry of health still remains the supervisory body. To make matters even more complicated, yet another ministry (the ministry of labor and social affairs, or in Hungary the ministry of social and family affairs) has responsibility for maternity and parental leave benefits. This type of institutional arrangement makes it difficult to introduce de-familization policies, which require more comprehensive planning (coordination between nursery schools, kindergartens, parental leave insurance etc.). Market liberal policies, in contrast, require little governmental planning and coordination, while more conservative policies at least do not place the same demands on providing comprehensive childcare services.

In addition, the fact that the ministry of health has had responsibility for nursery schools, and even now personnel are nurses, sends a clear signal to parents: they cannot expect their children to receive qualified care, since the personnel do not have any training in pedagogy and psychology. Instead, the authorities look upon these children as health problems! Therefore, it is hardly surprising that nursery schools have poor reputations in Central Europe (Heitlinger 1996, Götting 1998: 228) and home care has been emphasized as superior to them in public discourse.

Not only can the institutional legacy from the communist era help explain the general move toward re-familization, it can also help explain the differences among the countries. Thus, Poland is the only country that has means-tested extended parental leave, which represents a continuation of the communist policies, as this benefit was means tested from the date of its incorporation in 1982 (Balcerzak-Paradowska 1991: 48). Given the country's debt crisis, not even social democratic governments have tried to replace an institutionalized income-tested policy with a more expensive universal benefit.

Meanwhile, Hungary, which had the relatively generous income-based childcare fee in the communist era, succumbed to economic pressures arising from the communist economic legacy and replaced the childcare fee with an income-tested benefit. However, after the economy began improving and the communist economic legacy lost some of its influence, the government decided to re-institute the communist-era childcare fee rather than introduce a new kind of parental leave benefit.

"Exit" and the Failure of Post-Communist Family Policies

Now that we have explained why family policies have generally moved toward re-familization, we can analyze the manner in which these policies interact with the needs and aspirations of the population. Here, we find that Havelková's (1996) differentiation between *abstract* and *concrete* citizenship is extremely usual for analyzing post-communist societies. She defines abstract citizenship as "an image of the system into which certain ideals are projected" (Havelková, 1996: 248). Meanwhile, concrete citizenship is "the attitudes that are rooted in the concrete knowledge and experiences of the individual within a particular social or political system" (Havelková, 1996: 248).

In the context of gender roles, we observe that because of the anti-feminist communist legacy, citizens of post-communist countries (including women) tend to be rather skeptical toward abstract, more theoretical feminist arguments concerning power relations in society and the ideal roles for men and women in society. However, at the concrete level, based on everyday experiences of balancing work and family, post-communist citizens (especially women) are much more supportive of increased equality. In other words, women have not been particularly engaged in debates about political power, power relations or notions about gender roles in society, but they are interested in increasing their possibility of having a career and they are also interested in achieving a more balanced division of labor within their own household.

We should note that although we use the terms "abstract feminism" and "concrete feminism" in line with Havelková's model, we are aware that many different kinds of feminisms exist. We are following the dominant tradition within Scandinavia in using "feminism" to designate support for gender equality, particularly the equality of or elimination of gender roles, which is not to deny that many feminists have other goals.

Abstract Feminism

The two most recent ISSP surveys on Gender and Family Roles from 1994 and 2002 provide data for comparing attitudes on abstract and concrete gender issues. The surveys were basically based on random samples, with some minor exceptions (see ISSP 2002 for details). Unfortunately, only one question posed in the ISSP survey is useful for measuring attitudes toward gender equality at the normative, abstract level. Respondents were asked whether they agree that "a man's job is to earn money; a woman's job is to look after the home and family". This statement is "abstract" in the sense that it asks about one's ideals as to what general roles men and women should have in society, rather than asking about concrete issues in the respondents' daily life. As Figure 1 shows, a great gap exists between the post-communist countries and the West European countries on the theoretical issue of what the role of women and men should be in society. Among the post-communist countries, only 25–35 per cent disagree that "a man's job is to earn money; a woman's job is to look after the home and family", while in conservative, familist western Germany over 61 per cent disagree and in social democratic, de-familist Sweden nearly 78 per cent disagree. Among the 11 western EU countries participating in the survey, nearly 65 per cent disagreed with the statement. This lack of support for gender equality at the abstract, theoretical level can explain why the post-communist governments could pursue re-familization policies without meeting much political protest. Nevertheless, it is worth noting that support for abstract feminism is increasing in all countries that participated in the last two surveys, which means that the potential is increasing for women to organize around feminist issues.

Concrete Feminism

Even if the majority of post-communist citizens still reject abstract feminist ideas about power and gender roles in society, at the concrete level questions exist about both the needs and aspirations of the population.

Figure 1. Percentage disagreeing that men should work and women should stay at home

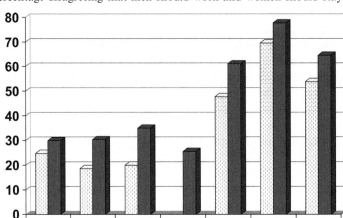

Note: for 1994 the ISSP survey includes the following EU countries: Western Germany (n = 2324), Great Britain (n = 984), Sweden (n = 1272), Austria (n = 977), Italy (n = 1018), the Netherlands (n = 1968), Ireland (n = 938) and Spain (n = 24949. Slovakia did not participate in the survey that year. For the Czech Republic n = 1024, H = 1500 and Poland n = 1597.

For the 2002 ISSP survey includes the following western EU countries: Western Germany (n = 936), Great Britain (n = 1960), Sweden (N = 1080), Austria (n = 2047), the Netherlands (n = 1249), Ireland (n = 1240), Spain (n = 2471), Portugal (n = 1092), Flanders (Belgium) (n = 1360), France (n = 1903) and Denmark (n = 1379). Italy did not participate in the survey that year. For the Czech Republic n = 1289, Hungary n = 1023, Poland n = 1252 and Slovakia n = 1133.

For calculating the EU-West average, we counted each country equally regardless of the number of respondents, so that those countries with more respondents did not influence the average more than those with fewer respondents.
Source: ISSP 1994, 2002.

On the issue of needs, the 1994 ISSP survey asks whether women must work in order to support the family. Although Slovakia did not participate in the survey, among the other three countries over 92 per cent of women answered in the affirmative. Thus, even if some women might have wanted to return to the home, virtually all of them believed that working was a financial necessity. Unfortunately, the 2002 survey did not repeat this question. Nevertheless, among female respondents 88 per cent of Czechs, 74 per cent of Poles, 80 per cent of Hungarians and 83 per cent of Slovaks think that both members of the family *should* contribute to the family income, which in practice means that they believe that women should work at least part-time. Post-communist women believe that they must and should work to support their families, whether they really want to work or not.

In order to examine attitudes toward family and gender relations in more detail, we conducted confirmatory factor analysis and found that at the concrete, daily level, attitudes toward gender roles have three dimensions: household equality, mother/child relations and state support for families (see Figure 2).

The results show that important differences in attitudes only exist for the second factor, mother/child relations. On the issue of household equality, post-communist

Figure 2. Percentage supporting gender equality

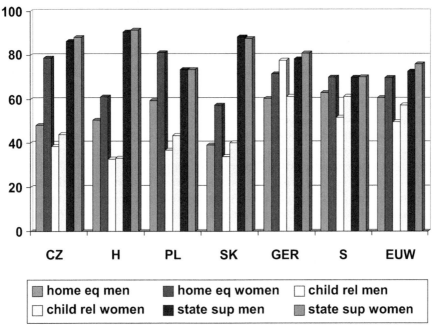

Note: for EUW the same 11 western EU countries are included as in Figure 1.
Note on the factors (where "men" = male respondents and "women" = female respondents):
HOME EQ = Household Equality, measured by two questions: 1) the percentage agreeing that men should do a larger share of the household work; and the percentage agreeing that men should do a larger share of child caring.
CHILD REL = Mother/Child Relations, measured by three questions: 1) Percentage agreeing that working mothers can have warm relations with their children; 2) percentage disagreeing that pre-school children suffer if their mother works; 3) the percentage disagreeing that "What women really want is home & kids".
STATE SUPPORT = State Support to Families, measured by two questions: 1) the percentage agreeing that working women should be paid maternity leave; and 2) the percentage agreeing that working parents should receive financial benefits.
Sometimes we counted the percentage disagreeing with a statement rather than agreeing with it, so that we would always measure the percentage of those who are most supportive of gender equality. The factors were testing using confirmatory factor analysis in Amos 5. All of the factors for all the countries met the minimum conditions of RMSEA < .05, AGFI and GFI > .92.
Source: ISSP 2002.

citizens are no less supportive of concrete feminism than West Europeans. In fact, Czechs and Poles are even more likely than West Europeans to argue that men should do a larger share of the household and childcare work.

It is also interesting that respondents in the post-communist countries are extremely positive toward state support for families and they are more supportive than those in the Western European countries. Poland provides the one exception, as Poles are less favorable to state support than western Germans, but more so than Swedes. Part of the difference in responses could be because of the unfortunate wording in the survey that asks about maternity leave rather than paternal or parental leave. Nevertheless, the results are still interesting, because they show that little support exists for the liberal, means-tested implicit familized policies which the post-communist governments have pursued in Poland and which the first socialist government pursued in Hungary (from 1994 to 1998).

The one factor where Central Europeans are clearly more conservative than Western Europeans is mother/child relations. Here the negative legacy of the communist nursery schools loom. For even if women feel that they must work for financial reasons and even if many women want to work in order to pursue the new career opportunities that opened up with the collapse of communism, they still fear that the state cannot provide high quality daycare for young children. Instead of using the "voice" option, parents have willingly abandoned the nursery schools and quietly tried to get their children placed in kindergartens.

The survey also indicates that Central Europeans are starting to rethink the issue of daycare, as the percentage of those believing that mother/child relations will *not* suffer has increased in all of the countries compared to the 1994 survey. Moreover, regression analysis for the factor mother/child relations shows that in all four countries, age and educational level significantly influence the belief that mothers can work without harming their relationship with their children (see Figure 2 for a listing questions for each factor). The more educated one is and the younger one is, the greater one's belief that mothers can work without damaging their children. This means we can expect support for working women to increase, since educational levels are rising in all four countries, thanks to a sharp increase in the number of colleges and universities. Meanwhile, the generational factor indicates that the newer generation is more supportive of the working women than previous ones and we can expect this trend to continue.

Conclusion: The "*Wrong*" Kind of Exit

We have shown that in contrast to recent trends in Western Europe, the post-communist countries have explicitly or implicitly tried to persuade women to leave the labor market by pursuing re-familization policies. EU accession has not greatly influenced policies in the fields of part-time work and childcare, which have been largely neglected. The EU's main influence so far has only been on the rather formal incorporation of EU legislation on equal treatment in employment and pay.

As Table 3 shows, the cost of childbearing is quite high for women, as their position in the labor market significantly decreases once they have children, while the position of men actually improves. In addition, this decrease is much higher than the EU average. However, our discussion of attitudes shows that women feel that they must work whether they want to or not. In addition, although support for abstract, theoretical feminism is rather low (but increasing), great support exists for gender equality at the concrete, daily level. The lack of support for theoretical feminism has hindered the emergence of a strong feminist movement that could challenge the re-familization policies. Rather than choosing "voice" by organizing politically, Central European women have largely chosen "exit", by refusing to have babies. Rather than leaving the labor market, they have quite simply left the reproductive market. Thus the change in women's employment rates has been rather modest as female employment as a share of total employment has remained rather high (see Table 3). Women comprise a higher share of unemployed than they do of employed (except for Hungary, where female inactivity rate is still extremely high). This indicates that women generally face a higher risk of unemployment then men.

As Figure 3 shows, in the 1980s fertility rates were much higher in the Central European countries than in Western Europe. One year after the communist regimes fell, fertility rates were still higher than in conservative, familist Germany. Throughout the decade birthrates fell by around half and now are lower than in Germany. Meanwhile, fertility rates have been rising in Sweden after an initial fall during its economic crisis in the 1990s.

The fact that fertility rates could rise in Sweden, while declining in the post-communist countries and conservative, familist Germany, indicates that the familist policies constitute a major cause of the decline. If the decline were merely part of a general international trend, then fertility rates could not increase in Sweden. We do not deny that the economic crisis also played a role as living standards decreased for many families. However, the economic crisis did not cause declining birth rates during the communist era, when policies were less familist. In addition, in contrast to Sweden, fertility rates have not increased in the post-communist countries during periods in which economic conditions have improved. So, as Strohmeier (2002: 351) notes, family policies do influence fertility rates.

Figure 3. Fertility rates

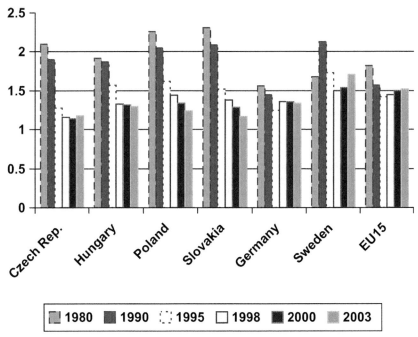

Source: EUROSTAT 2004, available at http://epp.eurostat.cec.eu.int/portal/page?_pageid= 1996,39140985&_dad=portal&_schema=PORTAL&screen=detailref&language=en&product= Yearlies_new_population&root=Yearlies_new_population/C/C1/C12/cab12048

The Central Europe countries contradict Esping Andersen et al.'s (2002) and Castles' (2003) observations that the previously negative correlation between fertility rates and employment rates has transformed into a positive correlation. Post-communist women exhibit persistently high employment, while their fertility rates have dropped radically. However, our results confirm Castles' conclusion about the causal mechanism: the employment prospects of women greatly influence family formation, because values have changed. Today women believe that they have the same right and need to work as men and that they must combine having children with the demands of working life.

Similarly, our findings support McDonald's (2000a, 2000b) incoherence theory. He shows that in the industrially advanced countries the conflict between norms supporting high levels of gender equity in individual-oriented social institutions (like education system and labor market) and sustained gender inequality in family-oriented social institutions (in caring and nurturing and household maintenance) has caused fertility rates to drop. Post-communist family policies have increased rather than dampened this conflict.

Acknowledgments

This study was written with the support of the Czech Ministry of Education (project MSM 0021622408 "Reproduction and Integration of the Society").

Note

1. Re-familization differs from familization in that familization policies are the general policies that a regime pursues, while re-familization connotes a direction. It implies that a country that once has carried out policies which to some extent have deviated from familization policies has now moved back toward policies that encourage increased familization.

    As Hantrais (2003: 204) writes about post-communist countries: "Family policy can be said to have been refamilialised. This does not mean that formal institutional structures for managing family policy are non-existent, or that they are not legitimised. It does mean they are underfunded, that support for families is often rhetorical rather than practical and that the state is not trusted to deliver good quality and reliable services."

    We use the term "re-familization" because before the war the Central European Countries pursued familist conservative social policies. Their policies were based on the conservative Bismarckian model: all family benefits were insurance-based including maternity benefits which were a part of sickness insurance that depended on the woman's employment record. Maternity benefits were limited to mothers and were only paid for 12 weeks (24 weeks in Hungary) at a replacement rate of 100 per cent (50 per cent in Poland). These countries did not introduce child benefits until after the war (except Hungary, where child allowance for state servants and low income groups existed in the pre-war period, and in Czechoslovakia, where they were only available for civil servants), and child care services did not exist. All in all, childbearing costs as well as child care have been assumed to be completely a family responsibility while caring duties were imposed on women due to the predominating male breadwinner model of the family.

References

Balcerzak-Paradowska, B., 1991, Urlop wychowawczy w Polsce. Kontekst socjalny i demograficzny, in: D. Graniewska, B. Balcerzak-Paradowska and D. Staszewska (Eds) *Okresowa dezaktywizacja kobiet wychowujacych dzieci jako element polityki rodzinnej* (Warszawa: IPiSS).

Castle-Kanerova, M., 1992, Social policy in Czechoslovakia, in: B. Deacon (Ed.) *The New Eastern Europe. Social Policy Past, Present and Future* (London: Sage), pp. 91–117.

Castles, F. G., 2003, The world turned upside down: below replacement fertility, changing preferences and family-friendly public policy in 21 OECD countries. *Journal of European Social Policy*, 13(3), 209–227.

Čermáková, M., 1997, Postavení žen na trhu práce. *Sociologický časopis*, 33(4), 389–404.

Dabrowska-Caban, Z. 1997, Partnerstwo w rodzinie i na rzecz rodziny. *Problemy rodziny*, 37(5), 21–28.

EIRO, 2003, National centres' answers to study questionnaire on "family and parental leave provision and collective bargaining" (November 2003), available at http://www.eiro.eurofound.eu.int/2004/03/word/cs_parental_annex.doc

Esping-Andersen, G., 1990, *The Three Worlds of Welfare Capitalism* (Princeton: Princeton University Press).

Esping-Andersen, G., 1999, *Social Foundations of Postindustrial Economies* (Oxford: Oxford University Press).

Esping-Andersen, G., Gallie, D., Hemerijck, A. and Myles, J., 2002, *Why We Need a New Welfare State?* (Oxford: Oxford University Press).

European Commission, 2003, *Employment in Europe* (EC: Brussels).

European Commission, 2004, *Indicators for Monitoring the Employment Guidelines 2004–2005 Compendium*. Second Version, latest update 22/92004 (EC: Employment and Social Affairs DG).

Eurostat, 2003/1, *Employment and Labour Market in CEC* (Brussels: EC).

EUROSTAT, 2004, available at http://epp.eurostat.cec.eu.int/portal/page?_pageid=1996,39140985&_dad=portal&_schema=PORTAL&screen=detailref&language=en&product=Yearlies&_new_population&root=Yearlies_new_population/C/C1/C12/cab12048

Flam, H. (Ed.), 2001, *Pink, Purple, Green: Women's, Religious, Environmental, and Gay/Lesbian Movements in Central Europe Today* (Boulder: East European Monographs/Columbia University Press).

Fuszara, M., 1991, Will the abortion issue give birth to feminism in Poland?, in: M. Maclean and D. Groves (Eds), *Women's Issues in Social Policy* (London: Routledge), pp. 205–228.

Fuszara, M., 1994, Market economy and consumer rights: the impact on women's everyday lives and employment. *Economics and Industrial Democracy*, 15(1), 75–87.

Gornick, J. C. and Meyers, M. K., 2003, *Families that Work: Policies for Reconciling Parenthood and Employment* (New York: Russell Sage Foundation).

Götting, U., 1998, *Transformation der Wohlfahrtsstaaten in Mittel- und Osteuropa* (Opladen: Leske & Budrich).

Gucwa-Leśny, E., 1995, Which role the more difficult – the situation of women in the household. *Bulletin: no. 1, Women: The Past and the New Roles* (Center for Europe, Warsaw University), pp. 125–137.

Hantrais, L., 2003, *Family Policy Matters* (Bristol: Policy Press).

Havelková, H., 1996, Abstract citizenship? Women and power in the Czech Republic. *Social Politics*, 6(1), 243–260.

Heinen, J., 1997, Public/private: gender – social and political citizenship in Eastern Europe. *Theory and Society*, 26, 577–597.

Heitlinger, A., 1996, Framing feminism in post-communist Czech Republic. *Communist and Post-Communist Studies*, 29(1), 77–93.

ISSP, 2002, *Family and Changing Gender Roles III* (Koeln: GESIS, Zentralarchiv für Empirische Sozialforschung).

McDonald, P., 2000a, Gender equity, social institutions and the future of fertility. *Journal of Population Research*, 17(1), 1–16.

McDonald, P., 2000b, Gender equity in theories of fertility transition. *Population and Development Review*, 26(3), 427–439.

MISSCEEC II, 2004, *Mutual Information System on Social Protection in the Central and Eastern European Countries. Bulgaria, Czech Republic, Estonia, Hungary, Latvia, Lithuania, Poland, Romania, Slovak Republic and Slovenia. Situation at 1 January 2002*. Available at http://europa.eu.int/comm/employment_social/missceec/index_en.html

MISSOC, 2003, 2004, *Mutual Information System on Social Protection in the Member States of the European Union* (Brussels: EC Publication of Directorate General V), available at http://europa.eu.int/comm/employment_social/missoc/index_en.html

MONEE database, 2004, TransMONEE database (Florence: UNICEF ICDC).

Nowakowska, U. and Swedrowska, A., 2000, Women in the labor market, in: U. Nowakowska (Ed.) *Polish Women in the 1990s* (Warsaw: Women's Rights Center), pp. 41–75.

OECD, 1999, 2001, 2003, *Employment Outlook* (Paris: OECD).

OECD, 2002, *Taxing Wages. Special Feature: Taxing Families* (Paris: OECD).
Pestoff, V. A., 1995, Citizens as co-producers of social services: from the welfare state to the welfare mix, in: V. A. Pestoff (Ed.) *Reforming Social Services in Central and Eastern European Eleven Nation Overview* (Cracow: Cracow Academy of Economics), pp. 11–28.
Potůček, M., 1999, *Křižovatky české sociální reformy* (Prague: Slon).
Sainsbury, D., 1996, *Gender, Equality and Welfare States* (Cambridge: Cambridge University Press).
Robinson, J., 1995, Women, the state, and the need for civil society, in: D. M. Stetson and A. Mazur (Eds) *Comparative State Feminism* (Thousand Oaks: Sage), pp. 203–220.
Sainsbury, D. (Ed.), 1999, *Gender and the Welfare States Regimes* (Oxford: Oxford University Press).
Saxonberg, S., 2001a, In the shadow of amicable gender relations, in: H. Flam (Ed.) *Pink, Purple, Green: Women's, Religious, Environmental, and Gay/Lesbian Movements in Central Europe Today* (Boulder: East European Monographs/Columbia University Press), pp. 33–46.
Saxonberg, S., 2001b, *The Fall: A Comparative Study of the End of Communism in Czechoslovakia, East Germany, Hungary and Poland* (Amsterdam: Harwood Academic).
Saxonberg, S., 2003, *The Czech Republic Before the New Millennium: Politics, Parties and Gender* (New York and Boulder: Columbia University Press).
Siemienska, R., 1994, The contemporary dilemma of the Polish family and its genealogy. *The European Journal of Women's Studies*, **1**, 207–225.
Šiklová, J., 1998, Why western Feminism isn't working. *The New Presence. The Prague Journal of Central European Affairs* (January), pp. 8–10.
Standing, G., 1996, Social protection in Central and Eastern Europe: a tale of slipping anchors and torn safety nets, in: G. Esping-Andersen (Ed.) *Welfare States in Transition. National Adaptations in Global Economies* (London: Sage Publications), pp. 225–255.
Strohmeier, K. P., 2002, Family policy – how does it work?, in: F. X. Kaufmann, A. Kuijsten, H.-J. Schulze and K. P. Strohmeier. *Family Life and Family Policies in Europe*, Vol. 2 (Oxford: Oxford University Press), pp. 321–362.
Steinhilber, S., 2003, Women's views on social security reform: qualitative survey, in: E. Fultz, M. Ruck and S. Steinhilber (Eds) *The Gender Dimension of Social Security Reform in Central and Eastern Europe: Case Studies of the Czech Republic, Hungary and Poland* (Budapest: ILO), pp. 315–325.
Vývojová ročenka školství 2003 (Praha: MŠMT).
Vlemickx, K., 2002, The proliferation of part-time work, family employment and household income security, in: R. Muffels, P. Tsakloglou and D. G. Mayes (Eds) *Social Exclusion in European Welfare States* (Cheltenham, UK and Northampton, MA: Edward Elgar), pp. 98–134.
Wiktorow, A., 1996, Kobiety w ubezpieczeniu społecznym w Polsce. *Polityka Społeczna*, **23**(8), 27–29.
Wolchik, S. L., 1995, Women and the politics of transition in the Czech and Slovak Republics, in: M. Rueschemeyer (Ed.) *Women in the Politics of Post-communist Eastern Europe* (Armonk, NY: M. E. Sharpe), pp. 3–27.

Comparative Analysis of Governmental Accounting Diversity in the European Union

ROSA MARIA DASÍ, VICENTE MONTESINOS, & SANTIAGO MURGUI

ABSTRACT *Comparability of governmental financial reporting in the EU presents important problems, as long as the preparation of budget information is not harmonized and National Accounts works as the only reference to verify compliance with stability objectives. Understanding the differences between the magnitudes indicative of budgetary discipline and the diversity of accounting policies is of paramount importance, especially for the Eurozone. This paper quantifies and analyzes the differences between financial and budgetary reporting policies of EU members, identifies the main factors that determine their diversity and analyzes the results in light of the different traditions of public administration and accounting policies.*

Introduction

This research aims to deepen the determination and analysis of the budget deficit in the European Union, currently one of the most important economic indicators, as a key measure for decision-making in the European Community, crucial to the identification and monitoring of convergence criteria such as the Protocol on the Excessive Deficit Procedure (EDP) and the Stability and Growth Pact (SGP) agreements.

At the EU level there is a single concept of deficit, enshrined in the Maastricht Treaty and the SGP standards, on the basis of the European System of National and Regional Accounts 1995, ESA 95 (Statistical Office of the European Communities, EUROSTAT, 1996 and 2002). Despite this, different budgetary systems exist in the EU, which define and determine the budgetary deficit according to different methodologies. This diversity of budgetary systems derives from social, economic, historical and legal frameworks in Europe and the analysis and explanation of their concrete features and processes are beyond the scope of this paper (see Lüder and Jones 2003; Lienert and Moo Kyung 2004; Ernst & Young 2012). This requires a reconciliation between the magnitudes of deficits resulting from the budget systems of each country (micro-accounting level) and the concept of deficit based on the ESA95 (macro-accounting level).

On the other hand, an effective harmonization of accounting standards applied by the member states (MSs) (http://epp.eurostat.ec.europa.eu/portal/page/portal/government_finance_statistics/documents/1_EN_ACT_part1_v5.pdf) would allow stakeholders to analyze the financial position and performance of governments and the long-term sustainability of public finances; enhance transparency, comparability and cost efficiency; provide the basis for improving governance in public sector (see European Commission 2013); and make it possible to derive the main EDP indicators (deficit and debt) directly from micro-accounting systems.

The EDP Notification Tables developed by the European Communities Statistics Office (EUROSTAT), serve as the starting point of this work to identify and analyze the methodological differences between budgetary figures and ESA95 information. The main objective of this paper is to analyze the link between macro and micro public accounting systems in the EU countries and the differences and necessary adjustments between them, in order to improve comparability, support the harmonization process and provide a better understanding of the relationship between budget information and statistical bases of financial reporting.

Specifically, this study attempts to answer the following research questions:

1. What are the most relevant features of the adjustments for differences between national accounts and the budgetary accounts of each country in determining the deficit? And what is their impact on both in the time frame and the different countries?
2. Is it possible to find differential behavior in terms of convergence between the two systems in the 27 EU countries and among adjustments in each country? And to what extent is it possible to verify whether administrative and accounting traditions and management styles in the public sector affect in a significant way the convergence between governmental reporting systems in any country?

The paper is divided into five sections. After the Introduction, we review previous literature in section two. The third and fourth sections present the empirical study, describing the information submitted to EUROSTAT by MSs, focusing on the reconciliation of the non-financial budgetary result of each country and their net borrowing (–)/lending (+) in EDP terms, data collection, methodology and some relevant results. Finally, we present the findings and concluding remarks of the paper.

Literature Review

As noted by Brusca (2010), the differing approaches between governmental and national accounting is a relevant research area in the field of governmental accounting, but has been little studied. The importance of this analysis has been highlighted by authors such as Cordes (1996), Jones and Lüder (1996), Lande (2000), Lüder (2000), Jones (2000, 2003), Montesinos and Vela (2000) and Keuning and Tongeren (2004).

Regarding these different approaches, the International Public Sector Accounting Standards Board (IPSASB) has developed a program of work on the convergence of the International Public Sector Accounting Standards (IPSAS) with national accounting systems, and in 2005 a research report was issued (IPSASB 2005) with the aim of identifying differences in the information provided by national accounts and financial information reported under IPSAS, making recommendations for convergence activities.

Recently, the IPSASB Conceptual Framework for General Purpose Financial Reporting (GPFRs) by Public Sector Entities (IPSASB 2013), points out that the information provided by GPFRs may be useful for compiling national accounts, as input to statistical financial reporting models, although IPSASB acknowledges that GPFRs are not developed specifically to respond to the needs of national accounting systems.

Moreover, in the context of the economic crisis and fiscal discipline, Council Directive 2011/85/UE on requirements for budgetary frameworks of member states notes in article 3 that "MSs shall have in place public accounting systems comprehensively and consistently covering all sub-sectors of general government and containing the information needed to generate accrual data with a view to preparing data based on the ESA 95 standard". In addition, MSs shall publish a detailed reconciliation table showing the methodology of transition between cash-based data (or the equivalent figures from governmental accounting if cash-based data are not available) and data based on ESA95 criteria. It thereby acknowledges the essential incoherence between public sector accounts, which only record cash flows, and the fact that EU budgetary surveillance is based on ESA95 accruals data. In this context, the Council Directive requested the Commission to assess the suitability of the IPSAS for the MSs.

The European Commission has forwarded its assessment on this issue to the Council and European Parliament, concluding that, even if IPSAS cannot be implemented in EU MSs as it stands currently, the Standards represent an indisputable reference for the potential development of European Public Sector Accounting Standards (EPSAS), based on a strong EU governance system. The existence and quality of comparable and coherent upstream accruals data at micro-accounting level are preconditions for the high quality of debt and deficit data at the accruals-based macro-accounting level. Micro public-sector accounting in the MSs has many variants, making comparisons difficult both within and between countries.

It is worth noting that the differences between national and micro-level accounting systems call into question the reliability and comparability of the aggregate financial decisions that sustain the EU (Lüder 2000; Bastida and Benito 2007; Benito et al. 2007; Benito and Bastida 2009). Many accounting standards setters are making efforts towards harmonization between national and financial accounting, that is between micro- and macro-information. Among these, we need to mention firstly the IFAC, which issued the IPSAS 22, "Disclosure of Financial Information about the General Government Sector", whose goal is to harmonize the statistical and financial reporting requirements of governments and which recognizes that the disclosure of appropriate information about the general government sector can enhance the transparency of financial reports, and provide for a better understanding of the relationship between financial statements and statistical bases of financial reporting. It is also notable the Australian experience, where the AASB 1049 (AASB 2007) has been issued with the intention of harmonizing general government financial reporting and government financial statistics.

Most studies on the classification of accounting systems are based on explanatory variables such as the socio-economic environment and the accounting practices of measurement and presentation of financial information. However, this research does not focus on these concepts, but on the analysis of the convergence between budgetary and national accounting figures, through the information of each country according to EDP requirements. Thus, we can highlight the work of Jesús and Jorge (2010, 2011a, 2011b) analyzing differences between governmental and national accounting in Portugal and the adjustments in the April 2010 EDP notification tables in Portugal and Spain. We also highlight the work of Fontes Lima and Craig (2005) in measuring the convergence of national accounting in Portugal with International Standards in the period 1977–2003.

To compare the distributions associated with the EU countries, we used the Euclidean distance, as in works such as Archer et al. (1996), Garcia and Gandia (1998), Torres et al. (1998), Aisbitt (2001); Garrido et al. (2002) or Fontes et al. (2005).

In any case, this analysis has to be placed within the framework of international comparability research in the field of public accounting, developed, by authors such as Lüder (1989), Montesinos et al. (1998), Brusca and Condor (2002), Pina and Torres (2003), Balaguer et al. (2003) and et al. (2007); Pina et al. (2009), Christiaens et al. (2010).

This research on the convergence of public and national accounting covers a greater spatial and temporal scope than those previously studied. As we shall see in the next section, our object of study is all EU MSs in the period 1995–2009. Furthermore, this analysis does not focus on specific differences between the two accounting information systems, but all the adjustments are studied by differences established by EUROSTAT in the EDP Notification Tables. Therefore we believe that the research contributes to the process of EU accounting harmonization as it facilitates understanding and comparability of financial reports and key magnitudes of MSs, in order to analyze the financial situation of the EU, both globally and in particular for each country.

Empirical Study of the Differences between Budgetary and National Accounting in the EU Countries

Information on Stability and Fiscal Balance of MSs' Public Finances: Study of the Complete Universe Data

The information obtained corresponds to the EDP Notifications Tables of 27 countries of the EU provided by EUROSTAT and gathered in its database on Governmental Statistics relative to Reporting of Government Deficits and Debt Levels.

As the Commission itself does not produce data directly, there are notification procedures whereby each country provides the Commission with twice yearly deficit and debt levels, along with other related data.

The Reporting of Government Deficits and Debt Levels contains four tables:

- EDP Table 1 "Reporting of government deficit/surplus and debt levels and provision of associated data", provides a summary view showing the net lending/net borrowing for general government and sub-sectors, the general government debt, interest payable and gross fixed capital formation, as well as the GDP of the reference year.
- EDP Table 2 "Provision of the data which explain the transition between the public accounts budget balance and the deficit/surplus" provides the link between the working balances (as reported nationally to parliament) and the ESA95 net lending/borrowing for each sub-sector.
- EDP Table 3 "Provision of the data which explain the contributions of the deficit/surplus and the other relevant factors to the variation in the debt level" makes the link between the net lending/net borrowing and the change in debt.
- EDP Table 4 "Provision of other data in accordance with the statements contained in the Council minutes of 22/11/1993" shows supplementary information.

From all that information presented by MSs, this study focuses on Table 2, which reflects the differences between governmental accounting and national accounts for net lending/borrowing, and allows us to study the differences between the two measures through appropriate adjustments, as well as to indicate in each case the recognition criteria of the working balance: cash, accrual, mixed or other.

Figure 1. Grouping analytical adjustments for EDP.

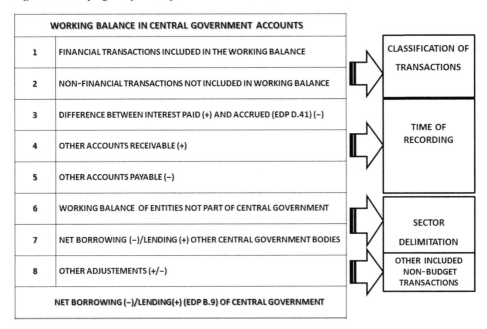

The "working balance" should be adjusted for net lending/borrowing. As shown in Figure 1, these adjustments can be classified into eight groups. In order to facilitate the analysis and interpretation of the data, the adjustments have been classified into four categories:

1. Adjustments resulting from differences in the *classification of transactions* between financial or non-financial public budget and national accounts (1 and 2).
2. Adjustments resulting from differences in the *time of recording, basis of recognition and the time period* (3, 4 and 5).
3. Adjustments resulting from differences in the *delimitation of the sector* (6 and 7).
4. *Other* adjustments (8).

At the time of this study, with respect to the temporal dimension, we had complete and definitive data from 1995 to 2009, and provisional data for the year 2010. The study is based on the definitive data set running from 1995 to 2009. Concerning the space dimension, the available information corresponds to the EU MSs individually, the euro area aggregates, as well as Croatia, Macedonia, Turkey, Norway, Iceland, Switzerland, Canada, the United States and Japan. In our study, the information selected comes from all the countries belonging to the EU, regardless of whether or not they are in the Eurozone.

We must take into account the different stages in the formation of the current EU. There has been a gradual incorporation of countries to reach the EU-27. In some cases this fact affects the period of data available in the database, as already indicated, ranging from 1995 to 2009. In the case of Belgium, Hungary, Malta, Portugal, Spain, Slovenia and the

UK, the available data covers the entire period. However, in other cases, either for reasons of joining the EU, or for other reasons, the available data corresponds to a shorter period.

We should also note that the information offered is in millions of euros, national currency and as a percentage of Gross Domestic Product (GDP). In order to carry out our study we have obtained the information in euros for all countries, regardless of whether or not they belong to the Eurozone.

When there was missing data on adjustments to the working balance for some periods, the amounts have been assigned according to the proportion of these adjustments in local currency in those years in which this information was available. Generally, the ratios represent the average of the years for which data is available, but sometimes the ratio used was from the year closest to the one for which we lacked information. On the other hand, our study has focused on information from the central government sub-sector (sector S.1311) that has greater weight in general government net borrowing/lending.

As noted above, among all the information in the EDP's Notifications, the study has focused on Table 2. Among the 27 EU countries, only Spain and UK declare an accrual basis as a recognition criterion in the budget, while Belgium, Denmark, Cyprus, Luxembourg and Finland declare a mixed basis and the rest of the countries declare a cash basis.

Objectives and Methodology of the Empirical Analysis

According to the research questions set up in the Introduction, in this study we have considered three main objectives:

- Objective 1: To assess the global magnitude of each adjustment, its evolution over time and its relevance for each country.
- Objective 2: To analyze the structure of the adjustments, both globally and in each country, identifying extreme cases and possible concordances.
- Objective 3: To analyze the position of countries according to the structure of the adjustments and their classification in light of the administrative and accounting traditions and management styles in the public sector.

The recorded data of the adjustments between the working balance and net borrowing/lending in EDP terms have three dimensions:

- SPACE: the unit of reference is the 27 countries of the EU.
- TIME: the years with available data.
- COMPONENTS: the adjustments between the working balance and the net borrowing/lending are classified into eight adjustments, with the global adjustment being the result of its integration into a single indicator.

After assessing the aggregate magnitudes of the adjustments in global terms, we make a first approach to their evolution over time. Similarly, we determine the average values in each country for the period for which data is available, highlighting the most remarkable similarities and differences. Finally, in order to quantify some aspects of the structure of the accumulated global adjustment, we provide an indicator of the degree of concentration of the adjustments and the distance between the different EU countries.

The statistical tools used in the study are appropriate to the objectives of the research, and mainly take the form of: designing mechanisms to measure and aggregate the adjustments that ensure uniformity and consistency of results; the construction of a concentration index of the adjustments; and the definition of a distance between the countries to display their relative position and classification.

Classification of the Member States of the EU

One of our main objectives is to specify the methodological differences between the accounting systems of any country in the EU and the ESA95. Likewise, another important objective of the paper is to verify whether administrative and accounting traditions and management styles in the public sector affect in a significant way the convergence between governmental reporting systems in any country.

In order to do this, it is necessary to use a classification of the MSs, selected "a priori" as a frame of reference for analytical purposes. In Table 1, four styles of government are included, representing the different cultural and administrative traditions, generally accepted by literature, as presented by authors like Dunleavy and Hood (1994), Pollitt and Bouckaert, (2004), Montesinos (2004), Benito and Brusca (2004a and 2004b), Torres (2004), Pina et al. (2009) and Nobes (2011). These models are: (1) Anglo-Saxon; (2) Nordic; (3) Continental; and (4) Eastern countries, the second of them considered as a mixed form of the Anglo-Saxon and Continental models.

Table 1. Classification of countries according to the styles of public management and accounting tradition (public sector accounting models)

1. Anglo-Saxon	United Kingdom
	Ireland
	Cyprus
	Malta
2. Nordic	Holland
	Finland
	Denmark
	Sweden
3. Continental	Belgium
	Luxembourg
	France
	Greece
	Italy
	Portugal
	Spain
	Austria
	Germany
4. Eastern	Estonia
	Hungary
	Latvia
	Lithuania
	Poland
	Bulgaria
	Czech Republic
	Romania
	Slovenia
	Slovakia

Results of the Study: Assessment of the Adjustments between Non-Financial Budgetary Balance and Net Borrowing/Lending

Global Assessment

In order to determine the aggregate values of the data that will measure the overall impact of the adjustments, some corrections were necessary so as to facilitate the consistency and comparability of the proposed aggregations. First, because of the great heterogeneity in the data, we have considered that it was necessary to standardize it, dividing the data by the total general government revenue (non-financial resources) as done by Anessi-Pessina and Steccolini (2007) and Brusca and Montesinos (2009). In addition, since the adjustments show discrepancies between two different information systems, all data was to be considered in absolute values, so that the aggregates correspond to accumulated values.

Moreover, to facilitate the manipulation and interpretation of the results, the value of the standardized data was multiplied by 10,000. This data transformation has no impact on the empirical study and has been done to facilitate the reading and interpretation of the data. It is not relevant in comparative terms but should be qualified when we raise other objectives.

The aggregation has been developed in two directions: spatial and temporal. In both cases it was necessary to introduce a weighting determined by non-financial resources to normalize outliers. In the case of aggregating adjustments of the same country over the period, such weighting may not be necessary; however, to ensure consistency between aggregations in space and time, we have finally decided to apply the weight in all cases.

Formally, if we call A_{jit} the recorded amount of adjustment j in country i in the year t, and R_{it} the amount of non-financial resources in that country for the same year, the corresponding relativized adjustment will be determined by:

$$AR_{jit} = \frac{|A_{jit}|}{R_{it}} \times 10000 \tag{1}$$

The adjustment j relativized and aggregated to all the countries in t will be:

$$AR_{jt} = \sum_{i=1}^{27} AR_{jit} \frac{R_{it}}{R_t}. \tag{2}$$

where:

$$R_t = \sum_{i=1}^{27} R_{it} \tag{3}$$

Similarly, the adjustment j relativized and aggregated for a period of T years in a country is:

$$AR_{ji} = \sum_{t=1}^{T} AR_{jit} \frac{R_{it}}{R_i}. \tag{4}$$

where:

$$R_i = \sum_{t=1}^{T} R_{it} \qquad (5)$$

As a result, the global adjustment j for all countries and T years may be determined by:

$$AR_j = \sum_{t=1}^{T} AR_{jt} \frac{R_t}{R} \qquad (6)$$

or

$$AR_j = \sum_{i=1}^{27} AR_{ji} \frac{R_i}{R}. \qquad (7)$$

Where:

$$R = \sum_{i=1}^{27} R_i = \sum_{t=1}^{T} R_t \qquad (8)$$

aggregates non-financial resources for all the countries and the whole period under analysis.

Overall, the incidence of each adjustment calculated as an aggregate for all the countries and over the analyzed period is presented in Table 2. The values included in Table 2 allow the inference that the adjustment with the highest incidence over the period studied is adjustment 1, which is related to the government's budget strategy, as expressed objectives of the different public policies. This budget strategy is different for every country and for each year. Following in incidence is adjustment 8, which generally achieves important values in all countries except Ireland, where its impact is practically nil.

The last positions correspond to adjustment 2, whose value is 23, and adjustment 6 with a value of 0.4. Adjustment 2 was introduced on the EDP's Tables in 2009 and previously was included in adjustment 8. This provides a possible explanation for the low relative importance of adjustment 2 during this period. Meanwhile, adjustment 6 is almost zero for all countries, and is related to the delimitation of the sector. The sector has a very stable structure, and it is consistent with this that the zero adjustment is maintained over time.

Table 2. Aggregate impact of the adjustments for the years available

Adjustments	Average
1. Financial transactions included in the working balance	183
2. Non-financial transactions not included in the working balance	23
3. Difference between interest paid and accrued	30
4. Other accounts receivable	46
5. Other accounts payable	36
6. Working balance of other entities that are not part of central government	0,4
7. Net borrowing/lending of other central government bodies	50
8. Other adjustments	136

Temporal Analysis: Evolution of Adjustments between 1995 and 2009

We now consider the temporal evolution of the adjustments between 1995 and 2009, years for which final data are available. We have taken into account the representation reflected in Figure 2, in which, we represent the years (horizontally) and the values of the adjustments (vertically). This graphic can be complemented with some relevant data from the tendency equation, the values of which are shown in Table 3.

Some relevant results can be highlighted from this information. First, we note the great stability of adjustment 6, which is very consistent given that it is conceptually related to the delimitation of the sector that remains stable. The adjustments related to the accrual basis, which are adjustments 3, 4 and 5, exhibit fairly regular behavior. The adjustment that has the greatest fluctuation is adjustment 1, which is mainly due to the values from

Figure 2. Temporal evolution of the adjustments.

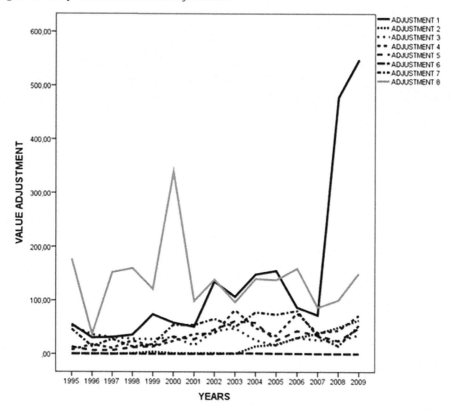

Table 3. Slope of the tendency equations of the aggregated adjustments

Adjustments	AJ. 1	AJ. 2	AJ. 3	AJ. 4	AJ. 5	AJ. 6	AJ. 7	AJ. 8
Slope	25.11	3.96	−0.78	3.97	2.62	0.031	2.01	−1.73

2008 and 2009. This result is very consistent from a conceptual point of view, since this adjustment is related to the budgetary strategy of the different countries, which changes over time.

Apart from the high variations observed in adjustment 1, we emphasize the fluctuations of adjustment 8. This adjustment does not present a significant evolution as seen through its slope. However, it has a strong random component probably due to its very strong residual character. The slope is negative for adjustments 3 and 8, which means a decreasing incidence over time, although the values found are not particularly relevant. Most significant in the analysis of the temporal evolution of the aggregated adjustment is the behavior of adjustment 1 in recent years, which has increased very sharply.

Space Analysis: Incidence of Adjustments by Country

In order to assess the differential impact of various adjustments on the EU countries in the period, we proceeded to calculate the aggregate AR_{ji} of each country for the referenced period. The results are shown in Table 4.

An analysis of the values included in Table 4 reveals the following interesting results:

Table 4. Relativized adjustments to non-financial resources for each country

Country	ADJU1	ADJU2	ADJU3	ADJU4	ADJU5	ADJU6	ADJU7	ADJU8
Austria	252	32	33	71	24	0	14	148
Belgium	735	0	5	48	39	0,16	19	116
Bulgaria	10	0	50	102	119	31	124	302
Cyprus	821	0	11	69	18	0	27	40
Czech Rep.	126	18	21	277	27	4	177	332
Denmark	75	5	10	81	130	12	25	90
Estonia	59	0	2	141	104	0	107	144
Finland	281	0	96	42	6	0	103	87
France	150	29	13	37	52	0	169	27
Germany	323	0	15	40	11	0	66	69
Greece	61	84	77	166	125	0	17	447
Hungary	227	0	82	96	94	0	181	344
Ireland	49	0	47	75	38	0	393	2
Italy	223	0	68	83	65	0	0	141
Latvia	85	26	59	249	252	0	68	702
Lithuania	115	154	25	187	242	0	154	114
Luxembourg	88	0	17	113	165	0	305	69
Malta	109	106	14	49	59	0	213	74
Holland	760	0	62	83	44	0	7	100
Poland	63	485	63	169	106	0	89	90
Portugal	115	0	88	71	105	0	100	215
Romania	364	0	36	130	186	0	303	404
Slovakia	39	485	73	155	30	0	335	298
Slovenia	43	20	34	146	196	0	197	153
Spain	63	86	89	0	0	0	35	686
Sweden	355	0	29	156	58	0	16	151
United Kingdom	0	0	0	0	0	0	0	57
Total	183	23	30	46	36	0.40	50	136

1. The exceptional nature of the United Kingdom should be noted, in which none of the adjustments have an effect except adjustment 8.
2. Adjustment 6 has a zero incidence in almost all countries, with the exception of Bulgaria and Denmark, in which a significant effect is detected.
3. Adjustment 2 exhibits irregular behavior among the countries, and in fact has a zero incidence in 15 of the 27 countries while also reaching very high values in six of them.
4. In the case of Spain, there is a null value for adjustments 4 and 5, related to the recognition criteria. These can be connected to the implementation of accrual basis in determining the working balance.

Considering that one objective of this paper is to determine the possible link between accounting tradition and public management styles of the EU countries, and the level of incidence of the adjustments, an aggregation of adjustments for the four groups of countries set out in Table 1 was carried out. The aggregation process was performed, as previously described, using the weights that define the non-financial resources. The results are shown in Table 5.

An analysis of the values given in Table 5 highlights some observations:

- In Anglo-Saxon countries we note, as expected, the small size of the adjustments related to the implementation of accrual basis, while adjustment 7, which relates to the sector delimitation, and mainly adjustment 8, have the greatest weight, with the latter being the only adjustment collected in the UK.
- In the Nordic group, the situation of adjustments relating to the classification of operations is highlighted, so that adjustment 1 is the most important of all the adjustments in this group, while adjustment 2 has the smallest impact. Additionally, this group presents the highest average value for adjustment 6 related to the sector delimitation, because, as already noted, the value reported by Denmark is significantly higher, due to the fact that this value is zero for all the other countries in this group.
- The Continental Group is the one with an average value of the adjustments closest to the values obtained for the whole EU. This is quite possibly due to two circumstances: first, a number of very high aggregate financial resources and, secondly, the absence of statistically unique countries.
- In the Eastern countries, the importance of the adjustments related to the recognition criteria, adjustments 3, 4 and 5, are higher than in the other groups of countries. It is also worth noting the importance of adjustment 2 on the classification of operations, which has little impact on other groups.

Table 5. Aggregated adjustments for groups of countries with the same administrative and accounting tradition

	Adjust 1	Adjust 2	Adjust 3	Adjust 4	Adjust 5	Adjust 6	Adjust 7	Adjust 8
Anglo-Saxon	5	0.3	2	3	2	0.0	15	55
Nordic	498	1	48	95	59	2.2	22	108
Continental	231	24	42	50	44	0.0	70	190
Eastern	139	194	53	161	114	1.9	166	243
Total	183	23	30	46	36	0.4	50	136

Structure of Accumulated Adjustment and Positioning of Countries

In this section, the focus is on the integrated effect of all the adjustments as a unique magnitude resulting from the accumulation of the eight components, with an emphasis on the vector determined by the weight corresponding to each adjustment.

Our interest in discovering the different behaviors among the countries and between the adjustments in each country leads us to focus on the structure of the accumulated adjustment in each country for the entire period, regardless of the initial values in each adjustment.

In order to increase the statistical robustness of the results, aggregated calculations were performed on all the years for which data was available, something that certainly could be revised if the intention were to give greater prominence to the temporal domain.

For our purposes, given a reference period that includes T years and a country i, the relative weight of the adjustment j is identified through the expression p_{ji}, which is defined by the ratio of the corresponding aggregated adjustment for the years available and the accumulative aggregated adjustment for the same years for each country.

This is formally defined as:

$$p_{ji} = \frac{\sum_{t=1}^{T} |A_{jit}|}{\sum_{t=1}^{T} AG_{it}} \times 100 \qquad (9)$$

in which A_{jit} is the value defined in section 7, AG_{it} is the accumulative adjustment in country i in year t, and T is the number of years for which data is available, verifying that:

$$\sum_{j=1}^{8} p_{ji} = 100 \qquad (10)$$

Similarly, for a period of T years, we define the weight of adjustment j in the whole universe comprised by the 27 countries studied and is named p_j. The relative weight of adjustment j in all these countries is determined by the expression:

$$p_j = \frac{\sum_{i=1}^{27} \sum_{t=1}^{T} |A_{jit}|}{\sum_{i=1}^{27} \sum_{t=1}^{T} AG_{it}} \times 100 \qquad (11)$$

verifying that:

$$\sum_{j=1}^{8} p_j = 100 \qquad (12)$$

In order to facilitate the analysis of the structure of the adjustments in each country, we calculated an indicator of the degree of concentration of the adjustments. For each country, we seek to determine whether the incidence of adjustment is more or less uniform, or, if not, whether the accumulated adjustment is concentrated in a small number of components. The indicator that we propose can be stated as the Euclidean distance between the weight vector associated with each country and the vector 0 representing the absence of adjustments. Its expression is:

$$CR_i = D(i,0) = \sqrt{\sum_{j=1}^{8} p_{ji}^2} \tag{13}$$

Alternatively, the distance could have been established based on the uniform distribution, which is characterized by the vector (100/8) * 1, where 1 represents the unit vector of dimension 8. However, the results would be equivalent to those obtained by referring to the vector 0.

The concentration ratio CR has a range between a minimum value of 35 in the case of uniform distribution and a maximum value of 100 in the case of a country for which only one adjustment has been registered. The highest degree of CR means the highest convergence between the two accounting information systems. Table 6 provides the CR of the accumulated adjustment for each country obtained as proposed.

Some relevant results from the values shown in Table 6 are as follows:

1. Predictably, the UK has the maximum concentration, since this country is only affected by adjustment 8.
2. There are some countries with high levels of concentration and similar magnitude, such as Ireland, Cyprus and Spain. However, the structure of their adjustments is

Table 6. Concentration ratios

Country	Concentration ratio
Austria	50
Belgium	51
Bulgaria	45
Cyprus	76
Czech Rep.	48
Denmark	45
Estonia	49
Finland	55
France	51
Germany	58
Greece	55
Hungary	46
Ireland	67
Italy	50
Latvia	54
Lithuania	41
Luxembourg	51
Malta	47
Holland	49
Poland	46
Portugal	44
Romania	45
Slovakia	48
Slovenia	44
Spain	69
Sweden	50
United Kingdom	100

different because, in each case, the concentration is located on different components. In Cyprus the maximum weight is located on adjustment 1, in Ireland on adjustment 7 and in Spain on adjustment 8.

3. Countries with the lowest concentration of the accumulated adjustment are Lithuania, Portugal, Romania, Bulgaria and Denmark. We conclude that the accounting implications of the differences between government accounting systems and national accounts are similar in the eight concepts set out in Figure 1.

Returning to the aim of analyzing the possible link between accounting adjustments and the administrative and accounting tradition of the countries, we have proceeded to calculate CR for the four groups presented in Table 1. The results are shown in Table 7.

We want to emphasize the high degree of concentration on the Anglo-Saxon group and the low concentration on the Eastern group (bear in mind that the minimum concentration corresponds to 35). The Anglo-Saxon group, as noted, polarizes all differences into one accumulative adjustment, while the latter group has weights distributed among all the adjustments or components. The Nordic and Continental groups have an intermediate concentration index.

We found that the CR of the Continental group is 49, which is similar to 48, the adjustments for aggregates for all EU countries. This finding strengthens the result in Table 5, in which the Continental group has a structure closer to that corresponding to the EU overall.

The CR obtained for the different countries allowed us to establish comparisons between them, but are insufficient to analyze their relative positioning with respect to the structure of the adjustments. For example, Ireland and Spain have a similar rate, but the adjustments with higher incidence are different. In Ireland the higher incidence corresponds to adjustment 7 and in Spain it corresponds to 8.

In order to complement the perspective offered by CR, we have proceeded to establish a criterion of similarity between countries based on the distance between their adjustments. We have chosen the Euclidean distance, which between two countries i and i' is defined by the expression:

$$D(i, i') = \sqrt{\sum_{j=1}^{8} (p_{ji} - p_{ji'})^2} \qquad (14)$$

The analysis of the distances provides some interesting results:

– The UK has a structure far away from other countries, being its average Euclidean distance to the rest of 88.7.

Table 7. Concentration ratios in the groups of countries with the same administrative and accounting tradition

Countries	Concentration ratios
Anglo-Saxon	70
Nordic	63
Continental	49
Eastern	40

Table 8. Average distances between the structures of the countries with the same administrative and accounting tradition

	Anglo-Saxon	Nordic	Continental	Eastern
Anglo-Saxon	0	78	49	50
Nordic	78	0	31	53
Continental	49	31	0	28
Eastern	50	53	28	0

- Other countries with a structure of adjustments away from others are Cyprus, Ireland and Spain. In fact their average distances are 64.9, 64.6 and 59.2. They should all be considered as atypical, since the distances between them are very high.
- The greatest similarities in the structure of adjustments are located between Holland, Belgium, Italy and Sweden. We also found some reduced distances, such as in the case of Portugal and Hungary.

In order to establish the possible identifying singularities of the groups that determine the administrative and accounting tradition, we have also calculated the distances between the four groups of countries. The results are shown in Table 8.

Table 8 shows that Anglo-Saxons and Nordics have very distant structures, which was shown by the corresponding CR.

Groups with a similar structure of adjustments are the Eastern and Continental groups, and to a lesser degree the Continental and the Nordic countries. However, consistent with what is suggested by CR, the most relevant is the proximity between the Continental group and the other two groups, while the distance between the Eastern and Nordic groups is high.

Conclusions

The aim of this paper is to contribute to the analysis of governmental accounting harmonization in EU MSs, as a useful tool to improve the comparability of financial reports and provide a better understanding of the relationship between budget information and statistical bases of financial reporting. The analysis and classification of differences between budgetary and economic and financial information have been carried out for individual countries and groups of them, as well as for the EU as a whole.

From the EDP Notification Tables, we carried out a statistical analysis aimed at measuring aspects of the discrepancy between the non-financial budgetary result and net borrowing/lending. The major conclusions derived from this analysis are:

1. In global terms, for the entire group of countries analyzed and the period between 1995 and 2009, the specific adjustments with the greatest impact are adjustment 1, related to differences in the classification of operations, and adjustment 8 "Other adjustments", while adjustment 6, related to the delimitation of the sector, is the lowest incidence adjustment.
2. From the analysis of the temporal evolution of adjustments, we note that accruals have a quite regular behavior along the period. On the other hand, adjustment 1 is the

one with greater fluctuations, an observation that is consistent from a conceptual standpoint, since this setting is related to the budgetary strategy of the different countries.
3. From the space analysis we can highlight that:
   - In the Anglo-Saxon countries, the insignificance of the adjustments related to the implementation of accrual basis stands out, while the 7th and especially the 8th adjustments, respectively related to sector delimitation and other adjustments, have the greatest weight.
   - In the Nordic countries, adjustments 1 and 6 stand out, related to the classification of operations and sector delimitation.
   - The Continental group has an incidence of adjustments closest to the overall average across the EU. Among the causes, we highlight the high value of the non-financial resources aggregate and the absence of singular values between the components of the adjustment.
   - In the Eastern countries, we underline the relative importance of the adjustments that have little impact in the other groups. Particularly, the adjustments related to recognition criteria and adjustment 2 on the classification of operations.
4. The construction of a Concentration Ratio of the adjustments allows us to know the convergence degree between the two accounting information systems. It has revealed polarized behavior in the Anglo-Saxon group, where the magnitude of the adjustment is located on a single different component for each country. This points out the small difference between the two information systems and highlights the important influence of the Anglo-Saxon environment in the international public accounting and the national accounting systems. On the other hand, the Eastern group presents a greater distribution of adjustment between different concepts. This means that the member countries of this group have the greatest divergence between the two information systems.
5. In general, as regards the nature of the discrepancy between the accounting systems, it appears that the Anglo-Saxon group has considerable distance from other EU countries, while the countries in the Continental group occupy an intermediate position that is more or less equidistant from the groups that form the Nordic and Eastern countries.

At the end of the day, this study shows the existence of significant diversity among the EU budgetary reports, as concluded in the paper, after a sound interpretation of adjustments. The harmonization of national financial reporting by means of international accounting standards will be, no doubt, the next step for an effective implementation of financial transparency and comparability in Europe.

References

Aisbitt, S., 2001, Measurement of Harmony of Financial Reporting within and between countries: the Case of the Nordic Countries. *European Accounting Review*, **10**(1), 51–72.

Anessi-Pessina, E. and Steccolini, I., 2007, Effects of Budgetary and Accruals Accounting Coexistence: Evidence from Italian Local Governments. *Financial Accountability & Management*, **23**(2), 113–131.

Archer, S., Delvaille, P. and Mcleay, S., 1996, A Statistical Model of International Accounting Harmonisation. *ABACUS*, **32**(1), 1–29.

Australian Accounting Standard Board, AASB, 2007, Whole of Government and General Government Sector Financial Reporting. AASB 1049.

Balaguer Coll, T., Fuertes Fuertes, I. and Illueca Muñoz, M., 2003, La Armonización Contable en las CCLL. Europeas: La Influencia del Entorno. *Institut Valencià D'investigacions Econòmiques (Ive)*. Documentos de Trabajo. Serie EC. Nº 13.

Bastida, F. J. and Benito, B., 2007, Central Government budget practices and transparency: an international comparison. *Public Administration*, **85**(3), 667–716.

Benito, B., Brusca, I. and Montesinos, V., 2007, The harmonization of government financial information systems: The role of the IPSASs. *International Review of Administrative Sciences*, **73**(2), 293–317.

Benito Lopez, B. and Bastida Albaladejo, F. J., 2009, Budget Transparency, fiscal performance and political turnout: an international approach. *Public Administration Review*, **69**, 403–417.

Benito López, B. and Brusca Alijarde, I., 2004a, International Classification of Local Government Accounting Systems. *Journal of Comparative Policy Analysis: Research and Practice*, **6**(1), 57–80.

Benito López, B. and Brusca Alijarde, I., 2004b, Análisis comparativo de la contabilidad pública a nivel internacional. *Presupuesto y Gasto Público*, **37**, ISSN 0210–5977, 189–210.

Brusca Alijarde, I., 2010, Treinta años de investigación en Contabilidad y Gestión Pública en España. *Revista de Contabilidad*, **13**(2), 175–210.

Brusca Alijarde, I. and Condor Lopez, V., 2002, Towards the harmonisation of local accounting systems in the international context. *Financial Accountability & Management*, **18**(2), 129–162.

Brusca Alijarde, I. and Montesinos Julve, V., 2009, Accrual versus cash basis in the public sector: where are the differences in practice?. *12th biennial Comparative International Governmental Accounting Research (CIGAR) Conference*, Módena, May 2009.

Christiaens, J., Reyniers, B. and Rollé, C., 2010, Impact of IPSAS on reforming governmental financial information systems: A comparative study. *International Review of Administrative Sciences*, **76**(3), 537–554.

Cordes, U., 1996, The 1995 European System of National Accounts (ESA), Governmental Accounting Reforms and the Government Sector´s Micro-Macro Link. In Lüder, K. (ed.) *"Recent Developments in Comparative International Governmental Accounting Research"*. Speyer, Forschungsinstitut für Öffentliche Verwaltung bei der Hochschule für Verwaltungswissenschaften Speyer: 3–20.

Dunleavy, P. and Hood, C. C., 1994, From Old Public Administration to New Public Management. *Public Money and Management*, **14**(2), 9–16.

Ernst & Young, 2012, *Overview and Comparison of Public Accounting and Auditing Practices in the 27 EU Member States*. Final Report prepared for Eurostat. Available at http://epp.eurostat.ec.europa.eu/portal/page/portal/government_finance_statistics/documents/study_on_public_accounting_and_auditing_2012.pdf (accessed 15 March 2013).

European Commission, 2013, Towards implementing harmonised public sector accounting standards in the MSs. Available at http://epp.eurostat.ec.europa.eu/portal/page/portal/government_finance_statistics/documents/1_EN_ACT_part1_v5.pdf (accessed 17 March 2013).

Fontes, A., Lima, L. and Craig, R., 2005, Measuring convergence of National Accounting Standards with International Financial Reporting Standards. *Accounting Forum*, **29**, 415–436.

Garcia Benau, M. A. and Gandía Cabedo, J. L., 1998, Análisis del grado de armonización europeo basado en los sistemas contables. *Revista Española de Financiación y Contabilidad*, **XXVII**(97), 951–978.

Garrido, P., Leon, A. and Zorio, A., 2002, Measurement of formal harmonization progress: The IASC experience. *The International Journal of Accounting*, **37**, 1–26.

International Public Sector Accounting Standards Board (IPSASB), 2005, *International Public Sector Accounting Standards (IPSASs) and Statistical Bases of Financial Reporting: An Analysis of Differences and Recommendations for Convergence*. Research Report, New York.

International Public Sector Accounting Standards Board (IPSASB), 2012, IPSAS 22 – Disclosure of Financial Information About the General Government Sector.

International Public Sector Accounting Standards Board (IPSASB), 2013, Conceptual Framework for General Purpose Financial Reporting by Public Sector Entities (Chapters 1–4), New York.

Jesús, M. A. and Jorge, S., 2010, From Governmental Accounting to National Accounting: implications on the Portuguese Central Government Deficit. *Revista Notas Económicas*, **31**, pg. 2 4–47, Faculdade de Economia da Universidade de Coimbra.

Jesús, M. A. and Jorge, S., (2011a), Adjustments from Governmental Accounting to National Accounts: Impact on the Iberian Countries' Central Government Deficit. *XIII Accounting and Auditing Congress*, Oporto.

Jesús, M. A. and Jorge, S., (2011b), Governmental Accounting versus National Accounts –implications of different accounting bases on EU member-States Central Government deficit/surplus, in: *13th Biennial CIGAR Conference.*

Jones, R., 2000, National Accounting, Government Budgeting and Accounting Discipline. *Financial Accountability & Management*, **16**(2), 101–116.

Jones, R., 2003, Measuring and Reporting The Nation's Finances: Statistics and Accounting. *Public Money & Management*, **23**(1), 21–28.

Jones, R. and Lüder, K., 1996, The relationship between National Accounting and Governmental Accounting: state of the art and comparative perspectives. *Research in Governmental and Non-profit Accounting*, **9**, 59–78.

Keuning, S. and Tongeren, D., 2004, The Relationship between Government Accounts and National Accounts, with special reference to Netherlands. *Review of Income and Wealth*, **50**(2), 167–179.

Lande, E., 2000, Macro Accounting and Accounting Relationships in France. *Financial Accountability and Management*, **16**(2), 151–165.

Lienert, I. and Moo Kyung, J., 2004, The Legal Framework for Budget Systems: An International Comparison. *OECD Journal of Budgeting*. Special Issue, **4**(3).

Lüder, K., 1989, *Comparative Government Accounting Study: Interim Summary Report, Revised ed.* (Speyer: Speyerer Forschungsberichte) No. 76.

Lüder, K., 2000, National Accounting, Governmental Accounting and Cross-country Comparisons of Government Financial Condition. *Financial Accountability & Management*, **16**(2), 117–128.

Lüder, K. and Jones, R. (Eds), 2003, *Reforming Governmental Accounting and Budgeting in Europe* (Frankfurt am Main: Fachverlag Moderne Wirtschaft).

Montesinos Julve, V., 2004, Rapport sur la situation de la comptabilité et son processus d´harmonisation dans les pays de la région méditerranéenne. In *Programme regional pour la promotion des instruments el mécanismes du Marché euro-méditerranéen*. Volumen II. European Institute of Public Administration/Institut Européen d ´Administration Publique- Centre Européen des Régions, pp. 145–164.

Montesinos Julve, V. and Vela Bargues, J. M., 2000, Governmental accounting in Spain and the European Monetary Union: a critical perspective. *Financial Accountability & Management*, **16**(2), 267–4424.

Montesinos Julve, V. Pina Martínez, V., Torres Pradas, L. and Vela Bargues, J.M., 1998, Análisis comparado de los principios y prácticas contables de los sistemas contables públicos de los países de la OCDE: una aproximación empírica. *Revista Española de Financiación y Contabilidad*, **XXVII**(96), 787–820.

Nobes, C., 2011, IFRS Practices and the Persistence of Accounting System Classification. *ABACUS*, **47**(3), 267–283.

Pina, V. and Torres, L., 2003, Reshaping public sector accounting: an international comparative view. *Canadian Journal of Administrative Sciences*, **20**(4), 334–350.

Pina, V., Torres, L. and Royo, S., 2010, Is E-Government Promoting Convergence Towards More Accountable Local Governments?. *International Public Management Journal*, **13**(4), 350–380.

Pina, V., Torres, L. and Yetano, A., 2009, Accrual Accounting in EU Local Governments: One Method, Several Approaches. *European Accounting Review*, **18**(4), 65–807.

Pollitt, C. and Bouckaert, G., 2004, *Public Management Reform: A Comparative Analysis* (Oxford: Oxford University Press).

Statistical Office of the European Communities (EUROSTAT), 1996, *European System of National and Regional Accounts* (ESA95), Luxembourg.

Statistical Office of the European Communities (EUROSTAT), 2002, *Manual on Government Deficit and Debt.* Available at http://europa.eu.int/.Luxemburgo: Oficina de Publicaciones Oficiales de las Comunidades Europeas. 5th ed. published in 2013. Available at http://epp.eurostat.ec.europa.eu/portal/page/portal/product_details/publication?p_product_code=KS-RA-13-001 (accessed 19 March 2013).

Torres Pradas, L., 2004, Trajectories in public administration reforms in European Continental countries. *Australian Journal of Public Administration*, **63**(3), 99–112.

A Comparative Study of Asset-based Policy in Asia: Korea, Singapore, and Taiwan

CHANG-KEUN HAN

ABSTRACT *Asian countries have implemented inclusive asset-based policies. Using a theoretical framework, this study evaluates the extent to which the asset-based policies in Korea, Singapore, and Taiwan are inclusive. The framework of 'inclusiveness' of asset-based policy has four components such as universal, progressive, life-long, and adequate. The study found that, compared to asset-based policies in Korea and Taiwan, those in Singapore have strengths in universality and life-long feature. However, asset-based policies in Singapore have a weakness in progressiveness. This paper concludes by presenting policy implications for inclusive asset-based policy.*

Introduction

Over the last two decades, many countries around the world have adopted 'inclusive' asset-based policies (OECD 2003). 'Inclusive' asset-based policy can be defined as social policy providing institutional opportunities of saving to not only the haves but also the have-nots. Advocates for inclusive asset-based policy claim that the institutional opportunities should be universal, progressive, life-long, and adequate (Sherraden 2005: 2; Han 2009b).

Originating from the western context, 'inclusive' asset-based policies have been recently experimented with in Asian countries where saving rates are generally high. Asian countries have high saving rates compared to countries in the other regions (World Bank 1999; Adams and Prazmowski 2003; Baharumshah, Thanoon and Rashid 2003). The possible explanations for the high saving rates in Asia may be the combination of culture, demographics, government policies, financial institutions, and high interest rates (Adams and Prazmowski 2003). Despite the high average saving rates, wealth in Asian countries is also highly skewed to the right, which means that assets are concentrated to the haves. In addition, a large percentage of people in Asian countries have few assets or negative net worth because total debts exceed total assets. For example, in South Korea (hereafter Korea), the top 10 per cent of households holds about 52 per cent of total net wealth in the society in 2006. In addition, it was estimated that the top 20 per cent of the income distribution hold 7.3 times the amount of financial assets compared to the bottom 20 per cent in Korea (Sherraden and Han 2007).

It is noteworthy that inclusive asset-based policies and programs have been recently adopted in Asian countries such as Korea, Singapore, and Taiwan. However, each country has a different history and development stage of inclusive asset-based policies. In addition, they have different institutional features which may influence different impacts on saving and asset accumulation. This study aims to examine inclusive asset-based policies in Korea, Singapore, and Taiwan in terms of the extent to which the policies in each country meet the four conditions (universal, progressive, life-long, and adequate) of inclusive asset-based policy suggested by Sherraden (2005). For a balanced understanding of inclusive asset-based policies, this paper also provides critics and limitations of asset-based policies, and discusses future directions for more inclusive asset-based policies in Asian countries.

Asset Building as Social Policy

The primary function of income support policies is to maintain the consumption of people without sufficient income. Income support, on its own, has been an effective policy when the economy provided stable jobs in the long term. Income support policies, however, were not designed for development and capabilities. In short, income support is a passive social policy supporting citizens' consumption, but not designed to increase their capabilities (Sherraden 2003, 2005). Furthermore, it has been a major oversight of the traditional social policies that building the assets of people at the bottom has been largely ignored (Sherraden 1991).

Asset building matters to individuals, families, and communities for a variety of reasons. Assets buffer economic shocks, break the cycle of intergenerational poverty, and promote economic and social development. Asset ownership may increase feelings of financial security and enhance future orientation that likely results in behavioral changes. Michael Sherraden, a proponent of inclusive asset-based policy, discusses asset effects concisely by saying, "While income feeds people's stomachs, assets change their heads" (Sherraden 1991: 6).

The idea of asset-based policies is not new. Countries have initiated asset-based policies promoting ownership of pensions, housing, business, and land. However, existing asset-based policy often fails to reduce a growing asset gap between the rich and the poor. Making it worse, the current forms of asset-based policies have contributed to exaggerating asset inequality. Sherraden (2002) explains asset inequality through regressive tax policies where the well-off get most of the tax benefits for asset building. Therefore, it will be a policy challenge to introduce inclusive asset-based policies providing asset-building opportunities for disadvantaged populations in particular.

Theory and Progress of Inclusive Asset-based Policy

Institutional Saving Theory

Institutional features of policy and program influence savings outcomes. Several institutional features influencing asset accumulation have been proposed: access, expectations, information, incentives, facilitation, and restrictions (Beverly and Sherraden 1999; Schreiner and Sherraden 2007). Easy *access* to banking institutions can significantly improve savings outcomes by decreasing transaction costs. People with knowledge (*information*) of how to save are inclined to behave differently from those without (Lusardi 2003). For example, people with knowledge of saving are aware of their financial choices and their outcomes (Schreiner and Sherraden 2007). Matching grants, tax-free earnings, and rebates can be types of *incentives* stimulating more savings (Clancy et al. 2006). Positive relationships between matching incentives and saving outcomes are found in retirement pension accounts (Munnell, Sunden and Taylor 2001/2002) and 529 savings plans (Clancy et al. 2006). *Facilitation* means assistance encouraging active participation and savings. Schreiner and Sherraden (2007) regard facilitation as a key feature of contractual saving programs. The goal of savings (*expectations*) can be institutionalized. The match cap is regarded as a target savings amount, which often becomes a goal for participants (Schreiner and Sherraden 2007). Compared to other institutional factors, *restrictions* limit certain types of actions or impose limits so that participants are more likely to achieve saving goals.

Empirical evidence supports the hypothesis that institutional features matter for saving. Using data from low-income participants in individual development accounts in the US, studies have found that institutional features in IDAs have stronger explanation power in savings than other socioeconomic characteristics and social stratification (Curley, Ssewamala and Sherraden 2005; Han and Sherraden 2009).

Progress

Since Sherraden's (1991) proposal, there has been modest progress toward more inclusive asset-based policies in many countries. Two types of asset-based policies have been developed. First, IDAs for working poor have been initiated in the US in the 1990s. Key features of IDAs include match rates that range from 1:1 to 8:1, financial education, matching caps, designated saving purposes such as buying a house, investing in education, and starting a small business. Influenced by the preliminary success of IDAs in the US, IDA-type programs have now been adopted in many countries including Canada, Australia, Peru, Uganda, Taiwan, and Korea (OECD 2003).

Second, a more universal asset-based policy for children in general began in the UK in 2005. In 2001, former Prime Minister Tony Blair proposed the Child Trust Fund for all children, with progressive funding. Canada, Singapore, and Korea have comparable asset-based policies for children (Loke and Sherraden 2008). In the US, universal and progressive accounts for children at birth are now being tested in a demonstration project, the Saving for Education, Entrepreneurship, and Downpayment (SEED) initiative (Loke and Sherraden 2008).

Key Features of Inclusive Asset-based Policy

Inclusive asset-based policy can be justified in that asset ownership can lead to the development of individuals, families, and community. Indeed, asset accumulation is the way families improve their well-being over time and across generations. Reflecting these positive functions of asset building, the best alternative social policy will move beyond the idea of consumption as well-being toward what Amartya Sen (1999) identifies as capabilities. Building people's assets is one policy pathway to increase capabilities and reduce the trade-off between economic growth and social development.

Four principles guide 'inclusive' asset-based policies (see Table 1). First, opportunities for asset accumulation should be open to all people, regardless of income, age, race/ethnicity, gender, etc. In addition to public awareness emphasizing the importance of saving and asset accumulation, social policies should decrease barriers to saving. In particular, since low-income households are likely to be excluded from the opportunities of saving and asset ownership, more attention should be paid to expanding access to saving opportunities for low-income households. Second, asset-based policy should be *progressive* in that greater incentives and benefits should be provided to low-income households and minorities. Progressive mechanisms include matched savings by participants, tax-free earnings, and rebates. Third, saving is a *life-long* process. When saving starts as early as possible, life chances for economic and social development will be brighter. Children in households with home and other types of assets (e.g. financial and non-financial assets) were found to have more positive child outcomes in mental health and education than asset-poor children (William Shanks et al. 2010). These findings support the introduction of Child Development Accounts (CDAs) in several countries. The life-long process of asset accumulation also suggests that saving continues from birth to death, and that assets should be portable across the life-course. Last, *adequacy* is more complicated because it is not easy to determine how much of savings are adequate for saving purposes (e.g. buying a house, starting a business, etc.). Rather, saving programs should help people save enough to achieve self-determined goals.

Limitations of Asset-based Policy

Before the study explains key features of asset-based policies in Asia, it is necessary to briefly review several criticisms and limitations of asset-based policy. Some

Table 1. Framework of inclusive asset-building policy

Universal	Progressive
• Equal opportunities for asset accumulation • Open access (decrease barriers) • Increase scale	• Incentives for low-income households • Matching • Tax exemption or low tax

Life-long	Adequate
• From birth to death • Portability • Continuity	• Adequacy for future investment • Adequacy for economic development • Adequacy for social development

scholars have discussed critiques of asset-based welfare (Gamble and Prabhakar 2005; Gokhale and Tanner 2006; Prabhakar 2009). Although this study does not intend to cover all the critiques in detail, several critical issues need to be addressed for a balanced view of inclusive asset-based policies. More importantly, the critiques suggest that advocates need to provide robust empirical evidence supporting inclusive asset-based policies.

First of all, this study focuses on four fundamental critiques of asset-based welfare. First, there is a controversial question about whether the poor actually can save. Since the poor struggle to make ends meet, they are likely to have no money left over for saving. Sherraden (1991: 208) said, "When the incentives are right, and the institutional mechanisms are present, at least some people will find a way to save." However, many critics still question the possibility of saving among the poor.

Second, rationales for inclusive asset-based policies are founded on asset effects which suggest that owning assets is likely to lead to better outcomes in thinking and behaviors (Sherraden 1991). However, "The most obvious question is whether such an effect actually exists, and evidence is important for assessing this" (Prabhakar 2009: 57). Although empirical evidence has been accumulated to support positive asset effects in recent decades (e.g. Scanlon 2001; Zhan and Sherraden 2003; Meyer, Masa and Zimmerman 2010), Prabhakar (2009) still argues that definitive judgments about asset effects cannot be made.

Third, funding for asset-based policies for all has remained a real problem. Sherraden (1991) suggests that regressive government subsidies should be reduced and used for asset policies for all. However, it is true that a universal asset-based policy is expensive. For example, to implement the KidSave account program awarding $2,000 seed money to families in the name of each newborn child in the US, it was projected to cost $8 billion in 2006 and $266 billion during the next 75 years (Gokhale and Tanner 2006). The estimated cost would be considerable political pressure and may hamper the introduction of the asset-based policy.

Last, a critical challenge of inclusive asset-based policy is whether poor countries can afford asset-based policies for the huge numbers of poor people. It is true that even developed countries have struggled to expand inclusive asset-based policies to all citizens. Indeed, the scope of IDAs and CDAs in the US is small compared to the total population. Underdeveloped countries may face more challenges in adopting inclusive asset-based policies in terms of not enough budgets, underdeveloped infrastructure for social policy, and unstable politics. However, some inclusive asset-based policies experimented with in developing countries, despite the small scales, can have significant impacts on the expansion of asset-based policies in underdeveloped countries (Meyer et al. 2010).

Here, this study presents a few empirical findings suggesting limitations of asset-based policies. First, voluntary self-selection into a saving program may be a key feature of inclusive asset-based policy. While it seems that all eligible persons participate in a saving program, it was found that some applicants for a saving program may not join at the end. Using a sample of IDA participants, Rothwell and Han (2010) found that the presence of a child, negative net worth, and vehicle non-ownership are related to second thoughts preventing persons eligible for a saving program enrolling in the program. The findings suggest that relatively advantaged persons in terms of asset ownership are more likely to use the opportunities of saving in inclusive asset-based policies.

Second, who can actually save? Participants who opened accounts may face difficulties in saving. Schreiner and Sherraden (2005) examined who has a higher probability of dropping out, defined by someone who saved less than $100 during the IDA participation. They found that education and marital status matter for the likelihood of dropping out. Persons with higher education and married couples are likely to save more. They also found that participants with checking accounts, their own homes, and cars are less likely to drop out of the program. These findings may suggest that participants who have a better financial situation are more likely to get benefits from inclusive asset-based policies.

Last, insecure job status among low-income household may prevent saving. Using longitudinal data of IDA participants, Han (2009b) found that participants who experienced unemployment during the four-year participation period saved less than their counterparts who were employed throughout the period. The unemployed may struggle to make ends meet and face financial strains. As a result, the unemployed cannot find resources available to deposit in a savings program (Han 2009b).

Inclusive Asset-based Policies in Asia

Despite some possible challenges and limitations of asset-based policies, the policies have been expanded worldwide. Here, the study focuses on asset-based policies in three Asian countries: Korea, Singapore, and Taiwan.

Korea

Since the 1990s, Korean social policy has undergone significant changes. Two phenomena may explain these changes: the 1997 financial crisis and the advent of a more politically liberal administration. Under these circumstances, policy makers have paid increasing attention to social investment strategies which have features of integration of social policy and economic policy, development of human potentials, preventive policies, and employment-oriented policies (Han 2006). Policymakers in Korea assume that asset-based policies may play an important role in creating conditions and opportunities for both economic and social development (Han 2006; Sherraden and Han 2007).

Asset-based policies were first discussed at the 56th Korean National Meeting in November 2004. Since their introduction, enthusiasm for asset-based policies has grown steadily in Korean government circles (Han 2006; Sherraden and Han 2007). In particular, CDAs implemented in April 2007 were viewed not only as a mechanism for encouraging asset accumulation for low-income households, but also as a policy for increasing equal opportunities through development of individual capabilities. While CDAs were introduced as part of broader efforts to tackle asset inequality, polarization in the labor market, and plummeting birth rates in Korea, potential policy effects of CDAs may include human capital investment and an increase in economic participation (Han 2006; Sherraden and Han 2007; Sherraden et al. 2008).

Child Development Accounts. CDAs started targeting children on welfare, children without parents, and children with disabilities. In the long term, the Korean government planned to encompass all children born into low- and middle-income households, approximately 50% of all Korean newborns (Sherraden et al. 2008). Parents and/or sponsors contribute to the CDA. The maximum matching deposit into a CDA is approximately US$30. Contributions are then matched 1:1 by the Korean government. In total, the maximum monthly deposit is $80. Savings above the match cap earns higher interest. At age 18, children can withdraw their CDA savings for postsecondary education fees, home ownership, or small business ventures.

Two features of Korean CDAs are noteworthy. First, to encourage children in the welfare system to save, Korean CDAs adopted sponsorship programs which organize pooled contributions and distribute sponsorship into children's CDA accounts (Nam and Han 2010). Sponsorship was found to significantly influence total savings in CDAs (Kim, Kim and Hong 2007). Another feature is strong inter-organizational collaboration. The central government (Ministry of Health and Welfare), local municipalities, a private bank (Shinhan Bank), and a non-profit organization (Korea Federation of Child Welfare) worked together to design and administer CDAs. The strong collaborations are evaluated as a key feature contributing to the successful start of CDAs (Nam and Han 2010).

Evidence suggests that participants are taking advantage of the opportunity. By the end of 2007, 31,828 children had opened accounts (Kim et al. 2007). Account monitoring data indicated that 98.1 per cent of eligible children have made at least one deposit into a CDA account. Contributions have also been relatively high: the average monthly saving of $29 has been very close to the pre-established match cap ($30). Furthermore, 21 per cent of children saved more than the match cap. The preliminary findings suggest that these disadvantaged children can save if given institutional opportunities for saving.

Seoul Family Development Accounts. In collaboration with the Seoul City government and private funding companies, the Seoul Welfare Foundation started a three-year SFDA demonstration program in 2007. The SFDA program aims to provide opportunities of asset accumulation for poverty alleviation with financial education to encourage saving and self-support. In the pilot project, 100 working poor families saved for home buying, education, or microenterprise. Each SFDA participant deposits a maximum of 200,000 Korean Won (US$200) per month for three consecutive years. Savings are then matched 1.5:1 (Sherraden et al. 2008). Mentoring, financial education, and online networking among participants are key features of SFDA. Program evaluation of the SFDA is underway. Recently, the other local governments have also initiated saving programs similar to SFDA.

Singapore

Singapore is characterized as a nation where asset-based institutions and policies have been developed systematically and comprehensively to advance social development and economic growth (OECD 2003; Sherraden 2003). According to a report of the Boston Consulting Group (2008), Singapore has the highest density of the richest persons in the world. It was reported that one out of 10 households in Singapore owns more than $1 million. Additionally, the home ownership rate in Singapore is high: 92 per cent of resident households in 2005. Average home equity among Housing Development Board (HDB) households is about S$154,000, which is three times their annual household income (Chia 2008).

The Central Provident Fund (CPF) and HDB are two primary policy mechanisms that promote asset accumulation among Singaporeans over the life course (Han 2010). CPF is a compulsory and defined contribution savings for retirement income. More significantly, CPF savings can be withdrawn for down-payments and mortgage payments for the purchase of HDB housing units. Approximately 95 per cent of those who withdrew CPF funds in 2006 used the money to buy public housing (Chia 2008). Since the 1980s, governmental policy has been further liberalized so that CPF savings are used to finance purchase of private housing (Bardhan et al. 2003; Phang 2004).

Given that Singapore is a small country where people are its only resource, social policy is oriented toward human capital development. In particular, asset-based policies have been developed targeting children who are the country's greatest assets. There are three types of CDAs in Singapore, depending on different life stages of childhood (Loke and Sherraden 2008; Ng and Nair 2008). First, the Child Development Co-Savings Scheme covers children from birth to six years. The Co-Savings Scheme is part of the Baby Bonus Scheme which was introduced in 2001 to encourage marriage and to tackle low birth rates. Parents receive cash gifts of S$4,000 each for the first and second child and S$6,000 each for the third and fourth child. Further, a CDA account can be opened for each child and deposits into the account by parents are matched by 1:1 up to a cap. In 2001, CDA match caps were applied only to the second (S$6,000) and third (S$12,000) child. In 2008, the caps expanded as follows: S$6,000 for the first and second child; S$12,000 for third and fourth child; and S$18,000 for the fifth and beyond. Savings in CDAs can be used for childcare, health care, early years education, and other medical expenses. Savings left over at the age of six can be rolled over to the Post-Secondary Education Account (PSEA) (Han 2010).

The second type of CDA is the EduSave Scheme (ES). Opened in 1993, the ES was the first child development account in the world. The ES targets school-going children aged 6–16 and can be used for enrichment programs such as study trips, sports, school equipment fees, and other expenses. Unused savings balances can be transferred to the child's PSEA (Loke and Sherraden 2008; Han 2010).

Third, in 2007 the PSEA was introduced to support investment in continued tertiary education. Balances in CDAs and ES are eligible to be rolled over to PSEA. Parents can contribute to the PSEA until a child reaches the age of 18. The contribution is matched by the government only if previous deposits in CDAs had not reached the match caps of CDAs. Unused PSEA balances are transferred into the child's CPF at the age of 30 (Loke and Sherraden 2008; Han 2010).

Taiwan

Global economic downturns since the late 1990s have stunned the fast-growing economy of Taiwan. The economy witnessed falling real wages, rising unemployment rates, and rising income and wealth gaps between the rich and the poor. In particular, while income gaps between the rich and the poor increased from 4.2 in 1980 to 6.4 in 2001, wealth gaps in 2001 were double those (16.8) in 1991. Politically, with the development of democracy, policymakers were able to undertake and experiment with a series of economic and social policy initiatives responding to the rapidly changing needs of people (Cheng 2003). In particular, after rethinking existing anti-poverty policy in Taiwan, policymakers realized the limitations of anti-poverty systems in enhancing life chances for future development. In addition, the income support system, in some senses, prevents low-income families from achieving economic self-sufficiency because of means tests removing incentives to save (Cheng 2003).

The first inclusive asset-based policy in Taiwan is the Taipei Family Development Accounts (TFDA). The TFDA was launched to help low-income households in Taipei save for investment in home, microenterprise, or education (Cheng 2003). Similar to IDAs in the US, the program provides matching incentives to encourage saving.

The TFDA was designed to target the working poor. Participants make deposits ranging from NT$2,000 to NT$4,000 (US$1 = NT$33), which are matched throughout the 36-month demonstration. All participants are required to attend financial education classes on planning, budgeting, investment in home or small business. Similarly, the matched savings in the account can be withdrawn at the end of the demonstration. Interestingly, since working poor have high chances of unemployment, TFDA prepared principles for long-term unemployment which often result in drop-out from the program. If participants are unemployed for up to three months, then they are referred to occupational assistance. Savings and matching are designed to resume only after they are reemployed (Cheng 2003).

Performance in these programs has been promising. By 2003, 69 out of 100 households completed the three-year program with an average of NT$286,019 (US$1 = NT$33) per account. Furthermore, TFDA helped participants accumulate assets: 12 first homebuyers, 22 small business owners, and 31 children's college or graduate school enrollment. Considering that participants are welfare recipients, the saving and investment performance are significant and noteworthy (Cheng 2007).

Evaluation of Inclusive Asset-based Policies in Korea, Singapore, and Taiwan

Since countries highlighted in this paper are at different stages of inclusive asset-based policies, it is difficult to evaluate their summative effectiveness. However, the evaluation is expected to provide policy directions and implications for further development of inclusive asset-based policies. This study uses the framework of inclusive asset-based policy discussed previously (see Table 1). Summary findings of the analysis are presented in Table 2.

First, Singapore was evaluated as a country which is mostly close to the exemplary model of inclusive asset-based policy (OECD 2003; Sherraden 2003). Singapore asset-based policies are universal and comprehensive in that they cover most children. Furthermore, asset-based policies in Singapore have been developed systematically to cover the whole stage of life course from birth to retirement. The

Table 2. Comparison of inclusive asset-building policies in Korea, Singapore, and Taiwan

	Korea		Singapore		Taiwan
	CDAs	SFDA	CDAs	CPF	TFDA
Universal	△	X	○	○	X
Progressive	○	○	X	X	○
Life-long	△	X	○	○	X
Adequate	△	△	△	△	△

Notes: CDAs: Child Development Accounts; SFDA: Seoul Family Development Accounts; SIDA: Singapore Individual Development Accounts; TFDA: Taipei Family Development Accounts.
°denotes fully satisfied.
△denotes moderately satisfied.
ˣdenotes poorly satisfied.

key feature means that a person is institutionalized to save and accumulate assets throughout the lifespan. In addition, asset-based policies in Singapore were modeled to promote not only intra-generational, but also intergenerational development of asset building (Lee 2000). However, it is questionable whether all citizens are utilizing the saving opportunity. According to a CPF board report, only 1.6 million out of 3.3 million Singaporeans owning CPF accounts are active in contributing to their accounts for at least the last three months (CPF Board 2011). In addition, Single-parent families are not included in CDAs and poor households tend to receive fewer benefits because, by and large, they cannot save up to the match caps of CDAs (Ng and Nair 2008). Regarding housing, it is also true that there are families giving up their flats due to their inability to service their loans. These findings throw up questions regarding the 'universality' of asset-based policies in Singapore. It also leads to the regressive outcomes of the policies. While Singaporeans with secure jobs may contribute to CPF accounts and CDAs regularly, workers with a low income or in the informal labor market may struggle to make ends meet and save little in the accounts (Han and Chia 2012). The Singapore government favors top-up cash-outs to existing saving accounts (e.g. CDAs) with larger top-ups for low-income households (Ng and Nair 2008). However, the top-ups are too irregular and small to achieve progressiveness of asset policies. Although asset schemes are open to all, disadvantaged members of the population may not save, resulting in increases in asset inequality. Adequacy of asset-based policies is another challenge in Singapore. In particular, CPF can be used for housing, education, health, and private investment. This diversification of CPF savings may cause insufficient retirement income. To back up the multiple usage of CPF money, Singapore introduced the CPF minimum sum: CPF members should own S$123,000 at age 55. However, it was found that only 40 per cent of CPF members meet the minimum sum requirement in 2010 (Cai 2011).

The Taiwan FDA program has progressiveness in some aspects. The policy targets the working poor with a progressive matching rate, which participants perceived as a key factor influencing savings in TFDA (Cheng 2007). Private and public funds were used to fund the match. In addition, savings in TFDA were found to be adequate for future investment. As discussed before, a significant proportion of participants achieved saving goals of investing in small business, education, and homeownership (Cheng 2007). These findings suggest that the seed money in the accounts played a significant role in achieving future investment. However, the adequacy of savings in TFDA is still questionable depending on the saving goals. Savings in TFDA may be too small to buy a new home or start a new business. A critical challenge of asset-based policies in Taiwan is the scale. Many community-level asset-based policies are covering a small group of residents. Although not yet realized, there is potential for universality since the success of the TFDA pilot program in Taipei has emerged as a central social policy theme in Taiwan. Additionally, 15 municipalities on the island are initiating new TFDA-type programs (Cheng 2007). Time limit is another weakness. The three-year duration of the program may be too short to help the working poor accumulate assets for their life course. To reach their full potential, policymakers need to discuss how current short-term policies are connected to asset-building processes in the long term.

Third, development of asset-based programs in Korea is more dynamic. First, the less universal coverage of inclusive asset-based policy is a priority issue. Korean CDAs were originally proposed to expand to children in low- to middle-income households but no additional budgets for the expansion have been allocated. Still, children in the child welfare system are the target population of CDAs (Nam and Han 2010). KFDA also has a limited scope because only a small proportion of low-income households are covered by the program. An important feature of CDAs and KFDA are their progressiveness. Both programs provide saving incentives such as matching savings for low-income households. It is premature to evaluate whether the Korean asset-based system satisfies the life-long approach. However, if CDAs are connected with the national pension system, Korean asset-based policies have potential to create life-long asset-based systems. It is crucial that participants save regularly and develop sufficient assets to purchase a home, start a small business, or pursue post-secondary education. In other words, savings should be adequate for future investment, which increases the likelihood of self-reliance. Children in CDAs will accumulate about $39,000 (including contribution, interest, earnings, and matches) if they save the maximum monthly deposit ($80) for 18 years (Nam and Han 2010). It is expected that this accumulated sum will be adequate for seed money for future investment in housing, education, and small business. However, savings in inclusive asset-based schemes are voluntary, which means that adequacy depends on how much participants actually save into their accounts.

Implications and Discussion

Inclusive asset-based policies primarily aim for development and capacity building which can empower individuals and families, and contribute to the economy and society (Loke and Sherraden 2008; Han 2010). Remarkably, empirical results suggest that the poor can save if they participate in saving programs and they are provided with incentives and information (Cheng 2007; Schreiner and Sherraden 2007; Nam and Han 2010). This article concludes by presenting several policy implications.

First, inclusion should be a priority for national asset-based policies. Inclusion can happen in two ways. First, progressive saving plans can target low-income households. As another pathway to future inclusiveness, policies can expand access to those currently excluded from existing asset-based policies by providing low-income households with more incentives. For example, workers in underground or informal markets are today unlikely to participate in retirement pension plans. Through providing some combination of incentives and enforcement, the excluded will have increased opportunities to save for retirement income (Han 2006; Sherraden and Han 2007).

Second, as discussed in the Korean and Taiwanese FDAs, collaboration between private and public sectors are a key factor influencing the success of inclusive asset-based policy (Cheng 2007; Nam and Han 2010). Each entity or agent specializes in sponsoring, monitoring, managing, and implementing asset-based policy. Without the collaboration, it would be not easy to implement saving programs and to achieve policy goals. Government's roles, in particular, are critical in adoption as well as expansion of inclusive asset-based policy.

Third, it should be noted that asset-based policy is not to replace income-maintenance policy. Income-maintenance policy serves a number of purposes for social welfare. It can be said that only when the two policies cooperate to cater to diverse needs of the poor, can goals of social policy such as economic sufficiency and social development be achieved. Therefore, implementation of inclusive asset-based policy has the potential to complement existing income support policies to promote development of individuals, families, and communities (Han 2006; Sherraden and Han 2007).

Fourth, further research is needed to examine saving patterns and outcomes of participants in inclusive asset-based policies. However, currently there are a number of barriers to data collection for evaluation. Just as inter-organizational cooperation is necessary for the implementation of policies, researchers and policy stakeholders should cooperate for the execution of evidence-based social policy.

Last, the accumulation of evidence on asset effects and policy impacts can provide rationales for expanding inclusive asset-based policies. The evidence may reduce criticism of asset-based welfare. Specifically, advocates need to collect robust evidence on whether the poor can save, how they overcome economic distress, and which asset effects can be achieved from asset accumulation. Positive evidence from policy evaluation studies can provide political supports to expand inclusive asset-based policies. Furthermore, the evidence will be helpful to reorganize and restructure asset-based policies to encourage the poor to maximize the institutional opportunities of saving.

Korea, Singapore, and Taiwan have begun to implement inclusive asset-based policies. But these policies are in the early stages of definition, implementation, and evaluation (Sherraden and Han 2007). It is crucial for those countries to discuss long-term plans. Specific policies must be carefully designed, and research will be fundamentally essential. Recent economic downturns across the world have enormous impacts on asset accumulation through declining housing prices, plummeting stocks, and increasing credit card liabilities. Private sectors adjust these crises by reducing consumption or changing consumption patterns. In many countries, governments tend to adopt policies stimulating domestic consumption. In addition to these short-term economic boosting policies, policymakers should endorse long-term initiatives such as inclusive asset-based policies for the general population.

References

Adams, G. F. and Prazmowski, P. A., 2003, Why are saving rates in East Asia so high? Reviving the life cycle hypothesis. *Empirical Economics*, **28**(2), pp. 275–289.

Baharumshah, A. Z., Thanoon, M. A., and Rashid, S., 2003, Saving dynamics in the Asian countries. *Journal of Asian Economics*, **13**(6), pp. 827–845.

Bardhan, A. D., Datta, R., Edelstein, R. H. and Kim, L. S., 2003, A tale of two sectors: Upward mobility and the private housing market in Singapore. *Journal of Housing Economics*, **12**(2), pp. 83–105.

Beverly, S. G. and Sherraden, M., 1999, Institutional determinants of saving: Implications for low-income households and public policy. *Journal of Socio-Economics*, **28**(4), pp. 457–473.

Boston Consulting Group, 2008, Global Wealth 2007 (Boston: Boston Consulting Group). Available at http://www.bcg.com/impact_expertise/publications/publication_search.jsp (accessed 12 December 2008).

Cai, H., 2011, More CPF members meeting minimum sum requirement. *The Straits Times*, 19 February, p. B12.

Central Provident Fund Board, 2011, General information on CPF. Available at http://mycpf.cpf.gov.sg/Members/Gen-Info/mbr-Gen-info.htm (accessed 6 October 2011).

Cheng, L.-C., 2003, *Developing Family Development Accounts in Taipei: Policy innovation from income to assets*. CSD working paper 03-09 (St. Louis, MO: Washington University, Center for Social Development).

Cheng, L.-C., 2007, *Asset-based policy in Taiwan: Demonstration and policy progress*. Policy update (St. Louis: Washington University, Center for Social Development).

Chia, N. C., 2008, Home ownership and income security in old age. Paper presented at IPS-TSAO Foundation Conference on Successful Ageing in Singapore: Older Men and Women in a Society of Longevity, Institute of Policy Studies and TSAO Foundation, Singapore.

Clancy, M., Han, C.-K., Mason, L. R. and Sherraden, M., 2006, *Inclusion in college savings plans: Participation and saving in Maine's matching grant program*. CSD Research Report (St. Louis, MO: Washington University, Center for Social Development).

Curley, J., Ssewamala, F. and Sherraden, M., 2005, *Institutions and savings in low-income households*. CSD Working Paper No. 05-13 (St. Louis, MO: Washington University, Center for Social Development).

Gamble, A. and Prabhakar, R., 2005, *Assets and poverty*. Asset-based Welfare and Poverty Reduction-2005. ESRC End of Award Report from RES-000-23-0053 Nominated Output 2.

Gokhale, J. and Tanner, M., 2006. *KidSave: Real problem, wrong solution*. Policy Analysis No. 562 (Washington, DC: Cato Institute).

Han, C.-K., 2006, Asset-based policy and its implications for Korea, in: S. H. Ahn (Ed.) *Challenges of economic and social policy in Korea* (Seoul, Korea: Korean Labor Institute), pp. 446–453. [In Korean].

Han, C.-K., 2009a, Unemployment, financial hardship, and savings in Individual Development Accounts. *Journal of Poverty*, **13**(1), pp. 74–95.

Han, C.-K., 2009b, Asset-building policy in Korea, Singapore, and Taiwan: A comparative perspective. Paper presented at an International Conference Co-Sponsored by Association of Public Policy and Management (APPAM), Singapore, 9 January.

Han, C.-K., 2010, Asset-building policy throughout the life course: Lessons from Singapore. Paper presented at the 7th East Asian Social Policy (EASP) Conference, Seoul, Korea, 21 August.

Han, C.-K. and Chia, A., 2012, A preliminary study on parents saving in the Child Development Account in Singapore. *Children and Youth Services Review*. **34**(9), pp. 1583–1589.

Han, C.-K. and Sherraden, M., 2009, Do institutions really matter for saving among low-income households? A comparative approach. *The Journal of Socio-Economics*, **38**(3), pp. 475–483.

Kim, M., Kim, H. and Hong, M., 2007, *Effective operation of Child Development Accounts in Korea*. KIHASA Policy Report 2007-85 (Seoul: Korea Institute for Health and Social Affairs). [In Korean]

Lee, K. Y., 2000, *From Third World to First. The Singapore Story: 1965–2000* (New York: HarperCollins).

Loke, V. and Sherraden, M., 2008, *Building assets from birth: A global comparison of Child Development Account policies*. CSD working paper 08-03 (St. Louis, MO: Washington University, Center for Social Development).

Lusardi, A., 2003, *The impact of financial education on savings and asset*. Working Paper wp061 (Ann Arbor, Michigan: Michigan Retirement Research Center, University of Michigan).

Meyer, J., Masa, R. D. and Zimmerman, J. M., 2010, Overview of Child Development Accounts in developing countries. *Children and Youth Services Review*, **32**(11), pp. 1561–1569.

Munnell, A., Sunden, A. and Taylor, C., 2001/2002, What determines 401(k) participation and contributions? *Social Security Bulletin*, **64**(3), pp. 64–76.

Nam, Y. and Han, C.-K., 2010, A new approach to promote economic independence among at-risk children: Child Development Accounts (CDAs) in Korea. *Children and Youth Services Review*, **32**(11), pp. 1548–1554.

Ng, K. H. and Nair, S., 2008, Child Development Accounts in Singapore. Paper presented at the Symposium of Child Development Accounts, St. Louis, MO, USA, 12–14 November.

OECD, 2003, *Asset building and the escape from poverty: A new welfare policy debate*. Local Economic and Employment Development (LEED) Programme (Paris: Organization for Economic Co-operation and Development).

Phang, S.-Y., 2004, House prices and aggregate consumption: Do they move together? Evidence from Singapore. *Journal of Housing Economics*, **13**(2), pp. 101–119.

Prabjakar, R., 2009, The asset agenda and social policy. *Social Policy and Administration*, **43**(1), pp. 54–69.

Rothwell, D. W. and Han, C.-K., 2010, Second thoughts: Who almost participates in an IDA program? *Journal of Social Service Research*, **36**(2), pp. 107–117.

Scanlon, E., 2001, *Toward a theory of financial savings and child well-being: Implication for research on a children and youth*. CSD Research Paper 01-11 (St. Louis, MO: Washington University, Center for Social Development).

Shreiner, M. and Sherraden, M., 2005, Drop-out from Individual Development Accounts: Prediction and prevention. *Financial Services Review*, **14**(1), pp. 37–54.

Schreiner, M. and Sherraden, M., 2007, *Can the poor save? Savings and asset building in Individual Development Accounts* (New York: Aldine de Gruyter).

Sen, A., 1999, *Development as freedom* (New York: Knopf).

Sherraden, M., 1991, *Assets and the poor: A new American welfare policy* (Armonk, NY: M. E. Sharpe, Inc.).

Sherraden, M., 2002, From a social welfare state to a social investment state, in: C. Kober and W. Paxton (Eds.) *Asset-based welfare and poverty: Exploring the case for and against asset-based welfare policies* (London: Institute for Public Policy Research), pp. 5–8.

Sherraden, M., 2003, Individual accounts in social security: Can they be progressive? *International Journal of Social Welfare*, **12**(2), pp. 97–107.

Sherraden, M., 2005, *Inclusion in asset building: Testimony for hearing on "Building assets for low-income families" Subcommittee on Social Security and Family Policy Senate Finance Committee*. CSD Perspective 05-24 (St. Louis, MO: Washington University, Center for Social Development).

Sherraden, M. and Han, C.-K., 2007, Social investment state and asset-based policy: Implications for Korean social policy. Paper presented at the International Symposium of Social Investment Strategy in Korea, Seoul Welfare Foundation, Seoul, Korea, 14 November.

Sherraden, M., Nam, Y., Zou, L., Han, C.-K., Kim, Y. and Han, W., 2008, *Asset-based policy in South Korea*. CSD Policy Update (St. Louis, MO: Washington University, Center for Social Development). Available at http://gwbweb.wustl.edu/CSD/Publications/GAP_Updates/Korea_Update.pdf (accessed 27 December 2008).

William Shanks, T., Kim, Y., Loke, V. and Destin, M., 2010, Assets and child well-being in developed countries. *Children and Youth Services Review*, **32**(11), pp. 1488–1496.

World Bank, 1999, Why do savings rates vary across countries? *World Bank Policy and Research Bulletin*, **10**(1), pp. 1–4.

Zhan, M. and Sherraden, M., 2003, Assets, expectations, and children's educational achievement in female-headed households. *Social Service Review*, **77**(1), pp. 191–211.

The Challenges of Implementing Merit-Based Personnel Policies in Latin America: Mexico's Civil Service Reform Experience

MAURICIO I. DUSSAUGE LAGUNA

ABSTRACT *Implementation of Merit Based Personnel Policies (MBPP) continues to be a highly problematic endeavour in Latin American countries. According to the literature, this is usually caused by the politico-administrative inheritances that characterize this region, such as patronage, corruption, centralism and the lack of effective accountability mechanisms. By looking at Mexico's recent Civil Service reform process, this article shows that the development of new MBPP has been certainly constrained by some of those factors. However, the article also shows that a number of issues faced during the Mexican reform process can be linked to "simpler" issues of policy design and implementation. The article thus concludes that while "patronage", "amiguismo", illegality, and other traditional features of Latin American (and Mexican) administrative systems remain a central impediment for developing well-functioning MBPP, academics and practitioners should probably pay more attention to policy design issues (e.g. policy co-ordination; time and resources availability; institutional framework design), which contribute to better explaining and understanding why MBPP implementation remains such a challenging task in this region.*

> ... today is an historic day for Mexico, today the Executive Power signs the decree which enacts the law that establishes the Servicio Profesional de Carrera in the Federal Public Administration, a government innovation of broad impact and relevance because with this law we reach a democratic ideal, and ideal that Mexico has been looking forward to see for decades.
>
> Vicente Fox, Presidential Speech, April, 9 2003

Public personnel policies are commonly assumed to be a key variable for developing a high performing public sector (Ingraham et al. 2003, GAO, 2004, Klitgaard and Light 2005). Furthermore, while the relevance of "classic" civil service systems *à la* Weber has been contested in recent decades by New Public Management-oriented reforms (Wright 1994, Hood 1991, Pollitt and Bouckaert 2004), it is still widely accepted that apolitical, "merit-based" personnel policies (MBPP) are essential for guaranteeing adequate public services provision; promoting economic growth; and reducing corruption (World Bank 1997, Evans and Rauch 1999, OECD 2005, 2008).

However, the design and implementation of MBPP continues to be highly problematic in many developing countries, including the Latin American ones. During the twentieth century, MBPP were a frequent component of administrative reform strategies across the region (Spink 1999, Kliksberg 2005). In fact, some nations succeeded in introducing government-wide MBPP (for example Chile, Brazil, Costa Rica). On the other hand, "patronage" and partisan considerations still strongly influence bureaucratic appointments. In some jurisdictions (for example Peru, Mexico, Bolivia), merit-based recruitment and promotions exist, but only within a limited number of agencies or policy fields (tax revenue, diplomatic corps, central banks; see Echebarría and Cortázar 2007). Therefore, the development of a well functioning civil service structure continues to be "a democratic ideal" for most Latin American countries.

The question of why implementing MBPP in this region is so difficult has attracted significant academic attention (Geddes 1994, Klingner 1996, Arellano et al. 2003, Martínez 2005, Ramió and Salvador 2005, Echebarría 2006, Villoria 2007, Longo and Ramió 2008). This has been partly due to the number of administrative reform waves that have taken place across Latin America during the past two decades (Moctezuma and Roemer 1999, Spink 1999, Barzelay et al. 2003, Ramió and Salvador 2008). But perhaps more importantly, the fact is that we still know relatively little about the specific challenges of MBPP implementation in this region.

This article will seek to offer a policy analysis of Mexico's recent civil service reform process. As expressed in the quote by former President Vicente Fox, the "Ley del Servicio Profesional de Carrera" of 2003 (Civil Service Law, hereafter CSL-2003) represented an historic institutional change for Mexico. The law introduced merit for the first time as the guiding principle for managing personnel policies across the federal government agencies, just like the UK's Northcote-Trevelyan reforms, or the US Pendleton Act did. However, only a few years after its enactment, the new civil service system had been repeatedly subject to numerous criticisms by academics, public servants and political parties alike.

The analysis of the Mexican experience thus offers an excellent opportunity to look at why implementation of MBPP remains difficult in Latin America. Mexico is the second largest country of the region in economic and bureaucratic terms, and has been traditionally perceived as a regional leader. In recent years, the Mexican administrative reforms have been supported by international aid agencies – such as the US Agency for International Development (USAID), the British Council and the Agencia Española de Cooperación Internacional para el Desarrollo (AECI, Spain). Furthermore, the Mexican initiatives have been closely monitored/advised by the World Bank and the Inter-American Development Bank (SFP 2005, Pardo 2009, Dussauge 2008), because the country is perceived to be a key jurisdiction for testing the feasibility and effectiveness of reforms (Interviews I1, I2). Similarly, Mexico shares with most other Latin American countries a common "administrative tradition", characterized by patronage, corruption, centralist tendencies and the lack of effective accountability mechanisms (Méndez 1997, Nef 2003). Therefore, while the Mexican experience is interesting on its own, it also represents a relevant case of study from which useful insights might be obtained for refining our theories about MBPP in the region (Rueschemeyer 2003, George and Bennett 2005, Yin 2009). Furthermore, the revision of the Mexican experience might also contribute to the ongoing international "comparative conversation" (Page 1995) on public personnel and administrative reform policies.

The article will argue that implementation of the MBPP introduced by the CSL-2003 has been problematic for various reasons. First, the constraints imposed by the values, routines and informal norms of the "Mexican administrative tradition" (Merino 1996, Méndez 1997, Arellano 1999, Peters 2008). In this sense, these pages will support the commonly held view that the adoption and, above all, implementation of MBPP in Latin American countries has been affected by the politico-administrative inheritances that characterize this region (Nef 2003, Ramió and Salvador 2005, Villoria 2007, Parrado 2008). However, the article will also argue that implementation of MBPP has been difficult because of other factors, which are not generally discussed in the literature. In particular, broader attention will be paid here to policy design issues, such as the way in which personnel policies were originally drafted in both the CSL-2003 (SFP 2003) and the first "Reglamento" of 2004 (or Code of Regulations, hereafter CR-2004; SFP 2004). Therefore, in line with the vast academic literature that has long underlined the links between policy design and policy implementation (Pressman and Wildavsky 1973, Hood 1976, Ingraham 1987, May 2003), the article will suggest that issues associated with the design of MBPP deserve further analysis.

The remainder of the article is divided into four sections. The first briefly discusses the "Mexican administrative tradition" and the origins of the civil service reform of 2003. The second analyzes key implementation issues that the new MBPP faced between 2004 and 2007. The third presents the rationale, contents and limitations of the regulatory reforms of 2007. Finally, the article will offer some concluding remarks regarding the Mexican case and its broader implications for other Latin American countries seeking to "draw" or "extrapolate" lessons from this particular "exemplar" of civil service reform (Rose 2005, Barzelay 2007).

The analysis has been based on a combination of academic and non-academic sources. First, official reports, government publications, legislation and secondary regulations published by the Secretaría de la Función Pública (Ministry of Public Administration, MPA), which is the federal entity in charge of managing the new Servicio Profesional de Carrera (Professional Career Service, PCS). Second, international reports, academic articles, newspaper notes and reflections from practitioners directly involved in managing and implementing the new MBPP. Fourth, seven semi-structured interviews (conducted in January of 2009) with public servants that had been directly involved in the design and/or implementation stages of the MBPP.

From the "(Quasi) Spoils" System to the *Servicio Profesional de Carrera*

This section is structured around two main topics. First, it will provide an overview of the "Mexican administrative tradition", which is closely associated to the Latin

American one. This is relevant to set the civil service reform of 2003 in its broader historical perspective and to better understand the politico-administrative inheritances encountered by the new MBPP. The section will then briefly describe the CSL-2003 contents.

The "Mexican Administrative Tradition"

As in the case of any country, Mexico's administrative system reflects a set of characteristics, values and relationships among public institutions which have developed throughout history and have formed a certain "administrative tradition" (Peters 2008). In particular the "Mexican administrative tradition" has been the product of at least two huge political transformations. First, the Spanish domination until the early nineteenth century, which left behind a set of political inheritances (Méndez 1997, Nef 2003). The most commonly cited example of this is the so-called *"obedézcase, pero no se cumpla"* principle ("obey this, but do not comply with it"), by which orders from the Spanish colonial authorities were legally expressed and communicated to the administrative corps in the "New World", but were not always implemented. Similarly, another relevant political inheritance, frequently mentioned in the literature, was the practice of "patrimonialism" by which public resources were regularly used by officials as their own private property, without necessarily raising accountability issues or legal consequences.

These traits would later be reinforced by the political transformations of the early twentieth century. As a result of the social revolution of 1910–1920, an authoritarian and highly centralized state developed in Mexico. In this scenario, the President of the Republic and his political party would become key institutions of the politico-administrative system for the following 70 years (Arellano and Guerrero 2003). Furthermore, until the mid-1990s/early 2000s, when the "transition to democracy" process culminated with the first presidential triumph of an opposition party in 2000, the legislative and judiciary powers remained subordinate to the political control of the federal executive. This impeded the development of effective accountability and anti-corruption mechanisms until the end the twentieth century (Dussauge 2010).

As a result, the executive branch became the field where political power and bureaucratic promotions were sought after by several "camarillas", that is groups of political appointees and public servants formed around a promising political leader (see Grindle 1977). These "camarillas" rotated within the federal government during important political junctures, particularly after electoral periods when the new president would distribute the "spoils" (public positions) among his supporters on a discretionary and strategic way. Top political appointees (for example secretaries and undersecretaries of state, heads of agencies) would in turn do the same, filling subordinate positions with members of their own groups. This highly politicized environment, governed by informal rules, generated an organizational culture in which personal loyalties and group commitments were seen as the most important administrative values (Merino 1996, Arellano 1999).

There certainly were some exceptions to this "spoils system", and thus it might be possible to think about a "quasi-spoils system" (Arellano 2008). First, while merit and open competition did not exist as legally binding principles for managing human resources (recruitment, promotion, or dismissals) within the federal government, political appointees did take into account some informal assessments of personal effectiveness for hiring/firing personnel (Hernández 2000). Second, the internal rotation of "camarillas" took place every few years and frequently within the same policy field, thus allowing their members to acquire certain levels of policy expertise and managerial experience, while at the same time guaranteeing a minimum of institutional memory. Most importantly, in a number of highly technical policy sectors, professional expertise and specialized knowledge were as important as political considerations. In areas such as telecommunications, tax collection, central banking, or health services, some informal "career systems" emerged. In these, recruitment and promotion were conducted informally (albeit regularly) on a rather meritocratic basis (Interviews I1, I3, I7). Similarly, informal career paths did exist, and were well known among public servants within these policy fields. However, it should be stressed that these were exceptions, and that political patronage and "amiguismo" (personal friendship considerations) remained as the key government-wide principles for starting, developing and ending a professional career in the federal public administration.

The Civil Service Law of 2003

The pitfalls of the Mexican government's public personnel policies had long been criticized (Merino 1996, Moctezuma and Roemer 1999, Méndez 2000, Pardo 2000), but gained further attention as the "transition to democracy" progressed. During the 1980s, the idea of introducing a civil service system received some political consideration, but the need to solve the economic crisis implied that only short-term, efficiency-oriented measures were discussed and implemented (Cejudo 2003). In addition, public sector unions had expressed their opposition to any civil service law that could imply a loss of power for them (Guerrero 1998, Pardo 2005). In the mid-1990s, the idea would re-enter the government agenda, apparently as a result of Mexico's admission as a member of the Organization for Economic Co-operation and Development (OECD; Pardo 2003). However, the government of President Ernesto Zedillo (1994–2000) would not able to complete its plan for introducing a merit-based civil service law. This happened as a result of significant disagreements between the Ministry of Finance (MoF) and the then Ministry of Administrative Development (currently the Ministry of Public Administration, MPA), which had been designated as co-sponsors of the reform project (Arellano and Guerrero 2003). The former had co-ordinated the reform initiatives during the 1980s, and had even created a "Civil Service Unit" within its organizational structure; but from the mid-1990s the latter was in charge of administrative modernization. Because of their institutional functions, both agencies had different perspectives on how to design the new civil service system, including its personnel management subsystems and the degree of system decentralization. Both also had a clear interest in retaining control over the system (Pardo 2009). In the end, the reform failed as a result of both these disagreements and a loss of presidential interest on the topic.

The need to establish a merit system returned to the agenda during the 2000 election, when the topic was included in all party manifestos (Sosa 2000). After Vicente Fox won the presidential election, a number of policy experts discussed in various forums the potential benefits that new government-wide MBPP would bring.

They showcased international examples and the national experiences that existed (such as the Diplomatic Service and the Federal Electoral Institute). At the same time, legislators from each of the three major political forces introduced draft civil service laws. Finally, a number of international agencies (for example USAID, British Council and the Spanish AECI), which understood that the idea was gaining prominence, decided to further support the initiative (Interviews I1, I3, I7). They funded various publications and conferences in which national scholars and public servants debated the advantages of the reform (Méndez 2008, Martínez 2009). Experts from the UK, US, New Zealand and France were also invited to Mexico City in order to participate in the conferences and meet with advisors from the newly created Presidential Office for Government Innovation, the MPA and other federal ministries.

The product of this process would be the "Ley del Servicio Profesional de Carrera en la Administración Pública Federal" (CSL-2003). The law was published on April 10, 2003, after months of negotiations between political parties, key members of the President's office and a small group of senior public personnel experts from the federal government (Interviews I1, I2, I7). The law sought to establish "a mechanism for guaranteeing equal opportunity of access to the public administration based on merit and with the goal of advancing the development of public administration for the benefit of society" (art. 2, SFP 2003). While the MBPP included in the CSL-2003 would have government-wide application, in practice the new personnel policies would only apply to a limited number of agencies (about 76 out of some 240 in total) and to a minority of federal public servants (numbers have varied between 40,000 and 37,000, from a total of about 1.5 million). The law's main objective was to cover the so-called "servidores públicos de confianza" within the "centralized public administration", that is the group of public servants who had been traditionally appointed and dismissed at the discretion ("confianza" or "trust") of their supervisors. Furthermore, the law would not cover street-level bureaucrats to avoid blockage from public sector unions (as happened in the 1980s); nor would it cover federal institutions within the so-called "decentralized public administration". Table 1 presents the main features of the CSL-2003:

The CSL-2003 introduced new MBPP in the areas of planning, recruitment and selection, promotions, performance appraisals, training and dismissals, all of which would be fleshed out throughout 2003–2004. A supplementary "Reglamento", or Code of Regulations (the CR-2004), would be published on April 2, 2004. Further norms and criteria for each subsystem would also be prepared during the rest of that year.

The CSL-2003 was widely celebrated by President Vicente Fox, but also by political leaders, academics and public servants alike. The leader of the Chamber of Deputies said the law was a "qualitative advancement" for the Mexican state reform. The Senate's President expressed that it showed "willingness to do things right for the benefit of the country" (Ruiz 2003). Public policy scholars remarked the CSL-2003 implied a "historical step in the institutional and democratic consolidation of Mexico" (María del Carmen Pardo, see Ruiz 2003); perhaps the "biggest ever institutional change within the federal executive branch" (Merino 2004); and the "best means to achieve the Mexican society's objectives" (Méndez 2004: 11). Public

Table 1. Main institutional features of the SPC

Feature	Content of the law
Institutions covered	• Federal government*: a) 14 "Secretarías de Estado" (federal ministries), and b) 62 "órganos desconcentrados" (semi-autonomous agencies)
Institutions exempted	• Presidential Offices • Ministries involved in national security and public safety functions • Ministry of Foreign Affairs
Job positions covered	• About 37,000 policy analysts, middle-level, and high-level management positions*: a) Director General b) Deputy Director General c) Director of Aread d) Deputy Director e) Chief of Department f) Administrative officers ("enlaces")
Job positions exempted	• About 1.5 million positions in the federal government**, including a) Senior political positions (such as Secretaries of State, Undersecretaries of State, and Heads of Unit) b) Private secretaries and political advisors ("gabinetes de apoyo", or "cabinets") c) Street-level bureaucrats d) Public servants in decentralized (semi-autonomous) agencies e) School teachers and health services
Governance of the system	• MPA (through its newly created Civil Service Unit) is accountable for the whole system, particularly normative and control functions • Federal agencies are accountable for implementing merit principles • Advisory council offers policy and management recommendations (integrated by Chief Administrative Officers ("oficiales mayores"), and one participant from each the private, academic, and social sectors)
HRM subsystems	• Human Resources Planning • Hiring (Recruitment and Selection) • Performance Appraisal • Training and Competency Certification • Professional Development • Dismissals • Control and Evaluation

Source: Based on Dussauge (2006); *SFP (2008); **CIDE (2007a).

servants commented they had been expecting this policy for a long time (Herrera 2004, Casas 2005).

However, a few years (even months) after its enactment, things changed radically. A number of newspaper articles (Otero 2004, 2006, Reséndiz 2004, Ramos 2007, Téllez 2007, Velasco 2007, López 2008, Solís 2007); practitioner perspectives (Cedillo 2006, 2007, Sánchez 2007, Herrera 2008); academic assessments (Pardo, 2005, Merino 2006a, 2006b, 2008, Valverde, 2007, Dussauge 2008, Méndez 2008); and preliminary evaluations carried out by the Supreme Audit Institution (ASF 2006) and a prestigious public research centre (CIDE 2007a, 2007b) would raise a number of criticisms regarding implementation of the new MBPP. What happened in such a short period of time? Was it all due to implementation problems? If so, what kind of problems and why?

From Merit Principles to Administrative Realities

This section analyzes the main issues the new MBPP have faced during their introduction into the Mexican bureaucratic environment. The main time period covered in the section is from April 2004 (when the first supplementary regulations were published), to September 2007 (when the second "reglamento" was introduced), albeit significant events outside those dates are included when relevant. The analytical point of departure will be the implementation literature (Pressman and Wildavsky 1973, Hill and Hupe 2002), with specific attention paid to issues related to the idea of "perfect implementation" first introduced by Hood (1976) and later elaborated by Hogwood and Gunn (1984). This particular approach is used for two main reasons. First, the difficulties that MBPP have faced in Latin American countries have been generally framed as an "implementation problem" (Villoria 2007, Longo and Ramió 2008). Second, by using this analytical perspective it might be possible to look at "pure" implementation issues, but also at the links between policy implementation and policy design (Ingraham 1987, May 2003), and between implementation and institutional constraints. This approach is thus theoretically relevant and analytically useful, albeit other implementation approaches (such as backward mapping), or policy literatures (for example policy failures/fiascos) might be productively employed as well for similar purposes.

External Circumstances

One of the key issues that might undermine implementation of a new policy is the presence of crippling external forces (Hogwood and Gunn 1984: 199; Ingraham 1987: 618–619). In the case of the new MBPP introduced in 2004, it seems as though a number of external pressures have certainly affected this "perfect implementation" condition.

A first pressure that has been present from the very beginning is how to retain political attention on the MBPP. During the Fox government (2000–2006), MBPP were perceived as an important topic (Interview I2). Key presidential advisors actively participated in the design of the CSL-2003 and were involved in the congressional negotiations that led to its approval. The president himself supported the topic and perceived it as an important politico-administrative reform. Furthermore, until the end of the administration, implementation of the new MBPP remained as one of the six components of the so-called Good Government Agenda. On the other hand, the mere existence of the latter implied that administrative and political attention (inside presidential offices and across the federal government) had to be divided up between various administrative modernization efforts, including e-government tools, citizen charters, cost containment measures and anti-corruption strategies (Dussauge 2008, Pardo 2009). Additionally, the symbolic appeal of the PCS obviously diminished once the CSL-2003 was approved in 2003, particularly as criticisms towards MBPP implementation mounted throughout 2005–2006 (Interviews I2, I4, I5).

During the administration of President Felipe Calderón (2006–2012), MBPP have faced an even harder time. The government agenda has been focused on public security and drug-trafficking issues, and other policy topics (particularly those related to administrative reforms) have become secondary. In fact, in contrast to his predecessor, President Calderón has never considered MBPP as a topic worth fighting for (Interview I2). On the contrary, this is perceived as a time-consuming activity, from which little political gain might be obtained. Given the present political and economic conditions, administrative modernization efforts during this administration have been mainly focused on cost-containment measures, such as reducing contracting out costs and cutting salaries of top level political appointees and public servants (Poder Ejecutivo 2006). Last but not least, the federal ministry (MPA) in charge of ensuring the appropriate implementation of MBPP has shifted its institutional attention and currently prioritizes performance management and policy evaluation over public personnel management (Sosa 2008).

Further external pressure has come from various congressional initiatives that have attempted to reform the CSL-2003. During the 2006 presidential election, one of the main opposition parties introduced a bill proposing that all director-general and deputy director-general positions (the most senior administrative levels of the bureaucratic structure) should be removed from the civil service structure (*El Universal* 2006). A similar initiative was introduced in 2007 by another opposition party (Martínez 2009). Although both initiatives have so far failed to gain the necessary congressional support, these political attacks have shown the fragility of the new civil service system, while at the same time they have distracted the attention of those responsible for its implementation.

These external pressures provide some, albeit not absolute, support to the view that implementation of MBPP in countries like Mexico is constrained by political factors that are a "legacy of the past". The legal reform attempts show that political parties are seeking changes which, in the event of a future presidential triumph (first in 2006 and now in 2012), would provide them with substantial "spoils" (for example government positions) for their supporters. This is certainly in line with the "patronage" oriented political culture of the past. But the external pressures described above also point to other issues. First, the issue of how political priorities change over time, something that could affect any country (whether Latin American or not). Second, they also point to issues related to the original design of the policy: the CSL-2003 mandates the use of MBPP for all middle-level and senior management positions in 76 federal agencies. Therefore, after decades of a "quasi-spoils" system, the new legislation perhaps went too far in too short a time, as it left very limited room for political parties to make partisan appointments within the bureaucratic structure.

Time and Resources

A second key issue for achieving "perfect implementation" is that related to the availability of adequate time and resources (Hogwood and Gunn 1984: 199–200, Ingraham 1987: 620). However, the experience of the PCS during its initial years seems to show that none of these elements has been in place to ensure an adequate implementation of the MBPP.

Regarding timeframes, the CSL-2003 was somehow ambiguous. According to its article 69, implementation of new MBPP should have been gradual, taking into consideration the particular features and conditions of each federal agency. Yet the law also established in its transitional article 4 that full implementation should not exceed three years (meaning 2006). Since the supplementary Code of Regulations was not published until April 2004, the MPA and all other agencies that are part of the system had only two years to get ready for the process.

The huge limitations of this original timeframe become clearer when the administrative implications of the reform are taken into account. Although the new PCS applies to a relatively small part of the federal government, its coverage includes a huge diversity of administrative positions (policy analysts, senior executives, middle-level bureaucrats and administrative staff); bureaucratic structures (large ministries, small agencies); policy fields (health, urban development, communications, education, agriculture, among many others); and professional specialization areas (such as engineers, lawyers, administrators, scientists, political scientists). Time pressures were further aggravated by transitional article 3 of the CSL-2003, which established that every public servant taking a position in the new civil service structure would need to pass a set of tests before acquiring tenured ("carrera") status. The CR-2004 then introduced additional conditions for completing this transition (SFP 2004, Pardo 2005, Martínez 2006). In the end, not only did the new MBPP have to be tailored to suit a wide variety of bureaucratic environments, but attention and resources were also divided up to fulfil both the general requirements of setting up a new civil service system and those specifically needed to co-ordinate the transition of public servants from "servidores públicos de confianza" (that is non-tenured officials), to "servidores públicos de carrera" (that is the tenure track).

In terms of resources availability, the picture is a bit more complex. International agencies (such as the British Council, USAID, AECID) provided significant funding to the Mexican government for developing its merit system (Interviews I2, I6). A considerable amount of federal resources was also available to participating agencies (about $100 million for 2007; CIDE 2007a: 27). These resources allowed the acquisition of expensive IT tools, such as the "TrabajaEn" system used for advertising vacancies and recruiting applicants; the "@CampusMexico" platform, an e-learning system with training courses and academic examinations; and the "RHNet" system for managing HRM subsystems information (Martínez 2009, Pardo 2009).

On the other hand, it is the lack of broader administrative conditions and capacities which probably has had a deeper impact on the implementation process. For instance, a study carried out by the MoF and the MPA showed that before implementation of the CSL-2003, there were "huge normative, organizational and salary gaps that would need to be overcome" (SFP 2005: 52). The same diagnostic study showed that, prior to 2003, only 18 per cent of the federal agencies used to publish job vacancies, and 51 per cent openly admitted that hiring decisions were discretionally made by supervisors; less than 50 per cent of the agencies developed induction courses; almost none certified professional competencies; only 13 per cent conducted performance appraisals on a regular basis; and just 44 per cent said they had put in place administrative mechanisms to control personnel management activities (Martínez 2006: 462). In other words, merit principles and policies were new to most federal agencies, their human resources offices and those public servants who would now become involved in position classification, hiring, performance appraisal, training and dismissal activities (Dussauge 2005, Pardo 2005).

By looking at time and resources considerations we obtain, again, some mixed conclusions regarding why MBPP implementation has been difficult. It is clear that the three-year timeframe was defined on the basis of political considerations, so that the full implementation cycle of the CSL-2003 coincided with the end of the Fox administration in 2006 (Interview I2). The high level of politicization that has historically conditioned policy decisions in Mexico thus certainly played a crucial role. At the same time, however, it is less clear to what extent those same political considerations defined the scope and specific positions covered by the CSL-2003, as well as the requirements established for managing the transition of public servants to a full career (tenured) status. In fact, some interviewees suggest that these decisions were taken on the basis of technical considerations (Interviews I1, I7). Similarly, it remains unclear whether information about the state of administrative capacities in federal agencies (particularly regarding the management of public personnel) was ignored when detailing the new MBPP because of political pressures, or because policy designers did not adequately assess its potential effects.

Understanding of, and Agreement on, Policy Objectives

A clear and continuous understanding of, and agreement on, policy objectives could be seen as a third key premise for "perfect implementation" (Hogwood and Gunn 1984: 204, Ingraham 1987: 618–620). Regarding this point, the situation of the CSL-2003 offers contrasting evidence. Politicians, academics and public servants alike did seem to understand what a merit system was, and how it could improve government functions. Furthermore, the law was unanimously approved by all political forces. Yet some evidence points to a rather ambiguous situation.

A first element of confusion originated from the way in which the new civil service system was structured in the law. Despite being a "Servicio Profesional de Carrera", or "Career Professional Civil Service", the PCS is actually closer to position-based systems such as the American one, rather than to career-based systems like the European ones (OECD 2008). According to the law (arts. 23 to 28), vacancies within the PCS should be filled through open competition procedures. Civil servants should only have formal preference over external competitors when examination results are tied. However, the CSL-2003 also introduced elements of a "career-based" system (Dussauge 2005, Cedillo 2006). Articles 35 to 39, for instance, describe a "Professional Development Subsystem", which explains how tenured civil servants are supposed to get hierarchical and monetary promotions within the system. In addition, this subsystem mandates the definition of "promotion-trajectories" as well as the design of "career plans". Yet article 37 then states that promotions should follow the same open competition procedures established for hiring purposes. In the end, open competition has been the rule for both hiring and promotions, whereas "career plans" and related activities have been relegated. This has had profound implications for the internal management of public personnel policies in ministries as "informal career paths" had existed for a long time, and hierarchical promotions were basically reserved for internal candidates. Public servants that were hoping the CSL-2003 would allow them to pursue a career within their ministries suddenly faced an "open competition" principle (Interviews I4, I5). Similarly, supervisors that previously had certain margins to decide on hierarchical promotions now had to coordinate with their ministry/agency's personnel office a public announcement for each new vacancy, even when suitable candidates existed within the same agency.

A second question that shows the apparent lack of agreement regarding the essence and objectives of the new system can be found within the very organization in charge of its implementation. Since its establishment in 2003, the MPA's Civil Service Unit has already had four Heads of Unit. While one of these changes could be attributed to the presidential transition of 2006–2007, the others would seem to be linked to other questions, including intra-bureaucratic conflicts about how to translate MBPP principles into administrative decisions (Méndez 2008, Interviews I1, I7). Similarly, during this same time period, the CSU was renamed three times: from the original "Unidad del Servicio Profesional y Recursos Humanos" (Civil Service and Human Resources Unit), to "Unidad de Recursos Humanos y Profesionalización" (Human Resources and Professionalization Unit), to "Unidad de Política de Recursos Humanos en la Administración Pública Federal" (Federal Public Administration Human Resources Policy Unit). In fact, the PCS nowadays occupies only a General Direction within the original Unit, reflecting both a change in institutional priorities and its diminished position in the government agenda.

A third issue that shows the lack of agreement about the objectives of the newly established MBPP is the persistence of "patronage" appointments across the federal government. According to a leading public policy scholar, "the traditional [hiring] methods are still alive and the majority of public administration positions are still being distributed among loyal people" (Merino 2008). This was also pointed out by a recent article that asserted almost 9,000 appointments had been made using article 34 of the CSL-2003 (López 2008). This article was originally introduced to allow for non-competitive, temporary appointments, needed in case of emergencies and other exceptional circumstances. If the numbers are correct, this would represent about 24 per cent of the whole PCS structure. While it is difficult to confirm that all of these appointments have been decided on purely political grounds, all interviewees agreed that discretion, personal loyalties and even party affiliations continue to play a significant role in hiring and promotion decisions.

The former points provide some interesting insights regarding why implementation of MBPP has been so complex. First of all, they certainly point to political inertia and bureaucratic resistance. The weight of the "Mexican administrative tradition" can be clearly observed in the latter issue, related to patronage-based appointments. A similar case could be argued with regard to the changing names of the bureaucratic unit in charge of the MBPP, as this has certainly reflected political resistance both inside and outside the MPA against the advancement of merit principles (Interviews I2, I6). Finally, the rotation of heads of the CSU could be also interpreted as a situation in which the traditionally high level of politicization of the Mexican government has affected administrative decisions. However, the influence of the "legacy of the past" could not be reduced to questions of patronage and politicization. A clear example of this has been the introduction of "position-based" system practices in federal ministries that had previously developed informal "career-based" system practices. In this case, the resistance to developing "open-competition" procedures (or its manipulation) and the use of article 34 have sometimes been linked to non-political considerations (Interviews I1, I3, I7), such as the lack of suitable external candidates for highly specialized positions; the desire to reward/promote internal candidates with a long record of high performance; or the need to nurture institutional *esprit de corps*. This particular issue leads back to the design aspects of the MBPP, as the decision to establish an "open" system, instead of a "closed" one, was less a product of past policies or political arrangements than a desire to build a "modern" civil service that avoided the "pitfalls" of "traditional" civil service models (Interviews I1, I7).

Dependency Relationships and Co-ordination

A fourth set of premises for achieving "perfect implementation" as discussed by Hogwood and Gunn (1984: 202–206; and see Ingraham 1987: 619–620), but also by many other authors in the implementation literature (Pressman and Wildavsky 1973, Hood 1976, Hill and Hupe 2002), are those related to the number of dependency relationships and co-ordination effectiveness among relevant actors.

A key feature of the Mexican system has been the high number of actors involved in implementation tasks from the beginning, a fact that has certainly complicated the process. The following provides a list of actors and their main roles:

a. The MPA (including the Secretary, the Undersecretary for Public Administration and the Head of the CSU), accountable for normative and control functions.
b. The Ministry of Finance, responsible for clearing budgetary resources.
c. About 76 federal ministries and agencies. Within each one, the number of key actors actually increases when both relevant political appointees (secretaries/undersecretaries/chief administrative officers) and administrative actors (HR director-generals) are taken into account.
d. The former Presidential Office of Government Innovation, which played a crucial role until 2006.
e. About 35,000 or so public servants with various HRM responsibilities, who have had to participate simultaneously in various activities to acquire tenured status.
f. Consulting firms and education centres, which have been contracted out for preparing various hiring, training and competency certification tools.

Obviously, the number and variety of actors described above has increased the complexity of MBPP implementation.

Adequate co-ordination has been further complicated by a number of reasons, such as the initial centralizing tendency assumed by the MPA with regard to key policy decisions (Pardo 2005, CIDE 2007a, Méndez 2008). According to the CSL-2003, a "shared responsibilities" system (see Ingraham et al. 2003) was established. In this system, the MPA plays two key roles: a "normative" one, for developing regulations, guidelines and other government-wide directives; and a "control" one, for enforcing merit principles and ensuring correct functioning of the PCS. Federal agencies were supposed to be responsible for two main activities: day-to-day implementation, including hiring procedures; and development of additional norms, procedures and decisions required by specific agency conditions. However, the CR-2004 drafted by the MPA's CSU assigned to the latter additional responsibilities over hiring, training and performance appraisals, many of which were beyond the original intentions of the CSL-2003 (CIDE 2007a, Interviews I3, I7). The then Undersecretary for Public Administration said "the strategy we have decided to follow is to centralize at the beginning some of the most important procedures. As [federal] institutions show maturity, procedures will be becoming more flexible, so that institutions can make increasingly more independent decisions" (Mesta 2004: 23–24). The issue was that agencies frequently had to wait for decisions made by the MPA, something that slowed down implementation in key personnel management areas such as position classification, which serves as a basis of all open-competition procedures (Pardo 2005, Martínez 2006).

Co-ordination issues appear to have been further affected by the lack of effective inter-agency communication channels (Dussauge 2006, Iacovello et al. 2006). Following the publication of the CSL-2003, the MPA launched a series of meetings to discuss practical implementation issues related to the new MBPP. A second round of meetings took place once the supplementary CR-2004 was published. According to some interviewees (Interviews I1, I3, I7), numerous HR director-generals attended both rounds of meetings, but they became increasingly disappointed because they thought their opinions were not influencing key decisions. As a consequence, agencies began to send lower-level representatives, or simply stopped attending the meetings. Agency representatives also criticized a certain lack of transparency among the CSU team, particularly after its second leadership change took place in 2006–2007.

MBPP implementation has been also affected by the involvement of external consultants and education centres. These have been contracted out at various points for developing HRM tools. According to the CSL-2003, tenured civil servants need to periodically certify their professional competencies (arts. 44 and 52). The CR-2004 also added that competency certification, training and hiring activities should be based on the assessment of "managerial competencies" (arts. 54 and 25). The problem was that the Mexican government lacked expertise in these matters (Pardo 2005, Cedillo 2007). As a consequence, the MPA and most federal agencies would need to rely on consultants and education centres, some of which did not have adequate expertise on these subjects either (Interviews I3, I5). New hiring tools, on-line training courses and competency certification examinations were developed, or adapted for public service organizations from their previous use in the private sector (Pardo 2009). These dependency relationships increased co-ordination problems between the MPA and federal agencies, as tools were not always available on time. More importantly, federal managers frequently complained about the quality and applicability of the new tools, and would often blame these for problems during hiring processes (for example, between 2004 and 2009 30–40% of the "open-competition" procedures did not have a winner; CIDE 2007a, Méndez 2008, Martínez 2009).

By looking at these co-ordination and dependency relationship issues, additional insights can be obtained about the Mexican case. It is possible to note again that Mexico's "administrative tradition" has constrained implementation. This was particularly the case with the "centralizing tendencies" of the MPA, which would seem to reflect past authoritarian practices by which control is held at the centre. However, other issues described above would seem to be linked to specific policy design flaws. This was particularly the case with the "managerial" competencies used for hiring purposes, which had not been originally included in the CSL-2003. Instead, these requirements were the product of technical decisions made by officials within the MPA, who considered that the Mexican civil service system should contain these and other components (for example performance appraisals) discussed in contemporary debates, despite the limited administrative capacities and experience throughout the federal government. The need to hire external consultants was thus left as the only choice to solve the conundrum of how practically to develop all these HR tools that promised so many benefits in theory. These issues would then deepen after the leadership changes in the MPA's CSU during 2003–2004, as the new team (mainly integrated by people from the private sector) would further support the use of both private sector consultants and HR tools originated in private sector personnel management environments (Interviews I1, I3, I6, I7, Pardo 2009).

Reforming the Reform: The New Code of Regulations of 2007

The series of implementation problems faced by the new MBPP between 2004 and 2007 would eventually lead to a revision of the initial supplementary regulations. This section will briefly describe the main purposes and contents of this second round of reforms, and will provide a provisional assessment of how it sought to pave the way for a better implementation. It will also suggest that the new code of regulations of 2007 (CR-2007), which substituted the CR-2004, still fails to solve all the original issues described above.

After the presidential transition of 2006, the new Secretary for Public Administration introduced changes to the regulatory framework that governed the federal MBPP. The decision was made after a series of meetings with Chief Administrative Officers ("Oficiales Mayores") from the federal agencies, who repeatedly expressed their dissatisfaction with the implementation process (Interview I1). Inside the MPA, the need to change the status quo was also recognized by the then Undersecretary (and current Secretary) for Public Administration, who was accountable for overseeing the work of the ministry's Civil Service Unit. According to him, there was

> a completely centralized procedure which implied that all Professional Career Service procedures needed to pass through the Undersecretary, [and] through a Unit in the Undersecretary; this implied not only long-during processes...; these procedures did not guarantee at all what we want...: that the best men and women have access to the public service. (Sosa 2008: 102)

As a result, the MPA launched a revision of the merit system in mid-2007, which ended up in the publication of a second code of regulations on September 7, 2007.

This reform was jointly conducted by a group of academic experts and policy analysts from the MPA's CSU. The team thoroughly analyzed previous implementation shortcomings, as reported in policy reports by the MPA, the Supreme Audit Institution and the Inter-American Development Bank, as well as by senior human resources officials (CIDE 2007a, 2007b, 2007c, Martínez 2009).

The CR-2007 introduced some significant changes (SFP 2007). First, it redistributed authority among participant agencies, seeking to establish a more decentralized system. This implied both a return to the CSL-2003's original intentions, as well as a reduction of dependency relationships between the agencies and the MPA. Second, it provided additional requirements for using article 34 of the CSL-2003, in order to limit the number of non-competitive appointments that were apparently being made for partisan reasons in most cases. Third, it deleted the concept of "managerial competencies" from the code of regulations to reduce complexities during hiring and training activities. Fourth, it attempted to reinforce the weight of the "professional development subsystem" so that agencies could develop hiring and promotion activities more in line with "career-based" principles, if deemed appropriate for their organizational needs. Finally, it also introduced the participation of inspector-generals (the MPA's division in charge of internal control and anti-corruption measures) as observers of personnel management decision-making processes.

Despite the relevance of some of these regulatory changes, a number of practical issues remained. By mid-2009, more than a year after the CR-2007 had been published, detailed rules for recruitment and selection, and for the new "professional development subsystem" had yet to be published (Fócil 2009). For all practical purposes, this meant that implementation of these HR subsystems had to follow the original rules of 2004 for a while. A second issue was that decentralization of authorities increased risks of "patronage" appointments. This point was raised by the interviewees, who also underlined that the MPA had not put in place adequate measures to ensure accountability of the federal agencies (Interviews I1, I2, I3). Thirdly, an issue that was basically ignored during this second round of reforms was how to limit problems of "asymmetrical implementation" due to differences in administrative capacity and expertise among participating agencies (Martínez 2005). Similarly, the question of how to reduce the dependency of government agencies (particularly the smaller ones) on consultants and education centres regarding the development of HR tools and solutions was not addressed either (Martínez 2009).

This brief analysis of the second round of reform offers additional insights regarding the introduction of MBPP in Mexico. The new regulations explicitly showed that a number of implementation issues could be directly linked to flaws in the original policy design, particularly in specific details introduced by the CR-2004. Therefore, the CR-2007 sought to correct these design features, at least at the level of secondary regulations. On the other hand, the reasons behind the reform, as well as the level of actual enforcement of the new CR-2007, also bring back to the picture the "legacy of the past". While recent decentralization efforts would seem to go against the traditional centralizing tendencies of the Mexican administrative system, they are actually a reflection of other traits of the country's "administrative tradition". The reform was set in motion more as a political response to bureaucratic conflicts within the federal government than as a way to promote flexible implementation. Thus, the decentralization of authorities was less a technical solution than a negotiated political strategy by which the MPA sought to return control to federal agencies over personnel management decisions (Interviews I2, I3). The lack of monitoring and enforcement of the merit principles by the MPA, even in the face of dubious hiring and promotion practices inside the civil service structure (Ramos 2007), would seem to respond to the same logic. More importantly, the loss of presidential attention regarding the new MBPP regulations, and the persistence of patronage-based appointments across government positions reserved for merit-based entry (Merino 2008), would seem to show that the traditional politicization of administrative affairs and the primacy of partisan affiliations and personal loyalties (albeit now under a different governing party) still constrain the consolidation of MBPP in Mexico.

Concluding Remarks

The analysis of the Mexican experience would seem to prove that implementation of MBPP certainly represents a difficult endeavour for Latin American countries. It would also seem to confirm that, despite recent democratic transitions, the "administrative tradition" that has characterized the region (for example high politicization of administrative affairs, patronage and "amiguismo", centralism and illegality) has not faded away. In fact, it continues to strongly constrain the development and consolidation of well-functioning merit-based civil service systems and policies. On the other hand, the analysis developed here demonstrates that the question of why developing MBPP remains so difficult in Mexico (and perhaps other Latin American countries) cannot be answered by a simple consideration of institutional and political inertias. In the end, the Mexican case has proved to be useful for better understanding the causal mechanisms that are behind unsuccessful MBPP implementation, and thus provides valuable insights for refining our theoretical ideas and propositions on this topic (Rueschemeyer 2003, George and Bennett 2005, Yin 2009).

In particular, there are at least five main conclusions that might be drawn from the Mexican experience, all of which might be relevant for analyzing other countries in the same region. Firstly, the analysis has made clear that political factors linked to the Mexican or Latin American "administrative traditions" can affect the development of new MBPP both *before and after* implementation has begun. In other words, high politicization might damage the impartiality and legality of actions by which implementation of MBPP takes place (for example by following partisan considerations, instead of merit principles, for hiring purposes). Yet it might also influence its institutional or administrative dimensions beforehand (for example by tying policy timeframes to electoral cycles, as in the case of the three-year limit for implementing the new PCS). In doing so, the "legacy of the past" is actually affecting the implementation of new MBPP twice: by conditioning policy design features, which delineate the future implementation process; and by constraining the actual implementation process.

Secondly, however, the case also demonstrates that not all institutional resistance necessarily reflects practices inherited from the past, even if these take the form of bureaucratic politics. Given the considerable number of new civil service appointments made under article 34 of the CSL-2003 (which allows for temporal, non-competitive entry under exceptional conditions), it would be naive to ignore the persistence of "patronage". Yet it might be equally inadequate to attribute to patronage every single action affecting the consolidation of MBPP. As mentioned above, within the Mexican public administration the "spoils system" coexisted with informal merit-based promotions and informal career paths, which in some policy sectors were followed in quite a regular way. Therefore, some federal agencies and public servants might be resisting implementation of new MBPP not because they are against the introduction of merit principles *per se*. Perhaps they do so because the new system (for example open-competition principle for recruitment and promotions in all federal agencies) do not fit well with past organizational practices (such as promotion limited to internal candidates).

Thirdly, it should be noted that not all implementation problems faced by the Mexican government have been political problems (either in the partisan or in the bureaucratic sense). Past problems of co-ordination, lack of resources, time constraints, administrative capacity restrictions (all of which have appeared in one way or the other during these years) can happen anywhere. Questions of partisan advocacy, deliberate mistakes, or even favouritism in tendering procedures or the management of external consultancies certainly might have occurred (Interviews I2, I3). Yet it would be difficult to attribute all implementation problems to political issues, or to a particular (Mexican) "administrative tradition". On the contrary, inadequate decisions regarding external consultants; erroneous assumptions about the applicability of HR tools; or untimely adjustments to HR guidelines or formats might have been originated in a lack of knowledge and expertise on public personnel management questions.

Fourthly, the Mexican experience also seems to show that not all issues faced in the introduction of new MBPP are necessarily "implementation" issues. The previous pages have shown that a number of these problems might be better explained by looking at flaws or limitations in the particular design of the civil service policy. In this sense, they might be representative of the Mexican case only, and not of other Latin American countries. Some examples of "policy design" issues are the inclusion of "position-based" *and* "career-based" systems' features in the general architecture of the PCS; or the additional details introduced by the first code of regulations of 2004 (for example the use of "managerial competencies" for hiring purposes) which had not been originally considered by the CSL-2003. Although it is true that these decisions were made under political pressure, those involved in the process also had a considerable degree of autonomy. These features thus reflected technical considerations about what might be a "best practice", as well as aspirations regarding what a "modern" civil service system should look like.

The previous pages have shown that MBPP in Mexico have not necessarily received adequate levels of political attention and support. In this sense, the question of how to persuade Latin American political leaders about the long-term administrative and societal benefits that MBPP might bring to their countries certainly remains to be answered. However, the revision of the Mexican experience also demonstrates that a number of issues faced when introducing new MBPP mainly relate to policy design and policy implementation matters. These are issues that could have been avoided in the Mexican case, and thus do not need to happen in other Latin American countries as well. A clearer civil service framework; a better fit between the general structure of civil service system and the particularities of each participant agency; a more careful sequencing of implementation stages; an easier transition from non-tenured to tenured status for those public servants with relevant experience and academic background; and a stronger development of personnel management capacities are but a few areas in which appropriate administrative, regulatory and policy measures might be taken beforehand. By looking at Mexico's civil service reform experience, Latin American (and other) countries might thus draw relevant lessons for learning how to overcome the challenges of developing and implementing their own merit-based personnel policies in the future.

Acknowledgements

The author would like to thank Alex Turrini, Victor Bekkers, Greta Nasi, Salvador Parrado, Richard Huff, Harald Sætren and the other participants in the "Fifth International Comparative Policy Analysis Forum Workshop" (Milano) for their very helpful comments on a first draft of this article. Interviewees in Mexico generously shared with the author their invaluable knowledge about the Mexican reform process, something that is much appreciated. María del Carmen Pardo, Rafael Martínez Puón, Mauricio Merino, Alfredo Muñoz, David Arellano and Maira Vaca kindly read the manuscript and provided additional information, interesting ideas and most encouraging comments, all of which were essential for preparing this final draft. Last but not least, the constructive criticisms offered by two JCPA anonymous reviewers were extremely useful for refining the article's argumentation and theoretical approach, and are thus gratefully acknowledged.

Interviews

I1. Director-General for Human Resources, Federal Ministry, January 8, 2009.
I2. Director of Area, PCS tenured member, Civil Service Unit, MPA, January 9, 2009.
I3. Former Head of the Civil Service Unit, A, January 13, 2009.
I4. Director of Area, PCS tenured member, MPA, January 13, 2009.
I5. Director of Area, PCS tenured member, MPA, January 13, 2009.
I6. Former Head of the Civil Service Unit, B, January 14, 2009.
I7. Former Director-General for Human Resources, Federal Ministry, January 20, 2009.

References

Arellano, David, 1999, Mexican public sector reform: patrimonialist values and governmental organisational culture in Mexico. *International Review of Public Administration*, **4**, 67–77.

Arellano, David, 2008, La implementación de un servicio civil meritocrático: ¿un asunto técnico? El Caso de México, in: Francisco Longo and Carles Ramió (Eds) *La profesionalización del empleo público en América Latina* (Barcelona: Fundació CIDOB), pp. 143–169.
Arellano, David, Egaña, Rodrigo, Oszlak, Oscar and Pacheco, Regina, 2003, *Retos de la profesionalización de la función pública* (Caracas: CLAD).
Arellano, David and Guerrero, Juan Pablo, 2003, Stalled administrative reforms of the Mexican state, in: Ben Ross Schneider and Blanca Heredia (Eds) *Reinventing Leviathan. The Politics of Administrative Reform in Developing Countries* (Miami: North South Center Press), pp. 151–179.
Auditoría Superior de la Federación (ASF), 2006, *Informe del Resultado de la Revisión y Fiscalización Superior de la Cuenta Pública 2005* (Mexico: Auditoría Superior de la Federación).
Barzelay, Michael, 2007, Learning from second-hand experience: methodology for extrapolation-oriented case research. *Governance*, 20, 521–543.
Barzelay, Michael, Gaetani, Francisco, Cortázar, Juan Carlos and Cejudo, Guillermo, 2003, Research on public management policy change in the Latin America region: a conceptual framework and methodological guide. *International Public Management Review*, 4, 20–41.
Casas, Antonio, 2005, El Servicio Profesional de Carrera: un sistema complejo pero impostergable para la consolidación del buen gobierno. *Servicio Profesional de Carrera*, 3, 67–76.
Cedillo, Miguel Ángel, 2006, El desafío de una nueva normatividad, in: Mauricio Merino (Ed) *Los desafíos del Servicio Profesional de Carrera* (Mexico: CIDE), pp. 147–186.
Cedillo, Miguel, Ángel, 2007, Un largo y sinuoso camino: La evaluación de dos subsistemas del Servicio Profesional de Carrera desde el punto de vista del Modelo y su Implementación. *Servicio Profesional de Carrera*, 8, 51–67.
Cejudo, Guillermo M., 2003, Public management policy change in Mexico, 1982–2000. *International Public Management Journal*, 6, 309–325.
CIDE, 2007a, Asesoría para la reforma del Servicio Profesional de Carrera en la Administración Pública Federal (Mexico: CIDE).
CIDE, 2007b, Elementos operativos para la transición al nuevo modelo de Servicio Profesional de Carrera (Mexico: CIDE).
CIDE, 2007c, Recomendaciones operativas para la puesta en marcha de los 29 puntos críticos del SPC (Mexico: CIDE).
Dussauge Laguna, Mauricio, I., 2005, Sobre la pertinencia del Servicio Profesional de Carrera en México. *Foro Internacional*, 182, 761–794.
Dussauge Laguna, Mauricio, I., 2006, Diferencias estructurales, retos comunes: los servicios profesionales de México y Estados Unidos en una perspectiva comparada, *Servicio Profesional de Carrera*, 5, 147–186.
Dussauge Laguna, Mauricio, I., 2008, Paradoxes of public sector reform: the Mexican experience, 2000–2007. *International Review of Public Management*, 9, 56–75.
Dussauge Laguna, Mauricio I., 2010, Combate a la corrupción y rendición de cuentas: avances, pendientes y retrocesos, in: José Luis Méndez (Ed) *Políticas Públicas* (Mexico: El Colegio de México), pp. 207–252.
Echebarría, Koldo (Ed) 2006, *Informe sobre la situación del servicio civil en América Latina* (Washington, DC: Inter-American Development Bank).
Echebarría, Koldo and Cortázar, Juan Carlos, 2007, Public administration reform and public employment reform in Latin America, in: Eduardo Lora (Ed) *The State of State Reform in Latin America* (Washington, DC: Inter-American Development Bank-Stanford University Press), pp. 123–155.
El Universal, 2006, Vuelven amiguismo y compadrazgo, editorial page of *El Universal*, March 30.
Evans, Peter and Rauch, James E., 1999, Bureaucracy and growth: a cross-national analysis of the effects of Weberian state structures on economic growth. *American Sociological Review*, 64, 748–765.
Fócil, Mario, 2009, Servicio Profesional de Carrera en México de "Esperando a Godoy" al "Gatopardo". *Buen Gobierno*, 6, 151–165.
Fox, Vicente, 2003, Palabras del Presidente Vicente Fox Quesada durante el acto de firma del Decreto por el que se expide la Ley del Servicio Profesional de Carrera en la Administración Pública Federal, April 9.
Geddes, Barbara, 1994, *Politician's Dilemma*, Berkeley: University of California Press.
General Accounting Office, 2004, *High-Performing Organizations* (Washington, DC: GAO).
George, Alexander and Bennett, Andrew, 2005, *Case Studies and Theory Development in the Social Sciences* (Cambridge, MA: MIT Press).

Grindle, Merilee, 1977, Patrons and clients in the bureaucracy: career networks in Mexico. *Latin American Research Review*, **12**, 37–66.
Guerrero, Juan Pablo, 1998, Un estudio de caso de la reforma administrativa en México: los dilemas de la instauración de un servicio civil a nivel federal, CIDE, Documento de Trabajo de Administración Pública, no. 61.
Herrera, Alejandro, 2004, Algunas consideraciones en la implementación del Servicio Profesional de Carrera en México para hacer frente a la globalización. *Servicio Profesional de Carrera*, **1**, 95–110.
Herrera, Alejandro, 2008, Hacia un balance del Servicio Profesional de Carrera en México a cinco años de la publicación de la Ley. *Servicio Profesional de Carrera*, **9**, 25–32.
Hernández, Rogelio, 2000, Los altos mandos de la administración pública mexicana, in: José Luis Méndez (Ed) *Lecturas básicas de administración y políticas públicas* (Mexico: El Colegio de México), pp. 465–476.
Hill, Michael and Hupe, Peter L., 2002, *Implementing Public Policy* (London: Sage).
Hogwood, Brian W. and Gunn, Lewis A., 1984, *Policy Analysis for the Real World* (Oxford: Oxford University Press).
Hood, Christopher, 1976, *The Limits of Administration* (London: Wiley).
Hood, Christopher, 1991, A public management for all seasons? *Public Administration*, **69**, 3–19.
Iacovello, Mercedes, Rodríguez, Ana Laura and Orozco, Ivania de la Cruz, 2006, Síntesis del diagnóstico Caso México, in: Koldo Echebarría (Ed) *Informe sobre la situación del servicio civil en América Latina* (Washington, DC: Inter-American Development Bank), pp. 319–355.
Ingraham, Patricia W., 1987, Toward more systematic consideration of policy design. *Policy Studies Journal*, **15**, 611–628.
Ingraham, Patricia, W., Joyce, Philip and Donahue, Amy, K., 2003, *Government Performance. Why Management Matters?* Baltimore, MD: The Johns Hopkins University Press.
Kliksberg, Bernardo, 2005, Public administration in Latin America: promises, frustrations and new examinations. *International Review of Administrative Sciences*, **71**, 309–326.
Klingner, Donald E., 1996, Public personnel management and democratization: a view from three central republics. *Public Administration Review*, **56**, 390–399.
Klitgaard, Robert and Light, Paul C., 2005, *High Performance Government* (Santa Monica, CA: RAND Corporation).
Longo, Francisco and Ramió, Carles (Eds), 2008, *La profesionalización del empleo público en América Latina* (Barcelona: Fundació CIDOB).
López, Ángel, 2008, La reforma del servicio profesional de carrera. ¿Cambiar para quedar igual? *Política Digital*, **46**, 46.
May, Peter, 2003, Policy design and implementation, in: B. Guy Peters and Jon Pierre (Eds) *Handbook of Public Administration* (London: Sage), pp. 223–233.
Martínez Puón, Rafael, 2005, *Servicio Profesional de Carrera ¿Para qué?* (Mexico: Miguel Ángel Porrúa).
Martínez Puón, Rafael, 2006, Alcances y resultados del Servicio Profesional de Carrera en México. *Gestión y Política Pública*, **XV**, 455–482.
Martínez Puón, Rafael, 2009, La nueva fisonomía del Servicio Profesional de Carrera. *Reforma y Democracia*, **43**, 177–206.
Méndez, José, Luis, 1997, The Latin American administrative tradition, in: *International Encyclopaedia of Public Policy and Administration* (Boulder, CO: Westview).
Méndez, José Luis, 2000, La profesionalización del Estado mexicano: ¿olvidando o esperando a Godot?, in: José Luis Méndez (Ed) *Lecturas básicas de administración y políticas públicas* (Mexico: El Colegio de México), pp. 477–501.
Méndez, José Luis, 2004, Retos inmediatos del Servicio Profesional de Carrera en México. *Servicio Profesional de Carrera*, **1**, 5–12.
Méndez, José Luis, 2008, Diseño, aprobación e implementación del Servicio Profesional en México. Lecciones y retos. *Servicio Profesional de Carrera*, **9**, 9–24.
Merino, Mauricio, 1996, De la lealtad individual a la responsabilidad pública. *Revista de Administración Pública*, **91**, 5–18.
Merino, Mauricio, 2004, Inadvertido Servicio Profesional de Carrera. *El Universal*, April 3.
Merino, Mauricio (Ed), 2006a, *Los desafíos del Servicio Profesional de Carrera* (Mexico: CIDE).
Merino, Mauricio, 2006b, Otra regresión cínica. *El Universal*, April 1.
Merino, Mauricio, 2008, Puros leales. *El Universal*, September 17.

Mesta, Jesús, 2004, Ley del Servicio Profesional de Carrera en la Administración Pública Federal. *Servicio Profesional de Carrera*, **1**, 13–26.

Moctezuma, Esteban and Roemer, Andrés, 1999, *Por un gobierno con resultados* (Mexico: FCE).

Nef, Jorge, 2003, Public administration and public sector reform in Latin America, in: B. Guy Peters and Jon Pierre (Eds) *Handbook of Public Administration* (London: Sage).pp. 523–535.

OECD, 2005, *Modernising Government. The Way Forward* (Paris: OECD).

OECD, 2008, *The State of the Public Service* (Paris: OECD).

Otero, Silvia, 2004, 'Pobre', la capacitación a servidores públicos. *El Universal*, October 22.

Otero, Silvia, 2006, Critican que omitan concursos para elegir a funcionarios. *El Universal*, March 30.

Page, Edward C., 1995, Comparative public administration in Britain. *Public Administration*, **73**, 123–141.

Pardo, María del Carmen, 2000, El servicio civil de carrera en México: un imperativo de la modernización, in: José Luis Méndez (Ed.) *Lecturas básicas de administración y políticas públicas* (Mexico: El Colegio de México), pp. 445–464.

Pardo, María del Carmen, 2003, La modernización administrativa zedillista, ¿más de los mismo? *Foro Internacional*, **XLIII**, 192–214.

Pardo, María del Carmen, 2005, El Servicio Profesional de Carrera en México: de la tradición al cambio. *Foro Internacional*, **XLV**, 599–634.

Pardo, María del Carmen, 2009, *La modernización administrativa en México* (Mexico: El Colegio de México).

Parrado, Salvador, 2008, Las estrategias de implantación de una profesionalización del empleo público en Centroamérica y el Caribe, in: Francisco Longo and Carles Ramió (Eds) *La profesionalización del empleo público en América Latina* (Barcelona: Fundació CIDOB), pp. 219–259.

Peters, B. Guy, 2008, The Napoleonic tradition. *International Journal of Public Sector Management*, **21**, 118–132.

Poder Ejecutivo, 2006, Decreto que establece las medidas de austeridad y disciplina del gasto en la Administración Pública Federal. *Diario Oficial*, December 4.

Pollitt, Christopher and Bouckaert, Geert, 2004, *Public Management Reform*, 2nd edition (Oxford: Oxford University Press).

Pressman, Jeffrey and Wildavsky, Aaron, 1973, *Implementation* (Berkeley: University of California Press).

Ramió, Carles and Salvador, Miquel, 2005, *Instituciones y Nueva Gestión Pública en América Latina* (Barcelona: Fundació CIDOB).

Ramió, Carles and Salvador, Miquel, 2008, Civil service reform in Latin America: external referents versus own capacities. *Bulletin of Latin American Research*, **27**, 554–573.

Ramos, Jorge, 2007, Desdén al servicio Profesional de Carrera. *El Universal*, March 10.

Reséndiz, Francisco, 2004, Anular nombramientos ilegales de funcionarios, pide la Cámara a Fox. *Crónica*, December 6.

Rose, Richard, 2005, *Learning from Comparative Public Policy* (London: Routledge).

Rueschemeyer, Dietrich, 2003, Can one or a few cases yield gains?, in: Dietrich Rueschemeyer and James Mahoney (Eds) *Comparative Historical Analysis in the Social Sciences* (Cambridge: Cambridge University Press), pp. 305–336.

Ruiz, José Luis, 2003, Firman Ley del Servicio Profesional de Carrera. *El Universal*, April 10.

Sánchez, Alejandro, 2007, El Servicio Profesional de Carrera: una crítica constructiva al diseño e implementación en México. *Servicio Profesional de Carrera*, **7**, 39–55.

Secretaría de la Función Pública (SFP), 2003, Ley del Servicio Profesional de Carrera en la Administración Pública Federal, Diario Oficial de la Federación, April, 10.

Secretaría de la Función Pública (SFP), 2004, Reglamento de la Ley del Servicio Profesional de Carrera en la Administración Pública Federal, Diario Oficial de la Federación, April, 2.

Secretaría de la Función Pública (SFP), 2005, *Transparencia, Buen Gobierno y Combate a la Corrupción en la Función Pública* (Mexico: Fondo de Cultura Económica).

Secretaría de la Función Pública (SFP), 2007, Reglamento de la Ley del Servicio Profesional de Carrera en la Administración Pública Federal, Diario Oficial de la Federación, September, 6.

Secretaría de la Función Pública (SFP), 2008, Informe Anual de Operación del Servicio Profesional de Carrera en la Administración Pública Federal 2007 (Mexico: Secretaría de la Función Pública).

Solís, Juan, 2007, CONACULTA pasa por alto ley de SPC, *El Universal*, February 21.

Sosa, José, 2000, Gobierno y Administración Pública en México: apuntes para una discusión abierta, *Foro Internacional*, **XL**, 522–551.

Sosa, José, 2008, La modernización del gobierno mexicano a partir de la mejora de su gestión: entrevista a Salvador Vega Casillas, Secretario de la Función Pública. *Revista de Administración Pública*, **115**, 97–111.

Spink, Peter, 1999, Possibilities and political imperatives: seventy years of administrative reforms, in: Luiz Carlos Bresser Pereira and Peter Spink (Eds) *Reforming the State. Managerial Public Administration in Latin America* (Boulder, CO: Lynne Rienner Publishers), pp. 91–114.

Téllez, Cecilia, 2007, Acusan al Gobierno de violar la Ley de Servicio Profesional de Carrera, *Crónica*, March 5.

Valverde, Miguel Ángel, 2007, El Servicio Profesional de Carrera en la Administración Pública Federal en México: consideraciones sobre su implementación. *Servicio Profesional de Carrera*, **7**, 25–38.

Velasco, Elizabeth, 2007, Reprueban al servicio profesional de carrera. *La Jornada*, May 15.

Villoria, Manuel, 2007, *El Servicio Civil de Carrera en Latinoamérica*. Madrid: INAP.

World Bank, 1997, *The State in a Changing World*. Washington, DC: The World Bank.

Wright, Vincent, 1994, Reshaping the state: the implications for public administration. *West European Politics*, **17**, 102–137.

Yin, Robert K., 2009, *Case Study Research*, 4th edition (London: Sage).

Public Personnel Policies and Problems in the New Democracies of Central and Eastern Europe

TIINA RANDMA-LIIV and JANE JÄRVALT

ABSTRACT *The development of personnel policies in the new democracies of Central and Eastern Europe (CEE) may be divided into three periods: institution building and introduction of modern personnel policies in the 1990s; Europeanization of personnel policies before acceding to the EU; and making further adjustments after accession. The development of selected personnel policies in new CEE democracies is analyzed. The paper concludes by recommending that, in modernizing their personnel policies, countries going through similar changes should (1) keep a strategic view; (2) pay close attention to the details of implementation; and (3) recognize the key role of top public servants.*

Introduction

The relationship between personnel policies and organizational performance has been thoroughly discussed in both academic and applied organizational settings (for example, Evans and Rauch 1999). Yet the question of whether people management contributes to a more professional and better-performing public service, and helps to reform the structure of public administration, remains highly relevant – especially in environments characterized by sweeping political, social and economic changes.

Public management reforms in new European democracies have already been studied by a number of researchers (Ridley 1995, Hesse 1996, Verheijen 1998, Drechsler 2000, Goetz 2001, Meyer-Sahling 2004). Yet the personnel management component of these reform attempts has so far not received sufficient academic attention. The paper at hand proposes to make up for that deficit by highlighting and exploring a selection of key personnel policies within the public services of the Central and East European (CEE) countries that have acceded to the European Union. Although there are important differences among those, they still appear to share a number of common developments, opportunities and risks.

The paper draws on the records and commentary concerning key aspects of public service reforms, including reports of the World Bank and OECD (Support for Improvement in Governance and Management (SIGMA)), and various government websites of the countries in question. Where possible, the authors have expanded the above-mentioned material by considering applicable legislation, previous country studies, and their personal experience and observations. Employing a broad range of information sources has allowed the authors to gain an insight into two dynamic decades of fundamental political and administrative reforms and an opportunity for generalization.

The success of any government is determined largely by its ability to attract and retain a high-quality and high-performance workforce. Governments of all CEE countries have attempted to develop personnel policies in which decisions regarding an individual's selection and progress are guided by comparative merit or achievement, and in which the conditions and rewards of performance contribute to the competency and continuity of the public service (Goetz and Wollmann 2001). Three periods are distinguished in the development of personnel policies in CEE countries: (1) institution building and introduction of modern personnel policies in the 1990s; (2) efforts to reform public personnel policy before acceding to the EU; and (3) fine-tuning the reforms after joining the EU in 2004 and 2007. In addition, four key areas of personnel policy that affect the movement of people into, through and from the public service are examined: recruitment and career management, training and development, performance management and rewards. In this paper, the focus is exclusively on central government. The paper concludes with specific policy recommendations for designing and implementing personnel reforms in countries which are undergoing processes of transition and Europeanization similar to those experienced by CEE states.

Development of Public Personnel Policies in CEE Countries

The 10 CEE states that have to date acceded to the EU (the Czech Republic, Estonia, Hungary, Latvia, Lithuania, Poland, Slovakia and Slovenia in 2004, and Bulgaria and Romania in 2007) have gone through major changes in the last two decades. These changes were a response to the challenges of post-communist transition, to the development from candidate status to full membership of the EU and to making further adjustments in personnel policies after joining the EU. The development of personnel policies in the CEE countries has been influenced by broadly similar societal, legal and economic factors. Therefore, an examination of the background and underlying dynamics of the personnel reform efforts of those countries allows us to sketch a set of common features reflecting developments in the policy design and legislation as well as in the actual implementation of personnel policies.

Institution Building and Introduction of Modern Personnel Policies in the 1990s

Several authors (Ridley 1995, Hesse 1996, Verheijen 1998, Drechsler 2000, Goetz 2001) have observed that the absorption of decision makers in urgent economic, political and social problems of post-communist transition tends to downgrade administrative reforms to a lesser priority. Although public service reform is usually ranked among the so-called "second generation" reforms of transition (Verheijen 2003), the governments of CEE countries understood the necessity of reforming their administrative apparatuses. It was clear already in the 1990s that an underdeveloped public service shaped by inconsistent and inadequate personnel policies was likely to jeopardize the continuation of political and economic reforms, and make further stabilization unlikely (Beblavy 2002). Lucking (2003) has argued that the fact that CEE countries had to go through early stages of transition without the benefit of a system of general personnel policy guidelines, led to lower efficiency, higher costs and poorer services.

One of the main problems in public personnel management in CEE countries stemmed from a tradition of not regarding public servants as a category apart from other types of employees. Thus, at the beginning of the 1990s, public servants in post-communist CEE countries (with the exception of Poland), were subject to general labour codes, and enjoyed no special status, or any particular social guarantees. The public services in former communist countries were a clear example of a patronage (spoils) system with no regard for merit principles. Contrary to developments in many old democracies, which in the 1990s took steps to reduce differences in the general employment arrangements applicable in the public and private sectors, the CEE countries all passed public service laws (see Table 1), granting public servants a special status and deliberately emphasizing the distinction between public and private employees.

Although this legislation was not fully implemented in all countries (World Bank 2006), the enactment created a basis for the development of merit principles in the public service. Through that, all subfields of personnel policies (for example, recruitment, training, career or incentive systems) were fundamentally challenged, and in most cases also reformed.

At the beginning of transition, no strong bureaucratic constraints existed in the CEE countries to endanger public personnel reforms, as they did in Western countries with long public service traditions and well-established administrative cultures. Yet the countries in question had to contend with a Communist legacy that included patronage networks and considerable ideological influence. The positive role of public servants could not be taken for granted in CEE countries that lacked an established tradition and experience of democratic governance. The absence of a positive concept of the state and the resulting lack of a sense of ownership on the part of the citizens led to serious problems. Among other things, these included a negative image of public service careers, a lack of loyalty on the part of citizens, rivalries between government units, ebbing commitment among public servants, an absence of a common administrative culture and a lack of co-operation within the public service (Drechsler 2000, Verheijen 2003, Riigikantselei 2008).

The early years of transition coincided with a period of Western thinking about the state that was dominated by neo-liberal concepts of public management. The New Public Management (NPM) fashion also prevailed in the international organizations (for example, the World Bank and the International Monetary Fund (IMF)) and countries that had served as models for CEE reforms, especially the USA and the UK (Verheijen 2003: 490). The NPM ideology sat well with CEE countries that did not like big state apparatuses, and were carrying out large-scale privatizations as a part of a radical reworking of their one-sector economies. In

Table 1. Adoption of public service legislation in selected CEE countries

Country	Year of adoption of Public Service Act(s)
Bulgaria	1999
Czech Republic	2002
Estonia	1995
Hungary	1992
Latvia	1994, 2000
Lithuania	1995, 1999
Poland	1982, 1996, 1998
Romania	1999
Slovakia	2001
Slovenia	1990, 2002

Sources: Beblavy (2002), Boussaert and Demmke (2003), Meyer-Sahling (2004).

personnel policies, this led to solutions based on deregulation and decentralization, as well as on "letting the managers manage". However, the introduction of merit principles in "deregulated" public service settings has proved difficult, as demonstrated in the following sections.

Finally, the dilemma between continuity and change in the public service became an important issue during the early years of transition. In most CEE countries, for example in Bulgaria and Romania as well as in Hungary, a majority of the old cadre remained in office as governments did not initiate replacement of civil servants (Drechsler 2003, Meyer-Sahling 2004). However, in other countries the *nomenklatura* problems were not so severe. For example in Estonia changes in personnel were especially marked in 1992-93, when 37 per cent of public servants were replaced (Drechsler 2003). By 2000, the proportion of Estonian public servants who had worked in the public service for less than 10 years reached 76 per cent (Riigikantselei 2001). A rapidly developing private sector created many new jobs that required new qualifications and provided interesting opportunities for personal growth. As several authors (Jasaitis 1999, Randma 2001) have demonstrated, in a time of increasing career opportunities, the public sector was losing out to the private sector, which was preferred by labour market "winners" on account of higher salaries and better growth prospects. This, in turn, became an obstacle in designing and implementing public personnel reforms (Beblavy 2002, World Bank 2006).

"Europeanization" of Personnel Policies before Accession to the EU

A key challenge faced by governments in transitional environments is one of maintaining a strategic view in the context of constantly changing political frameworks. However, the history of public administration development in CEE tells a mixed story of piecemeal and ill-sequenced attempts to reform existing systems (Verheijen 2003). In the late 1990s and the beginning of the 2000s, the European integration process was one of the few stable strategic goals that provided the backbone for administrative reforms. It also created an important motive for systematic development of personnel policies (Grabbe 2001, Viks and Randma-Liiv 2005). Although public personnel management *per se* was not part of the *acquis communautaire* to be formally incorporated into a country's legal framework in order for the country to join the EU, entrants were required to have a functioning administrative system. The legalistic nature of the *acquis* mainly focused the accession process on changes in the legal framework, yet to an extent also spilled over into substantive public service reform (Beblavy 2002).

The European Commission was rather successful in pushing through major formal institutional instruments (such as the adoption of Public Service Laws in some candidate countries, most notably in the Czech and Slovak Republics), but it was much less successful in influencing the actual content of change and the implementation of new legislation (Beblavy 2002, Meyer-Sahling 2009). The implementation gap between the adoption of formal acts and procedures, and their realization, has been a serious problem in most CEE countries (Verheijen 1998). Researchers have revealed ample evidence of continuing patronage in a number of accession countries that possessed a legal framework ostensibly creating the necessary preconditions for a democratic public service and public personnel management (Jasaitis 1999: 305–307, Verheijen 1999: 98). For instance, it was observed in Latvia that although most vacancies were announced as essentially "open", their openness was in many cases effectively negated by the specifics of decentralized selection procedures (Simanis 1999). Moreover, the Czech public service law had not become effective by 2006 yet (World Bank 2006).

Therefore, it could be argued that in the Europeanization process too much reliance was placed on legislation as the main reform instrument. As for the "softer" European values behind personnel reforms, the goal of developing a "European Administrative Space" operating by a set of common principles including the rule of law, openness and transparency, accountability, efficiency and effectiveness, was well known in CEE countries during the accession process. It is unclear, though, if this had any actual influence on the reality of personnel reforms and practices.

Adjustments in Personnel Policies after Joining the EU

While transition and EU accession could be seen as periods of "project management" characterized by a series of clear targets and deadlines, the ensuing membership period has brought with it permanent demands for managing complex processes. This requires careful attention to structural defects in personnel policies, which may have been neglected during the rush of transition and accession. As EU compatibility could be seen as the benchmark for evaluating new member states' administrative arrangements, the significance of external pressure and expectations in shaping the path of reforms has decreased following accession. EU policies towards the new member states all but neglect developments in their public services, which means that the sustainability of personnel reforms essentially depends on the domestic factors (Meyer-Sahling 2009).

One of the widely recognized obstacles to root-and-branch reform is political instability. Frequent political swings have effectively reduced the prospects of reform continuation in several countries. Government changes in Poland, Slovakia, the Czech Republic and Slovenia between 2004 and 2006 meant that the public service reforms negotiated and initiated before accession were put on the back-burner (see Meyer-Sahling 2009). Indeed, those in charge of drafting important reform legislation are rarely in office for long enough to oversee (and responsibly care for) its implementation. The work of previous governments is often rejected on principle, and any institutions and functions created by them are subject to almost automatic reshuffles. A lack of consensus in the direction of personnel reforms leads to a lack of continuity. In addition, frequent cabinet changes tend to result in changes in personnel, especially at the top level. Although the reasons for these changes have been widely different, such turbulence in high public offices makes trust building, serious commitment and enhancement of co-operation difficult, especially considering the fact that top officials usually play a key role in developing and implementing strategic personnel policies.

Despite the fact that the Europeanization process has contributed to the general development of co-ordination culture in CEE governments (Viks and Randma-Liiv 2005), insufficient policy co-ordination has resulted in uneven development and fragmentation of personnel policies within individual countries (Verheijen 2003). Albeit there are certain "islands of success", these tend to be limited and, as a rule, cannot be considered instances of irreversible progress (Verheijen 2003). These "success stories" tend to co-exist with essentially unreformed public institutions and personnel policy practices, which makes a generalized assessment of reform results complicated. Better co-ordination could help to prevent the introduction of conflicting regulations and policies by different public organizations. In reality, however, horizontal management systems such as central public service agencies or departments have in several cases been weakened or removed – most conspicuously in Poland, Slovakia and the Czech Republic. Hungary and Estonia also lack a central authority to coordinate their personnel policies (see Table 2). This, in turn, increases the risks of politicization, problems with equal opportunities and the decreasing transparency of personnel policies (Lucking 2003, Meyer-Sahling 2004, Randma-Liiv 2005).

Chronic resource shortage, be it financial, organizational or human, has also been pointed out as an obstacle to effective implementation of reforms (Goetz 2001, World Bank 2006). It remains to be seen to what extent the economic and financial downturn of 2008 reduces investments in the public service personnel, or whether it can provide new incentives for personnel development and promote discussions of the quality and effectiveness of the public service. Shortage of economic resources might be a possible constraint on the pace of reform, but should not prevent a strategic approach (Lucking 2003).

There are a number of challenges facing the public services of CEE that cannot be implemented by decree. Making amendments in the public service laws can only be a precondition for improving the everyday practice of personnel management. Whereas the two first periods of personnel development tended to focus on policy making by ensuring the presence of a modern legal and institutional framework, the challenge of the third period lies in the constant improvement of policy implementation through permanent reflection, feedback and evaluation of personnel policies.

Key Personnel Policies – Problems and Prospects

Fundamental public service reforms in all CEE states have, with greater or lesser success, addressed four key areas of personnel policy. Although the overall starting platform as well as the direction of reform has been the same – to move from a

Table 2. Responsibility for co-ordination and management of the public service in selected CEE countries

Country	Authority
Central authority	
Lithuania	Civil Service Department under the Ministry of Interior, established in 2002
Latvia	State Chancellery, responsible for public service since 2003
Slovenia	Ministry of Public Administration, established in 2004
Fragmented or partial authority	
Hungary	Government Centre for Public Administration and Human Resource Services under the Prime Minister's Office, established in 2007
Estonia	Ministry of Justice, Ministry of Finance and State Chancellery, responsibilities divided since 1995
No central authority	
Czech Republic	No institution with central public service management authority
Poland	Civil Service Office abolished in 2006, some responsibilities in the Civil Service Department within the Prime Minister's Office
Slovakia	Civil Service Office abolished in 2006, some responsibilities left in the Ministry of Labor and the Government Office

Sources: Meyer-Sahling (2009), World Bank (2006).

Communist patronage to merit principles – actual implementation has resulted in various unexpected side-effects in most CEE countries.

Recruitment and Career Management

In the core of recruitment and career management has been the development of a merit-based system in which an official's selection and progress is determined by his or her comparative merit or achievement, and in which the conditions and rewards of performance contribute to the competency and continuity of the public service. An important precondition for merit-based systems is the establishment of formal recruitment procedures. By 2008, announcement of public service vacancies has been made mandatory in most CEE countries (Meyer-Sahling 2009). Yet the presence of merit-based procedures does not necessarily mean their automatic implementation. Replacing the Communist public service by merit principles is not simply a matter of passing relevant legislation and reforming the corresponding institutions. It also requires a fundamental shift in the values, attitudes and beliefs of politicians, public managers and individual public servants who determine day-to-day personnel decisions. Several authors have identified serious implementation problems in recruitment and selection in CEE, especially in the 1990s. For instance, the Bulgarian system of announcing public service vacancies remained vestigial, and many public servants were recruited in an informal way, by means of private contacts (Verheijen 1999). There were cases in Lithuania where undesirable applicants were informally intimidated or discouraged from pursuing their applications, and there were also cases where selection procedures were influenced by ideological considerations and personal ties (Jasaitis 1999). There is, however, some evidence to suggest a gradual recognition of merit values in CEE. For example, in the Czech Republic the advertisement of public service vacancies is not compulsory, yet most positions are actually advertised and the merit principle is widely accepted (Meyer-Sahling 2009). It could be argued that the general competitive environment has contributed to a shift to merit-based recruitment.

CEE countries which do not have long state traditions, high prestige or a distinctive social status for the public service, face difficulties in building their public services upon a long-term "career contract" between an official and the state. Instead, short-term gains of position-based public service systems tend to dominate over long-term benefits of a career system. A classical career system presumes societal and organizational stability and continuity, whereas CEE public administrations suffer from social and political as well as structural and legal instability. Moreover, unlike many old democracies whose personnel policies are in need of more flexibility, the personnel policies of CEE states primarily require stability and predictability. In theory, these could be provided by the development of a classical career system. Yet none of the CEE countries has been able to develop one (Drechsler 2005), although the governments of Poland, Hungary and Slovenia have over the last two decades tried to boost systematic career management (Drechsler 2003). In the majority of CEE countries, public service laws do not provide for an "automatic" rise in rank or position, nor do they guarantee life-long tenure (Meyer-Sahling 2009). Although most CEE countries recognize the special status of public servants, declare them to be employed for indefinite terms and proclaim public service employment security, the actual practice could be rather different. Dismissal of public officials is easy and widely used, making a mockery of formal declarations of permanent tenure (Verheijen 1999). Consequently, in most cases it is possible to enter the public service at any level of the hierarchy, attempts to manage officials' careers are random and depend on the will of individual public institutions and managers (Rees et al. 2005).

Such practices tend to weaken CEE public services and lay them open to political influence (Verheijen 1999). Politicization of the public service is a serious problem in CEE (see Table 3). For instance, Verheijen (1999: 118) claims that although professional competency is an important qualification requirement in the Bulgarian public service, professional criteria can sometimes be sacrificed to political interests. Another study shows that Hungary, Poland and Slovenia experienced a trend towards increased politicization in top-level appointments even after accession to the EU (World Bank 2006). There are also examples of re-institutionalization of political appointments, for example in Poland, Slovakia and Hungary (World Bank 2006).

Another important question to be considered in relation to recruitment and career development policies is the degree of centralization. The experience with over-centralization under Communist rule made decentralization very attractive to CEE citizens. The decentralization of traditionally centralized recruitment procedures in several Western countries in the 1990s has also had a substantial impact on the organization of public services in CEE. A number of CEE governments have decentralized their personnel policies to a considerable degree. For example, the Czech as well as Estonian governments allow their individual agencies a high degree of discretion in the recruitment and selection of personnel (Vidláková 1999,

Table 3. Degree of politicization of the senior civil service in selected CEE countries

Low politicization	Medium politicization	High politicization
Estonia, Latvia, Lithuania	Czech Republic, Slovenia	Bulgaria, Hungary, Poland, Romania, Slovakia

Sources: Meyer-Sahling (2004, 2009).

Randma-Liiv 2005, Meyer-Sahling 2009). Only Poland, Lithuania and Slovakia are characterized by partly centralized selection procedures – initial selection in the form of standardized exams is carried out by a special unit of the public service (Meyer-Sahling 2009). A high level of discretion in personnel management may prove risky if practised in countries characterized by an insufficiently developed legislative framework, high incidence of corruption, inexperienced top and mid-level managers, a lack of democratic values in administrative culture and insufficient control mechanisms. Verheijen (1998) has argued that liberalization of employment conditions in the CEE context may lead to further politicization, is likely to enhance rather than eliminate instability and could boost favouritism. In addition, when a central government works with an internal labour market that consists of loosely connected mini-markets, government units may develop their particular cultures and recruitment traditions, potentially leading to rivalries between individual public organizations.

Training and Development

The performance of organizations in rapidly changing environments depends by and large on the qualities of their members and on the organizations' ability to learn and adapt. The development of new knowledge and skills has been particularly crucial for CEE countries, whose newly democratic public services were initially composed of officials who had served under the Communist system, or of complete public service newcomers. Whereas in Western countries, public service training traditionally revolves around skills and competencies, training efforts in CEE countries are expected, in addition to skill development, specifically focus on the role and values of the public service, because in spite of the fact that two decades have elapsed since democratic reforms in CEE, democratic values cannot be taken for granted yet.

There is evidence that CEE countries increasingly provide systematic training programmes for new public servants. For instance, Hungary and Slovenia require new public servants to follow a mandatory in-service training programme (Meyer-Sahling 2009). Although several other CEE countries have also introduced mandatory training programmes for new entrants, this practice has not been sustainable. For example, Jasaitis (1999) demonstrates that although a mandatory training period was prescribed in the Lithuanian Law on Public Officials, it was not offered in practice because of budget restrictions and the unwillingness of managers to release critical personnel for training activities. The usual practice in most CEE countries is that officials are provided with an opportunity for both general public service training as well as specific training for certain posts. However, it should be noted that the training processes have at times been random, fragmented and unconnected to organizational or public service goals (Lucking 2003, Verheijen 2003, Randma-Liiv 2005). A positive exception to this practice was the pre-accession period when most CEE states sought to improve the knowledge of their public servants of the EU institutions and policies by organizing systematic training programmes (Lucking 2003).

The key question in the personnel development now, more than ever before, is the need for highly qualified top public servants. The competence and ethical standards of senior public servants and their personal example in forming and promoting modern public service values throughout the public service has become crucial for further development of public service personnel. Senior public servants in CEE countries either have a long public service experience from the Communist period or, alternatively, represent relatively young people who have joined the public service only recently. In both cases, the public servants in question may lack managerial and/or professional qualifications, as well as an experience of democratic governance. Top public servants play a substantial role in initiating and maintaining democratic changes (or resisting these) and therefore their development requires special attention, and probably even a specific personnel policy. Estonia and Lithuania have systematically invested in the development of senior public servants (Meyer-Sahling 2009). Based on the competency framework of top officials, multi-staged development programmes, specific training events, master classes and workshops as well as individual activities such as mentoring or consulting have been put in place for senior public servants in Estonia since 2005 (Järvalt 2007).

Performance Management

Performance-orientedness has been a central value in the rhetoric of personnel reforms in CEE due to the general popularity of NPM ideas. However, CEE countries have no success stories of performance management so far. Although Hungary, Latvia and Lithuania have made the most progress in this area by introducing performance evaluation systems, this has not occurred without problems, which include cases of unfairness and of weak links between strategic goals and evaluation (Meyer-Sahling 2009). The Estonian example of pay-for-performance has also received criticism, mostly because of the poor management experience of public sector leaders (Randma-Liiv 2005). Public managers in CEE often have insufficient managerial experience, and will therefore find it difficult to pick up problems and failures related to performance management. Managers with too little experience tend to over-quantify performance indicators that are easy to measure and that may look more "objective" and understandable than qualitative data (Mintzberg 1994). This way the technique may easily triumph over the purpose of performance management. An additional CEE-relevant problem is the lack of trust between managers and public servants due to a high level of politicization – which may make the appraisal process less "counselling" and more a controlling exercise.

Most of the NPM ideas are rooted in bundles of various concepts that often embody contradictions (Peters 2001). Several "democratic" goals such as transparency, representativeness, equal opportunities and fairness of procedures can be in conflict with the "technocratic" or "rational" goals such as efficiency, value-for-money or fast decision making. For instance, in Latvia, management contracts with defined performance bonuses for senior staff became rather unpopular due to their lack of transparency (World Bank 2006). The quality of Slovenian and Slovakian initiatives has been criticized because of the legal uncertainty in their performance evaluation systems (Meyer-Sahling 2009). Such contradiction in values is particularly hard to solve in CEE countries, where democratic values are not as deeply held as in old democracies.

CEE governments can thus fall into the trap of adopting cost-concerned and efficiency-oriented approaches that are likely to sideline democratic values. The concept of accountability to the general public with the multiple dimensions may easily change to accountability for financial outcomes. The situation will be even more complicated if limited financial resources bring pressure to bear on governments to give precedence to "technocratic" goals. Finding a balance between democratic and technocratic goals will have implications for the development of a variety of personnel policies and tools, which is why this field is expected to become one of the greatest challenges in the years to come, especially in the context of sharply decreasing economic growth.

Rewards

Successful recruitment and retention of public servants depends on traditional labour market factors such as the relative attractiveness of the public service and the conditions of public employment. In order to have a realistic chance of attracting and maintaining highly talented people in a situation where public service employment conditions are increasingly compared to those in the private sector, public service pay and benefits are expected to be reasonably competitive, although the specific motivators of the public service, such as contribution to the public good and socially meaningful accomplishment, may compensate for salary disparity to a certain extent.

Insufficient competitiveness of public service pay in CEE countries is a far-reaching problem (World Bank 2006). In addition, government and the state do not evoke positive associations for many citizens of the CEE countries, leading to a lack of respect for public administration. This means that the presence of the solidary motivators of the public service (see Clark and Wilson 1961) can also be questioned. As this is coupled with uncertain public service tenure, it is very difficult to attract and maintain qualified public servants.

The situation is further complicated by the need for compensation policies to be perceived as fair by public servants and the public alike. A growing number of countries (for example, the Czech Republic, Latvia, Lithuania and Slovakia) have opted for broadbanding, it is, grouping jobs into job families and salary brackets to achieve more flexibility and discretion (World Bank 2006, Meyer-Sahling 2009). Estonia and Poland have decentralized their public sector salary systems to a large extent, leaving a considerable degree of discretion to individual organizations and managers. It has been expected that a high level of discretion will enable the flexible consideration of specific environmental factors surrounding each organization which is particularly important in a highly dynamic context of transition and

Europeanization. However, decentralization might also have considerable disadvantages. If every government unit develops its particular working conditions, public organizations can find themselves in a situation where instead of co-operation they have to compete with each other. For example, in Estonia this has led to a situation where each ministry and agency is responsible for the remuneration of its staff and individual salaries vary to a large extent due to the effects of pay differentiation and "add-ons", negotiated for each organization and individual. In 2007, the average salary in the best paid institution was 3.2 times higher than that in the lowest paid institution (Riigikantselei 2008).

Bonus payments – often in the form of pay-for-performance – have attracted considerable attention in the last decade in CEE. Some politicians and public sector managers look upon pay-for-performance as a quick and easy fix for serious performance problems. Although certain positive results have been reported in Latvia and Lithuania, the use of pay-for-performance has met with only limited success in the region (World Bank 2006). On the one hand, pay-for-performance is a valuable tool to encourage high-quality performance of public servants, and to motivate the best officials. On the other hand, complexities of performance appraisal have set limits to the use of pay-for-performance. The primary problem that managers encounter is not one of knowing who are the best performers, but of measuring and documenting performance differentials (Perry 1990). For example, a Slovakian bonus-based performance system has been criticized for the lack of transparency and subjectivity (World Bank 2006). If pay-for-performance is poorly designed or managed, it may produce an effect contrary to what was intended, and eventually harm productivity and organizational culture. This has, for instance, been demonstrated in relation to Estonia (Randma-Liiv 2005).

Conclusion and Policy Recommendations

Two decades after the fall of Communist regimes, public personnel reforms in the new democracies of Europe are still struggling with weak strategic planning and insufficient policy co-ordination, reform delays, failures of implementation and a lack of political commitment. Certain achievements have been reported in developing training programmes and creating merit-based systems in recruitment by means of institutionalization of open competitions and fair treatment of applicants. Yet these efforts have remained insufficient to build a personnel policy that allows to attract and retain highly qualified staff. Such a mixed record in the implementation of personnel policies appears to be due to a lack of headway in the reform of reward systems and limited progress in the use of performance-based management tools.

Each country of the region is characterized by a mix of problems affecting the general public service level and of more promising examples in individual organizations. Common features were more frequent in the personnel management of the CEE countries at the beginning of the 1990s because of the similarity of their Communist legacy and the directions of personnel reforms. While it is relatively easy to describe common negative features of public services, the current diversity makes it more difficult to discern solutions that would apply to all CEE countries. Although there are some limits to the generalizability of the findings and further constraints on their applicability to other countries and settings, several lessons can still be learned from the experience of the new CEE democracies.

The first lesson concerns a strategic approach to personnel policies which is a necessary precondition for ensuring the success and sustainability of any modernization programme. The strategic direction, developed and maintained by politicians, top public servants and central personnel institution(s) is particularly needed in the time of structural reforms. Especially after accession to the EU, governments in CEE countries seem to be at a loss for a basic consensus regarding the direction of public personnel reforms and apparently there are no new, sufficiently powerful drivers for change. It remains to be seen what will be the impact of the economic and financial crisis on developments in public service reform, and whether the crisis will create new incentives to drive personnel reforms strategically. The experience of CEE countries shows that instability in the public service, combined with high levels of decentralization and weak co-ordination systems, is a major risk to effective policy design and implementation. Therefore, it is important to achieve a healthy balance between the decentralization of functions and the central steering of personnel policies.

Secondly, public servants of transition countries are accustomed to the role of a policy *maker* as opposed to that of a policy *implementer*. Whereas most CEE countries were involved in the development of a legislative framework and institution building in the 1990s, more attention has been paid to the managerial, or "softer" issues of public personnel management in the past decade. The legalistic approach to personnel policy has gradually been replaced by a focus on management problems that have been encountered during the implementation. As the implementation gap between legislation and reality remains a problem in CEE, future modernization efforts are expected to pay particular attention to implementation issues as well as to both *ex ante* and *ex post* policy evaluation. The biggest challenge for effective implementation, however, is the need for a systematic development of democratic public service values such as the rule of law, transparency, openness and accountability.

Thirdly, the role of top public servants cannot be emphasized enough, especially in the context of fundamental personnel reforms. On the one hand, top public servants can substantially influence the design of personnel policies and, even more importantly, their actual implementation in individual public organizations. They are also crucial in developing modern values in their respective organizations and throughout the public service, in ensuring fair treatment of public servants and in setting a personal example. On the other hand, well-developed personnel policies help to make the public service an attractive place for the most qualified people in the labour market. Once there is a critical mass of new and democratically minded public managers in place, this *per se* adds to the comparative attractiveness of a public service career. Consequently, merit recruitment, high-level training and career management as well as competitive reward packages are of particular importance in the case of top public servants.

Finally, the study has several implications for policy learning. CEE countries started out their state-building efforts with an insistent demand to be like the West. The Europeanization process as well as the worldwide NPM fashion of the 1990s both left their footprints on the personnel policies of CEE countries. Nevertheless, considering Western countries as role models is highly problematic as the success of policy transfer depends on the substitutability of institutions and the equivalence of resources between model and recipient (Rose 1993). In addition, several "Western solutions" to personnel problems such as deregulation and decentralization presume a considerable experience of democratic governance, a high level of trust and the presence of professional public managers. It is thus questionable whether West European or Anglo-American models provide the best lessons for new and fragile democracies, which still experience political instability and inconsistent strategic management, have relatively high corruption levels, deficient accountability and co-ordination mechanisms and insufficient management experience. It is also significant that the new EU member states are gradually changing from policy searchers to policy providers. An analysis of the successes but also of mistakes made in Central and Eastern Europe may help the countries of the Balkans, the Caucasus or Central Asia to modernize their personnel policies. The analyzed countries themselves could benefit from a greater cross-national comparison and lesson-drawing, given their proximity and the similarity of their problems.

Acknowledgements

The study was supported by the Estonian Target Financing grant no. SF0140094s08 and by the Estonian Science Foundation grant no. 7441.

References

Beblavy, Miroslav, 2002, Management of civil service reform in Central Europe, in: Gabor Péteri (Ed) *Mastering Decentralization and Public Administration Reforms in Central and Eastern Europe* (Budapest: OSI – LGI), pp. 55–72.
Boussaert, Danielle and Demmke, Christoph, 2003, *Civil Services in the Accession States: New Trends and the Impact of the Integration Process* (Maastricht: European Institute of Public Administration).
Clark, P. M. and Wilson, J. Q., 1961, Incentive systems: a theory of organizations, *Administrative Science Quarterly*, **6**, 129–166.
Drechsler, Wolfgang, 2000, Public administration in Central and Eastern Europe: considerations from the "state science" approach, in: Leonardo Burlamaqui, Ana Celia Castro and Ha-Joon Chang (Eds) *Institutions and the Role of the State* (Cheltenham and Northampton: Edward Elgar), pp. 267–279.
Drechsler, Wolfgang, 2003, *Managing Public Sector Restructuring: Public Sector Downsizing and Redeployment Programs in Central and Eastern Europe* (Washington, DC: Inter-American Development Bank).
Drechsler, Wolfgang, 2005, The re-emergence of "Weberian" public administration after the fall of new public management: the Central and Eastern Europe perspective. Halduskultuur. *Administrative Culture*, **6**, 94–108.
Evans, Peter and Rauch, James E., 1999, Bureaucracy and growth: a cross-national analysis of the effects of "Weberian" state structures on economic growth. *American Sociological Review*, **64**, 748–765.
Goetz, Klaus H., 2001, Making sense of post-communist central administration: modernization, Europeanization or Latinization? *Journal of European Public Policy*, **8**(6), 1032–1051.
Goetz, Klaus H. and Wollmann, Helmut, 2001, Governmentalizing central executives in post-communist Europe: a four-country comparison, *Journal of European Public Policy*, **8**(6), 864–887.
Grabbe, Heather, 2001, How does Europeanization affect CEE governance? Conditionality, diffusion and diversity. *Journal of European Public Policy*, **8**(6), 1013–1031.
Hesse, Joachim J, 1996, Rebuilding the state: public sector reform in Central and Eastern Europe, in: Jan-Erik Lane (Ed) *Public Sector Reform. Rationale, Trends and Problems* (London: Sage), pp. 114–146.

Jasaitis, Edwardas, 1999, Lithuania: a civil service system in transition, in: Tony Verheijen (Ed) *Civil Service Systems in Central and Eastern Europe* (Cheltenham: Edward Elgar), pp. 299–327.

Järvalt, Jane, 2007, What does professionalisation mean to Estonian top officials? A paper presented at the EGPA conference in Madrid, available at: http://soc.kuleuven.be/io/egpa/HRM/madrid/Jarvalt2007.pdf

Lucking, Richard, 2003, Civil service training in the context of public administration reform: a comparative study of selected countries from Central and Eastern Europe and the former Soviet Union (1989 to 2008) (UNDP BiH).

Meyer-Sahling, Jan-Hinrik, 2004, Civil service reform in post-communist Europe: the bumpy road to depoliticisation. *West European Politics*, **27**(1), 71–103.

Meyer-Sahling, Jan-Hinrik, 2009, Sustainability of civil service reforms in Central and Eastern Europe five years after EU accession. Sigma paper No. 44.

Mintzberg, Henry, 1994, *The Rise and Fall of Strategic Planning* (New York: Prentice Hall).

Peters, B. Guy, 2001, *The Future of Governing*, 2nd edition (Kansas, TX: University Press of Kansas).

Perry, James L., 1990, Compensation, merit pay, and motivation, in: Steven W. Hays and Richard C. Kearney (Eds) *Public Personnel Administration*, 2nd edition (Englewood Cliffs, NJ: Prentice Hall), pp. 104–115.

Randma, Tiina, 2001, A small civil service in transition: the case of Estonia. *Public Administration and Development*, **21**, 41–51.

Randma-Liiv, Tiina, 2005, Performance management in transitional administration: introduction of pay-for-performance in the Estonian civil service. *Journal of Comparative Policy Analysis*, **7**(1), 95–115.

Rees, Christopher, J., Järvalt, Jane and Metcalfe, Beverly, 2005, Career management in transition: HRD themes from the Estonian civil service. *Journal of European Industrial Training*, **29**(7), 572–592.

Ridley, F. F., 1995, Civil service and democracy: questions in reforming the civil service in Eastern and Central Europe. *Public Administration and Development*, **15**, 11–20.

Riigikantselei (The Estonian State Chancellery), 2001, *Avaliku teenistuse aastaraamat 2000* [Public Service Yearbook 2000] (Tallinn: Riigikantselei).

Riigikantselei (The Estonian State Chancellery), 2008, *Avaliku teenistuse aastaraamat 2007* [Public Service Yearbook 2007] (Tallinn: Riigikantselei).

Rose, Richard, 1993, *Lesson-Drawing in Public Policy: A Guide to Learning across Time and Space* (New Jersey: Chatham House).

Simanis, Mara, 1999, *Civil Services and State Administrations. Country Report: Latvia* (Paris: SIGMA).

Verheijen, Tony, 1998, NPM reforms and other Western reform strategies: the wrong medicine for Central and Eastern Europe? in: Tony Verheijen and David Coombes (Eds) *Innovations in Public Management: Perspectives from East and West Europe* (Cheltenham: Edward Elgar), pp. 407–417.

Verheijen, Tony, 1999, The civil service of Bulgaria: hope on the horizon, in: Tony Verheijen (Ed) *Civil Service Systems in Central and Eastern Europe* (Cheltenham: Edward Elgar), pp. 92–130.

Verheijen, Tony, 2003, Public administration in post-communist states, in: G. B. Peters and J. Pierre (Eds) *Handbook of Public Administration* (London: Sage), pp. 489–499.

Vidláková, Olga, 1999, *Civil Services and State Administrations. Country Report: Czech Republic* (Paris: SIGMA).

Viks, Külli and Randma-Liiv, Tiina, 2005, Facing the challenges of EU accession: development of coordination structures in Estonia. *International Journal of Organization Theory and Behavior*, **8**(1), 67–102.

World Bank, 2006, *Administrative Capacity in the New Member States: The Limits of Innovation?* Report 36930-GLB.

The Missing Dimension: A Comparative Analysis of Healthcare Governance in Central and Eastern Europe

MONIKA EWA KAMINSKA

ABSTRACT *Post-1989 healthcare in Central and Eastern Europe countries (CEEC) is often classified as Bismarckian following the adoption of social health insurance (SHI). The article provides evidence that in CEEC healthcare regulation is state-dominated, with a weak role of corporate partners, which differs from Western European SHI countries where corporatist arrangements underlie healthcare regulation. The weakness of corporatist arrangements in CEEC is explained by communist legacies and ideas prevailing in the post-communist transition. Moreover, despite commonalities, CEEC display heterogeneity in the modes of healthcare regulation. The article contributes to the comparative literature on healthcare regulation and CEEC healthcare, and illuminates the impact of regulation on healthcare provision and policy-making.*

Introduction

The post-1989 healthcare systems in Central and Eastern Europe countries (CEEC) are often classified as Bismarckian (Marree and Groenewegen 1997, Hacker 2009) or social health insurance (SHI) (Dubois and McKee 2004; Hassenteufel and Palier 2007; Österle 2007) following the adoption in CEEC of statutory health insurance based on social contributions. This article argues that most CEEC healthcare systems are characterized by a state-hierarchical mode of regulation and a very weak role of corporate partners in healthcare governance, and as such they cannot be classified in the same group as the Western European SHI countries where corporatist arrangements continue to constitute the basis of healthcare governance, despite a growing role of state regulation and market mechanisms. The article explains the weakness of corporatist arrangements in CEEC healthcare by embedding healthcare regulation and governance in the context of communist legacies and ideas that prevailed in the post-communist transition. Moreover, the article takes issue with the implicit assumption in the literature of CEEC healthcare systems' homogeneity and provides evidence of heterogeneity in the modes of healthcare regulation.

Applying one of the objectives defined by Marmor et al. (2005) for comparative analysis in health policy to the study of healthcare systems, this contribution makes factual adjustments in national portraits of regulation and governance structures in CEEC healthcare systems. To avoid misdescription and superficiality, and to deliver on the promise of a comparative cross-national study (see Marmor et al. 2005: 331), the article examines regulation and governance of healthcare in six CEEC that have introduced SHI: Czech Republic, Estonia, Hungary, Poland, Slovakia, and Slovenia. The sample allows for a proper comparative analysis thanks to its six cases but is limited enough to present a detailed portraiture of national solutions and their contexts. The selection ensures the cases' comparability and presents the institutional diversity in CEEC. The six countries share a communist history and joined the EU in the 2004 enlargement, which suggests similar achievements in the transition and democratization. Their OECD membership indicates comparable levels of economic development. Yet they display diversity in terms of historical background, models of capitalism and industrial relations (Bohle and Greskovits 2007a, b).

The focus on the dimension of regulation in CEEC healthcare systems follows, methodologically, from the recommendation by Marmor and Wendt (2012) to concentrate on a pre-select dimension in comparative analysis of healthcare systems; empirically, from regulation being the healthcare dimension displaying most dissimilarities between CEEC and Western European countries with SHI; and, finally, from the absence of analysis of healthcare regulation in CEEC in existing studies. The article fills this gap in the comparative literature on CEEC healthcare and lays the ground for further work on its classification. Moreover, it contributes to the still scarce literature on healthcare regulation. Finally, it illuminates the impact of healthcare institutional setting on the quality of provision and policy-making.

The next section reviews the literature on healthcare regulation and governance with a focus on Bismarckian healthcare systems in Western Europe. Against this background, section three discusses the framework for comparative analysis of healthcare regulation and governance in CEEC. Section four presents the case studies, while section five discusses the findings. Section six concludes.

Healthcare Regulation and Governance in Bismarckian Healthcare Systems

Freeman and Frisina (2010) reveal that the most widely accepted typology of healthcare systems is a trichotomous classification into national health services, social health insurance systems and private health insurance systems. Classification of healthcare systems should be based on their three basic functions: financing, provision of healthcare goods and services, and regulation of the interactions between funding agencies, service providers and (potential) beneficiaries (Wendt et al. 2009; Rothgang et al. 2010). Yet, due to "the priority given to financing mechanisms", the literature displays "relative paucity of attention given to the matter of regulation" (Freeman and Frisina 2010: 172).

Still, issues of healthcare regulation have been increasingly discussed. Giaimo and Manow (1999) refer to modes of financing, provision and access to identify the main drivers of regulation, and distinguish between state-led, market-driven and corporatist-governed systems, though they do not further distinguish between the "configurations of actors and the forms of interaction" (Rothgang et al. 2010: 15). Tuohy (2003) theorizes modes of healthcare regulation based on the idea of accountability and indicates three such modes: agency (the state delegates the tasks of healthcare regulation and distribution to the medical profession); contract (the state both finances and purchases healthcare services); and "governance" (actors operate in networks and the boundaries between public and private are blurred). Moran (2000) analyses the interests that dominate consumption, provision and production, and distinguishes, accordingly, the entrenched command-and-control state (the government dominates the three areas), the supply state (provider interests dominate all areas), the corporatist state (domination of corporate actors) and the insecure command-and-control state (the state dominates formally but fails to ensure proper coverage and access). Freeman (2000) refers to different dimensions of delivery, financing and regulation, and under the latter he distinguishes between markets, hierarchies and networks. Rico et al. (2003) apply the same distinction in discussing the forms of coordination without, however, considering the actors involved. Wendt et al. (2006) consider healthcare regulation as hierarchical, self-regulated or market-driven and define objects of regulation as relationships between financing agencies, providers and beneficiaries. Wendt et al. (2009: 79) state explicitly: "The concept of regulation [in healthcare] can be applied not only to state regulation but also to self-regulation by non-governmental actors and to regulation by market mechanisms." Rothgang et al. (2010), apart from the objects of regulation, identify the actors involved in regulation and the modes of interaction between them. The two latter elements can be dominated by the state, self-regulation, or the market. Accordingly, three pure regulatory types emerge: state-hierarchical regulation, societal self-regulation, and private-competitive regulation (Rothgang et al. 2010: 14).

For decades, Bismarckian healthcare systems in Western Europe have been self-regulated by corporate actors with a semi-public status and pivoted on a corporatist model of negotiations (Saltman 2004; Hassenteufel and Palier 2007; Rothgang et al. 2010; Agartan et al. 2013). The objects of self-regulation in SHI systems include compensation of providers, payment schedules, quality of care, benefit packages, patient volumes. The state shares public space with the stakeholders (see Crouch 1986). It provides legislation that ensures the binding character of self-regulation and brings stakeholders together for structured negotiations, with the aim of establishing public consensus and nurturing social solidarity. The stakeholders include employees (represented by trade unions), and associations of professionals, employers, insurers and patients. The interactions between these actors are based on participation in shared governance arrangements and collectively setting the rules of the game (Chinitz et al. 2004: 158).

Self-regulation hinges, first, on the internal authority of the organizations representing different stakeholders and their mandate to take binding decisions on their members' behalf. Such peak organizations encompass different interests and are able to represent and discipline members (see Hassenteufel and Palier 2007). Second, they depend on recognition by the state and other corporate actors as partners to ensure a semi-public status in the policy process (see Offe 1981).

Obviously, differences between SHI systems in Western Europe (Germany, Austria, Belgium, France) exist. For instance, in Germany, professional and supervisory boards that usually consist of employees' and employers' representatives administer health insurance funds (HIFs). Panel doctors' associations serve as negotiating partners in the provision of ambulatory care (Agartan et al. 2013) and their membership is compulsory. Since the 1980s the doctors' representatives have participated in the negotiation of health expenditure budgets (Hassenteufel and Palier 2007: 579). In France, negotiations between HIFs and numerous and divided doctors' trade unions also concern the fee levels, but the state's role is more pronounced and no agreement can be signed without its approval (Hassenteufel and Palier 2007: 580). The ability of the social partners to administer the social insurance schemes is more limited and "unions are oppositional more than management-oriented"; this can be explained by different national historical legacies and political contexts in Germany and France (Steffen 2010: 145–147).

Undeniably, the last two decades in Western Europe have witnessed "a decreasing role of corporatist self-government in favour of state hierarchy and market competition" (Schmid et al. 2010: 470) following reforms of governance aimed at increasing the efficiency of SHI systems (Hassenteufel and Palier 2007: 582). They involved introducing (more) competition between health suppliers and between health insurers, principles of managerialism, creation of state agencies, reorganization of medical care (GPs as gate keepers, health networks, integrated care) and institutional reforms of HIFs, which weakened the role of corporate partners (Hassenteufel and Palier 2007: 581–582). Even in Germany competition and government intervention have increased simultaneously (Rothgang et al. 2010). However, these changes have not altered the core of healthcare regulation in SHI countries which continues to be characterized by a pronounced role of corporate actors and self-regulation (Hassenteufel and Palier 2007: 593–594). While section three presents a framework for further analysis, section four demonstrates that healthcare regulation in CEEC differs substantially from Western Europe and in most cases is characterized by a lack of corporatist arrangements.

Analytical Framework and Data

The analytical framework for discussing healthcare regulation in CEEC builds on Wendt et al. (2009) and Rothgang et al. (2010). As it is difficult to use quantitative indicators to study healthcare regulation (Rothgang et al. 2010), the article qualitatively analyses data drawn from scholarly articles and books, the WHO European Observatory, the European Industrial Relations Observatory, and the Mutual Information System on Social Protection database to answer the following questions. First, it focuses on a selection of three objects of regulation (see Wendt et al. 2009: 80; Agartan et al. 2013), examines whether it is the state, self-regulation or the market that regulates i) the level of contributions that finance healthcare, ii) provider compensation mechanisms in ambulatory care, and iii) the content and range of services offered to patients in the selected countries, and establishes if the regulation of at least two out of these three relations is dominated by one actor.

Second, it examines actors (including health ministries and other governmental agencies, HIFs, employers' associations, trade unions, and professional associations), their competences and configurations in healthcare governance. It discusses whether: HIFs are self-governed and have semi-public status in the policy process or are state-controlled; trade unions and medical associations are capable of representing and disciplining members, enjoy recognition by the state and participate in policy-making; the state shares public space with the stakeholders, and enables and promotes self-regulation.

Third, through a careful qualitative assessment, the article establishes whether interactions between the actors are based on hierarchy ("a clear domination–subordination relationship"); collective negotiations ("actors operating on equal terms enter into long-term agreements"); or competition ("a competitive relationship between the actors prevails") (Rothgang et al. 2010: 14–15).

Finally, as these questions are answered, the main mode of healthcare regulation is identified: state-hierarchical (comprehensive planning and tight control by the state); corporatist self-regulation (legal framework and some state control); or market transactions between private actors (limited state regulation) (see Rothgang et al. 2010).

Empirical Evidence from CEEC

The post-1989 transition to democracy and a market economy required an overhaul of social policies, including healthcare. Nine (Bulgaria, Czech Republic, Estonia, Hungary, Lithuania, Poland, Romania, Slovakia, and Slovenia) out of the ten CEEC have introduced compulsory SHI (Latvia has maintained tax-based financing). SHI rather than a tax-funded model was preferred in CEEC mainly because of the dramatically decreasing healthcare budgets and SHI's political attractiveness because of its "dissimilarity to the former system" (Sitek 2010: 578).

The comparative literature on post-1989 healthcare in CEEC has focused on the financing dimension of reforms. Consequently, the CEEC healthcare systems have been classified as Bismarckian due to the adoption of health insurance contributions.

The regulation and the role of corporate actors in CEEC healthcare have not been considered, and their analysis is missing in the literature (Maree and Groenewegen 1997; Busse 2002; McKee et al. 2004; Aspalter et al. 2009; Hacker 2009), with the exception of Sitek's (2008, 2010) insights on Czech Republic, Hungary, and Poland. Yet the absence of the medical professionals and other stakeholders in the reform and policy processes can be regarded as the most salient feature distinguishing post-communist healthcare from advanced welfare states of Western Europe (Sitek 2008: 47). This study fills that gap. Before presenting the national cases, the article discusses the post-1989 conditions in which CEEC healthcare regulation has been developing.

The established governance structures that in the healthcare states of Western Europe have accommodated the negotiation and implementation of reforms (Moran 1999) were missing in the post-communist transformation (Sitek 2010). In the pre-1989 system, professional self-government was discouraged or abolished, although the doctors retained autonomy in the area of clinical expertise (Wlodarczyk 1986). After 1989, self-governing professional bodies were re-established but have often struggled to find recognition among medical professionals and remained unclear about their role (Healy and McKee 1997). The post-1989 trade unions were also facing difficulties. Within the previous system, all healthcare employees were generally represented by a single union. After 1989 new industrial relations structures were developing and from "corporations with compulsory membership" unions had to become "voluntary associations of employees" (Kohl 2008: 108). A common perception of unions as remnants of communism undermined their identity and legitimacy and led to massive drops in membership (which in all the studied countries is now voluntary), also in the healthcare sector. Moreover, diverse economic interests of healthcare employees have led to union fragmentation and competition.

The weakness of social actors has been matched by the state's dominating position. First, healthcare reforms were often designed and implemented by senior bureaucrats, many of whom were opposed to radical changes that would imply loss of state control over healthcare. Second, any empowerment of social partners, especially organized labour, was in conflict with the neoliberal reform agenda which prevailed in most CEEC (Nemec and Kolisnichenko 2006). Third, since 1989 the public has continued to expect the state to operate as a "comprehensive, general insurance institution" (Kornai and Eggleston 2001: 139). A majority of CEEC public opinion is still in favour of state responsibility for healthcare: 80 per cent in Slovenia, 71 per cent in the Czech Republic, 70 per cent in Hungary, and 69 per cent in Poland, against 52 per cent in France and 50 per cent in Germany (Kikuzawa et al. 2008).

The following offers detailed national accounts of the six cases and presents commonalities and variance in healthcare regulation and governance arrangements.

Czech Republic

As of 2009, ten HIFs existed in the Czech Republic. Though formally semi-public and self-governed, they are supervised by the government. The General Health Insurance Fund, the first to be established (in 1992) and currently the largest, covering 63 per cent of the population, is guaranteed by the state and functions as a safety net for members of funds that close or go bankrupt, which further enhances its dominant position among HIFs (Bryndova et al. 2009). Ten members of its board of trustees are nominated by the Health Ministry and appointed by the government, while the other 20 are elected by the Chamber of Deputies and proportionally represent the political parties. The composition of the boards of the other funds is based on tripartite representation (Bryndova et al. 2009).

The purchasing of health services by the HIFs and the relationship between the HIFs and providers is regulated by the state. The level of contributions is defined by the parliament. Until 2007 the chambers of physicians and dentists participated in annual negotiations with other stakeholders on a fee schedule that defines services covered by SHI during the following year. In 2008 the negotiations were abolished and a Health Services Working Group, based at the Health Ministry and excluding chambers, was created instead. The Group includes associations of hospitals, HIFs, general practitioners and ambulatory care specialists without veto power; a consensus procedure is in place. A fee schedule is issued annually by the Health Ministry. The benefits are mostly regulated by state legislation (1997 Act on Public Health Insurance). Lists of covered pharmaceuticals are defined by the State Institute for Drug Control administered by the Health Ministry. Annual negotiations between HIFs and providers, directed by the Health Ministry, produce amendments to the long-term contracts between funds and providers. The Ministry is also responsible for licensing health professionals (Bryndova et al. 2009).

Only public facilities (70 per cent of inpatient care) are unionized, with a unionization level at around 30 per cent. The four trade unions in the hospital sector compete with each other, though there have been instances of cooperation (Veverkova 2011b). Ambulatory care (98 per cent private) remains non-unionized. Employers' organizations do exist in inpatient facilities but do not participate in collective bargaining; collective agreements are signed at company level only (Veverkova 2011b). The professional associations include the Medical Chamber, the Dental Chamber and the Chamber of Pharmacists; membership is compulsory for every practising physician, dentist, and pharmacist, respectively.

Medical professionals played an important role in the instituting of change through parliamentary legislation adopted in 1991 in Czechoslovakia. Their leverage relied on their informal position in the policy-making structures, thanks to their membership of the Civic Forum, the political movement behind the Velvet Revolution (Sitek 2008). Most policy documents were designed by the newly established Czech Medical Association and included solutions that were beneficial to that professional group, which led to conflicts of interest and undermined the effectiveness of reforms (Lawson and Nemec 2003). In the 2000s relations between the Health Ministry and professionals, unions in particular, deteriorated, especially after the 2006 electoral victory of right-wing parties. Conflicts have erupted into strikes and collective handing in of resignation notices by 3500 doctors protesting against the situation in the sector and the government ignoring the professionals' voice (Veverkova 2011a, 2011b). Emigration of medical graduates and medical specialists is rising. The number of vacancies doubled between 2007 and 2010 (Oborna et al. 2010).

In the last decade, despite a general agreement that the healthcare system needs reforming due to unsustainable financing, no government has found enough political support to introduce radical changes (Veverkova 2011a). Medical associations and unions have blocked reform attempts based on the claim that they were non-professional and unsystematic (Veverkova 2009). The legislation eventually implemented by the government has introduced "cosmetic" modifications rather than important changes (Veverkova 2011a).

Estonia

Political stability in the early transition years enabled a relatively smooth implementation of healthcare reform. As the focus was on economic and political transformation (Atun et al. 2006), changes in healthcare benefited from "a window of opportunity for policy-makers to introduce the reforms with minimal opposition from politicians" (Hsiao and Done 2009: 13).

The Estonian Health Insurance Fund (EHIF) obtained the status of a public independent legal body in 2001, replacing the Central Sickness Fund and its 17 regional branches, and is now the core purchaser of healthcare services. Actual payment methods, service prices, and benefits package are not determined through contract negotiations, but regulated in a single government-approved health service list (MISSOC 2011). The tax contribution rate is also specified by the government; the tax is collected by the Estonian Tax and Customs Board and transferred to EHIF (Koppel et al. 2008). The government nominates members to the EHIF Supervisory Board which includes representatives of the state, employers' and patients' organizations, and is chaired by the Minister of Social Affairs. An agency of the Ministry, the Healthcare Board, licenses healthcare providers and registers health professionals.

Three trade unions are active in the hospital sector; union density is estimated at 65 per cent. Cooperation among unions is rather weak as they focus on different objectives (Osila and Nurmela 2011). The Estonian Medical Association (EAL), with voluntary membership, is the largest association, representing around half of Estonian doctors. In the 1990s it played an important role in the initiation and implementation of health insurance reform (Atun et al. 2006). EAL has taken on a trade union role and has been very active during recent years, together with a union representing nurses, in successfully negotiating minimum wages (Koppel et al. 2008); the minimum wages for healthcare workers nearly doubled between 2003 and 2006. However, following the 2009 budget cuts, salaries of doctors and nurses were reduced by 8 to 10 per cent, which led to protests by the unions and professional associations (Osila and Nurmela 2009).

The unions signal lack of cooperation on the part of the Ministry and the Estonian Hospitals' Association, the only employer association. They claim that the government avoids consultations with social partners. Unions' shared positions on issues regarding financing and organization of hospital services, cost of health services, wages, and the workload of doctors are not considered by the government (Karu and Nurmela 2009). Social dialogue and collective bargaining are rather weak, as reflected in the sectoral-level minimum wage agreements that have often ended with a labour dispute and conciliation procedure. Problems in relation to social partnership and representativeness persist due to conflicts and competition between the social partners themselves (Karu and Nurmela 2009).

Over the past decade, unsatisfactory wages and working conditions have forced around 20 per cent of doctors and nurses into other economic sectors and triggered emigration of healthcare professionals producing labour shortages (Wismar et al. 2011).

Hungary

The central government has almost exclusive power to define strategic directions and regulate healthcare, and its role as funder and purchaser has consistently increased (Gaal et al. 2011). The compulsory health insurance contributions are collected by the Tax Office and pooled in a single HIF. Since 1993 the HIF has been administered by the National Health Insurance Fund Administration (NHIFA) which is the sole payer in the system. The governance of the NHIFA has been increasingly placed under direct central control, which has "reduced stakeholder participation and exposed the system to political pressure, thus leading to less transparent and unpredictable funding arrangements" (Gaal et al. 2011: XXVII). Currently, NHIFA is directly supervised by the State Secretariat for Healthcare and is headed by a person appointed by the Prime Minister. It has "no discretion over revenue collection or budget setting, and has only limited discretion over purchasing decisions" (Gaal et al. 2011: XX) because the state administers provider payment methods. Purchasing is based on a contract model and the terms of contract are determined by the national assembly (Gaal et al. 2011). The assembly also legislates annually the final size of the HIF budget (administered by the Ministry of Economy) and the contribution rates. The package of benefits is defined by the central government (there is no regular mechanism for its revision).

Between 1993 and 1998, the HIF was self-regulated by a board comprising representatives of unions and employers' associations but "this corporatist experiment failed": the board was in constant conflict with the government over the HIF's deficit (Sitek 2008: 49). As a cost-containment measure, the HIF's rights over budgetary decisions were curtailed in 1996. Self-government was completely abolished in 1998 after the electoral victory of the conservative right (Gaal et al. 2011). In 2005, a board comprising representatives of social partners was re-established but it has limited responsibilities (Sitek 2008).

The Medical Chamber with voluntary membership was re-established in 1988, and in 1994 it began to operate on a self-regulatory basis, with compulsory membership. Also in 1994, the Chamber of Pharmacists with compulsory membership was established. Yet the government saw the professional associations as the main opposition to healthcare reforms and terminated their compulsory membership as of 2007, to weaken their power (Sitek 2008). Some disciplinary rights of the Medical Chamber were also withdrawn, while the regulatory rights of the Chamber of Pharmacists were limited following the liberalization of the pharmaceutical retail market in 2006–2007 (Gaal et al. 2011).

Ten trade unions represent different professions and constituencies within the sector (Rindt 2011). The estimated union density in the hospital sector is 31 per cent (Kaminska and Kahancova 2011). Fragmentation and divisions following type of employment, specialty, or profession, have fuelled rivalry between different representative organizations (Balint et al. 2009). Employers' organizations are also fragmented; the limited availability of financial and human resources generates rivalries and competition (Rindt 2011).

The conflicts of the medical professionals with the government have, on some occasions, erupted into industrial (protests and strikes) and political (referenda) actions that have blocked or reversed major policy changes. For instance, a referendum co-organized by the social partners nullified the government's plan to introduce co-payment schemes (Edelenyi 2008). Dissatisfaction with wage levels and working conditions has triggered emigration of doctors and nurses leading to labour shortages (Kaminska and Kahancova 2011; Wismar et al. 2011).

Poland

In the past two decades the state has reasserted its regulatory, budgetary, and managerial powers. The single National Health Fund (NHF) is controlled by the Health Ministry. The Fund's President is appointed by the Prime Minister upon recommendation of the Health Minister and so is its Board (only two out of the ten Board members are recommended by the Tripartite Commission for Socio-Economic Affairs). Contribution rates are established by a political decision influenced by the Finance Ministry. In ambulatory care, although formally fees are defined through negotiations between doctors and the HIF's regional branches (MISSOC 2011), the basic rate is centrally determined and has been contested by the providers as too low since the introduction of SHI. The benefit package is defined by the Health Minister, who is supposed to consult, apart from specialized state agencies, the Supreme Medical Council of the Chamber of Physicians and Dentists. Yet the Minister is entitled to ignore their recommendations. In practice, the package has been defined without proper consultation by copying and pasting earlier NHF President's decisions which had often been questioned by the providers (RMF FM 2009).

Chambers of Physicians and Dentists, of Nurses and Midwives, and of Pharmacists license practices and monitor professional conduct, and membership is compulsory for the relative professions, but they have suffered from internal divisions and diverging interests of different specialisms (Sitek 2008). Their position as interlocutors of policy-makers has been undermined by trade unions which developed institutionalized links to political parties. In turn, unions, with an estimated density in the hospital sector at 53 per cent (Kaminska and Kahancova 2011), are fragmented and compete with each other on ideological grounds related to their historical origins either in the Communist Party or in the Solidarity movement and have been captured in an inverse dependency relationship with political parties (Avdagic 2005). Their voice in the policy-making process is weak. Diverse economic interests of different professional constituencies have led to further fragmentation. As a consequence, the unions have failed to present common positions on policy issues (Kaminska and Kahancova 2011).

Employer organizations represent private healthcare providers, while trade unions are present only in the public sector. A common platform for sectoral-level negotiations is missing. Regional and local governments which manage most of the public healthcare entities are unwilling to enter into collective bargaining (Mrozowicki 2011). Sectoral social dialogue is very weak.

The government has been unwilling to encourage self-regulation in the sector and involve social partners in policy-making. Attempts by the social partners to influence the policy process have been ignored, which has often led to unrest among healthcare professionals. Strikes have been very frequent (113 in 2007; 80 in 2008). The government has responded with ad hoc solutions, mostly wage increases, rather than structural changes (Sitek 2008; Kaminska and Kahancova 2011).

The non-involvement of social actors in the sector's governance and politicization of the policy-making have led to poor quality legislation, unclear competences, informational and organizational chaos. The lack of institutional continuity, where alternating ruling coalitions introduce different and sometimes conflicting reform agendas, has required many "corrections" of the malfunctioning system. Consequently, rather than coherent reform process, Polish healthcare has been subject to change and attempts to reverse the change by subsequent governing coalitions. Healthcare professionals do not feel responsible for the adopted solutions and disregard the regulations by signing fictitious contracts to meet NHF staffing requirements or performing procedures which are unnecessary but well paid. The emigration of healthcare professionals (6–7 per cent of physicians left between 2004 and 2008) has caused labour shortages (Kaminska and Kahancova 2011).

Slovakia

Post-1989 Slovak governments were unstable and short-lived, both at the republican level within Czechoslovakia and at the national level after 1992. Yet there were no significant changes among the senior health bureaucrats (in general risk averse and opposed to policy change) who designed and implemented healthcare reforms. Moreover, a majority of the Slovak population, apprehensive about the social costs of transformation, believed that limited changes of social policies would suffice. Consequently, in the 1990s Slovak healthcare witnessed a high degree of continuity with communist social policies (Lawson and Nemec 2003). The institutional and regulatory framework was "weak and plagued by corruption", leading to increasing debts and bankruptcies (Szalay et al. 2011). The political context, marked by the weakening of liberal democratic institutions due to the rule of a nationalist-conservative party, was not conducive to effective reforms. The healthcare system plunged into a crisis. In contrast, the 2000s were marked by frequent paradigm shifts in reforming healthcare. The 2002–2006 reforms, introduced by a centre-right coalition, were part of a larger neoliberal reform agenda (Fisher et al. 2007). They imposed individual responsibility, "managed competition", and a more decentralized and contractual system (Szalay et al. 2011). This paradigm was strongly resisted by medical professionals and the public (Fisher et al. 2007). The 2006 electoral victory of social democrats brought a halt to the neoliberal reforms in favour of more direct state involvement, which was approved by the public. However, following the earlier neoliberal changes the state's ability to steer the healthcare system directly was limited (Szalay et al. 2011). The return of a centre-right coalition after the 2010 elections partially revived the pro-market reforms.

Following the 2002–2006 changes aimed at containing costs, HIFs are joint stock companies operating under private law. Currently there are three funds. One is state-owned and, as it receives the government's contributions for non-wage earners, it has the dominant position (68 per cent market share) and strongly influences the entire health insurance market (Szalay et al. 2011). Since 2004 the HIFs have acted as both payers and purchasers, based on selective contracting. The HIFs' autonomy is limited, given that the government defines reimbursement policy, accessibility conditions for minimum provider networks, maximum waiting lists, and application of user fees. The basic benefit package is also set centrally, although with some participation of HIFs' representatives. The SHI contribution is calculated based on the contribution rate defined by law and the annual assessment base. The government decides on additional resources for healthcare financing by changing the contribution rate for the state-insured (Szalay et al. 2011). While 90 per cent of outpatient care is private, the state owns the largest hospitals and HIFs must contract state-owned healthcare facilities, regardless of their quality and effectiveness, which – critics argue – gives them an unfair competitive advantage (Szalay et al. 2011: 13–14). The fact that the state regulates both providers and the HIF that it owns generates conflicts of interests (Szalay et al. 2011).

Since 2003 prices and payment mechanisms have been gradually deregulated. Currently, the Health Ministry defines, among other things, maximum prices for pharmaceuticals, medical devices in outpatient care, and first aid medical services. Prices of emergency services are fixed; prices and payments for other health services are negotiated between HIFs and providers, though payment mechanisms still represent mostly a modification of the original models (Szalay et al. 2011).

Since 2004, the Healthcare Surveillance Authority has supervised health insurance, healthcare purchasing and provision markets, but its independence is limited because the government has the competence to withdraw its chairman (which happened in 2010) and the Authority's board is elected by parliament (Szalay et al. 2011).

Two unions are active in the sector: the bigger, the Trade Union of Healthcare and Social Services, negotiates collective contracts with the employers' representatives. Union density in the hospital sector reaches 51 per cent (Kaminska and Kahancova 2011). The four professional chambers (of physicians, dentists, pharmacists, and nurses and midwives) register and license professionals, and provide opinions on ethical issues related to the profession. Since 2005 membership in the chambers has been voluntary, and chambers cannot impose obligations on non-members. Nevertheless, they have maintained a large membership base (Szalay et al. 2011). Professional organizations participate in the negotiations with HIFs but usually without the members' mandate to negotiate on their behalf. Employers are relatively well organized into four associations. Collective bargaining is well developed. Employees' and employers' representatives participate in the tripartite Healthcare Sector Economic and Social Council (Cziria 2009). However, "their mutual agreement is not needed to continue the legislative process" and their recommendations "carry relatively little political weight" (Szalay et al. 2011: XIX). In recent years industrial actions (strikes, strike alerts, and protest actions) have intensified, expressing discontent with working conditions and wages (Kahancova 2011). Between 2004 and 2008 around 3.5 per cent of healthcare staff emigrated (Kaminska and Kahancova 2011).

Slovenia

The adoption of SHI in Slovenia implied a shift in the control over the healthcare budget away from the Health Ministry to the single Health Insurance Institute of Slovenia (HIIS). While in principle HIIS acts rather independently on the state's behalf, its autonomy is limited by the state's tight control over the budget and its planning through the activities of the Finance Ministry that involves and commits the HIIS in the preparation of the national budget (Albreht 2010). Moreover, parliament takes the final decision on the contribution rates. Also, HIIS' statute is bound by approval of the Health Ministry. The government is involved in defining the scope of benefits and the financial plan, and confirming the elected general manager (Albreht et al. 2009). Corporate actors are integrated in HIIS management. In 2005–2006 the Health Ministry tried to expel representatives of corporate partners from the HIIS governing body and abolish the institute's autonomy. The attempt was successfully countered by trade unions through negotiations (Skledar 2007). The internal distribution of funds is negotiated between HIIS, corporate partners, and the Health Ministry that monitors, influences, and is able to overturn the collective decisions, though this happens rarely (Albreht 2010).

Slovenia is the only country in the sample where a state-controlled SHI system has been officially installed and no mass privatization in the sector has taken place

(Albreht 2010). Providers are mostly state- or municipality-owned, together employing over 75 per cent of the total health workforce (Albreht et al. 2009).

Healthcare personnel may practise as employees of public providers, private providers with concession within public healthcare, or private providers outside public healthcare. Employees are public servants and are salaried from the HIIS and voluntary health insurance under the conditions of collective agreements for each professional group. As the sector is publicly owned, the employer side is represented in the negotiations by the Health Ministry and the Ministry of Labour, Family and Social Affairs. Collective bargaining takes place at the national level, with the coverage rate reaching almost 100 per cent (Plachtej 2011). Providers with a concession are paid based on the contract negotiated with the HIIS. Private providers are paid directly by the patients. The prices for private services are set by the Medical Chamber and confirmed by the Health Ministry.

Unionization in the sector reaches 80 to 90 per cent (Pavlin and Plachtej 2009) and relations among the unions are rather cooperative. As most administrative and regulatory functions are performed centrally, the unions and medical chambers also operate at the state level (Plachtej 2011). The Medical Chamber with compulsory membership for medical doctors and dentists manages postgraduate training, medical audits, continuous medical education and licensing. It keeps the medical manpower low to ensure a limited availability of health professionals and enough provider competition to attract them (Albreht 2010). The position of stakeholders in the sector is rooted in pre-1989 legacies. An exception in the sample, Slovenia had "a long experience of relatively autonomous self-management" and "participatory decision-making" (Bohle and Greskovits 2007a: 452). Its transition was built on a consensus among "employers, employees, experts, [and] major political parties that had been institutionalized in neo-corporatist bodies" (Bohle and Greskovits 2007b: 109).

While no tripartite body for the healthcare sector exists, social dialogue used to function well until the recent financial crisis but according to union leaders it has been faltering recently. Strikes have been held over working time issues and salaries, cuts in healthcare spending and privatization (Pavlin and Plachtej 2009). On their part, government representatives consider some of the unions' demands unrealistic (Plachtej 2011).

Discussion of Empirical Findings

Unlike in the Bismarckian healthcare states in Western Europe, corporatist governance arrangements are mostly missing in CEEC healthcare systems (see Sitek 2008). In the six cases the state has maintained its dominant position in healthcare regulation and governance. Its willingness to share public space with other stakeholders is limited. Even in Slovenia, despite collective bargaining structures and a formally autonomous HIF, the state dominates the sector.

In most countries, unions and medical associations have little say in regulating and governing healthcare. Divergence of interests of different professional groups and providers results in limited cooperation and conflicting agendas. Medical associations usually have compulsory membership. Their functions include licensing and monitoring professional conduct but not real co-decision on policy issues. Unions lack unity and recognition by the state as partners in policy-making. Although unionization levels are high compared to other economic sectors, only the hospital sector (state-owned) is unionized. The exception is Slovenia where primary care is state-owned and unionized. The relations between professionals (associations and unions) and the sphere of politics are conflicting rather than cooperative (see Sitek 2008: 48–49). The exclusion of social partners from policy-making and conflicts over wages and working conditions have led to industrial and political action, and not infrequently blocked reforms. The governments enter negotiations only once open conflicts erupt, but their responses are ad hoc rather than collectively agreed long-term solutions (see Kaminska and Kahancova 2011). Recently, in the wake of the financial crisis, this has been the case also in Estonia and Slovenia where industrial relations used to be consensual.

HIFs are either explicitly state-controlled or tightly supervised by the government. In Estonia, Hungary, Poland, and Slovenia a single HIF exists and operates under central control. In the Czech Republic and Slovakia more HIFs are operative, but the state-controlled fund holds the dominant position and strongly influences the insurance market. Despite formal appearances, the actual status of HIFs is far from semi-public, perhaps with the exception of the private funds in Slovakia and Czech Republic. In all six countries, benefits and contribution levels are almost exclusively regulated by the state. Also the remuneration of doctors in ambulatory care is in most cases regulated centrally, with the exception of Slovakia. The interactions between the state and corporate partners are based on a domination–subordination relationship. Thus, the dominant mode of regulation across the sample is state-hierarchical, although elements of competition and corporatist self-regulation can also be detected. Despite common features, variance across the sample is visible in the degree of social partners' involvement in policy-making, their effective organization, and the state's dominance over the sector. This is attributable to "persistent patterns of continuity in national models of healthcare" (Marmor et al. 2005: 336) consistent with legacies rooted in the pre-1989 communist experience, and the dynamics of post-1989 politics.

The exclusion of social partners has consequences observable in at least two areas. Limited possibilities of influencing the unsatisfactory wages and working conditions, or the lack of "voice", result in numerous healthcare professionals "exiting" the system (see Hirschman 1970): they move to other economic sectors (in Estonia, Czech Republic, and Poland) or emigrate (from all countries in the sample with the exception of Slovenia), which generates labour shortages. Second, the politicization of policy-making, present especially in Poland, Slovakia, Hungary, and the Czech Republic, leads to frequent shifts in reform agendas, lack of policy continuity in the sector causing policy inconsistencies, or indeed an impossibility to implement reforms.

Conclusions

Conclusions about regulation and governance in CEEC healthcare systems can be drawn in terms of these systems' classification and the impact of regulation and governance arrangements on the quality of policy-making and provision.

First, in contrast to the Western European tradition of Bismarckian social insurance, self-regulation and corporatist governance arrangements are mostly missing in CEEC healthcare systems where the state has maintained its dominant position, while social actors' roles are limited. This finding contradicts Marree and Groenewegen's (1997: 9) claim that in CEEC "state-regulated healthcare systems lost their dominant position".

Second, given that in CEEC healthcare regulation does not present features consistent with the Bismarckian model of SHI and lacks arrangements that inhabit the social space between public and private modes of healthcare organization (see Chinitz et al. 2004), the CEEC healthcare systems cannot be classified in the same group as SHI systems in Western Europe.

Third, CEEC healthcare systems emerge as institutional hybrids, representing a "mix of change and continuity" (Sitek 2010: 572), where a new institutional element (financing mechanisms) has been cast against a framework of a dominant role of the state and subordinate position of societal actors, which is rooted in the communist legacies and the post-communist transition neoliberal paradigm. Interestingly, the developments in healthcare systems in Western Europe discussed above, although displaying different causes and extent, suggest that hybridization of healthcare systems is a common trend and call for further research comparing Western Europe and CEEC healthcare systems. This has rarely, if ever, been done systematically in the literature.

Fourth, and in line with findings by Hacker (2009), the existence of a single post-communist healthcare system type cannot be detected: despite the common features specified above, the cases display variance in involvement of social partners in decision-making, effective organization of social partners, and state dominance over the sector. This variance merits further investigation which this article cannot provide for reasons of space.

Finally, most CEEC healthcare systems appear to be developing into a pure mixed type (see Wendt et al. 2009), where predominantly societal financing (contributions constitute the greatest share of resources) and mostly private provision (following privatization of primary care and part of the hospital sector in most CEEC) is accompanied by state-dominated regulation.

The issue of impact of the modes of regulation and governance on the system outcomes has been given scant consideration in the literature and policy documents (including in the 2010 Joint Report on Healthcare Systems by the European Commission). Yet the lack of "voice" of the stakeholders in policy-making in CEEC has serious negative implications for the quality of reforms and for the stability of the system.

First, the article offers a different interpretation of the CEEC healthcare reforms from Marree and Groenewegen (1997: 9), who conclude that "the current pattern of health systems is not the result of independent, multiple inventions, but rather the result of deliberate take-over and adaptation". In fact, in most CEEC the paths of healthcare reforms have been rather patchy and have lacked institutional continuity due to a high level of politicization and contrasting paradigms used by alternating ruling coalitions from different sides of the political spectrum. This is, at least partly, attributable to the exclusion of social partners from policy-making. As a result, healthcare policies often display inconsistencies and their logic and effectiveness are questioned by healthcare staff who resort to industrial or political action to block the changes. As governments design and introduce policies unilaterally, such policies – enjoying no support from the professionals – are often reversed after elections (cases of re-election have been rare in CEEC). Moreover, governments hold full responsibility for the outcomes, as they cannot share the blame for potential failures with the social partners. They might try and avoid introducing reforms that are desirable but unpopular with the public and may produce electoral losses (for similar conclusions see Pierson 1994 on NHS reforms under Thatcher and Visser and Hemerijck 1997 on the role of neo-corporatism in reform sustainability and policy learning in Western Europe).

Second, and consistent with earlier studies (Kaminska and Kahancova 2011) the lack of "voice" in policy-making and the limited autonomy of medical professionals in defining their wage and working conditions generates dissatisfaction leading to "exits" of professionals into other economic sectors and emigration. This trend produces labour shortages and has the potential of undermining these systems' stability by generating losses of public investment in medical education and limiting access to care for patients.

Acknowledgments

The author thanks Jelle Visser, two anonymous reviewers, and the participants at the workshop "Healthcare Systems: Change and Outcomes. Ideas, Institutions, Actors, and Reforms" (Centre for Social Science and Global Health, University of Amsterdam, November 2011), in particular Rudolf Klein, Ted Marmor, Claus Wendt, Ralf Götze and Achim Schmid for their insightful comments.

References

Agartan, T. I., Kaminska, M. E. and Wendt, C., 2013, Social Health Insurance without Corporate Actors. Forthcoming in *Social Science and Medicine*.

Albreht, T., 2010, Slovenian health care in transition, Doctoral dissertation, National Institute of Public Health of Slovenia, Ljubljana.

Albreht, T., Turk, E., Toth, M., Ceglar, J., Marn, S., Pribakovic, Brinovec, R. and Schaefer, M., 2009, Slovenia: Health system review. *Health Systems in Transition*, **11**(3), pp. 1–168.

Aspalter, Ch., Jinsoo, K., and Sojeung, P., 2009, Analysing the Welfare State in Poland, the Czech Republic, Hungary and Slovenia: An Ideal-Typical Perspective. *Social Policy and Administration*, **43**(2), pp. 170–185.

Atun, R. A., Menabde, N., Saluvere, K., Jesse, M. and Habicht, J., 2006, Introducing a complex health innovation – Primary health care reforms in Estonia (multimethods evaluation). *Health Policy*, **79**(1), pp. 79–91.

Avdagic, S., 2005, State–labour relations in East Central Europe: Explaining variations in union effectiveness. *Socio-Economic Review*, **3**(1), pp. 25–53.

Balint, A., Illes, M. and Neumann, L., 2009, Representativeness of the European social partner organisations: Hospitals – Hungary. Available at http://www.eurofound.europa.eu/eiro/studies/tn08020 17s/hu0802019q.htm (accessed 19 October 2011).

Bohle, D. and Greskovits, B., 2007a, Neoliberalism, embedded neoliberalism and neocorporatism: Towards transnational capitalism in Central-Eastern Europe. *West European Politics*, **30**(3), pp. 443–466.

Bohle, D. and Greskovits, B., 2007b, The state, internationalization, and capitalist diversity in Eastern Europe. *Competition and Change*, **11**(2), pp. 89–115.

Bryndova, L., Pavlokova, K., Roubal, T., Rokosova, M. and Gaskins, M., 2009, Czech Republic: Health system review. *Health Systems in Transition*, **11**(1), pp. 1–x222.

Busse, R., 2002, Health care systems in EU pre-accession countries and European integration. *Arbeit und Sozialpolitik*, **5–6**, pp. 41–50.

Chinitz, D., Wisma, M. and Le Pen, C., 2004, Governance and (self-)regulation in social health insurance systems, in: R. B. Saltman, R. Busseand, J. Figueras, (Eds) *Social Health Insurance Systems in Western Europe* (Buckingham: Open University Press), pp. 155–169.

Crouch, C., 1986, Sharing public space: States and organized interests in Western Europe, in: J. Hall (Ed.) *States in Societies* (Oxford: Blackwell), pp. 179–200.

Cziria, L., 2009, Representativeness of the European social partner organisations: Hospitals – Slovakia. Available at http://www.eurofound.europa.eu/eiro/studies/tn0802017s/sk0802019q.htm (accessed 19 October 2011).

Dubois, C. A. and McKee, M., 2004, Health and health care in the candidate countries to the European Union: Common challenges, different circumstances, diverse policies, in: M. McKee, L. MacLehose and E. Nolte (Eds) *Health Policy and European Union Enlargement* (Buckingham: Open University Press), pp. 43–63.

Edelenyi, M., 2008, Government performs unexpected U-turn on health reform bill. http://www.eurofound.europa.eu/eiro/2008/06/articles/hu0806029i.htm (accessed 19 October 2011).

European Commission, 2010, Joint report on healthcare systems. Occasional Papers 74. Directorate-General for Economic and Financial Affairs. Available at http://europa.eu/epc/pdf/joint_healthcare_report_en.pdf (accessed 19 October 2011).

Fisher, S., Gould, J. and Haughton, T., 2007, Slovakia's neoliberal turn. *Europe–Asia Studies*, **59**(3), pp. 977–998.

Freeman, R., 2000, *The Politics of Health in Europe* (Manchester: Manchester University Press).

Freeman, R. and Frisina, L., 2010, Health care systems and the problem of classification. *Journal of Comparative Policy Analysis*, **12**(1–2), pp. 163–178.

Gaal, P., Szigeti, S., Csere, M., Gaskins, M. and Panteli, D., 2011, Hungary: Health system review. *Health Systems in Transition*, **13**(5), pp. 1–266.

Giaimo, S. and Manow, P., 1999, Adapting the welfare state: The case of health care reform in Britain, Germany and the United States. *Comparative Political Studies*, **32**(8), pp. 967–1000.

Hacker, B., 2009, Hybridization instead of clustering: Transformation processes of welfare policies in Central and Eastern Europe. *Social Policy and Administration*, **43**(2), pp. 152–169.

Hassenteufel, P. and Palier, B., 2007, Towards neo-Bismarckian health care states? Comparing health insurance reforms in Bismarckian welfare systems. *Social Policy and Administration*, **41**(6), pp. 574–596.

Healy, J. and McKee, M., 1997, Health sector reform in Central and Eastern Europe: The professional dimension. *Health Policy and Planning*, **12**(4), pp. 286–295.

Hirschman, A., 1970, *Exit, Voice and Loyalty: Responses to Decline in Firms, Organizations, and States* (Cambridge, MA: Harvard University Press).

Hsiao, W. C. and Done, N., 2009, *Implementation of Social Health Insurance in Estonia* (Washington, DC: Harvard University Press).

Kaminska, M. E. and Kahancova, M., 2011, Emigration and labour shortages: An opportunity for trade unions in the new member states? *European Journal of Industrial Relations*, **17**(2), pp. 189–203.

Kahancova, M., 2011, Slovakia: Industrial relations in the health care sector. Available at http://www.eurofound.europa.eu/eiro/studies/tn1008022s/sk1008029q.htm (accessed 19 October 2011).

Karu, M. and Nurmela, K., 2009, Representativeness of the European social partner organization: Hospitals – Estonia. Available at http://www.eurofound.europa.eu/eiro/studies/tn0802017s/ee0802019q.htm (accessed 19 October 2011).

Kikuzawa, S., Olafsdottir, S. and Pescosolido, B.A., 2008, Similar pressures, different contexts: Public attitudes toward government intervention for health care in 21 nations. *Journal of Health and Social Behavior*, **49**, pp. 385–399.

Kohl, H., 2008, Where do trade unions stand in Eastern Europe today? Stock-taking after EU enlargement. *Internationale Politik und Gesellschaft*, **3**, pp. 107–130.

Koppel, A., Kahur, K., Habicht, T., Saar, P., Habicht, J. and van Ginneken, E., 2008, Estonia: Health system review. *Health Systems in Transition*, **10**(1), pp. 1–230.

Kornai, J. and Eggleston, K., 2001, *Welfare, Choice, and Solidarity in Transition. Reforming the Health Care Sector in Eastern Europe* (Cambridge: Cambridge University Press).

Lawson, C. and Nemec, J., 2003, The political economy of Slovak and Czech health policy: 1989–2000. *International Political Science Review*, **24**(2), pp. 219–235.

Marmor, T. R. and Wendt, C., 2012, Conceptual frameworks for comparing healthcare politics and policy. *Health Policy*, **107**, pp. 11–20.

Marmor, T. R., Freeman, R. and Okma, K., 2005, Comparative perspectives and policy learning in the world of health care. *Journal of Comparative Policy Analysis*, **7**(4), pp. 331–348.

Marree, J. and Groenewegen, P.P., 1997, *Back to Bismarck: Eastern European Health Care in Systems Transitions* (Aldershot: Avebury).

McKee, M., MacLehose, L. and Nolte, E. (Eds) 2004, *Health Policy and European Union Enlargement* (Buckingham: Open University Press).

MISSOC, 2011, Mutual information system on social protection, online database. Available at http://ec.europa.eu/employment_social/missoc/db/public/compareTables.do (accessed 19 October 2011).

Moran, M., 1999, *Governing the Health Care State. A Comparative Study of the United Kingdom, the United States and Germany* (Manchester: Manchester University Press).

Moran, M., 2000, Understanding the welfare state: The case of health care. *British Journal of Politics and International Relations*, **2**(2), pp. 135–160.

Mrozowicki, A., 2011, Poland: Industrial relations in the health care sector. Available at http://www.eurofound.europa.eu/eiro/studies/tn1008022s/pl1008029q.htm (accessed 19 October 2011).

Nemec, J. and Kolisnichenko, N., 2006, Market-based health care reforms in Central and Eastern Europe: Lessons after ten years of change. *International Review of Administrative Sciences*, **72**(1), pp. 11–26.

Oborna, I., Licenik, R. and Mrozek, Z., 2010, Health care in the Czech Republic. *The Lancet*, **375**(9731), pp. 2071–2072.

Offe, C., 1981, The attribution of public status to interest groups, in: S. Berger (Ed.) *Organizing Interests in Western Europe* (Cambridge: Cambridge University Press), pp. 123–154.

Osila, L. and Nurmela, K., 2009, Healthcare workers protest against cuts in spending. Available at http://www.eurofound.europa.eu/eiro/2009/11/articles/ee0911029i.htm (accessed 19 October 2011).

Osila, L. and Nurmela, K., 2011, Estonia: Industrial relations in the health care sector. Available at http://www.eurofound.europa.eu/eiro/studies/tn1008022s/ee1008029q.htm (accessed 19 October 2011).

Österle, A., 2007, Health care across borders: Austria and its new EU neighbours. *Journal of European Social Policy*, **17**(2), pp. 112–124.

Pavlin, S. and Plachtej, B., 2009, Representativeness of the European social partner organisations: Hospitals – Slovenia. Available at http://www.eurofound.europa.eu/eiro/studies/tn0802017s/si0802019q.htm (accessed 19 October 2011).

Pierson, P., 1994, *Dismantling the Welfare State? Reagan, Thatcher and the Politics of Retrenchment* (New York: Cambridge University Press).

Plachtej, B., 2011, Slovenia: Industrial relations in the health care sector. Available at http://www.eurofound.europa.eu/eiro/studies/tn1008022s/si1008021q.htm (accessed 19 October 2011).

Rico, A., Saltman, R. B. and Boerma, W. G. W., 2003, Organizational restructuring in European health systems: The role of primary care. *Social Policy and Administration*, **37**(6), pp. 592–608.

Rindt, Z., 2011, Hungary: Industrial relations in the health care sector. Available at http://www.eurofound.europa.eu/eiro/studies/tn1008022s/hu1008021q.htm (accessed 19 October 2011).

RMF FM, 2009, Newsroom of RMF FM Radio. Available at http://www.rmf24.pl/fakty/polska/news-ustawa-koszykowa-wspoltworzona-przez-nfz-eksperci-sa,nId,132979 (accessed 19 October 2011).

Rothgang, H., Cacace, M., Frisina, L., Grimmeisen, S., Schmid, A. and Wendt, C., 2010, *The State and Healthcare. Comparing OECD Countries* (Basingstoke: Palgrave Macmillan).

Saltman, R.B., 2004, Social health insurance in perspective: The challenge of sustaining stability, in: R. B. Saltman, R. Busse and J. Figueras (Eds) *Social Health Insurance Systems in Western Europe* (Buckingham: Open University Press), pp. 3–20.

Schmidt, A., Cacace, M., Götze, R. and Rothgang, H., 2010, Explaining health care system change: Problem pressure and the emergence of "hybrid" health care systems. *Journal of Health Politics, Policy and Law*, **35**(4), pp. 455–486.

Sitek, M., 2008, Politics and institutions in the reforms of health care in the Czech Republic, Hungary and Poland. *Polish Sociological Review*, **1**(161), pp. 39–53.

Sitek, M., 2010, The new institutionalist approaches to health care reform: Lessons from reform experiences in Central Europe. *Journal of Health Politics, Policy and Law*, **35**(4), pp. 569–593.

Skledar, S., 2007, Trade unions defend autonomy of health insurance institute. Available at http://www.eurofound.europa.eu/eiro/2007/01/articles/si0701019i.htm (accessed 19 October 2011).

Steffen, M., 2010, Social health insurance systems: What makes the difference? The Bismarckian case in France and Germany. *Journal of Comparative Policy Analysis*, **12**(1–2), pp. 141–161.

Szalay, T., Pazitny, P., Szalayova, A., Frisova, S., Morvay, K., Petrovic, M. and van Ginneken, E., 2011, Slovakia: Health system review. *Health Systems in Transition*, **13**(2), pp. 1–200.

Tuohy, C., 2003, Agency, contract, and governance: Shifting shapes of accountability in the health care arena. *Journal of Health Politics, Policy and Law*, **28**(2–3), pp. 195–215.

Veverkova, S., 2009, Representativeness of the European social partner organisations: Hospitals – Czech Republic. Available at http://www.eurofound.europa.eu/eiro/studies/tn0802017s/cz0802019q.htm (accessed 19 October 2011).

Veverkova, S., 2011a, Czech Republic: Industrial relations in the health care sector. Available at http://www.eurofound.europa.eu/eiro/studies/tn1008022s/cz1008029q.htm (accessed 19 October 2011).

Veverkova, S., 2011b, Hospital doctors' resignation campaign. Available at http://eurofound.europa.eu/eiro/2011/01/articles/cz1101019i.htm (accessed 19 October 2011).

Visser, J. and Hemerijck, A., 1997, *A Dutch Miracle* (Amsterdam: Amsterdam University Press).

Wendt, C., Kohl, J. and Thompson, T., 2006, Modes of regulation and their effects on financing and service provision in OECD health care systems. MZES Working Paper, 95.

Wendt, C., Frisina, L. and Rothgang, H., 2009, Health care system types. A conceptual framework for comparison. *Social Policy and Administration*, **43**(1), pp. 70–90.

Wismar, M., Maier, C. B., Glinos, I. A., Dussault, G., Figueras, J., 2011, Health professional mobility and health systems. Observatory Studies Series, 23.

Wlodarczyk, C., 1986, In search of economic rationality: The experience of the Polish National Health Service. *Health Policy*, **7**, pp. 149–162.

Made to Measure? Europeanization, Goodness of Fit and Adaptation Pressures in EU Competition Policy and Regional Aid

CARLOS MENDEZ, FIONA WISHLADE and DOUGLAS YUILL

ABSTRACT *The measurement of Europeanization and adaptational pressures can be facilitated by three elements: an EU-wide perspective to enable a comparative assessment of impacts and outcomes; using a clear example of a new European-level policy initiative that impacts on all member states simultaneously; and a detailed knowledge of the ex ante and ex post situation in each country. This article incorporates these elements in a comparative case study of adaptational pressures and policy change under EU regional state aid policy, which casts doubt on the utility of goodness-of-fit propositions.*

Introduction

The impact of the EU on national public policies has been a central theme in European integration theorizing, not least amongst the early North American-led scholarship which launched the sub-discipline. Haas's (1958) seminal study of the European Coal and Steel Community devoted a whole chapter to the operation of the common market, focusing on the impacts of ten ECSC policy areas[1] on the founding members, exploring the adaptation pressures confronted and subsequent reactions (Haas 1958: 60–110).

A decade later, two prominent integration theorists criticized the absence of systematic research on EU policy implementation arguing that it was an "area which must receive more attention in the years to come... if we are really to understand the 'new Europe'" (Lindberg and Scheingold 1970: 66). A similar deficiency was highlighted by Puchala, who coined the term "post-decisional politics"

(Puchala 1975: 497–498) – paralleling recent definitions of Europeanization over 30 years ago! – to refer to "[th]e transmission downward and outward of regional directives from Brussels to the national peripheries, and the problems, pitfalls and impacts involved".

Further and more substantive empirical treatment of EU public policies was provided by European scholars, particularly by Wallace *et al.* (1977, 1982). In setting out the analytical framework, Wallace *et al.* (1982: 44) stressed "the intrusion of Community issues into the policy processes of the member states – and their political repercussions".[2] Research co-ordinated by Siedentopf and Ziller (1988) was perhaps the first to provide a systematic analysis of EU policy impacts across all EU member states and a range of policy areas. This was followed by an explosion of policy studies throughout the 1990s, notably on EU cohesion, environmental and transport policies.

The main objective of this paper is to contribute to the understanding of the Europeanization of public policy through a cross-national study of the impact of EU state aid policy on the EU-15. Definitional debates relating to Europeanization are addressed elsewhere in this special issue. This article adopts the standard approach of treating the EU as an independent variable that impacts on the policies, polities and politics of the member states (in the definitional sense of Ladrech 1994: 70, Börzel 1999: 574 and Olsen 2002: 932).

The paper makes three key contributions. In theoretical terms, it provides an empirical critique of goodness-of-fit propositions (Risse *et al.* 2001). Hitherto, the focus of such critiques has been on cases where Europeanization pressure is less coercive (e.g. through the transposition and implementation of directives). However, goodness-of-fit arguments are considered to offer most analytical leverage in policy areas where the mode of EU governance is hierarchical and compliance driven (Knill and Lehmkhul 1999, 2002, Bulmer and Radaelli 2004: 10). EU regional state aid policy provides a critical test given the highly Europeanized nature of the policy domain in which extensive legislative and executive autonomy is vested in the Commission. By using a "most likely case" (Eckstein 1975) for goodness-of-fit propositions, this article provides a more compelling critique of the theory.

A second gap in the existing scholarship relates to the methodological challenge in measuring Europeanization (Saurugger 2005). This article aims to show that well-known methodological techniques (bottom-up/top-down research designs; counter-factual reasoning; comparative approach) can help to address the challenge of measuring causality in the empirical analysis of Europeanization.

The final contribution is empirical. EU state aid policy remains under-researched (Allen 1977, 1983, Lavdas and Mendrinou 1995, McGowan 2000). Where it has been the object of scholarly enquiry, the focus has been on policy change at the EU level (e.g. Smith 1996, 2001, Cini 2000) or on the impacts of different EU decisions on single national cases, such as France (Le Galès 2001), Italy (Gualini 2003, 2004) and Germany (Thielemann 2000). There has been no systematic comparative research exploring the impact of a single EU state aid policy initiative on all member states.

The paper is in six further sections. The next section presents the research design for the empirical analysis. Section three describes the historical development of regional aid control, culminating in the application of EU regional aid guidelines for 2000–2006. To determine the adaptational pressures placed on member states by the new guideline approach, section four reviews the degree to which traditional approaches to regional aid mapping could be expected to fit within the guideline model. The following section then measures the adaptational responses of the member states. Section six moves beyond the initial map development phase to consider the extent to which policy can be viewed as having been Europeanized. A final section draws together conclusions.

The Design – Methodological Approach

The key methodological challenge confronting empirical research on Europeanization lies in isolating the "net" impact of the EU on domestic institutions and policies, particularly in terms of separating and disentangling global (Berger and Dore 1996, Keohane and Milner 1996, Friedman 1999) and domestic factors from European pressures (Wallace 2000, Hurrell and Menon 2003). A second empirical challenge is to generalize findings across time and space.

A number of methodological techniques can help address these challenges. Following the recommendations of a number of scholars (Radaelli 2003, Börzel 2005), this study explicitly incorporates a bottom-up research design, drawing on well-established approaches in the policy implementation literature (Lipsky 1971, Barret and Fudge 1981, Hjern and Porter 1981). More specifically, it combines "backward mapping" and "forward mapping" research techniques as proposed by Elmore (1979). The latter approach "begins at the top of the process, with as clear a statement as possible of the policy-maker's intent.... At the bottom of the process... a satisfactory outcome would be... measured in terms of the original statement of intent" (Elmore 1979: 602). The former perspective, on the other hand, "begins... with a statement of the specific behaviour at the lowest level of the implementation process which generates the need for policy" (Elmore 1979: 604).

The empirical analysis that follows is top-down in that it examines the extent to which EU-level policy objectives were met and explores the intervening factors which account for policy responses and outcomes. However, it is also strongly informed by backward mapping techniques as it begins with a comprehensive analysis of the starting conditions for designating regional aid areas in each member state. A key advantage of this approach is that it allows relative precision in specifying goodness of fit and also in assessing the degree of Europeanization resulting from the new policy rules. Furthermore, "it does not assume that policy is the only – or even the major – influence on the behaviour of people engaged in the process" (Elmore 1979: 604). The bottom-up approach is also apparent through the focus on how member states have responded to EU pressures and in seeking to understand the internal reasons for these reactions, including whether member state (as opposed to solely EU) objectives were met.

The value of "process tracing" techniques (Bennett and George 1997) are well recognized (Risse *et al.* 2001: 4, Radaelli 2003: 48). This study places a particular focus on the sequencing of map changes. Following the overview of historical approaches to area designation, which provides the context for the latest policy initiatives, the analysis of adaptation responses and outcomes is disaggregated into three stages: the initial submission of regional aid maps to the Commission; negotiations with the Commission; and the final map submissions and outcomes.

The aim is to produce a fine-grained analysis of adaptation and policy change across all member states that is sensitive to process dynamics.

A further strategy to demonstrate the causal importance of the EU is the use of counterfactual reasoning (Haverland 2005: 4–6). To more fully capture the degree of Europeanization, the penultimate section tries to create a counterfactual scenario. It compares the initial submissions with the final outcomes and explores whether underlying domestic policy preferences were really challenged.

Last, this paper responds to Radaelli's (2000: 19) call for an intensification of "comparative public policy analysis" in the study of Europeanization. Comparative methods can help overcome some of the aforementioned methodological challenges. In particular, they allow for the testing of hypotheses and controlling of variables e.g. by assessing whether cases with a similar goodness of fit (independent variable) produce similar policy responses (dependent variable). Related, comparative policy analysis can facilitate the development of causal inference by placing member state responses to the EU within the broader domestic and global context. The examination of a single public policy change across all member states provides analytical leverage in measuring the independent influence of the EU, particularly, in the case selected, since the policy decision marked a significant departure in almost all member states. Further, by increasing the number of observations, the validity of the conclusions drawn is enhanced. Finally, the comparative study of the EU-15 can help in understanding differences in the scope and substance of major EU policy impacts affecting all member states, enabling us to overcome "culture bound generalisations" (Rose 1972: 70) and broaden our depth of understanding of Europeanization beyond the usual suspects (e.g. the UK, France and Germany).

The analysis is based on a detailed examination of published and unpublished documentation and on more than 50 semi-structured interviews with high-level policy makers involved in developing and negotiating aid area maps under the guidelines, as well as in DG Competition and DG Regio. The interviews covered all the member states except Greece[3] and took place annually between 1999 and 2002. Intercoder reliability was employed to ensure the robustness of the analysis.

The Model – EU Regional Aid Control

The legal basis and general background to the competition policy control of state aid have been described in detail elsewhere.[4] The essence of the Treaty provisions is that, although Article 87 provides for a general ban on state aid, there are two regional policy exceptions to this prohibition. Article 87(3)(a) allows aid in areas where the "standard of living is abnormally low or where there is serious underemployment"; Article 87(3)(c) enables aid for the development of certain activities or areas, where trade is not affected "to an extent contrary to the common interest". These provisions have been extensively interpreted by the European Commission, mainly through published guidelines and communications.

The development and application of these rules has not been smooth. Early on, Commission scrutiny was rather tentative, but in the 1970s the Commission adopted a series of communications on the "co-ordination" of regional aid which introduced a number of principles that remain central to regional aid control: targeting aid at disadvantaged regions; calibrating aid levels to regional disparities; and requiring aid values to be measurable and comparable across countries.

From the early 1970s, the Commission began to intervene directly in the design of regional aid policies. This was partly based on the Treaty requirement that member states gain prior approval for any plans to offer aid or change existing schemes (Article 88(3)) and partly on the Commission's role in keeping state aid "under constant review" (Article 88(1)). However, there was no *detailed* published justification for Commission action until 1988 when the Commission outlined the method underlying its decisions to authorize or outlaw member state regional aid proposals.[5] Under the 1988 Communication, Article 87(3)(a) regions were defined as NUTS II[6] areas with GDP(PPS) per head of less than 75 per cent of the EU average for the last five years for which data were available, while Article 87(3)(c) areas were principally determined by national disparities in GDP per head and unemployment rates.

The Commission's decision to publish its methodology met with a mixed response; where previously member states had attacked the lack of transparency in the Commission's approach, now arguments shifted to substantive issues. Around this time, the Commission had to review German aid map proposals following reunification. German regional policy relations with the Commission had always been problematic and the map discussions were expected to be difficult. However, the Commission recognized the domestic challenges created by reunification and allowed considerably more flexibility in the selection of aid areas than previously – provided that the agreed population coverage of the map (as a percentage of the national population) was not exceeded. This approach departed significantly from the 1988 Communication: instead of focusing on *which areas* should be designated, the *population coverage* of the designated areas became the key element of regional aid discipline.

Given the success of this approach in Germany, DG Competition began informally to pilot it in subsequent map negotiations. In parallel it devised proposals for approving the selection of areas within the agreed population quota. It took the view that some further discipline over *how* areas were chosen was necessary to ensure that assistance was focused on meaningful areas of genuine need.[7] Reflecting the federal domestic context, the German area designation system was transparent: it involved ranking labour market areas according to a set of agreed indicators. The Commission considered that imposing a similar model on all member states would introduce the desired level of discipline and transparency; this philosophy underpinned the 1998 regional aid guidelines.

There were three main features to area designation under the guidelines.[8] First, the *duration* of aid area maps was limited. The authorization of current maps was to expire at the end of 1999 and the new maps would apply for a fixed period (2000–2006),[9] co-ordinated with the phasing of Structural Funds programmes.[10] This time-limited approach differed from the previous system under which new maps were drawn up at the initiative of the member states or where aspects were revised at the instigation of the Commission.

Second, an EU-15 *population ceiling* (42.7 per cent) was introduced for national aid area coverage; the Commission considered that this would allow coherence between national and Structural Funds areas while restricting coverage to less than half the anticipated enlarged EU population. Within this ceiling, broadly the same definition of Article 87(3)(a) areas was applied as before – NUTS II regions with GDP(PPS) per head of less than 75 per cent of the EU average (the definition of Objective 1 areas under the Structural Funds). The remaining population (under Article 87(3)(c)) was shared between member states via a "quota" for each country. The global ceiling reduced overall aid area coverage significantly; prior to 1999, 46.7 per cent of the EU-15 population was contained within the designated aid areas.

Third, while previously the Commission had focused on whether the selection of a particular area was justified, the 1998 guidelines made each member state responsible for designating Article 87(3)(c) areas within its population quota. However, certain parameters constrained the *method* by which eligible areas could be determined:

- the *methodology* had to be "objective", and presented in a manner which enabled the Commission to assess its merits;
- the *indicators* (up to five could be used) had to be objective, relevant and based on time series of at least three years; in addition, regions with a population density of less than 12.5 per km^2 could also qualify;
- the *building blocks* were to be NUTS III or, where justified, an alternative unit (such as labour market areas). Only one type of unit could be used; moreover, designated areas had to have a minimum population of 100,000;
- the list of eligible regions had to be arranged on the basis of the chosen indicators;
- regarding Structural Funds *coherence*, Objective 2 regions could be included in addition to areas chosen using the methodology, subject to the population ceiling and the 100,000 population rule (but not the building block requirement). This became known as the Structural Funds derogation.

Finally, the guidelines laid down rate of award ceilings and indicated that award rates would be modulated to reflect the severity of the problem.

The Expected Fit – Previous National Approaches to Regional Aid Mapping

To review how far national approaches could be expected to fit within the Commission model, the three main aspects of the model are considered: the timing of area designation exercises; map coverage; and the methodology for designating Article 87(3)(c) areas. A final section discusses expectations with respect to goodness of fit and adaptational pressures.

Timing and Timescales

Prior to the 1998 guidelines, the Commission operated a rolling map review programme. Map revisions could also be initiated by member states, but this was not common since any new map had then to be approved by the Commission (which often sought to reduce coverage). Only in Denmark, Germany and the Netherlands were there regular area re-designation exercises. However, whereas the Danish and German reviews involved well-established designation systems, the Dutch approach was specific to each review.

During the 1980s, Commission pressure for aid area cutbacks was countered by lengthy transitional provisions and special pleading by member states. Just a few maps were processed by the Commission each year. Only at the start of the 1994–99 Structural Funds period was a concerted effort made to review virtually all maps. This alignment of review cycles culminated in the requirement that the Commission approve all maps from the start of 2000. Member states faced an end-1999 cut-off, after which regional aid was unlawful until a new map was agreed. This increased the pressures to adapt to the Commission's designation requirements, especially in countries with no domestic tradition or established machinery for reviewing aid areas.

In terms of timing and timescales, member states can be divided into three groups: those where few problems were anticipated, either because a time-limited approach and established review procedures already existed (as in Denmark and Germany) or because the whole country was eligible for support (Greece, Ireland and Portugal); conversely, many were expected to face challenges (Austria, Belgium, Finland, France, Italy, Luxembourg, Spain, Sweden and the United Kingdom) since map reviews had been so infrequent; and last, although there was no established designation machinery in the Netherlands, there was at least a tradition of regular map review.

Coverage

From a Commission perspective, population coverage became an important measure of regional aid discipline from the early 1990s. For the member states it had always been a background issue. Moreover, up until 1999, population reductions had generally been relatively modest (Yuill *et al.* 1999). Set against this, the cutbacks demanded by the 1998 guidelines were significant. Only in Finland, Greece, Ireland, Portugal and Spain did overall population coverage remain stable or increase slightly. In contrast, Austria, Luxembourg and the United Kingdom experienced cutbacks of more than 20 per cent. All but one of the remaining member states faced 10–15 per cent reductions. The exception was Germany where the cutback was just over 7 per cent. In addition, the Article 87(3)(c) quotas in Italy, the Netherlands and Sweden were very low, all below 16 per cent.

Area Designation Methodologies

As noted earlier, the 1998 guidelines were developed around the German area designation system. The two approaches were not, however, identical. While the German system had an objective methodology, up to five indicators and a common unit of assessment (labour market regions), it also contained a qualitative element which allowed the *Länder*, by means of exchange, to include other regions with acute structural problems. The Commission, concerned about enforcing coverage discipline, removed the qualitative component from the final version of the guidelines (Wishlade 2003: 81). In Denmark, too, an objective methodology, combining five indicators to rank 59 groups of planning region in a single listing, was complemented by qualitative inputs from an interministerial advisory group. Nevertheless, in both countries, quantitative aspects were central to the designation decision.

This suggested that Germany and Denmark would have few methodological problems with the 1998 guidelines. The same was true of Finland and Sweden because of the special provisions for sparsely populated areas. Greece, Ireland and Portugal also had no methodological issues since their entire territory was eligible for support.

In other member states, methodological concerns were expected to be more prominent. In some, such as Austria, Luxembourg, the Netherlands and the United Kingdom, statistics were traditionally used to obtain an overview of the problem, but not in the explicit formalized way specified in the guidelines. In the remaining countries – Belgium, France, Italy and Spain – designation approaches were even more qualitative, creating obvious methodological challenges in compliance.

Expected Adaptational Pressures

Based on the above review, certain conclusions emerge about the broad goodness of fit of the 1998 guidelines with previous designation practice and the associated adaptational pressures on member states (see Table 1). Arguably the most important issue relates to the coverage cutback demanded. However, account also has to be taken of the extent to which previous designation systems were time-limited and had well-established designation procedures; and the methodological challenges posed by

Table 1. Expected adaptational pressures across the member states

	Timing-related	**Coverage-related**	**Methodology-related**	**Overall**
Austria	High	High	Med	High
Belgium	High	Med	High	High
Denmark	Low	Med	Low	Low
Finland	High	Low	Low	Low
France	High	Med	High	High
Germany	Low	Med	Low	Low
Greece	Low	Low	Low	Low
Ireland	Low	Low	Low	Low
Italy	High	Med	High	High
Luxembourg	High	High	Med	High
Netherlands	Med	Med	Med	Med
Portugal	Low	Low	Low	Low
Spain	High	Low	High	Med
Sweden	High	Med	Low	Med
UK	High	High	Med	High

Key:
Timing: Low = Time-limited approach with established procedures; plus countries where no area designation required; Med(ium) = Regular domestic reviews, but not time-limited or with established procedures; High = Occasional reviews, no time limits.
Coverage: Low = No cutback; Med = Cutback of between 7 per cent and 15 per cent; High = cutback of over 21 per cent.
Methodology: Low = Single rankings based on explicit indicators *or* no area designation requirement; Med = Overt, statistics-based systems with qualitative inputs; High = Essentially qualitative systems.
Overall: Low = Combined score of 3–5 (with Low = 1, Med = 2 and High = 3); Med = Combined score of 6–7; High = Combined score of 8–9.

the guidelines. Bringing these arguments together, overall adaptational pressures were expected to be low in Denmark, Finland, Germany, Greece, Ireland and Portugal; medium in the Netherlands, Spain and Sweden; and high in Austria, Belgium, France, Italy, Luxembourg and the UK.

The Adjustments – Measuring Adaptational Responses

This section analyses the initial map submissions under the 1998 guidelines to establish whether the anticipated adaptational pressures and responses (summarized in Table 2) held true. Drawing on the Europeanization literature (Héritier et al. 1996, Borzel and Risse 2001, Schmidt 2001, Radaelli 2003), member state responses are divided into three groups: resistance, transformation and absorption. Responses fall under the *resistance* heading where submissions fail to comply with the guideline requirements, with member states either retaining their original approach or adopting a revised approach which does not meet the guideline stipulations. Regarding *transformation*, member states respond to the changes required under the guidelines in their submissions. Finally, where there is *absorption*, guideline demands are accommodated without any significant change of approach.

Measuring Adaptational Pressures and Responses

One overall measure of adaptational pressures is the time taken to submit map proposals; this can be viewed as a proxy for the ease with which maps were devised under the guidelines. Set against the end-March 1999 target date, there were clear submission difficulties in Italy, Luxembourg and Sweden (delays of seven months or more), and in Austria and the United Kingdom (four- to five-month delays). Only in Luxembourg was the delay (partially) attributable to factors external to the guidelines (a change of government in June 1999). In contrast, there were no significant delays in Denmark, Finland, Germany, Greece, Ireland and Spain.[11] In broad terms, the delays reflect the pattern expected from Table 2. The main exception is Sweden, where concern at the (unexpectedly) low population quota (which in effect restricted map coverage to areas of sparse population) meant that no map was submitted until October. During this time, the Swedish authorities argued (unsuccessfully) for more generous treatment.

Submission delays are, of course, a relatively crude measure of adaptational pressures. At a more detailed policy level, Table 3 assesses the initial map

Table 2. Expected adaptational pressures and responses

Expected adaptational pressures (see Table 1)		Expected adaptational responses (policy change)
High	Austria, Belgium, France, Italy, Luxembourg, UK	Resistance (Low)
Medium	Sweden, Netherlands, Spain	Transformation (High)
Low	Denmark, Finland, Germany, Greece, Ireland, Portugal,	Absorption (Low)

Table 3. Goodness of fit – measuring adaptational responses

	Timing	Coverage	Unit	Use of unit	Indicators	Composite ranking	Award rates	Overall
Austria	T	T	A	R	A	A	T	R TTT AAA
Belgium	T	R	R	R	R	R	R	RRRRRR T
Denmark	A	T	A	A	A	A	T	TT AAAAA
Finland	T	A	A	R	A	R	T	RR TT AAA
France	T	T	T	R	T	R	R	RRR TTTT
Germany	R	R	A	R	A	A	R	RRRR AAA
Greece	T	A	A	A	A	A	T	TT AAAAA
Ireland	T	A	A	A	A	A	R	R T AAAAA
Italy	T	T	T	R	R	R	T	RRR TTTT
Luxembourg	T	R	A	A	T	R	T	RR TTT AA
Netherlands	T	T	R	T	R	R	R	RRRR TTT
Portugal	T	A	A	A	A	A	R	R T AAAAA
Spain	T	A	A	A	R	R	R	RRR T AAA
Sweden	T	T	A	A	A	A	R	R TT AAAA
UK	T	R	R	R	A	R	R	RRRRR T A

Key: R = Resistance (failure to comply); T = Transformation (policy change); A = Absorption (no need to change).

submissions in relation to the key requirements under the guidelines. It shows that *timing* issues were relatively uncontroversial. All but two countries moved to time-limited approaches covering the 2000–2006 period (transformation). The exceptions were Denmark (which absorbed the change by adjusting its time limits) and Germany (which resisted the seven-year period specified in the guidelines); instead, Germany submitted a 2000–2003 map and scheduled a 2004–2006 review in line with previous domestic practice.

Regarding *coverage*, most countries submitted maps that complied with their population quotas. For Finland, Greece, Ireland, Portugal and Spain, this represented absorption since the ceilings were either unchanged or higher; in contrast, the acceptance of lower ceilings by Austria, Denmark, France, Italy, the Netherlands and (after delay) Sweden represented transformation. However, in Belgium, Germany, Luxembourg and the United Kingdom, the guideline ceilings were exceeded (resistance). In Belgium, it proved impossible for the regions to agree on the subdivision of the new national ceiling; instead, they made separate submissions which, in combination, exceeded the quota on the assumption that the Commission would arbitrate. In Luxembourg, the ceiling was exceeded by 0.2 per cent of the population; the Luxembourg authorities (wrongly) anticipated that the Commission would agree to such flexibility. In the United Kingdom, ambiguity about the status of Northern Ireland was exploited; this led to the province being *added to* rather than *included within* the UK quota. Finally, in Germany, there was a rejection *in principle* of the new ceiling and the way in which it had been determined; this ultimately led to a case being brought before the European Court of Justice.

Regarding *methodology*, the guidelines proved to be unproblematic for Denmark, Greece, Ireland, Portugal and Sweden – and could be absorbed within the domestic approach to designation. In contrast, in Belgium, Italy, the Netherlands and the UK, the submissions infringed the guideline methodology in all or almost all respects (as measured by the Commission).[12] In a final group – Austria, Finland, France, Germany, Luxembourg and Spain – the submission reflected the methodology in most but not all respects.

Finally, with respect to *rates of award*, nine countries made submissions which exceeded the guideline stipulations. Only Austria, Denmark, Finland, Greece, Italy and Luxembourg submitted maps with award ceilings in line with the guidelines. While this may seem a high level of resistance, the guidelines were unclear on responsibility for setting rates and historically this task had fallen to the Commission. The French decision to submit higher rates than those specified in the guidelines was not resistance *per se* but rather the desire to leave unpopular arbitration to the Commission.

Set against the expectations of Table 2, the predominant pattern in Table 3 is broadly as anticipated for Denmark, Greece, Ireland and Portugal (where absorption was the standard response). It is also as expected for Belgium and the United Kingdom, where high adaptational pressures were anticipated, as well as in France and Italy. Less predictable was the relatively low resistance in Austria, Luxembourg and Sweden – though, in each case, this followed significant submission delays. Finally, resistance was much higher than anticipated in Germany and the Netherlands. The marked German resistance is especially noteworthy given that the guidelines were modelled on the German approach.

Explaining the Unexpected

How can the unexpected outcomes in respect of Germany, the Netherlands, Sweden, Austria and Luxembourg be explained? One explanation lies in the national significance of the policy area. Levels of regional aid expenditure help explain the particular importance of the issue to Germany and its relative lack of significance to Austria, Sweden and Luxembourg (Yuill *et al.* 1999). However, the relatively low level of spend in the Netherlands leaves the Dutch resistance (as measured by Table 3) unexplained.

Another explanation concerns the nature of the coverage change required by the population quotas. Although the *percentage* cutbacks in the Netherlands and Sweden fell within the medium group in Table 1, the *absolute* quota for both countries was very low – just 15 per cent in the Netherlands and 15.9 per cent in Sweden – significantly increasing the designation challenge. Sweden was also negatively influenced by the fact that the quota was much lower than had been implied by the pre-guideline consultations. This factor was also important in Germany where policy makers had expected coverage to *increase*, but actually faced a (moderate) cutback. The resulting sense of injustice exacerbated German resistance to the guidelines.

A further explanatory factor derives from the ambiguity of the guidelines and, associated, the timing of map submissions. Some of the resistance recorded reflects a different understanding of the guidelines to that of the Commission (as, for instance, in the UK). Moreover, amongst early submitters (including the Netherlands) there was a belief that, as under the 1988 Communication, it would be possible to negotiate a compromise solution. In practice, this was not to be; on the contrary, the Commission was keen to highlight early instances where the guidelines were not met (to encourage the others). This, combined with Commission reluctance to set precedents, led to the Netherlands being characterized as a "resister" (see Table 3), even though the map was not contentious domestically. Conversely, the late submissions from Austria, Sweden and Luxembourg – made after the rules of the game had become clearer – allowed maps to be submitted which were broadly acceptable to the Commission.

Underlying member state reactions was the fact that, for most, the key driver was the *outcome* of the exercise – that is, the areas actually designated for support: the central question was whether a guideline-derived approach could deliver "sensible" maps. Whether member states resisted, accepted or absorbed the changes was directly related to the extent to which their overall policy objectives could be accommodated. This underpinned the resistance in Germany where, despite the fact that the German model inspired the Commission's approach, that approach failed to meet key German goals. This was most obvious with respect to the population quota, but the lack of domestic "fine-tuning" under the guidelines (the qualitative stage of the German methodology) also created difficulties for the German authorities.

The Final Cut – Measuring Europeanization

This section considers the extent to which policy can be viewed as having been Europeanized. The emphasis is on assessing the degree of change imposed by the Commission in relation to the pre-1999 position. In practice, however, the initial submissions of the member states cannot be ignored when measuring Europeanization. Although clearly tempered by the guidelines, these submissions also reflected member states' preferences at the time – while the pre-1999 maps were often an important starting point for the 2000–2006 designations, changing socio-economic circumstances meant that, by 1999, member state preferences were not necessarily embodied in the existing maps.

Table 4 relates the final outcomes of the negotiation process to the pre-1999 position. It takes the same approach as Table 3 but, importantly, because of the need for Commission approval prior to implementation there is no scope for *resistance*; instead, where there had previously been resistance, the negotiations led either to policy *transformation* on the part of the member state or *compromise* (rule stretching) by the Commission.

Regarding *timing*, there was a clear Europeanization of the scheduling of map reviews. Previously, only Denmark and Germany had domestically set expiry dates. Now, the same (EU-determined) expiry dates apply everywhere. There was initial resistance in Germany to moving away from a three- to four-year review. However, the Commission thwarted the planned 2004–2006 review, following which Germany too has indicated that it will accept a seven-year review period. As mentioned earlier, a key characteristic of the pre-1999 period was the use of lengthy transitional provisions to phase out aid area status; for 2000–2006 DG

Table 4. Europeanization – measuring policy change

	Timing	Coverage	Methodology Unit	Use of unit	Indicators	Composite ranking	Award rates	Outcome
Austria	T	T	A	C	A	A	T	C TTT AAA
Belgium	T	T	T	T	T	C	T	C TTTTTT
Denmark	A	T	A	A	A	A	T	TT AAAAA
Finland	T	A	A	C	A	C	T	CC TT AAA
France	T	T	T	C	T	C	C	CCC TTTT
Germany	A	T[1]	A	T	A	A	T	TTT AAAA
Greece	T	A	A	A	A	A	T	TT AAAAA
Ireland	T	A	A	A	A	A	C	C T AAAAA
Italy	T	T	T	T	T	C	T	C TTTTTT
Luxembourg	T	T	A	A	T	C	T	C TTTT AA
Netherlands	T	T	C	T	A	C	T	CC TTTT A
Portugal	T	A	A	A	A	A	C	C T AAAAA
Spain	T	A	A	A	C	C	A	CC T AAAA
Sweden	T	T	A	A	A	A	T	TTT AAAA
UK	T	C	T	T	A	C	T	CC TTTT A

Notes: [1]There was a small concession to Germany in allowing coverage to rise slightly under Article 87(3)(c) to compensate for population decline in east Germany.
Key: C = Commission compromise (rules stretched); T = Transformation (policy change); A = Absorption (no need to change).

Competition succeeded in imposing immediate terminal dates, in contrast with the arrangements for the Structural Funds and to the frustration of some member states, notably France.

On *coverage*, the Commission was extremely successful in imposing population ceilings on the member states. The principal exception is the United Kingdom which, as noted, exploited the sensitivities surrounding the Northern Ireland peace process to gain inclusion of the province *in addition* to the UK allocation. This increased the UK quota by 3 per cent of the national population. In Germany, the pressure to ensure that at least some areas could receive regional aid from 1 January 2000 led to the submission of a revised map which *did* respect the ceiling. A subsequent attempt to challenge the ceiling before the European Court of Justice was unsuccessful.

The outcome for *area designation methodologies* is more mixed and more difficult to assess. Prior to 1999, only Denmark and Germany operated single rankings of areas based on explicit indicators; whereas Denmark had no difficulty adjusting to the guideline methodology (absorption), Germany eventually had to forgo the qualitative part of its methodology (transformation). In Greece, Ireland and Portugal, no methodological issues arose (since they were eligible in their entirety) and in Sweden, too, the methodology was straightforward given that nearly all the quota was accounted for by sparsely populated areas. For the remaining countries, the Commission soon appreciated that a wholly statistics-driven approach based on uniform units of assessment and culminating in a single ranking was untenable. Rule stretching was almost universal with respect to composite rankings, and is apparent in Austria, Finland, France and the Netherlands in terms of units of assessment.

Although timing, coverage and methodology are the core elements of change implied by the 1998 guidelines, a "technical" assessment of the implementation of the new rules gives only a partial view of their impact in terms of Europeanization. A consideration of the role of the pre-1999 maps in devising the initial submissions is also relevant, as is an assessment of the difference between the initial submissions and final outcomes.

In a number of countries, fieldwork reveals that policy makers took the pre-1999 map as the basis for the 2000–2006 designation. In Spain, for example, the decision was taken not to de-designate any areas, but to consult with the Autonomous Communities on which areas should be added to the map to use up the additional population quota; the key task then was to find the combination of indicators which would deliver that result under the guideline methodology. In the Netherlands, the existing map was also central – with two small exceptions, the initial proposal did not include any new areas, but simply removed areas from the existing map to come within the population ceiling. In both cases, the prescribed methodology was essentially reverse-engineered to produce a map corresponding to domestic policy needs while meeting the population ceilings. In this sense, some apparent transformation from a technical perspective conceals a high degree of absorption with respect to map outcomes.

For several countries, there were protracted negotiations between the initial submission and the final map (see Table 5). In some cases, the Commission opened the formal investigative procedure; in others, the process was informal. For a majority of countries, more than one map was submitted. However, the length and

Table 5. Timing, procedures, proposals and the significance of change

	Months from initial submission to approval	Article 88 investigative procedure	Number of maps submitted	Significance of change
Austria	10		3	Not significant
Belgium	16	Y	2	**Significant**
Denmark	7		1	None
Finland	7		1	None
France	9	Y	2	Not significant
Germany	12	Y	2	**Significant**
Greece	8		1	None
Ireland	6		1	None
Italy	9	Y	2	Not significant
Luxembourg	7		2	Not significant
Netherlands	16	Y	3	Not significant
Portugal	13	Y	1	None
Spain	12		1	None
Sweden	5		1	None
UK	12		2	**Significant**

Note: Significance of change refers to the differences between the initial proposal and the approved map.

heat of the negotiations, the number of submissions made and the depth of formal scrutiny are not necessarily indicative of the scale of change wrought by the Commission.

Only in Belgium, Germany and the United Kingdom were the changes required by the Commission significant. For Belgium, the initial submission had essentially comprised three distinct proposals (one from each region) which neither respected the population quota nor met the single methodology requirement; the ultimate proposal was therefore significantly different, imposing a unified designation methodology on a country where there is no national-level responsibility for regional policy. In the German case, as noted, the national authorities ultimately surrendered to pressure to respect the population ceiling – a cutback of over 4 million people. In addition, DG Competition refused to allow the splitting of units (the qualitative stage of the traditional German methodology), even through the use of the Structural Funds derogation (which it permitted, and even encouraged, elsewhere). In the United Kingdom, DG Competition opposition to the initial proposals resulted in a major reworking of the statistical analyses to increase the "compactness" of the map, involving a transfer of around 1 million people between the original and the amended maps.

A more qualitative indicator of Europeanization may be gleaned from policy maker perceptions. For some countries, the process of agreeing an aid area map with the Commission seems to have been regarded as tiresome, rather than troublesome; for example, in Austria and France policy makers characterized the negotiations as long, rather than difficult. By contrast, in Germany the changes imposed by the Commission were regarded as a serious interference in domestic policy. German resistance to Europeanization pressures was strengthened by the unexpected decrease in the German quota to allow increases elsewhere whilst retaining global discipline. The perceived inequity of this led to the already mentioned European Court of Justice case, an indicator of the strength of German feeling on this point. Finally, in the United Kingdom the original map was considered to be a successful attempt to combine the Commission guidelines with the labour market aims of UK regional policy, while the revised map was viewed as a substantial compromise of national regional policy objectives (DTI *et al.* 2000).

Some measure of Europeanization may also be established by considering to what extent the Commission's priorities were met. Clearly, there was a high level of compliance regarding timing and coverage but, with respect to area designation methodologies, the picture is more nuanced. Moreover, there is widespread evidence of member states exploiting the Structural Funds derogation to gain approval for national priority areas which did not meet the guideline requirements on uniform geographical units. This in turn raises the question of "whose Europeanization is it anyway"? DG Regio had given a high priority to the "coherence" of assisted areas – in this instance meaning that Structural Funds areas should also be eligible for national regional aid; in contrast, DG Competition never viewed this as an important objective. The compromise Structural Funds derogation came to be used by member states for national rather than European ends, with areas designated for Structural Funds purposes just so that they could be included in domestic regional aid maps.

A complication in measuring Europeanization is the degree of discretion exercised by the Commission. Some negotiations forced member states to change their proposals to fit the guidelines and compromised national preferences – as in the UK and Germany. In others, the emphasis was on finding ways of accommodating proposals within the guidelines, especially through the Structural Funds derogation – as in Finland, France and Spain; however, use of the derogation was explicitly denied to Germany. The uneven application of the guidelines partly explains the differing timescales for decision making, with potentially controversial precedents being held back. More pertinent, the measurement of Europeanization is clearly more complex in circumstances where European constraints are not imposed uniformly.

Conclusions

This article has examined the application of the 1998 regional aid guidelines to gain comparative insights into how and to what extent Europeanization has taken place and can be measured. It has also considered the degree to which the adaptational pressures which member states experience can be measured in practice and the relevance of goodness of fit to predicting adaptational responses.

The analysis has established that goodness-of-fit propositions provide relatively poor predictive capacity with respect to adaptation responses. Further aspects which need to be taken into account include: the significance of the policy area for the member state; member state expectations regarding the new policy; the level of understanding of Commission requirements; the clarity of policy objectives; and the fit with overarching domestic policy priorities.

This article has shown that a number of well-established techniques can help address the challenge of measuring causality in empirical research. These include bottom-up research designs, process tracing, counterfactual reasoning and the use of more systematic comparative methods. Nevertheless, an over-emphasis of those aspects of policy that are susceptible to measurement runs the risk of bogus precision.

The reality is that the policy environment is neither static nor uniform. The 1998 regional aid guidelines did not emerge from a vacuum but rather have evolved since the 1970s: each EU enlargement has affected the regional aid policies of the acceding countries; as important, each enlargement has altered EU regional aid control policy. The guidelines are therefore a *landmark* in an ongoing process, rather than an endpoint against which final outcomes can be measured. Moreover, the substantive results confirm the role of bottom-up processes in shaping outcomes (Méndez et al. 2006). Of key importance, a thorough analysis of the process demonstrates not only that application of the guidelines by DG Competition was uneven on key issues, but also that DG Regio objectives were partially subverted, raising wider issues about the "ownership" of Europeanization.

Most of the Europeanization literature attributes the differential impact of Europe to a set of intervening variables at the level of the member state (i.e. domestic institutions). This paper identifies another source of variation which has so far received little attention. The analysis shows that the independent variable itself (the EU pressure) may also vary across member states (independently of the degree of fit with member state policies and institutions), thus rejecting the uniformity-of-pressure assumption in much of the top-down literature. While recent scholarship has emphasized the domestic "usage" of European pressures (Jacquot and Woll 2003) as an explanation of differential European impacts, the analysis presented here draws attention to the ability of European institutions to strategically utilize Europeanization to advance their own goals and preferences in a dynamic fashion during the adaptation process.

These characteristics make the measurement of Europeanization akin to the pursuit of a mobile and metamorphosing target. The measurement of Europeanization *can* be facilitated by adopting a comparative assessment of impacts and outcomes, the use of a clear policy initiative that impacts on all member states simultaneously and a detailed knowledge of the *ex ante* and *ex post* situation in each member state. However, perhaps perversely, such a comprehensive and forensic approach also reveals the limitations of essentially reductionist methods of measuring policy change. A qualitative understanding of the complexities and dynamics of policy, and of the wider context, is an indispensable complement to quantitative approaches; policy researchers ignore this at their peril.

Acknowledgements

The authors gratefully acknowledge the financial support provided by the UK Economic and Social Research Council under its Future Governance programme (ESRC Award No. L216252050). Thanks are also due to EPRC's EoRPA regional policy research consortium for broader regional policy research funding (see http://www.eprc.strath.ac.uk/eorpa/). The views expressed are solely those of the authors who are responsible for all errors of fact or judgement.

Notes

1. It is particularly fitting in the context of this study that one of the policy areas examined by Haas was the "elimination and reduction of subsidies" (Haas 1958: 85–88), arguably the first scholarly account of the Europeanization of state aid policy.
2. Having said this, most of the chapters were mainly concerned with policy change at the EU level, which, as noted by Bulmer (1983: 349), "overshadowed some of the equally important findings concerning policy-making in the member states".
3. Greece was excluded from the interviews since the whole country remained eligible, with no regional differentiation in the map.
4. See generally D'Sa (1998) and, on regional aid specifically, Wishlade (2003).
5. Commission Communication on the method for the application of Article 92(3)(a) and (c) to regional aid, OJEC No. C 212 of 12 August 1988.
6. NUTS refers to the European Nomenclature of Statistical Units which are defined across the EU at up to five different levels. NUTS II is equivalent to a French or Italian region or a Spanish Autonomous Community.
7. Ideally through standard geographical building blocks (i.e. NUTS III or labour market areas); it wanted to outlaw the pin-pointing of areas (like industrial estates) with economic activities but, often, no resident population.
8. OJEC No. C74 of 10 March 1998
9. Although there was scope for mid-term review if a member state so desired.
10. More generally, the Commission wished to see "coherence" between aid maps designated for national and EU regional policy purposes, ensuring in particular that all areas eligible for EU Structural Funds should also be eligible for national regional aid.

11. The slightly delayed (April) submissions for Greece, Ireland and Spain reflected the fact that EU agreement on the EU budget for 2000–2006 (which impacted directly on the nature and coverage of regional policy in these countries) was not reached until the Berlin European Council (25 March 1999).
12. Commission reservations were set out in formal notices, press releases and in communications with the member states. In some instances, the member states believed their submissions were in line with the guideline methodology and, indeed, this was their explicit aim. The UK, for instance, consulted regularly with the Commission services seeking confirmation that its proposals were compliant. It was not until the map was submitted that it became apparent that the approach was not acceptable – to the considerable frustration of the UK authorities.

References

Allen, David, 1977, Policing or policy-making? Competition policy in the European Communities, in: Helen Wallace, William Wallace and Carole Webb (Eds) *Policy-Making in the European Communities* (London: John Wiley & Sons), pp. 91–112.

Allen, David, 1983, Managing the Common Market: the Community's competition policy, in: Helen Wallace, William Wallace and Carole Webb (Eds) *Policy-Making in the European Communities* (London: John Wiley & Sons), pp. 209–236.

Barrett, Susan and Fudge, Colin (Eds), 1981, *Policy and Action* (London: Methuen).

Bennett, Andrew and George, Alexander L., 1997, Process tracing in case study research. Paper presented at MacArthur Foundation Workshop on Case Study Methods, 17–19 October.

Berger, Suzanne and Dore, Ronald (Eds), 1996, *National Diversity and Global Capitalism* (Ithaca: Cornell University Press).

Börzel, Tanja, 1999, Towards convergence in Europe? Institutional adaptation to Europeanization in Germany and Spain. *Journal of Common Market Studies*, **39**(4), 573–596.

Börzel, Tanja A., 2005, Europeanization: how the European Union interacts with its member states, in: S. Bulmer and C. Lequesne (Eds) *The Member States of the European Union* (Oxford: Oxford University Press), pp. 45–69.

Börzel, Tanja A. and Risse, Thomas, 2000, When Europe hits home: Europeanization and domestic change. *European Integration Online Papers*, **4**(15), available at http://eiop.or.at/eiop/texte/2000-015a.htm (accessed February 2005).

Bulmer, Simon, 1983, Domestic politics and EC policy making. *Journal of Common Market Studies*, **21**(4), 349–363.

Bulmer Simon, J. and Radaelli, C. M., 2004, The Europeanisation of national policy. *Queen's Papers on Europeanisation*, No.1/2004, Queen's University, Belfast.

Cini, Michelle, 2000, From soft law to hard law? Discretion and rule-making in the Commission's state aid regime. *EUI Working Papers*, RSC No.2000/35, European University Institute, Florence.

D'Sa, R., 1998, *European Community Law on State Aid* (London: Maxwell & Sweet).

DTI, DETR, Welsh Office and Scottish Office, 2000, *Amendments to the Government's Proposals for New Assisted Areas* (London: DTI, URN 00/776).

Eckstein, Harry, 1975, Case study and theory in political science, in: F. Greenstein and N. Polsby (Eds) *Strategies of Inquiry: The Handbook of Political Science*, Vol. 7 (Reading, MA: Addison-Wesley), pp. 79–138.

Elmore, Richard, 1979, Backward mapping: implementation research and policy decisions. *Political Science Quarterly*, **94**(4), 601–616.

Friedman, Thomas, 1999, *The Lexus and the Olive Tree: Understanding Globalization* (London: HarperCollins).

Gualini, Enrico, 2003, Challenges to multi-level governance: contradictions and conflicts in the Europeanization of Italian regional policy. *Journal of European Public Policy*, **10**(4), 616–636.

Gualini, Enrico, 2004, *Multi-level Governance and Institutional Change: The Europeanization of Regional Policy in Italy* (Ashgate: Aldershot).

Haas, Ernst B., 1958, *The Uniting of Europe: Political, Social, and Economic Forces 1950–1957* (Stanford, CA: Stanford University Press).

Haverland, Markus, 2005, Does the EU cause domestic developments? The problem of case selection in Europeanization research. *European Integration Online Papers*, **9**(2), available at http://eiop.or.at/eiop/texte/2005-002a.htm (accessed February 2005).

Héritier, Adrienne, Knill, Christoph and Mingers, Susanne, 1996, *Ringing the Changes in Europe* (Berlin, New York: Walter de Grutyer).

Hjern, Benny and Porter, David O., 1981, Implementation structures: a new unit of administrative analysis. *Organisation Studies*, **2**, 211–227.

Hurrell, Andrew and Menon, Anand, 2003, International relations, international institutions and the European state, in: J. Hayward and A. Menon (Eds) *Governing Europe* (Oxford: Oxford University Press).

Jacquot, Sophie and Woll, Cornelia, 2003, Usage of European integration – Europeanization from a sociological perspective. *European Integration Online Papers*, **7**(12), available at http://eiop.or.at/eiop/texte/2003-012a.htm (accessed February 2005).

Keohane, Robert O. and Milner, Helen V. (Eds) 1996, *Internationalization and Domestic Politics* (Cambridge: Cambridge University Press).

Knill, Christoph and Lehmkuhl, Dirk, 1999, How Europe matters. Different mechanisms of Europeanization. *European Integration Online Papers*, **3**(7), available at http://eiop.or.at/eiop/texte/1999-007.htm (accessed February 2005).

Knill, Christoph and Lehmkuhl, Dirk, 2002, The national impact of European Union regulatory policy: three Europeanization mechanisms. *European Journal of Political Research*, **41**(2), 255–280.

Ladrech, Robert, 1994, Europeanization of domestic politics and institutions: the case of France. *Journal of Common Market Studies*, **32**(1), 69–88.

Lavdas, Kostas and Mendrinou, Maria, 1995, Competition policy and institutional politics in the European Community: state aid control and small business promotion. *European Journal of Political Research*, **28**(1), 171–201.

Le Galès, Patrick, 2001, Est maître des lieux celui qui les organise: how rules change when national and European policy domains collide, in: A. Stone-Sweet, W. Sandholz and N. Fligstein (Eds) *The Institutionalisation of Europe* (Oxford: Oxford University Press), pp. 137–154.

Lindberg, Leon N. and Scheingold, Stuart A., 1970, *Europe's Would-Be Polity: Patterns of Change in the European Community* (Englewood Cliffs, NJ: Prentice-Hall).

Lipsky, Michael, 1971, Street level bureaucracy and the analysis of urban reform. *Urban Affairs Quarterly*, **6**, 391–409.

McGowan, Francis, 2000, Competition policy, in: H. Wallace and W. Wallace (Eds) *Policy Making in the European Union* (Oxford: Oxford University Press), pp. 115–147.

Méndez, Carlos, Wishlade, Fiona and Yuill, Douglas, 2006, Conditioning and fine-tuning Europeanization: negotiating regional policy maps and the EU's competition and cohesion policies. *Journal of Common Market Studies*, **44**(3), 581–605.

Olsen, Johan P., 2002, The many faces of Europeanization. *Journal of Common Market Studies*, **40**(5), 921–952.

Puchala, Donald J., 1975, Domestic politics and regional harmonization in the European Communities. *World Politics*, **2**(4), 496–520.

Radaelli, Claudio, 2000, Whither Europeanization? Concept stretching and substantive change. *European Integration Online Papers*, **4**(8), available at http://eiop.or.at/eiop/texte/2000-008a.htm (accessed February 2005).

Radaelli, Claudio, 2003, The Europeanization of public policy, in: K. Featherstone and C. Radaelli (Eds) *The Politics of Europeanization* (Oxford: Oxford University Press), pp. 27–56.

Risse, Thomas, Green Cowles, Maria and Caporaso, James, 2001, Europeanization and domestic change: introduction, in: M. G. Cowles, J. Caporaso and T. Risse (Eds) *Transforming Europe. Europeanization and Domestic Change* (Ithaca, NY: Cornell University Press).

Rose, Richard, 1972, Comparing public policy. *European Journal of Political Research*, **1**, 67–94.

Saurugger, Sabine, 2005, Europeanization as a methodological challenge: the case of interest groups. *Journal of Comparative Policy Analysis*, **7**(4), 291–312.

Schmidt, Vivian A., 2001, Europeanization and the mechanics of economic policy adjustment. *European Integration Online Papers*, **5**(6), available at http://eiop.or.at/eiop/texte/2001-006a.htm (accessed February 2005).

Siedentopf, Heinrich and Ziller, Jacques, 1988, *Making European Policies Work* (London, Newbury Park and New Delhi: Sage Publications).

Smith, Mitchell P., 1996, Integration in small steps: the European Commission and member-state aid to industry. *West European Politics*, **19**, 563–582.
Smith, Mitchell P., 2001, How adaptable is the European Commission? The case of state aid regulation. *Journal of Public Policy*, **21**(3), 219–238.
Thielemann, Eiko R., 2000, Institutional limits of a "Europe with the regions": EC state-aid control meets German federalism. *Journal of European Public Policy*, **6**(3), 399–418.
Wallace, Helen, Wallace, William and Webb, Carole (Eds), 1977, *Policy-Making in the European Communities* (London: John Wiley & Sons).
Wallace, Helen, Wallace, William and Webb, Carole (Eds), 1982, *Policy-Making in the European Communities*, 2nd edition (London: John Wiley & Sons).
Wallace, Helen, 2000, Europeanisation and globalisation: complimentary or contradictory trends? *New Political Economy*, **5**(3), 369–382.
Wishlade, Fiona G., 2003, *Regional State Aid and Competition Policy in the European Union* (The Hague: Kluwer Law International).
Yuill, Douglas, Bachtler, John and Wishlade, Fiona, *European Regional Incentives 1999*, 18th edition (London: Bowker Saur).

Overfishing in Southern Africa: A Comparative Account of Regime Effectiveness and National Capacities

MARTIN SJÖSTEDT & AKSEL SUNDSTRÖM

ABSTRACT *The international community has in recent decades supported the installment of formal regulations and institutions for monitoring, control, and surveillance to decrease illegal, unreported, and unregulated fishing in African nations. Yet, few studies have investigated the effectiveness of these reforms. By conducting a systematic comparison of the enforcement of fisheries regulations in five Southern African Development Community (SADC) countries, we illustrate how the effectiveness of international agreements and regional commitments is fundamentally conditioned by national capacities. The empirical investigation also provides some tentative insights into the general dynamic process and mechanisms through which this can be understood.*

Introduction

Millions of small-scale fishermen around the world depend on fish and fishing for income and nutrition. Yet many fisheries suffer seriously from overexploitation and ecological stress, endangering the livelihoods of some of the poorest segments of society, putting pressure on public finances, and also threatening the overall health of the oceans (Myers and Worm 2003; World Bank 2004; FAO 2006). The scholarly community – as well as policymakers and donors – have in recent decades mainly attributed these challenges to institutional failures (Bailey 1988; Alcock 2002). In the vast literature on common pool resource management, one such crucial institutional aspect is in turn argued to be systems of monitoring, control, and surveillance (MCS) (Gibson et al. 2005).

Consequently, international organizations have supported developing countries in their efforts to install MCS systems. For example, in Southern Africa – which is in focus in this article – the EU and the United Nations Food and Agriculture Organization (FAO) have in the last decade supported the Southern African Development Community (SADC) in its efforts to install MCS systems and a regional commitment to combat illegal, unreported, and unregulated (IUU) fishing activities (FAO 2001). Yet while all SADC countries have agreed on the regional Protocol on Fisheries and its action plan, there are few studies investigating how the effectiveness of this regional commitment, informed by an international agreement to counter illegal fishing and install MCS measures, is affected by the respective country's national capacity to implement the agreements. This paper aims to fill this gap by conducting a systematic comparison of the enforcement of fisheries regulations in five SADC countries (Angola, Mozambique, Namibia, South Africa, and Tanzania). More specifically, we aim to illustrate how the effectiveness of international commitments and regional agreements are fundamentally conditioned by national capacities and how the rules to combat overfishing play out in practice.

By investigating how a global norm travels from the international level to national legislation and then to rules in practice, this study contributes primarily to the research conducted within the field of implementation and policy studies (Pressman and Wildavsky 1973; Lundqvist 1980; Finnemore 1996; Checkel 1999). In addition, it adds to recent policy developments within natural resource management where MCS systems have been agreed internationally while their effectiveness and relationship to national capacities have been overlooked. The study also contributes with an explicit comparative approach, implying a potential to generate general knowledge beyond the particularities of specific cases.

Natural Resource Management and Enforcement

Overexploitation of fisheries resources comes as no surprise to scholars of institutional theory and natural resource management (Demsetz 1967; Hardin 1968). For example, in line with the well-known *tragedy of the commons* and *logic of collective action*, research within social science has repeatedly shown that resource users who expect that others are overharvesting natural resources tend to engage in overuse themselves (Ostrom et al. 2002). But institutional theory also provides remedies, and various forms of institutional arrangements such as protected areas, quotas, etc. have been put forward as silver bullets in managing marine resources.

Yet while institutional theory has largely been occupied with issues of institutional design – i.e. different types of institutional arrangements – enforcement mechanisms and institutions of MCS have been largely overlooked. More recently, however, the role of MCS systems and the role played by such surrounding institutional frameworks in which resource systems and the arrangements that govern their use are embedded have been highlighted (Anderson 1989; Gibson 1999; Burton 2003; Gibson et al. 2005). Accordingly, outcomes in natural resource management can hence potentially be explained by differences in enforcement capacities.

The standard definition of MCS systems – guiding most policy efforts and reforms in fisheries management – is formulated by the FAO as follows:

- *Monitoring* involves the collection, measurement, and analysis of fishing activities and includes catch and species composition, fishing effort, bycatch, discards, area of operations, etc.
- *Control* includes the specification of the terms and conditions under which resources can be harvested.

- *Surveillance* includes the regulation and supervision of fishing activities aimed to ensure that legislation, conditions of access, and management measures are adhered to (FAO 1997).

The growing focus on MCS also shines through in contemporary policy developments. One example is the International Plan of Action to Prevent, Deter and Eliminate Illegal, Unreported and Unregulated Fishing (IPOA-IUU), which was developed as an instrument within the Code of Conduct for Responsible Fisheries. It was adopted by the Committee on Fisheries (COFI) in March 2001 and was later endorsed by the FAO Council. The objective of the IPOA-IUU is to prevent, deter, and eliminate IUU fishing by providing all states with comprehensive, effective, and transparent measures by which to act. These measures focus, for example, on state responsibilities, coastal state measures, port state measures, and internationally agreed market-related measures.

The IPOA has in turn inspired the SADC Protocol on Fisheries, which is a statement of commitment on IUU fishing by SADC ministers responsible for marine fisheries, signed in Windhoek, Namibia, in July 2008. In this protocol, the ministers declare they would strengthen fisheries governance and legal frameworks to eliminate illegal fishing and strengthen MCS capacity – and resolve to commit to effective implementation of existing MCS measures.

However, although MCS is now at the forefront of both research and policy developments, there has been a tendency to take enforcement capacities for granted. Hersoug and Paulsen (1996, p. 87) argue:

> In all manuals prescribing modern (western) fisheries management, the authority of the state is taken for granted. This is, at least in an African context, a gross oversimplification. Even if the fisheries administration has a strong central presence, its power and capacity out in the provinces and at the local level may still be weak or non-existent.

To conclude, while the scholarly and policy interest in the role of MCS certainly has increased, there is still a lack of knowledge and systematic comparative accounts of how these measures have been implemented in practice as well as of how country-specific differences have impacted on this implementation. In fact, although more than two decades have passed since Paul Sabatier (1991) urged scholars to develop better theories and empirics for understanding the policy process, public policy can still be said to suffer from the absence of a "commonly accepted, clearly articulated, and empirically verified body of theory" (Sabatier 1991, p. 153). In particular, while there have been great contributions as regards the specifics of different policy sub-systems – such as bureaucrats, legislative personnel, and interest groups – more knowledge is needed on how country-specific characteristics impact on the diffusion and implementation of international norms (Finnemore 1996; Checkel 1999). Admittedly, such diffusion has been the subject of renewed attention in recent years, but the importance of country-specific differences and capacities has largely been neglected. For example, Checkel (1999, p. 86) argues: "the role of agency within the adopter population is largely ignored or assumed away with simplifying assumptions. It is therefore not surprising that one interdisciplinary summary of the state of diffusion research concluded that, while the 'nature of the adoption environment is central to the diffusion process,' (Hugill and

Dickson 1988: 270–271) it remains poorly understood". The theoretical ambition of this article is to contribute to such an understanding.

Monitoring, Control, and Surveillance of Fisheries in Five SADC Coastal Countries

The countries chosen for this investigation all belong to the SADC and hence share important geographical and cultural features. Fisheries are important in all countries, and overexploitation has serious repercussions for poverty eradication in the region. Moreover, the countries have all been subject to a global norm and resulting international efforts to improve MCS, and have signed a regional protocol where they commit to combat IUU fishing. Yet, although this particular setting provides ample opportunities for systematic comparative investigations, research within the field of policy analysis and natural resource management has previously been dominated by single-case studies (Duit, forthcoming) (For exceptions, see Campbell 2010). A systematic comparative approach, we argue, can significantly contribute to our understanding of fisheries management and enforcement dynamics as well as to our theoretical understanding of how "norms 'out there' in the international system get 'down here' to the national arena and have constitutive effects" (Checkel 1999, p. 85).

The framework and organizing questions of the comparative account in this article focus on the relationship between international regime effectiveness and country-specific national capacities to implement and enforce. The dependent variable is conceptualized as effectiveness of the national regime to prevent, deter, and eliminate IUU fishing, and is here proxied by levels of IUU fishing and overfishing in each country. As these phenomena are inherently difficult to measure, we have tried our best to use the most recent estimates from existing literature on the topic. The independent variable is national capacities to implement and enforce measures to address IUU fishing. This includes rules on paper, but in particular how these rules play out in practice and the factual implementation of MCS measures to combat IUU fishing. The five cases we analyze are arranged along four themes. The first section of each case discusses the *outcomes* of overfishing and IUU fishing in the specific country. Focusing on the possibilities of governing fisheries resources in each country, the *tractability* of the sector is then described. Proceeding to define the regulations of the sector, the *formal policy* of fisheries management is discussed. The final section of each case is focused on the policy output, analyzing how and to what extent MCS measures to enforce the formal policy have been *implemented*. In all, each case illustrates how the effectiveness of these rules on paper is conditioned by national capacities.

Angola

Angola faces a significant challenge of IUU fishing with foreign vessels often pinpointed as offenders (Pramod et al. 2008, p. 12). Illegal activities include fishing without license, in closed areas, in areas only permitted for artisanal actors, and with illegal methods (Stop Illegal Fishing 2008e). Overfishing is described as having "significantly reduced fish stocks, threatening some species with extinction" (UNEP 2008, p. 83), and there are indications of a decline in commercial fish stocks and in total fish biomass of all fish groups except sardinella (Pramod et al. 2008, p. 3; du Preez 2009).

Fisheries are mainly artisanal and the sector is important for ensuring food security (Sowman and Cardoso 2010, p. 3). The Angolan Ministry of Fisheries is responsible for managing marine resources and the Aquatic Biological Resources Act from 2005 regulates fisheries (BCLME 2005, pp. 43–48). A total allowed catch (TAC) is set for different species on an annual basis, of which a portion is allocated to the artisanal subsector (du Preez 2009, p. 11). Moreover, fisheries are managed through inheritable and transferable fishing rights, gear restrictions, closing of fisheries, and size regulations (FAO 2004; INFOSA 2010, p. 8). Protected and reserved areas exist to some extent (Earthtrends 2003; Wood 2007). Whereas foreign actors have to lease their vessels to Angolan enterprises or form joint ventures to fish in Angola, subsistence fishers are allowed considerable catches without licenses (BCLME 2005; Sowman and Cardoso 2010, p. 3). There are references to co-management systems (e.g., IPS/IFEJ 2009), yet the extent or quality of these regimes has been questioned. Community observers are appointed as monitors, but are not salaried (Amador 2004, pp. 23, 40; du Preez 2009). Vessels are responsible for maintaining records and for reporting on positions and catches, and the administration is authorized to verify data from vessel monitoring systems (VMS) and logbooks (BCLME 2005, pp. 55–56). A division is made between "serious" and "common" offenses, with increasing fines for repeated offenses (Amador 2006, pp. 4–5).

Measures for MCS were implemented late and gradually, with little infrastructure available (Pramod et al. 2008, p. 11). The possibility to use judicial appeal has created incentives for offenders to contest decisions in court, prolonging judicial procedures (Amador 2006, p. 5), and the officers within the enforcement regime are not granted police powers (BCLME 2005, p. 56). Financing is a further problem. Initially it was constructed as a prerequisite for a fisheries agreement with the EU, but this agreement has since been canceled (Pramod et al. 2008, p. 11). Moreover, the responsible authority faces internal challenges. In many cases evidence of malpractice is not reported due to the knowledge that violating boats are co-owned or operated by government officials. The vested interests of politicians and civil servants have thus led to the suspicion that enforcement is deliberately kept low, with funding restricted, and diligent inspectors marginalized (Cederrand 2004, cited in Standing 2008). In sum, the enforcement capacity in Angola is comparatively low. No observer scheme exists and no formal catch inspection scheme is reported (Pramod et al. 2008, pp. 11–12). Although ten new patrol vessels were bought some years ago, measures undertaken to ensure that regulations are complied with are generally inadequate (Stop Illegal Fishing 2008e). An evaluation of the UN Code of Conduct for Responsible Fishing rates the country at the lower end in regard to compliance to the code (Pitcher et al. 2008). According to recent assessments, "Angola has very low offshore sea patrol capacity due to absence of a designated patrol vessel for this purpose" and dockside inspections are limited as navy, police, and port authorities do not cooperate in joint MCS activities (Pramod 2011, p. 12).

Mozambique

Around 100 IUU vessels are estimated to operate in the Mozambican channel (Stop Illegal Fishing 2008b, pp. 47–48). Mozambique has a history of high under-reporting of catches, mainly due to the neglect of the catches from the artisanal sector. Artisanal fishermen often fish during closed season and in protected areas (Stop Illegal Fishing 2008a, p. 30). It is evident that national fish stocks are under great pressure and many fisheries show signs of overexploitation, and the shallow coastal waters are severely overfished (Jacquet et al. 2010, pp. 203–204).

The fisheries sector, spread over 700 landing sites, is an important provider of employment and nutrition (FAO 2007a, p. 7). The Marine Fisheries Regulation was adopted in 2003, and the Ministry of Fisheries is now the responsible authority (Lux Development 2005, p. 10). Management measures mainly cover the commercial sector and consist of a combination of quotas and TACs together with effort restrictions (Virgilio Omar 2006; FAO 2007a, p. 16). Although mentioned as an example of where ITQs are used (Arnason 2002, p. 373; Hatcher et al. 2002, p. 54), license limitation is still the principal measure to control fishing effort. Further measures include gear regulations and closed seasons (Amador 2005, p. 83). The strongest management scheme is found in the shallow water shrimp fisheries (Afonso 2004, p. 19). There exists a strategy of protected areas (Wood 2007), some of which are co-managed (Johnstone 2004). Enforcement officers are authorized to conduct inspections, employ onboard observers, and require catch and effort reports (Lux Development 2005, p. 10; Stop Illegal Fishing 2008b). One report describes how "control of the artisanal fisheries is addressed through co-management", but concludes that they are still "largely monitored by provincial fisheries officers" (Stop Illegal Fishing 2008b, p. 31). The legislation distinguishes between "regular" infringements, more serious infringements, and recurring offenders (Cacaud et al. 2003).

Measures for MCS were implemented late and with few resources available (Afonso 2004, p. 19). Legal infraction processes have often been delayed, and unpaid fines amassed (Kelleher 2002, p. 18; Amador 2005). Moreover, corruption remains a serious challenge. The current president has economic interests in fishing companies that have been accused of being privileged in the acquisition of quotas (Mosse 2005, p. 435), and there have been incidences of corruption within the fisheries ministry (Kelleher 2002, p. 31). There is no permanent budget for MCS activities, onboard inspectors are not considered to be effective, and no VMS exists for the approximately 130 foreign tuna boats in the EEZ (Exclusive Economic Zone) (Lux Development 2005; Pramod et al. 2008; Stop Illegal Fishing 2008b, pp. 24–25). In 2005, inspectors were based in a majority of the nation's districts and also responsible for licensing artisanal vessels. A VMS was installed in the prawn and linefish fisheries but neither aerial surveillance nor offshore patrol boats exist (Afonso 2004). Although a patrol boat for near-coast activities has been introduced in recent years (Stop Illegal Fishing 2008d, p. 31), one evaluation expresses that "due to nearly non-existent surveillance, there is weak knowledge of ongoing activities in EEZ" (Lux Development 2005, p. 4).

Foreign vessels detained for illegal fishing have still been able to escape. In 2006, the collision of two foreign vessels exposed that authorities were unaware of their presence in the EEZ (Stop Illegal Fishing 2008b, pp. 47–48). Artisanal fisheries have in practice been considered as "open-access" (Afonso 2004, p. 418) and offenses are common: "artisanal fisheries are operated generally without management, landings data from this sector are incomplete, and there is not enough control in this sector" (Lux Development 2005, p. 11). In all, regulations are poorly enforced: "75 percent of fisheries are theoretically managed, but a very small part is effectively managed" (Cunningham and Bodiguel 2005, p. 76).

Namibia

Namibia has been relatively successful in minimizing IUU fishing. Persisting problems relate to violation of the EEZ, piracy of unlicensed vessels, and unreported discards. Demersal fisheries have had low violation rates. The economically less important midwater fishery has faced more violations (Bergh and Davies 2004, p. 297). A recent evaluation states, "There is virtually no illegal fishing by unlicensed vessels ... Generally, levels of compliance by licensed vessels appear high. This means that there is a good evidential basis for the validation of landings" (Megapesca 2009, pp. 24–25). While Namibia's most important commercial fish stocks certainly are under pressure, studies hold that marine ecosystems are in balance and that management is responsive to changes in fish stocks (BCLME 2005; Stop Illegal Fishing 2008a, p. 32).

Fisheries are predominantly industrial and have two major landing ports. While this increases the prospects for successful management, marine resources were mismanaged before independence in 1990 (van Zyl 2002; Kleinschmidt 2006; FAO 2010, p. 61). The Ministry of Fisheries and Marine Resources is responsible for regulating fisheries (Nichols 2004, p. 320). The fisheries are managed with a rights-based system. While fishing rights are granted for longer periods, the TACs are set annually for specific species. Individual quotas are then distributed among the rights-holders (Winter 2009, p. 171). These quotas were made non-transferable in order to support previously disadvantaged groups (Stewart 2004, p. 88). The use of protected or closed areas is limited but growing (Wood 2007; Pramod et al. 2008). Moreover, there have been closed seasons in certain fisheries (Boyer and Boyer 2005, pp. 19–20). Management measures are financed by the fishing industry itself through fees, ensuring that the treasury collects a positive net income (Arnason 2002, pp. 36–37). Transshipping fish at sea between vessels is prohibited and vessels must supply daily effort and position reports. Unauthorized fishing is a criminal offense subject to fines (Rukoro 2009, p. 181).

After independence, the fisheries management was rebooted in accordance with an "aggressive policy to promote the recovery of the resources to previous levels" (Boyer and Boyer 2005, p. 4). The administration forcefully arrested foreign actors and seized their vessels (Rukoro 2009, p. 178). Currently, the MCS strategy consists of an observer scheme, the collection of scientific data, sea and air patrols, as well as monitoring of landings by onshore inspectors (Boyer and Boyer 2005, p. 3). No sanction is prescribed for repeat offenders and goals of compliance are somewhat hampered by the low fines and the delay between crime and punishment (Amador 2006, p. 10; Rukoro 2009). Yet Namibia's MCS is hailed as a role model in the region. In an evaluation of compliance with the UN code of conduct on responsible fishing, Namibia receives top scores in most aspects. The observer scheme and the catch inspections scheme are largely deemed efficient (Pramod et al. 2008, pp. 17–19). Another evaluation of compliance to the UN code of conduct notes that, though there is clearly room for improvement, Namibia is one of the top ranking countries in the world in this respect (Pitcher et al. 2008). The merits of the regime also include that the cost of MCS has corresponded to the value of the fisheries sector (Winter 2009, p. 309). Currently, observers cover 91.5 per cent of all vessels in Namibian waters and nearly 85 per cent of the total fishing fleet is equipped with VMS (Pramod 2011, pp. 137–138).

South Africa

The widespread IUU fishing in South Africa is estimated to cost US$815 million annually (Moolla 2010). There is inadequate control of no-take zones and large-scale poaching has occurred in protected reserves (Pramod et al. 2008, p. 190). Heavy poaching of lobsters is also a major problem (Mail & Guardian 2011). Significant levels of illegal fishing exist in linefish and abalone fisheries (Pramod 2011, p. 181). This has in turn had an impact on the health of marine ecosystems. In fact, according to the IUCN (the International Union for Conservation of Nature) red list, almost 70 fish species are threatened (UNEP 2008, p. 301). Accordingly, "the majority of South African fisheries are described as fully exploited, with little room for further development" (Stop Illegal Fishing 2008c, p. 31).

Few major companies control the largely industrial fisheries. Fisheries are not crucial for food security but constitute an important employer in certain areas (FEIKE 2008). Fisheries management has taken some steps away from the top-down approach of the apartheid era (see Hersoug and Holm 2000), but although certain areas use co-management committees to assess stocks, the system has been described as being "in its infancy" (Hauck and Sowman 2001, p. 183). The Marine Living Resources Act from 1998 regulates marine resources (Branch and Clark 2006, p. 4) and there are regulations for specific fisheries (DEAT 2005, pp. 15–18). Commercial fisheries are managed through the allocation of fishing rights and quotas as well as effort controls. Tools for management include TACs and catch and gear restrictions (Cunningham and Bodiguel 2005; Feike 2008; Moolla et al. 2008a). In a regional comparison, South Africa has an ambitious program of protected areas. While only South Africans are allowed to hold fishing rights, foreign vessels can act in cooperation with domestic actors (Pramod et al. 2008, p. 190). Violation of the MLRA is treated as a criminal offense (Republic of South Africa 1998, p. 28). Measures to increase regulatory compliance have also included efforts to create trust among fishermen and delegation of authority (Hauck and Kroese 2006, pp. 78–79).

After a gradual implementation of MCS measures, the regime's record in countering IUU fishing peaked in the middle of the last decade. Since then, the funding for MCS has declined (Kleinschmidt 2006, p. 82). In 2002, resources for monitoring activities were unevenly distributed along the coast (Lux Development 2002, pp. 12–14). Yet the responsible department had ambitious plans (DEAT 2001). MCS measures included an investigation unit, joint investigations with the navy, an environmental court, international cooperation, and anti-corruption efforts (Hauck and Kroese 2006, pp. 78–79). In 2003 and 2004, high-profile arrests were made and an anti-poaching unit was created (Steinberg 2005). Accordingly, these efforts were successful: "compliance in South Africa has improved in recent years with an increasing number of convictions" (Japp 2004, p. 442). Another evaluation concluded: "IUU fishing is probably at a low level in South Africa as a result of the high levels of MCS" (MRAG 2005, p. 40). However, this momentum was lost from 2005 when funding for environmental courts was ended and the anti-poaching unit closed: "[MCS] has lost some of its efficiency due to administrative and funding problems in recent years, resulting in a relatively weak monitoring of the main fisheries" (Pramod et al. 2008, pp. 22–23). Subsistence fisheries are now managed "on an ad hoc basis and in certain instances considered to be 'open access' system" (Kleinschmidt 2006, p. 102). In 2006, only two inshore patrol vessels and one offshore patrol vessel had been delivered (Hauck and Kroese 2006, pp. 78–79). One of the large patrol vessels was later sold (PMG 2008). The responsible department also faced problems, with a budget dependent on the selling of confiscated abalone (Moolla 2010, p. 20). Moreover, the responsible minister stated that the fishing industry has its tentacles in the department (PMG 2010). Violations have ballooned since 2005, and accordingly "this has been directly linked to the institutional collapse" of the responsible department (Moolla 2010, p. 36). Recent findings indicate that since inspectors from this department are often perceived as corrupt, the willingness to comply with regulations among small-scale fishermen from various sectors is low. One evaluation concludes: "[South Africa] presently does not have any monitoring, control and surveillance strategy in place to prevent, deter or eliminate illegal fishing" (Moolla 2010, p. 41). Other evaluations are less drastic, describing South Africa as being "moderately equipped to patrol fishery resources within the EEZ" (Pramod 2011, p. 180).

Tanzania

IUU fishing is said to continue in the Tanzanian EEZ, especially by foreign actors (World Bank 2008, p. 37). Though infringements by non-licensed foreign vessels have decreased in recent years, few comply with the ban on discards, and illegal gear is still in use (Pramod et al. 2008). Fish catches are decreasing across a number of reef and inshore species (MRAG 2003; Verheij et al. 2004; UNEP 2008, p. 317), and dynamite fishing and poisoning are targeted as particular threats (World Bank 2008; Wells 2009, p. 36).

The mainly artisanal fisheries are dispersed over 1,000 landing sites and are important for livelihsood security (FAO 2007b, p. 5). In mainland Tanzania, the Ministry for Natural Resources and Tourism is the responsible authority and the Fisheries Act from 2003 is the current legislative document. In Zanzibar, the Fisheries Act from 1988 deals with fisheries (Cunningham and Bodiguel 2005, p. 6). The main regulatory measure is licensing. Owners of vessels pay annual fees, where it is more expensive to register a foreign vessel (Wilson 2004, p. 5). Management tools include restrictions of mesh size of gill nets and trawl nets (FAO 2007b, p. 14). The industrial prawn fisheries are regulated through specific measures (Lokina 2006, p. 16). Artisanal fishermen face restrictions such as closed areas and gear restrictions, but not restrictions on time, catches, or capacity (Cunningham and Bodiguel 2005, p. 10). At least four marine parks have been established and several small islands are declared protected (Hatton year unknown: v; McClanahan and Arthur 2001, p. 560). There have been initiatives to create co-management through the establishment of Village Environment Committees and Beach Management Units (BMUs) (Mngulwi 2003; MRAG 2003, p. 56). Although it is difficult to assess the extent to which BMUs have been implemented, they have been deployed in some fisheries (FAO 2007b, p. 12). There are both sanctions for criminal acts and certain administrative sanctions applied by officers (Amador 2006, p. 14).

MCS measures were implemented slowly and were heavily dependent on donor funding (Lokina 2006, p. 26). The weakness of this situation is exemplified in a project to counter dynamite fishing, which rapidly lost effect when external support was phased out (Wells 2009, p. 20). MCS measures include coordination with onboard observers and other divisions and countries (MRAG 2003, pp. 49–50). Each vessel must communicate three times daily with authorities to enable monitoring (Lokina 2006, p. 16). There has been surveillance organized by communities and BMUs (Verheij et al. 2004, p. 313; Kimani et al. 2009, p. 10). The record of MCS however has been quite weak. Although an observer program has been implemented, it is not clear how surveillance operations are sustained (Mngulwi 2003, p. 450; Lokina 2006). A lack of formal property rights over fish resources on many islands, often being regarded as open fishing grounds, has hindered the creation of protected areas (World Bank 2008, pp. 35–36). Moreover, legal processes have a poor record. Many offenders pay smaller fines instead of being prosecuted in a court, offenses are not graduated according to their degree of seriousness, and violators who are prosecuted are rarely punished (Amador 2006; Shauri 2006; Pramod et al. 2008). Moreover, since many of the data collectors were laid off in the 1990s, the calculations of catches are not working satisfactory and there is hence a "serious information gap on fisheries statistics nationwide" (MRAG 2003, p. 19). Taken together, the MCS measures are weak. Surveillance activities include inspections but these are crippled: "arresting [illegal fishers] has been hampered by the low speed of the patrol vessel currently used by the MNRT" (Lokina 2006, p. 23).

Discussion

The five countries in this study have all been subject to an international norm pushing them to counter illegal fishing and install MCS measures. Yet their responses in formulating and implementing related policies have been significantly different. Table 1 schematically summarizes the main findings of the comparative analysis. The section below synthesizes our analysis across the countries we study, using the four themes introduced above as a structure and attempt to discuss how these findings could be understood.

Regarding *outcomes* it is clear that the five countries stand in contrast to each other in how well they have managed to address the problem of IUU fishing. As indicated, Namibia has clearly been the most successful case. Moreover, while Tanzania and Mozambique seem to have problems related to foreign actors in their EEZ, South Africa's problems relate more to widespread non-compliance among domestic actors. Material and geographical conditions also seem to affect the capacity for successful implementation. The *tractability* of the successful case of Namibia clearly illustrates that it is easier to monitor two harbors than the dispersed landing sites of, for example, Angola or Mozambique. Analyzing the *formal policy* of fisheries regulations in the five countries, it is evident that they all have quite far-reaching legislation in place. However, there are considerable differences in what type of measures are prescribed, ranging from rights-based approaches to licensing systems and varying degrees of protected areas. It is apparent that the five countries also differ in the *implementation* of these policies, and they have adopted MCS measures with a varying degree of firmness. While the approach by Namibia was characterized by a steadfastness in terms of allocated resources to monitoring and punishment of offenders, Angola is an example of a country where MCS measures where implemented gradually and late, with few resources available for monitoring and where sanctions were not functioning as intended.

In all, it is evident that national capacities to implement and enforce the existing regulations fundamentally condition their effectiveness. Our analysis has illustrated how the country-specific characteristics discussed above impact on the diffusion and implementation of the international norm in focus in this article, and show how the rules to combat overfishing play out in practice. As such, we contribute to well-established literatures within international relations and policy studies (Lundqvist 1980; Checkel 1999). Moreover, the comparative analysis also contributes to a literature arguing that outcomes in natural resource management are fundamentally affected by differences in

Table 1. Regime effectiveness and national capacities to enforce fisheries regulations in the five SADC countries

	Angola	Mozambique	Namibia	South Africa	Tanzania
Outcomes of overfishing and IUU fishing	Significant challenge of IUU fishing, especially from foreign fleets. A majority of fish stocks show a declining trend.	High presence of IUU vessels and a history of underreporting of catch from the artisanal sector. Artisanal actors often violate regulation and many fisheries are overexploited.	Low levels of IUU fishing. Although unreported discards occur and certain stocks are under pressure, fisheries are quite well managed.	Significant levels of illegal fishing in numerous sub-sectors and low compliance among poaching artisanal actors. Many species are threatened and exploitation is near a maximum.	Presence of foreign IUU vessels in the EEZ. Use of illegal gear and methods by artisanal actors. Fish catches are decreasing across a number of species.
Tractability	Mainly artisanal, relatively dispersed. Fisheries important for livelihood security.	Mainly artisanal, highly dispersed. Fisheries important for livelihood security.	Mainly industrial, centered only on two ports. Fisheries not important for livelihood security.	Largely industrial, relatively dispersed. Fisheries not important for livelihood security.	Mainly artisanal, highly dispersed. Fisheries important for livelihood security.
Formal policy	Regulatory measures include a rights-based system with catch restrictions for certain species.	Main regulatory measure is licensing.	Regulatory measures include a rights-based system with individual non-transferable quotas.	Regulatory measures include a combination of effort and catch controls with extensive protected areas.	Main regulatory measure is licensing.

(continued)

Table 1. (*Continued*)

	Angola	Mozambique	Namibia	South Africa	Tanzania
Policy outputs	MCS measures implemented late, gradually, and with little infrastructure available. Funding for MCS is lacking and the observer scheme is not working as intended. Dockside inspections as well as patrol vessels are limited.	MCS measures implemented late and with little infrastructure available. Few cases of offenses have led to convictions. Corruption is a problem. Responsible authority not sufficiently equipped to detain foreign illegal vessels. A majority of the artisanal actors are not regulated in practice.	MCS measures implemented firmly with significant infrastructure available and financing based on revenues from fishing industry. Foreign illegal actors have been prosecuted with force. Fisheries observers cover most of the vessels and nearly 85% of the fleet are equipped with VMS.	MCS measures implemented gradually, initially with significant infrastructure available. After a period of increasing capacity in the early 2000s, the responsible authority faced numerous challenges. MCS measures are now significantly weaker.	MCS measures implemented slowly, largely dependent on donor funding. Violators are rarely punished. Capacity of catch estimations is low. Infrastructure of monitoring authorities deemed to be insufficient for patrolling the EEZ.

enforcement capacities (Anderson 1989; Gibson 1999; Burton 2003; Gibson et al. 2005). However, we urge scholars to unpack the concept of enforcement capacity theoretically as well as to challenge how we understand success and failure in this respect. In this analysis we have found indications that corruption in government as well as lack of funding in responsible agencies are crucial aspects of the implementation failures. We urge scholars to continue this research and to focus explicitly on these two phenomena.

Conclusions

This paper set out to explore the relationship between regime effectiveness and national capacities to implement and enforce – in five countries belonging to the South African Development Community (SADC). More specifically, we show how international rules on paper play out differently in different national contexts, i.e. that MCS reforms have had widely different outcomes in different countries. The empirical investigation also provides some tentative general insights into the dynamic process and mechanisms through which this can be understood.

Firstly, this investigation reveals that variation in national capacities seems to fundamentally condition outcomes in terms of IUU fishing and overfishing. For example, the comparatively high capacity of Namibia's enforcement system has made IUU fishing less frequent and the overall health of its marine ecosystem is generally perceived as higher than in countries with lower MCS capacity. This finding in turn implies that international organizations and donors should take national context and national capacities seriously. Secondly, as argued by Hersoug and Paulsen (1996), it is evident that in the international efforts to install MCS measures, state capacity is more or less taken as a given. More specifically, this study shows that the reforms undertaken predominantly focus on formal institutional arrangements and legislation, while informal institutions and fundamental issues of power and resources are overlooked. Finally, the variation in capacities and outcomes identified here implies that there are reasons to focus more closely on the underlying and fundamental drivers of overexploitation (Alcock 2002; Ostrom et al. 2002). This includes looking more closely at the relationship between the state and society, and also investigating how the character of this relationship fundamentally conditions enforcement and compliance dynamics in any given resource system.

References

Afonso, P. S., 2004, Country review: Mozambique, in: D. Young (Ed) *Review of the State of World Marine Capture Fisheries Management: Indian Ocean*. FAO Fisheries Technical Paper. No. 488 (Rome: FAO).

Alcock, F., 2002, Bargaining, uncertainty and property rights in fisheries. *World Politics*, **54**(3), pp. 437–461.

Amador, T., 2004, *Review and audit of the legal provisions and institutional arrangements that impact on the artisanal fisheries sector in the BCLME region*, final report for IPA, Artisanal Fishing Institute of Angola.

Amador, T., 2005, Elements for harmonization of fisheries legislation from an MCS perspective. Working paper no. 36, 1st legal workshop, the SADC-EU MCS programme, South African Development Community: Namibia.

Amador, T., 2006, Enforcement procedures, offenses and sanctions in the SADC region. Legal assessment and review. Working paper no. 48, the SADC-EU MCS programme, South African Development Community: Namibia.

Anderson, L. G., 1989, Enforcement issues in selecting fisheries management policy. *Marine Resource Economics*, **6**(3), pp. 261–277.

Arnason, R., 2002, *A review of international experiences with ITQs. CEMARE Report 58, Annex to Future options for UK fish quota management*, Report to the Department for the Environment, Food and Rural Affairs.
BCLME, 2005, An analysis of fisheries management protocols in the BCLME countries. BCLME Project LMR/SE/03/03.
Bailey, R., 1988, Third world fisheries: Prospects and problems. *World Development*, **16**(6), pp. 751–7.
Bergh, P. E. and Davies, S., 2004, Against all odds. Taking control over Namibia's fisheries, in: U. R. Sumaila, D. Boyer, M. D. Skogen and S. I. Steinshamn (Eds) *Namibia's Fisheries: Ecological, Economic, and Social Aspects* (Netherlands: Eburon).
Boyer, D. C. and Boyer, H. J., 2005, Sustainable utilization of fish stocks – is this achievable? A case study from Namibia, in: J. Swan and D. Gréboval (Eds) *Overcoming Factors of Unsustainability and Overexploitation in Fisheries: Selected Papers on Issues and Approaches*, FAO Fisheries Report. No. 782 (Rome): FAO).
Branch, G. M. and Clark, B. M., 2006, Fish stocks and their management: The changing face of fisheries in South Africa. *Marine Policy*, **30**(1), pp. 3–17.
Burton, P. S., 2003, Community enforcement of fisheries effort restrictions. *Journal of Environmental Economics and Management*, **45**(2), pp. 474–491.
Cacaud, P., Kuruc, M. and Spreij, M., 2003, *Administrative Sanctions in Fisheries Law*, FAO legislative study 82, FAO: Rome.
Campbell, H. E., 2010, A comparative framework for analyzing urban environmental policy. *Journal of Comparative Policy Analysis*, **12**(4), pp. 373–394.
Checkel, J. T., 1999, Norms, institutions, and national identity in contemporary Europe. *International Studies Quarterly*, **43**, pp. 83–114.
Cunningham, S. and Bodiguel, C., 2005, Subregional review: Southwest Indian OCEAN, in: D. Young (Ed) *Review of the State of World Marine Capture Fisheries Management: Indian Ocean*, FAO Fisheries Technical Paper. No. 488 (Rome: FAO).
DEAT, 2001, Business Plan 1 April 2001–31 March 2002. Department of Environment Affairs and Tourism. Available at www.info.gov.za/otherdocs/2003/notused/deatstrat.pdf, accessed the 28th of August, 2013.
DEAT, 2005, General policy on the allocation and management of long term commercial fishing rights. Draft general policy, Department of Environment Affairs and Tourism, South Africa.
Demsetz, H., 1967, Towards a theory of property rights. *American Economic Review*, **57**, pp. 347–359.
Duit, A., forthcoming, *State and Environment: The Comparative Study of Environmental Governance* (Cambridge, MA: MIT Press).
du Preez, M. -L., 2009, Fishing for Sustainable Livelihoods in Angola: The Co-operative Approach. SAIIA Occasional Paper, No 45, October 2009.
Earthtrends, 2003, Biodiversity and protected areas – Angola. Available at http://rmportal.net/library/content/frame/angola-biodiversity.pdf, accessed the 28th of August, 2013.
FAO, 1997, "Fisheries management", *FAO Technical Guidelines for Responsible Fisheries* no 4 (FAO: Rome).
FAO, 2001, *International Plan of Action to Prevent, Deter and Eliminate Illegal, Unreported and Unregulated Fishing* (Rome: FAO).
FAO, 2004, Information on fisheries management in the republic of Angola. Available at http://www.fao.org/fi/oldsite/FCP/en/ago/body.htm, accessed the 28th of August, 2013.
FAO, 2006, *The State of World Fisheries and Aquaculture 2006* (Rome: FAO).
FAO, 2007a, National fishery sector overview: The republic of Mozambique. *ftp://ftp.fao.org/fi/document/fcp/en/FI_CP_MZ.pdf*, accessed the 28th of August, 2013.
FAO, 2007b, *Fishery Country Profile: The United Republic of Tanzania* (Rome: FAO)
FAO, 2010, Fishery and Aquaculture Country Profiles, Namibia. Available at http://www.fao.org/fishery/facp/NAM/en, accessed the 28th of August, 2013.
FEIKE, 2008, South African fisheries. Available at http://www.feike.co.za/rightsAllocations.html (accessed 24 June 2010).
Finnemore, M., 1996, Norms and international relations theory. *International Organization*, **50**, pp. 325–348.
Gibson, C. C., 1999, *Politicians and Poachers. the Political Economy of Wildlife Policy in Africa* (Cambridge: Cambridge University Press).
Gibson, C. C., Williams, J. T. and Ostrom, E., 2005, Local enforcement and better forests. *World Development*, **33**(2), pp. 273–284.
Hardin, G., 1968, The tragedy of the commons. *Science*, **162**(3859), pp. 1243–1248.

Hatcher, A., Pascoe, S., Banks, R. and Arnason, R., (2002). "Future options for UK fish quota management." CEMARE Reports no. 58. Portsmouth: Centre for the Economics and Management of Aquatic Resources (CEMARE) University of Portsmouth.

Hatton, J., (year unknown), "Policy, legal and Institutional Framework: Mozambique", WWF Eastern African Marine Ecoregion Programme, Dar Es Salaam: Tanzania. Available at http://www.wiomsa.org/index.php?option=com_content&view=article&id=348&Itemid=388, accessed the 28th of August 2013.

Hauck, M. and Kroese, M., 2006, Fisheries compliance in South Africa: A decade of challenges and reform 1994–2004. *Marine Policy*, **30**, pp. 74–83.

Hauck, M. and Sowman, M., 2001, Coastal and fisheries co-management in South Africa: an overview and analysis. *Marine Policy*, **25**, pp. 173–185.

Hersoug, B. and Holm, P., 2000, Change without redistribution: An institutional perspective on South Africa's new fisheries policy. *Marine Policy*, **24**, pp. 221–231.

Hersoug, B. and Paulsen, O., 1996, *Monitoring, Control and Surveillance in Fisheries Management* (Windhoek, Namibia: University of Namibia).

Hugill, P. and Dickson, B., 1988, *The Transfer and Tranformation of Ideas and Material Culture* (College Station, TX: Texas A&M University Press).

INFOSA, 2010, Angola country profile. www.infosa.org.na/dloads/restrict/country%20profile/Angola.pdf

IPS/IFEJ, 2009, "Fighting for the right to fish", By Patrick Burnett, the 21st of February 2009. Available at http://www.ipsnews.net/2009/02/environment-fighting-for-the-right-to-fish/, accessed the 28th of August 2013.

Jacquet, J. L., Motta, H., Fox, H., Ngusaru, A. and Zeller, D., 2010, Few data but many fish: Marine small-scale fisheries catches for Mozambique and Tanzania. *African Journal of Marine Science*, **32**(2), pp. 197–206.

Japp, D., 2004, Country review: South Africa (Indian Ocean), in: D. Young (Ed) *Review of the State of World Marine Capture Fisheries Management: Indian Ocean*, FAO Fisheries Technical Paper. No. 488 (Rome: FAO).

Johnstone, G., 2004, Artisanal Fisheries Co-management in Mozambique: Quirimbas Archipelago. Working Paper No. 22, SADC Monitoring Control and Surveillance of Fisheries Activities Programme, Windhoek: Namibia.

Kelleher, K., 2002, "Planning cost-effective fisheries monitoring control and surveillance in Mozambique", Ministry of Fisheries Mozambique.

Kimani, E. N., Okemwa, G. M. and Kazungum, J. M., 2009, Fisheries in the Southwest Indian Ocean: Trends and Governance Challenges, in: E. Laipson and A. Pandhya (Eds) *The Indian Ocean: Recourse and governance challenges*, The Henry L. Stimson Centre.

Kleinschmidt, H., 2006, "Research paper on the exploitation and management of the marine resources in the SADC region", FEIKE Natural Resource Management Advisors.

Lokina, R. B., 2006, *Economic Aspects of MCS, Tanzania: Profile of National Fisheries, MCS Assets and Activities*, Report 1, for SADC regional MCS Project, MCS Programme supported by Lux Development.

Lundqvist, L. J., 1980, *The Hare and the Tortoise: Clean Air Policies in the US and Sweden* (Ann Arbor, MI: University of Michigan Press).

Lux Development, 2002, SADC Monitoring, control and surveillance of fisheries activities programme. Working paper no. 9, the SADC-EU MCS programme, South African Development Community: Namibia.

Lux Development, 2005, National Management Structures for MCS. Working Paper No. 33, EU-SADC Monitoring Control and Surveillance of Fisheries Activities Programme, Windhoek: Namibia.

Mail & Guardian, 2011, "Fishing experts put red alert on lobsters", published the 18th February 2011, avilable online http://mg.co.za/article/2011-02-18-fishing-experts-put-red-alert-on-lobsters/.

McClanahan, T. R. and Arthur, R., 2001, The effect of marine reserves and habitat on population of east African coral reefs. *Ecological Applications*, **11**(2), pp. 559–569.

MegaPesca, 2009, Analysis of Expected Consequences for Developing Countries of the IUU Fishing Proposed Regulation and Identification of Measures Needed to Implement the Regulation – Phase 2, Final Report: FPA 15/IUU/08, May 4, 2009, 157 p.

Mngulwi, B. S. M., 2003, Country review: United Republic of Tanzania, in: A. de Yong (Ed) *Review of the State of the World Marine Capture Fisheries Management: Indian Ocean*, FAO fisheries technical paper 488 (Rome: FAO).

Moolla, S., 2010, Illegal fishing of marine resources in South African waters: In search of solutions. Draft paper, Institute for Security Studies.

Moolla, S. and Kleinschmidt, H., 2008a, Fishinc: A guide to the South African commercial fishing industry. Feike Natural Resource Management advisors, Cape Town.

Mosse, M., 2005, "Can Mozambique's new president lead the fight against corruption? *Review of African Political Economy*, **32**(104/105), pp. 431–436.

MRAG, 2003, "Review of Marine Fisheries for Tanzania", Annex 1.1. of FMSP Project R8196: Understanding Fisheries Associated Livelihoods and the Constraints to their Development in Kenya and Tanzania, London, UK.

MRAG, 2005, *Review of Impacts of Illegal, Unreported and Unregulated Fishing on Developing Countries*. Final Report, London: MRAG.

Myers, R. A. and Worm, B., 2003, Rapid worldwide depletion of predatory fish communities. *Nature*, **423**, pp. 280–283.

Nichols, P., 2004, Marine fisheries management in Namibia: Has it worked?, in: U. R. Sumaila, D. Boyer, M. D. Skogen and S. I. Steinshamn (Eds) *Namibia's Fisheries: Ecological, Economic, and Social Aspects* (Netherlands: Eburon).

Ostrom, E., 1990, *Governing the Commons* (Cambridge: Cambridge University Press).

Ostrom, E. Dietz, T. Dulsak, N. Stern, P. C. and Stonich, S., (eds), 2002, *The Drama of the Commons* (Washington, DC: National Academy Press).

Pitcher, T. J., Kalikoski, D., Pramod, G. and Short, K., 2008, *Safe Conduct? Twelve Years Fishing Under the UN Code* (Switzerland): WWF, Gland).

PMG, 2008, Marine Living Resources Fund 2006/07 Annual Report. Parliamentary Monitoring group, 26 Mars 2008. Available at http://www.pmg.org.za/report/20080326-marine-and-living-resources-fund-mlrf-briefing-200607-annual-report, accessed the 28th of August, 2013.

PMG, 2010, Marine Coastal Management: Minister and Departmental Briefing. Parliamentary Monitoring group, 1 June 2010. Available at http://www.pmg.org.za/report/20100601-minister-and-departmental-briefing-marine-coastal-management, accessed the 28th of August, 2013.

Pramod, G., 2011, Evaluations of Monitoring, Control and Surveillance in marine fisheries of 41 countries, MCS Case Studies Report, Fisheries Centre, University of British Columbia, Canada, 222 p.

Pramod, G., Pitcher, T. J., Pearce, J. and Agnew, D., 2008, *Sources of Information Supporting Estimates of Unreported Fishery Catches (IUU) For 59 Countries and the High Seas Fisheries*, Research Report 16 Number 4, Fisheries Centre, University of British Columbia: Canada.

Pressman, J. and Wildavsky, A., 1973, *Implementation* (Berkeley, CA: University of California Press).

Republic of South Africa, 1998, *Marine Living Resources Act*, Act No. 18 of 1998, Government Gazette, South Africa 1998; 395 (18930).

Rukoro, R. M., 2009, Promotion and management of fisheries in Namibia, in: G. Winter (Ed) *Towards Sustainable Fisheries Law. A Comparative Analysis* (Switzerland: IUCN, Gland).

Shauri, D. V., 2006, Enforcement procedures, offenses and sanctions in Tanzania: Legal assessment and review. Working paper no. 42, South African Development Community: Namibia.

Sowman, M. and Cardoso, P., 2010, Small-scale fisheries and food security strategies in countries in the Benguela Current Large Marine Ecosystem (BCLME) region: Angola, Namibia and South Africa. *Marine Policy*, **34**(6), pp. 1163–1170.

Standing, A., 2008, Corruption and industrial fishing in Africa. U4 Anti-Corruption Resource Centre, U4 Issue 2008:7.

Steinberg, J., 2005, The illicit abalone trade in South Africa. Institute for Security Studies, Occasional paper no 105. Available at http://www.issafrica.org/publications/papers/iss-paper-105-the-illicit-abalone-trade-in-south-africa-jonny-steinberg, accessed the 28th of August, 2013.

Stewart, C., 2004, Legislating for property rights in fisheries. FAO legislative study 83, for the Development Law Service (Rome: FAO).

Stop Illegal Fishing, 2008a, Country Profiles: Namibia, in: *Stop Illegal Fishing in South Africa*, report by the Stop Illegal Fishing programme, Gaborone: Botswana.

Stop Illegal Fishing, 2008b, Country Profiles: Mozambique, in: *Stop Illegal Fishing in South Africa*, report by the Stop Illegal Fishing programme, Gaborone: Botswana.

Stop Illegal Fishing, 2008c, Country Profiles: South Africa, in: *Stop Illegal Fishing in South Africa*, report by the Stop Illegal Fishing programme, Gaborone: Botswana.

Stop Illegal Fishing, 2008d, Country Profiles: Tanzania, in: *Stop Illegal Fishing in South Africa*, report by the Stop Illegal Fishing programme, Gaborone: Botswana.

Stop Illegal Fishing, 2008e, Country Profiles: Angola, in: *Stop Illegal Fishing in South Africa*, report by the Stop Illegal Fishing programme, Gaborone: Botswana.

UNEP, 2008, Environmental atlas: Angola. Available at http://na.unep.net/atlas/profiles/english/Angola.pdf

Van Zyl, B. J., 2002, Managing Namibia's marine fisheries. A decade of rebuilding. Available at https://www.cbd.int/doc/nbsap/fisheries/VanZyl%28summary%29.pdf, accessed the 28th of August, 2013.

Verheij, E., Makoloweka, S. and Kalombo, H., 2004, Collaborative coastal management improves coral reefs and fisheries in Tanga, Tanzania. *Ocean & Coastal Management*, **47**(7–8), pp. 309–320.

Virgilio Omar, M. I., 2006, Overview of fisheries resources: Mozambique. Presented at the "Workshop on Fisheries and Aquaculture in Southern Africa: Development and Management", Windhoek, Namibia, 21st–24th August 2006.

Wells, S., 2009, Dynamite fishing in northern Tanzania – pervasive, problematic and yet preventable. *Marine Pollution Bulletin*, **58**(1), pp. 20–23.

Wilson, J. D. K., 2004, *Fiscal Arrangements in the Tanzanian Fisheries Sector*. FAO Fisheries Circular No. 1000, FIPP/C1000, (Rome: FAO).

Winter, G., 2009, Towards a legal clinic for fisheries management, in: G. Winter (Ed) *Towards Sustainable Fisheries Law. A Comparative Analysis* (Switzerland: IUCN, Gland).

Wood, L. J., 2007, MPA Global: A database of the world's marine protected areas. Sea Around Us Project, UNEP-WCMC & WFF.

World Bank, 2004, *Saving Fish and Fishers: Toward Sustainable and Equitable Governance of the Global Fishing Sector*. Report No. 29090-GLB (Washington, DC: World Bank).

World Bank, 2008, *Putting Tanzania's Hidden Economy Into Work: Reform, Management ?and Protection of Its Natural Resources Sector* (Washington, DC: World Bank).

A Legal Perspective on "Privateness" and "Publicness" in Latin American Higher Education

ANDRÉS BERNASCONI

ABSTRACT *This paper considers how the law conceptualizes what is public and what private in higher education, and the legal consequences of those definitions. Following the institutionalist perspective, our interest is in the law as a source of coercive isomorphism. From the evidence gathered from seven countries in Latin America, exhibiting private sectors of varying dimension and degrees of maturity, it appears that the law assigns the same comprehensive mission to the two sectors, and expects from both the same all-encompassing repertoire of functions, regardless of the degree of development of private higher education. Yet, the law allows greater autonomy to the public sector, and delineates separate oversight and coordinating systems for private and publics, even where all of higher education is governed by the same law.*

Introduction

The law is pervasive in the lives of organizations. The law regulates how organizations are born and extinguished, the powers at their disposal, the manner in which they can exert them, and the relationships with their employees, stakeholders, clients, and overseers (Edelman and Suchman 1997: 480). Moreover, the scope and reach of the law over society continues to expand (Barnes and Burke 2006: 493) as a result of the growing complexity of social exchange and the retreat of traditional and charismatic modes of social control. Indeed, it has been argued that organizations – not individuals – are nowadays the preeminent target of the law. Conversely, the law is predominantly the output of organizations, not individuals. Insofar as the law, together with personnel and money, is one of the key instruments of public policy, organizations often find themselves an object of public policy through the dispositions of the law.[1]

Yet the interplay between the law and public policy based on it is far from straightforward. There is the matter of the difficulty in ascertaining the impact of laws on the achievement of policy goals (Rodgers 1973), and the well studied distance that exists between the "law-on-the-books" and the "law-as-implemented" (Rose 1986: 297). Often the law is seen as a redundant variable in policy analysis, one that is merely the formal expression of bureaucratic politics or interest group dynamics (Rose 1986: 299; Komesar 1994).

Notwithstanding these analytical difficulties, there is one dimension of legislation that cannot be overlooked in policy studies: the law as a *constitutive* environment for organizations. In its constitutive role, the law defines organizations, classifies them, and gives them their nature and attributes (Edelman and Suchman 1997: 483). In its constitutive guise, among other definitions the law determines which organizations are to be deemed private and which public, and seeks to delineate the consequences that follow from each organizational nature, such as the kind of law applicable to each one, their form of access to staff and other resources, and the manner of their interaction with the government. In this volume, Pachuashvili (2011) provides an apt example: in her discussion of the relationship between the legal and regulatory framework and the status of private higher education in post-communist nations, private higher education growth is linked to the varying degrees of permissiveness of that framework, among other factors.

The public–private distinction as set forth by the law, and the legal consequences of it, are the constitutive definitions of interest for this paper. As I shall explain below, and Levy (2011, in this issue) makes clear in his global analysis of higher education policy (in this volume), many differences exist between private and public higher education that have little or nothing to do with the law, but those differences are not the subject of this work.

Higher education makes for an appropriate case study because the subject of private–public differentiation in higher education has been a matter of considerable scholarly interest since the mid-1980s, fuelled in part by the growth of private sectors of higher education in many areas of the globe.[2]

The question of what defines private sectors of higher education, as opposed to public ones, has been treated systematically in only a subset of the works on private higher education (Geiger 1986; Levy 1986 a, 1986b, 1987, 1992, 2006a, 2006b; Teixeira and Amaral 2001; Bernasconi 2006). From these sources we know that private and public sectors of higher education in most of the world tend to differ in dimensions that we can group along the axes of institutional mission, finance, and institutional governance and administration. The sources of these differences, where they exist, and have been examined, include nationalism, religion, politics, business interest, extent of market coordination, social stratification patterns, ideology, funding and other governmental policy, demographic trends, and the law.

These differences are rarely as clear cut as ideal types may suggest (Marginson 2007). Often private sectors present attributes characteristic of public institutions (for instance, the provision of public goods, such as research or teacher training), while public institutions have come to acquire, especially in recent times, features commonly associated with the private sphere (such as income generating endeavors). For this reason, it has been observed that the law, insofar as it defines institutions of higher education as either private or public, can be used as the only unambiguous criterion for the public–private distinction (Levy 1987: 258). Indeed, it is hard to even speak about private or public higher education without beginning the analysis with a reference, explicit or not, as to which institutions the law classifies on either camp.

In spite of the inevitability of this reference to the constitutive dimension of the law, the way in which it defines what is public and what is private has been largely neglected in the mainstream higher education literature.[3] This is unfortunate, given the importance of the law for some of the factors of differentiation between the public and private spheres mentioned above.

The Latin American nations are fertile ground for comparative analysis[4] because of their common Iberian colonial past, and their adoption in the twentieth century of a similar idea of the university as a social institution (Bernasconi 2008). The presence of a private sector of higher education, however, now a common feature across the region (with the exception of Cuba), emerged at different points in the post-independence evolution of the region's higher education systems, spanning a century between Chile, the earliest example of private provision of higher education, and Uruguay, the latest. In addition, while in some countries most post-secondary students are enrolled in the private sector, in others private provision remains marginal compared to enrollments in public institutions. Different levels of maturity of private initiative in higher education within a common cultural background allow for intriguing possibilities of comparative analysis across the Latin American nations.

In the context of Latin America's higher education, the focus of this article shall be on the role of the law in constituting the realms of the public and the private. The influence of the law – or more generally, of the State, for which the law is an instrument – in defining the form and functions of educational organizations, has been examined in the context of the new institutionalism in organizational studies[5] (most recently, and focusing on education, Levy 1999, 2006a; Meyer and Rowan 2006). Organizational institutionalists stress similarities across organizations operating in the same sector ("isomorphism"), and explain them as a consequence of the values, norms, habits, and meanings their members share. Homogeneity also arises as a result of organizations' common quest for the legitimacy that comes embedded in rules and structures that are taken for granted as proper and necessary building blocks for them. Thirdly, isomorphism results from external deliberate pressure to conform, typically in the form of laws and regulations (coercive isomorphism).

Given that the law defines what is public and what private and lays out the consequences of each status, it can either foster differentiation or push for homogeneity. The institutionalist perspective would expect the law to operate as a source of coercive isomorphism in higher education. Furthermore, if homogenization is, as postulated by the institutionalist viewpoint, the long term thrust, the law ought to partake more strongly in this trend as private sectors consolidate over time.

Therefore, our central questions in this paper shall be:

1) Is there a pattern in the Latin American nations' laws crystallizing a single set of formal structures and rules for higher education, or has the law, rather, defined a different set for the private sector?
2) Is the legal treatment of private higher education compared to its public counterpart affected by the maturity and size of the private sector?

In keeping with the institutionalist hypothesis that the law is deployed as the normative expression of the institutional field of higher education, providing organizations in the field with the common framework of functions, principles, norms, and procedures needed for the unity of the higher education field, two hypotheses can be derived that will guide our research:

a) the law has crystallized a single set of formal structures and rules for higher education, rather than a different set for the private sector, and it demands or expects the same functions from it, compared to the public sector, so that in fact it defines a single environment of legitimacy for private and public higher education in Latin America; and
b) this common framework is oblivious to the degree of consolidation of the private sector, and can be similarly found in countries with recently established private sectors and in countries where private provision has been a feature of higher education for decades, and in nations where most students attend private institutions as well as in countries where enrollments concentrate in the public sector.

Data and Themes

Our data come from the current constitutional and statute law bearing on higher education in Argentina, Bolivia, Brazil, Chile, Costa Rica, Mexico and Uruguay. These countries were selected because as a group they capture the variation in maturity and size of private higher education of interest for our hypotheses (see Table 1, below). In addition to constitutional and statute law, where universities are authorized to promulgate their own bylaws as equivalent in force to an act of the legislature, as in Bolivia and Costa Rica, I have considered those bylaws too.

Although the number of private universities surpasses that of public ones in every country, since the former are generally much smaller that preeminence does not

Table 1. Private higher education foundation and enrolment in selected countries in Latin America

	Date of establishment of first private university (a)	Private enrolment as % of total enrolment in 1975 (b)	Private enrolment as % of total enrolment in 2006 (c)	Private universities as % of total number of universities in 2006 (d)
Chile	1888	35	74	75
Brazil	1940	65	72	69
Mexico	1935	15	33	65
Costa Rica	1976	0	55	92
Argentina	1959	12	21	55
Bolivia	1967	3	16	73
Uruguay	1985	0	10	80

Sources: (a) Levy (1986a: 4), except for Uruguay: Chiancone and Martínez (2006: 8), (b) Levy (1986a: 5), (c) CINDA (2007: 111), (d) Calculation based on CINDA (2007:74).

obtain in enrollments: only in Chile, Brazil and Costa Rica does one find more students in the private sector than in the public system. The data provided in Table 1 allow us to distinguish four groups of countries, and to deploy them in a two-way matrix (Table 2) that captures the dimensions of interest for our hypotheses – maturity and size of private higher education. In effect, private higher education is a more recent phenomenon in Bolivia, Costa Rica and Uruguay than in the other four nations, which by the mid-1970s already had a significant private sector. On the other hand, private institutions capture a majority of students in Costa Rica, Brazil and Chile.[6]

I have studied the legal texts directly, as primary sources, but since I am not expert on the legal systems of every country, I have considered also the reports on the laws of higher education in 15 Latin American and Caribbean countries commissioned in 2002 by UNESCO's Institute of Higher Education for Latin America and the Caribbean (IESALC). These studies were carried out by national experts on the law of higher education of each nation, and I used them to validate my identification of the relevant bodies of law and my interpretations of their contents.[7] I have further checked through the respective web sites of the national ministries or departments of education to ascertain which norms are currently in force, and find the up-to-date sources of the law.[8]

I shall report on what the law says about private and public higher education in seven countries of Latin America, to discover how higher education policy is constructed through the constitutive dispositions of the law. Consistent with the dimensions of possible differentiation between the private and public spheres set forth by the higher education literature, the analysis is organized in three themes: mission and functions of higher education, the extent of institutional autonomy (usually a limit to the policymaking powers of governments in higher education), and the organization of the higher education system.

Table 2. Maturity and size of private higher education in selected countries of Latin America

Maturity	Size	
	Majority	Minority
Old	Brazil	Argentina
	Chile	Mexico
New	Costa Rica	Bolivia
		Uruguay

Notes: The exercise of locating the rest of the countries of Latin America in the cells of this matrix would place all the other South American nations in the "old" quadrants, with only Colombia and Ecuador in the "majority" cell. The republics of Central America and the Caribbean saw their first private universities in the early1960s and significant enrollments in the private sector by the mid-1970s, which places them closer to the "old" group, but only the Dominican Republic is majority private nowadays. There is, therefore, a margin for the choice of different cases of old private systems. In choosing Brazil, Argentina, Mexico, and Chile as my examples I have kept with previous comparative work based on those countries (Bernasconi 2008), which are also the most studied higher education systems in the region. For the "new" quadrants, however, there are no alternative cases: only the three countries considered in Table 2 can be considered as instances of recent development of a private higher education sector.

Mission and Functions

The fundamental legislation on higher education of Argentina, Brazil, Chile, and Mexico, our older private systems, define the same mission and goals for all of higher education, irrespective of the public or private nature of the institutions. Typically, these missions and goals speak of education for the professions; research for the creation and transmission of knowledge and its application to solving the problems of society; artistic creation; scientific, economic, cultural, democratic, and social development; integration with and improvement of the other levels of education; the promotion of national identity, cohesion, and solidarity; the promotion of sustainable development and the preservation of the cultural heritage of the country.

As to functions, private and public sectors of higher education have the same legally mandated tasks: teaching, research, and service, within the scope allowed to each type of institution (greater for university than for non-university entities). Moreover, the protection of academic freedom, the classes of institutions (such as universities, technical universities, vocational schools, and the like), the types of degrees offered by each, general requirements for admission of students (such as having completed secondary education for the first university degree) and graduation (such as producing a dissertation for a doctoral degree), as well as student transfer regulations are generally the same across sectors.

In the cases of Bolivia and Costa Rica, the law does not legislate on the mission and functions of higher education, possibly as a result of a notion of university autonomy that, as shall be elaborated below, leaves such definitions to the sole discretion of the universities.

In the case of Uruguay, where no general higher education law exists, the legal framework for the sole public university in the country, the University of the Republic, is set by its *Organic Law*, passed by Congress in 1958. Article 2 of this Act defines the mission of the university as public higher education, training for professions, cultural, artistic and scientific development, and the defense of moral values, the principles of justice, freedom and social welfare, human rights and democracy. Private universities, in turn, emerged in the 1980s under the freedom of education clause of the Constitution, and the recognition of Law 15,661. Enacted in 1985 by the military government, Law 15,661 recognized the validity of degrees issued by private universities licensed by the government, as equal to those granted by the public university. Executive Decree 308 (1995), a complement to the 1985 law and juridical framework for private higher education, also conceptualizes the role of private higher education in terms of teaching, research and extension, but omits the reference to the defense and promotion of moral and civic values found in the Organic Law.

In general, then, the law forgoes prescribing for private sectors of higher education missions and functions different from those laid out or allowed to emerge in the public sphere. Therefore, the source of mission differentiation between the private and public institutions which manifests itself empirically in the region has to be found elsewhere. This is not necessarily to say that it has to be found outside of the law, because even if legislation homogenizes the ends, it may well be the case that it differentiates the means through which those ends are to be pursued, or that it allows for this differentiation to occur naturally. The law, for instance, could establish different degrees of freedom and self-determination between the two sectors, or rule that the public and the private sectors, although equal in mission and functions, are to be nonetheless organized as two distinct systems of higher education. I turn now to the examination of these other possibilities of legally induced organizational behavior, namely, the extent of the autonomy recognized to different types of institutions, and whether the structure of the higher education system is single or dual.

Autonomy

Autonomy is generally defined in the Constitutions and laws examined here as the sum of the rights of self-governance including the selection of leadership and the right to dictate the institution's bylaws and regulations, free administration of the institution's resources, and freedom to create programs of study, define the curriculum, grant valid degrees, undertake research, admit and teach students, and hire faculty and staff. In other words, autonomy has governance, academic and administrative implications.

The main legal difference between sectors rests on the source of the bylaws of private and public institutions. While the former result from articles of association privately convened between the founders of the institution and later approved by the executive branch of government if they conform to the framework defined by the law, the latter are either sanctioned by an act of the legislature, or approved by the governing bodies of the institution acting on a delegation of legislative authority from Congress. As a consequence, public institutions enjoy more latitude as to the contents of their bylaws compared to privates, the bylaws of which must conform to a single blueprint legally defined, usually based on public forms. On the other hand, while private institutions are allowed to organize their internal governance as they see fit, public institutions, especially universities, are expected to conform to collegial and participatory modes of authority. It is important to stress, however, that such expectation is not a juridical mandate, but rather an expression of the values and traditions of the university community, to which the legislature defers as a matter of autonomy (Bernasconi 2008).

In Chile, Argentina, and Brazil, once a private institution of higher education attains full certification (after a probationary licensing period of six years in Argentina, and up to 11 in Chile), it becomes fully autonomous and no difference exists in the extent of this autonomy compared to that of the public sector institutions. Exceptions to the academic autonomy of universities, such as the mandatory evaluation and accreditation of some degree programs in Argentina or Chile, or the periodic renewal of the license to operate in Brazil, are shared by the two sectors. Other restrictions on autonomy, pertaining to the granting of degrees, are indeed imposed only on private universities, but they are temporary, while they obtain full recognition as mature institutions.

The Constitution of Mexico of 1917, a federal system, defers to the law the question of who shall have autonomy, but private institutions have to be authorized by the state to operate (art. 3, VI). Public universities are autonomous according to their own organic laws, passed by the federal Congress for the federal universities, or by the competent state Congress, in the case of state universities (Torres Mejía 2003: 38, 39). Private institutions can grant valid degrees if they are "incorporated" with a public institution and teach the same curriculum in the same conditions, or if they are authorized by the federal or state government (Torres Mejía 2003: 45).

Among countries with "new" private sector, the legislation of Bolivia can be cited as an example of a differentiated approach to autonomy. Its Constitution of 2004 grants autonomy only to public universities. In Bolivia autonomy means freedom to administer resources, choose and appoint faculty, rector, and administrators, establish internal regulations, set budgets, define study plans, and issue academic degrees and professional titles with nationwide validity (arts. 185 and 186 of the Constitution). Unlike with public universities, the Executive Branch has the permanent power to approve or reject the articles of association of privates and their modifications, and the same with undergraduate and graduate programs' study plans, and their modifications, or new campus locations. Private universities have to be recognized by the executive branch in order to issue valid academic degrees, but nationally valid professional titles can only be issued by the state, never by the private university itself, whereas public universities can issue professional titles without further ado (Daza Ordanza 2003: 38).

Similarly, Costa Rica's Constitution of 1949 only gives autonomy ("independence", in the Costa Rican case) to public universities. The limitations to private autonomy consist in the requirement that they submit their new programs to an oversight council for private higher education, under the authority of the Ministry of Education, program offerings that must conform to the standards of the public sector. Following the norm for the public *University of Costa Rica*, students must be represented by no less than a 25 per cent share in the organs of collegial governance, and study plans must be equivalent to those of the public sector (Law 6,693 of 1981).

Lastly, Uruguayan private institutions must submit their new programs to approval of the Ministry of Education, even after they have completed their initial probationary period.

In sum, countries with relatively newer systems of private higher education seem to bestow autonomy less liberally on private institutions than nations with more mature private sectors. Control by the licensing agencies is tighter, possibly a reflection of a less than complete confidence on the part of the legislature in the capacity or willingness of private institutions to abide by the legal framework set for them. Over time, as private institutions consolidate and gain political clout, it could be hypothesized, they obtain for their sector an autonomy status generally equal to that of public institutions. Alternatively, tighter control over privates in newer systems may be a consequence of less favorable political conditions for the development of private initiative in higher education in these nations in recent times. The private-friendly political economy of the 1980s and early 1990s in Latin America seems to have subsided, partly replaced by more "statist" mores. Yet, the Costa Rican strict regulation of privates dates from 1981, while the Brazilian legislation on private higher education, relatively more lenient, is as recent as 2001. On the other hand, the authoritarian or democratic nature of the regime seems not to be a factor here, since most legislation considered here emanated from democratic rule.

System Organization

Is higher education organized as one integrated system, or is it legally conceptualized, rather, as the sum of two distinct systems, private and the public higher education? There is a single system when higher education is governed and coordinated either by a national Ministry of Education with similar authority over the public and the private sectors, or through a decentralized coordinating body with membership from both sectors. In dual systems, on the other hand, there is no attempt to coordinate the two sectors for the purpose of policy development or implementation. Indeed, most policy is directed only to public institutions, or delegated to public universities. Thus defined, Argentina and Brazil appear closer to the idea of a single system, whereas Bolivia, Uruguay, Chile, Costa Rica, and Mexico represent examples of dual systems.

Powerful ministries are a feature of integrated systems. In Brazil, a federal country, the Constitution of 1988 (art. 211) gives the government of the Union the jurisdiction over the federal educational system, which according to the 1996 *Law of guidelines and bases of national education* (N° 9,394), includes not just the educational institutions maintained by the Union, but also "the higher education institutions created and maintained by private initiative" (art. 16). Moreover, it falls to the Union to elaborate a national educational plan, "ensure a national process of evaluation of institutions of higher education", "establish general norms for undergraduate and graduate programs", and "authorize, recognize, license, supervise and evaluate" both higher education institutions and their programs (art. 9). Argentina, also a federal nation, in addition to a strong Ministry, features a common advisory and coordinating body for the two sectors: the *Council of Universities*. Non-university higher education in Argentina falls within the jurisdiction of the provinces, while universities are under the policymaking powers of the federal government.

Bolivia, Uruguay and Costa Rica, on the contrary, maintain the private and the public sectors in separate systems. In Bolivia the *Educational Reform Law* creates a national system only for technical and technological education, composed of public and private institutes, but at the university level public institutions are responsible solely for their affairs, and regulate themselves through their periodic National Congresses that congregate representatives of all public universities in the country to discuss and approve common regulations on organization, academics, students, graduate programs, evaluation and accreditation, and the like. Private universities in Bolivia are authorized and overseen in perpetuity by the Ministry of Education, which has defined a set of very detailed prescriptions and standards to which private universities must conform to attain and renew their license.

Costa Rica's Constitution states that there shall be a national plan for public higher education, elaborated by the coordinating body for public universities. This is the *National Council of Rectors*, composed only of the four public universities (Law N° 6162, of 1977). In addition, an agreement for coordination reached by the public universities in 1982, with force of law, allows the publics to function as a system and allocate funding among them. Its decisions have to have the approval of all four universities. It provides for student transfer, approval of new programs, homogeneity of degree structure and names, and since 1993, an accreditation system. Private universities are overseen by a Council operating under the authority of the Ministry of Education, which approves bylaws, new programs, and tuition charges.

Uruguay, where the public sector of higher education at the university level is composed of only one institution,[9] recognizes the autonomy of the public *University of the Republic* to govern itself within the rules of organization set in its Organic Law. Private institutions, for their part, are placed under the supervision of the Ministry of Education.

Mexico, a federal country, lacks unified legislation for higher education. Although the so called *Law for the coordination of higher education* of 1978 declares that it is a responsibility of the state to coordinate higher education, the licensing of private institutions is in Mexico, unlike Brazil, a competence of the state governments, and the only higher education policy tool at the disposal of the federal government is program funding, not available to private institutions, except for research and on a competitive basis. There is not in Mexico a single coordinating body for higher education, but two: ANUIES, for publics, and FINPES, for the privates (Torres Mejía 2003: 40–45).

Chile's 1990 *Organic Law of Education* deals with higher education mostly to organize the licensing system for new private institutions. Only the public sector has a representative Council of Rectors, a coordinating mechanism created by an Act of Congress of 1954. No such coordinating body exists in the private sector and once fully licensed, private universities attain the same autonomy as public institutions.

In sum: binary systems are the norm, even if the law defines the same mission and demands the same functions of both sectors. The law seems to recognize that there is sufficient difference between the public and private sectors to warrant separate coordination and oversight mechanisms. Yet whether a country has organized higher education as a single system, or maintains separate coordination for public and private institutions seems not to be correlated with the maturity or size of the private sector: binary systems can be found in all four quadrants defined in Table 2. Federalism as an explanation does not seem to fit the data either: while federal Argentina and Brazil are, from the point of view of their higher education, unitary systems, Mexico, also a federal republic, is dual. The structuring of higher education as a single system seems, rather, to correlate with the presence of a common evaluation (Brazil) or accreditation (Argentina) mechanism for public and private institutions. No such legally mandated mechanisms exist in Costa Rica, Mexico, and Uruguay. In Bolivia accreditation for all universities was legislated in 1994 but forcefully resisted by public universities and successfully challenged on constitutional grounds. In the case of Chile, accreditation was only legislated in 2006, but participation in it is voluntary for institutions.

Conclusions: Does the Law Make a Difference?

The questions put to the law of higher education throughout this paper were, first, if it embodied a single framework of structures and rules for higher education, or rather, a different set for the private sector, and whether the size and maturity of the private sector had any influence over the legal treatment of private institutions.

From the evidence gathered from seven countries in Latin America, exhibiting private sectors of varying dimension and degrees of maturity, it appears that the law assigns the same comprehensive mission to the two sectors, and expects from both the same all-encompassing repertoire of functions, regardless of the degree of development of private higher education. To some degree, this reflects the unrealistic grandiosity of legislators when only words are at stake, but it is important nonetheless that both sectors are covered under such rhetoric.

On the other hand, legal directives allow greater autonomy to the public sector (even while in practice their autonomy may be undercut by politics or financial pressures from which the privates are largely free). Indeed, the prerogatives included in public universities' autonomy serve as the benchmark upon which the autonomy of the privates is defined: while established private sectors enjoy autonomy rights roughly equal to those of the public sectors, newer systems find their autonomy limited with respect to their public counterparts. Put differently: while public universities are born autonomous, for private institutions autonomy appears as an acquired condition to which they grow and which they attain, presumably, if they develop according to the expectations set forth in the law. A probationary period, therefore, exists not just for individual private institutions in national systems to earn their autonomy rights, but could also be hypothesized for private sectors as a whole as they grow in status sufficiently to be granted autonomy equal to the public sector.[10]

Additionally, the law sees sufficient difference in how the sectors are to carry out that mission and functions to commonly delineate separate oversight and coordinating systems for one and the other, even where all of higher education is governed by the same law: unitary systems were found to be the exception. Typically, the law is concerned with creating a forum facilitating coordination among public universities, or the dialog between them and the government (after all, public institutions are a part of public administration, writ large), and leaves the private sector free to create and maintain its own coordination platforms.

This survey of national legal systems suggests that, as anticipated by our theoretical discussion of the new institutionalism, a long term trend may exist towards legal homogeneity and a single institutional framework of definitions of higher education covering both its public and private forms, at least in Latin America. This is not to say that the there are no differences between the sectors, but that the impetus for diversity is to be more fruitfully investigated outside of the constitutive dimension of the law: in public policy, for instance, including its implementation, or in the operations of the various higher education markets. It is appropriate to stress here that since our focus has been on this dimension of the law, and not on its regulatory (policy) or procedural roles, it may well be the case that substantive and procedural norms do establish differences between sectors that have gone unnoticed here. Funding (also an element of the legal environment) is an example: homogeneity does not extend to finance, because while public resources are assigned almost exclusively to public institutions in this region (as in most), privates fund themselves almost solely through tuition. When institutionalism has been contrasted with this more ample array of influences over private sectors, it has been found wanting in its ability to account for the degree of differentiation empirically observed between public and private sectors (Levy 2006a). Still, it is remarkable that even when it comes to funding the most consolidated private sectors – Argentina, Brazil, Chile, Mexico – can variously claim public funds on a competitive basis for research, cultural programs, and student aid. These funds, while not as significant as direct transfers of public funds to public universities, carry substantive definitional and policy implications.

The exploration of legal frameworks presented here suggests areas for further research. If, as I have argued above, the law is one expression of public policy, a fundamental question concerns the elements that lie behind the emergence of the particular legal forms characteristic of Latin American higher education.[11] Also of interest are the political dynamics by which these common forms were widely adopted. Beyond higher education and Latin America, there is the more general issue of the role of the law in public–private differentiation or lack thereof. The "dimensional" approach to the public/private question, that is, the idea that publicness (or privateness) is present in variable degrees in public and private organizations independent of legal status (Scott and Falcone 1986; Haque 2001: 66; Pesch 2008),[12] risks overlooking the effect of the law in shaping organizations' capacities and limits. The dimensional approach has produced insightful analyses in higher education (for instance, Levy 1986b; Marginson 2007), but needs not leave behind the still important core distinctions between the public and the private (Scott and Falcone 1986: 140).

So, what is private higher education from a constitutive legal standpoint? Brazil's law N° 9,394 of 1996 gives us an instance of the no frills, most fundamental response: private institutions are those maintained and administered by natural or legal persons of private law, while publics are those created or incorporated, maintained, and administered by the public authority (art. 19). There are, of course, legal consequences to this fundamental distinction, some of which have been noted here – for instance, "created by the public authority" means, in several countries, that public universities must be created and organized by an act of Congress – but these consequences are not, in themselves, enough for the law to shape privates into institutions different from publics.

Notes

1. See Rose (1986: 298–305), Edelman and Suchman (1997: 480), Barnes and Burke (2006: 495).
2. For global perspectives, Altbach (1999), and Altbach and Levy (2005).
3. This is not to say that the law has not been examined with regard to higher education. Certainly in the United States (Kaplin and Lee 1995), but also in China (Kui 2006), the Federal Republic of Germany (Mushaben 1984), Central and Eastern Europe (Tomusk 1998, 2001), Latin America (Bernasconi 2007), and Spain (Irujo 1999). But these works do not focus on the definitional role of the law with respect to the public and private nature of the institutions of higher education.
4. Latin America is no exception to the dearth of research on higher education and the law. Two exceptions are Lucio's (1995) original, but nowadays dated piece on the political processes leading to higher education bills in Colombia, Brazil, Argentina, Chile and Mexico, and Bernasconi (2007), where the Constitutions of Latin America are examined from the point of view of the reform agenda propounded in the late 1990s by the World Bank and the Inter-American Development Bank.
5. Meyer and Rowan (1977), DiMaggio and Powell (1983), Zucker (1983, 1987), Scott (1987), Powell and Di Maggio (1991).
6. I will not deal in this article with the differences in regulation between not-for-profit and profit-seeking private universities. The different status of private institutions with regard to profit is of no consequence for the legal dimensions of interest here.
7. The studies are available at www.iesalc.unesco.org.ve.

8. As of October 2008. Legislation no longer in force, in spite of its value for discovering trends in the evolution of higher education legal systems, will not be considered here, given that my interest here is on law as an expression of the contemporary social understanding in each country of the nature and role of private higher education. The comparison between the precepts of the law and the actual features of the national private and public sectors will not be attempted here either.
9. The public sector of higher education in Uruguay also features teacher training schools and vocational and technical institutes.
10. I found no examples of regulation of international branch campuses (see Lane 2011, in this issue), or of other forms of transnational provision of higher education, in the legislation considered for this study. In Latin America, generally, the law assumes that all higher education is provided by locally established institutions.
11. The degree of similarity found across Latin American nations in their legal treatment of the mission and functions for higher education, and in their notions of university autonomy, and even in the basic structure of their higher education systems, points to factors both historical and ideological: a common Hispanic heritage, with independence achieved at roughly the same time in the early nineteenth century; and post-colonial ideals about the university that found currency most everywhere in the region (Bernasconi 2008). Brazil, however, a Portuguese dominion until late in the nineteenth century, has always been a bit of an outlier with respect to Latin America's patterns in higher education, both historically and ideologically.
12. For an application of this approach to the public or private nature of charter schools in the United States, see Mead (2003: 375).

References

Altbach, P. G. (Ed.), 1999, *Private Prometheus: Private Higher Education and Development in the 21st Century* (Westport, CT: Greenwood Press).

Altbach, P. G. and Levy, D. C. (Eds), 2005, *Private Higher Education: A Global Revolution* (Rotterdam: Sense Publishers).

Barnes, J. and Burke, T., 2006, The diffusion of rights: From law on the books to organizational rights practices. *Law and Society Review*, **40**(3), pp. 493–523.

Bernasconi, A., 2006, Private universities' institutional affiliations as a source of differentiation in Chilean higher education. *Higher Education*, **52**(2), pp. 303–342.

Bernasconi, A., 2007, Constitutional prospects for the implementation of funding and governance reforms in Latin American higher education. *Journal of Education Policy*, **22**(5), pp. 509–529.

Bernasconi, A., 2008, Is there a Latin America Model of the University? *Comparative Education Review*, **52**(1), pp. 27–52.

Chiancone, A. and Martínez, E., 2006, *La Educación Superior en Iberoamérica 2006: Informe de Uruguay*. Report prepared for CINDA.

CINDA, 2007, *Educación Superior en Iberoamérica: Informe 2007* (Santiago: Centro Interuniversitario de Desarrollo).

Daza Ondarza, M., 2003, *Estudio evolutivo de la legislación en educación superior de la República de Bolivia. Principales aspectos y transformaciones del sistema educativo (de la Legislación Política impuesta hacia la Formación de Políticas de Estado Consensuadas)*. Report prepared for UNESCO's Instituto de Educación Superior para América Latina y el Caribe, IESALC, 2006, Informe sobre la educación superior en América Latina y el Caribe 2000–2005. La Metamorfosis de la educación superior (Caracas: IESALC), CD-ROM Annex.

DiMaggio, P. J. and Powell, W. W., 1983, The iron cage revisited: Institutional isomorphism and collective rationality in organizational fields. *American Sociological Review*, **48**(2), pp. 147–160.

Edelman, L. B. and Suchman, M. C., 1997, The legal environments of organizations. *Annual Review of Sociology*, **23**, pp. 479–515.

Geiger, R., 1986, *Private Sectors in Higher Education: Structure, Function and Change in Eight Countries* (Ann Arbor, MI: University of Michigan Press).

Haque, M. S., 2001, The diminishing publicness of public service under the current mode of governance. *Public Administration Review*, **61**(1), pp. 65–82.

Irujo, A. E., 1999, The legal framework of private universities in Spain. *European Journal for Higher Education Law and Policy*, **3**(2), pp. 89–109.

Kaplin, W. A. and Lee, B. A., 1995, *The Law of Higher Education*, 3rd ed. (San Francisco, CA: Jossey-Bass).

Komesar, N. K., 1994, *Imperfect Alternatives: Choosing Institutions in Law, Economics and Public Policy* (Chicago: University of Chicago Press).

Kui, S., 2006, Rule of law and public higher education institutions. A perspective on school student relationships. *Chinese Education and Society*, **39**(4), pp. 11–57.

Lane, J. E., 2011, Importing Private Higher Education: International Branch Campuses. *Journal of Comparative Policy Analysis: Research and Practice*, **13**(4).

Levy, D. C., 1986a, *Higher Education and the State in Latin America: Private Challenges to Public Dominance* (Chicago: University of Chicago Press).

Levy, D. C., 1986b, "Private" and "public": Analysis amid ambiguity in higher education, in: D. C Levy (Ed.) *Private Education: Studies in Choice and Public Policy* (New York: Oxford University Press), pp. 170–192.

Levy, D. C., 1987, A comparison of private and public educational organizations, in: W. W. Powell (Ed.) *The Nonprofit Sector. A Research Handbook* (New Haven: Yale University Press), pp. 258–276.

Levy, D. C., 1992, Private institutions of higher education, in: B. Clark and G. Neave (Eds) *Encyclopedia of Higher Education*, Vol. 2 (Oxford: Pergamon), pp. 1183–1195.

Levy, D. C., 1999, When private higher education does not bring organizational diversity, in: P. G. Altbach (Ed.) *Private Prometheus: Private Higher Education and Development in the 21st Century* (Westport, CT: Greenwood Press), pp. 15–43.

Levy, D. C., 2006a, How private higher education's growth challenges the new institutionalism, in: H. D. Meyer and B. Rowan (Eds) *The New Institutionalism in Education: Advancing Research and Policy* (Albany, NY: SUNY Press), pp. 143–162.

Levy, D. C., 2006b, The unanticipated explosion: Private higher education's global surge. *Comparative Education Review*, **50**(2), pp. 217–240.

Levy, D. C., 2011, Public Policy for Private Higher Education: A Global Analysis. *Journal of Comparative Policy Analysis: Research and Practice*, **13**(4).

Lucio, R., 1995, La legislación sobre la educación superior en América Latina: tendencias recientes de reforma. *Universidad Futura*, **6**(18), pp. 69–78.

Marginson, S., 2007, The public/private divide in higher education: A global revision. *Higher Education*, **53**(3), pp. 307–333.

Mead, J. F., 2003, Devilish details: Exploring features of charter school statutes that blur the public/private distinction. *Harvard Journal on Legislation*, **40**(2), pp. 349–394.

Meyer, H. D. and Rowan, B. (Eds), 2006, *The New Institutionalism in Education* (Albany, NY: SUNY Press).

Meyer, J. W. and Rowan, B., 1977, Institutionalized organizations: Formal structures as myth and ceremony. *American Journal of Sociology*, **83**(2), pp. 340–363.

Mushaben, J. M., 1984, Reform in three phases: judicial action and the German Federal Framework Law for Higher Education of 1976. *Higher Education*, **13**(4), pp. 423–438.

Pachuashvili, P., 2011, Governmental Policies and Their Impact on Private Higher Education Development in Post-Communist Countries: Hungary, Latvia, Lithuania and Georgia, 1990–2005. *Journal of Comparative Policy Analysis: Research and Practice*, **13**(4).

Pesch, U., 2008, The publicness of public administration. *Administration & Society*, **40**(2), pp. 170–193.

Powell, W. W, and DiMaggio, P. J. (Eds), 1991, *The New Institutionalism in Organizational Analysis* (Chicago: The University of Chicago Press).

Rodgers Jr., H. R., 1973, Law as an instrument of public policy. *American Journal of Political Science*, **17**(3), pp. 638–647.

Rose, R., 1986, Law as a resource of public policy. *Parliamentary Affairs*, **39**(3), pp. 297–314.

Scott, P. G. and Falcone, S., 1986, Comparing public and private organizations: An exploratory analysis of three frameworks. *The American Review of Public Administration*, **28**(2), pp. 126–145.

Scott, R. W., 1987, The adolescence of institutional theory. *Administrative Science Quarterly*, **32**(4), pp. 493–511.

Teixeira, P. and Amaral, A., 2001, Private higher education and diversity: An exploratory survey. *Higher Education Quarterly*, **55**(4), pp. 359–395.

Tomusk, V., 1998, Developments in Russian higher education: Legislative and policy reform within a Central and East European context. *Minerva*, **36**(2), pp. 125–146.

Tomusk, V., 2001, Higher education reform in Estonia: A legal perspective. *Higher Education Policy*, **14**(3), pp. 201–212.

Torres Mejía, D., 2003, *Informe nacional sobre la educación superior en México. Secretaría de Educación Pública, Subsecretaría de Educación Superior e Investigación Científica.* Report prepared for UNESCO's Instituto de Educación Superior para América Latina y el Caribe, IESALC, 2006, Informe sobre la educación superior en América Latina y el Caribe 2000–2005. La Metamorfosis de la educación superior (Caracas: IESALC), CD-ROM Annex.

Zucker, L. G., 1983, Organizations as institutions. *Research in the Sociology of Organizations*, **2**, pp. 1–47.

Zucker, L. G., 1987, Institutional theories of organization. *Annual Review of Sociology*, **13**, pp. 443–464.

Watching the Watchers: Transgovernmental Implementation of Data Privacy Policy in Europe

ABRAHAM L. NEWMAN

ABSTRACT *The governance of data privacy in Europe increasingly transpires through networks of transgovernmental actors – data privacy authorities. While research has demonstrated how such networks shape the policy agenda, little work has examined issues of implementation. This article, thus, explores the growing role that pan-European networks of data privacy authorities play in the enforcement of regional privacy rules. It first surveys the different networks and their participants before identifying their implementation efforts – information sharing, standards harmonization, and joint enforcement. The article notes how such regional enforcement co-operation has itself become a political leverage point for data privacy authorities seeking to expand their authority. In comparing across networks and their functions, the article isolates a regional dimension to privacy implementation and more generally suggests a novel form of networked governance within Europe.*

Introduction

With the rise of global digital networks, personal information increasingly passes across borders (Castells 1996, Rosenau 2002, Zysman and Newman 2006). Multinational corporations transfer detailed customer and personnel data; governments share terrorism watchlists and information on transnational criminals; individuals engaged in global activism, friendship, or commerce exchange financial data and intimate photographs. As such information exchange transcends national boundaries, data protection regulations developed domestically to protect individual privacy are put to the test. What and whose rules should be followed? Who should monitor and enforce them? This has produced a series of regional and international agreements concerned with the global regulation of privacy, with the European Data Privacy directive amongst the most far-reaching. In 1995, the European Union mandated that all member states adopt data privacy legislation for the public and private sector and establish an independent regulator empowered to monitor and enforce these rules. These rules have spread widely across the globe and produced a series of heated disputes between Europe and its allies (Newman 2008a).

Despite a growing literature interested in the politics driving and resulting from regional regulatory efforts within Europe (Swire and Litan 1998), very little attention has been paid to the cross-border implementation and enforcement of these rules.[1] In addition to traditional national enforcement questions, global digital networks pose an increasing number of issues that span jurisdictions and complicate regulatory oversight. Issues of on-line authentification, transatlantic financial data, and SPAM are just some of the most hotly contested. At the same time, regional collaboration has the potential to enhance and change national enforcement. How then has the regulation of data privacy within Europe adapted to cross-border enforcement and how has international collaboration shaped domestic implementation?

Examining regional efforts, I argue that a system of transgovernmental co-ordination has emerging in the area of data privacy implementation. Linking up with their peer regulators in other member states, data privacy authorities share best practices, harmonize standards for international concerns, and conduct joint enforcement activities. In contrast to a centralized, hierarchical system of regulation centered at the supranational level, European data privacy regulation relies on a network of national regulators embedded within a pan-European co-operative structure to oversee and monitor data privacy rules (Eberlein and Newman 2008). Such transgovernmental efforts draw on national expertise pooled regionally that can then be implemented by regulators endowed with national authority and ties to local actors. While research has increasingly mapped how these networks were formed and their agenda-setting capabilities, little work has looked at issues of cross-border policy implementation.

The goal of this essay is then two-fold. First, it describes transgovernmental initiatives within Europe targeted at promoting the enforcement of data privacy rules. Second, it examines how these efforts are being used at the political level recursively to lobby for expanded enforcement authority both within Europe and across the globe (Sabel and Zeitlin 2010).

The findings of the paper contribute to several critical empirical and theoretical public policy debates. For those interested in the day-to-day work of data privacy authorities, transgovernmental enforcement signals a new page in the regulatory rulebook, whereby sanctions and investigations will be a prominent part of cross-border implementation strategies. Theoretically, the case of data privacy offers an important example of a novel form of networked governance that is increasingly being proposed in a range of sectors (most notably the call for a College of Supervisors in response to the financial crisis). At the same time, it highlights how such novel forms of governance may have unanticipated feedback effects on the resources and goals available to the political actors involved (Pierson 1993).

The paper proceeds in five parts. It begins by presenting the transgovernmental framework. The second part of the paper details the different institutional sites for regional cross-border implementation co-operation. The third section takes a closer look at several examples of the three core areas of transgovernmental co-operation – information exchange, standards harmonization, and joint enforcement. This is followed by a brief exploration of how such efforts are feeding back into the political process as a basis for lobbying activity. The final section of the paper concludes with some implications for privacy regulation within Europe and transgovernmental efforts more generally.

Trangovernmental Co-ordination

Starting in the 1970s, scholars identified a growing number of international interactions among substate officials such as regulators, legislators, and judges (Russell 1973, Hopkins 1976). Such efforts were particularly striking as they frequently occurred outside of the purview of foreign ministries and were conducted informally without the backing of standard international treaty law. Keohane and Nye (1974) argued that transgovernmental co-ordination, in which networks of national officials collaborating across borders could help manage transnational issues and provide collective goods. Proponents of such networks argue that they coupled two important governance resources – expertise and authority. Given considerable national and technical knowledge, these actors come to the international or regional table with on-the-ground experiences of rule development and implementation; this contrasts sharply with negotiators from the executive branch that might have little day-to-day experience with a policy area. At the same time, substate actors are frequently endowed with domestic authority, which eases the implementation of international agreements. In contrast to information networks or epistemic communities (Haas 1992, Majone 1997), these actors enjoy power resources beyond information and expertise. While treaties must frequently proceed through cumbersome and politically volatile ratification procedures, national regulators may employ existing delegated powers to quickly translate transgovernmental agreements into domestic policy (Raustiala 2002).

Extending these arguments, scholars developed the concept of transgovernmental co-ordination, delineating a range of functions such co-operation might serve. In particular, this work distinguished between information provision, standards harmonization, and joint enforcement (Slaughter 2004). Information provision focuses on learning efforts by network participants and typically includes sharing of best practices, case-based tutorials, and updates concerning national developments. Standards harmonization requires a greater level of co-ordination, whereby transgovernmental actors agree to common interpretations of rules and regulations. Such harmonization is particularly powerful as individual participants frequently enjoy the authority to implement and enforce these policies domestically. Finally, joint enforcement includes collective efforts at the transgovernmental level among the participants to review policy implementation, conduct audits, and assist members in the prosecution of non-compliance. Clearly, these functions often overlap but the distinction serves as a helpful heuristic device to identify the level and intensity of co-operation.

At the same time, Keohane and Nye (1974) distinguished between transgovernmental co-ordination and transgovernmental coalitions. In the former, substate actors are primarily engaged in resolving governance challenges and managing the frictions that arise from greater international interdependence. In the latter, by contrast, transgovernmental actors forge coalitions with likeminded peers in other jurisdictions to lobby governments and international organizations in order to alter the policy landscape (Newman 2008b, Thurner and Binder 2009). Put bluntly, substate actors collaborate cross-nationally when their preferences conflict with their home governments. While transgovernmental coalition building focuses on the politics of rule development, transgovernmental co-ordination centers on the implementation and enforcement of those rules.

The Proliferation of Transgovernmental Co-operation in Data Privacy

Transgovernmental co-operation in the area of data privacy has a long and rich tradition. Starting with the first meeting of the International Conference of Data Protection Commissioners in Bonn in 1979, data privacy authorities have met annually to discuss national experiences and develop policy priorities for regional and international co-operation (see Transnational Data Report 1979). This effort was complemented by the European Data Protection Commissioners Conference and working groups dealing with a range of issues such as telecommunications and children's privacy. These initial transgovernmental efforts focused primarily on information provision and standards harmonization. In particular, European data privacy authorities developed and lobbied for regional regulations that would harmonize rules across the European Union (Newman 2008a).

Since the 1990s and the passage of the European Data Privacy directive, however, transgovernmental co-ordination has intensified, with information provision, standards harmonization, and joint enforcement focusing equally on rule implementation as rule development. Here a number of organizations play a particularly important role. The most well established and influential is the Article 29 Working Party. Created as part of the European Data Privacy directive, the Working Party consists of the national data privacy authorities from the member states, the European Data Protection Supervisor, and a representative from the European Commission. The directive tasks the group with several key responsibilities in Article 30. These include monitoring the uniform application of the directive under national law, evaluating protection levels in the Community and in other countries, advising the Commission on additional data protection legislation, and making recommendations concerning new and emerging data protection issues. Members elect a chair and a vice chair who serve to organize and lead the meetings of the group. While the Commission sits in on meetings, its primary responsibilities include drafting documents, providing language services, preparing meetings, and managing travel for participants. The Working Party works on a consensus basis, with different national authorities frequently shepherding an issue and then circulating drafts of recommendations and opinions among members. There are some 15 subgroups, where civil servants from the authorities meet to co-operate on more specific issues, including a working group on enforcement (Interview with Commission Official on the Secretariat, Brussels, June 2007).

In addition to the Working Party, there are complementary groups that have been active in areas concerning police and judicial co-operation. Because the original data privacy legislation was passed under the First Pillar of the European Union concerned with the internal market, the authority of the Article 29 Working Party was long circumscribed to internal market issues (Wallace et al. 2005). To fill this regulatory void, a number of transgovernmental groups have been created in the Third Pillar concerned with home and justice affairs. These include the Joint Supervisory Authority (JSA) for Schengen Information System, the Joint Supervisory Authority for Europol, and the Joint Supervisory Authority for Customs. Similar to the Article 29 Working Party, these bodies include representatives from national authorities and monitor the implementation of data privacy issues within their respective issue areas. To complement the Article 29 Working Party, national data privacy authorities have formed an overarching body to monitor Third Pillar issues named the Working Party on Police and Justice (Interview with member of the Working Party, Brussels, June 2007).

In addition to these European Union groups, there are a number of subregional and transregional bodies that engage in cross border enforcement co-operation. One of the more established is the Central and Eastern European Personal Data Protection Commissioners, which was founded in 2001.[2] Some 13 jurisdictions attend annual meetings, including candidate countries, where a broad set of issues from children's privacy to biometric data have been discussed. A similar group, known as the Ibero-American Data Protection Network, was created in 2003 between Spain and 12 Latin American Data Protection Authorities (see Ibero-American Data Protection Network, 2003, Eisenhauer 2006). Hundreds of officials attend the annual meetings, where regulators share best practices. More generally, the members have committed to information exchange between authorities. Spain has also signed an individual co-operative agreement (a Memorandum of Understanding) with the Federal Trade Authority in the United States concerning issues related to SPAM. The agreement provides a framework for the two authorities to co-operate on enforcement issues and investigate abuses that violate data privacy provisions. Between the EU Working Parties and these additional subregional initiatives, there are a host of transgovernmental actors working to monitor and implement cross-border regulations.

Regional Implementation Co-operation – Information Sharing, Harmonization, Joint Enforcement

Given the extensive institutional development of transgovernmental data privacy networks in Europe, this section offers initial empirical examples of the different implementation strategies employed by transgovernmental actors. Before detailing these strategies it is important to underscore that the central focus of the paper is not national enforcement of national laws but rather transgovernmental implementation efforts. European integration efforts have clearly resulted in a significant convergence among national enforcement regimes. Nevertheless, legal traditions continue to vary and on-the-ground practices differ across the member states (Bignami forthcoming). Additionally, it is useful to establish a baseline for such enforcement efforts. While critics frequently cite the limited use of sanctions by data privacy authorities, studies of compliance frequently stress the alternative mechanisms of implementation aside from coercion. Given the costs and frequent failure of coercive tools, regulators often look for less confrontational tactics and thus the number or extent of sanctions may significantly underestimate implementation success. At the regional level, it is even more striking that there should be any co-operation on such day-to-day efforts. The fact that data privacy breaches persist in countries with data privacy rules should not be the metric of implementation but rather the costs to an organization of violating a regulatory norm (Chayes and Chayes 1995). The following review indicates that authorities are actively pursuing regional regulatory co-operation on the enforcement side. These activities range from *ex ante* preventative strategies, which attempt to minimize compliance failures, to *ex post* sanctions, which in addition to punishing privacy breaches have an important symbolic effect.

Information Sharing

Information sharing is perhaps the easiest form of transgovernmental co-ordination as it imposes few costs on participants and does not require regulators to alter their behavior. Instead, it contributes to a learning environment whereby regulators are positioned to improve their own performance by exchanging experiences from other markets. It is therefore not surprising to find evidence that transgovernmental actors engage in extensive information sharing concerning implementation issues. Nevertheless, it is worthwhile to note that these efforts have been significantly formalized and routinized in Europe over the last two decades. Starting in 2000, the Article 29 Working Party under the auspices of the working group on enforcement holds a semiannual International Complaints Handling Workshop. Data privacy authorities meet to discuss case management and emerging implementation and complaint trends. Using case-based learning, data privacy authorities work through recent examples that presented challenges and from which they hope to share experiences and get advice from other authorities. The workshops have covered a broad range of issues including health data, transborder exchanges, financial services, and personnel data. Similarly, the Central and Eastern European Data Protection Commissioners have developed a web portal focused on information exchange and advice. Individual members may post recent cases or questions to the group. Both the Complaints Workshop and the web portal offer important examples of how national data privacy authorities leverage transgovernmental co-operation to enhance national and cross-border implementation.

Standards Harmonization

In addition to sharing of information and best practices, regulatory data privacy networks in Europe, particularly the Article 29 Working Party, have begun making joint decisions regarding privacy standards. While often not legally binding, these soft law statements have considerable force in the implementation process. On the one hand, they reduce legal uncertainty for firms, offering a focal point around which companies can converge. More coercively, they set an important precedent that has been used by local courts as they enforce privacy regulations. In some cases, common standards developed regionally can be directly enforced by national privacy officials.

The importance for policy implementation of transgovernmental standards is well demonstrated in the debate over on-line authentication services. More and more on-line services require consumers to log into virtual stores. This allows companies to charge for services, monitor customer behavior, and enhance marketing. Major technology companies have begun to explore ways that might help consumers manage the explosion of logins and centralize customer behavior profiling across on-line stores. One solution, favored by Microsoft, would have consumers log into a single trusted service, known as .NET Passport, which would then authenticate its customers across a range of service providers. Microsoft would then be in a position to provide profiling data to the various companies that participated in its program. Such a system naturally involves a tremendous amount of data transfers containing personal data (see New York Times 2002).

In July 2002, the Article 29 Working Party released a preliminary opinion concerning on-line authentication in which it raised several objections to a system under development by Microsoft. The Working Party was particularly concerned with the lack of information given to consumers over how personal information would be used as well as the lack of input given to consumers over which profiling data could be exchanged and under what conditions. The Working Party then developed over a six-month period a more detailed framework for considering data privacy concerns for such authentication systems (Article 29 Data Protection Working Party 2003). After the release of the non-binding opinion, Microsoft agreed to change its program in order to address the privacy concerns of the Working Party and avoid any public relations scandal. The far-reaching effect of such opinions is seen in the fact that Microsoft decided to integrate the new privacy enhancing features not only in Europe, but globally (see Loney 2003). Far from an isolated instance, the Working Party has released similar opinions on a range of issues including data retention and Radio Frequency Identification (RFID) technology, which have shaped actual business practices of major multinational corporations.

As national regulators and courts frequently look to the opinions of the Article 29 Working Party in their national implementation decisions, these standards have an important effect on the local behavior of firms and other organizations. National courts have, for example, employed the decisions of the group to determine EU-level legislative intent (see UNICE 2002). Companies, thus, turn to law firms to examine the opinions of the Working Party and offer compliance advice. Professional services that seek to protect their clients from uncertainty, then, bolster the authority of the Working Party's decisions. Firms often conclude that it is in their best interest to comply with the Working Party's opinions and avoid litigation in national courts or regulatory penalties, even though the opinions have no direct regulatory application.[3] Multinational firms integrate the opinions of such advisory bodies into their global best practices, limiting the costs of maintaining multiple policy standards across interdependent affiliates.

Joint Enforcement

In addition to scanning for emerging regulatory challenges and setting common standards, transgovernmental data privacy co-operation has begun to engage in joint national enforcement. As these groups identify particular enforcement issues that need to be addressed, members can use their nationally delegated power to investigate and sanction. Such efforts may occur informally as national regulators learn from the group and then go back to their home jurisdiction and implement best practices. But in an increasing number of cases, data privacy authorities are working together regionally to formally conduct joint investigations and audits.

Since 2004, the Article 29 Working Party has stepped up its focus on enforcement issues, initiating a series of joint enforcement practices. This issue of joint enforcement was first identified in the Working Party Strategy Document, where the Working Party explicitly underscored harmonized compliance as a key goal of the group (Article 29 Working Party 2004b). Under the auspices of the Working Party's subgroup on enforcement, a framework was developed for joint exercises. Firing a shot across the bow of organizations that might have grown complacent, these efforts were not to be limited to awareness raising and sharing of best practices but focus on investigations and audits. The Working Party explains:

> The Working Party is of the view that awareness raising activities, the provision of guidance and advice to both data subjects and data controllers, the promotion of codes of conduct, etc, are no doubt important means for achieving compliance ... Nevertheless, additionally, enforcement actions in a narrow sense, including the imposition of sanctions, are also a necessary, and often last resort, means to ensure compliance. By applying enforcement and sanctions, data protection authorities discourage non-compliance with the law and encourage those who effectively comply to continue doing so. The Article 29 Working Party believes that enforcement is an important instrument in the compliance "toolbox", and it therefore, aims to contribute to a more proactive stance towards enforcement of data protection legislation within the European Union. (Article 29 Working Party 2004a: 4)

Here it is important to note that the Working Party acknowledges the symbolic effect of sanctions and investigations. Rather than assessing implementation by the aggregate number of investigations or sanctioning activity, they view such efforts as a deterrence tool, which sends a signal to data controllers. The objective of joint enforcement activities, then, is not to root out all breaches of data privacy but rather to understand patterns of non-compliance, which can be corrected, and reinforce self-regulatory behavior by individual organizations. This, then, reinforces the lion's share of data privacy authority implementation efforts, which are preventative in nature.

In order to prepare for such a stepping up of enforcement activities, the Working Party first surveyed its members to examine a range of recent national efforts (Article 29 Data Protection Working Party 2005). Over the course of 2005 and 2006, the Working Party prepared for its first formal joint investigation. In such investigations, the Working Party first develops a common strategy to examine the sector or issue area. A questionnaire and audit model is constructed. Each national regulator, then, conducts an investigation nationally, which is reported back to the group. After an evaluation of the results, the Working Party identifies a series of implementation recommendations which are then carried out nationally. The first such initiative focused on the health insurance sector and was conducted in the 25 member states plus Norway and Iceland. Each national regulator conducted a survey of implementation in their respective markets. The survey was developed jointly by the data privacy agencies and took the better part of a year to construct. The results of the survey form the basis for a comprehensive compliance report in the sector and give notice to firms active in health insurance that regulatory oversight of data privacy issues is important (Article 29 Data Protection Working Party 2007). A second investigation concerning data retention policies of telecommunications firms was authorized in 2008 and is now being conducted (Article 29 Working Party 2008). More generally, joint enforcement is singled out as one of the key priorities in the Working Party's 2008–2009 Work Program. While active enforcement and sanctions have long been in the background of national data authorities' compliance strategies, it is clear that regionally the Working Party has elevated co-operative enforcement to one of its central concerns.

In addition to the work of the Article 29 Working Party, other transgovernmental groups are involved in similar activities. The Joint Supervisory Authority of the Schengen Information System, for example, conducts periodic reviews of the system. The Schengen agreement facilitates the movement of individuals across borders in European countries by removing many internal customs controls. In order to facilitate the oversight of the Schengen borders, the countries involved constructed a joint database where customs data is housed and exchanged. This raised many data privacy concerns and thus the Joint Supervisory Authority was established to monitor the use of the Information System. Composed primarily of technical experts from national data privacy authorities, the Joint Supervisory Authority complements the work of the Article 29 Working Party. In its most far-reaching implementation exercise, the Joint Supervisory Authority investigated the use of Article 96 Alerts. These alerts are flagged by customs officials when third country nationals are refused entry to a Schengen country. The Joint Supervisory Authority had received complaints that these were being used inappropriately and thus undertook a joint review. In a similar process to the Working Party, the JSA developed a common evaluation criteria including a questionnaire and two inspection modules. These were conducted in the member states. The results demonstrated that there were a series of problems with the implementation process including improper data retention, alerts on EU nationals, and unwarranted alerts. The JSA made a set of implementation recommendations to improve the system (Joint Supervisory Authority of Schengen 2005). National data privacy authorities, then, investigated individual cases and followed up with their respective governments. The Danish data privacy authority, for example, examined the 443 alerts entered by Danish authorities and found 22 inappropriate alerts. Working with the National Commissioner of Police, the Danish privacy authority got the inappropriate alerts corrected and helped revise the alert procedure (Joint Supervisory Authority of Schengen 2006).

This overview highlights the transformation in regulatory oversight occurring in data privacy regulation. Collaborating with their peers transgovernmentally, data privacy authorities are both leveraging the experiences of their fellow regulators to improve domestic oversight and working regionally to manage cross-border data flows.

The Political Feedbacks of Transgovernmental Enforcement Co-operation

The move towards cross-border implementation co-operation cannot be completely decoupled from national enforcement authority. Since the inception of modern data privacy regulation in the 1970s, many data privacy authorities in Europe had only limited powers to investigate and sanction rule breaches (Bennett 1992). Research on early efforts frequently cited weak enforcement and disparities among regulators as a potential barrier to effective protection (Flaherty 1989). Interestingly, cross-border implementation efforts have produced an important focal point for data privacy authorities to demand an expansion of their domestic authority. In short, transgovernmental co-ordination on data privacy rules for Europe forged a transgovernmental coalition supporting expanded regulatory powers.

Such political feedback occurs when government policies alter the resources and goals available to specific interest groups. Well documented in the social policy literature, public policies such as veteran's benefits or social security create incentives for citizens to mobilize and offer these groups a clear agenda to organize behind (Skocpol 1992, Campbell 2003, Pierson 2004). Similarly, public policy can shape the identity and resources available to bureaucratic actors, who may then use these new identities and resources to change future policy.

The first and most dramatic instance of such a policy feedback occurred during the debate over the European Privacy Directive. After the failure of initial proposals that sought to centralize oversight in the hands of the European Commission, data privacy authorities pushed for the creation of the Article 29 Working Party (Bignami 2005). This maintained their role in pan-European policy and quickly won favor with national governments which feared excessive delegation to the European Commission. National regulators warned, however, that disparities in sanctions and investigation authorities would cripple a federated oversight system and thus lobbied for an equalization of enforcement powers. Article 28(3) of the directive, thus, stipulates that data privacy authorities should have a range of powers, including the authority to investigate, intervene, and sanction or engage in legal proceedings. National authorities thus used the new responsibility of joint implementation to push for expanded authority (Newman 2008b).

While there is of course variation in the usage of such authority, it is clear that this lobbying effort has transformed on-the-ground enforcement efforts.[4] In Spain, for example, the data privacy authority received 2,000 complaints in 2006 and conducted over 1,000 investigations (see Ortuno and Perez 2007). In 2005, over 200 cases received financial sanctions. This activism is particularly striking as the Spanish agency did not exist prior to the EU Privacy Directive. Similarly, France created an auditing department in 2001 in the wake of the directive and is targeting to conduct 150 random inspections per year. Additionally, the CNIL investigates roughly one in four individual complaints (see Girot 2006). In most areas of market governance, regulators act pre-emptively to give advice and establish clear procedures so as to avoid harsh sanctions and costly investigations. Nevertheless, the expansion of national authority under the guise of cross-border harmonization has had very real national implications.

Interestingly, European data privacy authorities have used international fora on cross-border implementation to further promote and lobby for the expansion of enforcement authority for their peers. At the 27th International Conference of Data Protection Commissioners in Montreux, Switzerland, the officials published a declaration calling for greater co-operation on cross-border issues. One of the key elements of the Declaration is the creation of parallel data privacy authorities in other jurisdictions with investigatory powers and "to intensify in particular the exchange of information, the co-ordination of their supervisory activities, the development of common standards" (International Conference of Data Protection and Privacy Commissioners 2005: 3). The Article 29 Working Party has reinforced these statements as it conducts its own joint enforcement efforts. In its Declaration on Enforcement, the Working Party argues, "Of course, adequate powers and sufficient resources are a prerequisite for performing effective enforcement actions. The Article 29 Working Party therefore calls upon Member States to ensure that the supervisory authorities are sufficiently empowered and resourced at a national level" (Article 29 Working Party 2004a: 4).

Similarly, in a recent effort by the OECD to investigate cross-border efforts, European data privacy officials used the opportunity to lobby for their counterparts to receive expanded authority. In presentations to the study representatives from both Spain and France made this an explicit part of their suggestions. When describing the necessary elements of international enforcement co-operation, the Spanish regulator listed three key ingredients: harmonized legislation, similar enforcement tools, and the ability to communicate (see Ortuno 2006). A representative from the French authority emphasized that it is "more comfortable to co-operate with DPAs or enforcement authorities with similar powers" and underscored the challenges of working with countries with "no identified enforcement authority" (see Girot 2006: 15). Their basic argument follows that from the previous European debate, cross-border co-operation is easiest when the participating parties have similar enforcement powers. The final OECD recommendations mirror their demand, arguing that in order to facilitate cross-border enforcement nations should "improve their domestic frameworks for privacy law enforcement to better enable their authorities to co-operate with foreign authorities" (OECD 2007: 7). In particular, the recommendations call for "providing effective powers and authority" including the authority to "deter and sanction violations of laws protecting privacy; permit effective investigations, including the ability to obtain access to relevant information, relating to possible violations of laws protecting privacy; permit corrective action to be taken against data controllers engaged in violations of laws protecting privacy" (OECD 2007: 9). This is a sharp break from earlier OECD statements that tended to stress regulatory diversity. Given that the report was focused on cross-border enforcement, it is also striking that a significant portion of its recommendations focused on the expansion of domestic enforcement powers. While it is too soon to know the effect of such transgovernmental coalition building, it is clear that the push for greater cross-border implementation co-operation has been coupled politically to an expansion of enforcement powers.

Conclusion

Since the mid-1990s, data privacy implementation and enforcement has taken on an increasingly transgovernmental character. Regulators from multiple jurisdictions actively collaborate across borders to share best practices, develop common standards, and conduct joint investigations. This collaboration takes place at the regional level in a range of fora including the Article 29 Working Party, Third Pillar Supervisory Authorities, and subregional bodies such as the Central and Eastern European Personal Data Protection Commissioners. In contrast to expert networks that populate international meetings and organizations, data privacy authorities come to these discussions with substantial national authority. With the power to investigate and audit domestic organizations, the individual members of these bodies simultaneously co-ordinate transgovernmentally and implement locally.

It is important to caution that such cross-border efforts do not and cannot eliminate breaches of personal privacy. The intent of modern data privacy legislation is to create a balance between an individual's privacy rights and the needs of organizations to process personal information. As such, they create a framework in which data is collected and exchanged. There will inevitably be bad actors, mistakes, and oversights. Bureaucracies such as data privacy authorities will suffer all of the limitations of government agencies tasked with overseeing complex business and public sector environments. But at the same time that these limitations and criticisms are raised, it is important to highlight the innovative efforts (such as transgovernmental networks) that have been developed to overcome the difficult task of monitoring and implementing policy in a multi-level polity such as the European Union.

This novel networked form of co-ordination exemplifies an important governance alternative to traditional hierarchical command and control structures. While the European Union has centralized oversight powers in a few sectors such as competition policy, sovereignty concerns and national politics frequently limit complete delegation to the supranational level (Dehousse 1997). As a result, federated transgovernmental networks of national regulators are often embedded within EU policy oversight. In sectors ranging from financial services to energy, parallel institutions to the Article 29 Working Party have been created (Eberlein and Newman 2008, Posner 2009, Sabel and Zeitlin 2010).

These transgovernmental networks need not be viewed, however, as a second-best solution. The initial review of their collaboration in the data privacy field suggests that they have taken on a host of responsibilities and actively engage the task of pan-European oversight. Each member of the network enjoys unique relationships with local actors and distinct monitoring capacities. While many of these initiatives are still in their infancy, it is clear that national regulators have left the domestic realm and are actively seeking to learn from their colleagues and construct regional enforcement structures.

At the same time, the move into cross-border enforcement has created a political platform for further empowerment of regulatory bodies and the diffusion of European regulation globally. As policy makers turn increasingly to international privacy concerns, such as airline passenger name records or personnel data for multinational corporations, institutional inequalities among national regulators continue to hinder further co-operation (Farrell 2003) . European regulators have used these frictions to lobby for the creation of peer institutions in other countries endowed with equal investigatory powers. The debate on cross-border implementation started in Europe thus opens a political opportunity for institutional change globally.

Notes

1. For an exemplary description of the various governance tools available see Bennett and Raab (2006).
2. See Central and Eastern European Personal Data Protection Commissioners, *Final Declaration*, Warsaw, December 17, 2001. For information on the group see http://www.cecprivacy.org

3. The power of the Group's opinions over business behavior was echoed by numerous European trade associations representing the telecommunications, banking, and direct marketing industries. Interviews were conducted in 2003.
4. For a comprehensive study of enforcement powers across country, see OECD (2006).

References

Article 29 Data Protection Working Party, 2003, Working document on on-line authentication services. Brussels: European Union.
Article 29 Data Protection Working Party, 2004a, Declaration of the Article 29 Working Party on Enforcement. Brussels: European Union, pp. 1–5.
Article 29 Working Party, 2004b, Strategy document. Brussels: European Union, pp. 1–10.
Article 29 Data Protection Working Party, 2005, Recent examples of enforcement actions carried out by data protection authorities. Brussels: Article 29 Working Party.
Article 29 Data Protection Working Party, 2007, First joint enforcement action: Evaluation and future steps, June 20. Brussels: European Union, pp. 1–19.
Article 29 Working Party, 2008, Mandate to the Enforcement Subgroup to proceed to the 2nd joint investigation action. Brussels: European Union, pp. 1–2.
Bennett, C., 1992, *Regulating Privacy: Data Protection and Public Policy in Europe and the United States* (Ithaca, NY: Cornell University Press).
Bennett, C. and Raab, C., 2006, *The Governance of Privacy: Policy Instruments in Global Perspective* (Boston: MIT Press).
Bignami, F., 2005, Transgovernmental networks vs. democracy: the case of the European Information Privacy Network. *Michigan Journal of International Law*, **26**, 806–868.
Bignami, F., Forthcoming, Cooperative legalism and the non-Americanization of European regulatory styles: the case of data privacy. *American Journal of Comparative Law*.
Campbell, A., 2003, *How Policies Make Citizens: Senior Political Activism and the American Welfare State* (Princeton, NJ: Princeton University Press).
Castells, M., 1996, *The Rise of the Network Society* (Oxford: Blackwell).
Chayes, A. and Chayes, A., 1995, *The New Sovereignty: Compliance with International Regulatory Agreements* (Cambridge, MA: Harvard University Press).
Dehousse, R., 1997, Regulation by networks in the European Community. *Journal of European Public Policy*, **4**(2), 246–261.
Eberlein, B. and Newman, A., 2008, Escaping the international governance dilemma? Incorporated transgovernmental networks in the European Union. *Governance*, **21**(1), 25–52.
Eisenhauer, M., 2006, Developments in Latin America privacy laws. *Privacy and Security Law*, **5**(15), 521–523.
Farrell, H., 2003, Constructing the international foundations of e-commerce: the EU–US safe harbor arrangement. *International Organization*, **2**, 277–306.
Flaherty, D., 1989, *Protecting Privacy in Surveillance Societies* (Chapel Hill: University of North Carolina Press).
Girot, Clarisse, 2006, CNIL's powers under the new French DP Act: Strategy, findings, challenges. Presentation at the OECD Roundtable on Privacy Law Enforcement Cooperation, London, November 1.
Haas, P., 1992, Introduction: epistemic communities and international policy coordination. *International Organization*, **46**(1), 1–35.
Hopkins, R., 1976, The International Role of "Domestic" Bureaucracy. *International Organization*, **30**(3), 405–432.
Ibero-American Data Protection Network, 2003, *La Antigua Declaration,* Guatemala, June 6.
International Conference of Data Protection and Privacy Commissioners, 2005, Montreux Declaration: The protection of personal data and privacy in a globalised world, a universal right respecting diversities. Montreux: International Conference of Data Protection and Privacy Commissioners.
Joint Supervisory Authority of Schengen, 2005, Article 96 inspection. Brussels: Schengen.
Joint Supervisory Authority of Schengen, 2006, Schengen Joint Supervisory Authority activity report 2004–2005. Brussels: Schengen.

Keohane, R. and Nye, J., 1974, Transgovernmental relations and international organizations. *World Politics*, **27**(October), 39–62.
Loney, M., 2003, Microsoft passport compromise after EU scrutiny with global consequences, available at: http://www.silicon.com/management/cio-insights/2003/01/31/microsoft-passport-compromise-after-eu-scrutiny-10002697/.
Majone, G., 1997, The new European agencies: regulation by information. *Journal of European Public Policy*, **4**(2), 262–275.
New York Times, 2002, Microsoft faces European Commission inquiry on privacy concerns, *New York Times*, available at: http://query.nytimes.com/gst/fullpage.html?res=9904E0DC133BF93BA15756C0A9649C8B63.
Newman, A., 2008a, *Protectors of Privacy: Regulating Personal Data in the Global Economy* (Ithaca, NY: Cornell University Press).
Newman, A., 2008b, Building transnational civil liberties: transgovernmental entrepreneurs and the European Data Privacy Directive. *International Organization*, **62**(1), 103–130.
OECD, 2006, *Report on the Cross-Border Enforcement of Privacy Laws* (Paris: OECD).
OECD, 2007, *OECD Recommendation on Cross-Border Cooperation in the Enforcement of Laws Protecting Privacy* (Paris: OECD).
Ortuno, M., 2006, Privacy law enforcement cooperation: the perspective of the Spanish Data Protection Agency. OECD Roundtable on Privacy Law Enforcement Cooperation, London, November 1.
Ortuno, M. and Perez, J., 2007, Reflecting on a long established enforcement experience, by the Spanish Data Protection Agency. Presented at the Workshop on Enforcement organized by the European Data Protection Supervisor, Brussels, April 24.
Pierson, P., 1993, When effect becomes cause: policy feedback and political change. *World Politics*, **45**(4), 595–628.
Pierson, P., 2004, *Politics in Time: History, Institutions, and Social Analysis* (Princeton, NJ: Princeton University Press).
Posner, E., 2009, Making rules for global finance: transatlantic regulatory cooperation at the turn of the millennium. *International Organization*, **63**(4), 665–699.
Raustiala, K., 2002, The architecture of international cooperation: transgovernmental networks and the future of international law. *Virginia Journal of International Law*, **43**, 1–92.
Rosenau, J., 2002, Information technology and the skills, networks, and structures that sustain world affairs, in J. Rosenau and J. Singh (Eds) *Information Technology and Global Politics* (Albany, NY: SUNY Press), pp. 275–288.
Russell, R., 1973, Transgovernmental interaction in the international monetary system, 1960–1972. *International Organization*, **27**(4), 431–464.
Sabel, C. and Zeitlin, J., 2010, *Experimentalist Governance in the European Union: Towards a New Architecture* (Oxford: Oxford University Press).
Skocpol, T., 1992, *Protecting Soldiers and Mothers: The Political Origins of Social Policy in the United States* (Cambridge, MA Harvard University Press).
Slaughter, A.-M., 2004, *A New World Order* (Princeton, NJ: Princeton University Press).
Swire, P. and Litan, R., 1998, *None of Your Business: World Data Flows, Electronic Communication, and the European Privacy Directive* (Washington, DC: Brookings).
Thurner, P. and Binder, M., 2009, European Union transgovernmental networks: the emergence of a new political space beyond the nation-state? *European Journal of Political Research*, **48**(1), 80–106.
Transnational Data Report, 1979, European data production chiefs to meet in Bonn, *Transnational Data Report*, volume 2(1), p. 1.
UNICE, 2002, Comment on the Implementation of Directive 95/46/EC on the Protection of Individuals with regard to the processing of personal data and on the free movement of such data of 24 October 1995, August 30 (UNICE: Brussels).
Wallace, W. et al., 2005, *Policy-Making in the European Union* (Oxford: Oxford University Press).
Zysman, J. and Newman, A., 2006, *How Revolutionary was the Digital Revolution: National Responses, Market Transitions, and Global Technologies* (Palo Alto, CA: Stanford University Press).

Managing Urban Growth in Asia

CLAY G. WESCOTT and L. R. JONES

ABSTRACT *This article provides perspectives on some key issues countries need to consider in rethinking their priorities to achieve greater social, environmental and economic sustainability from increasing urbanization in Asia. It discusses three areas where such new thinking is needed: improved governance requiring clearer assignment of responsibilities, more extensive use of information and communications technology, and performance and results management to increase urban government productivity. The advantages of establishing a more competitive business climate and increased reliance on markets and market mechanisms for problem solving in Asian cities also is emphasized. The importance of increased infrastructure investment and development are noted, followed by conclusions and recommendations.*

Introduction

Cities in Asia confront difficult challenges when attempting to establish safe, poverty free and well-managed urban development. Despite their differences, many Asian cities have two common challenges. First, hazardous environmental conditions have arisen as a result of rapid industrialization, rapid urbanization and the growth of vehicle population in the cities combined with the absence of sound land use planning and management. These are seriously damaging the environment in urban areas of Asia – air and water pollution, solid waste management, and transport-related forms of environmental stress (congestion, toxic gases, etc.) – by affecting the entire population and creating serious health problems and financial costs.

For example, in urban areas in the People's Republic of China (PRC) and in other large Asian cities, urban air quality has fallen dramatically as a result of industrialization and huge increases in automobile, bus and truck traffic. Urban traffic congestion already is a serious problem in Beijing, Shanghai and other Chinese cities despite the fact that these locales are served by subway and other rapid transit systems with state subsidized low prices to encourage usage. The private automobile is a major status symbol in PRC and Asia generally, and with the number of automobiles in private ownership in the PRC projected to increase by as much as tenfold in the next decade or so the twin problems of urban traffic gridlock and increased air pollution are formidable. Indian cities also are confronted by projections of increased car ownership and similar problems are faced by other Asian cities and urban areas where rapid industrialization has occurred causing the emergence of a sizable middle income class cohort that can afford to buy automobiles.[1]

Secondly, many Asian cities face common challenges related to urban poverty, including patterns of urbanization, creating jobs and providing housing, utilities and social infrastructure for the poor. Despite widely acknowledged significant economic growth in Asia in recent decades, the region, especially in urban areas, remains beset by high levels of poverty (see ADB 1994, 2001a). As noted by ADB,

> Urban poverty has many causes. Some of these are the willingness of new migrants to take low paid jobs in the city, increases in the cost of land, long journeys to work, less support from an extended family network, exposure to greater environmental risk, and greater vulnerability to changes in market conditions in urban areas... Poverty is not only related to low income, it involves poor health and education, deprivation in knowledge and communications, inability to exercise human and political rights, and low self-esteem... Most Asian cities have grown and diversified economically well ahead of their capacity to manage development. (ADB 1999: 5–6)

The political will and fiscal ability to address urban poverty and its associated problems across the region varies considerably, but remains a challenge in most cities in Asia.

This article sets out three areas that countries need to address in rethinking their priorities to achieve greater social, environmental and economic sustainability from increasing urbanization: 1) good governance, including transparency, high quality of services, and low transaction costs; 2) competitive business climate, including sound regulations and land use policies, and 3) public-private partnership in building efficient, affordable, and commercially sustainable infrastructure.

Good Governance

The sustainable development of Asia's cities is only possible with good governance, defined as the sound management of a city's social and economic resources. Three aspects are of central importance: 1) the need for clear assignment of responsibilities among levels of government, while providing for a range of competitive service providers to help ensure efficiency and citizen choice; 2) extensive use of information and communications technology to drive down costs and provide for maximum transparency, and 3) incorporation of various approaches to enhance performance and results management of city governments.

Clear Assignment of Responsibilities

Across Asia, one common feature of policy and institutional packages applied by governments keen to foster growth alongside poverty reduction has been to assign state powers, responsibilities and resources to urban and other sub-national authorities and to private and civil society agencies under various forms of contracts, partnerships and other principal-agent arrangements. Decentralization has become a catch-all term for what proves in practice to be a highly differentiated, and differently motivated, range of practices and institutional forms. Yet a clear lesson from regional experience is that each level of government needs a clear assignment of responsibilities, and adequate human and financial resources to meet them.

It is presumptuous and misleading to assume that decentralization always results in an inexorable policy progression from 'more' to 'less' centralized governance structures. Some services (quasi-public goods) are best delivered at the national level, including defense and monetary policy. Many regulations are best set at the national level (e.g., environmental protection, air and water resource management) because of spillover effects across subnational jurisdictions. Some taxes are more efficiently collected by national government due to economies of scale such as customs and VAT.

Some policy objectives can best be achieved with intergovernmental transfers, such as reducing disparities between rich and poor localities. By conventional measures, decentralization is in its early stages of adoption in Asia, despite commitments in most countries to intensify it, and the fact that various instances and types of 'devolution' are underway (Wescott and Porter 2005).

In addition, decentralization is not necessarily a spatial concept requiring reassignment of service delivery responsibilities from higher to lower orders of administration, although this often is the case. Cohen and Peterson (1999: 61) emphasize that it is rather the broadening of institutions producing and providing needed goods and services to the public at more efficient cost, wherever they are located and whether they are public, quasi-public or private. Indeed, that devolution often manifests itself in a plurality of agencies, public and private, operating at different scales of jurisdiction providing overlapping services. This circumstance gives rise to debate about the consequences of devolution in terms of economic efficiency, the extent and consequences of increased public agency and market competition, clarity of accountability where mandates are devolved creating overlap of roles and responsibilities, and fiscal effects on subordinate governments.

However, there is evidence that clear devolution of responsibilities to well governed cities and municipalities can increase public access to the affairs of government; bring about greater responsiveness and accountability of locally elected leaders, better match resources for public services with locally defined and often highly specific needs, and support the commitments made by central governments in the region to poverty reduction and sustainable economic growth.

For example, Philippine survey data has been examined for evidence of improved performance linked to devolution, and there are some positive indicators. Fifty-eight per cent of those surveyed say health care has improved with decentralization, while only 8 per cent think it has worsened. Another survey found a much higher perception of corruption at the national level than at the local level, although the results could be affected by better media coverage of the former. Some local government units (LGUs) have been increasingly tapping their own revenue sources. For example, Tagaytay Municipality has reduced its dependence on intergovernmental transfers to 23 per cent (compared to an average 63 per cent for all LGUs) by introducing new local taxes, and investing in four hotels and an international convention center to generate income (Rufo 2005: 28). There is also anecdotal evidence that performance management systems being introduced, and recognition of local government excellence through the annual Galing Pook and Magsaysay awards may have spurred better performance in some LGUs (Campos and Hellman 2005: 246–250, ADB and World Bank 2005: 44–47, Wescott and Jones 2005). However, there are still major concerns regarding LGU capacity to (i) prepare comprehensive urban development plans; (ii) effectively link the local planning exercise with public investment plans and expenditure surveys; (iii) join into more efficient economic planning units, (iv) organize effective participatory consultation; and (v) re-engineer local bureaucracies and develop quantitative indicators to measure the efficiency and effectiveness of local institutions.

Achieving good governance of Asia's cities requires partnerships of government, private sector and civil society. In addressing the challenge of poverty, the traditional instruments used to hold governments accountable, such as audit and legislative oversight, have proved ineffective. The evidence suggests that citizen report cards could be an important instrument to hold public servants accountable and improve the quality of public services. The Public Affairs Centre (PAC), a non-profit organization in Bangalore, India, pioneered the Bangalore Citizen Report Card (CRC) to assess the satisfaction level of citizens with regard to public services in Bangalore and ranked public service agencies (water, power, transport, housing, communications, health care and other municipal services) in terms of their service performance. The first survey was conducted in 1994 with a random sample of households and assessed various dimensions of public satisfaction with respect to staff behavior, quality of service, information provided, and corruption. The survey found that level of public satisfaction with the quality and efficiency of public services were low, the public agencies were not responsive to citizens and they lacked customer orientation, corruption was widespread and negatively affected the public service delivery. The second survey was conducted in 1999 and revealed some improvement in public satisfaction with public services.

As Ravindra (2004) suggests, in general the CRCs had a positive impact on public service delivery by increasing client orientation and improving the quality of services. The use of CRC information by the media and by civil society increased public awareness of the quality of services, stimulated citizen groups to demand better services and influenced key officials in understanding the perceptions of ordinary citizens and the role of civil society in city governance. As a result, following the CRCs, the local government and public agencies launched some important reforms to improve the infrastructure and services in the city, including property tax reform through self-assessment schemes, streamlining internal systems and procedures of public service agencies and the Bangalore Agenda Task Force.

Widespread, Accessible Information

One of the keys to effectively managing Asian urban growth is providing widespread, accessible information to all. An important tool for this is e-government: the use of information and communication technology (ICT) to promote more efficient and cost-effective government, facilitate more convenient government services, allow greater public access to information, and make government more accountable to citizens. E-government is expanding in the region on the back of rapid increase in penetration of ICT. There are over 250 million Internet users in Asia-Pacific, more than any other region, and growing at close to 40 per cent a year. There are 560 million mobile phone subscribers, more than twice the number in 2000. The Republic of Korea is ranked number one in the world in broadband use, with Hong Kong and Taipei in China and Japan also in the top seven (International Telecommunications Union 2004).

There is strong anecdotal evidence of positive results from e-government in Asian cities. For example, the Beijing city government's website allows visitors to select from categories such as government services, laws and regulations, a news center, links to other government departments. Users can join an electronic forum to get answers to questions such as how to move one's official residence to Beijing to work there. In the Philippines, Naga City is internationally recognized for a range of governance innovations. An extensive e-government system goes beyond that in many other jurisdictions to inform citizens on budgets, bidding documents, legislation and procedures. Since many citizens do not have access to the Internet, the city also provides a hard copy of the Naga City Citizen Charter containing essential information that is also on the website on how to access city services.

The Hyderabad (India) Metropolitan Water Supply and Sewerage Board use its Single Window Cell (SWC) to reduce corruption for new connections. The application process is centralized in one public place, with applications recorded on computers that are difficult for corrupt officials to alter. Staff are motivated to provide good service with distinctive uniforms, modern offices and individual computer terminals. The service improvement has been praised extensively in the media, which further helps staff motivation.

In many cities, land market data is often not freely available, resulting in increased costs to the potential developer and often the need for payment of bribes. This problem is being addressed as computer-based land information systems facilitate the storage and dissemination of data and as the benefits of freely available data are realized. Such ICT systems also show promise in helping to raise public revenue. In India, for example, urban areas contribute 55 per cent of GDP, but municipal revenue is only 0.6 per cent of GDP. A property tax collection system integrating cadastral GIS with billing and financial accounting has been developed by a foundation linked with Infosys, Inc. The introduction of the system in Bangalore has contributed to an increase between 2001 and 2004 of over 20 per cent in assessed properties, and 50 per cent in property owners paying property tax (Nadhamuni 2005).

Jurisdictions such as Singapore and Hong Kong, China have comprehensive systems where a web-portal or smart card integrates information and services from various government agencies to help citizens and other stakeholders get seamless service without needing to know about the responsible government agency. Thus, users can obtain services across different geographic levels of government within the same functional area, and across different functions. As an example of the latter, a citizen can submit a change of address on their driving license, and the change is automatically registered with the health, elections, and tax departments, thus avoiding the need for multiple filings (Wescott 2005).

One challenge facing many cities is that English is the lingua franca of ICT; there are an estimated 2200 languages used in Asia, and only 20 per cent of Asians can use English. Making e-government widely accessible to citizens requires addressing this challenge. Asian writing systems are varied and far more complex than English, and designing digital fonts for any one of them a massive challenge. Yet progress is being made. For example, in 2003 a character-based font was released for the Urdu language. This potentially allows 60 million speakers in 20 countries to use their language in computer applications.

Performance and Results Management

A number of initiatives are in progress to strengthen city performance and results management including improving intergovernmental fiscal relations, anti-corruption initiatives, use of improved information technology in financial management, accounting and other areas, and use of public scorecards on performance (Wescott 2005).

In the Philippines, major initiatives have been undertaken to develop results-based budgets. A proposal to adopt this approach is underway and is to be submitted to Congress in late 2005. In addition, ADB and the World Bank recently issued a report on decentralization in the Philippines that states, "Measuring and managing LGU performance assume special importance in the context of the issues examined in this report." The report notes that performance management for cities and other local government units has advanced at two levels in the Philippines; national government and partner organizations have shown. "interest in nationally standardized tools that could be used to assess LGU performance and provide incentives to high performing units and capacity building to others. The result is that a wide array of such tools are in use". Some measures apply to measurement of cash management of revenues and expenditures while others are applied to evaluate LGU performance on specific normative criteria and also permit comparison between local governments. Some of the measures are directed at rule compliance while others measure "development outcomes". The report also notes that some of the performance tools are used by the LGUs themselves "to measure costs and ongoing performance" (ADB and World Bank 2005).

At the same time, a highly visible initiative has continued to be used by the Department of the Interior and Local Government (DILG) in the form of a Local Productivity and Performance Measurement System (LPPMS). LPPMS was initiated in the 1980s for monitoring of LGU service delivery and with the legal enactment of LGUs in 1991 it has proven useful to monitor the substantial devolution of powers and functions authorized in law. More recently, the LPPMS has been employed as more than a central agency monitoring instrument; it is now used as a management mechanism by some LGUs to measure and assess their performance, for instance in planning and budgeting. Other national government departments have developed LGU performance monitoring systems. For example, the Bureau of Local Government Finance, with assistance from US Agency for International Development (USAID), has created and maintains an online database of 126 distinct features of LGU finance and the idea of linking this data into the LPPMS is under consideration. Other government national agencies have databases that might be similarly linked, such as the Department of Budget and Management, the Commission on Audit, and the Civil Service Commission.

In addition, a Citizen Satisfaction Index System (CSIS) is in place in the Philippines to score and evaluate a variety of areas of devolved service delivery responsibility and to increase citizen participation and influence in local governance in areas including agriculture, health, social services, the environment and natural resources. In augmentation of these efforts an internet based Local Development Watch (DevWatch) system has also been deployed to evaluate the level of development in LGUs and to focus on and make more visible highest priority needs in underserved local governments.

One evident question about the orientation of these monitoring systems is what purposes they are used for. Monitoring often leads to control, which in the case of the Philippines, given the degree of devolution established in the law in 1991, could result in excessive influence of central agencies over LGUs. On the other hand, good monitoring systems can be used to steer resources to areas of highest need both in terms of location and sector.

A different type of monitoring is being fostered by the Clean Air Initiative for Asian Cities.[2] By demonstrating innovative ways to improve the air quality through partnerships and sharing experiences, this group seeks to promote better practices in monitoring, modeling, emissions inventories, mobile and stationary sources, education and awareness (Karim 1999, Kaginalkar and Dalvi 2004). A conference of 800 air quality policy makers, experts and scientists was held in Yogyakarta, Indonesia in September 2006 to explore new ways to reduce air pollution in Asian cities.

Competitive Business Climate and Increased Reliance on Markets

Closely related to good governance is the second essential feature for Asian cities: a competitive business climate. Two aspects should be stressed here. First, as cities are engines of growth for their countries, they need a sound regulatory framework that facilitates new business startups and expansion of existing businesses, including adequate contract law, dispute procedures, and clear allocation of responsibilities. Secondly, many cities are corporatizing, privatizing or outsourcing public facilities and services to reduce costs, improve effectiveness, and to attract private capital. Also, Asian city governments are using techniques from the private sector such as demand management in the areas of service tariff reform, charges and restrictions to improve use of limited road space, regulation of groundwater use, and market discipline in project design.

As an example of the first point, new systems allow direct access to transaction or customer accounts held in different parts of a city government. For example, Ho Chi Minh City in Viet Nam has taken the lead in that country in working to simplify administrative procedures faced by businesses, as a way of promoting investment. A "one-stop shop" for business license applications has been established, whereby businesses can apply once online, and thereby initiate action from all the concerned agencies. These ICT-enabled reforms have inspired simplification of administrative procedures in many other districts and communes throughout the country through "one-stop, one-door" models. Citizens benefit by spending less time waiting and traveling, and having better information provided to them.

Other cities have introduced innovations that can reduce opportunities for corruption by helping to measure performance better, facilitate outsourcing and contestability of public functions, reduce transaction costs, enforce rules more strongly, reduce discretion and increase transparency. For example, in Seoul, Republic of Korea, the On-line Procedures Enhancement for Civil Applications (OPEN) system helps to get transparency in city administration by preventing delays in processing of licenses and other government documents. Prior to the introduction of the system, applicants often had to pay speed money; now processing is a matter of public record, on the web. If officials are unnecessarily delaying documents, citizens can complain and disciplinary action is taken.

The PRC is a prime example of a developing nation that is experimenting with market solutions to public service supply within a system that evidences a high degree of fiscal and policy devolution. This pathway is pursued under the authority of a highly centralized national political and governance framework, but one that permits a significant degree of provincial and local economic experimentation and innovation. Performance is enhanced through a combination of hierarchy, given the nation's well-developed civil service system, and performance rewards associated with non-bureaucratic approaches, such as individual leadership and managerial rewards in terms of career enhancement opportunity for successful teamwork and organizational goal achievement. And the emergence of private financing for urban area projects ranging from tourism and hotel facilities to industrial plants has increased the influence of and reliance on private markets in PRC and elsewhere in Asia.

Another area of great importance to cities, which can only be mentioned briefly due to length limitations, is the necessity for reform of state and private banking and lending institutions and systems to embrace market principles and practices. Provision of capital is critical to economic growth as capital formation typically is one of the most difficult problems faced by established as well as smaller entrepreneurial businesses. Whether the problem is availability of quick liquidity for residents of Viet Nam and Cambodia or availability of longer term credit in the Greater Mekong Development Corridor, the Philippines or elsewhere, reform of money lending systems and arrangements is critical. Asian capital investment markets have evolved and matured significantly, but reform of state banks and banking regulations and practices has lagged behind in many Asian nations, with important implications for capital formation and infrastructure investment in urban areas (Estache and Sinha 1995).

Infrastructure Investment and Development

To quote ADB's Urban Sector Strategy:[3]

> While initial capital requirements for infrastructure may be greater in urban than in other areas, the payoff from such investment can also be high. Urbanization brings health and social benefits that could only be achieved in rural areas at far greater costs. Residential infrastructure costs may be higher in cities, but households are also better serviced with piped water, solid waste collection, and electricity – all of which contribute to better health and welfare.

Additionally, economic returns to industrial and commercial investments also tend to be higher in cities than in small towns and rural regions. More productive jobs can be created in cities, due in part to the fact that workers have more complementary capital inputs to increase productivity... Yet potential improvements in the provision and maintenance of urban infrastructure and services are constrained by poor urban governance, management, and finance. Outdated legal, institutional, and governance traditions, as well as inadequate reform measures have constrained the pace of development. (ADB 1999: 4)

Among many examples of such challenges is ADB's Eastern Islands Urban Development Sector Project in Indonesia. Although the civil works constructed improved the quality of urban infrastructure and service delivery in at least some of the districts, the uniform approach taken did not address the variable capacity evident at the local level. This is a key constraint since local governments will be responsible for future maintenance. Furthermore, these local governments were unable to secure the planned subsidiary loan agreements, and will not in the future until they demonstrate much greater capacity in revenue collection, and in persuading their citizens to pay for the cost of providing services. In particular, wastewater treatment failed in the project, and needs clear responsibilities for management, and setting and collecting user charges (ADB 2004).

Despite the numerous challenges confronted by cities in Asia, there has been progress in some areas. For example, effective law enforcement, regular vehicle inspections with up-to-date equipment, and responsible driving are essential to the effective use of road facilities. Road safety is typically the joint responsibility of many agencies and departments; thus a co-ordinated approach is generally more effective than individual agency efforts (ADB 2001b: 3; and ADB 2000). For example, an inter-ministerial meeting in Lao PDR in 1998 found that police and regulators were unaware of key issues, undermined by special exceptions granted by transport authorities, and faced by ambiguous and conflicting regulations and lack of co-ordination among concerned departments. A survey in Vientiane found that 85 per cent of all trucks were overloaded. In a pilot enforcement project in Vientiane, local authorities were allowed to keep part of the fine revenue collected to pay for weighing scales, vehicles, training and overtime costs. By training and working together, the better equipped regulators and police could enforce regulations more effectively. The pilot team went on to train other provinces and districts (Chagnan *et al.* 2002: 40, 58).

The environmental problems in urban areas, such as air pollution, cannot be solved by local government efforts alone. The solution requires coherent collaboration between national and local governments in setting air quality standards, issuing environmental laws and regulation, enforcing those laws and standards, installing equipment to control emission from vehicles, improving and campaigning for using public transportation, creating urban green areas, and so on. Evidence suggests that a successful collaboration between the national government (especially Ministry of Natural Resources and Environment) and the local government (the Bangkok Metropolitan Administration) during the past 10–15 years has led to significantly reduced air pollution and improved air quality in the city.[4] The national government included the improvement of air quality in Bangkok in the policy on protection of public health formulated within the 7th National Economic and Social Development Plan (1992–1996) (see further Thavisin 2001). The measures included an increase in the number of roads, traffic improvement, development of public transport systems, reducing lead content in gasoline, and improvement of fuel quality. In 1999 the nationwide use of unleaded gasoline was introduced. These measures were further developed in the 8th Plan and the 5th Bangkok Development Plan (1997–2001) and shared the objectives of the National Plan regarding regulation of urban growth and development, improvement of quality of life and the environment. In 1999, the Bangkok Metropolitan Administration introduced 13 measures for reduction of air pollution, including setting up check-points, mobile inspection units, motorcycle units, pollution free roads, air quality reporting, engine inspection and tuning services, campaigning and public relations, strictly enforcing covering sheets at construction sites and by tracks, improvement of road verges, inspection of motorcycles for white smoke, car free roads, and improvement of fuel quality. Effective collaboration of national and city authorities resulted in developing a coherent and transparent air quality management system in Bangkok. Currently, information regarding the quality of air in Bangkok is available online (http://www.pcd.go.th/AirQuality/Bangkok/), which provides information regarding various measures (CO_2, NO_2, CO, Ozone, and so on) of air quality.

Conclusions

At all levels of government and governance, it is evident that successful public management reform of the type noted here is dependent upon leadership and sustained support from elected and appointed officials in the political process. Many of the observations of Wildavsky (1964, 1979), and Caiden and Wildavsky (1974, 1980) about the politics of the budgetary process and budgeting in poor nations are relevant to the present circumstances of Asian cities. Wildavsky noted, for example, that cultivation of constituencies is critical to empowerment in political systems. Caiden and Wildavsky demonstrated that revenue and expenditure forecasts in developing nations are weak predictors of actual fiscal results.

With respect to Wildavsky's assertion, cultivation of a strong clientele base is essential for urban area politicians in Asia, perhaps even more so than elsewhere. In the more democratic political systems in Asia, key constituents tend to play strong roles in establishing political power and leverage to enable the effectiveness and influence of politicians. However, effective democracy requires more than power brokers, particularly in smaller urbanizing cities and where increased emphasis has been placed on citizen participation from the national level to local governments as in the Philippines, Viet Nam, Mongolia, Thailand and even Cambodia. In nations with less democratic political systems (for example the PRC) or those where democratic practices are only emerging, as in Cambodia, Lao PDR and other Southeast Asian nations, citizen support remains a relevant source of power and influence in urban settings. For example, in the PRC such a tradition has long been present in many municipalities. In Thailand, where this far less a part of cultural tradition relative to governance, participation is growing as citizen interest groups seek to influence urban policy, planning and budgeting. Thus, under political systems that are at either end of the spectrum of democracy, cultivation of a supportive constituency is critical for political survival and, relative to the recommendations in the analysis presented here, necessary to support the types of reform we believe is needed.

Experience with Asian public budgeting suggests that Caiden and Wildavsky's finding about the failures of fiscal planning and forecasting is valid in the region to varying degrees. This is due in part to dependence on uncertain revenues, failure to reform tax systems, dependence on external assistance (either from national or provincial governments or international banks and aid agencies), and to inadequate budget and accounting systems and processes and staff capacity weaknesses. The changes that seem most important for urban areas in Asia are those to correct these and related problems so that revenue and expenditure forecasting becomes more stable, accurate and reliable.

While the challenges of urbanization in Asia sometimes seem almost insurmountable, this article has attempted to demonstrate the number of measures either in place or in progress to improve urban management and problem resolution in the region. Many of these measures and prescriptions are not unique to Asia – they are applicable in both developing and developed nations. What is distinctive about the Asian circumstance appears to be a double-sided coin. On one side is the magnitude of the problems faced by urban decision makers, managers and citizens. On the other is the demonstrated capability of many of the nations and cities in the region to mobilize capital required for rapid economic expansion. If this same energy and level of resources are directed to solve the problems of urbanization, then in 20 years or less, many of the cities in the region could become examples of progress for the rest of the world.

Acknowledgements

The views expressed are those of the authors, and not necessarily those of the Asian Development Bank. The authors wish to thank Kamil Akramov and K. E. Seetharam for their comments and inputs. This article draws on materials presented at an Expert Group Meeting on Managing Urban Growth in Asia, 28 – 29 July 2005, and from ADB (1999).

Notes

All URLs accessed 4 April, 2006.
1. The World Health Organization (WHO) calculated that in the early 1990s, 12 of the 15 cities in the world with the highest levels of particulates, and six with the highest levels of sulfur dioxide in the atmosphere were in Asia. Since then air quality has grown much worse in most Asian cities. While the focus of environmental concerns has previously been on large cities, increasing attention is now directed to secondary cities, as in Malaysia and Thailand (ADB 1999: 5).
2. As examples of the studies promoted by this initiative, see "Welcome to the Clean Air Initiative for Asian Cities", available at http://www.cleanairnet.org/caiasia/1412/channel.html.
3. The strategy highlights the operational objectives of (i) maximizing the economic efficiency of urban areas; (ii) reducing urban poverty; (iii) improving quality of life; and (iv) achieving more sustainable forms of urban development. These objectives are to be achieved through the promotion of urban sector policies for (i) encouraging good governance; (ii) improving urban management; (iii) mobilizing financial resources; (iv) reducing urban poverty; and (v) addressing urban development subsectors: water supply, sanitation, and solid waste management; land management; transport; and housing.

Good governance includes the principles of accountability, predictability and transparency, as well as policies and mechanisms for decentralization, community participation, and increased private sector involvement (ADB 1999: 1).
4. Interview with Supat Wangwongwatana, the Chair of the Clean Air Initiative for Asian Cities, with David Kruger, available at http://www.adb.org/Documents/Periodicals/ADB_Review/2003/vol35_4/cleaning_air.asp.

References

ADB, 1994, *Urban Poverty in Asia: A Survey of Critical Issues* (Manila: Ed. Ernesto M. Pernia).
ADB, 1999, *Urban Sector Strategy* (Manila: ADB), available at http://www.adb.org/Documents/Policies/Urban_Sector/urban0700.asp
ADB, 2000, *Developing Best Practice for Promoting Private Sector Investment in Infrastructure: Roads* (Manila: ADB).
ADB, 2001a, *Asian Cities in the 21st Century: Contemporary Approaches to Municipal Management, Vol. 5. Fighting Urban Poverty* (Manila: ADB).
ADB, 2001b, *Performance Audit Report on Selected Technical Assistance in Road Safety* (Manila: ADB).
ADB, 2004, *Project Performance Audit Report on the Eastern Islands Urban Development Sector Project in Indonesia,* available at http://adb.org/Documents/PPARs/INO/ppar-ino-24206.pdf
ADB and World Bank, 2005, *Decentralization in the Philippines: Strengthening Local Government Finance and Resource Management in the Short Term* (Washington, DC: World Bank, March 31), available at http://siteresources.worldbank.org/INTEAPDECEN/Resources/dc-full-report.pdf
Caiden, N. and Wildavsky, A., 1974, *Planning and Budgeting in Poor Countries* (New York: John Wiley & Sons).
Caiden, N. and Wildavsky, A., 1980, *Planning and Budgeting in Poor Countries,* 2nd edition (Somerset, NJ: Transaction Press).
Campos, J. and Hellman, J., 2005, Governance gone local: does decentralization improve accountability? in: *East Asia Decentralizes: Making Local Government Work* (Washington, DC), available at http://siteresources.worldbank.org/INTEAPDECEN/Resources/dc-full-report.pdf
Chagnan, J., Gansberghe, D. V., Vongphasouk, B. and Rumpf, R., 2002, *Looking Back to See Forward – Consultations about Good Governance and Participatory Development in the Lao PDR* (Vientiane: Swedish International Development Cooperation Agency).
Cohen, J. and Peterson, S., 1999, *Beyond Administrative Decentralization Strategies for Developing Countries* (West Hartford, CT: Kumarian Press).
Estache, A. and Sinha, S., 1995, Does decentralization increase public infrastructure expenditure?, in: A. Estache (Ed) *Decentralizing Infrastructure: Advantages and Limitations,* Discussion Paper No. 290 (Washington, DC: The World Bank).
International Telecommunications Union, 2004, *Asia Pacific Telecommunication Indicators 2004* (Geneva: ITU).
Kaginalkar, A. and Dalvi, M., 2004, *Design of operational air quality management information systems,* Centre for Development of Advanced Computing (C-DAC), paper presented at BAQ 2004, Agra, India, available at http://www.cleanairnet.org/baq2004/1527/article-59253.html
Karim, M. M., 1999, Traffic pollution inventories and modeling in metropolitan Dhaka, Bangladesh. *Transport and Environment,* **4**(5), 291–312.
Nadhamuni, S., 2005, *Enhanced Property Tax System through Municipal Egovernance and GIS* (Bangalore: eGovernments Foundation), available at http://www.adb.org/Documents/Events/2005/Managing-Urban-Growth/presentation-nadhamuni.pdf
Ravindra, 2004, An assessment of the impact of Bangalore Citizen Report Cards on the performance of public agencies, The World Bank, OED, ECD Working Paper Series 12, available at http://lnweb18.worldbank.org/oed/oeddoclib.nsf/DocUNIDViewForJavaSearch/D241684DF81FCE2785256EAD0062DE10/$file/ecd_wp_12.pdf
Rufo, A., 2005, Tagaytay shows the way. *Newsbreak,* Aug. **1**, 28.
Thavisin, Nathanon, 2001, Management of air quality in Bangkok metropolitan, available at http://www.cleanairnet.org/asia/1412/articles-35509_recurso_1.pdf

Wescott, C. G., 2005, Fiscal devolution in East Asia, Asian Development Bank, working paper prepared for Training Workshop on Optimizing Local Revenue Generation for Local Governments and Development, Makati City, Philippines, Oct. 5.

Wescott, C. G. and Jones, L. R., 2005, Strengthening performance in public sector management, Working Paper, Asian Development Bank, Oct. 26.

Wescott, C. and Porter, D., 2005, Fiscal decentralization and citizen participation in East Asia, in: I. Licha (Ed) *Citizens in charge: managing local budgets in East Asia and Latin America*. Washington: Inter-American Development Bank, available at http://www.adb.org/Governance/fiscal_decentralization.pdf

Wildavsky, A., 1964, 1979, *The Politics of the Budgetary Process*, 1st and 3rd editions (Boston, MA: Little Brown).

Governance for Sustainability in East Asian Global Cities: An Exploratory Study

MEE KAM NG

ABSTRACT *This paper explores the state of governance for sustainability in East Asian global cities. Most conceptualizations on the governance of sustainable development are based on Western democratic contexts with a market-based economy and an active citizenry. Capacity in fostering partnerships and consensus building among different stakeholders is often identified as an essential quality in implementing sustainable development. The four East Asian cities discussed in this paper are fundamentally different: they all have a "strong" government exerting major direct or indirect influences on market sectors that are at varying stages of development and their civil societies are relatively immature, if not inactive. Given the central role played by the state in these political economies, this paper argues that capturing the government's perceptions of and commitments towards sustainable development is instrumental in understanding their sustainability practice. A small-scale benchmarking exercise is carried out to verify this proposition.*

Introduction

Many authors have suggested prescriptive modes of governance for sustainable development (Ayre and Callway 2005, Bressers and Rosenbaum 2003, Evans *et al.* 2005, Ginther *et al.* 1995, Hyden 2001, Jaskolski 2004, Voss *et al.* 2006). However, very few studies have explored the relationships between an existing mode of governance and sustainable development efforts undertaken in a particular place. There are a few published works (Astleithner and Hamedinger 2003, European Consultative Forum on the Environment and Sustainable Development 2000, OECD 2002) but they are based on Western contexts. No publication so far has investigated the relationships between governance and sustainability efforts in Asian cities. This paper is a small first step in that direction.

The following section first discusses the unique modes of governance in the four East Asian global cities. Unlike their Western counterparts where there seems to be a positive correlation between sustainability efforts and democratic governance that emphasizes multi-stakeholder participation (Arce 2003, Roseland 2000, Vonkeman

2000), the state-centred mode of governance found in Asia (Boyd and Ngo 2006, Brodsgaard and Young 2000, Drysdale 2000, Johnson 1995, Kwon 2005, Woo-Cumings 1999) means that the perception and commitment of the government to sustainable development is the key to understand a city's sustainability practice. This latter argument is further developed in section three where the sustainable development rhetoric and actions in the four cities are explored and compared. The concluding remarks summarize this exploratory essay.

Modes of Governance in Asia

Based on the European context, Baker *et al.* (1997: 8–18) have worked out "a ladder of sustainable development" ("treadmill" development, weak or strong sustainable development and ideal sustainable development).[1] Synthesizing this framework with existing literature (Astleithner *et al.* 2003, Ayre and Callway 2005, Bressers and Rosenbaum 2003, Ginther *et al.* 1995, OECD 2002), different "modes of sustainability governance" reflecting varying power relationships among the public, business and third sectors and their diverse perceptions and hence responses towards sustainable development can be identified (Table 1). For instance, "treadmill" development is very likely to be found in the pro-growth market-oriented mode of governance where technology is believed to have the power of fixing all environmental problems. Moving up the ladder from weak, strong to ideal sustainable developments, stakeholders will appreciate that sustainability issues are larger and more complicated than just environmental concerns and the realization of sustainable development requires concerted efforts. While this framework may help us understand sustainable rhetoric and actions in some Western cities, it may not be particularly useful in understanding sustainability practices in East Asia, where the modes of governance are very different from the Western democratic setting. One thing that is unique to Asian cities is the central role played by governments in the development process. This argument is different from adopting wholesale the perspective of the developmental state (Johnson 1995). As argued by Whitehead (2006: 178), "the really existing states of contemporary Asia present us with a colorful menagerie that is far removed from the standardized attributes of stateness commonly found in Western-originated social theory". As can be seen below, the state-centred modes of governance vary in form and substance in the four cities.

Before examining in detail the modes of governance in the four East Asian global cities, a brief overview is warranted. The economic performance of these four cities may pale in comparison to existing world cities, but they all share similar visions of becoming a hub of the rapidly globalizing economy and at the same time pursuing some kind of sustainable development. The four cities are mega cities by population standard[2] (Table 2). Shanghai has the largest population (13.3 million), but as reflected in the city area, since the city boundary includes extensive rural counties. Shanghai is almost six times the size of Hong Kong, which has a population of 6.8 million. Population density in Hong Kong has been very high because only 20 per cent of land is developed for urban uses. Contrary to the general impression, Hong Kong has over 40 per cent of its country park conserved whereas the conservation area in Singapore constitutes only 4 to 5 per cent of its total land area.

Table 1. A synthesized framework for understanding sustainable development and governance

A ladder of sustainable development[1]	Mode of governance	Roles of different stakeholders		
		Government	Private sector	Civil society
"Treadmill" development.	Pro-growth, market-oriented governance: faith that technology will fix all environmental problems.	Government plays a pivotal managerial role in promoting economic growth rather than providing a regulatory framework to achieve social and environmental sustainability.	Still focuses on profit maximization and pays scant attention to its social and environmental responsibilities.	Relatively weak and powerless. Probably not awakened to its role towards sustainable development.
Weak sustainable development.	Economic growth-led governance: environmental problems can be resolved by economic means.		Forced by regulations to deal with negative externalities. Reactive rather than proactive.	
Strong sustainable development (1): focus on resources management and economic growth.	Ecological modernization-led governance: public and private sectors work together to reflect ecological priorities & greening of social & corporate values & practices.	Government plays a proactive role in partnering with the market to promote environmental and to a certain extent social sustainability. Economic growth depends not just on exploitation bur rather enhancement of environment.	Plays a proactive role to assume corporate social and environmental responsibilities and to ensure clean and green product life cycles.	Civil society is also active in partnering with the public and private sector to further sustainability goals.
Strong sustainable development (2): concerns also distribution and equity issues.	"Reflexive modernity",[2]-led governance:	Government to be self-reflective of its role & proactive in fostering three-way partnership in urban governance.	Private sector playing proactive role in partnership with others to minimize uncertain socio-economic & environmental impacts.	Active citizenry demanding a central role to monitor & decide city futures.
Ideal sustainable development.	Ecology-centered governance.	Three-way partnership to manage and nurture earth's ecological resources.		

[1]The concept of a ladder of sustainable development is first put forward by Baker *et al.* (1997: 8–18).
[2]For reflexive (radical or second) modernity, Beck (1997: 24, 31–32) refers to a new ecological democracy where 'politics and morality gain priority over shifting and inherently uncertain science' (Hills and Ng 2000: 15).
Source: Author's synthesis of various sources.

Table 2. Background information of the four East Asian global cities

	Hong Kong[a]	Singapore[b]	Taipei[c]	Shanghai[d]
Population (million)	6.8	4.4	2.6	13.3
Area (km^2)	1,101	699	272	6,341
Population density in densely built up (metropolitan) areas (persons/km^2)*	26,279	10,352	21,366	21,402
GDP/capita (US$)	29,961	28,340	13,139 (Taiwan)	4,486
GDP by industries (%):				
• Primary	0.1	n.a.	1.8	1.3
• Secondary	9.9	32	30.6	50.8
• Tertiary	90	62.7	67.6	47.9

*In Singapore, the figure for metropolitan area (425 km^2) was advised by the Urban Renewal Authority through email in August 2003. For the figure in Shanghai, if Pudong is included, the population density will decrease to 10,148.
Sources:
[a]Figures on Hong Kong are from: YOD: 2005. Census and Statistics Department, http://www.censtatd.gov.hk/home/index.jsp, and *Hong Kong in Figures*, http://www.censtatd.gov.hk/FileManager/EN/Common/hkinf.pdf, both viewed in May 2006.
[b]Figures on Singapore are from: YOD: 2005. Department of Statistics, http://www.singstat.gov.sg/, viewed in May 2006.
[c]Figures on Taipei are from: YOD: 2005. Department of Budget, Accounting and Statistics, Taipei City Government, http://english.taipei.gov.tw/dbas/index.jsp, viewed in May 2006. Figures on per capita GDP and GDP by industries are from: Taiwan Yearbook (2005).
[d]Figures on Shanghai are from: YOD: 2004. Shanghai Municipal Statistics Bureau (2005).

In terms of economic strength, Hong Kong and Singapore are more or less in the same league, followed by Taipei and then the rapidly growing Shanghai, the GDP per capita of which is less than one-sixth of Hong Kong's. While Hong Kong, Singapore and Taipei have been dubbed Asia's "tigers" since the 1980s, Shanghai's transition from a centrally planned economy to a socialist market economy is a relatively recent phenomenon. Hong Kong is now basically a tertiary economy with most of its industrial production activities relocated to the China mainland. Singapore and Taipei retain a considerable amount of industrial production (about 30 per cent of GDP) and the tertiary sector constitutes about two-thirds of the city's GDP. Shanghai is still primarily an industrial city (industrial production contributed to 51 per cent of GDP in 2004).

Based on these statistics, one can postulate that sustainability issues in the tertiary economy-based high-density Hong Kong should be very different from those found in Singapore and Taipei. As a transitional and primarily industrial city, Shanghai faces yet another set of sustainable development issues. Given the central role of the state in Asia, it is postulated that sustainable development practices in the four cities are closely linked to the perception and understanding of and commitments to sustainable development by the governments. The following examine in further detail the role of the state in the four political economies.

Hong Kong: Strong Executive-led Government Leading an Economics-first City

Hong Kong had been a British colony from 1842 to 1997. However, the city's economic take-off did not take place until the 1950s and 1960s when capitalists and laborers from the China mainland fled to Hong Kong to escape communist rule, thus fueling the transformation of the entrepot port into a manufacturing power-house. "A borrowed-place with a borrowed-time", residents in Hong Kong then abhorred politics and preferred to focus on pursuing economic growth. Colonization has also perpetuated a sense of territorial alienation among Hong Kongers, sometimes described as "a rootless generation". Nevertheless, the 155 years of British rule allowed Hong Kong to become a society ruled by law.

Hong Kong as a British colony was never a democratic polity and this has remained so since it became a Special Administrative Region (SAR) in 1997. In fact, in many respects, democratic development has moved backward after 1997.[3] The HKSAR government is now headed by the Chief Executive (CE) who was elected by an 800-member Election Committee. The CE is advised on major policy decisions by the Executive Council, members of which are appointed by the CE from among the principal officials of the executive authorities, members of the Legislative Council and public figures. From July 1, 2002, the membership of the Executive Council comprises 14 Principal Officials appointed under the Accountability System and five non-officials. Members' appointment or removal under the Accountability System is decided by the CE[4] (HKSAR Government 2003).

The CE decides on what matters should be put before the Executive Council. The CE is required by the Basic Law to consult the Council before making important policy decisions, introducing bills into the Legislative Council, making subordinate legislation or dissolving the Legislative Council (HKSAR Government 2003). As argued by Raj-Kumar (2003), the current electoral system produces a weak and fragmented legislature. The system was designed to facilitate the operation of an "executive-led" political system in the HKSAR. Yep (2003) asserts that Hong Kong's political parties remain underdeveloped and often lack resources and a mature organizational structure. He suggests that this is due primarily to the de-politicization process in Hong Kong during the colonial period which provided few opportunities for public participation in decision making, resulting in low public interest in political activity.

As the territory's dominant landowner, the government has strong interests in land related economic developments, particularly the property and financial sectors. Compared with industrialists, players in these sectors seem to be able to exert more significant impacts on various policy decisions regarding the city's future development. Masked by the rhetoric of "minimum intervention and maximum support", the government indeed has exercised selective intervention in the territory's economic development. For instance, over half of the city's population is living in public housing estates and the government controls the land market, and between 1998 and 2000 the government intervened in the housing market by setting an annual production target of 85,000 units.

Given the historical and institutional setting, people in Hong Kong cannot be described as active citizens. While the Hong Kong-born generations have regarded Hong Kong as home and show genuine concern about its development, the busy city values dedication to work and money-making endeavors over community participation and empowerment. Nevertheless, there has been a slow awakening to civic rights and aspirations towards democratic development (Cheng 2005).

In a word, the strong executive-led government and its role as almost the sole land owner in the territory have given the administration a unique position in shaping development trajectories in a law-based society.

Singapore: People's Action Party-led State Taking Care of Market and Society

Similar to Hong Kong, Singapore had been a British colony. Britain assumed sovereignty over Singapore in 1824 (Haas 1999) and Singapore became an independent state in 1965. Unlike the pragmatic migrants in Hong Kong, the Singaporeans under British rule had been very active in fighting for internal self-governance which they finally gained in 1958. While Singapore had briefly joined the Federation of Malaysia in 1963, the merger proved to be a failure. With the withdrawal of the British force in 1968, the new Singaporean government had no choice but to adopt a two-pronged development strategy: an increasingly active role of the government in the economic arena and the creation of a favorable investment climate to lure foreign investment (Ng 1999: 14).

Singapore's economic policy has been highly interventionist though a free market system is adopted (The Economist Intelligence Unit 2003). The government plays important roles not only by providing the legislative framework but also infrastructure such as the Economic and Trade Development Boards and manpower training (Ministry of Trade and Industry 2003). Furthermore, individual industries have been encouraged and the government is deeply involved in economic development through its macro- and micro-economic policies and its ownership of firms in many sectors (Ministry of Trade and Industry 2003). Although the Singaporean government has begun reversing the trend of "nationalisation and expansion of state enterprises" since the 1980s, only "limited privatisation" or "managed competition" (Heracleous 1999 cited in Haque 2004: 232) was carried out. Up to 1996, there were still close to 600 government-linked companies in Singapore (Low and Haggard 2000 cited in Haque 2004: 232). The justification for the government's heavy intervention in the economy are to "substitute for the weak private sector, ensure rapid industrialization and maintain political and economic stability" (Lam 2000: 404 cited in Haque 2004: 230).

Consequently, Singapore's industrial base is dominated by foreign multinationals and a few large domestic firms with strong government links. Small and medium-sized enterprises (SMEs) play only a minor role, in spite of government efforts to encourage their development (The Economist Intelligence Unit 2003). According to one estimate, by 1989 foreign investors controlled some 73 per cent of total assets in all sectors of Singapore's economy, amounting to S$685 billion. Some 80 per cent of Singapore's exports, 40 per cent of employment and 26 per cent of gross domestic capital formation are directly or indirectly accounted for by foreign transnational corporations (Yeung *et al.* 2001: 163).

Domestic industries in Singapore were historically small in size and weak in organizational capacity. The development strategy of the government, which centered on the expansion of state-owned and multinational enterprises, have hampered the growth of domestic entrepreneurship. The characteristics of such an economic structure means that it would be difficult for the "private" sector to be a significant political force in Singapore (Zhang 2003).

More so than executive-led Hong Kong, Singapore's executive branch dominates the legislative and judicial branches, and the prime minister (PM) within the executive government has all along enjoyed predominant authority (Ho 2000). Singapore is a parliamentary democracy led by the People's Action Party (PAP). Since the independence of Singapore in 1965, the PAP has dominated politics in the country and its intolerant approach to opposition politicians has prevented the development of a combative multiparty legislature (The Economist Intelligence Unit 2003). The president, as the head of state, appoints the PM (i.e. the leader of the political party who secures the majority of seats in parliament). On the advice of the PM, the president also appoints other members from among the elected members of parliament to form the Cabinet.

The Cabinet is responsible for all government policies and the day-to-day administration of the affairs of the state. The Cabinet is responsible collectively to the parliament (Parliament of Singapore 2003). The Singapore Parliament has a single house (i.e. House of Parliament) and together with the directly elected president of Singapore is known as the legislature (Parliament of Singapore 2003). Meritocracy is one of the foundations of Singapore's mode of governance and the ruling PAP has repeatedly claimed that its legitimacy is rooted in performance. Besides "meritocracy, survivability and social peace", Singapore seems to have little space for alternative discourse on human rights and individual civil liberties (Subramaniam 2001). In Singapore "the boundaries and space for civil society have been set by the state and government". From a "civic" perspective, citizens tend to exhibit a general unwillingness to become members of civil society interest groups or to volunteer in social work as "the final word always rests with the authorities". "Political and or public participation in Singapore is at best partial and at worst pseudo, but never full" (Lee 2002: 108).

Nevertheless, in recent years participation and involvement of "as many Singaporeans as practical in the political process" have been encouraged through established channels so that the government can hear alternative viewpoints and build consensus with the people on major urban living issues (Ho 2000: 108).

Taipei: Government-led "Planned Market" and Political Democratization

Taiwan had been a Japanese colony from 1895 to 1945, serving as the island nation's agricultural appendage. Unlike Hong Kong where indigenous population is a minor proportion when compared to mainland migrants, native Taiwanese have been living in the island for a long time. This helps to explain the historically deep-rooted conflicts between native Taiwanese and those who went from the Mainland to Taiwan after the Nationalist Party lost their civil war in 1949. In fact, the historical hatred between the native Taiwanese and the corrupt Nationalist Party that led the government had exacerbated the traditional Chinese culture of paying little respect to rules and regulations which have been perceived as state instruments of repression (Ng 1999: 18).

Today, Taipei City is a special municipality under the direct jurisdiction of the central government. Unlike the Hong Kong Special Administrative Region, the central government in Taipei has a tighter and closer control of policies and developments in Taipei, especially when currently the two levels of government are controlled by two opposing political parties. Martial law was terminated in 1987 and the temporary provisions during the period of communist rebellion was ended in 1991. Since the passage of the Municipal Self-governance Law in 1994, city mayors of Taipei and Kaohsiung have been directly elected by their citizens (Taipei City Government 2003). Prior to 1994, city mayors were nominated by the premier and appointed by the president of the republic. Taipei city councilors are also elected through the ballot box. Councilors have four-year tenure of office and are eligible for re-election. In 1996, for the first time in China's history, the president of Taiwan was elected. Currently, Taipei city government operates under a mayor (member of Koumintang (KMT)) and vice mayor with 16 bureaux, eight departments and seven commissions (Government Information Office 2003).

As a result of the democratization process, more and more liberal-minded citizens demand participation and empowerment in urban governance. Coupled with intensified parliamentary divisions and different patterns of political alliances, urban governance in Taiwan is bisected by politics amongst various factions within and between the governments, the parliament, the business sector and the civil society (Ng 1999: 21). Tang (2003: 1050), borrowing from Rose and Shin (2001), describe the situation as "democratization backwards", that is, a reverse process of democratization when competitive elections come before the establishment of the basic institutions of a modern state. This explains why in contemporary Taipei politics, "gold-power" alliance, corrupt practice and political clientelism can still be found amongst an active political community and a maturing civil society.

Through various land and economic reforms back in the 1950s and 1960s (Selya 1995), the mainlander-dominated government in Taipei had developed intensive involvement in the city's economic development. As argued by Chu (1999: 301), "the state was relatively strong vis-à-vis the private business because the state was endowed with a centralized political authority, an oversized military and administrative apparatus, and a huge array of state-owned enterprises". One means is the government's heavy involvement in the banking sector to "suppress" interest rates so that capital resources can be directed to economic sectors "desired" by the government (Ho and Lee 2001). This has not only created a dual financial market but also led to a situation when bank loans are sometimes decided by political decisions (Ho and Lee 2001). However, with China's open door policy, Taiwanese investment in the Mainland has also surged. The intensification of economic restructuring and liberalization has nurtured the growth of an economic elite that has challenged the government's hegemonic rule and hence diminishes the government's control over policy outcomes (Ng 1999: 18).

Shanghai: Chinese Communist Party-led Urban Governance amidst Economic Reforms

Similar to Singapore, China is ruled by a dominant party, the Chinese Communist Party (CCP). The structure of the CCP at all levels runs parallel to and supervises that of the government and the legislature (i.e. the National People's Congress, NPC). In fact, there is overlapping membership of the government and the CCP at all levels.

The government of Shanghai municipality, as the first-level local state administrative organ in the PRC, is directly under the central government. It must accept the leadership of the State Council (SC) which is the highest executive body of state administration and has the power to decide on the division of power and functions between the central government and the state administrative organs of Shanghai municipality; and to change or reverse decisions and orders made by the government of Shanghai municipality. The municipal government of Shanghai has the right to exercise unified leadership over the work of the districts, counties, townships and towns; and exercise unified administration over economic, social and cultural affairs in areas under its jurisdiction (CIIC 2003).

The mayor and vice mayors are elected by the people's congress of the municipality. Officially, the city has three administrative levels in its urban area: the municipal government, urban districts and "street offices" (Zhang 2002: 485). Before China's open door policy in the late 1970s, Shanghai, as a coastal industrial powerhouse, had been used by the central government as an economic base to support development in other parts of the country (Cheung 1996). In 1984, Shanghai was selected as one of the 14 coastal cities to receive foreign investments and adopt foreign technology and management skills (Zhang 2000). Although financial reforms were introduced in 1985, it was in 1988 that greater financial autonomy was granted to Shanghai with the favorable policy of the contract responsibility system (Chan 1996). Yet Shanghai's strong re-emergence onto the world stage has to do with the development in Pudong in 1990 (Jacobs 1997). With Deng's southern tour in 1992, Shanghai's administration was further simplified and decentralized to districts and counties. The strategy was to have a market system in the economic arena while politically retaining a socialist system. The separation of politics from the enterprise aims to reduce power of the government by enlarging the role played by the market (Tsao 1996: 98). Ways to achieve this include function consolidation among government units or commercialization of most of the activities of the bureaux by setting up companies, while retaining some of their administrative functions (Tsao 1996: 98). This partial reform strategy has led to the coexistence of contradictory old and new elements in the administrative system (Tsao 1996: 103). Nevertheless, the new form of urban governance is characterized by more decentralized, fragmented, ambiguous and constantly refined power relationships among various levels and branches of government (Wu 2000: 1366).

Although public ownership is still the main form in China's economy, the non-public sectors are growing. Various forms of non-public ownership today include collectively owned, privately owned, share holding, sole foreign ownership, jointly owned (by non-state domestic owners), and joint ventures (with foreign partners) (Zhang 2002: 484). Measured by percentage of total gross output value, the share of state-owned enterprises dropped from 49 per cent in 1993 to 23 per cent in 1999. In 1993, a total of RMB17.25 billion was spent on urban infrastructure (Chan 1996). By the end of 1997, there were more than 2,600 Chinese and foreign financial institutions in Shanghai, including 51 foreign banks and financial companies and 163 representative offices (Shi and Hamnett 2002). As claimed by Mr Chen Liangyu, Secretary of the CCP Shanghai Municipal Committee, "foreign capital has been integrated deeply in Shanghai's economy". The cumulative foreign investment in Shanghai had topped US$70 billion by the end of July 2003, accounting for one-fifth of the city's investment in fixed assets and one-third of its profits and tax revenues (Xinhua News Agency 2003).

Facing more than 75 per cent of industrial production by the non-public sectors, the municipal government has to seek views from the emerging non-public-owned industries in making development decisions (Zhang 2002: 485). While the growing non-public sectors have joined the "growth machine", it has remained as a "little brother". And Zhang (2002) opines that community groups are the weakest players in urban development in China. He further argues that in a socialist country such as China government manages much of the day-to-day life of a community and NGOs, as a new concept to many Chinese scholars, have little space to thrive (Zhang 2002: 496).

The Central Role of the State in the Development of East Asian Cities

These four cities are characterized by the existence of a strong municipal government: the administration or bureaucracy has set up the development agenda, formulates policies, employs resources in policy implementation and in some cases, influences the direction of economic growth and development. This statement, however, needs to be qualified because, except for Singapore, central government policies do have an impact on the relative autonomy of local states. Nevertheless, all the four city governments have either major stakes in or "interesting" relationships with the economy, and the public-private partnership often overshadows the existence of the civil society. Such modes of governance would seem hopeless for mainstream sustainable development enthusiasts who advocate participatory democracy and collective decision making by different stakeholders. However, this paper argues that, unlike their Western counterparts, perhaps a "mode" of sustainable development (as defined by these municipal governments) is still possible in the East Asian global cities. The following section reviews sustainability practice in the four cities, followed by a brief statistical analysis to explore the results of the municipal governments' efforts in promoting and operationalising the concept.

Planning for Sustainable Development in East Asian Global Cities: Rhetoric and Actions

Since all four cities have state-centered modes of governance, it is postulated that capturing the governments' rhetoric and commitments towards sustainable development is the key to understanding the city's sustainability practice. The following paragraphs first examine what the four cities have done with reference to sustainable development. Then sustainability indicators are employed to assess the performance of each city.

Hong Kong: Wide-ranging Rhetoric? Fragmented Action?

During the years of breakneck economic growth from the mid-1980s to the mid-1990s, "sustainable development" seemed to be such a remote concept that Hong Kongers could hardly understand its meaning in relation to their city. Perhaps this is why the government did not send any representative to the first Earth Summit in 1992. Although the term "sustainable development" was first mentioned in the 1993 *Third Review of Progress of the 1989 White Paper: Pollution in Hong Kong – A Time to Act* (PELB 1993), it was not until 1998 that the then first chief executive, in his Policy Address, called for the initiation of a *Sustainable Development for the 21st Century Study (SUSDEV 21)* (HKSAR Government 1998: 34). Indeed, concerns over sustainable development have risen since the late 1990s: after the enactment of the Environmental Impact Assessment Ordinance in 1999; the study of the SUSDEV 21; the involvement of strategic environmental assessment in the Territorial Development Strategy Review; and in other strategic proposals relating to sewage disposal, waste to energy incineration and power generation policies (Briffett *et al.* 2003: 177). However, people then tended to confine sustainable development to environmental concerns.

With the absence of a comprehensive sustainable development strategy and a comprehensive environmental policy, and insufficient coordination among different government departments (Briffett *et al.* 2003: 179), it is very difficult for all parties concerned to assess or estimate sustainability impacts of development projects in the territory. Another downside of this lack of an overall strategy is that the government is able to find reasons to compromise with the effects on the environment for the sake of "essential" development (Briffett *et al.* 2003: 179).

Not too long after the chief executive's 1999 policy speech, the *SUSDEV 21* was completed in 2000 and provides a local definition of sustainability (Planning Department 2000: 72): "Sustainable Development in Hong Kong balances social, economic, environmental and resource needs, both for present and future generations, simultaneously achieving a vibrant economy, social progress and a high quality environment, locally, nationally and internationally, through the efforts of the community and the government" (Planning Department 2000: 21).

The question, of course, is who is going to balance these needs? Whose needs should be balanced and what kinds of efforts are required by the community and the government in the balancing act? *SUSDEV 21* has also produced a Computer-aided Sustainability Evaluation Tool (CASET)[5] to provide a technical mechanism for the evaluation of sustainability implications of policy and project proposals (Planning Department 2000: 89). Since December 2001, all policy bureaux and executive departments are required to carry out sustainability assessments of new strategic initiatives or major programmes which may have noticeable or persistent implications for the economic, environmental and social conditions of Hong Kong (SDU 2006). Since December 2003, the government has encouraged bureaux and departments "to set out the main sustainability assessment findings of their major proposals in the relevant public consultation documents to help facilitate better informed public discussion and building of community consensus" (SDU 2006). However, the indicator-driven tool is not particularly helpful in directing government officials to adopt an integrated approach to deal with sustainable development issues, nor does it provide "a verdict as to whether a proposal is sustainable" (Planning Department 1999: B5 quoted in Ng 2005: 476). In fact, such an assessment is absent in many recent planning controversies such as the debates on the construction of the cultural district and central Harbour reclamation (Ng 2005, 2006).

A Council for Sustainable Development was formed in 2003 by the CE "to advise the government on the priority areas in promoting sustainable development; the preparation of an integrative development strategy; to facilitate community participation and to promote public awareness and understanding of the principles of sustainable development" (SDU 2004). Members of the council are appointed by the CE and they are experts in the environmental, social and business sectors, as well as senior government officials. The council is currently chaired by the chief secretary for administration.

In 2001 for the first time in Hong Kong's history the principle of sustainable development was incorporated as one of the key objectives in a territorial development plan – *Hong Kong 2030: Planning Vision and Strategy* (HKSAR Government 2001). In 2004–2005, through rather widespread consultation and engagement, the Sustainable Development Council came up with a sustainable development strategy which was confined to solid waste management, renewable energy and urban living space. The 18-page document does not discuss the inter-relationships of these three sectors and most of the 15 initiatives outlined are rather general. The initiatives have been taken up by individual departments but the strategy does not seem to have created a wider impact within government or beyond.[6] There also seems to be no follow-up or monitoring of the implementation of these initiatives.

The Business Environment Council Limited (BEC) is a non-profit environment organization set up by the private sector to undertake environmental projects that indirectly or directly benefit the community.[7] Its vision is to enable the business in Hong Kong "a model for sustainable development in Asia through the integration of environmental and social responsibility into existing business practices" (BEC 2006). Another group of businessmen formed a "Vision for Hong Kong" study group (2002) with the assistance of Hong Kong Coalition of Service Industries and Hong Kong General Chamber of Commerce. They put forward a lot of recommendations, addressing problems of inter-governmental co-ordination and co-operation. It is, however, interesting to note that a lot of the problems identified are seen to be solvable by the government and few roles, if any, are identified for the community. While there are quite a few active green groups such as the Conservancy Association and Friends of the Earth, not many NGOs are interested in or knowledgeable about sustainable development. In September 2003, a group of non-government delegates who attended the second Earth Summit and were impressed by people's councils elsewhere, decided to set up a Hong Kong People's Council for Sustainable Development. While this group is dedicated to and passionate about sustainable development in Hong Kong, they face severe financial constraints in the course of advocating the concept.

Singapore: Environmental Qualities, Social Creativity but no Sustainability Rhetoric...

It is interesting to note that "sustainable development" as a multidimensional concept is not deliberated in the Singaporean government's policy discourse. However, environmental qualities are closely guarded in the Lion City to maintain its appeal to foreign direct investment. To the Singaporean Government, their Green Plan is equivalent to Agenda 21.[8] According to Ooi (2002: 459), since the 1960s government agencies have planted some two million trees in the city and developed parks in every neighborhood in the planned new town as part of the planning framework to develop Singapore into a garden city. Indeed, ironically, the development and management costs of these parks and trees are high compared to those for nature reserves (Ooi 2002: 459).

The past colonial economy and the current modern city-state have single-mindedly focused on economic growth and the maximum possible exploitation of land resources to develop the supporting infrastructure for such growth (Ooi 2002: 460). Substantial loss of natural habitat has occurred and much of the residue is still under the threat of future development pressure (Briffet et al. 2003: 183). The general approach of government ministries is still an engineering one relying on the use of technical solutions to protect the environment. While the achievement of a well-landscaped and clean urban environment is a laudable achievement in Singapore, the environment is often regarded as a secondary factor in favor of economic, social and technical issues (Malone-Lee 1993, Perry et al. 1997). In fact, Singapore's ecological footprint[9] is the highest among the four cities, 7.2 ha/person[10] (The Earth Council 1997).

The concern about environmental qualities is not translated into legislation that makes Environmental Impact Assessments (EIAs) compulsory for major developmental projects in Singapore. Instead, the Master Plan Commission has required EIAs of developmental projects which may pollute the environment. Regarding foreign investments, projects using or storing large quantities of hazardous substances are required to engage a third-party consultant to conduct EIAs to support the establishment of a plant in Singapore (UNESCAP 2003). Despite the absence of legislation requiring mandatory EIAs, Singapore has used the comprehensive planning process to ensure that industries are properly sited and environmental guarantees solicited from project proponents.

Although Singapore does not have a comprehensive Agenda 21 as specified in the First Earth Summit, they do have Trade 21, Industry 21 (I21), Productivity Action 21 (ProAct21), National Science and Technology Plan 2000, Technopreneurship 21, Construction 21, Franchise 21, Manpower 21 and SME 21 and Singapore 21 Report which was published in 1999. These various vision statements prove again that Singapore's primary focus in its development trajectory is economic growth. Nevertheless, as mentioned, the government has recently produced the *Singapore Green Plan 2012* (SGP2012). In preparing the SGP2012, Singapore launched a National Preparatory Process (NPP)[11] in 2001. Singaporeans from the "people, private and public" (3P) sectors contributed many ideas and suggestions. Released in 2002, the *Singapore Green Plan (SGP) 2012* is Singapore's blueprint towards environmental sustainability for the next decade. According to the Ministry of Environment (2003a), the SGP 2012 goes beyond green and clean and emphasizes the sustainability of the Singapore development process. Three "key thrusts" are identified in SGP 2012: "quality living environment" which includes "setting new air pollution policies; promoting the use of natural gas; maintaining the quality of coastal and inland water; reducing the need for landfill through recycling; and keeping down ambient noise levels"; "working in partnership with the community"; and "doing our part for the global environment" through work to "enhance international and regional environmental governance".

The government has also been active in promoting environmentally friendly innovations. The Innovation for Environmental Sustainability Fund provides assistance through grants to encourage and assist Singapore-registered companies to undertake innovative environmental projects which can help to meet the government's goal of environmental sustainability (National Environment Agency 2003a). A 3P Partnership Fund is also set up to facilitate the implementation of 3P partnership efforts between National Environment Agency and members of the "people, private and public" (3P) sectors in "environmental education; promotion of community participation in environmental activities; enhancement of environmental services or infrastructure; research on environmental issues; and activities which tap on the partners" expertise to solve problems or come up with innovative strategies" in order to achieve a sustainable, quality environment in Singapore (National Environment Agency 2003).

In this new economy era, the government also recognizes that creativity and collective wisdom in society should be valued. In the Singapore 21 Report, the government acknowledged that they have run too "tight a ship since independence". "While this has earned it a good reputation for being able to make decisions quickly and to respond nimbly to changing situations", the Report contends, "the 21st century brings a population increasingly different from the old one. They want more consultation, more say in setting directions. This can only come about if citizens play their part by contributing effort, initiative and ideas" (Singapore 21 Committee 1999: 48). Through various established channels such as the Town Council, the community centre, the Residents' Committees and the Community Development Councils, the government has urged the public to put forward suggestions, views and participation so that the people and public sectors can work in partnership, pooling their energies. The public sector is also urged to share more information with the community, thus facilitating an equal dialogue (Singapore 21 Committee 1999: 53–54). These will no doubt lead to an increased delegation of powers and a greater public involvement in taking responsibilities for running their own affairs including environmental protection (Briffet *et al.* 2003: 185). In fact, some local citizenry and citizen groups have been fighting for the carrying out of environmental impact assessment on the biodiversity in nature reserves (Ooi 2002). For instance, Nature Society (Singapore) (NSS) was founded as the Singapore branch of the Malayan Nature Society (MNS) in 1954. It became an independent society in 1991 (Goh 2001: 14). The society produced the *Master Plan for the Conservation of Nature in Singapore*. In the URA's Concept Plan, 90 per cent of the specified 3,000 ha of nature areas for conservation are sites proposed in the NSS Master Plan (Malone-Lee 1993: 5).

Taipiei: Strong Government Rhetoric and Innovative Community Actions

One can argue that Taiwan has, perhaps not conscientiously, adopted a "grow first, clean up later" strategy in its industrialization drive after the Second World War. After a long period of natural resource exploitation and ignorance of the negative consequences of development activities, endemic diseases and health problems prevailed around the sites of many state-owned enterprises and big companies (Tang 2003: 1036). However, it was not until the late 1980s, when the economy had moved beyond a mid-income level and the polity had begun to undergo democratization that governments, civil groups and economic enterprises began to undertake more rigorous environmental conservation efforts (Tang and Tang 2004: 176). The environmental movement in Taiwan has evolved in tandem with the democratization process (Tang and Tang 2000: 82). In 1987, the year the Brundtland Report was published, a cabinet-level Environmental Protection Agency was established and "sustainable development" was declared an official goal. Since then, a spate of environmental regulations has been enacted; personnel for environmental protection grew by more than 20 per cent; and environmental protection budgets doubled (Tang and Tang 2000: 83). In 1997, the National Council for Sustainable Development (NCSD) was established.

In May 2000, President Chen Shui-bian declared in his inauguration speech that Taiwan would be developed into "a sustainable green silicon island",[12] with the "emphasis on Green rather than Silicon, as Green symbolizes culture, sincerity and respect for the environment" (NCSD 2003). In the same year, the NCSD drafted the Agenda 21 of Taiwan: National Sustainable Development Strategy Guidelines (NCSD 2004). The NCSD has been set up "to enhance the protection of the environment and ecology, guarantee social fairness and justice, promote economic development, and establish a green silicon island, so as to promote citizens' living standards and pursue national sustainable development". The vision put forward by the NCSD is: "To create a safe, healthy, comfortable, beautiful, and sustainable living environment; build a pluralistic, harmonious, flourishing, vital and vigorous society, and be a responsible citizen of the global village" (National Sustainable Development Network: http://ww2.epa.gov.tw/nsdn/TWSIGN/content-E.htm).

It is interesting to see that key words such as economic growth or prosperity are not built into this vision. Instead words such as "flourishing, vital and vigorous" are used. Eight working groups have also been set up to pursue specific areas of sustainable development: sustainable vision; water and land resources; technology and industries; biodiversity; life and production; international environmental protection; health risks and sustainable education. These working groups are to work with other relevant public agencies. In 2002, the NCSD also produced the Taiwan Sustainable Development Action Plan which included 264 items of concrete action to serve as guidelines for the nation to enforce and carry out sustainable development.

Given the Taiwanese government's efforts in promoting sustainable development, the city government of Taipei has also focused on promoting sustainability in the course of economic development. The 2002 White Paper of Taipei's Urban Development championed the promotion of sustainable development as one of its seven objectives. The vision for urban development in Taipei is to make the city "an international metropolis with pluralistic orientation and high competitiveness". It is recognized that in doing so issues of sustainable development must be considered:

> Faced with the increasing international and regional competition, as well as the changing political and economic climate at home, Taipei City has to reinforce its interaction with the international community in order to boost further economic growth potentials. Under the impacts of globalization, of rapid information exchanges, of the growing local autonomy, of the rising community awareness, and *the need for sustainable development*, Taipei City must re-orientate itself as a pluralistic and international metropolis for the 21st century. (Department of Urban Development 2004, emphasis added)

To the Taipei City government, the goals are to "shape Taipei into a global city" and "to promote the city as one with advanced accessibility, comfortable pedestrian environment, ecological awareness, high living quality, and strong-flow of networks with other major cities of the world" (Department of Urban Development 2004). Seven goals and strategies of urban development, embracing elements of sustainable development are put forward to turn Taipei into "an accessible city; a pedestrian city; an eco-city; a humanistic city; a cyber-city; a global city; and a people's city". In January 2004, the Taipei City Sustainable Development Council was established to create "a world class capital city" encompassing "cyclic symbiosis of environment and resources", "progress sharing in secure society", and "intelligent growth of economy and technologies".[13] The current mayor has declared that "the City is fully determined to integrate sustainable development thinking into the planning and budgeting process, and strive to overcome the temporal and spatial limitations, in order to achieve the Sustainable Taipei visions through organizational innovation and re-creation, as well as continuous progress and improvement".[14] The vision of a "sustainable Taipei" consists of the following dimensions: "*Sustainable Taipei*: urban development with sustainable land use; *Eco-Taipei*: fully recycled and diversified urban ecology; *Clean Taipei*: urban environment with low energy consumption and pollution; *Secure Taipei*: safe, healthy and respectable urban living; *Cultural Taipei*: urban community with overall culture creation; *Knowledgeable Taipei*: urban production based on clean knowledge; *Network Taipei*: city with convenient and barrier-free urban network."[15] Altogether, 46 strategies, 96 action plans and 282 work items have been identified to implement Taipei's *Strategic Plan for the Sustainable Development of Taipei City – Agenda 21 for Taipei City* (Taipei City Government 2004: 11–12).

Regarding the social aspect of sustainability, Taipei residents and the city government have both been proactive in making joint planning decisions. In fact, compared to Hong Kong, the civil society in Taipei is much more active in promoting sustainable development as Taiwan's democratization proceeds. Many exciting things happened in 1989, two years after the lifting of the Emergency Decree and martial law. Initiated by a group of homemakers who were concerned about social and environmental issues of Taipei, the Homemaker's Union and Foundation was established and registered. Since its establishment, the Foundation has contributed to various community building and environmental protection initiatives (such as recycling used cooking oil to make soap and producing compost from kitchen waste) (Homemaker's Union and Foundation 2004). In the same year, a grassroots organization called "Citizen Solidarity against Urban Speculation" (or "Snails without Shells") summoned more than 10,000 people for a sleep-in demonstration at the most expensive section of real estate in Taipei to protest against high housing prices as a result of speculation by a few rich corporations. The event was organized by a group of primary school teachers and was supported by architects and city planning professionals. The organization later developed into two different social organizations: the Tsuei Ma Ma Housing and Community Service Association (TMM) and the Organization of Urban Re-s[16] (OURS) to champion social reform ideals (TMM Foundation for Housing and Community Service 2004). In fact, in 1994, the Council of Cultural Development established a "Comprehensive Community Rebuilding" program to fund participatory local community projects, thus helping to facilitate grassroots community development.

The Taiwan Business Council for Sustainable Development (BCSD) was created in December 1995 when its 13 founding companies joined the Earthplace Foundation. In 1997, 31 member companies officially and independently launched an enlarged and refocused BCSD Taiwan (http://www.bcsd.org.tw/eng/eng01.htm). Even though BCSD Taiwan is in place, most companies have not yet adopted long-term plans to reduce pollution (Lin and Wu 2003: 152). According to a survey by BCSD Taiwan, almost 80 per cent of business respondents know very little or do not know what constitutes corporate social responsibility (Lin *et al.* 2004). Nevertheless, there are individual companies which are carrying out socially and environmentally responsible projects as detailed in the Business Sustainable Development Newsletter.[17]

Shanghai: Top-down Initiatives – Sustaining Economic Growth through Resources Management

Similar to Taipei, Shanghai is subject to a national Agenda 21. China is among the world's first nations to produce a national Agenda 21. Part of the reasons for China's swift response to the call for concerns over environment and development in the first Earth Summit is that after more than a decade of open door policy, the environment in China has been rapidly degraded. The Chinese government realizes that if it does not manage resources utilization well, economic growth will soon hit the environmental limits (Ng *et al.* 2003). Hence, to China, sustainable development is more about utilizing ecological resources while the part on intra- and inter-generation equity is comparatively played down. In China, the promulgation and implementation of the country's Agenda 21 is through various sectoral plans and five-year socio-economic plans that all levels of governments have to prepare. As stated in Shanghai's Tenth Five Year Plan (FYP) (2001–2005), the "implementation of sustainable development strategy, improvement of urban ecological environment and cooperative development among economic, social, population, resources and environmental factors" are the key objectives of the FYP (SMDRC 2003).

Besides socio-economic FYPs, the goal of the second-round Three-Year Environmental Action Plan (2003–2005) is to build Shanghai to be a national green city, one of the most livable cities in the world with its clean air, clear water and green spaces. Four principles are involved: 1) *Implement sustainable development strategy*: enhance Shanghai's integrated competitiveness; improve urban environmental quality and protect citizens' health; and adopt ideas of "environmental priority, green civilization and sustainable development"; 2) *Roles of different stakeholders*: developers protect; polluters pay; manufacturers recycle; and users bear cost; 3) *High quality environmental planning*: high standards of pollution prevention, control and environmental infrastructure; and high-level environmental management; and 4) *Innovative institutional reform, policy or mechanism*: coordinated development in Shanghai's economic, social and environmental sectors.

Shanghai has published *China's Agenda 21: Shanghai's Plan of Action* in 1999 and the document has become a guidebook on sustainable development in Shanghai (LGICA21SH 1999). Similar to China's Agenda 21, the emphasis is on conservation and management of natural resources in the production process. The Action Plan covers the overall strategy, agriculture, industrial and energy production, pollution aspects, natural resources conservation, consumption patterns, population, city construction and capacity building issues.

In 2004, China established its Business Council for Sustainable Development.[18] The Council became the 48th member of the World Business Council for Sustainable Development's Regional Network in 2004 (CSR Newswire Service 2004). China BCSD is the result of a joint effort with the China Enterprise Confederation (CEC). Unlike the other three cities where civil societies have in one way or another promoted sustainable development, little is known about sustainability initiatives local community groups have undertaken in Shanghai.

Sustainability at a Glance

Having reviewed the rhetoric and commitments of these four cities, the following paragraphs examine what has happened on the ground.

In the executive government-led polity of economics-first Hong Kong, sustainability rhetoric has been in place, but instead of integrated actions the first sustainable development strategy is fragmented into three areas, the implementation of which is resourced through the existing compartmentalised administrative set-up. The third sector is enthusiastic in promoting sustainable development and joined-up governance but has suffered from shortage of resources and marginalization in the executive government-led commercial society. In the state-centered polity of Singapore, the government has deliberately avoided the controversial rhetoric of sustainable development. The paternalistic government, however, has pursued a "green and clean" environment to appeal to foreign investment and has encouraged the private and non-governmental sectors to engage in promoting environmentally friendly innovations. After all, Singapore is run like an "incorporated company". In the rapidly democratizing Taipei, the concept of sustainable development has gained political currency. Concerns by politicians are translated into government actions and civil society activism in the course of formulating plans, strategies, projects and community-based actions. In Shanghai, where sustainable development has become national development strategy, sustainability efforts have primarily been resource management-related, top-down and state-centered, with minor inputs from the "market" or civil society, if any.

Can we then postulate that Taipei should be the most sustainable city among the four as Taipei has formally launched a comprehensive sustainable development strategy? Naturally, one would expect industrial Shanghai to have more environmental problems than the other three cities as reflected in *Shanghai's Agenda 21* which addresses resources management, rather than multidimensional sustainable development issues. Although the Singaporean government has avoided the rhetoric of sustainable development, its tight control over politics, economy and society should place it in a unique position to build a model "green and clean" city. One may speculate that Hong Kong, while more vibrant and dynamic, probably would be inferior to the Lion City especially in environmental terms. Table 3 presents comparative economic, social and environmental data of the four cities.[19]

Table 3. Sustainable development at a glance

	Hong Kong	Singapore	Taipei	Shanghai
Cost of living ranking (2005)[a]	9th (2005)	34th (2005)	29th (2005)	30th (2004)
Government expenditure on:				
• Environment	3.9	2.4	4.4	n.a.
• Social welfare	13.0	n.a.	8.3	3.6
• Infrastructure/public works (% of total expenditure)[b]	11.2	8.5	12.5	22.5
Gini coefficient of income distribution (%, national figure)[b]	53	48	33	43
% of households receiving social security assistance[b]	13.0	0.01	1.6	2.6
% of population holding post-secondary qualification[b]	28.2	57.8	31.6	11.4
Proportion of work trips using public transport[c]	87	63	41	30
% of household expenditure on medical services[d]	2.2	3.3	8.4	6.0
Average living space (m² per household)[e]	37.6 (public rental housing)	104.4	102.4	88.0
No. of listed buildings[f]	77	42	64	181
Ecological footprint (ha/person) (national figure)[g]	6.1	7.2	4.7	1.6
% of wastewater with secondary treatment[h]	16.5	100	6.7	53.3 (1st level treatment)
TSP in microgram per cubic metre[i]	74	31	52	108
No. of noise complaints received per 100,000 population[j]	184	120	312	124
Per capita annual garbage production (kg)[k]	358	332	226	451

Sources:

[a]Mercer Human Resources Consulting, *Global/World Cost of Living Rankings 2005–2006*, http://www.finfacts.ie/costofliving.htm, viewed in May 2006. According to the website, "Mercer's survey covers 144 cities across six continents and measures the comparative cost of over 200 items in each location, including housing, transport, food, clothing, household goods and entertainment".

[b]*Hong Kong*: YOD: 2005. Census and Statistics Department, http://www.censtatd.gov.hk/home/index.jsp, and *Hong Kong in Figures*, http://www.censtatd.gov.hk/FileManager/EN/Common/hkinf.pdf, both viewed in May 2006.
Singapore: YOD: 2005. Department of Statistics, http://www.singstat.gov.sg/, viewed in May 2006.
Taipei: YOD: 2005. Department of Budget, Accounting and Statistics, Taipei City Government, http://english.taipei.gov.tw/dbas/index.jsp, viewed in May 2006. Figures on per capita GDP and GDP by industries are from: Taiwan Yearbook (2005).
Shanghai: YOD: 2004. Shanghai Municipal Statistics Bureau (2005). Gini coefficient is from: Wong (2003).

[c]*Hong Kong*: YOD: 2002, Transport Department (2003). Figure refers to the proportion of work trips using public transport and the details are as follows: franchised bus (37%); MTR (22%); KCR (6%); public light bus (PLB) (13%); taxi (3%); LRT (2%); tram (2%) and ferry (2%).
Singapore: YOD: 2000, Email contact with Mrs Geraldine Chan, Deputy Manager of Publicity and Programs, Corporate Communications Department of Land Transport Authority on Feb. 18, 2004. Figure refers to the percentage of all journeys to work made on public transport. The proportion of journeys to work using public transport is as follows: public bus (27%); company bus (7%); MRT (24%) and taxi (5%).
Taipei: YOD: 2003, Email contact with Mr Jason Tse-Ying Lin of Department of Transportation, Taipei City Government on Dec. 22, 2003. Figure refers to the usage rate of public transportation in Taipei metropolis which is collected from series of questionnaire surveys by Department of Transportation, Taipei City Government.

(*continued*)

(Continued)

Shanghai: YOD: 2001, Email contact with Mr Yifeng Cai of the Shanghai City Comprehensive Transportation Planning Institute on Feb. 18, 2004. Figure refers to the percentage of work trips using public transportation (transit – 26%, railway – 2.6% and taxi – 1.5%).
[d]*Hong Kong*: YOD: 1999–2000, Census and Statistics Department (2001).
Singapore: YOD: 2003, Singapore Department of Statistics (2003a).
Taipei: YOD: 2002, Department of Budget, Accounting and Statistics (2003). Figure refers to average monthly expenditure on medical and health care.
Shanghai: YOD: 2001, Shanghai Municipal Statistics Bureau (2002a). Figure refers to annual urban household expenditure on medical and health care.
[e]*Hong Kong*: YOD: 2002, Hong Kong Housing Authority and Housing Department (2003). Figure refers to the average living space per Housing Authority Public Rental Household of Hong Kong in 2002.
Singapore: YOD: 2000, Ministry of Trade and Industry (2000) and Singapore Department of Statistics (2000: 2, 17).
Taipei: YOD: 2002, Department of Budget, Accounting and Statistics (2003b).
Shanghai: YOD: 2001, Shanghai Municipal Statistics Bureau (2002b).
[f]*Hong Kong*: YOD: 2002, Leisure and Cultural Service Department (2002).
Singapore: YOD: 2003, Ministry of Information, Communications and the Arts (2003).
Taipei: YOD: 2003, Taipei City Government (2003b).
Shanghai: YOD: 2001, Shanghai Culture Year Book (2002).
[g]*Hong Kong and Singapore*: YOD: 1997, The Earth Council (1997).
Taipei: YOD: 1998, Forestry Bureau (2005).
Shanghai: YOD: 2002, Ecological footprint and biocapacity, downloaded from the Ecological Footprint webpage under The European Environment Agency, http://org.eea.europa.eu/news/Ann1132753060, viewed in May 2006.
[h]*Hong Kong*: YOD: 2003, Email contact with Ms Carmen Wong, Community Relations Officer of Drainage Services Department of the HKSAR Government, on Oct. 28, 2003.
Singapore: YOD: 2003, Email contact with Mr Tan Yok Gin, assistant director for director of Water Reclamation Department, Public Utilities Board of Singapore on Oct. 29, 2003.
Taipei: YOD: 2003, Email contact with Mr Lee Shu-Chuan, director of Sewerage System Office of Taipei City Government, Republic of China on Dec. 29, 2003.
Shanghai: YOD: 2001, Shanghai Municipal Statistics Bureau (2002c). Figure refers to the percentage of treated urban wastewater.

(*continued*)

(Continued)

[i] *Hong Kong*: YOD: 2002, Environmental Protection Department (2002). Figures are the averages of all stations.
Singapore: YOD: 2000, Ministry of the Environment (2000: 20–22). Conversions were made for SO_2 and NO_2 from microgram per cubic meter to ppm based on the NAAQS standards. The available CO data is of annual average rather than the standard 8-hour 2nd maximum reading.
Taipei: YOD: 2002, Department of Environmental Protection (2002). Conversions were made for SO_2 and NO_2 from ppb to ppm based on the NAAQS standards. The available CO data is of annual average rather than the standard 8-hour 2nd maximum reading.
Shanghai: YOD: 2002, Shanghai Environmental Protection Bureau (2003).

[j] *Hong Kong*: YOD: 2002, Information Services Department (2002: 493, Appendix 6).
Singapore: YOD: 2001, Email contact with Mr Charles Lee for head of Pollution Department of National Environmental Agency on Nov. 1, 2003; National Environmental Agency (2002) and Singapore Department of Statistics (2003b: Table 1.8). Figure is obtained by dividing the total number of noise complaints received (4984 in 2001, of which 192 are those from factories and 4792 are those from construction sites) by the total population of Singapore (4.131 million in 2001).
Taipei: YOD: 2002, Department of Budget, Accounting and Statistics (2003c: Table 261). Figure is obtained by dividing the number of petition cases on noise (8,252 in 2002) by the total population of Taipei (2.642 million in 2002).
Shanghai: YOD: 2002, Environmental Protection Bureau (2002) and Shanghai Municipal Government (2003).

[k] *Hong Kong*: YOD: 2006, *Monitoring of Solid Waste in Hong Kong – Waste Statistics for 2006* (Hong Kong: EPD).
Singapore: YOD: 2004, Ministry of Environment and Water Resources (2005).
Taipei: YOD: 2005, Taipei City Government (2006).

While Hong Kong has the highest GDP per capita among the four cities, it also ranks highest among the four in terms of the cost of living index (9th) and Gini coefficient (53 per cent), suggesting that social polarization is a major issue. In fact, unlike the other three cities, 13 per cent of its households are receiving social security assistance, which is considerable. Although a wealthy city by any standard, only 28 per cent of its population possesses post-secondary education. Hong Kong has done particularly well in terms of the public transportation network, which supports 87 per cent of work trips, and medical services, which cost a mere 2.2 per cent of household expenditure. However, in terms of the built and natural environment, there is much room for improvement when compared to, say, Singapore. Singapore's per capita GDP is close to that of Hong Kong but its cost of living index ranking is lowest among the four: 34th. In many respects, Singapore has outdone Hong Kong as a more livable and egalitarian society: average living space is much higher (104 m^2 compared to the average of public housing space of 38 m^2 in Hong Kong); 100 per cent of its wastewater is treated (compared to 16 per cent in Hong Kong); total suspended particulates (TSP) in air is 31 ug/m^3 (the figure for Hong Kong is 74 ug/m^3, almost 50% over the United States Environmental Protection Agency (USEPA) standard of 50 ug/m^3); the Gini-coefficient is 48 per cent; and 58 per cent of its population has post-secondary qualifications. Singaporeans also produce less per capita garbage (332 kg) when compared to Hong Kong (358 kg). Yet in terms of ecological footprint Singapore has a higher figure (7.2 ha/person) than Hong Kong (6.1 ha/person). In other words, the "clean and green" city is resource-intensive to build.

Taipei has a similar economic structure to Singapore (one-third industrial and two-thirds tertiary) though average per capita GDP is lower in Taiwan. Population density is much higher in Taipei (21,366 persons/km^2) than Singapore (10,353 persons/km^2). They rank 29th in the cost of living index. While one may speculate that Taipei's Gini coefficient should be higher than the national average of 33 per cent, the figure would probably be lower than that of Singapore. This can be confirmed by the fact that only 1.6 per cent of households are receiving social welfare assistance. About one-third of its population has post-secondary education, a figure higher than Hong Kong but lower than Singapore. While the population of Taipei city is only 2.6 million, there are over one million motorcycles. Car and motorcycle ownership rates are 276/1,000 and 393/1,000 population respectively.[20] Hence, only 41 per cent of the population use public transport and TSP level is 52 ug/m^3. The city also receives a large number of noise complaints. Nevertheless, Taipei has launched a very successful "waste reduction" program and municipal waste has been cut by 55 per cent in 2005 when compared to 1999, with a 38 per cent recycling rate and the closing down of two incinerators.[21] Taiwan's ecological footprint is also lower than Hong Kong and Singapore and stood at 4.67.

Shanghai's per capita GDP is the lowest among the four cities (only 15 per cent of Hong Kong) but its cost of living ranking is 30th, higher than Singapore, the per capita GDP of which is more than six times of Shanghai's. In many respects, data on Shanghai reflects the limitation of China's narrow interpretation of sustainable development as resources management in economic growth. We can see that more than one-fifth of the city's GDP in 2004 went to fixed capital investment. Its Gini coefficient, though lower than Singapore and Hong Kong, is considerable: 43 per cent. Only 11.4 per cent of its population has post-secondary qualifications. Only half of its wastewater receives some kind of treatment and the TSP in air doubles the USEPA standard: 108 ug/m^3. Its per capita garbage production almost doubles that of Taipei: 451 kg. We cannot get a city-level ecological footprint figure for Shanghai but one can assume that while the figure probably would be lower than the other cities, it should be much higher than the national average of 1.6 ha per person.

These statistics have painted a very interesting picture: the Government of Singapore, determined to build a "clean and green" city, has managed to provide a better quality of life for its citizens with a rather large ecological footprint; the Government of Taipei and its community have worked hard to try to transform a largely motorcycle and car-dependent society into a sustainable community with "zero-waste"; Hong Kong, with its loose rhetoric on sustainable development, has produced a society bisected with environmental problems and social polarization; and in Shanghai the strong emphasis on resources management has yet to make an impact on the rather appalling environmental scene not atypical of rapidly industrializing cities.

Concluding Remarks

The level of economic growth affects a city's social, economic and environmental performance as can be seen in Table 3 (Ng and Hills 2003). This paper, however, argues that the state of growth in these cities hinges on the perceptions, definitions and commitments of the government towards sustainable development. This is because all four cities have state-centred political economies. Although Hong Kong, Singapore and Taipei have supposedly free market economies, the government of Singapore is heavily involved in economic development and marketing the city to foreign investors. To a certain extent, this is also true of Taipei because of the legacy of the government's traditional role in "orchestrating" economic growth. The Hong Kong government has never explicitly "guided" the direction of economic growth but its dual role as the biggest land owner and development decision maker puts it in a unique position in "influencing" the city's path of development. As an unfolding socialist market economy with the strong legacy of a centrally planned economy, the Party-led government of Shanghai plays a hugely important role in the city's development.

The city of Taipei seems to exhibit the greatest dedication to the notion of sustainable development and government rhetoric and community actions should put it on a par with many Western cities having local Agenda 21 and promoting other sustainable development initiatives. However, while the rhetoric is strong, the statistics listed in Table 3 prove that a lot has yet to be done on the ground to move the city towards sustainable development. While Shanghai has signed most of the international conventions or protocols on the environment, it still considers economic growth as fundamental (a prerequisite) in sustainable development and resources management is the license to achieve it (Ng et al. 2003). Such an eclipsed understanding of sustainable development may do more harm than good in the longer term development of the city.

The Singaporean government relies basically on technical solutions to tackle its sustainability issues. The case of Singapore also reminds us that there is a fine distinction between being "green and clean" and being environmentally sustainable.

While Singapore has done an excellent job in terms of greening and sanitation, the city is far from sustainable, as indicated by its ecological footprint and the amount of garbage production. Hong Kong as an economics-first city has been paying rather tokenistic lip service to the ideas of integrated sustainable development. The government has been slow in putting rhetoric into action and so far the city has suffered from the lack of a sustainable development strategy or Agenda 21. The four state-centred cities have displayed a wide range of sustainability rhetoric and practices: from endorsing sustainable development in integrated policy making to reducing sustainable development to environmental policy concerns. These cities help us appreciate how difficult it is to ensure that everyone is speaking the same "language" when sustainability is at stake. In the case of CCP-led Shanghai, sustainable development is about ecological utilization of natural resources rather than inter- and intra-generational equity. For PAP-led Singapore, the priority is to have a green, clean, creative and innovative environment that can propel further growth. Taipei as a rapidly democratizing polity has adopted mainstream sustainable development rhetoric and actions. To a certain extent, this is also true for executive government-led Hong Kong, though in the economics-first city rhetorical commitments overwhelm real actions. All in all, these four cases prove that in order to "crack the sustainability practice codes" in state-centered Asian cities, understanding the perceptions, rhetoric and commitments of the governments towards sustainable development should be the first step.

Acknowledgement

The author would like to thank the three anonymous reviewers for their valuable and persistent comments. Financial support provided by the Research Group on Sustainable Cities of the University of Hong Kong and the University Development Fund in this project is also gratefully acknowledged.

Notes

1. For a brief overview of the evolution of the concept of sustainable development, please see introduction to this volume, 'Sustainable Development and Governance in East Asian World Cities'.
2. Unless stated otherwise, the sources of the information for the statistics cited below are listed in the tables.
3. For instance, in 1997, the Provisional Legislative Council passed the Legislative Council Bill. The Bill significantly reduced the number of voters from 2.6 million to only 18,000 for the nine seats of functional constituencies. It also changed the composition of the election committee from comprising 280 district councilors to 800 government appointed members. The proportional representation voting system was adopted (Yuan 2003: 33).
4. The main administrative and executive functions of the government are carried out by 11 policy bureaus in the government secretariat, and 67 departments and agencies, mostly staffed by civil servants. With the implementation of the accountability system for principal officials on July 1, 2002, the Chief Secretary for Administration, the Financial Secretary, the Secretary for Justice and 11 Directors of Bureaus are the most important officials within the government (HKSAR Government 2003). The principal officials are no longer civil servants. Instead they are political appointees who are accountable to the CE for the success or failure of their policy initiatives and the most senior civil servants are now called permanent secretaries (Cheung 2003).
5. The CASET has adopted eight guiding principles and 41 sustainability indicators. They can be downloaded from the SDU website: Guiding principles: http://www.susdev.gov.hk/html/

en/su/GuidingPrinciples_e.pdf; Sustainability Indicators: http://www.susdev.gov.hk/html/en/su/SustainabilityIndicators_e.pdf.
6. A copy of the progress report can be found in the SDU website: http://www.susdev.org.hk/en/pdf/InformationNoteA.pdf, viewed in May 2006.
7. See Business Environment Council webpage: http://www.bec.org.hk/general/e_home.php, viewed in May 2006.
8. See http://www.un.org/esa/agenda21/natlinfo/counter/singapore/inst.htm, accessed in December 2003.
9. "The Ecological Footprint is a measure of the 'load' imposed by a given population on nature. It represents the land area necessary to sustain current levels of resource consumption and waste discharge by that population" (http://www.sustaindane.org/main/EF1.htm).
10. According to the IMD (2003), Singapore's ecological footprint is 12.4. However, we cannot verify this figure in the original source cited (WWF 2002) which specified that they had inadequate data to calculate the city's ecological footprint. Hence, we have to discard this even higher figure.
11. To prepare for the World Summit on Sustainable Development (WSSD), the National Environment Agency (NEA) formed a WSSD National Preparatory Committee (NPC) to demonstrate national efforts to co-ordinate sustainable development activities. Three Focus Groups were set up to assist the NPC in making detailed preparations and recommendations in consultation with various stakeholders: one on "economic development issues"; one on "regional and international issues" and one on "environment and public health issues". The NPC and Focus Groups comprised members from the public, private and third sectors. They included representatives of professionals, businesses and NGOs with the government providing personnel to assist the focus groups in their work. Collectively, the work of the NPC and focus groups were known as the National Preparatory Process (NPP). The NPP served as a platform to involve local interest groups on environmental sustainability issues (Ministry of the Environment 2003b).
12. On May 20, 2000, President Chen declared, "at present, we need to immediately improve social order and environmental protection, which are important indicators of the quality of life. Building a new social order, we will let the people live and work in peace and without fear. Finding a balance between ecological preservation and economic development, we will develop Taiwan into a sustainable green silicon island" (NCSD 2003).
13. Goals and visions in the Sustainable Taipei Eco-city website: http://www.epb.taipei.gov.tw/tsd/english/goals.htm, viewed in May 2006.
14. Mayor's Declaration and Commitment in the Sustainable Taipei Eco-city website: http://www.epb.taipei.gov.tw/tsd/english/declaration.htm, viewed in May 2006.
15. Strategies and action plans in the Sustainable Taipei Eco-city website: http://www.epb.taipei.gov.tw/tsd/english/strategies.htm, viewed in May 2006.
16. Organisation of Urban Re-s stands for Organization of Urban Reformers, Revolutionaries, etc.
17. See note 18.
18. The WBCSD is a coalition of 170 international companies united by a shared commitment to sustainable development via the three pillars of economic growth, ecological balance and social progress. Its activities reflect the belief that the pursuit of sustainable development is good for business and business is good for sustainable development (CSR Newswire Service 2004).
19. Unless stated otherwise, the sources of information for the figures cited below are listed in Table 3.
20. Figure obtained from the Taipei City Government at the 2005 *Taipei International Sustainable Development Conference* held in International Conference Hall, Chinese Culture University, Taipei, Taiwan, November 2005.
21. Ibid.

References

Arce, A., 2003, Value contestations in development interventions: community development and sustainable livelihoods approaches, *Community Development Journal*, **38**(3), 199–213.
Astleithner, F. and Hamedinger, A., 2003, Urban sustainability as a new form of governance: obstacles and potentials in the case of Vienna, *Innovation*, **16**(1), 51–75.
Ayre, G. and Callway, R., 2005, *Governance for Sustainable Development [electronic resource]: A Foundation for the Future* (London and Sterling, VA: Earthscan).

Baker, S., Kousis, M., Richardson, D. and Young, S. (Eds), 1997, *The Politics of Sustainable Development: Theory, Policy and Practice within the European Union* (London: Routledge).

Beck, U., 1997, Global risk politics, in: M. Jacobs (Ed) *Greening the Millennium? The New Politics of the Environment* (Oxford: Blackwell Publishers), pp. 18–33.

Boyd, R. and Ngo, T.-W. (Eds), 2006, *State Making in Asia* (London: Routledge).

Bressers, H. T. A. and Rosenbaum, W. A., 2003, *Achieving Sustainable Development: The Challenge of Governance Across Social Scales* (Westport, CT and London: Praeger).

Briffet, C., Obbard, J. P. and Mackee, J., 2003, Towards SEA for the developing nations of Asia, *Environmental Impact Assessment Review*, **23**, 171–196.

Brodsgaard, K. E. and Young, S. (Eds), 2000, *State Capacity in East Asia: Japan, Taiwan, China and Vietnam* (Oxford: Oxford University Press).

Business Environment Council, 2006, http://www.bec.org.hk/general/e_home.php, viewed in May 2006.

Census and Statistics Department, HKSAR Government, 2001, *Hong Kong Statistics: 1999/2000 Household Expenditure Survey Average Monthly Household Expenditure by Commodity/Service Section/Group*, available at http://www.info.gov.hk/censtatd/eng/hkstat/fas/hes/hes_index.html, viewed on Feb. 12, 2004.

Chan, R. C. K., 1996, Urban development and redevelopment, in: Y. M. Yeung and Y. W. Sung (Eds) *Shanghai: Transformation and Modernization under China's Open Policy* (Hong Kong: The Chinese University Press).

Cheng, J. Y. S. (Ed), 2005, *The July 1 Protest: Interpreting a Historic Event* (Hong Kong: City University of Hong Kong Press).

Cheung, C. Y., 2003, Pamphlet on *Discussing Democratic Development: The Civil Service and Political Reform* (Hong Kong: Civic Exchange).

Cheung, P. T. Y., 1996, The political context of Shanghai's economic development, in: Y. M. Yeung and Y. W. Sung (Eds) *Shanghai: Transformation and Modernization under China's Open Policy* (Hong Kong: The Chinese University Press).

China Internet Information Centre (CIIC), 2003, *China's Political System*, available at http://www.china.org.cn/english/index.htm, viewed Nov. 26, 2003.

Chu, Y.-H., 1999, The institutional foundation of Taiwan's industrialization: exploring the state-society nexus, in: G. Ranis, S.-C. Hu and Y.-P. Chu (Eds) *The Political Economy of Taiwan's Development into the 21st Century* (Cheltenham: Edward Elgar), pp. 285–310.

Corporate Social Responsibility (CSR) Newswire Service, 2004, China now among WBCSD regional partners, *The Corporate Social Responsibility Newswire Service*, http://www.csrwire.com/article.cgi/2409.html.

Department of Budget, Accounting and Statistics, Taipei City Government, 2003a, *The Statistical Abstract of Taipei City for 2003: Family Income and Expenditure*, available at http://www.dbas.taipei.gov.tw/stat/abstract/Family_I.htm, viewed Sept. 4, 2003.

Department of Budget, Accounting and Statistics, Taipei City Government, 2003b, *Key Statistics Express*, available at http://www.dbas.taipei.gov.tw/state/express/E27-1.xls, viewed Dec. 11, 2003.

Department of Budget, Accounting and Statistics, Taipei City Government, 2003c, *The Statistical Abstract of Taipei City 2003: Environmental Protection*, available at http://www.dbas.taipei.gov.tw/stat/abstract/Environmental_P.htm, viewed Oct. 27, 2003.

Department of Environmental Protection, Taipei City Government, 2002, *Diagram of Air Quality of Taipei City in 2002*, available at http://www.epb.taipei.gov.tw/english/official/air_quality.htm, viewed Jan. 26, 2004.

Department of Urban Development, Taipei City Government, 2004, http://www.planning.taipei.gov.tw/TCDB/, viewed June 1, 2004.

Drysdale, P. (Ed), 2000, *Reform and Recovery in East Asia: the Role of the State and Economic Enterprise* (London: Routledge).

Environmental Protection Bureau, Shanghai City, 2002, *Shanghai Environmental Report 2002: Public Participation*, available at http://www.sepb.gov.cn/gongbao/linian2002.asp, viewed Nov. 2003.

Environmental Protection Bureau, Shanghai City, 2003, *2003 Shanghai Environmental Bulletin*, available at http://www.sepb.gov.cn/gongbao/inian2002.asp, viewed Nov. 7, 2003.

Environmental Protection Department, 2002, *Air Quality in Hong Kong 2002*, http://www.epd.hk/epd/tc_chi/environmentinhk/air/air_quality/files/aqr02c.pdf, viewed Jan. 27, 2004.

European Consultative Forum on the Environment and Sustainable Development, 2000, *Sustainable Governance: Institutional and Procedural Aspects of Sustainability* (Luxembourg: Office for Official Publications of the European Communities).

Evans, B., Joas, M., Sandback, S. and Theobald, K., 2005, *Governing Sustainable Cities* (London and Sterling, VA: Earthscan).

Forestry Bureau, 2005, Sustainability Index, http://www.forest.gov.tw/web/English2/ESI.htm, viewed in May 2006.

Ginther, K., Denters, E. and de Waart, P. J. I. M., 1995, *Sustainable Development and Good Governance*, (Dordrecht: M. Nijhoff).

Government Information Office, The Republic of China (Taiwan), 2003, *Taiwan Yearbook 2003: Government*, available at http://www.gio.gov.tw/taiwan-website/5-gp/yearbook/chpt04.htm, viewed Oct. 16, 2003.

Goh, D. P. S., 2001, The politics of the environment in Singapore?, *Asian Journal of Social Science*, **29**(1), 9–34.

Haas, M., 1999, A political history, in: M. Haas (Ed) *The Singapore Puzzle* (Westport, CT and London: Praeger).

Haque, M. S., 2004, Governance and bureaucracy in Singapore: contemporary reforms and implications, *International Political Science Review*, **25**(2), 227–240.

Heracleous, L., 1999, Privatisation: global trends and implications of the Singapore experience, *International Journal of Public Sector Management*, **12**(5), 432–444.

Hills, P. and Ng, M. K., 2000, Pathways to sustainability: a critical review of the sustainable development paradigm, *Asia-Pacific Development Monitor*, **2**(1), 1–31.

HKSAR Government, 1998, *1998 Policy Address*, available at http://www.policyaddress.gov.hk/pa98/english/speech.htm, viewed Dec. 22, 2004.

HKSAR Government, 2001, *Hong Kong 2030: Inception Report*, available at http://www.info.gov.hk/hk2030/hk2030content/inception/inception_cover.htm, viewed May 21, 2004.

HKSAR Government, 2003, *Hong Kong: The Facts: Government Structure*, available at http://www.info.gov.hk/hkfacts/govtstru/pdf, last updated April 2003.

Ho, K. L., 2000, Prime ministerial leadership and policy-making style in Singapore: Lee Kuan Yew and Goh Chok Tong compared, *Asian Journal of Political Science*, **8**(1), 91–123.

Ho, S.-Y. and Lee, J.-C., 2001, The political economy of local banking in Taiwan, *National Policy Foundation*, http://www.npf.org.tw/English/Publication/FM/FM-R-090-069.htm, viewed in May 2006.

Homemaker's Union and Foundation, 2004, *An introduction to the Homemaker's Union and Foundation*, available at http://forum.yam.org.tw/women.backinfo/recreation/bulletin/int01.htm, viewed April 1, 2004.

Hong Kong Housing Authority and Housing Department, 2003, *Housing in Figures 2002: Living Space of HA PRH Tenants; Population; and Land Domestic Households*, available at http://www.housingauthority.gov.hk/en/aboutus/resources/figure2002/0,,1-2519-4421,00.html, viewed Feb. 2, 2004.

Hyden, G., 2001, Operationalizing governance for sustainable development, *Journal of Development Studies*, **17**(2), 14–31.

IMD, 2003, *IMD World Competitiveness Yearbook 2003*, (Switzerland: IMD).

Information Services Department, HKSAR Government, 2002, *Hong Kong Yearbook 2002*, (Hong Kong: Information Services Department of the HKSAR Government).

Jacobs, J. B., 1997, Shanghai: an alternative centre?, in: D. S. G. Goodman (Ed) *China's Provinces in Reform: Class, Community and Political Culture*, (London: Routledge).

Jaskolski, M., 2004, In pursuit of sustainability? Challenges for deliberative democracy in a Tasmanian local government, *Environment and Planning B: Planning and Design*, **31**(2), 311–325.

Johnson, C., 1995, *Japan: Who Governs? The Rise of the Developmental State* (New York and London: W. W. Norton & Co.).

Kwon, Huck-ju (Ed), 2005, *Transforming the Developmental Welfare State in East Asia* (New York: Palgrave Macmillan).

Lam, N. M. K., 2000, Government intervention in the economy: a comparative analysis of Singapore and Hong Kong, *Public Administration and Development*, **20**(5), 397–421.

Lee, T., 2002, The politics of civil society, *Asian Studies Review*, **26**(1), 97–118.

Leisure and Cultural Service Department, HKSAR, 2002, *Antiquities and Monuments Office – Declared Monuments*, available at http://www.lcsd.gov.hk/CE/Museum/Monument/eng/declared/index.html, viewed Sept. 1, 2003.

Lin, S.-M., Li, X.-J. and Lin, J.-X., 2004, Survey on the market and potential of SRI in Taiwan, powerpoint presentation available from http://www.bcsd.org.tw/images/doc/701/20031024.htm, viewed Nov. 2003.

Lin, S.-L. and Wu, S.-S., 2003, The effects of corporate environmental performance and environmental capital investment on stock market valuation in Taiwan, in: J. A. Batten and T. A. Fetherston (Eds) *Social Responsibility: Corporate Governance Issues* (Amsterdam and Boston: JAI).

Local Group on the Implementation of China's Agenda 21 in Shanghai (LGICA21SH), 1999, *China's Agenda 21 – Shanghai's Plan of Action*, (Shanghai, China: Shanghai Translation Press).

Low, L. and Haggard, S., 2000, *State, Politics and Business in Singapore*, Working Paper Series, Singapore: Department of Business Policy, National University of Singapore.

Malone-Lee, L. C., 1993, Environmental planning, in: C. Briffett (Ed) *Action Proposals Environmental Issues in Development and Conservation*, School of Building and Estate Management, National University of Singapore (Singapore: SNP Publisher).

Ministry of the Environment, Singapore Government, 2000, *Annual Report 2000*, available at http://www.nea.gov.sg/cms/ccird/pg_18_23.pdf, viewed Jan. 28, 2004.

Ministry of the Environment, Singapore Government, 2003a, *The Singapore Green Plan 2012: Beyond Clean and Green, Towards Environmental Sustainability*, available at http://www.env/gov.sg/sgp2012/, viewed Sept. 25, 2003.

Ministry of the Environment, Singapore Government, 2003b, *The Singapore Green Plan 2012: Singapore's National Preparatory Process for WSSD*, available at http://www.env.gov.sg/sgp2012/national.htm, viewed Nov. 18, 2003.

Ministry of Environment and Water Resources, 2005, *Key Environmental Statistics 2005* (Singapore: MEWR).

Ministry of Trade and Industry, Singapore Government, 2003, *Economic Management: Philosophy*, available at http://www.mti.gov.sg/public/ECM/frm_ECM_Default.asp?sid=16&cid=78 and http://www.mti.gov.sg/public/ECM/frm_ECM_Default.asp?sid=17, viewed Nov. 24, 2003.

Ministry of Information, Communications and the Arts, Singapore Government, 2003, *National Monuments*, available at http://www.mita.gov.sg/pmb2.htm, viewed Sept. 30, 2003.

Ministry of Trade and Industry, Singapore Government, 2000, *News Room: Speeches – Speech by DPM Lee Hsien Loong at Key Hand-over Ceremony to 800,000th Homeowner*, available at http://www.mti.gov.sg/public/NWS/frm_NWS_Default.asp?sid=39&cid+373.

National Council for Sustainable Development (NCSD), 2003, *Action Plan: Taiwan Sustainable Development Action Plan*, available from National Sustainable Development Network at http://ivy2.epa.gov.tw/NSDN/en/project/index.htm, viewed Oct. 16, 2003.

National Council for Sustainable Development (NCSD), 2004, *Taiwan Agenda 21*, available from National Sustainable Development Network at http://sta.epa.gov.tw/NSDN/en/agenda/index.htm, viewed Oct. 2007.

National Environment Agency, Singapore Government, 2003a, *Innovation for Environmental Sustainability (IES) Fund*, available at http://app.nea.gov.sg/cms/htdocs/category_sub.asp?cid=42, viewed Nov. 2003.

National Environment Agency, Singapore Government, 2003b, *3P Partnership Fund*, available at http://app.nea.gov.sg/cms/htdocs/article.asp?pid=2160, viewed Nov 24, 2003.

National Environmental Agency, Pollution Control Department, 2002, *Environmental Protection Division Annual Report 2002*, available at http://www.nea.gov.sg/cms/pcd/PollutionControlReport2002.pdf, viewed Nov. 3, 2003.

Ng, M. K., 1999, Political economy and urban planning: a comparative study of Hong Kong, Singapore and Taiwan, *Progress in Planning*, **51**(1), 1–90.

Ng, M. K., 2005, Governance beyond government: political crisis and sustainable world city building, in: J. Y. S. Cheng (Ed) *The July 1 Protest Rally: Interpreting a Historic Event* (Hong Kong: City University of Hong Kong Press), pp. 469–500.

Ng, M. K., 2006, Globalisation and the making of Asian world cities, Introduction to a Special Issue on Asian World Cities in *Town Planning Review*, **77**(3), 251–256.

Ng, M. K. and Hills, P., 2003, World cities or great cities? A comparative study of five Asian metropolises, *Cities*, **20**(3), 151–165.

Ng, M. K., Chan, K. and Hills, P., 2003, Sustainable development in China: from knowledge to action, *International Journal of Environment and Sustainable Development*, **2**(1), 36–61.

OECD, 2002, *Governance for Sustainable Development: Five OECD Case Studies* (Paris: OECD).
Ooi, G.-L., 2002, The role of the state in nature conservation in Singapore, *Society and Natural Resources*, **15**, 455–460.
Parliament of Singapore, 2003, *Welcome to the Singapore Parliament*, available at http://www.parliament.gov.sg/AboutUs/Htdocs/aboutus-main.html, viewed Oct. 9, 2003.
Perry, M., Kong, L. and Yeoh, B., 1997, *Singapore: a Developmental City State*, World City Series (Singapore: Wiley).
Planning, Environment and Lands Bureau (PELB), 1993, *The Hong Kong Environment: A Green Challenge for the Community (Third Review of Progress of the 1989 White Paper: Pollution in Hong Kong – A Time to Act)* (Hong Kong: Government Printer).
Planning Department, 1999, *Study on Sustainable Development for the 21st Century: Background Information*, Unpublished materials distributed during an expert session on CASET.
Planning Department, 2000, *Study on Sustainable Development for the 21st Century: Final Report*, Hong Kong, prepared by Environmental Resources Management.
Raj-Kumar, C., 2003, Pamphlet on *Discussing Democratic Development: Electoral Systems* (Hong Kong: Civic Exchange).
Rose, R. and Shin, D. C., 2001, Democratization backwards: the problem of third-wave democracies, *British Journal of Political Science*, **31**, 331–354.
Roseland, M., 2000, Sustainable community development: integrating environmental, economic and social objectives, *Progress in Planning*, **54**(2), 73–132.
Selya, R. M., 1995, *Taipei* (Chichester: John Wiley).
Shanghai Culture Year Book, Editorial Department, 2002, *Shanghai Culture Yearbook 2002* (Shanghai, China: Zhong-guo da bai ke quan shu chu ban she) (in Chinese).
Shanghai Municipal Development and Reform Commission (SMDRC), 2003, *Shanghai's Tenth Five-Year Plan (2001–2005)*, available at http://jhw.sh.gov.cn/, viewed Sept 29, 2003.
Shanghai Municipal Government, 2003, *Shanghai Information: Population*, available at http://www.shanghai.gov.cn/gb/shanghai/node2314/node3766/node3783/node3784/index.html, viewed Nov. 7, 2003.
Shanghai Municipal Statistics Bureau, 2002a, *Shanghai Statistical Yearbook 2002, Statistics on Urban Household Expenditure 1980–2001*, available at http://www.chinainfobank.com, viewed Sept. 8, 2003 (in Chinese).
Shanghai Municipal Statistics Bureau, 2002b, *Shanghai Statistical Yearbook 2002*, Statistics on 2001 Housing Market in Shanghai, available at http://www.chinainfobank.com, viewed Nov. 18, 2003 (in Chinese).
Shanghai Municipal Statistics Bureau, 2002c, *Shanghai Statistical Yearbook 2002*, Statistics on Environmental Management in Shanghai (1998–2001), available at http://www.chinainfobank.com, viewed Oct. 28, 2003 (in Chinese).
Shanghai Municipal Statistics Bureau, 2005, *Shanghai Statistical Yearbook* (Shanghai: Statistics Bureau).
Shi, Y. and Hamnett, C., 2002, The potential and prospect for global cities in China: in the context of the world system, *Geoforum*, **33**, 121–135.
Singapore 21 Committee, 1999, *Singapore 21 Report*, available at http://www.singapore21.org.sg/s21_reports.pdf, viewed April 19, 2004.
Singapore Department of Statistics, 2000, KeyStats: Census 2000 – Singapore Population, available at http://www.singstat.gov.sg/keystats/c2000/handbook.pdf, viewed Feb. 2, 2004.
Singapore Department of Statistics, 2003a, *Household Expenditure Survey 2002/2003*, available at http://www.singstat.gov.sg/press/hes.html, viewed in May 2006.
Singapore Department of Statistics, 2003b, *Yearbook of Statistics Singapore*, available at http://www.singstat.gov.sg/keystats/annual/yos/yos18.pdf, viewed Nov. 3, 2003.
Subramaniam, S., 2001, The dual narrative of "good governance": lessons for understanding political and cultural change in Malaysia and Singapore, *Contemporary Southeast Asia: A Journal of International and Strategic Affairs*, **23**(1), 65–71.
Sustainable Development Unit (SDU), 2004, *SDU website*, available at http://www.susdev.gov.hk/html/en/su/index.htm, viewed May 21, 2004.
Sustainable Development Unit (SDU), 2006, *SDU Website: Sustainability Assessment*, available at http://www.susdev.gov.hk/html/en/su/sus.htm, viewed in May 2006.
Taipei City Government, 2003a, *Taipei City Government: Leading Taipei into the New Millennium*, available at http:www.taipei.gov.tw/English/government/city_introduction.htm, viewed Oct. 16, 2003.

Taipei City Government, 2003b, *Understand Taipei: Monuments,* available at http://www.taipei.gov.tw/cgi-bin/classify/index.cgi?class_id=A02,B15, updated July 31, 2003, viewed Oct. 28, 2003 (in Chinese).

Taipei City Government, 2004, *Sustainable Taipei Eco-city: Strategic Plan for the Sustainable Development of Taipei City – Agenda 21 for Taipei City* (Taipei: Taipei City Government).

Taipei City Government, 2006, Chapter 17: environmental protection, *Statistical Yearbook of Taipei City 2006,* (Taipei: City Government).

Taipei City Sustainable Development (SD) Council, 2004, *Taipei City's Vision, Declaration and Commitment for Sustainable Development,* available at http://tsd.utrust.com.tw/hope/index.htm, viewed June 1, 2004.

Taiwan Yearbook, 2005, http://www.gio.gov.tw/taiwan-website/5-gp/yearbook/, viewed in May 2006.

Tang, C.-P., 2003, Democratizing urban politics and civic environmentalism in Taiwan, *The China Quarterly*, **176**, 1029–1051.

Tang, C.-P. and Tang, S.-Y., 2000, Democratizing bureaucracy: the political economy of environmental impact assessment and air pollution prevention fees in Taiwan, *Comparative Politics*, **33**(1), 81–99.

Tang, S.-Y. and Tang, C.-P., 2004, Local governance and environmental conservation: gravel politics and the preservation of an endangered bird specifies in Taiwan, *Environment and Planning A*, **36**(1), 173–189.

The Earth Council, 1997, *Ranking the Ecological Impacts of Nations,* available at http://www.ecouncil.ac.cr/rio/focus/report/english/footprint/ranking.htm, viewed in May 2006.

The Economist Intelligence Unit, 2003, *Country Profile 2003: Singapore,* available at http://db.ein.com/report_dl.asp?mode=pdf&valname=CPSGD201, viewed Oct. 31, 2003.

Transport Department, HKSAR Government, 2003, Chapter 3 Characteristics of Trips Made within the HKSAR by Hong Kong Residents, *Travel Characteristics Survey 2002: Final Report,* available at http://www.info.gov.hk/td/eng/publication/tcs/Section%203%20(Eng).pdf, viewed April 1, 2004.

Tsao, K. K., 1996, Institutional and administrative reform, in: Y. M. Yeung and Y. W. Sung (Eds) *Shanghai: Transformation and Modernization under China's Open Policy* (Hong Kong: Chinese University Press).

Tsuei Ma Ma (TMM) Foundation for Housing and Community Service, 2004, *Towards a City for Citizens: Two Community Organizations in Taiwan,* available at http://www.enpo.org.tw/www/tmmweb/tmm/story/hmm-eng01.htm, viewed March 18, 2004.

United Nations Economic and Social Commission for Asia and the Pacific (UNESCAP), 2003, *Administrative Implementation of Environmental Impact Assessment in Singapore,* available at http://www.unescap.org/drpad/vc/orientation/legal/2D_std_sgp.htm, viewed Sept. 25, 2003.

"Vision for Hong Kong" study group, Hong Kong Coalition of Service Industries, Hong Kong General Chamber of Commerce, 2002, *A Blueprint for the Hong Kong World City* (Hong Kong).

Vonkeman, G. H. (Ed), 2000, *Sustainable Development of European Cities and Regions* (Dordrecht: Kluwer Academic Publishers).

Voss, J.-P., Bauknecht, D. and Kemp, R. (Eds), 2006, *Reflexive Governance for Sustainable Development* (Cheltenham, UK and Northampton, MA: Edward Elgar).

Whitehead, L., 2006, Some states of Asia compared from afar, in: R. Boyd and T.-W. Ngo (Eds) *State Making in Asia* (London and New York: Routledge), pp. 162–181.

Wong, L., 2003, Review of "China's New Rulers", *Socialist Review*, February, available at http://www.socialistrevuew.org.uk/article.php?articlenumber=8332, viewed Jan. 29, 2004.

Woo-Cumings, M. (Ed), 1999, *The Developmental State* (Ithaca, NY and London: Cornell University Press).

World Wide Fund for Nature (WWF), 2002, *Living Planet Report,* available at http://www.panda.org/news_facts/publications/living_planet_report/1pr02/index.cfm, viewed May 2007.

Wu, F., 2000, The global and local dimensions of place-making: remaking Shanghai as a world city, *Urban Studies*, **37**(8), 1359–1377.

Xinhua News Agency, 2003, Foreign capital integrated into Shanghai's economy: mayor, *Xinhua News Agency*, Aug. 28, available at http://www.china.org.cn/english/government/73666.htm, viewed Nov. 27, 2003.

Yep, R., 2003, Pamphlet on *Discussing Democratic Development: Political Reform and Political Parties* (Hong Kong: Civic Exchange).

Yeung, W.-C., Poon, J. and Perry, M., 2001, Towards a regional strategy: the role of regional headquarters of foreign firms in Singapore, *Urban Studies*, **38**(1), 157–183.

Yuan, Q. (Ed), 2003, *Xianggang hui gui y laid a shi ji (Major Events after Hong Kong's Reversion to Chinese Rule), 1997–2002* (Xianggang: San lian shu dian) (in Chinese).

Zhang, T., 2002, Urban development and a socialist pro-growth coalition in Shanghai, *Urban Affairs Review*, **37**(4), 475–499.

Zhang, X., 2003, Political structures and financial liberalization in pre-crisis East Asia, *Studies in Comparative International Development*, **38**(1), 64–92.

Zhang, W. B., 2000, Shanghai: a gateway to China's economic modernization, in: A. E. Anderson and D. E. Anderson (Eds) *Gateways to the Global Economy* (Cheltenham; Northampton, MA: Edward Elgar).

Building Collaborative Emergency Management Systems in Northeast Asia: A Comparative Analysis of the Roles of International Agencies

NAMKYUNG OH, AYA OKADA, & LOUISE K. COMFORT

ABSTRACT *Without systems for collaboration, response systems in disaster operations are easily fragmented and often compound loss of life and property for the affected citizens. Due to historical conflicts and rivalries, building collaborative systems for disaster management in Northeast Asia has posed challenges to Korea, Japan, and China. This study uses a brokerage role framework to analyze the network of response organizations that emerged following the 2011 Japan disasters and explores whether agencies used structural embeddedness to enhance collaboration in the response system. Findings show that brokers facilitating international collaboration were rare, indicating the importance of social capital and organizational capacities to function as brokers in international emergency management systems.*

Introduction: Policy Problem

The occurrence of a disaster is a local event; however, the adverse impacts of large-scale disasters spread rapidly and pose significant threats to neighboring countries. Due to lack of resources and information, damage from large-scale disasters cannot be managed by single nations alone. Thus, organizations in a disaster response system can easily be isolated and, accordingly, have difficulties in collaborating with other organizations in an international, interdisciplinary disaster response network.

In recent disasters, countries in Northeast Asia have suffered from similar problems – isolation and a resulting failure in collaboration. Although the United Nations Office for the Coordination of Humanitarian Assistance (OCHA) is designed to facilitate international collaboration among nations in disaster events, it is activated only by the nation that has experienced the disaster. Consequently, the secondary effects of a disaster that may be damaging for neighboring nations are not necessarily considered. Without prior established international agreements, the responsibilities of emergency response may be limited to separate countries, leading to scattered responses that may cause significant loss of life and property in neighboring countries. Especially, the high economic interdependency and geographic closeness among Korea, Japan, and China create greater vulnerability to the rapid spread of adverse impacts from large-scale disasters. Thus, fostering systematic collaboration among the three countries for disaster risk reduction and management becomes a critical issue.

Through collaboration in the response network, the logistical needs of domestic agencies may be supplemented by pooled resources of international agencies, and agencies that are most in need can reach available resources and information more easily (Lai 2012). The need for such international collaboration in North Asia is demonstrated by actual events. In 2003, the Severe Acute Respiratory Syndrome (SARS) epidemic illustrated that building international systems for collaborative response to disasters is a compelling, but difficult, challenge for Korea, Japan, and China. The 2011 Japan earthquake and tsunami and resulting meltdown of nuclear power plants in Fukushima raised a serious question about whether any national emergency response system in this region could manage such a large-scale disaster without support from international partners. In the future, Korea, Japan, and China anticipate that other disasters, such as the spread of pandemic influenza or volcanic eruptions of Mt. Paekdu and Mt. Fuji, could disrupt the region. In addition, the possible collapse of the North Korea regime and resulting influx of refugees into neighboring countries may cause significant instability, requiring full-scale collaboration among the three countries. Yet, due to competing economic, military, and political interests, this task of building an international collaborative system has been difficult for Korea, Japan, and China. Particularly, deep-rooted rivalries and distrust from conflicts and competitions over the last century have prevented collaboration to address shared risk in this region.

The Asia Pacific Disaster Report 2010 evaluated the current status of collaboration in Northeast Asia as *progress without cooperation*, while acknowledging significant advances of individual countries toward risk reduction and response. Korea has successfully managed recurrent natural disasters such as typhoons and floods; Japan set an international standard of disaster management that culminated in the Hyogo Framework for Action (UNISDR 2005), and China has proactively reduced risks from massive earthquakes and floods (ESCAP and UNISDR 2010). Yet those advances were limited to the national-level actions. The collaboration and coordination for response to large-scale disasters remains ineffective. In an effort to address this problem of shared risk, the three countries held the Korea–Japan–China Trilateral Summit in 2008 and adopted a Joint Statement on Disaster Management in 2009. However, the three nations have yet to develop even a rudimentary general organization that would facilitate international collaboration during disasters (ESCAP and UNISDR 2010).

In this study, we examined empirical evidence for this assessment, *progress without cooperation*, and explored possible strategies to establish international collaborative emergency management systems in Northeast Asia. Specifically, we focused on the brokerage role of international agencies in facilitating collaboration and coordination. In extreme events, large numbers of agencies participate and interact in a response network, resulting in more agencies that are not directly connected to others. This absence of connections causes isolation and significantly interrupts the flow of information and resources through the response network. With entrepreneurial brokers that make connections for collaboration opportunities, countries in Northeast Asia may integrate available resources and information from supporting international agencies to mobilize a wider, more effective response system.

We conducted a brokerage roles analysis of the inter-organizational network that evolved following the 2011 Japan disaster to explore whether international agencies worked as brokers and, if so, in what context? Further, we sought to assess the conditions under which international agencies may be strategically utilized and strengthened to serve as mediating organizations for future disasters in this region.

Strategic Use of Brokers in Building Collaborative Emergency Response Systems

The joint efforts of three nations – Korea, Japan, and China – took meaningful steps forward; however, since those initiatives came from national government agencies, they were government-centric efforts posing significant challenges to developing substantive international collaboration in Northeast Asia. First, inter-agency collaboration includes highly complex dynamics among agencies from different levels of jurisdiction that cannot be governed by classic hierarchy (Comfort et al. 2009). Second, if only top public agencies are expected to play critical roles, contributions from local governments, private and nonprofit agencies would be easily undervalued. Third, when national-level governments do not consider external organizations as partners, it is difficult for them to build the professional trust which is critical for inter-organizational collaboration. Accordingly, the current top-down approach reveals weaknesses in managing collaboration among public, private, and nonprofit agencies which depends upon voluntary commitment to shared goals. This problem, in turn, causes ineffectiveness in utilizing resources and information from private and nonprofit actors that usually operate on the periphery of the government-centric network.

Given these constraints, the current top-down efforts need to be supplemented by some alternative strategies. The first strategy is to create strong ties[1] among all agencies, and accordingly to pursue a dense network[2] (Coleman 1990). In most cases, creating and maintaining strong ties with all other agencies is not possible due to excessive transaction costs (Williamson 1981). In contrast, the use of brokers as collaboration facilitators (Burt 1992), is a more feasible strategy for managing inter-organizational collaboration in response to extreme events. As Watts and Strogatz (1998) suggested, when network size increases with more participants, a dense network becomes sparser, creating structural holes as strategic positions (Burt 1992). In this less dense network, agencies create clusters or sub-groups in which they keep strong ties within clusters. Yet when clusters do not build ties with others, they face severe problems of isolation. In this situation, communication takes longer than usual and critical information circulates within groups before it circulates between groups, causing the distortion, rejection, or corruption of critical information.

This isolation problem generates greater needs for intermediaries (Granovetter 1973). As Burt (1992) said, if structural holes can be filled with competent and entrepreneurial brokers, the flow of information and resources becomes more efficient and effective since brokers identify unconnected individuals and create links for collaborative opportunities. In this analysis, we consider an international collaborative system as networked governance (Jones et al. 1997) in that multiple organizations create an interdependent structure where one unit is not merely the formal subordinate of the others in a networked arrangement (O'Toole 1997). Through dynamic interactions, organizations have specific embedded positions in a network, and this structural embeddedness creates both opportunities and limitations for organizations (Granovetter 1985).

There are four types of structural embeddedness in an emergency response network. Some agencies are isolated from others, others take leading positions and serve as coordinators, some are peripheral in that their interactions depend mostly on the coordination of brokering agencies, and others take brokerage roles and strategically use their embeddedness in the network to maximize individual or network benefits, using their strategic positions. When agencies are isolated, they have difficulty in getting available resources and information required for their operations, fail in fulfilling their duties as components of the system, and finally trigger the cascade of the entire system's collapse (Comfort et al. 2004; Boin and McConnell 2007). In contrast, if there are brokering agencies that facilitate the flow of resources and information, organizations can more easily collaborate to achieve the shared goal of the system. Brokers do not necessarily have their own resources and information. Rather, they have controls on the flow of resources and information among other actors, and they take advantage of their embedded positions in a network. Thus, the question for the strategic use of brokers in the emergency response context is how to make those brokers work for the shared goal of the whole emergency response system, instead of their own particular interests.

Augmenting the strategic use of brokers, social capital has been identified as a complementary factor for effective response to disasters (Quarantelli 1989; Kapucu 2006; Aldrich 2012). Social capital is a collective asset that forms and accumulates through social investments in relations (Lin 1999). When agencies build social capital within the systems, individual agencies gain access to valued resources and information, and leverage assets from other agencies in the systems (Baker 1990; Putnam 1995; Knoke 1999). Moreover, with social capital, agencies share a set of common values that serve as a base for effective collaboration (Coleman 1988). Yet, in the response systems operating in Northeast Asia, international and domestic organizations lack reliable, stable interactions and, accordingly, have difficulties in building collaborative relations with other organizations.

To operationalize brokerage roles of organizations that fill the structural holes in a network, Marsden (1982) defined any brokered exchange as a relation involving at least three actors, two of whom are the actual parties to the transaction and one of whom is the intermediary or broker. According to Gould and Fernandez (1989), there are five brokerage roles: coordinator, consultant, gatekeeper, representative, and liaison. For the identification of those roles, they suggested using ego-network[3] analysis as the methodological approach. By definition, ego is an agent connected to every other actor in an ego network. If others are not connected directly to one another, and if only ego has connections with other agencies, ego may serve as a broker. As such, ego falls on the paths between the other actors in the network (Hanneman and Riddle 2005). According to the typologies outlined by Gould and Fernandez (1989), the coordinator is an agent that brokers a relation between two members of the same group; the consultant mediates a relation between two members of the same group, but is not itself a member of that group;

Table 1. Typology of brokerage roles

Type of brokerage role	Conceptual diagram	Definition
Coordinator	A—B—C	Ego who is "brokering" (node B), and both the source and destination nodes (A and C) are all members of the same group.
Consultant	A—B—C	Ego B is brokering a relation between two members of the same group, but is not itself a member of that group.
Gatekeeper	A—B—C	Ego B is acting as a gatekeeper. B is a member of a group who is at its boundary, and controls access of outsiders (A) to the group.
Representative	A—B—C	Ego B is in the same group as A, and acts as the contact point or representative of the group to outsiders
Liaison	A—B—C	Ego B is brokering a relation between two groups, and is not part of either.

Notes:* Reorganized from Hanneman and Riddle (2005).
** Hanneman and Riddle used the conceptual typology of brokerage roles by Gould and Fernandez (1989).

the gatekeeper is a member of a sub-group who is at the boundary and controls access to the group for external actors; the representative is a member of a sub-group who represents that group in connection to external partners; and the liaison is an agent that connects a relation between two groups, but is not part of either. The various types of brokerage roles are visualized in Table 1.

Using brokerage analysis with the response network following the 2011 Japan disasters, we explored what organizations took what types of brokerage roles, under what conditions agents served as brokers, and what structural problems existed in the response systems.

Case Introduction

The most recent catastrophic event in Northeast Asia, the 2011 Tohoku, Japan triple disasters (2011 Japan disasters) serves as an actual case to analyze the interactions among Korea, Japan, and China in response to an extreme event. The severe impact of the cumulative 2011 Japan disasters warranted full-scale collaboration among Korea, Japan, and China to reduce disaster risk. The adverse effects, particularly the radioactive pollution from the Fukushima power plants, posed significant threats to Japan's neighboring countries. Occurring after the trilateral efforts among the three nations since 2008, the disasters provide a rare opportunity to assess whether any significant progress in collaboration has developed since that time.

The 2011 Tohoku disasters escalated as the cumulative consequences of interacting eco-socio-technical events. On March 11, 2011, a magnitude 9 undersea earthquake occurred off the coast of Oshika Peninsula in northeast Japan. This powerful earthquake triggered three massive tsunami waves that caused 15,883 deaths across 20 prefectures (National Police Agency of Japan as of July 10, 2013), and economic losses of US$169

Figure 1. Simulated diffusion of radioactive contamination toward neighboring countries

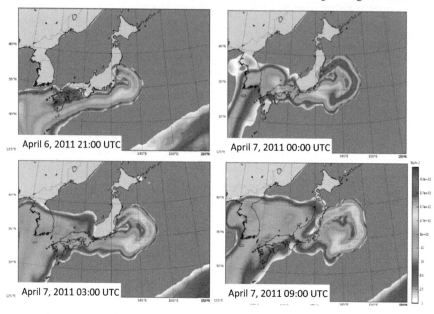

Source: Norsk Institutt for Luftforskning (NILU), Simulation analysis conducted on April 2, 2011.

billion (Cabinet Office of Japan 2011a). The worst incident occurred when the tsunami caused level 7 meltdowns (International Nuclear and Radiological Event Scale) at three reactors in the Fukushima Daiichi Nuclear Power Plant complex (Cabinet Office of Japan 2011b). This release of radioactive material brought about the unprecedented evacuation of residents within a 20 km radius of the Fukushima Daiichi Nuclear Power Plant (Cabinet Office of Japan 2011b).

Figure 1 shows simulated dispersion of radioactive contamination to Korea and China, based on local sea currents from Hokkai Island toward the East Sea (Sea of Japan). This release of toxic water into the Pacific Ocean caused significant concern to the governments and citizens of Korea and China. According to *Kyodo News* (August 7, 2013), the Government of Japan announced that 300 tons of toxic water have been flowing from the Fukushima plant into the Pacific Ocean daily since the disasters. Due to the sea contamination, the Korea government banned 49 items of sea food from eight prefectures; the China government prohibited all kinds of sea food from ten prefectures of Japan (*Donga Newspaper* August 1, 2013) and concerns for safety significantly reduced tourism and fisheries in Korea and China (KBS News, August 4, 2013).

The 2011 Japan disasters revealed weaknesses of the response systems in Northeast Asia. Historically, the most frequent and major disasters in this region were earthquakes, so earthquakes garnered the largest and most systematic investment in the nations' portfolio of disaster risk reduction actions, especially in Japan (Comfort et al. 2013). Compared to earthquakes, tsunamis and nuclear meltdowns have not been considered to be major risks, thus response operations were not well planned or exercised by the countries in this region. When the triple disasters occurred, the emergency response system of Japan was severely tested and overwhelmed, due to the low level of preparedness for tsunami and nuclear meltdown. Failure in response to the nuclear reactor breach at the Fukushima Daiichi Nuclear Power Plant was highlighted as a major concern among decision makers in Japan (Rebuild Japan Initiative Foundation 2012; National Diet of Japan 2012).

More importantly, the response to the triple disasters demonstrated that a single nation's disaster response system does not have sufficient capacity to cope with the domino effect of consecutive disasters in a very short time frame. However, Japan did not seek support from its international partners, and initially refused help that was offered by international actors (*Yomiuri*, March 18, 2011; Nakauchi 2011) until the situation rapidly degenerated to the point that the disasters seriously threatened the national security of Japan and neighboring countries. Although the formal UN OCHA system was activated upon the request of Japan's government, Japan did not request formal international assistance until March 24, 2011 (UN OCHA 2011).

Data Source and Analysis

To determine the interactions among participating actors in the 2011 Japan disasters response system, we used secondary data – structured data from content analysis of news reports that were coded and developed by Okada. Okada coded the reported interactions in *Yomiuri* newspaper articles from one day after the Tohoku earthquake and the following three weeks (March 12, 2011–April 1, 2011). The coded data from content analysis was used as an input to social network analysis (SNA). This three-week period covered essentially the response operations that were taken by local, national, and international public agencies, as well as those of business and nonprofit organizations. To run the brokerage roles analysis, we produced one-mode network (organization × organization) and identified five types of brokerage roles for individual agencies in the 2011 Japan disaster response system.

Findings from Analysis

With social network analysis, we first calculated descriptive features of the response system that formed following the 2011 Japan disasters. According to Table 2, 1,101 agencies participated in the response system. Among them, 689 organizations (62.6%) were isolated from other agencies. Thus, far less than half of the total number of organizations (412, 37.4%) built and maintained direct collaborative ties with other agencies in the system. Due to this significant degree of isolation, the entire network size is relatively small, with 644 total collaboration ties. The average number of ties for each agency is 1.563 and this reveals that each organization did not have more than two organizations as collaboration partners during their response operations.

Since the focus of this study is on the strategic use of international agencies as brokers in the response system, we explored how international agencies participated and interacted with others during response to the 2011 Japan disasters. Figure 2 shows the frequency distribution by source of funding and level of jurisdiction of participating agencies. There were 119 nonprofit (10.8 per cent), 392 private (35.6 per cent), and 590 public (53.6 per cent) organizations. Also, there were 166 international (15.1 per cent), 244 local/municipal (22.2 per cent), 173 prefectural/regional (15.7 per cent), and 518 national (47.0 per cent) agencies engaged in response operations within this system.

Table 2. Descriptive statistics of the 2011 Japan disaster response system

	Total number of actors	Number of non-isolated actors	Network size (total number of ties)	Average ties per non-isolated actor	Isolation (%)
2011 Japan Disasters	1,101	412	644	1.563	62.6%

Figure 2. Number of organizations by source of funding (left) and level of jurisdiction (right).

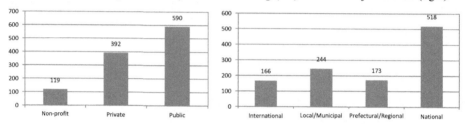

Judging from the dominant number of public and national organizations, this system is government-centric in that public agencies at the national level played the leading roles in this response system. The series of disaster management laws and plans in Japan primarily focus on public organizations, mainly at the national level, as key responders and decision makers. Nevertheless, there were still a significant number of nonprofit and private agencies from all levels of jurisdiction participating in response operations, so it was not an excessively government-centric system.

Figure 3 presents the network map of inter-organizational interactions in the system (all isolated agencies were removed from this network for ego-network analysis purposes) and shows limited evidence of the strategic use of international agencies as brokers in the system. Excluding totally isolated activities of international agencies, we identified three major interaction patterns of international agencies in the system.

First, in many cases, international agencies formed small sub-groups or clusters that were isolated from other sub-groups in the network. International agencies created and maintained collaborative ties to within-group partners, but did not develop connections to external sub-groups or leading coordinating agencies in the system. Consequently, the responding activities of isolated international agencies were not effectively coordinated with leading agencies in the domestic response system. For example, multiple international Red Cross agencies interacted with the Japan Red Cross, but the cluster of those interactions was not connected to brokering or leading agencies that took the central position in the network (refer to section #1, Figure 3).

Second, in contrast to the first type of interaction, some international agencies had brokers that connected them to others through coordinating agencies. For example, various types of international support from individual country governments reached Japanese domestic agencies through the Ministry of Foreign Affairs ("mofa_min" in highlighted section #2 of Figure 3). While these agencies had access to leading agencies due to their

Figure 3. Network map of the 2011 Japan disasters response system with ego network of the United States Army.

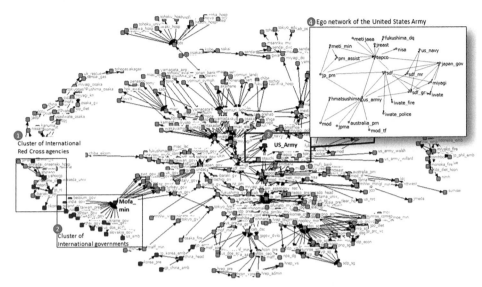

Notes: 1. This network map was created from Ucinet 6 software (Borgatti et al. 2002). 2. Isolated organizations were removed from this network map 3. Section #4 presents ego network of the United States Army with agencies within two-link distance. 4. The list of acronyms in ego network of the United States Army is available in the following table.

Acronym	Organization	Acronym	Organization
australia_pm	Office of the Prime Minister, Australia	meti_min	Office of the Minister of Economy, Trade, and Industry
fukushima_dq	Disaster Headquarter, Fukushima Prefecture	miyagi	Miyagi Prefecture
Hmatsushima	Higashi Matsushima City, Miyagi Prefecture	mod	Ministry of Defense, Japan
Iwate	Iwate Prefecture	mod_tf	Integrated Task Force, Minister of Defense
iwate_fire	Fire Department, Iwate Prefecture	nisa	Nuclear and Industrial Safety Agency
iwate_police	Prefectural Police, Iwate Prefecture	pm_assist	Office of the Assistant to Prime Minister, Japan
Jaea	Japan Atomic Energy Agency	sdf	Self Defense Force, Japan
japan_gov	Government of Japan	sdf_gr	Japan Ground Self-Defense Force
jp_pm	Office of the Prime Minister, Japan	sdf_mr	Japan Maritime Self-Defense Force
Jpma	Japan Pharmaceutical Manufacturers Association	tepco	Tokyo Electric Power Company
Jreast	East Japan Railway Company	us_army	United States Army
Meti	Ministry of Economy, Trade and Industry	us_navy	United States Navy

embedded peripheral positions in a network, they had too many connections to reach others. This complex situation caused significant corruption in information and delays in transactions. For both cases – isolated clusters of international agencies (highlighted #1) and peripheral agencies with connections through brokers (highlighted #2) – the structural positions of international agencies were not central, but isolated or peripheral, and their reachability to/from others was significantly lowered due to their embedded positions.

For the third type of interaction, some international organizations, even though rarely visible in this network, took central positions and served as leading agencies facilitating inter-agency collaborations in the network. As shown in Figure 3, the United States Army ("us_army" in highlighted section #3 of Figure 3) is located at the center of the network and actively moderated operations of various other agencies in the system. The strategic use of international agencies as brokers can enhance the competencies of the overall emergency response system, since they serve as channeling agencies for critical resources and information. However, except for the United States Army, no other international organization served as a brokerage agency in the 2011 Japan disaster response system.

Through intuitive interpretation of the network map, we identified the international agencies' roles and their structural embeddedness in the 2011 Japan disasters response network. The significant finding is that most international agencies and their operations were not effectively coordinated with Japanese domestic agencies, due to their peripheral status and the lack of brokers. Rather, the sub-groups of international agencies were disconnected from the central actors of the overall response system, and some international agencies did not develop mutual collaboration ties among the Japanese agencies, as they were moderating agencies. The distance (defined as the number of connections between two agencies in SNA) from international to leading agencies was too great, as the international agencies needed to pass through several mediating agencies to reach other domestic agencies. According to the distance analysis from Ucinet 6 software, even though this measure depends on the definition of centrality, international agencies roughly had 4.7 degrees of separation from major coordinating agencies in the system. This means that peripheral international agencies needed on average four to five connections to reach leading agencies. This distance caused significant delays in delivering resources to other agencies in the system.

To corroborate the lack of brokers in the system, we analyzed the ego network of international agencies and calculated the number of brokerage roles played by international agencies. "Ego" is an individual focal node in SNA, and the network map can be created centering on any specifically interested ego node (Borgatti 1997). Thus, the ego network analysis identifies the structural embeddedness of individual focal nodes. Because the ego network analysis puts each node at the center of the network, pairs of other nodes "go between" the focal ego node. This feature enables calculation of the number of brokerage roles that each ego node played during the response phase of the 2011 Japan disasters.

Table 3 presents the frequency distribution that was created from ego network analysis and G&F Brokerage roles analysis (refer to Table 1 for conceptual diagram). For the identification of membership, G&F Brokerage roles analysis requires a partition vector indicating the membership of an actor in a network. Based on each agency's membership, G&F Brokerage roles analysis creates clusters and calculates the type and frequency of brokerage roles by individual agencies. As a partition vector, this study used the level of jurisdiction.

Table 3. Top 19 brokering organizations in the 2011 Japan disasters response network

Name	Coordinator	Gatekeeper	Representative	Consultant	Liaison	Total
Office of the Prime Minister, Japan	104	159	165	66	180	674
Government of Japan	15	161	28	101	198	503
Tokyo Electric Power Company	1	15	19	76	71	182
Iwate Prefecture	1	10	13	66	73	163
Secretary General, Democratic Party of Japan	2	6	31	51	42	132
Miyagi Prefecture	15	19	12	5	9	60
Fukushima Prefecture	1	11	3	21	21	57
Office of the Chief Cabinet Secretary, Japan	0	0	0	13	29	42
Ministry of Land, Infrastructure, Transport and Tourism	12	6	8	1	3	30
Office of the Minister of Foreign Affairs	0	9	0	4	16	29
United States Army	**0**	**5**	**3**	**17**	**4**	**29**
Secretary General of Liberal Democratic Party	6	12	3	1	3	25
Self Defence Force, Japan	0	0	11	8	6	25
Ministry of Health, Labour and Welfare	0	9	0	7	6	22
Office of the Secretary General, New Komeito Party	6	6	4	1	3	20
Office of the Minister of Economy, Trade, and Industry	3	5	3	3	5	19
Japan Ground Self-Defense Force	2	4	4	2	4	16
Office of the Deputy Chief Cabinet Secretary, Japan	0	0	0	14	0	14
Office of the Defense Minister, Japan	8	0	2	0	0	10

Notes: 1. Created from Ucinet 6 software (Borgatti et al. 2002).
2. Cut point for choosing top 19 organizations is 10 brokerage roles.

From G&F brokerage role anaysis, this table shows the top 19 organizations that most actively played brokerage roles during the response to the 2011 Japan disasters. Major public agencies such as the Office of the Prime Minister, Iwate and Fukushima Prefecture governments, and the Self Defence Force of Japan took key brokerage roles in this network. In addition to various governmental departments and political parties, Tokyo Electric Power Company (TEPCO, 2012) also served as a major brokering agency in this network. Considering the severity of the Fukushima nuclear powerplant meltdown, TEPCO necessarily took a significant brokerage role. Specifically, the Office of the Prime Minister, the Government of Japan, TEPCO, Iwate Prefecture, and the Secretary General of Democratic Party were identified as the top five brokers who conducted the majority of brokering operations (73.8 per cent, 1,654 out of 2,240 brokerage roles).

When sorted by types of brokerage roles (Gould and Fernandez 1989), the Office of the Prime Minister played the most frequent brokerage role. Especially, during the response phase, the Office of the Prime Minister took the roles of coordinator, liaison, and representative, which shows its coordination of the majority of public sector operations. Similarly, the Government of Japan served as a critical broker for the types of gatekeeper, consultant, and liaison roles. This means that support and joint operations from external agencies needed to pass through the "gate" of the Government of Japan. At the same time, collaboration from all different levels of jurisdictions in the public sector (consultant role) and coordination among different groups of agencies (liaison role) were played within the National Center for Emergency Management of Japan. As revealed in Table 3, the major brokerage roles in this network were played by domestic public and private agencies, including TEPCO.

Regarding the brokerage roles played by international agencies, as shown in Figure 3 and Table 3, only rarely did international agencies serve as brokers in this network. Thus, the G&F brokerage analysis results are compatible with the previous interpretations of the network map. Most international agencies played only one or two brokerage roles in different categories. Some served as gatekeepers and others took liaison or consultant positions. If the operations of individual international agencies were well coordinated, the G&F brokerage analysis would show that a significant number of international agencies took coordinator, liaison, and representative roles in connecting to other agencies within the network. Moreover, Table 3 and Figure 3 empirically support the evaluation of the Asia Pacific Disaster Report 2010, "Korea, Japan, and China have yet to develop even a rudimentary general organization" to guide coordinated and collaborated operations in response to large-scale disasters in this region.

The highlighted section #4 of Figure 3 shows that, among 166 international agencies that participated in the system, only the United States Army ("us-army") played critical brokerage roles. Since the US Army is defined as an international agency by the partition vector, rather than a coordinator role, this agency would have taken other types of brokerage roles such as gatekeeper, representative, or liaison that connect international to domestic agencies in the response system. Yet, interestingly, it mostly played consultant roles (58.6 per cent, 17 out of 29 brokerage roles) when compared to the frequency of other brokerage roles such as gatekeeper, representative, or liaison. Also, the US Army did not play a coordinator role in this response network; that is, it did not keep a close collaboration with other international agencies.

According to the ego network map and table attached to Figure 3, we found that the United States Army mainly brokered response operations among Japanese agencies such as the Self Defence Force, the Office of the Prime Minister, and the Tokyo Electric Power Company. Clearly, through collaboration with Japanese agencies, the US Army played critical brokerage roles to address impending threats from the meltdown of nuclear power plants in Fukushima. It created connections for active interactions with domestic agencies (refer to section #4 of Figure 3 and attached table), and served as a major facilitator in promoting collaboration among domestic agencies. Not limited to the role of supporting agency, the United States Army took a leading position in the response network, or at least counted as a major actor, to deal with difficulties from the nuclear power plant meltdown.

Considering the reluctance of the Japanese government to accept interventions from international agencies, the consultant role played by the United States Army is a notable phenomenon. This case presents a possible use of competent international agencies as brokers in an international collaboration system. If any international agency has appropriate expertise and experience that domestic agencies do not have, that agency can be successfully integrated into the national-level emergency management system to coordinate and facilitate collaboration.

Discussion

The strategic use of international agencies as brokers is critical to build collaborative systems in Northeast Asia. Especially, the accumulating experience of international collaboration for humanitarian issues such as disaster management will provide a valuable base for further serious collaboration among Korea, Japan, and China. Applying brokerage role analysis to the disaster response system that emerged following the 2011 Japan disasters, we identified the major structural features of the system, explored what agencies acted as key brokers in the network, and assessed what conditions were critical to build collaborative systems among the countries in Northeast Asia.

Since the 2004 Sumatra Earthquake and Tsunami, the UN Office for the Coordination of Humanitarian Affairs (OCHA) has established the *cluster model* as a means of achieving the widest collaboration in facilitating international response to disasters. OCHA in theory acts as a broker between the nation that needs assistance and international organizations that have resources, knowledge, and skills to offer in response to extreme events. According to the 2005 Humanitarian Response Review (Adinolfi et al. 2005), the design is to develop clusters of organizations that share skills and interests in humanitarian relief, such as food, shelter, water and sanitation, health care at different levels of disaster operations that include both representatives of the disaster-afflicted country and international organizations.

To implement the cluster model, OCHA specifies the use of a lead UN organization to achieve system-wide efficiency in managing information and resources. OCHA emphasized the interoperability within each unit of the network (such as UN, Red Cross, and NGOs) and between networks. In terms of coordination, the cluster framework assumes that lead organizations take responsibility for coordination and collaboration at the sectoral, regional, and international levels. The OCHA coordinating system, while available through the United Nations, can only be activated by the nation requesting assistance. Since Japan did not request UN assistance until March 24, 2011 nearly two weeks after the triple disasters occurred, the cluster system was not actively engaged as the response system evolved.

The findings show that, except for the US Army, international agencies rarely played the brokerage roles to coordinate the scattered, isolated operations of individual agencies in the system. Consequently, when domestic agencies sought to collaborate with international agencies, it was difficult for them to identify contact points that could mediate their operations with international agencies. In some cases, we identified a small number of connections between domestic and international agencies. Yet, even for these cases, the distance and number of connections between two collaborating agencies was too far for any individual agent to reach other agencies easily.

One possible explanation regarding the lack of international agencies as brokers in the system is that the situation reflected the traditional attitude of the Japanese government in dealing with international actors in the emergency management context. The Japanese government has been reluctant to accept interventions from foreign agencies. This hesitant attitude toward international support partially came from inefficiency and ineffectiveness in coordinating international assistance that they experienced during the 1995 Kobe Earthquake (Kajiwara 2012). When several consecutive disasters hit Japan in 2011, the Japanese government initially refused the offer from the US to support the Fukushima crisis (*Yomiuri* Newspaper, March 18, 2011). Also, the Japanese government did not announce the precise nuclear fallout map that the US provided (*Asahi* Newspaper, June 18, 2012), and it took time for the Ministry of Foreign Affairs to carefully match the needs in disaster affected regions with the offers of assistance from international agencies (Nakauchi 2011).

This finding, a lack of international agencies as brokers, empirically confirms the Asia Pacific Disaster Report's (UNISDR 2010) evaluation, *progress without cooperation* in building collaborative emergency management systems in Northeast Asia. As confirmed by brokerage role analysis, there was no firmly established consensus on shared goals that could be activated to facilitate collaboration in the response network of the 2011 Japan disasters. Even though the 2011 Japan disasters occurred a year after this report, the progress has been only nominal, symbolic gestures from top-level politicians of three countries. Thus, international agencies could not work as brokers as outlined in the OCHA cluster model. Although OCHA specifies the use of a lead organization as a core coordinator in a clustered network, the role of coordinator is broadly defined, being limited to monitoring, training, reporting, and evaluating functions. From a brokerage role perspective, we argue that lead organizations should serve as brokers that facilitate collaboration among participating agents, using their social capital and specific expertise to build collaboration with target agencies.

In contrast, whereas there was no official agreement for collaboration in case of disasters, the US Army played the critical brokerage roles in the response system and actively participated, collaborating with the lead domestic agencies in the system. This sharp contrast reveals two critical conditions for serving as brokers in an emergency management network.

First, to achieve effective collaboration in actual disaster situations, major lead agencies need to build reliable, stable connections to cultivate social capital among agents prior to an extreme event. Since the 1950s, US Army and Self Defense Force of Japan (SDF in Section #4, Figure 3) have collaborated for the various national and regional security issues in Northeast Asia; thus they built sufficient social capital that could be utilized in response to the 2011 Japan disasters. As shown in Figure 3, the US Army and SDF kept strong ties for the coordination of individual operations, especially response to the nuclear related disasters. On the contrary, international agents from Korea and China did not have long-term relations and the resulting absence of social capital prevented them from serving as brokers in the system. Content analysis by Okada provides examples for the importance of social capital for inter-agency collaboration. When the Japanese government urgently needed external support, it selected the US Army as a collaboration partner[4] (*Yomiuri*, March 14, 2011), and established an Integrated Task Force and Japan–US Joint Coordination Office to strengthen partnership and critical information sharing between the two actors (*Yomiuri*, March 18, 2011).

Second, the US Army's specialized capacities to deal with nuclear related disasters enabled it to play critical brokerage roles in the system. According to the content analysis, the US Army provided special equipment to SDF and TEPCO such as high pressure water tanks, protective gear preventing exposure to radiation, and fire trucks to discharge two tons of water from the #3 reactor building in Fukushima Daiichi Nuclear Power Plant and experts to operate that special equipment (*Yomiuri*, March 19, 2011a, 2011b). These two conditions, social capital and organizational competencies, created a significant difference in the embedded positions of international agents in the system, revealing the importance of enabling agents to serve as brokers in the emergency management system.

Policy Implications and Limitations

Based on findings from the brokerage analysis, we propose four considerations to building collaborative systems in Northeast Asia. First is the strategic use of brokers in building an international emergency management system. The *strategic use* denotes the intentional creation of brokers to facilitate the flow of resources and information rather than depending on the accidental presence of brokers (Oh 2012). Toward this purpose, organizations may actively locate the weak ties or structural holes in a network and identify potential agents that could serve in brokerage roles and facilitate inter-agency collaboration.

Second is the conduct of substantial planning efforts beyond repetitive nominal agreements among Korea, China, and Japan to address the *progress without cooperation* problem. Thus, the OCHA cluster model needs to define clear roles and procedures that include options for neighboring nations that are threatened by secondary consequences of a major disaster to activate requests for assistance. This substantial planning effort requires that lead agencies take an active role in identifying available international agents for collaboration, explore their expertise and resources that can be mobilized in actual response situations, and, most importantly, support efforts to enable those agents to work together in the preparedness phase of disaster management. For example, since the 2004 Indian Ocean Tsunami and Earthquakes, regional countries – Indonesia, Malaysia, Thailand, India, and Philippines – have engaged in joint planning efforts to enhance the effectiveness of international collaboration (Telford and Cosgrave 2007).

The third implication is the significance of social capital among lead international agencies. For the cultivation of social capital, agents in the response system need to have stable, continuing interactions with partners as illustrated by the collaboration between the US Army and SDF. Before the 2011 disasters in Japan, the two agencies had already built and maintained a close, collaborative partnership. The US Army, as demonstrated in Hurricane Katrina response operations (US House of Representatives 2006), is well equipped to deal with disasters and has highly experienced personnel to advise operations in response to the nuclear power plant meltdown. In a disaster context, a joint planning approach is critical since it allows managers to locate partners, evaluate their specialties and resources, open communication channels, and build rapport with partnering personnel.

Lastly, the strategic use of brokers in building international collaborative systems requires the entrepreneurship of brokering agencies. Brokering agencies should be entrepreneurs that create public value from their operations. Entrepreneurs in collaborative systems in Northeast Asia should be brokers that search, define, and add value by expanding their reach to agents that are eager to share their valuable resources in a network (Moore 1997; Goldsmith and Eggers 2004). Consequently, the role of brokers in a network cannot be that of a mere deliverer of information and resources. Rather, brokers need to be critical value creators in a network that interprets the demands and culture of the multiple participants in an international emergency management system and coordinates the scattered efforts of agents to minimize the vulnerability of their system from disasters. In this regard, Burt (2005) argued for the development of an entrepreneurial network in which there is a large number of entrepreneurs who fill the structural holes of the network, and these entrepreneurial brokers mediate the flow of resources and information within the response system, recognizing the discrepancies among agencies.

Countries in Northeast Asia expect various types of natural or man-made disasters in the near future. For example, there is a high possibility of the abrupt collapse of the North Korea regime. Since there is no national system to manage this possibility, the security and living conditions of the North Korean people would deteriorate significantly and adverse effects would spread quickly to neighboring countries. Facing this situation, international agents in this region would be required to play leading roles in supporting the North Korean people. Under these conditions, the strategic use of international agents as brokers for collaborative and coordinated responses to future disasters would become even more essential. If there are agents that take brokerage roles for multinational and multi-sectoral collaboration in Northeast Asia, many unexpected disasters will be managed in a more effective and timely manner.

This study, using SNA, compared the roles of international agents to explore how to strategically build international collaboration systems in Northeast Asia and why the existence of brokers is critical. The application of SNA to emergency management has advantages in exploring structural features of networks and revealing locations for policy intervention (Carley 2004). Current studies applying SNA to emergency management face limitations in assessing the impact of different types of network on actual performance of disaster response, due to the lack of an empirical link between the structure of disaster response networks and their performance. Accumulating findings from applications of SNA to emergency management will provide an analytic opportunity to compare performance of different disaster response networks.

Acknowledgments

Financial support for this study was provided by a grant from POSCO Visiting Fellowship, East–West Center. The authors wish to thank Dr Denny Roy for his sincere support for the completion of this study.

Notes

1. Strong ties in a network means firmly established and direct connections between two agencies (nodes) through which they can communicate, interact, and collaborate.
2. Density is the ratio of the number of adjacencies that are present divided by the number of pairs. This means the proportion of all possible dyadic connections that are actually present (Hanneman and Riddle 2005).
3. *Ego* is an individual focal node in a network. *Neighborhood* is the collection of all other nodes to which ego has a connection at some path length. In social network analysis, the neighborhood is one step away from ego node; that is, it includes only ego and actors that are directly adjacent.
4. "US Army ships began providing relief activities for mega-earthquake in East Japan ... this is the first time the US Army is engaged in full emergency relief for a disaster that occurred within Japan" (Yomiuri, March 14, 2011).

References

Adinolfi, C., Bassiouni, D., Lauritzsen, H. and Williams, H., 2005, *Humanitarian Response Review*. Office for the Coordination of Humanitarian Affairs.
Aldrich, D. P., 2012, *Building Resilience: Social Capital in Post-Disaster Recovery*, (Chicago, IL, USA, University of Chicago Press).
Asahi Newspaper, 2012, Nuclear fallout map left unattended: US provided map not utilized for nuclear accident evacuations (in Japanese), page 2, 18 June.
Baker, W., 1990, Market networks and corporate behavior. *American Journal of Sociology*, **96**, pp. 589–625.
Boin, A. and McConnell, A., 2007, Preparing for critical infrastructure breakdowns: The limits of crisis management and the need for resilience. *Journal of Contingencies and Crisis Management*, **15**(1), pp. 50–59.
Borgatti, S. P., 1997, Structural holes: Unpacking Burt's redundancy measures. *Connection*, **20**(1), pp. 35–38.
Borgatti, S. P., Everett, M. and Freeman, L. C., 2002, *Ucinet for Windows: Software for Social Network Analysis*, (Harvard, MA: Analytic Technologies).
Burt, R. S., 1992, *Structural Hole*, (Cambridge, MA: Harvard University Press).
Burt, R. S., 2005, *Brokerage and Closure: An Introduction to Social Capital*, (New York: Oxford University Press).
Cabinet Office of Japan, 2011a, *Estimates of Damage in the Great East Japan Earthquake* (in Japanese). Available at http://www.bousai.go.jp/2011daishinsai/pdf/110624-1kisya.pdf (accessed 11 July 2013).
Cabinet Office of Japan, 2011b, *White Paper on Disaster Management* (in Japanese). Available at http://www.bousai.go.jp/kaigirep/hakusho/pdf/H23_zenbun.pdf (Accessed 11 July 2013).
Carley, K. M., 2004, Estimating vulnerabilities in large covert networks, in: *9th International Command and Control Research and Technology Symposium*, September 14 2004, Vienna, VA, Evidence Based Research.
Coleman, J. S., 1988, Social capital in the creation of human capital. *American Journal of Sociology*, **94**, pp. S95–S120.
Coleman, J. S., 1990, *Foundations of Social Theory*, (Cambridge, MA: Harvard University Press).
Comfort, L. K., Ko, K. and Zagorecki, A., 2004, Coordination in rapidly evolving disaster response systems: The role of information. *American Behavioral Scientist*, **48**, pp. 295–313.
Comfort, L., Oh, N. and Gunes, E., 2009, The dynamics of disaster recovery: Resilience and entropy in hurricane response systems 2005–2008. *Public Organization Review*, **9**(4), pp. 309–323.
Comfort, L. K., Okada, A. and Ertan, G., 2013, Networks of action in catastrophic events: The March 11, 2011 Tohoku disasters. *Earthquake Spectra*, **29**(s1), pp. S387–S402.
Donga Newspaper, 2013, Government just is advertising sea foods from Japan are safe, page 3, 1 August.
Goldsmith, S. and Eggers, W. D., 2004, *Governing by Network: The New Shape of the Public Sector*, (Washington DC: Brookings Institution).
Gould, R. V. and Fernandez, R. M., 1989, Structures of mediation: a formal approach to brokerage in transaction networks, in. *Sociological Methodology*, **19**, pp. 89–126.
Granovetter, M., 1973, The strength of weak ties. *American Journal of Sociology*, **78**(6), pp. 1360–1380.
Granovetter, M., 1985, Economic action and social structure: The problem of embeddedness. *American Journal of Sociology*, **91**, pp. 481–493.
Hanneman, R.A., and Mark, R., 2005, *Introduction to Social Network Methods*, (Riverside, CA: University of California Press).
Investigation Committee on the Accident at the Fukushima Nuclear Power Stations of Tokyo Electric Power Company, 2012, *Final Report*.
Jones, C., Hesterly, W. S. and Borgatti, S. P., 1997, A general theory of network governance: Exchange conditions and social mechanisms. *Academy of Management Review*, **22**(4), pp. 911–945.
Kajiwara, M., 2012, Overseas help part 3: Lessons learnt from Kobe on accepting international assistance (in Japanese). *The Asahi Shimbun Globe*, page 7, 23 October.
Kapucu, N., 2006, Interagency communication networks during emergencies boundary spanners in multiagency coordination. *The American Review of Public Administration*, **36**(2), pp. 207–225.
KBS News, 2013, Concerns for Radioactive Contamination: Continuing cancellation of Japan Tours (in Korean), 4 August.
Knoke, D., 1999, Organizational networks and corporate social capital, in: S. M. Gabbay (Eds) *Corporate Social Capital and Liability* (Boston, MA: Kluwer), pp. 17–42.
Kyodo News, 2013, 300 tons of toxic water flowing into sea from Fukushima plant daily: Gov't, page 4, 7 August.

Lai, A. Y. H., 2012, Towards a collaborative cross-border disaster management: A comparative analysis of voluntary organizations in Taiwan and Singapore. *Journal of Comparative Policy Analysis: Research and Practice*, **14**(3), pp. 217–233.

Lin, N., 1999, Building a network theory of social capital. *Connections*, **22**(1), pp. 28–51.

Marsden, P., 1982, Brokerage behavior in restricted exchange networks, in: P. V. Marsden and N. Lin (Eds) *Social Structure and Network Analysis* (Beverly Hills, CA: Sage Publications), 201–218.

Moore, M. ,H., 1997, *Creating Public Value: Strategic Management in Government*, (Cambridge, MA: Harvard Press).

Nakauchi, Y., 2011, Accepting international support for the great east japan earthquake: Responding to offers from over 190 countries and regions (in Japanese). *Rippo to Chosa*, **317**, pp. 65–69.

National Diet of Japan Fukushima Nuclear Accident Independent Investigation Commission (in Japanese), 2012, *Main Report*.

National Policy Agency of Japan, 2013, *Damage Situation and Police Countermeasures associated with 2011 Tohoku district – off the Pacific Ocean Earthquake* (in Japanese).

Oh, N.. 2012, Strategic uses of lessons for building collaborative emergency management system: comparative analysis of hurricane Katrina and hurricane Gustav response systems. *Journal of Homeland Security and Emergency Management*, 9(1), Article 10.

O'Toole, L. J., 1997, Treating networks seriously: Practical and research-based agendas in public administration. *Public Administration Review*, **57**(1), pp. 45–52.

Putnam, R. D., 1995, Bowling alone: America's declining social capital. *Journal of Democracy*, **6**, pp. 65–78.

Quarantelli, E. L., 1989, Conceptualizing disasters from a sociological perspective. *International Journal of Mass Emergencies and Disasters*, **7**, pp. 243–251.

Rebuild Japan Initiative Foundation, 2012, *Independent Investigating Committee for Fukushima Nuclear Accident Research Report (in Japanese)*, (Tokyo: Discover 21).

Telford, J. and Cosgrave, J., 2007, The international humanitarian system and the 2004 Indian Ocean earthquake and tsunamis. *Disasters*, **31**(1), pp. 1–28.

United Nations Economic and Social Commission for Asia and the Pacific (ESCAP) and UN International Strategy for Disaster Reduction (UNISDR), 2010, *Protecting Development Gains: Reducing Disaster Vulnerability and Building Resilience in Asia and Pacific*. Asia-Pacific-Disaster-Report 2010.

United Nations International Strategy for Disaster Reduction Secretariat (UNISDR), 2005, *Hyogo Framework for Action 2005-2015: Building the Resilience of Nations and Communities to Disasters*.

United Nations International Strategy for Disaster Reduction Secretariat (UNISDR), 2010, *Asia Pacific Disaster Report 2010: Protecting Development Gains*.

United Nations Office for the Coordination of Humanitarian Affairs (UNOCHA), 2011, *Japan Earthquake & Tsunami Situation Report No. 12*. 23 March 2011.

U.S. House of Representatives, 2006, *A Failure of Initiative: Final Report of the Select Bipartisan Committee to Investigate the Preparation for and Response to Hurricane Katrina*. Report no. 109–377, Washington, DC: US Government Printing Office.

Watts, D. J. and Strogatz, S. H., 1998, Collective dynamics of 'small-world' networks. *Nature*, **393**(6684), pp. 409–410.

Williamson, O. E., 1981, The economics of organization: The transaction cost approach. *American Journal of Sociology*, **87**(3), pp. 548–577.

Yomiuri Newspaper, 2011, *The great east Japan earthquake: US army carriers in action, assisting shipments* (in Japanese). 14 March.

Yomiuri Newspaper, 2011, *Fukushima daiichi nuclear accident: increasing distrust from the US Government* (in Japanese). 18 March.

Yomiuri Newspaper, 2011a. *Assistance: cooperation between Japan and the US expands* (in Japanese). 19 March.

Yomiuri Newspaper, 2011b. *Reactor #3 at Fukushima daiichi: watering continues for days* (in Japanese). 19 March.

Crucial Factors in Implementing Radical Policy Change: A Comparative Longitudinal Study of Nordic Central Agency Relocation Programs

HARALD SÆTREN

ABSTRACT *Why do public policies succeed or fail? The aim of this article is to contribute to answering this enduring research question in policy research through a comparative study of the variable efforts by Nordic governments to relocate their central agencies from the capital regions over a period of several decades. This was a radical redistributive policy program premised on a policy instrument – coercion – which was very alien to political systems characterized as consensual democracies. Hence, it is no surprise that only two out of seven relocation programs of any substance were successful. The really intriguing research question here is how any relocation program was achievable at all in a policy context where this was very unlikely. A broadly based multi-theoretical analytical framework linking interest groups, institutions, human agency in the form of policy entrepreneurship/design and situational factors is employed to solve this research puzzle. Findings from this study offer important contributions to the following research fields: comparative public policy, radical policy change and most specifically the so-called third generation of public policy implementation research.*

Theme, Research Question, Background and Motivation

How can we explain strikingly different results when three very similar countries are pursuing an identical policy – moving central agencies from their respective capital regions – even when two of them, Finland and Norway, are doing their best to draw lessons from the undisputed leader – Sweden – in terms of successful policy performance? The observed cross-national pattern in policy performance is also counterintuitive based on information about prior national legacies in this policy domain. This is the main research question this study attempts to answer.

Relocation programs in all three countries during the 1960s and 1970s were intended to alleviate a similar Nordic problem context: increasing regional imbalances due to heavy out-migration of people from peripheral rural areas and subsequent large in-migration to urban centers, affecting especially the capital regions (Stenstadsvold 1975; Nordrefo 1988, pp. 2–3; Isaksson 1989, pp. 14–23).

The study is motivated by a general interest in a more fundamental and enduring research question in political science with respect to policy change: what are the conditions under which public policies succeed or fail (Ingram and Mann 1980; Capano and Howlett 2009). Approaching an answer here requires investigation of cases with both types of policy results. Thus, this study includes both successful and failed attempts at adopting and implementing agency relocation programs. We find explaining policy change against unfavorable odds more intriguing than accounting for policy continuity as expected, even though these two foci are, of course, polar opposite aspects of the same issue. Policy change as the dependent variable in this respect is quite unambiguous in its simplicity and clarity: it is simply whether a relocation program is implemented or not after it has been endorsed by legislators. Our definition of the slippery and normatively laden terms, policy success or failure, are pragmatically defined likewise: i.e. relative to the political will and program goals expressed through majority votes in national legislatures.

Agency relocation programs of the type in focus here, being of a radical redistributive nature, are among the most difficult policies to adopt and implement (Lowi 1964; Ripley and Franklin 1982). They were radical in the sense that they were premised on a type of policy instrument – coercion – that is very unusual and alien to Nordic political systems characterized as consensual democracies because of their policy style emphasizing cooperation and consensus among stakeholders as means to produce legitimate compromise solutions (Elder et al. 1983; Lijphart 1984; Arter [1999] 2008). Hence, agency relocation programs should be ideally suited for our analytical purpose: explaining policy change against very unfavorable odds as a strategy to identify salient critical conditions under which policies succeed or fail more generally.

Methodology

Our comparison of agency relocation programs is based on a small-N qualitative and most-similar-systems research design both between countries synchronically and within each country diachronically and longitudinally (George and Bennett 2005). The advantage of this research design has been summarized by Lipset (1990, p. vi): "the more similar the units compared the more possible it should be to isolate the factors responsible for differences between them". Few countries in the world are more similar in so many respects as the Nordic countries (Lijphart 1984; Lane and Ersson 1994; Arter 1999). Hence, they are ideally suited for this particular research design.

At an earlier stage of this research project only Norway and Sweden were included in the cross-national comparison. Finland was included later for three reasons. First, to alleviate the over-determined research design caused by the familiar "too few cases, too many variables" syndrome (George and Bennett 2005) associated with small-N comparison by increasing the number of relocation programs from five to seven. Second, because this introduced more variation in one of the hypothesized key independent variables: type of political system and government. Third, because this provided a wider and hence tougher "testing ground" (see Stinchcombe 1968) regarding our main theoretical proposition explicated below.

This "testing" takes place in a crucial policy context – the Nordic countries – with the strongest organized interest groups worldwide (see Alvarez et al. 1991, p. 553), where chances of confirming an interest group politics type of explanation are maximized and conversely chances of confirming institutional explanations are minimized. This crucial case testing logic is an important integral part of our cross-national comparison intended to further enhance the explanatory power of this quite rigorous research design (Gerring 2007). Agency relocations are not representative policy cases. On the contrary they are deviant, extreme and revelatory cases (i.e. with respect to type of policy issue and inherent policy instrument, conflict intensity and bureaucratic politics at play), all of which make them optimally suitable for our analytical purpose – crucial case testing procedure – whose ambition is theoretical rather than empirical generalization (Yin 2009).

This study spans national policy processes going through two policy cycles in Finland and Sweden and three in Norway. Governmental efforts at the first policy cycle (1960s) with respect to agency relocation programs during the 1960s were clearly of a preliminary, tentative and less committed nature in all three countries. For this reason, as well as not to overwhelm the reader with too many detailed case histories, more attention is devoted to what happened in subsequent policy cycles – the 1970s (and the 2000s in Norway) – when governmental actions were of a more committed and serious nature.

With respect to data, the study relies heavily on the following sources of information: two doctoral dissertations from Finland and Norway (Sætren 1983; Isaksson 1989); a book and a journal article describing the third Norwegian policy cycle in quite unusual detail at the highest level of political decision making (Norman 2004; Meyer and Stensaker 2009) – two of these authors were key decision makers themselves; some quite thoroughly documented public evaluation reports from Sweden (Edstad 1980; Pettersson 1980). Finally, this author conducted some supplementary interviews in Stockholm in autumn 1983 with the top civil servant (Nils Finn) responsible for implementation of the Swedish relocation program after 1978.

Theoretical Framework and Derived Main Proposition

All central agency relocation program cases analyzed and compared in this study, not surprisingly, point clearly in the direction of a common critical bottleneck in the policy process – the cabinet as a formal political clearinghouse. This raises a more focused research question: why is there variation in cabinet performance on an identical policy program not just between but also within countries? Factors that make governments and their cabinets *strong* or *weak* in terms of policy making have been investigated by several policy scholars (Steinmo et al. 1992; Weaver and Rockman 1993; Olsen and Peters 1996; Pollitt and Bouckaert 2011; Doorenspleet and Pellikaan 2013). Thus, the historical-institutional (HI) approach expounded by these scholars (see e.g. March and Olsen 1984; Steinmo et al. 1992) presents itself as a logical primary theoretical starting point given our more precise research question. This choice may seem odd to some as the HI approach is generally credited with explaining policy continuity better than policy change. However, this interpretation is heavily premised on only one of the two faces of institutions – namely their constraining impact on the policy process. The other face, highlighting institutions' enabling and facilitating impact on policy making, is then ignored. In this study we recognize both faces of institutions, thus adopting a dynamic rather than static interpretation of the HI approach (Olsen 1992; Peters et al. 2005).

Nevertheless, even this more nuanced dynamic interpretation of institutional impacts has its clear limitations. Institutions may facilitate the policy-making process, but they do not

Table 1. Policy types by Wilson (1973) and their assumed related type of politics.

	Program benefits:	
	Widely distributed	**Narrowly distributed**
Program costs:		
Widely distributed	*Majoritarian politics* (Not relevant program design in this study)	*Client politics* (Not relevant program design in this study)
Narrowly distributed	*Entrepreneurial politics*: Politically *optimal**) program design Cell 1	*Interest group politics*: Politically *suboptimal**) program design Cell 2

Note: *programs are classified as optimal and suboptimal from the point of view of the majority of the legislators. There is a continuum here, not a dichotomy, from one term to the other. Optimal programs create few losers and many winners in the legislature while suboptimal programs produce many losers and few winners.

make decisions. People in them do! This strongly suggests that human agency must be an integral part of the institutional approach. Institutions combined with benign environmental circumstances may create opportunities for political action, but those opportunities must be recognized and capitalized on by some authorized decision makers using their personal will and skills as well as institutional capabilities and resources before windows of opportunity close. Kingdon (1984) referred to decision makers of this kind as *policy entrepreneurs*.

Wilson (1973), elaborating on Lowi's (1964) famous policy typology, had by then already hypothesized policy entrepreneurs to play a particularly critical role in redistributive policies of the kind we are studying. That is, programs where costs are narrowly concentrated on resourceful groups in the capital regions and benefits intended to be widely distributed to less resourceful areas outside the capital regions (see Table 1). Wilson's proposition is based on the assumption that redistributive policies of this type tend to target better-off segments of society, which must bear most of their costs. Hence, these citizens will tend to not only resent but also oppose such policies, and have many resources to succeed in this respect while those less well-off usually have fewer resources to defend policies that are supposed to benefit them. This imbalance in strategic resources between these two differently impacted target groups will tend to result in either no policy program at all or alternatively greatly reduced policy program benefits (and hence also costs) in terms of size and scope – i.e. *interest group politics* in Wilson's typological scheme. The more optimal agency relocation program from policy makers' point of view (narrowly concentrated costs and widely distributed benefits) supposedly requires the presence and actions of policy entrepreneurship. That is why Wilson attached the label *entrepreneurial* politics to the ideal-typical large-scale relocation program that this entails. Thus, Wilson's insight points towards the important role of deliberate design efforts in policy entrepreneurship with respect to organizing the policy process as a means to achieve the desired optimal policy program (Howlett 2011).

Figure 1 and Table 1 illustrate our multi-theoretical framework, whose basic elements stem from previous policy research (in particular Wilson 1973; Kingdon 1984; Olsen 1992; Weaver and Rockman 1993; Olsen and Peters 1996; Pollitt and Bouckaert 2011) as well as our own comparative study. Further elaboration and explanation of various constitutional-institutional arrangements and their policy-facilitating and -inhibiting

Figure 1. Multi-theoretical framework operationalized into different types of factors assumed to impact on policy-making performance

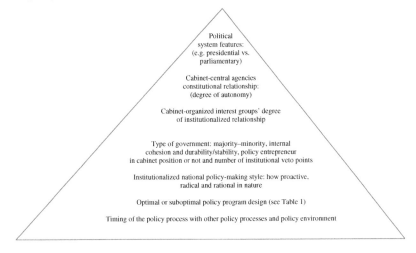

capabilities will, due to limited space, be dealt with below in the comparative section, where we try to explain differences in policy performance between as well as within countries. Table 2 briefly summarizes those efforts.

The sum of the above theoretical reasoning leads to three main propositions that will guide this comparative study:

Proposition 1: Agency relocation programs in cell 1 of Table 1 will be adopted by legislatures and subsequently implemented, while programs in cell 2 will be more frequently contested, opposed and rejected.

Proposition 2: Designing politically optimal relocation programs (cell 1) in the policy formulation stage requires political will, commitment and perseverance embodied in and executed by a institutionally well-positioned policy entrepreneur. Absence of a policy entrepreneur will lead to proposals of politically suboptimal relocation programs.

Proposition 3: Policy entrepreneurs operating within strong governments combined with other policies facilitating institutional arrangements and a beneficial situational context will be most effective in proposing politically optimal relocation programs, while weak governments with no policy entrepreneur and a less benign situational context will fail to achieve the same.

The Swedish Case History: 1957–1980/81

In May 1973 the Swedish parliament enacted the second and final part of a relocation program of unprecedented scope, totaling some 50 central governmental agencies located in Stockholm with more than 10,000 employees. The relocation program had a very well-balanced regional scope benefiting 16 cities located in all major regions outside the capital and a couple of other metropolitan areas. Hence, three out of four legislators voted in favor of this relocation program. This parliamentary decision was preceded by another in 1971 involving 30 central agencies with 6,300 employees.

Table 2. Summary of factors found to explain policy success and failure and their configuration across the three Nordic countries with respect to agency relocation programs during the 1970s (and 2000s in Norway).

Sweden	Norway	Finland
Mostly single party (SD) majority/minority governments 1945–1973/ 1973–1976. Majority coalition govt. of several center parties 1977–1982	Stable single (Labor) party minority governments 1973–1981. Coalition minority govt. of center parties 2001–2005. Multiparty cross-bloc majority coalition govt. 2005–2013	Many short-lived cross-bloc oversized multiparty coalition governments 1972–1983
Few institutional veto points	Few institutional veto points	Many institutional veto points
Exemption from ministerial rule and responsibility of central agencies	Ministerial rule and responsibility of central agencies apply	Ministerial rule and responsibility of central agencies apply
Very active policy entrepreneur (GS) in cabinet position 1969–1976	Policy entrepreneur (VN) in cabinet position 2001–2004 but none during the 1970s	Passive policy entrepreneur (president) in cabinet position
Proactive radical national policy style	Less proactive, radical national policy style	Less proactive, radical national policy style
Very strong, well-organized but self-disciplined relevant interest groups	Strong, well-organized, more aggressive and militant relevant interest groups	Strong, well-organized, less self-disciplined interest groups
Politically optimal program design	Politically suboptimal incomplete program design in 1970s, more optimal in 2000s	Politically optimal program design
Optimal timing of policy cycle relative to other parallel policy processes and external events more generally	Suboptimal timing of policy cycle relative to other policy processes and events. More optimal timing in 2000s	Suboptimal timing of policy cycle relative to other policy processes and events

A commission appointed by the government in 1969 to investigate which agencies were most suitable for relocation had proposed in two separate reports (SOU 1970, p. 29; SOU 1972, p. 55) a relocation program almost identical in content and scope. Commission membership was most noticeable for its lack of representation from political parties and interest organizations. They were for the most part, including the chairperson, civil servants close to and handpicked by the influential and powerful finance minister, Gunnar Straeng, with a clear mandate to propose substantial agency relocations as soon as possible. During its work the commission had fairly little contact with agencies under investigation and unions organizing their employees. Consultations only took place at the highest level involving a number of junior ministers.

The commission's reports were distributed widely for comments, as is customary in Sweden, to institutions, agencies and organizations of various sorts. The response to its proposals was overwhelmingly negative. The Federation of Trade Unions, with close ties to the ruling Social Democratic party, surprisingly endorsed the proposed relocation program. The other major unions organizing white-collar workers in the public and private sector did not support the relocation program, but they did not engage much in mobilizing their membership to oppose it. The government acted quickly, drafting its parliamentary bills in 1971 and 1973 without any further consultation, paying little heed to the flood of prior negative comments. Both the cabinet and the legislators not only endorsed but actually increased to some extent the number of agencies and new location sites proposed by the commission.

The challenge of implementing this large-scale and logistically demanding relocation program was solved through the typical Swedish style of meticulous organization and planning. The linchpin in this respect was an inter-ministerial coordinating group under the auspice of the Prime Minister's Office with secretarial assistance from a project/work group established within the Finance Ministry for this specific purpose. Thus, only few agencies exceeded the stipulated time frame for moving from the capital.

True to its thorough manner of doing things the Swedish government sponsored an impressive number of studies that were aimed at evaluating the various impacts of the relocation program (e.g. Edsta 1980; Petterson 1980). The results are too voluminous to be detailed here. As a general conclusion it is safe to say that many of its predicted positive effects were noted while most of the anticipated negative effects never materialized or turned out to be quite overstated. One example was the costs associated with this large-scale relocation program. They turned out to be 15 per cent lower than expected, resulting in estimated budgetary net savings in 1986/87 of 270 million kroner, mostly due to lower office accommodation costs. Only 20 per cent of employees relocated with their agencies. The effect of this was the creation of many thousands of new jobs in the new locations of the agencies. However, Stockholm also experienced a growth in total jobs during the 1970s, approximately equaling the number created elsewhere. Nevertheless, the proportion of central government employees in the capital decreased from 30.5 per cent in 1972 to 26.7 per cent in 1987 (NordRefo 1988).

This was not the first time the Social Democratic government considered the possibility of a fairly large-scale relocation of its central agencies in Stockholm. In 1957 it also appointed a commission (called *Lokaliseringsutredningen* in Swedish) to investigate its feasibility. The commission was well staffed in terms of secretarial resources and enlisted the assistance of external professional experts to investigate various aspects of a comprehensive relocation program. No concrete relocation program was proposed indicating which agencies should be moved to a specific location. Instead the commission outlined a very large-scale relocation program and an alternative more modest one.

The commission report was also then distributed widely for comments. A large majority of the responses were quite negative, especially from those agencies most directly affected by the suggested relocation plans. Perhaps in view of these mostly negative responses the government decided to abandon further work on this policy issue. Instead it opted to pursue another type of regional policy measure that had been investigated and proposed parallel to *Lokaliseringsutredningen*, called Active Location Policy. The latter program targeted private sector enterprises, offering them various types of incentives to relocate their businesses from overcrowded urban to more rural areas.

The Norwegian Case History: 1961–2007

In the early 1970s it would seem that Norway, not Sweden, was the undisputed leader in efforts at moving central governmental agencies from its capital, as it was the only Nordic country that had some success in doing so during the previous decade. But on closer scrutiny this proves to be much less the case. The relocation program proposed by a government-appointed commission in 1961 was not very ambitious. Nevertheless, by the time affected stakeholders, the cabinet and legislators had had their say on it, its size and scope, it had been depleted of even more substance, to such a degree – i.e. eight agencies totaling 400 jobs to five cities close to the capital – that it was rendered a mostly symbolic program.

Efforts by the same government to follow up on this limited relocation program with proposals for more substantial future relocations, which it had pledged to do during the parliamentary floor debate on its white paper in 1967, proved very hard to deliver. This was partly the result of widespread resistance in the governmental bureaucracy but also in no small part due to ambivalence and failure on the part of the government itself to support those entrusted with the task of delivering on its promises. Thus, by the early 1970s the relatively long lasting but internally weak center-right majority coalition government, led by a prime minister from the Center (former Agrarian) party, had achieved little if anything in terms of giving more substance to its previous mostly symbolic relocation program.

In view of these prior events it is somewhat surprising that the new but short-lived minority coalition government formed of center parties decided in 1973, a couple of weeks before the general election, to appoint a new commission to investigate the feasibility of a larger scale relocation program. The motivation seems to have been twofold: (1) pressure from the city government of Oslo to reinvigorate work on moving government agencies from the capital due to heavy net in-migration during the late 1960s and (2) probably both some embarrassment and also inspiration from what the Swedish government had accomplished in this policy area the same year with the enactment of its impressive and bold relocation program.

The new minority Labor government that won the general election in 1973 apparently shared the political commitment of its predecessor on this policy issue. In fact most political parties had pledged before that election to support the new initiative. The strategy now was obviously to try to emulate the successful policy process in Sweden. Thus, a new commission was asked to come up with some concrete relocation proposals relatively quickly in a first report that the cabinet could then submit to the parliament for its approval. This procedure was thought to give authority and legitimacy to both the commission and the government in their subsequent efforts to realize a Swedish-style agency relocation program.

The commission – hereafter named the Grande commission after its chairperson – did what it was asked to do. In its first report delivered in 1975 12 central agencies and parts of three others with approximately 1,000 employees were listed as suitable to be moved from Oslo, though without indicating where. The ministry appointing the commission had itself to decide on this politically sensitive issue. As before, the ministry distributed the report widely and received the same type of mostly negative responses. The ministry also wasted little time in drafting a white paper on the relocation issue based on the recommendations from the Grande commission. That is when things started to go awry. In a newspaper interview in late autumn 1975 a junior minister and associate member of the Grande commission revealed that concrete relocation proposals to be included in the parliamentary white paper had been met with considerable objections from ministers responsible for the central agencies in question. Hence, meetings between his lead ministry and these members of the cabinet were scheduled to secure their and the cabinet's approval of the proposed relocation program. It would take 2–3 years before the cabinet was able to submit a white paper on this issue to the parliament proposing moving 20 agencies with some 1,200 employees to some still undisclosed new locations outside Oslo. The parliament endorsed plans for such a relocation program but once again the government encountered heavy resistance within its own ranks as soon as it started work on implementation. A one-day strike among employees in affected central agencies organized by their unions in late autumn 1980 seems to have been the precipitating event causing the final collapse of the government's political will to pursue the relocation program. Announcement of this policy reversal by the lead minister in parliament in early January 1981 was met by legislators with a deafening silence. Hence, not only were the few relocation proposals in the parliamentary white paper abandoned, but more importantly so were subsequent substantial relocation proposals contained in the two most recent reports from the Grande commission submitted in 1977 and 1979, affecting in whole or in part more than 50 central agencies with close to 5,000 employees.

Contrary to what one might expect by now, this is not the end of the story on the relocation program in Norway. In June 2003, exactly 30 years after the Swedish parliament completed enacting its impressive relocation program, a clear majority in the Norwegian parliament endorsed moving seven central agencies with some 1,000 employees from Oslo to seven cities with a fairly balanced regional distribution. Even more noteworthy, in view of the prior policy history, is the fact that all agencies – despite substantial logistic challenges and heavy opposition in at least one case – were now moved to their new locations within the stipulated time frame of four years. While the scope of this relocation program pales in comparison with the Swedish one, the way in which it was achieved is much more remarkable.

It started with general election in autumn 2001 that resulted in a center-right minority coalition government (Bondevik II). The choice of Victor Norman (VN), an economics professor with no previous political experience, as minister of Labor and Government Administration (LGA) was a surprise to most observers and commentators. Being appointed with a specific mandate to modernize the public sector, he launched a new modernization program on behalf of his government in early 2002. Reorganizing and streamlining regulatory agencies in accordance with contemporary New Public Management (NPM) doctrines was a centerpiece of this modernization program. Relocating some of these agencies became part of the reform and turned out, not surprisingly, to be by far the most controversial issue in this respect. The latter idea was clearly the brain child of VN. He reasoned that since regulatory agencies were supposed to be largely politically autonomous and functionally independent there was less need for them to be located near other government institutions in Oslo. Hence, they were well suited to be part of a relocation program. Apparently VN did not consult or inform either the chairperson of his own political party (who was also a fellow cabinet minister) or his prime minister before, in January 2002, he announced the government's plan to relocate some regulatory agencies as part of the modernization program. This seems to have been a deliberate act on his part intended to lock his government into a policy position from which it could not retreat without losing considerable political face in the eyes of the public (see Norman 2004, p. 99).

The way Victor Norman organized the policy formulation process regarding the regulatory reform program was equally unconventional. He decided *not* to follow the standard procedure of appointing a public commission to investigate the policy issue and recommend possible solutions that various stakeholders then are invited to comment on before the cabinet eventually makes up its mind about whether and if so how to pursue it further with respect to the parliament. Instead VN chose to organize all work on the regulatory reform program within his own ministry in the form of a temporary project under his supervision. His junior minister (later his wife) supplemented by a political advisor and three LGA civil servants were given responsibility for coordinating the work together with two junior ministers from other ministries. This was intentionally a political project team. The junior ministers reported to their respective ministers thereby ensuring that all parties in the coalition government were involved. This meant that a number of other stakeholders both within and outside the government – such as the regulatory agencies, their labor unions, academic experts etc. – were excluded from the policy formulation process. Other civil servants in the LGA ministry and those from other ministries were also deliberately excluded at this stage of the policy process. The latter move was particularly controversial but nevertheless continued through most of the project before the cabinet decided they had to be included in its final stages.

This very exclusive political project team supervised by VN and his junior minister worked on the various elements of the regulatory reform program from April to late autumn 2002 with two exceptions. The junior ministers representing other ministries and governing political parties were so skeptical towards one reform idea (closer monitoring of local municipalities) that VN decided to take it off the project team's agenda. The other exception was the relocation issue, which was not on its agenda in the first place as VN did not trust even this handpicked political team to agree on concrete relocation proposals. Hence, most members of the project team did not know exactly which regulatory agencies would be part of the proposed relocation program until its final meeting when all reform elements had to be put together in its report. Just before this meeting cabinet members whose ministries were affected by the relocation program were informed about this fact. Surprisingly, in view of previous similar efforts, none of them objected this time. Shortly afterwards the full content of the planned relocation program was disclosed to the public.

The white paper submitted to the parliament in January 2003 reflected the fact that several changes and modifications had been made within the coalition government regarding clarification of roles/responsibilities and political autonomy/independence issues during the policy formulation process so far. Negotiations and further compromises on these issues with the opposition parties continued during parliamentary deliberations on the white paper. The exception here was the relocation program that was forwarded intact as initially proposed to the parliament. Though approved by a large majority of the legislators this did not happen without considerable opposition from some relocation program stakeholders. Especially the exclusion of affected agencies and their labor unions was highly controversial and caused a major uproar amongst their ranks, supported by the major national newspapers also located in Oslo. However, the mobilization against the relocation program began late due to the secrecy surrounding most of the policy formulation process. Hence, it was not very successful.

The Finnish Case History 1961–1976/77

The first investigative commission appointed in 1961 delivered its report as soon as late 1962. The commission and subsequently the cabinet in 1963 proposed a fairly modest and regionally very lopsided relocation program with only two cities outside the Helsinki region being included. Even worse was the fact that one of them was destined to receive four of the six agencies as well as 90 per cent of related jobs. Not surprisingly, the parliamentary bill proposing this relocation program ran into a lot of trouble once the legislators – who objected to its content – started dealing with it. Thus, after a complex, lengthy and very acrimonious deliberation process lasting for almost two years, the cabinet finally withdrew the bill altogether.

The second commission to investigate relocation of central agencies was appointed in 1972. Of its 12 members half were politicians and members of the parliament. They were from constituencies located in the middle and northern parts of the country some distance from the capital region in the south. Many of them apparently belonged to the Social Democratic party. It also had a secretarial staff of three persons at its disposal. The commission worked fast, thoroughly and effectively enlisting experts to carry out special investigations on its behalf. In two separate reports, submitted in 1973 and 1974 respectively, it recommended that some 30 central agencies totaling approximately 6,000 employees be moved to 12 different cities, of which four were located in the southern part, five in the middle part and three in the northern part of the country. In terms of jobs, their distribution towards regions farther away from the capital was even better, as the four agencies destined for the southern region had only 1,000 staff. The commission strongly advised that the cabinet should make a clear principled policy decision on its proposals detailing which agencies should be moved where, when and how.

The cabinet did make some sort of a policy decision in December 1974 but it was vague and non-committal in nature towards the proposed relocation program, emphasizing other alternative regional measures as preferable if they could achieve the same policy objectives. The cabinet also stressed that further work on these issues was to be based on cooperation with affected ministries and their subordinate agencies. A decentralization office, mandated to follow up this policy decision, was established within the administrative division of the Finance Ministry the next year (1975). Efforts by several subsequent, short-lived governments during the 1970s and into the 1980s to follow up on the commission's proposals by submitting some of them to the parliament were unsuccessful, again primarily due to the lengthy, complex deliberation process in the parliament. In autumn 1981 the Social Democrats suggested to their coalition partner of many years, the Center (former Agrarian) party, that the issue of relocating agencies should be dropped altogether. The suggestion was not appreciated by the latter party. After 1985, efforts to relocate agencies seemed to evaporate without any explicit policy decision having ever been made one way or the other regarding the proposed relocation program.

Explaining Differences in National Policy Performance

The overall constitutional political system features of our three countries are, as we said in the introduction, very similar. Hence, it follows from our comparative research design that we cannot explain differences in policy outcomes between or within countries with factors that are invariant. The exception here is Finland, which has a semi-presidential system with a politically much stronger head of state. Hence, we will discuss the implications of that fact for the Finish policy context. As for Norway and Sweden, we think, much like Weaver and Rockman (1993) found, that lower level political system features are much more important.

Sweden

Let us start with the puzzling success in the Swedish case. Why were the clearly best organized and most influential interest groups in the world (Alvarez et al. 1991, p. 553) – which had the most to lose from the proposed very large-scale relocation program – nevertheless also clearly least effective in blocking its realization? The answer to this paradox can to a large extent be found at lower institutional levels.

Type of Government and Institutional Veto Points. First of all Sweden had one of the strongest (single-party majority), most stable (see Appendix Table A1) and longest lasting governments in Europe (in power uninterruptedly from 1945) up until the enactment of the final part of its agency relocation program in 1973. The Social Democratic party ruled for another three years in a single-party minority government with negotiated support from opposition parties in parliament on vital political issues. This strong political regime was enhanced by a unicameral parliamentarian political system with a ceremonial-symbolic head of state and politically self-constrained judiciary amounting to very few institutional veto points.

Government-organized Interest Group Relations. This unprecedentedly long-lasting and strong Social Democratic regime impacted on Swedish politics and society in many ways. Political scientist Nils Elvander, an expert on Swedish interest groups, described one such regime impact which is of crucial importance to this study. Through comprehensive elite interviews with politicians, business and union leaders conducted in the early 1970s he found surprisingly strong consensus among all elite groups on some powerful self-constraining and disciplining behavioral norms regarding participation in public policy-making processes. Thus, the use of objective factual information and convincing arguments presented directly to decision-making institutions and refraining from threats, blackmail, heavy-handed pressure or agitation and appeals to public opinion were heavily stressed. Furthermore, those who violated these "rules of the game" risked damaging their reputation and hence also reducing their influence (Elvander 1974, pp. 41–42). Elvander's own interpretation was that Swedish associations of all kinds to a surprisingly large extent had adapted to these "rules of the game". This may explain the somewhat surprising consent to agency relocations by the Federation of Trade Unions and less aggressive actions by the white-collar unions.

A Unique National Policy-making Style. Elvander's findings are supported by other observers noting that Sweden at this time had a unique national policy style compared to many other countries in Western Europe, even the other Nordic countries. The unique feature of Swedish policy making was that it tended to be more proactive, rationalistic and radical (Anton 1969; Richardson 1982). This also explains why Sweden tended to be the innovative leader more generally in a Nordic policy context at this time (Karvonen 1981).

Relationship between Cabinet Ministers and Central Agencies. The very strong autonomous and independent role of central agencies in the policy-making process is another important institutional factor in our context. Paradoxically it became a *liability*, not an advantage, for them in this particular policy process. The reason for this is that the nearly universal ministerial rule and responsibility principle with respect to central government agencies does not apply in Sweden. The constitution actually prohibits cabinet ministers from interfering in how central agencies interpret and execute public policies in individual cases. Hence, it is the cabinet as a collective body to which central agencies are subordinate. We surmise that this Swedish institutional exceptionalism may actually have insulated individual cabinet ministers from strong lobbying and pressure group activity by central agencies, thus greatly facilitating unanimous cabinet decisions on a highly controversial and contested political issue.

Policy Entrepreneurship and Policy Design. The crucial role of policy entrepreneurs in promoting and ensuring policy change has been recognized by several policy scholars (Wilson 1973; Kingdon 1984). Our Nordic policy cases are no exception. The influential role of the long-serving and reputedly charismatic and strong-willed finance minister Gunnar Straeng during the 1960s and early 1970s is legendary. In our context it became evident how during the early 1970s he fronted the cabinet's uncompromising stance on the large-scale relocation program against various stakeholders, not the least with respect to affected agencies and their labor unions. As we saw, Straeng used his institutional position to organize key stakeholders out of the policy process at the important commission stage.

Additional Push and Pull Policy Facilitating Factors. Other circumstances – two "push" and one "pull" – probably also contributed to the impact of the above-mentioned factors. The first push factor was a shortage of office space in the Stockholm area that had lasted most of the post-war period – a situation that did not improve due to quite strict local government regulations on constructing new office buildings. The second push factor was the dramatic increase in migration of people to the capital during the late 1960s.

The pull factor had to do with a national regional policy measure intended to stem the flow of people and jobs towards the three largest urbanized centers (Gothenburg, Malmoe and Stockholm) by establishing a system of growth centers located at different administrative levels in other regions. The largest designated regional growth centers, of which there were some 20, were called primary centers or big city alternatives (Nilsson 1992). The political process of finalizing this alternative growth center system was remarkably synchronized with that pertaining to agency relocations of the 1970s. This greatly facilitated the politically thorny question of deciding which cities should receive the relocated agencies. Thus, of the 16 new locations to which agencies were relocated almost all were designated primary centers.

Timing of the Policy Process. The timing of the second Swedish policy cycle relative to other policy processes and changing political circumstances during the latter part of the 1970s probably also contributed to some extent to the remarkable success of the Swedish policy. Limited space does not allow us to elaborate too much on these other factors. Finalizing the relocation program the same year that marked the beginning of the end of the long-lasting and strong Social Democratic regime in 1973 and its demise in 1976 to be replaced by several short-lived non-socialist coalition governments into the early 1980s is one important factor. Since implementation of the relocation program was well on its way by then no efforts were made by subsequent governments to abort a policy program that some of the coalition partners had changed position on and opposed in 1973.

Another factor was the public debate and legislative initiatives to strengthen workplace democracy for employees in both the private and public sector that came onto the government's agenda around 1973 and was enacted by parliament in 1976, three years after the relocation program. There is no doubt that by 1973 the latter legislation had already started to undermine the legitimacy of agency relocations premised on a coercive policy instrument, though not yet seriously threatening its clear legislative majority.

A third factor was the dramatic worsening of Sweden's macro-economic performance from the early to the late 1970s, which resulted in a budget deficit during the implementation of the relocation program. Finally, the period of remarkable harmonious and peaceful coexistence between the government and unions in Sweden came to an end by the late 1970s, with worsening macro-economic performance and the emergence of some new quite controversial issues dealing with nuclear energy, pension funds and taxes.

Hence, in view of these emerging policy-inhibiting factors relative to Sweden's large-scale relocation program it is questionable whether it would have been seriously considered, proposed, adopted and implemented by the cabinet and parliament had the second policy cycle been delayed by just 4–5 years, starting in 1974/75 instead of 1969.

Norway

The dismal policy performance in Norway during the 1970s is also somewhat puzzling in view of its clearly leading regional policy legacy up until then. Being the only Nordic country that had succeeded to some extent in relocating central agencies from the capital during the 1960s adds to this paradox. Why then did the strongly worded, broadly based and apparently sincere political will to emulate Sweden's ambitious relocation program in the early 1970s evaporate so fast during the second policy cycle? Even more puzzling in view of this troubled past is the adoption and implementation of a relocation program some 20 years later. We think there are a handful of factors that together offer the best explanation for this mixed policy performance.

Type of Government and Institutional Veto Points. Governments during most of the 1970s were actually of the relatively strong type (single Labor party minority governments), though weaker than those in Sweden. During the 2000s two even weaker types of governments were in power. The first was the Bondevik II non-socialist minority coalition government from 2001 to 2004. The other one was the Stoltenberg across the socialist and non-socialist blocs majority coalition government from 2005 to 2013. Since Norwegian agency relocation programs – in the 1960s and 2000s – took place under weaker coalition governments and failed attempts were during stronger government in the 1970s we must look for other factors than type of government to answer this mixed policy performance.

Much like in Sweden, there are also few veto points in the Norwegian political system and this did not change during the time period under study. What about the two other constitutional-institutional features so salient in the Swedish case?

The Relationship between Cabinet Ministers, Central Agencies and Organized Interest Groups. In contrast to Sweden, in Norway (and Finland) the relationship between the cabinet and central agencies is based on the ministerial rule and responsibility principle. This implies much closer contact between the central agencies and cabinet ministers and their executive ministries. Thus, Norwegian central agencies at this time reported on average more than twice the frequency of contact with their parent ministries than the Swedish central agencies did. Even more importantly perhaps, contacts with more aggressive and militant interest organizations were generally three times more frequent among Norwegian central agencies than among the Swedish (see Appendix Table A2). The implication is that central agencies in Norway were in a more favorable strategic position to exert pressure on their superior ministries and cabinet ministers both directly and indirectly through their closer and more intimate contact patterns. Under the cross-pressure emanating from constitutional responsibility to respect and execute the will of the legislature on the one hand and obligations to protect and defend vested interests of subordinate central agencies on the other, cabinet ministers with few exceptions sided with the latter. They might at best agree to relocation programs as a general idea but nevertheless invariably object to those that included any of their subordinate agencies. Thus, opposition to any relocation program at cabinet level intensified the closer the decision process came to giving it real substance and political endorsement. The ministerial rule and responsibility principle with respect to central agencies and the presence and actions of more aggressive organized interest groups probably offer the best explanation for the government's policy reversal on this issue in the early 1980s as well as the hollow and symbolic relocation program of the late 1960s. However, as these institutional features did not change much in the 2000s we must look to other factors to explain what happened then.

Policy Entrepreneurship and Policy Design. Lack of a policy entrepreneur at cabinet level to champion the controversial relocation program combined with a more aggressive, militant and less self-disciplined role of labor unions in the policy process and an incomplete and underspecified relocation program design in terms of receiving regions and cities no doubt also contributed in no small part to its eventual demise during the late 1970s. The important fact about the Bondevik II government of the first half of the 2000s was not, as we have said above, its type of government, but rather that it had a policy entrepreneur – Victor Norman – in a cabinet position. It is hard to exaggerate the crucial precipitating role he played in realizing the politically optimal agency relocation program that everybody considered his pet project. We have detailed above how he achieved this remarkable feat against very unfavorable odds through deliberate policy design where he – much like Gunnar Straeng in Sweden – organized adversely affected stakeholders and other opponents out of the policy formulation process. He paid a heavy personal and institutional price, spending most of his political capital on a rather ruthless policy style where he used his constitutional prerogatives to the fullest. Hence, it is perhaps no surprise that he returned to his academic post before the government's time had expired but after the relocation program had been endorsed by the parliament.

Timing. Contrary to what we saw in Sweden, in Norway the timing of the 1970s policy process with other policy processes and external circumstance was clearly suboptimal. Though the process of institutionalizing workplace democracy for public employees started later in Norway than in Sweden it nevertheless came to parallel rather closely and adversely impact on the decision regarding the second relocation program because of the protracted policy cycle. The more Norwegian politicians got engaged in the debate on legislating for workplace democracy during the latter part of the 1970s the more ambivalent they became about supporting a program premised on the use of a coercive policy instrument. Hence, it is probably no coincidence that the cabinet's policy reversal on agency relocations happened approximately at the time when public employees' rights to co-determination on organizational issues pertaining to their workplaces had been substantially strengthened and legally formalized.

Agenda-setting circumstances were quite different during the early 2000s, as we described earlier. Now it was not inter-regional migration of people but modernization of regulatory agencies in an age of New Public Management reforms that brought the relocation issue back on the governmental agenda. Victor Norman saw this as window of opportunity, not only to modernize central regulatory agencies but also to relocate some of them. Other factors that were important during the 1970s seems to have been less significant due to his heavy-handed approach.

Finland

Finland, with the clearest and most consistent cases of policy failure, also constitutes a paradox in some respects. Net out-migration from rural peripheral areas and in-migration of people and hence agglomeration pressures of various sorts in the capital region were clearly at a higher level than in Norway and Sweden. All major political parties were represented in the second commission of inquiry that unanimously proposed the ambitious and large-scale relocation program. Furthermore, Finland had both the consistently broadest based governments and by far the politically strongest head of state in the president. He was from the Agrarian, later Center party, which most consistently and strongly advocated relocation of central agencies as a regional policy measure. Finland was also alone in creating a separate unit in the lead Ministry of Finance in 1975 to promote further work on decentralization measures. How could the proposed relatively large-scale and regionally well-balanced relocation program be defeated with these many apparently beneficial factors in favor of it?

Type of Government and Institutional Veto Points. The first and perhaps most important and surprising clue to an answer is the fact that Finland, contrary to what one might easily assume, had quite *weak* and short-lived governments during the 1970s and well into the 1980s (see Appendix Table A1). It has been observed repeatedly that oversized multi-party majority coalition governments spanning the divide between the socialist and non-socialist blocs can actually be weak, especially when dealing with radical and controversial policies. This is so because there is a good chance that interests which are adversely affected by and opposed to those policies are represented in the government (Weaver and Rockman 1993; Pollitt and Bouckaert 2011). This was very much the case in Finland where virtually all governments during the 1970s were dominated by the two largest coalition partners – the Center party and the Social Democrats – which had polar opposite views on the proposed relocation program. Hence, not only was the internal cohesion of Finnish governments low, so was their stability. Finland had no less than 11 very short-lived oversized majority multi-party coalition cabinets just during the second policy cycle of the 1970s. The Center party and the Social Democrats could only agree to disagree, resulting in cabinet stalemate on this thorny policy issue lasting for many years into the mid-1980s.

The main reason for these broadly based majority coalition governments was the "qualified majority rule" of the Finnish parliament which enabled one-third of the legislators to block the enactment of any government bill by suspending further deliberations and delay a vote on it until after the next general election. Another policy-constraining feature of the same body was the many standing committees and readings involved in deliberation on and final enactment of government bills (Arter 1999). Bills on proposed relocation programs were subject to these very complex and cumbersome parliamentary procedures both in the 1960s and late 1970s/early 1980s.

Why was it easier to reach political agreement on agency relocations in the commission than in the cabinet or parliament? We surmise that this is because it is easier to reach agreements on a recommendation in a commission where people work closely together for an extended period of time in isolation from the public and various adversely affected stakeholders. Other reasons are discussed in relation to the next factors in our analytical theoretical framework.

The Relationship between Cabinet Ministers and Central Agencies. We think the principle of ministerial rule and responsibility with respect to central public administration worked much the same way in Finland as in Norway by exposing cabinet ministers to strong pressure to oppose agency relocations from civil servants in affected ministries and their subordinate agencies. Additionally, the practice of political appointments of top civil servants by Finnish governments that evolved during this time period may actually have strengthened their influence within the ruling political parties on this particular policy area.

Policy Entrepreneurship. Lastly, but not least importantly: there was no policy entrepreneur at cabinet level to champion agency relocations as in Norway and Sweden. This is another puzzle, since Finland had a head of state – President Kekkonen – with far more political power and leverage than the constitutional and mostly symbolic heads of state (monarchs) in Norway and Sweden. By the mid-1970s Kekkonen had through an exceptionally long-lasting presidency (1956–1981) acquired a reputation as an all-powerful president (Arter [1999] 2008). He was not shy of wielding his powers on many policy issues. Nevertheless, and for whatever reason, even though he came from the Center party, he chose not to use his strong constitutional prerogatives as president to force his cabinet to adopt and implement the rather large-scale relocation program that his own party so strongly advocated. The role of unions, and in particular those organizing personnel in affected central agencies, was no doubt another major constraining factor on cabinet policy-making capability. Their politically fragmented and hence weaker organizational strength (Alvarez et al. 1991, p. 553) was probably more than compensated for by the quite fragile and weak governments, the many institutional veto points and the dominating presence of a labor-friendly party – the Social Democrats – in virtually all of them.

Conclusion: The Crucial Explanatory Factors

We formulated three propositions derived from our multi-theoretical framework specifying some factors and conditions that could explain why agency relocation programs either succeed or fail at the crucial policy adoption and implementation stages. Together they suggested that policy success in this respect depended on policy entrepreneurs using their skills and resources within constitutional and institutional arrangements with strong policy-making capabilities and benign situational policy contexts to fashion politically optimal program designs during the policy formulation process that would ensure their adoption and implementation.

We think our cross-national comparative and longitudinal study largely but not fully corroborates the validity of the three propositions. Sweden and Finland seem to offer the strongest confirmation here as respectively policy-facilitating versus inhibiting institutional arrangements combined with the presence or absence of policy entrepreneurs in cabinet positions within more and less beneficial policy environments all correlate clearly with their marked difference in policy performance.

Norway presents a somewhat different intermediate pattern here. The first mostly symbolic agency relocation program should, according to proposition 1 above, have been rejected by the legislators, as in Finland at the same time, rather than being adopted. The policy failure of the 1970s is also an intermediate case with relatively strong single-party minority governments but lacking a policy entrepreneur, combined with some other clear policy-inhibiting institutional arrangements (ministerial rule and responsibility principle of public administration system, and militant labor unions) and situational context. Finally, we have the unexpected and surprising Norwegian agency relocations of the 2000s, where the policy entrepreneur almost single-handedly within a relatively weak minority coalition government fashioned an optimal legislative program design – much as Wilson (1973) hypothesized – operating within a given window of opportunity that was recognized and forcefully utilized. The latter case suggests the "equifinality" often observed in comparative policy research: multiple causal paths to a given policy outcome (e.g. Weaver and Rockman 1993). This is just one of many aspects related to the complex, dynamic and contingent nature of institutional explanations.

In Appendix Table A3 we examine the potential role of some plausible, alternative and competing explanatory factors from previous comparative public policy research to those we started out with. The conclusion here is that national variations in terms of socio-economic, demographic factors as well as stable macro-political system features and public opinion cannot logically explain national differences in policy performance, thus enhancing the credibility and validity of those we have found to be the more crucial ones.

The conjunctural policy impacts of institutions, human agency and more or less random external events and parallel processes in this study point beyond traditional historical and rational choice institutionalism towards a modified expanded version of the garbage can model-inspired Multiple Stream Framework (Kingdon 1984; Sabatier 1999; Zahariadis 2002; Capano and Howlett 2009). Work in that direction has already started (Saetren 2013).

Relocating central agencies was an idea that entered government agendas at a time when increasing regional imbalances came to the attention of politicians and the public while adequate policy measures to deal with them were in their infancy and hence also scarce. This, combined with its potent symbolic value, made agency relocations an idea whose time had come. By the 1980s many other probably more effective regional policy measures had been adopted and implemented. Combined with legislation on workplace democracy in the public sector and other changes in the policy environment this meant that relocating agencies now was an idea whose time had passed. Nevertheless, as we saw in Norway in the 2000s, it was an idea not forgotten by its advocates patiently waiting for a new problem context to attach as a solution. This illustrates well the "garbage can" nature of this policy idea: i.e. its remarkable ability to present itself as a solution to new policy challenges. Perhaps governmental anti-terrorism policy will be the next area where relocating government agencies may appear to be a strategically opportune solution.

References

Alvarez, R. M., Garret, G., and Lange, P., 1991, Government partisanship, labor organization and macroeconomic performance. *The American Political Science Review*, **85**(2), pp. 539–556. doi:10.2307/1963174

Andersen, J. G., 1996, *Membership and Participation in Comparative Perspective*. Research Report, Aalborg: Department of Economics, Politics and Public Administration, Aalborg University.

Anton, T. J., 1969, Policy-making and political culture in Sweden. *Scandinavian Political Studies*, 4, pp. 88–102. doi:10.1111/j.1467-9477.1969.tb00521.x

Arter, D., [1999] 2008, *Scandinavian Politics Today* (Manchester: Manchester University Press).

Capano, G. and Howlett, M., 2009, Understanding policy change as an epistemological and theoretical problem. *Journal of Comparative Policy Analysis: Research and Practice*, **11**(1), pp. 7–31. doi:10.1080/13876980802648284

Doorenspleet, R. and Pellikaan, H., 2013, Which type of democracy performs best? *Acta Politica*, 48(3), pp. 237–267. doi:10.1057/ap.2012.35

Edsta, B., 1980, *Omlokaliseringens Effekter* [Effects of Relocations] (Stockholm: Budgetdepartmentet).

Elder, N., Thomas, A. H., and Arter, D., 1983, *The Consensual Democracies? The Government and Politics of the Scandinavian States* (Oxford: Martin Robertson).

Elvander, N., 1974, Interest groups in Sweden. *The ANNALS of the American Academy of Political and Social Science*, **413**, pp. 27–43. doi:10.1177/000271627441300104

George, A. L. and Bennett, A., 2005, *Case Studies and Theory Development in the Social Sciences* (Cambridge, MA: The MIT Press).

Gerring, J., 2007, Is there a (viable) crucial-case method? *Comparative Political Studies*, **40**(3), pp. 231–253. doi:10.1177/0010414006290784

Howlett, M., 2011, *Designing Public Policies: Principles and Instruments* (London: Routledge).

Ingram, H. and Mann, D. E., 1980, *Why Policies Succeed or Fail* (Beverly Hills, CA: Sage).

Isaksson, G.-E., 1989, *Resultatløs Omlokalisering*. [Failed Relocations] (Åbo: Åbo Academic Press).

Karvonen, L., 1981, Med vårt västra grannland som förebild, Phd dissertation, Åbo Academy.

Kingdon, J., 1984, *Agendas, Alternatives and Public Policies* (Boston, MA: Little Brown).

Lane, J.-E. and Ersson, S. O., 1994, *Politics and Society in Western Europe*, 3rd ed. (London: Sage).

Lijphart, A., 1984, *Democracies. Patterns of Majoritarian and Consensus Government in Twenty-One Countries* (New Haven, CT: Yale University).

Lipset, S. M., 1990, *Continental Divide. The Values and Institutions of the United States and Canada* (New York: Routledge).

Lowi, T. J., 1964, American business and public policy, case studies and political theory. *World Politics*, **16**, pp. 677–715. doi:10.2307/2009452

March, J. G. and Olsen, J. P., 1984, The new institutionalism: Organizational factors in political life. *American Political Science Review*, **78**(3), pp. 734–749. doi:10.2307/1961840

Meyer, C. B. and Stensaker, I. G., 2009, Making radical change happen through selective inclusion and exclusion of stakeholders. *British Journal of Management*, **20**(2), pp. 219–237. doi:10.1111/j.1467-8551.2008.00562.x

Nilsson, J.-E., 1992, Relocation of state agencies as a strategy for urban development: The Swedish case. *Scandinavian Housing & Planning Research*, **9**, pp. 113–118. doi:10.1080/02815739208730296

NordRefo, 1988, *De Nordiska Hovudstaderna: Drivkrefter eller skapare av regional ubalans? Fem studier* (Copenhagen: NordRefo report).

Norman, V. D., 2004, *Blue Notes* (Bergen: Vigmostad & Bjørke).

NOU 1977:3 *Utflytting av statsinstitusjoner fra Oslo*. Del II.

Olsen, J. P., 1992, Analyzing institutional dynamics. *Staatswissenschaft Und Staatspraxis*, Heft, **2**, pp. 247–271.

Olsen, J. P. and Peters, B. G., 1996, *Lessons from Experience. Experiential Learning in Administrative Reforms in Eight Democracies* (Oslo: Scandinavian University Press).

Peters, B. G., Pierre, J., and King, D. S., 2005, The Politics of Path Dependency: Political Conflict in Historical Institutionalism. *The Journal of Politics*, **67**(4), pp. 1275–1300. doi:10.1111/j.1468-2508.2005.00360.x

Petersson, O. and Valen, H., 1979, Political cleavages in Sweden and Norway. *Scandinavian Political Studies*, **2**(4), pp. 313–332. doi:10.1111/j.1467-9477.1979.tb00226.x

Petterson, R., 1980, *Omlokalisering av Statlig Verksamhet*. [Relocation of Governmental Organizations] (Stockholm: Government's Printing Office).

Pollitt, C. and Bouckaert, G., 2011, *Public Management Reform* (Oxford: Oxford University Press).
Richardson, J. J., 1982, *Policy Styles in Western Europe* (London: George Allen & Unwin Hyman).
Ripley, R. B. and Franklin, G. A., 1982, *Bureaucracy and Policy Implementation* (Homewood, IL: Dorsey Press).
Sabatier, P., 1999, *Theories of the Policy Process* (Boulder, CO: Westview Press).
Saetren, H., 1983, *Iverksetting av Offentlig Politikk.* [Implementation of Public Policy] (Bergen/Oslo: University Press).
Saetren, H. (2013) Lost in translation: Re-conceptualizing the Multiple Streams framework back to its source of origin to enhance its analytical and theoretical leverage. ECPR joint sessions conference paper, Mainz, March.
Saunders, P., 1985, Public expenditure and economic performance in OECD countries. *Journal of Public Policy*, 5(1), pp. 1–21. doi:10.1017/S0143814X00002865
SOU 1970: 29 *Decentralisering av statlig verksamhet. Rapport I.*
SOU 1972: 55 *Decentralisering av statlig verksamhet. Rapport II.*
Steinmo, S., Thelen, K., and Longstreth, F., 1992, *Structuring Politics: Historical Institutionalism in Comparative Analysis* (Cambridge: Cambridge University Press).
Stenstadsvold, K., 1975, Northern Europe, in: H. D. Clout (Ed.) *Regional Development in Western Europe* (London: John Wiley & Sons), pp. 245–271.
Stinchcombe, A. L., 1968, *Constructing Social Theories* (New York: Hartcourt, Brace & World).
Weaver, R. K. and Rockman, B. A., 1993, *Do Institutions Matter?* (Washington, DC: The Brookings Institution).
Wilson, J. Q., 1973, *Political Organizations* (New York: Basic Books).
Yin, R. K., 2009, *Case Study Research: Design and Methods* (London: Sage).
Zahariadis, N., 2002, *Ambiguity and Choice in Public Policy* (Washington, DC: Georgetown University Press).

Appendix

Table A1. Stability index score of Nordic governments 1955–1984.

Country	1955–59	1960–64	1965–69	1970–74	1975–79	1980–84
Sweden	59.4	94.2	87.4	92.8	71.0	73.4
Norway	83.0	64.8	89.2	39.8	64.0	52.6
Finland	30.6	41.2	48.0	45.8	30.8	66.4

Note: Note that the score does *not* measure internal *cohesion* of these governments, only their durability.
Source: Lane and Ersson (1994, p. 304).

Table A2. External contact patterns and contact frequencies of central agencies in Norway and Sweden in the early-to-mid 1970s.

	Sweden LQ	Sweden Median	Sweden UQ	Norway LQ	Norway Median	Norway UQ
Ministry	1	4	7	6	9	25
Other central agencies	4	8	12	5	9	18
Interest groups	4	8	15	13	12	22

Note: Frequency figures are based on registration of external contacts during a five-day period by personnel in a fairly large number of central agencies (some 30) that were assumed to be particularly dependent on inter-organizational networks.
Sources: SOU (1972, p. 55) and NOU (1977, p. 3).

Table A3. Factors that cannot logically explain national differences with respect to success and failure of relocation programs during the 1970s.

Sweden: Policy success	Norway: Policy failure	Finland: Policy failure
Politically weak head of state	Politically weak head of state	Very powerful head of state
Union membership among employed wage owners 1970 and 1980: 68% and 80%*	Union membership among employed wage owners 1970 and 1980: 51% and 57%*	Union membership among employed wage owners 1970 and 1980: 51% and 70%*
Population growth in capital region 1950–1975: 36%**	Population growth in capital region 1950–1975: 39%**	Population growth in capital region 1950–1975: 69%**
Weaker regional policy legacy	Strongest regional policy legacy	Weakest regional policy legacy
Earlier and stronger institutionalization of workplace democracy	Later and weaker institutionalization of workplace democracy	Later and weaker institutionalization of workplace democracy
Public opinion supporting/opposing relocation programs: 47%/21%***	Public opinion supporting/opposing relocation programs: 63%/9%***	No comparable data
Public opinion supporting/opposing workplace democracy: 73%/11%***	Public opinion supporting/opposing workplace democracy: 64%/13%***	No comparable data
Economic growth: 2.0%†	Economic growth: 5.6%†	Economic growth: 3.6%†
Budgetary surplus/deficit: 1974–1981: −0.2†	Budgetary surplus/deficit: 1974–1981: +3.3†	Budgetary surplus/deficit 1974–1981: +3.1†

Sources: *Andersen (1996); **NordRefo (1988); ***Petersson and Valen (1979); †Saunders (1985).

Comparative Statistics

Editor: FRED THOMPSON

Housing Conditions, States, Markets and Households: A Pan-European Analysis

MICHELLE NORRIS and HENRYK DOMAŃSKI

ABSTRACT *This article explores variations in housing outcomes in European Union member states that are measured in terms of the quality and affordability of accommodation. It reveals marked north/south and east/west inter-country variations in the outcomes considered. These variations are related to differences in housing inputs and outputs which are analyzed with reference to Esping-Andersen's (1999) distinction between the three main societal institutions that provide welfare services – states, markets and households. This analysis indicates that poor housing outcomes are associated with reliance on a single driver, i.e. state, market or household. Reliance on multiple drivers – states and markets for instance – is associated with better housing outcomes. However, household-driven housing systems, whether associated with another driver or not, generally result in poor outcomes.*

Comparative housing research has progressed significantly since Kemeny's (1992) *Housing and Social Theory* criticized both the lack of research in this field, the consequent ethno-centric nature of much housing research and the lack of an explicit and sound theoretical base for the majority of the comparative analyses that have been produced. Since then the first of these criticisms has largely been addressed and the last decade has seen the publication of many new significant instalments in the comparative housing literature (benchmark studies include: van Vliet and van Weesep 1990, Boelhouwer and van der Heijden 1992, Kemeny 1995, Golland 1998,

Angel 2000, Agus *et al.* 2002, Doling and Ford 2003, Allen *et al.* 2004, Ronald 2008). However, despite this progress, Kemeny's (1992) second criticism remains relevant and some methodological problems remain. For instance, many studies in this genre are based on the comparison of a limited number of (usually large, western European) countries, which raises issues about their comprehensiveness. With some important exceptions (Barlow and Duncan 1994, Balchin 1996) conceptual development in this field also remains slow compared to other comparative public policy genres. Several authors have drawn on typologies of other welfare services, such as Esping-Andersen's (1990) analysis of social security systems which is employed in Kurz and Blossfeld's (2004) comparative study of owner occupation. However the distinctiveness of housing as the "wobbly pillar" of the welfare state (Torgersen 1987) which, unlike social security provision, is funded mainly by markets and households rather than governments, indicates that this strategy may not always be appropriate. Most of the comparative housing studies conducted to date are also concerned with the analysis of housing *inputs* (such as government spending and housing policy regimes) and housing *outputs* (most commonly tenure structures) (e.g. Barlow and Duncan 1994, Golland 1998, Milligan 2003, Scanlon and Whitehead 2004). Although these factors are useful for categorizing inter-country similarities and differences between housing systems, their meaningfulness as indicators of populations' actual housing experiences is open to question.

Apart from conceptual development issues most of these deficiencies in the comparative housing literature are related to practical issues. These include: the lack of relevant, robust data sources and the complexity of systems of housing provision in developed countries, which as mentioned above generally involve action by some combination of states, markets and individual households, and due to the lumpy nature of housing investment usually necessitate very long term intervention in order to effect significant change in outcomes (Ploeger *et al.* 2001). Thus it would not be possible to address all or even the majority of these problems here. Rather our objective is to address some of them by taking advantage of recent improvements in the data available on housing in European Union (EU) member states to devise a comprehensive and multi-dimensional framework for comparing housing systems in these countries.

The starting point of this analysis is the most meaningful indicator of housing experiences – *housing outcomes*, which are measured using both objective and subjective indicators of housing conditions. This section of the article examines inter-country variations in this regard in all 27 current EU member states. The analysis then proceeds to assess the impact of three factors, encompassing both housing *inputs* and *outputs*, which are identified in the comparative housing literature as the most significant drivers of these differences in housing outcomes (Balchin 1996). These factors, which also reflect Esping-Andersen's (1999) distinction between the three main societal institutions that provide welfare services, are as follows:

- *States:* including housing policies, the tenure systems related to these policies and state provision and regulation of housing finance which is assessed using the concept of de-commodification, i.e. the extent to which living standards can be maintained independently of labour market participation.

- *Markets:* including recent and historic trends in GDP per capita and market provision of housing finance which is assessed with reference to the concept of commodification, i.e. the extent to which living standards are reliant on labour market participation.
- *Households:* including household structure and characteristics and expenditure on housing which is assessed using the concept of de-familization, i.e. the extent to which living standards can be maintained independent of relatives.

The conclusions to this article set out the findings of this analysis of the relationship between states, markets and household and variations in housing outcomes and reflect on the implications of these findings for housing policy.

Data and Methods

The primary source of data for this analysis is the European Quality of Life Survey (EQLS) which was conducted for the first time in 2003 and examined a wide range of issues relating to quality of life, including housing conditions in all 27 current EU member states (Donánski et al. 2003). The EQLS provides the most up-to-date and comprehensive source of information on housing in Europe and because of its wide range enables the comparison of housing issues with many other social and economic variables from a single and therefore comparable data source.

However, reliance on this dataset required some compromises. The broad range of issues covered in the EQLS necessitated the inclusion of relatively few questions addressing each topic, and in order to support the broad ranging analysis proferred here, these data had to be supplemented by information from other sources. Although the use of multiple sources of data was kept to a minimum in order to reduce problems of comparability, the use of more than one data source and the unavailability of longitudinal data on all of the issues under examination precluded the use of advanced statistical techniques in this analysis. Thus the investigation presented here was conducted principally by inspection of trends in these data and analysis of the relevant literature rather than by formal statistical testing.

Housing Conditions

Table 1 employs EQLS data to assess housing conditions in Europe. In order to do this it examines five "objective" measures of housing conditions: whether dwellings have at least one room per occupant, an indoor toilet and no reported shortage of space or rot in windows, doors or floors or damp or leaks. The first of these measures reflects the standard measure of overcrowding in most European countries, the remainder reflect several of the most commonly used self-reported measures of housing conditions (obviously many other key indicators of housing conditions require expert technical assessment of the dwelling) (Meijer 2002). Housing affordability is also a key indicator of housing conditions so this table employs the only two EQLS variables pertinent to this issue – whether households had missed a rent or mortgage payment in the last three months and the affordability of home heating. Following the growing use of subjective social indicators in, for instance, the quality of life research (Fahey and Smyth 2004), we also examine the proportion of

Table 1. Housing outcomes in European Union member states, 2003

Country	have at least one room per occupant in their dwelling	do not report shortage of space in their dwelling	do not report rot in windows, doors or floors in their dwelling	do not report damps or leaks in their dwelling	do not report the lack of an indoor toilet in their dwelling	can afford to keep their dwelling adequately warm	have not been in arrears in their rent or mortgage payments in the last 12 months	are satisfied with their level of accommodation (7–10)	do not report any of these problems	Ranking among EU member states (1 = highest = fewest households report problems)
Germany	93.8	89.5	96.1	90.2	99.1	95.7	95.0	82.6	66.6	1
Denmark	94.8	80.5	94.8	89.5	98.8	98.1	97.8	88.4	64.7	2
Austria	87.6	85.1	94.9	91.2	98.5	99.0	96.5	85.3	62.9	3
Sweden	89.8	80.2	97.1	93.9	98.8	98.8	95.9	82.2	62.9	4
Belgium	95.6	85.5	90.4	86.3	96.5	96.7	91.3	84.3	59.6	5
Netherlands	95.4	84.4	90.3	88.6	97.5	98.1	92.3	86.6	59.4	6
Finland	91.3	78.0	90.9	85.3	98.4	98.8	90.5	86.9	54.4	7
Ireland	83.1	83.0	91.1	87.3	98.0	93.3	87.5	82.2	53.2	8
France	92.9	78.8	89.0	85.5	98.8	92.7	91.8	72.8	52.6	9
Luxembourg	86.5	72.6	94.5	93.2	100.0	93.4	94.2	85.3	50.4	10
United Kingdom	89.7	78.3	92.8	91.8	98.9	93.0	89.9	76.8	47.9	11
Spain	82.3	85.6	94.6	86.4	98.1	85.7	94.5	73.9	47.0	12
Czech Republic	76.6	84.2	93.0	86.6	94.6	91.3	92.6	69.4	43.2	13
Cyprus	83.9	82.9	84.7	79.2	95.8	88.3	89.4	68.4	42.4	14
Slovenia	68.8	84.7	86.3	87.4	95.5	96.8	92.8	71.9	39.5	15
Greece	76.8	78.6	88.5	81.2	95.2	87.6	87.1	67.4	37.1	16
Malta	89.6	86.8	78.6	68.9	98.9	77.7	92.1	86.6	37.6	17
Italy	80.2	79.7	87.7	86.7	98.4	93.2	68.5	79.7	36.2	18
Hungary	62.6	81.7	75.5	84.4	91.1	88.4	88.2	60.6	30.7	19
Slovakia	66.6	85.7	59.2	86.3	92.3	82.5	85.9	58.7	25.7	20
Portugal	79.5	74.7	84.3	60.2	94.7	54.0	88.9	55.0	20.2	21
Poland	45.2	70.2	72.3	79.3	89.1	67.6	76.8	51.3	16.9	22

(*continued*)

Table 1. (*Continued*)

	Percentage of respondents who							
Country	have at least one room per occupant in their dwelling	do not report shortage of space in their dwelling	do not report rot in windows, doors or floors in their dwelling	do not report damps or leaks in their dwelling	do not report the lack of an indoor toilet in their dwelling	can afford to keep their dwelling adequately warm	have not been in arrears in their rent or mortgage payments in the last 12 months	are satisfied with their level of accommodation (7–10)	do not report any of these problems	Ranking among EU member states (1 = highest = fewest households report problems)
---	---	---	---	---	---	---	---	---	---	---
Estonia	79.8	68.5	58.8	68.3	82.9	65.9	86.8	53.5	16.2	23
Latvia	57.9	70.7	66.4	69.3	79.5	72.8	80.2	50.3	15.3	24
Bulgaria	65.7	78.5	80.3	75.0	70.1	48.6	83.6	51.6	10.1	25
Romania	68.6	72.0	69.8	70.5	60.7	49.8	82.5	71.1	9.7	26
Lithuania	61.7	74.1	64.4	79.7	75.1	41.6	85.7	41.4	8.9	27
Mean	82.3	81.0	87.7	85.3	94.7	86.8	87.4	74.0	44.7	

Source: Generated from the European Quality of Life Survey, 2003.

respondents who are satisfied with their level of accommodation (percentage who ranked it between seven and ten out of ten). Finally, the table details the proportion of respondents who did not report any of the aforementioned problems.

The last of these items may be regarded as a synthetic measure of housing outcomes in European countries. According to this ranking, in the top third in Europe are all north-western European countries which joined the EU prior to 2004 (hereafter: EU15 countries). These are, in descending order: Germany, Denmark, Austria, Sweden, Belgium, the Netherlands, Finland, Ireland and France. Those countries identified in Table 1 as having intermediate housing standards include a mix of EU15 countries and new EU member states which have acceded to membership since 2004 (NMS). With the exception of the UK and Luxembourg where housing conditions are at the top of the intermediate group, all of the other EU15 countries in this category are southern European countries (i.e. Spain, Greece and Italy), or NMS (the Czech Republic, Cyprus, Slovenia and Malta). Finally, in the bottom third of housing conditions in Europe are mostly former communist NMS (Hungary, Slovakia, Poland, Estonia, Latvia, Bulgaria, Romania and Lithuania) – Portugal is the only representative of the EU15 in this category.

State

In European countries state intervention relevant to housing conditions has principally involved: controlling housing tenure, housing output and housing design and standards (Balchin 1996). These policies have been operationalized by means of: direct state involvement in the provision of housing, subsidizing the provision of housing by others and regulating housing construction and standards (Norris and Shiels 2007). This section examines the impact of these factors on housing conditions in EU members.

The impact of public expenditure on housing outcomes in EU countries is examined in Figures 1 and 2. These graphs compare *direct* public expenditure on housing in 1990 and 2003 (which includes: social housing, rent benefits and means tested benefits) to housing outcomes in the latter year. Due to the lack of housing outcomes data for 1990 we have to rely on the 2003 EQLS for both points in time under the assumption that the international hierarchy of outcomes did not change significantly over this period. These graphs indicate that there is a broad relationship between public expenditure on housing and housing outcomes across the EU – particularly in Spain, Ireland, France, Italy, Malta and the Czech Republic – where the percentage of GDP devoted to public expenditure on housing rises so do housing outcomes (as measured in terms of the percentage of respondents not reporting problems). However, in the other EU members the relationship between these variables is weaker. Notably, Figure 2 indicates that in a large number of EU15 countries (specifically: Austria, Belgium, Denmark, Finland, Germany, Luxembourg, the Netherlands and Sweden) housing outcomes are better than would be expected in view of the proportion of GDP devoted to public spending on this area, whereas in several NMS (Estonia, Latvia, Lithuania, Slovakia and Hungary) and in Greece and the UK, the opposite is the case.

Housing is an inelastic good and many years of expenditure are required to effect a significant change in housing conditions. Therefore, the inter-country discrepancies

Figure 1. Comparison of public expenditure on housing as a percentage of GDP (1990) and housing outcomes (2003) in European Union member states

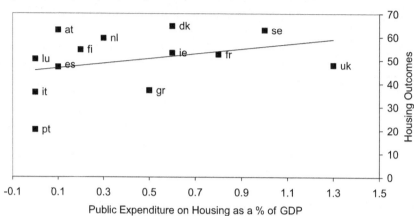

Sources: data generated from Eurostat (1990) and the European Quality of Life Survey (2003).
Notes: at = Austria; dk = Denmark; es = Spain; fi = Finland; fr = France; gr = Greece; ie = Ireland; it = Italy; lu = Luxembourg; nl = Netherlands; pt = Portugal; se = Sweden; uk = United Kingdom.
Data for: Belgium, Bulgaria, Cyprus, the Czech Republic, Estonia, Germany, Hungary, Latvia, Lithuania, Malta, Poland, Romania, Slovenia and Slovakia are not available.

Figure 2. Comparison of public expenditure on housing as a percentage of GDP (2000) and housing outcomes (2003) in European Union member states

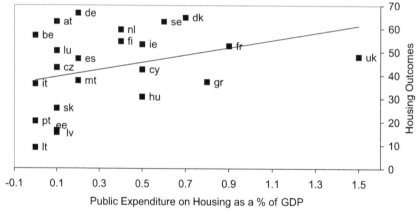

Sources: data generated from Eurostat (2000) and the European Quality of Life Survey (2003).
Notes: at = Austria; be = Belgium; cy = Cyprus; cz = Czech Republic; dk = Denmark; de = Germany; ee = Estonia; es = Spain; fi = Finland; fr = France; gr = Greece; hu = Hungary; ie = Ireland; it = Italy; lv = Latvia; lt = Lithuania; lu = Luxembourg; mt = Malta; nl = Netherlands; pt = Portugal; sk = Slovakia; se = Sweden; uk = United Kingdom. Data for Bulgaria, Slovenia and Romania are not available.

between state housing expenditure and housing conditions outlined above may be related to the long-term variations in direct government spending and indeed to differences in indirect expenditure (via for instance tax relief) – but no robust data are available to assess these issues. However, there is evidence that these discrepancies are also related to variations in the focus of housing policies and, as was mentioned above, tenure has traditionally been a key (explicit or implicit) focus of such policies.

Very broadly speaking, from the end of World War II until the 1980s, the literature identifies three housing tenure models which prevailed in the 27 current EU members (although other tenure models have been proposed they are less prominent in the literature). Among the EU15, Kemeny (1995) distinguishes between dual and unitary systems. In the dual system, which operates in Ireland and the UK, home ownership dominates and the social rented sector, which is largely state owned and managed, provides a safety net for the most disadvantaged households (see Table 2). In contrast, in the unitary systems that operate in countries such as Denmark, tenure patterns are driven by household preferences rather than government interventions, which are generally tenure neutral. Consequently, the owner occupied sector is generally smaller, the social rented sector is larger and less residualized than is the norm in countries which conform to the dual model (see Table 2).

In contrast, until the 1990s the former communist NMS countries adhered, with varying levels of definitude, to what Hegedüs and Tosics (1996) have termed the "East European housing model" (EEHM). The key characteristics of this model are:

- housing was defined as a state guaranteed social right, rather than a commodity;
- thus, there was state control over the production, consumption and allocation of most housing and the role of the market in this area was constrained;
- consequently, the level of homeownership was relatively low and a large proportion of the housing stock was state owned; and
- although this state owned rented housing tenure shared many of the characteristics of social housing in the EU15 (non-market allocation systems, rent regulation, subsidization) it was not necessarily allocated according to need.

However, it is important to stress that the degree of adherence to this model varied significantly among the countries in question and also over time. For instance, as a result of financial constraints, from the 1960s some countries, such as Hungary, began to diverge from the EEHM by introducing "marketization" reforms which involved the removal of barriers to the operation of the market in this sector and the re-privatization of housing (Pichler-Milanovich 2001).

Comparison of these housing tenure patterns with the data on housing outcomes (presented in Table 1) reveals that the vast majority of those countries where housing outcomes are in the top one-third in the EU employ the unitary system. In turn, most countries which followed the EEHM are in the bottom one-third.

In order to examine this issue in more detail, Table 3 compares housing tenure and housing outcomes using EQLS data. The latter are proportions of respondents who did not report problems with housing (see the last column of Table 1). It confirms that the large social rented sectors associated with the unitary housing systems are associated with relatively high housing standards, whereas among adherents to the EEHM, and in Spain, Portugal, Greece and Italy where tenure patterns conform to the dual model, housing outcomes among tenants are relatively low, which appears to have suppressed the mean housing outcome score for the countries in question.

Table 2. Occupied dwellings by tenure in European countries (%), 1990, 2000

Country	1990 Rented	1990 Owner occupied	1990 Co-operative	1990 Other	2000 Rented	2000 Owner occupied	2000 Co-operative	2000 Other
Austria	41	55	0	4	Nav	Nav	Nav	Nav
Belgium	33	67	0	0	32	68	0	0
Cyprus	13	64	0	23	14	68	0	18
Czech Republic	40	38	19	3	29	47	17	7
Denmark	40	45	5	1	39	52	7	2
Finland	25	72	0	3	32	64	0	4
France	39	54	0	7	39	55	0	7
Germany	58	42	0	0	Nav	Nav	Nav	Nav
Ex GDR	74	26	0	0	Nav	Nav	Nav	Nav
Greece	24	76	0	0	20	74	0	6
Hungary	26	74	0	0	7	92	0	1
Ireland	18	79	0	3	Nav	Nav	Nav	Nav
Italy	26	68	0	6	Nav	Nav	Nav	Nav
Latvia	79	21	0	0	30	70	0	0
Lithuania	Nav	Nav	Nav	Nav	7	91	0	0
Luxembourg	30	64	0	6	26	70	0	4
Netherlands	55	45	0	0	47	53	0	0
Poland	Nav	Nav	Nav	Nav	26	55	19	0
Portugal	28	67	0	5	21	75	0	4
Slovak Republic	28	49	22	1	21	75	0	4
Slovenia	28	49	22	1	9	74	15	2
Spain	15	78	0	7	10	84	0	6
Sweden	44	39	17	0	39	46	15	0
United Kingdom	35	65	0	0	31	69	0	0

Source: National Board of Housing Building and Planning, Sweden and Ministry for Regional Development of the Czech Republic (2004).
Notes: Nav means not available. GDR means German Democratic Republic. Data for the following countries are not available: Bulgaria, Estonia, Malta, Romania.

Table 3. Housing outcomes by housing tenure in European Union member states, 2003

	Housing outcomes by tenure					
	Owned without mortgage	Owned with mortgage	Private rented	Social rented	Rent free	Other
Austria	73.6	67.0	52.1	56.3	56.3	Nav
Belgium	72.3	67.4	30.6	31.2	52.2	69.6
Bulgaria	11.3	Nav	5.2	Nav	0.9	8.3
Cyprus	53.7	35.8	23.9	Nav	13.5	9.5
Czech Republic	54.1	51.0	27.7	36.1	29.8	46.4
Denmark	83.7	72.2	50.9	47.2	Nav	49.8
Estonia	17.0	16.7	13.5	10.0	23.6	8.4
Finland	63.7	54.0	39.9	47.9	7.4	74.6
France	71.9	62.4	35.9	40.2	38.9	17.8
Germany	83.4	72.3	55.7	54.7	73.2	32.6
Greece	41.5	34.5	30.6	9.9	17.5	30.7
Hungary	34.1	23.2	21.6	14.3	Nav	25.9
Ireland	62.4	63.2	34.6	18.9	51.0	49.2
Italy	37.0	52.5	29.5	30.2	11.9	Nav
Latvia	17.8	18.9	12.7	13.7	13.7	Nav
Lithuania	9.2	5.7	6.8	15.8	7.5	Nav
Luxembourg	54.0	62.5	35.0	Nav	25.9	43.0
Malta	43.0	32.6	21.4	13.4	33.5	51.4
Netherlands	65.5	69.2	47.9	51.1	49.4	48.9
Poland	21.8	Nav	Nav	7.8	15.6	6.3
Portugal	25.9	37.7	6.8	0.7	11.8	25.5
Romania	10.4	13.8	12.5	Nav	5.1	Nav
Slovakia	28.5	35.0	13.5	4.2	8.9	25.8
Slovenia	43.8	26.5	24.2	14.0	27.3	37.0
Spain	52.1	52.2	26.7	55.2	30.7	37.0
Sweden	76.4	69.7	47.4	56.3	34.1	41.0
United Kingdom	67.5	53.4	31.7	31.4	23.3	47.1
Mean	42.5	58.3	35.3	37.3	22.7	27.6

Source: Data generated from the European Quality of Life Survey, 2003.

In the EU15, large social housing sectors are broadly associated with higher housing standards, because in addition to addressing housing shortages, the key impetus behind the expansion of this sector was eliminating poor housing conditions by re-housing the occupants of the mainly private rented slum dwellings (Harloe 1995). In contrast, Allen *et al.* (2004) report that the social housing sectors of the southern EU15 states were generally too small to eliminate poor housing conditions and that state controls on private rents in these countries incentivized landlords to run down rather than maintain and improve their properties.

According to Hegedüs and Tosics (1996: 37), the tenure policy which underpinned the EEHM was the fundamental cause of poor housing standards because "housing was regarded as a social good but no society could really afford this". Tosics (1998: 227) also suggests that "even in the period of relatively high budget expenditures on housing" this model "was quite an inefficient way of allocating this money" because it was associated with over-centralized housing policies which did not reflect the needs of consumers or of different regions and, being completely dependent on the state budget, were often radically changed at the first sign of budget difficulties.

The period 1990 to 2000 saw marked changes in the tenure structure of many of the countries under examination. In many of the northern countries of the EU15 where public spending on housing was traditionally high, state capital subsidies for social housing construction were radically reduced and replaced, only in part, by housing allowances targeted at low-income households (Gibb 2002). The termination of these construction incentives effected a sharp decline in social house building and around the same time some countries, notably the UK and the Netherlands, also began to privatize the social rented stock by means of sales to tenants. The combination of these measures, coupled with rising household incomes and easier access to credit due to liberalization of mortgage lending, led to a diminution in this tenure usually accompanied by a rise in the level of owner occupation (van der Heijden 2002).

However, the changes in tenure patterns effected by the collapse of the EEHM in the early 1990s were far more dramatic. Although this system had been in crisis for the preceding decade – indeed Hegedüs and Tosics (1996) suggest since its inception – four developments signalled its eventual demise. These are:

- reform of property rights to provide for owner occupation and the introduction of market institutions in the housing sector;
- reform of the state owned sector, which generally involved transfer of ownership to local authorities;
- privatization of this stock by means of sales to tenants; and
- withdrawal of central government subsidies for the construction of state owned housing which resulted in the practical cessation of new building (Pichler-Milanovich 2001).

These developments did not occur evenly across the region, however. Roberts (2003) considers Hungary, Slovenia, Bulgaria, Romania and Lithuania "fast privatizers" because between 40 and 90 per cent of the state owned housing was privatized between 1989 and 1994, whereas in the Czech Republic, Poland, Slovakia, Estonia and Latvia between 1 and 9 per cent of relevant dwellings were privatized in this period.

These changes in tenure policy and patterns had very different implications for housing outcomes in the EU15 and the NMS. The withdrawal of capital subsidies for social housing construction in the former is of course linked to the ascendance of neo-liberal ideology and the "delegitimization" of the tenure (Dunleavy 1981). However, the fact that poor housing standards had been largely eradicated in many of these countries and, in the context of low population growth, the housing shortage resolved, was also an important impetus behind these reforms.

Recent tenure changes have had a more negative impact on housing outcomes in the countries that formerly employed the EEHM. Tosics (2003) reports that a large number of former tenants of state owned properties who purchased these dwellings have low incomes and cannot afford to pay the fees necessary for their upkeep. While the even lower incomes of those who have remained tenants in this sector makes it difficult for landlords to raise rents to pay for maintenance and upgrading (Tsenkova and Turner 2004). This is confirmed by the data presented in Table 3 which reveals low housing outcomes in the social rented sectors in many of these countries.

In addition to the focus of housing policies and the level of public spending on housing there is evidence that the inefficiency of state housing finance systems in those NMS that employed the EEHM until 1990 had negative implications for housing standards. As a result of state control over housing production, consumption and allocation for instance, in most countries in this category a large proportion of funding for housing construction and maintenance also emanated from the state. However the prioritization of investment towards industry led to underinvestment in housing between 1950 and 1975, which in turn effected persistent housing shortages and overcrowding in several countries (Sillince 1990). Although the post-1960 marketization reforms did help increase private sector housing output, their impact was lessened by the economic crisis of the late 1970s and early 1980s, which reduced the level of both private and public housing investment. Kozlowski's (1988, cited in Hegedüs and Tosics 1996) study of Poland reveals that in this context targets for state owned housing output were achieved by decreasing per unit costs by lowering average apartment sizes and decreasing specifications, particularly in terms of equipment and finishes. In addition, the rent determination method generally associated with EEHM also had negative implications for housing quality. Prior to the 1980s (by which time the rent setting regime in many of the countries in question had been liberalized), rents were generally set at between 2 and 5 per cent of average family earnings. This was far too low to generate sufficient income for the maintenance of dwellings, and as a result very little maintenance was carried out (Sillince 1990).

The state has also influenced housing outcomes via its role in regulating housing construction and influencing building systems and styles, although the available evidence indicates that the first of these areas has been the least influential in this regard. Although all EU members currently have nationwide building regulations, these vary widely. The regulations were introduced earlier and are more rigorous in northern countries of the EU15, which may have contributed to the higher quality of dwellings in these countries compared to their southern counterparts (Meijer 2002).

In relation to construction styles, the fashion for high-rise dwelling designs and semi-prefabricated or "system" building techniques which spread steadily across Europe from the 1960s, inspired by a widespread housing shortage, and the influence of modernist architects and advances in building technology, have had particularly significant implications for housing outcomes (Wassenberg *et al.* 2004). As is evidenced by the large proportion of high-rise estates in the EU15 that are currently subject to regeneration projects, this design type is commonly (but not universally in this part of Europe) associated with poor quality accommodation and management, and social problems (Power 1997). However the influence and durability of the high-rise trend varied considerably between the countries under examination here. In most of the northern EU15 countries high-rise residential construction was largely confined to the social rented sector and was abandoned by the mid-1970s, consequently, a relatively small proportion of dwellings in these countries are high-rise. However, in several of the southern EU15 states, most notably Spain and Italy, mass high-rise construction continued for long after this in the private sector, which has resulted in a relatively high proportion of high-rise dwellings. This building style was embraced with particular enthusiasm in the NMS from the 1960s onwards as a solution to shortages of dwellings, finance and employment for unskilled workers. Output levels were high and this type of construction continued until the 1990s (Wassenberg *et al.* 2004). As a result, high-rise dwellings make up 14.7 per cent all dwellings in the EU15 compared to 34.1 per cent in the NMS.

Andrews and Sendi (2001) argue that the quality of high-rise dwellings is particularly problematic in those countries which formerly employed the EEHM. The formerly state owned housing stock in these countries was built almost exclusively in this style, but due to the aforementioned funding problems their initial build quality was often poor. This problem was compounded by arrangements for building these dwellings which generally necessitated the establishment of large construction companies and factories to manufacture the concrete panels from which they were assembled. According to Sillince (1990: 50):

> Such organisations often exerted ... a strong monopolistic control over (and hence simplification of) design and price (amounting to protectionism of increasingly out-of-date technology and methods). The lack of participation of the eventual customers – the residents – [led to] ... poor quality work. The result was a higher demolition rate and even higher costs to repair poorly constructed dwellings.

Market

Sourcing data on the commodification of housing provision in Europe is challenging. Tenure patterns can paint a misleading picture in this regard, as the owner occupied and private rented tenures may be subsidized by government. For the purposes of this analysis, mortgage debt as a percentage of GDP was selected as the only available and suitable indicator of market investment. In Figures 3 and 4 trends in this type of investment in 1990 and 2000 are compared to the indicators of housing outcomes set out in Table 1.

Significantly, from the perspective of the discussion at hand, Figure 3 reveals that in those northern EU15 countries where public investment in housing was high in the early 1990s private investment was generally also high and vice versa. This is because until recent years the mortgage lending market was relatively underdeveloped in the southern EU15 states. Consequently house purchase was often funded by non-credit

Figure 3. Comparison of mortgage debt as a percentage of GDP (1990) and housing outcomes (2003) in European Union member states

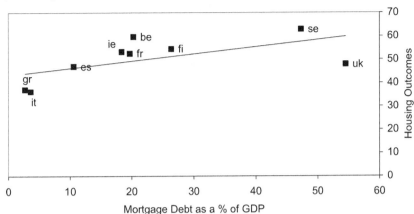

Sources: data generated from the European Mortgage Federation (1990) and the European Quality of Life Survey (2003).
Notes: be = Belgium; es = Spain; fi = Finland; fr = France; gr = Greece; ie = Ireland; it = Italy; se = Sweden; uk = United Kingdom. Data for: Austria, Bulgaria, Cyprus, the Czech Republic, Denmark, Germany, Estonia, Hungary, Latvia, Lithuania, Luxembourg, Malta, Netherlands, Poland, Portugal, Romania, Slovenia and Slovakia are not available.

Figure 4. Comparison of mortgage debt as a percentage of GDP (2000) and housing outcomes (2003) in European Union member states

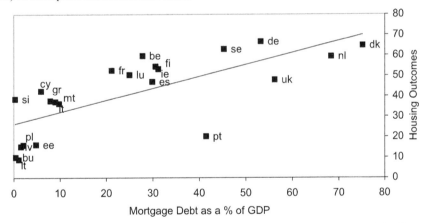

Sources: data generated from the European Mortgage Federation (2000) and the European Quality of Life Survey (2003).
Notes: be = Belgium; bu = Bulgaria; cy = Cyprus; dk = Denmark; de = Germany; ee = Estonia; es = Spain; fi = Finland; fr = France; gr = Greece; hu = Hungary; ie = Ireland; it = Italy; lv = Latvia; lt = Lithuania; lu = Luxembourg; mt = Malta; nl = Netherlands; pl = Poland; pt = Portugal; si = Slovenia; se = Sweden; uk = United Kingdom. Data for Austria, the Czech Republic, Hungary, Slovakia and Romania are not available.

methods such as self-building, personal savings and inheritance (Allen *et al.* 2003). These non-credit methods of funding such a bulky purchase as housing are associated with poorer housing standards and overcrowding because the initial investment is lower and in order to cope, strategies such as sharing with relatives or building a temporary dwelling, which is improved as funds allow, are often employed (Allen et al. 2003).

The availability of market funding for housing in the northern countries of the EU also reduced the potentially negative impact for housing outcomes of the cutbacks to state housing subsidies over the last two decades. By the mid-1990s, social landlords in Denmark, the Netherlands, France and Sweden derived the vast majority of their funding for the construction of new buildings from commercial borrowing (Priemus and Boelhouwer 1999).

In contrast, in several of the southern EU15 states the wider availability of mortgage credit since the mid-1990s as a result of market liberalization has helped to improve housing standards by increasing investment in new house building and renovation. In 2000, new house building rates in Spain and Portugal were 13.8 and 11.5 per 1,000 inhabitants respectively as compared to just 4.2 among the 20 current EU members for which data are available. This high output rate has improved housing outcomes by reducing overcrowding and because newer dwellings are more likely to include amenities such as indoor lavatories than their older counterparts. Thus, as a result of these developments, Ball (2005) argues that the longstanding gap between housing standards in the north and south of the EU15 has narrowed in recent years.

The collapse of the EEHM effected radical changes in housing finance systems in the relevant NMS countries. As mentioned above, subsidies for the construction of state owned housing, which had previously driven a large proportion of housing output, were largely withdrawn and although measures to support and regulate the development of private finance for housing were introduced, these have had mixed success. European Mortgage Federation data reveals that in 2000 the ratio of mortgage debt to GDP was 40.3 per cent in the EU15, but only 3.0 per cent in the NMS. Housing output in the NMS declined drastically during the first half of the 1990s, and has only recovered marginally since – in 2000 it averaged only 2.0 per 1,000 inhabitants, compared to 6.3 in the EU15 – which obviously has had negative implications for overcrowding and the quality of dwellings (Norris and Shiels 2004). Shinozaki (2005) attributes this occurrence primarily to underdevelopment of the mortgage lending system rather than to the macro-economy, lack of demand or the capacity of the construction industry. He argues that the mortgage lending systems in these countries are inefficient because they are dominated by a small number of commercial banks and thus have ologopolistic tendencies. These lenders often require high deposits and short repayment terms, which renders mortgages unaffordable for most households and discourages commercial builders from catering for this market (Norris and Shiels 2004).

Households

Esping-Andersen (1999) points out that the influence of the family on welfare is much more difficult to measure than that of states or markets because, unlike market supports, household self-servicing is not monitored and hence does not appear in national accounts, and unlike the state's role it is not mapped out in legislation or policy statements. In order to overcome this problem he suggests adopting an "eclectic methodological approach" which encompasses consideration of indirect measures such as data on intergenerational cohabitation and of the extent of welfare state and market non-provision, coupled with the direct data which are available in order to capture familialism or de-familization (Esping-Andersen 1999: 52). We follow this approach in the analysis presented below.

The first of these issues is examined in Table 4 which details the household status of households in the 18 to 34 age group in the EU. It reveals three distinct inter-country patterns of household formation among this population:

- In the north of the EU15 most young people live outside the parental home by the time they are 34, either alone (particularly if they are male), with a partner, or most commonly with a partner and children.
- By contrast in the south of the EU15 and in some NMS (such as Malta, Slovakia and Poland) a substantial proportion of males are still living in the parental home by the age of 34, whereas those living independently at this age are likely to have formed a partnership and, among females, to have children.
- Thirdly, in the other NMS and also in Ireland a significant minority of young people remain in the parental home after they form a partnership and/or have children or move to their partner's parental home.

These findings confirm the results of other research which has identified similar patterns in the living arrangements of young people, and despite widespread social change reveal no evidence of convergence of these patterns across Europe (Mayer 2001).

Cavalli and Galland (1996), relate the timing of exit from the parental home to internal and external factors. These are, firstly, the extent to which cultural values support or resist early exit and, secondly, the extent to which exit is facilitated or impeded by the labour and housing markets and state welfare provision. Detailed analysis of the import of the first of these factors is beyond the scope of this paper. However, earlier sections have examined the extent and efficiency of housing markets and state support for housing and comparison of this evidence with the data presented in Table 4 indicates that familial support for the housing of young people is much more common in countries where market and state supports are underdeveloped (i.e. the NMS and the south of the EU15) and less common in the northern EU15 countries where market and state supports are extensive and efficient. Interestingly, Saraceno et al.'s (2005) analysis of EQLS data indicates that housing may be the most significant of the external drivers of exit from the parental home. They found that the labour market participation does influence the timing of exit across the EU, but the significance of this factor varies between countries. Indeed, the proportion of young people at work is, on average, greater in those countries where young people leave the family home later.

This evidence regarding the extent of familialist housing solutions in the EU is further reinforced by Allen et al.'s (2004) research on the familialist housing strategies employed in the southern countries of the EU15. They identify three strategies of this type:

- patrimony: preservation of the stock of housing and land owned by the family rather than its sale and division among family members;

Table 4. Household status of people in the 18 to 34 age group in Europe, 2003

Country	Living with parents Male	Living with parents Female	Living alone Male	Living alone Female	Living as childless couple Male	Living as childless couple Female	Living as a couple with children Male	Living as a couple with children Female	Living as a childless couple in an extended household Male	Living as a childless couple in an extended household Female	Living as a couple with children in an extended household Male	Living as a couple with children in an extended household Female	Lone parent Male	Lone parent Female	Lone parent in an extended household Male	Lone parent in an extended household Female	Other kind of household Male	Other kind of household Female
Austria	29	13	35	23	14	26	13	18	4	1	0	2	2	12	1	2	2	4
Belgium	28	28	28	11	20	14	20	33	0	0	1	1	2	11	0	0	1	2
Bulgaria	50	23	11	3	3	13	23	25	4	8	6	19	0	4	0	2	4	3
Cyprus	43	29	16	6	9	20	19	30	7	7	2	1	2	2	0	1	3	5
Czech Rep	48	28	9	8	17	7	20	34	1	4	4	5	0	7	0	4	4	3
Denmark	17	8	33	28	28	28	20	21	0	0	0	1	0	9	0	0	1	5
Estonia	36	29	17	19	26	23	10	17	3	1	2	0	2	5	0	5	3	1
Finland	13	11	39	29	26	25	18	26	0	2	2	0	0	6	0	0	3	3
France	30	18	36	24	16	23	15	23	1	1	0	0	0	6	1	1	2	3
Germany	21	14	40	26	11	27	20	23	1	0	0	0	0	5	1	0	6	4
Greece	39	19	33	24	8	14	9	33	0	0	2	3	1	0	0	1	8	6
Hungary	47	32	13	5	10	14	16	25	9	5	2	11	1	3	0	1	2	5
Ireland	25	19	10	7	14	15	15	18	6	6	2	7	1	12	5	3	18	13
Italy	67	60	11	6	8	12	11	20	0	0	0	1	0	2	0	0	2	2
Latvia	39	22	14	13	13	20	21	24	3	3	6	4	2	6	0	5	3	4
Lithuania	41	18	9	8	8	14	34	35	1	1	7	8	0	10	1	3	0	4
Luxembourg	35	25	12	5	13	13	25	39	2	3	2	2	0	4	3	3	7	6
Malta	67	55	7	4	9	14	9	11	4	6	1	2	0	1	1	0	2	7
Netherlands	36	22	27	20	19	22	12	25	2	1	1	0	1	10	0	0	2	1
Poland	55	46	2	3	4	4	22	23	4	4	7	11	0	3	2	5	4	2
Portugal	48	33	7	5	8	10	28	30	1	3	3	8	0	9	0	1	5	2
Romania	51	19	6	11	12	18	11	20	11	10	5	6	1	2	2	2	4	12
Slovakia	57	41	4	1	4	421	21	31	2	2	10	11	1	3	0	4	2	2
Slovenia	53	43	10	6	10	11	17	26	3	1	2	8	0	3	1	0	5	3
Spain	45	34	5	5	22	16	13	26	3	1	2	3	0	2	0	2	9	10
Sweden	12	10	44	31	17	24	22	23	1	2	2	0	1	5	0	0	5	5
UK	19	12	33	14	22	36	8	19	4	1	0	0	1	13	0	1	12	4

Source: Generated from the European Quality of Life Survey, 2003.

- family: extended family contribution to house purchase or construction costs either in cash or in-kind (provision of land or labour); and
- self-promotion of housing: whereby the home owner provides the labour for the construction of the dwelling.

They also explain that these strategies are associated with poor housing outcomes, such as overcrowding due to late exit from the parental home and poor building standards due to the use of strategies such as constructing part of a dwelling which is completed as funds allow.

In some southern European countries there is evidence that the importance of familialist housing solutions has diminished in recent years as the extent of market investment has grown. Comparison of Figures 3 and 4 reveals that mortgage debt as a proportion of GDP rose dramatically in Spain between 1990 and 2000 and although 1990 data are not available for Portugal, in 2000 mortgage debt in that country was well above the EU average. Notably these graphs reveal no corresponding increase in this type of investment in Italy and Greece. While Figures 1 and 2 indicate in all of these four countries public expenditure on housing as a percentage of GDP remained relatively modest between 1990 and 2000.

Conclusions

This article opened with an examination of housing outcomes in EU member states in terms of the quality and affordability of accommodation. This revealed that these are generally poorer in the new EU members and to a lesser extent the countries in the south of the EU15, while housing outcomes in north-western Europe are better. In the main body of the article these inter-country variations in housing outcomes were linked to differences in housing inputs and outputs which were in turn related to the themes of state, market and household, which Esping-Andersen (1999) identifies as the main societal institutions that deliver welfare services.

Based on the results of the latter analysis, the position of the systems of housing provision of each of these 27 countries in Esping-Andersen's (1999) "welfare triangle" are plotted in Figures 5 and 6. In order to take account of the radical changes in housing inputs and outputs which took place around 1990 in European countries, particularly in the NMS, the first of these diagrams examines the pre-1990 period and the second focuses on the period since then. These diagrams also attempt to overcome the limitations of the "ideal type" categorization of countries presented in the preceding analysis by taking account of the extent to which housing outcomes are influenced by a combination of state, market and household related factors. This is important because the relevant literature indicates that these categories are indivisible in practice. Allen et al. (2004) point out for instance that familialist housing solutions common in the southern EU15 countries prior to 1990 were often necessitated by the absence or weakness of state interventions, while Shinozaki (2005) attributes the underdevelopment of the commercial mortgage lending system in the former communist NMS primarily to the absence or inefficiency of state regulation of this sector.

Figure 5, which examines housing systems prior to 1990, highlights a number of European countries that were reliant on a single "driver" of housing provision,

Figure 5. Typology of inputs and outputs in European Union member states, pre-1990

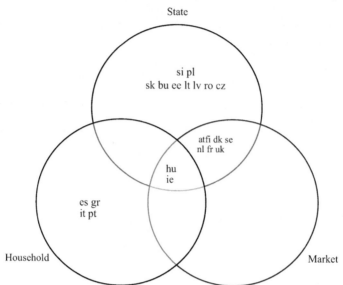

Notes: at = Austria; bu = Bulgaria; cz = Czech Republic; dk = Denmark; de = Germany; ee = Estonia; es = Spain; fi = Finland; fr = France; gr = Greece; hu = Hungary; ie = Ireland; it = Italy; lv = Latvia; lt = Lithuania; nl = Netherlands; pl = Poland; pt = Portugal; ro = Romania; si = Slovenia; sk = Slovakia; se = Sweden; uk = United Kingdom. Data are not available for the following countries: Belgium, Cyprus, Germany, Luxembourg and Malta.

i.e. on the state or market or household, rather than a combination of these. For instance, in the then communist NMS, most housing was provided by the state, while most southern EU15 countries operated familialist housing systems during this period. Comparison of this categorization with the data on housing outcomes presented in Table 1 indicates most countries where housing conditions were in the poorest one-third in the EU were reliant on a single driver of housing conditions. In contrast, in the mainly northern EU15 countries, where Figure 5 indicates housing provision is driven by a combination of factors (states and markets for instance), housing outcomes are above the European average according to the data presented in Table 1. However, this analysis also indicates that familialist housing solutions, whether associated with another driver or not, also generally result in poor outcomes. For instance, due to heavy reliance on self-provisioning of housing by individual households, housing outcomes in Spain were relatively poor during this period.

Figure 6 reveals that by the end of the 1990s the key drivers of housing outcomes had changed across most of the EU. Reliance on the state had largely ceased in the former communist NMS, but the underdevelopment of market drivers had resulted in increased reliance on familialist housing solutions, consequently housing outcomes here remain relatively poor compared to other EU members. In many northern EU15 countries the influence of the state on housing systems has declined since the early 1990s. However, most of these countries (Belgium and Germany are

Figure 6. Typology of housing inputs and outputs in European Union member states, post-1990

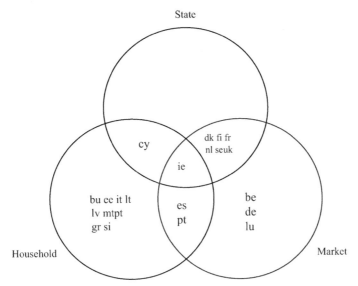

Notes: be = Belgium; bu = Bulgaria; cy = Cyprus; dk = Denmark; de = Germany; ee = Estonia; es = Spain; fi = Finland; fr = France; gr = Greece; ie = Ireland; it = Italy; lv = Latvia; lt = Lithuania; lu = Luxembourg; mt = Malta; nl = Netherlands; pl = Poland; pt = Portugal; si = Slovenia; se = Sweden; uk = United Kingdom. No data are available for the following: Austria, Czech Republic, Hungary, Romania and Slovakia.

exceptions) continue to employ a mixed housing model whereby states and markets are the most significant drivers of housing outcomes and familialist housing solutions are not widespread. As a result, housing conditions in these countries remain the best in the EU. However, in recent years improved efficiency of market supports for housing in the southern EU15 countries, particularly Spain and Portugal, is likely to have contributed to a north/south convergence in housing outcomes.

In terms of the implications of this analysis for housing policy, it indicates that state withdrawal from housing provision and consequent recommodification of this sector in the EU15 in recent years has not had the negative implications for housing outcomes which might have been expected. This is because of the increasing accessibility of market sector housing and finance for lower income households and the re-focusing of the remaining state housing investment towards neighbourhood regeneration measures intended to address the vestiges of poor quality dwellings in these countries. In the former communist new EU members, however, the picture is very different. Here market provision has largely failed to fill the vacuum left by the sharp withdrawal of government from the housing sphere in the early 1990s and housing outcomes have deteriorated as a result. This indicates that increased state intervention in housing in these countries may be necessary. Recently, this argument has formed the basis of a successful campaign by NMS governments to extend eligibility for EU Structural Funding (the main mechanism for redistribution of EU investment to disadvantaged regions) to include housing regeneration projects in these countries. This campaign was predicated on the concern that neither governments nor households in this part of Europe will be able to shoulder the cost of renovating high-rise housing, which is estimated to be over €350 billion (Netherlands Ministry of Housing Spatial Planning and the Environment 2004). However, in addition to public spending the analysis presented in this article indicates that more effective regulatory intervention by national governments could also help to improve housing outcomes at relatively minimal costs. For instance, Merrill and Kozlowski (2001) argue that introducing mortgage default insurance would enable the liberalization of lending criteria in these countries and Shinoazki (2005) suggests that better targeting of existing state home purchase supports at lower income households would invigorate these sections of the housing market which are currently dormant in many NMS.

Acknowledgements

The authors wish to acknowledge that the European Mortgage Federation supplied the data on mortgage debt which is employed in this paper.

References

Agus, Mohammed Razali, Doling, John and Lee, Dong-Sung, 2002, *Housing Policy Systems in South East Asia* (London: Macmillan).
Allen, Judith, Barlow, James, Leal, Jesús, Maloutas, Thomas and Padovani, Liliana, 2004, *Housing and Welfare in Southern Europe* (London: Blackwell).
Andrews, Kaliopa and Sendi, Richard, 2001, Large housing estates in Slovenia: a framework for renewal. *European Journal of Housing Policy*, **1**, 233–255.
Angel, Shlomo, 2000, *Housing Policy Matters: A Global Analysis* (Oxford: Oxford University Press).
Balchin, Paul (Ed.) 1996, *Housing Policy in Europe* (London: Routledge).
Ball, Michael, 2005, *RICS European Housing Review 2005* (London: Royal Institute of Chartered Surveyors).
Barlow, James and Duncan, Simon, 1994, *Success and Failure in Housing Provision: European Systems Compared* (London: Pergamon).
Boelhouwer, Peter and van der Heijden, Harry, 1992, *Housing Systems in. Europe: Part I. A Comparative Study of Housing Policy* (Delft: Delft University Press).
Cavalli, Alessandro and Galland, Olivier, 1996, *Youth in Europe* (London: Pinter).
Doling, John and Ford, Janet, 2003, *Globalisation and Home Ownership: Experiences in Eight Member States of the European Union* (Delft: Delft University Press).
Domański, Henryk, Ostrowska, Antonia, Przybysz, Dariusz and Romaniuk, Agatha, 2003, *First European Quality of Life Survey: Social Dimensions of Housing* (Dublin: European Foundation for the Improvement of Living and Working Conditions).
Dunleavy, Patrick, 1981, *The Politics of Mass Housing in Britain, 1945–1975: A Study of Corporate Power and Professional Influence in the Welfare State* (Oxford: Clarendon).
Esping-Andersen, Gosta, 1990, *The Three Worlds of Welfare Capitalism* (Princeton, NJ: Princeton University Press).
Esping-Andersen, Gosta, 1999, *The Social Foundations of Postindustrial Economies* (Oxford: Oxford University Press).
European Mortgage Federation, 2004, *Hypostat 2004* (Brussels: European Mortgage Federation).
Fahey, Tony and Smyth, Emer, 2004, Do Subjective Indicators Measure Welfare? Evidence from 33 European Societies. *European Societies*, **6**, 5–27.
Golland, A., 1998, *Systems of Housing Supply and Housing Production in Europe: A Comparison of the United Kingdom, the Netherlands and Germany* (Aldershot: Ashgate).

Gibb, Kenneth, 2002, Trends and Change in Social Housing Finance and Provision within the European Union. *Housing Studies*, **17**, 325–336.
Harloe, Michael, 1995, *The People's Home? Social Rented Housing in Europe and America* (Oxford: Blackwell).
Hegedüs, József and Tosics, Ivan, 1996, The disintegration of the East European housing model, in: David Clapham, József Hegedüs, Keith Kintrea, and Ivan Tosics (Eds) *Housing Privatization in Eastern Europe* (London: Greenwood), pp. 15–40.
Kemeny, Jim, 1995, *From Public Housing to the Social Market: Rental Policy Strategies in Comparative Perspective* (London: Routledge).
Kemney, Jim, 1992, *Housing and Social Theory* (London: Routledge).
Kurz, Karin and Blossfeld, Hans-Peter, 2004, Introduction: social stratification, welfare regimes and access to home ownership, in: Karin Kurz and Hans-Peter Blossfeld (Eds) *Home Ownership and Social Inequality in Comparative Perspective* (Stanford, CA: Stanford University Press), pp. 1–20.
Mayer, Ulrich, 2001, The paradox of global social change and national path dependencies: life course patterns in advanced societies, in: Alison Woodward and Martin Kohli (Eds) *Inclusions and Exclusions in European Societies* (London: Routledge), pp. 89–110.
Meijer, Frits, 2002, *Building Regulations in Europe – Part 1: Comparison of the Systems of Building Control in Eight European Countries* (Delft: Delft University Press).
Merrill, Sally and Kozlowski, Edward, 2001, Developing housing finance in a transition economy: the case of Poland. *Journal of Housing Economics*, **10**, 363–392.
Milligan, Vivienne, 2003, *How Different? Comparing Housing Policies and Housing Affordability Consequences for Low Income Households in Australia and the Netherlands*, Netherlands Geographical Studies No. 3 (Utrecht: University of Utrecht).
National Board of Housing Building and Planning, Sweden and Ministry for Regional Development of the Czech Republic, 2004, *Housing Statistics in the European Union, 2004* (KarlsKrona: Boverkert).
Netherlands Ministry of Housing, Spatial Planning and the Environment, 2004, *Sustainable Refurbishment of High-Rise Residential Buildings and Restructuring of Surrounding Areas* (The Hague: Ministry of Housing, Spatial Planning and the Environment).
Norris, Michelle and Shiels, Patrick, 2004, *Regular National Report on Housing Developments in European Countries: Synthesis Report* (Dublin: Stationery Office).
Norris, Michelle and Shiels, Patrick, 2007, Housing inequalities in an enlarged European Union: patterns, drivers and implications. *Journal of European Social Policy*, **17**, 59–70.
Pichler-Milanovich, Natasha, 2001, Urban housing markets in Central and Eastern Europe: convergence, divergence or policy "collapse". *European Journal of Housing Policy*, **1**, 145–187.
Ploeger, Ralph, Lawson, Julie and Bontje, Marco, 2001, The methodological challenge to comparative research. *Journal of Housing and the Built Environment*, **16**, 1–5.
Power, Anne, 1997, *Estates on the Edge: The Social Consequences of Mass Housing in Northern Europe* (Basingstoke: Macmillan).
Priemus, Hugo and Boelhouwer, Peter, 1999, Social housing finance in Europe: trends and opportunities. *Urban Studies*, **36**, 633–645.
Roberts, Andrew, 2003, Privatization and rent deregulation in Eastern Europe, in: Stuart Lowe and Sasha Tsenkova (Eds) *Housing Change in East and Central Europe: Integration or Fragmentation?* (Aldershot: Ashgate), pp. 45–62.
Ronald, Richard, 2008, *The Ideology of Home Ownership: Homeowner Societies and the Role of Housing* (London: Palgrave).
Saraceno, Chiara, Olagnero, Manuela and Torrioni, Paola, 2005, *First European Quality of Life Survey: Families, Work and Social Networks* (Dublin: European Foundation for the Improvement of Living and Working Conditions).
Scanlon, Kathleen and Whitehead, Christine, 2004, *International Trends in Housing Tenure and Housing Finance* (London: Council of Mortgage Lenders).
Shinozaki, Shigehiro, 2005, A comparative assessment of housing finance markets in transition economies, in: OECD, *Housing Finance Markets in Transition Economies: Trends and Challenges* (Paris: OECD Publishing), pp. 7–81.
Sillince, John, 1990, Housing policy in Eastern Europe and the Soviet Union, in: John Sillince (Ed.) *Housing Policies in Eastern Europe and the Soviet Union* (London: Routledge), pp. 12–25.

Torgersen, Ulf, 1987, Housing: the wobbly pillar under the welfare state, in: Bengt Turner, Jim Kemeny and Lennart Lundqvist (Eds) *Between State and Market: Housing in the Post-industrial Era* (Gävle: Almqvist and Wiksell International), pp. 116–127.

Tosics, Ivan, 1998, European integration and the East-Central European "outsiders", in: Mark Kleinman, Walter Matznetter and Mark Stephens (Eds) *European Integration and Housing Policy* (London: Routledge), pp. 275–299.

Tosics, Ivan, 2003, Comparative Perspectives on Urban Housing Conditions, in: Stuart Lowe and Sasha Tsenkova (Eds.), *Housing Change in East and Central Europe: Integration or Fragmentation?* (Aldershot: Ashgate), pp. 73–80.

Tsenkova, Sasha and Turner, Bengt, 2004, The future of social housing in Eastern Europe: reforms in Latvia and Ukraine. *European Journal of Housing Policy*, **4**, 133–149.

Van der Heijden, Harry, 2002, Social rented housing in Western Europe – developments and expectations. *Urban Studies*, **39**, 327–340.

Van Vliet, Willem and van Weesep, Jam, (Eds) 1990, *Government and Housing: Developments in Seven Countries* (London: Sage).

Wassenberg, Frank, Turkington, Richard, and van Kempen, Roland, 2004, Prospects for high-rise estates, in: Frank Wassenberg, Richard Turkington and Roland van Kempen (Eds) *High Rise Housing in Europe* (Delft: Delft University Press), pp. 280–324.

Regional Policy Agglomeration: Arctic Policy in Canada and the United States

PETER J. MAY, BRYAN D. JONES, BETSI E. BEEM,
EMILY A. NEFF-SHARUM and MELISSA K. POAGUE

ABSTRACT *Regional policies addressing urban policy, rural policy and policies with specific regional targets tend to evolve from the consideration of disparate issues that impact the designated region rather than as co-ordinated strategies. We label this aggregation of disparate policies as policy agglomeration. We examine this phenomenon for domestic aspects of Arctic policies in Canada and the United States. Arctic policy in each setting is comprised of a diversity of policy components with limited policy targeting for the Arctic region or populations. The greater targeting of Canadian policies with respect to both place and indigenous populations is explained by institutional and political factors.*

Introduction

When one thinks of Arctic policy, the big issues of grappling with implications of climate change, protection of biodiversity and non-renewable resources, and co-operation among nations that have interests in the Arctic typically come to mind. These issues have been addressed in various international forums and are subjects of international accords. From the perspective of the scholars who study these accords, Arctic policy emanates from the accords and the institutions that are created to implement them. However, there are also national perspectives on policy making that concern such things as development and land use, economic concerns, governance and legal systems, health and other social needs, and protection from environmental harms. These domestic policy considerations are within the province of individual nations and their subunits. These issues have had less attention in discussions of Arctic policy and politics.

We argue that Arctic policy is illustrative of regional policies addressing urban policy, rural policy, and policies with specific regional targets. Regional policies tend to evolve from the consideration of disparate issues that impact the designated region rather than as co-ordinated strategies. We label this aggregation of component policies as policy agglomeration. Two sets of issues are relevant for this aggregation. One consideration is the topical focus of the various policy components. Gaps in regional policy emphases arise from the selective attention to issues. For example, Browne (2001) identifies the dominance of attention to farm issues over other pressing needs as a key failure of rural policy in the United States.

Another consideration is the degree to which the component policies target relevant places or populations. Fragmented regional policies are less problematic if the policy components have consistent targeting. The policy impact is lessened, however, if the targeting of the component policies is dissipated. For example, Baumgartner and Jones (1993: 126–149) discuss how the urban policy of the 1960s in the United States was undermined by subsequent political pressures to provide federal fiscal subsidies to an expanding array of local governments.

This research addresses Arctic policy in Canada and the United States in order to illustrate regional policy agglomeration and the difficulties of regional policy targeting. Arctic policy is a good case to consider because it is less studied, provides a setting with a diversity of issues and interests, and has a relatively short history to recount. In discussing Arctic policies we consider the patterns of policy agglomeration and the degree of policy targeting. We show that the agglomeration of policy components to form Arctic policies is similar in the two settings. We also show that the targeting of Arctic regions and populations differs between the two settings.

Our discussion of these issues is organized as follows. We first discuss the conceptual foundations with attention to the relevance of the comparison of Arctic policies in Canada and the United States. From this discussion, we draw hypotheses about the targeting of Arctic policies and how they differ in each setting. We next consider the data that we collected and measures. Our findings are presented in several stages that include discussion of the basic contours of Arctic policies and differences in their targeting.

Conceptual Foundations: Policy Targeting and Agglomeration

Policies are often formed with the intent of changing the behavior, providing benefits, or administering burdens to a subset of the citizenry. The nature of this policy targeting, according to Schneider and Ingram (1993), is shaped by the political power and images of the affected groups. Regional policies constitute a particularly unique case of policy targeting because of the diffuseness of the issues that arise and the variation in the affected groups within the targeted region. For example, urban policy making entails consideration of housing, energy, health, economic development, employment, environmental, transportation and other issues. Rural policies concern rural development, agricultural support, rural health and so on. Policies about these aspects of urban or rural life have little in common other than the fact that they target urban or rural areas. Policies that target particular places such as the Arctic also address a diversity of issues.

The groups that are targeted by the various policy actions are also diverse. Although the populations share the common feature of living in a particular place, there may be little overlap among the concerns of the different groups within that setting. In the case of Arctic policy, for example, those groups concerned about getting human services directed at the Inuit do not overlap very substantially with those interested in exploring for energy in the Yukon. While both sets of activities can be classified as falling within Arctic policy, they call forth different sets of policy actors and are characterized by different forms of conflict and co-operation. In addition, the issues that impact Arctic regions typically involve groups that go beyond Arctic populations. This spillover of interests undermines policy targeting by diluting the constituency for a definable Arctic policy.

We suggest that regional policies are often little more than labels for an agglomeration of a diverse set of substantive policies that loosely target a given region. We label the various policy issue areas as *policy components*. We characterize these for Arctic policy to see whether one or more components dominate. We also consider the extent to which the components of Arctic policy specifically address Arctic regions and Arctic populations. This gets at the basic notion of targeting of regional policies. We develop a measure of *policy centrality* to allow a more precise way for characterizing the degree of policy targeting. The details of how we measure policy components and centrality are explained later in our discussion of data and measures.

Politics of Place: Defining the Arctic

The debate over what constitutes the Arctic is aptly characterized by Smith and McCarter (1997: xiii) who write that the Arctic is "an historical space where three powerful forces collide: cultural, political, and ecological". Historian Stephen Haycox (2001: 145) writes: "The questions of just where the Canadian North is, and of the appropriate placement of Alaska, are not as obvious as they might seem". The location of the Arctic has itself been an issue of policy debate, as is evident from the history of deliberations about the physical boundaries of the Arctic.

Instead of a single, obvious means of dividing Arctic from sub-Arctic regions, there are a number of potential scientific criteria including the tree line, continuous or discontinuous permafrost, and the latitude at which the sun does not set on the summer solstice (66°33') (see Huntington 2001: 11–12). In both the United States and Canada, the location of the Arctic is defined differently by various interests, depending on the specific purposes and goals of those groups for the region. This inconsistency is indicative of the diversity of interests that have a stake in Arctic policy making. This variability in definitions of the Arctic is apparent in both the United States and Canada.

The central issue in policy debates during the early 1980s in the United States, as reflected in the debates over the enactment of the Arctic Policy Research Act, was whether to define the Arctic in terms of narrow or broad geographic boundaries.[1] Representatives of some native corporations advocated for a definition based on the tree line, arguing that a broader definition would detract funds and attention from areas that had been harmed by resource development. They also claimed that a broad definition would allow special interests to use research funds to support resource development (energy, fisheries) in areas outside the Arctic. Others, including some industry representatives and government officials, supported broad boundaries to encompass locations for their resource development interests, including mineral wealth and fisheries resources in the Bering Sea. In short, this debate not only reflected the lack of a clear constituency with respect to Arctic policy, but its ultimate resolution – the adoption of an expanded definition – ensured that future policy debates involving the Arctic in the United States would involve a diverse range of problems and interests.

In Canada, variability in definitions of the Arctic has been less reflective of conflicts over the size of the region. Rather, different governmental and research organizations simply define the Canadian Arctic in different ways, employing context-specific variants of the definition articulated in the Canadian Polar Commission Act of 1991.[2] For instance, the Department of Indian Affairs and Northern Development restricts its jurisdiction to the Yukon Territory, Northwest Territories and Nunavut, while excluding the parts of Quebec and Labrador that fall within polar regions. In contrast, the Northern Dimension of Canada's Foreign Policy references a broader definition, including the Canadian "mid-North", comprised of large areas of British Columbia, Alberta, Saskatchewan, Manitoba, Ontario and Quebec.

Given variability in definitions of "the Arctic" in both Canada and the United States, we faced a challenge of establishing meaningful ways of describing the geographic target of Arctic policies. We employ definitions that best fit policy usage in order to identify as many potentially policy-relevant, domestic Arctic policy components in each setting as possible. This necessitated different designations for Canada and the United States. We delineate the Canadian Arctic as all land areas and social groups above the 60th geographic parallel. This includes the Northwest Territories, the Yukon Territory, the Nunavut Territory and the Nunavik region of Northern Quebec. Of particular policy import is that this definition embodies what the Canadian Department of Indian and Northern Affairs considers the Canadian North (the three territories: Northwest Territories, Yukon and Nunavut) and also includes important indigenous groups.

The policy-relevant definition of the US Arctic is easier to delineate than it is for Canada. We employ the definition provided by the Arctic Research and Policy Act of 1984 as constituting "all United States and Foreign territory north of the Arctic Circle and all United States territory north and west of the boundary formed by the Porcupine, Yukon, and Kuskokwim Rivers; all contiguous seas, including the Arctic Ocean and the Beaufort, Bering, and Chukchi Seas, and the Aleutian chain" (P.L. 98-373 Sec. 112). A complicating factor is that many provisions of American statutes concerning Alaska also potentially relate to the Arctic. Given the potential policy relevance of these Arctic-relevant provisions, we include policy components of Alaska-related statutes that specifically relate to the Arctic areas identified by the Arctic Research and Policy Act of 1984.

The Canadian and United States Comparison

We argue that Arctic policy making in both Canada and the United States illustrates regional policy agglomeration. To show this, we examine the differing Arctic-relevant policy components in each setting. We expect similar patterns of regional policy agglomeration involving a variety of substantive policy components in each setting. Consideration of these patterns serves as a limited test of our notion of regional policy agglomeration.

Our more refined hypotheses address differences in policy targeting. We are particularly interested in the extent to which Arctic policy components target Arctic regions and populations. The hypotheses that follow suggest differences in the degree of targeting in Canada and the United States. As elaborated upon below, two factors contribute to these differences. The first is the more paternalistic orientation of the Canadian central government toward the territories that constitute the Canadian North. The second factor is the greater political empowerment of Canadian indigenous populations.

Expectations about Targeting of Place

Hypothesis 1: Canadian policies target the Arctic region to a greater degree than US policies. More precisely, the Canadian Arctic region is expected to be more central to relevant Canadian policy components than the US Arctic is to American policy components. Two sets of considerations lead to this hypothesis. One is the more paternalistic orientation of Canadian government toward the Canadian North than the orientation of the American government toward Alaska. Until recently, territories in the Canadian North have had limited statutory authority. Even with expanded authority, the Northern Territories continue to rely heavily on the national government for both infrastructure development and financial aid to alleviate the high cost of living in northern regions. Historians Abel and Coates (2001: 10–11) characterize the implications of this dependence as follows:

> The Yukon, Northwest Territories (NWT), and Nunavut are all colonies of the federal state, and even with recent important steps toward regional autonomy, they remain subject to Ottawa's control ... Canadian authorities have a unique opportunity to define and impose the nation's will on a regional population ... In issues ranging from bilingualism (both the Yukon and NWT offer extensive services in French) to Aboriginal land rights (most of the modern treaties are in the northern regions), the federal government has imposed its views, policies, and assumptions on the region, attempting to make the Canadian North a reflection of Canadian aspirations.

A second factor suggesting greater targeting of the Arctic region in Canada is the type of political empowerment that has occurred in each setting. The relevant statute for the United States is the Alaska Native Claims Settlement Act of 1971. Among other provisions, the Act established a set of 12 regional corporations in charge of distributing funds to the village corporations and approving financial plans (Ongtooguk 1998: 16). These actions empowered a variety of groups – the individual native corporations, residents of affected villages and towns, and investors in the native corporations – which have differing political and economic agendas. Rather than advocating Arctic policy as a whole, these interests are more concerned with specifics of economic, employment, environmental and other policies that span more than just the Arctic.

In Canada, particularly in recent decades, indigenous groups of the Canadian Arctic have become increasingly involved in environmental conservation and development decisions within their respective territories as well as on the national level (Myers 2001). This has led to stronger political voices advocating for policies that are specific to the Canadian Arctic than the more diverse voices in the United States advocating policies that are less specific to the US Arctic.

Expectations about Targeting of Arctic Populations

Hypothesis 2: Canadian policies target Arctic indigenous populations to a greater degree than US policies. The expected greater attention to Canadian indigenous groups follows from the differences in the empowerment and treatment of indigenous populations in each setting. Native groups in both Canada and the United States have achieved degrees of economic and political empowerment largely as the result of settlement of major land and self-government disputes with their respective national governments. As discussed above, the key act in the United States is the Alaska Native Claims Settlement Act of 1971. The first of the land claims in Canada was for the Inuit. The James Bay and Northern Quebec Agreement of 1975 created the Nunavik territory. Other land claims involved the Inuvialuit in the Northwest Territories. The largest land claim settled by the Inuit was the creation of Nunavut as an independent territory in 1993.

The Canadian agreements have provided for stronger forms of political empowerment, in carving out separate territories with self-governing provisions, which are specific to different parts of the Canadian North. This fosters policy demands that are specific to First Nations' indigenous populations and enables more specific targeting of policies to those populations. In contrast, the indigenous populations in the United States have had less distinctive identities. Their political voice has been distributed across a number of villages and boroughs that, as with local governments in the American system more generally, are not politically powerful in national policy debates. The role of Arctic indigenous populations in the economy, which was to be greatly enhanced through the creation of native corporations, is blurred because the membership and operations of the native corporations span both Arctic and non-Arctic regions.

Also potentially relevant is the difference in the way that different groups are targets of policies in Canada and the United States. Radin and Boase (2000) suggest that the executive dominance of the Canadian federal structure permits a greater degree of enactment of redistributive programs that target particular populations than is possible in the United States. If identity-based targeting of policies (i.e., toward indigenous populations) are less contentious in Canada than the United States, we would clearly expect to see a greater degree of such policy targeting for the former.

Data and Measures

Statutes are by definition authoritative actions and as such they are a common basis for studying policies. The importance of provinces in the Canadian federal system normally would suggest that the study of Canadian policy needs to focus on the provinces. However, the policy dependence of the territories in the Canadian North upon Ottawa shifts attention for Arctic-related policy to the national level. As such, our primary comparison is patterns that we find in Canadian and US federal-level statutes that address Arctic regions or populations.

We were constrained in our search of statutes in each setting by several factors. One was the availability of searchable databases for studying statutes. We employed two different statute databases that have full text search capabilities. For the United States we used the Congressional Information Service (CIS), which allows full text searches of public laws from 1988 to 2002. For Canada we used Quicklaw America (QuicklawAmerica.com), for which the available period for full text searches of statutes is from 1996 to 2002. We undertook statistical tests to ensure that the differences in time periods do not bias our results.[3]

While our primary comparison is statutes in each setting, we also sought additional sources for characterizing Canadian policy makers' attention to the Canadian Arctic. The statutory data are limited when considering Arctic policy in Canada. The Canadian system generates less statutory based policy making than the United States. And, we had access to a shorter span of Canadian statutes than for the United States. Following the practice of Soroka (2002: 59–60) in his study of Canadian policy agendas, we also coded relevant question periods for Canadian parliamentary debates as recorded in the *Hansard*, the official documentation of the Canadian Parliament. Clearly, these data are not directly comparable to statutes or records of any other aspect of the federal legislative process in the United States. We use the findings from the Canadian question period analyses to buttress our findings concerning Arctic policy components in Canada.

We discuss in this section our selection of relevant statutes and the measures that we employ. The methodological appendix contains relevant details about coding decisions and inter-coder reliability measures. We also consider in this section the measures that we developed for examining our hypotheses about Arctic policy.

Selection of Statutes

We searched by keywords the full text of public laws in the United States enacted from 1988 to 2002. We searched by keywords the full text of "Annual Acts Assented To" in the Canadian Parliament from 1996 to 2002. The keyword searchers were identified separately for Canada and the United States based on the respective definitions of the Arctic for each country that we employed. For each setting, we identified keywords based on boundaries, political designations, key geographic features and social groups for the relevant areas. (These are listed in the methodological appendix.)

Based on these searches and subsequent culling, we identified for the United States 126 statutes that had some degree of Arctic policy relevance. Excluded from this count are appropriations-related bills and irrelevant items that happened to turn up the word "Arctic". (For example, one provision addressed an "Arctic blast" in referring to cold weather in the lower 48.) Following similar procedures, we identified 36 statutes in Canada that are Arctic-relevant.

We also characterize Canadian policy makers' attention to the Canadian Arctic based on topics raised in parliamentary question periods. For this, we also employed Quicklaw America to conduct full text searches of the record of question periods in the *Hansard*. We identified 822 question-items that were of relevance to the Canadian Arctic using the same search terms as were employed when identifying relevant Canadian statutes.

Measures and Coding

Our analyses revolve around two different aspects of Arctic policy: (1) policy components that are of relevance, and (2) the targeting of Arctic regions and populations as part of those components.

Policy components. Policy components refer to the substantive issues that are being addressed. Our coding of the subject matter of each of the Arctic-related statutes in Canada and the United States employed the procedures discussed by Baumgartner, Jones and Wilkerson (2002) for studying policy content as part of the Policy Agendas Project. This approach identifies a set of 19 content categories that allows for consistent identification of policy content across data sets and over time. The Arctic provisions of each statute were coded by two research assistants for the most applicable major subject code used in the Agendas Project. Differences in coding were resolved by discussion between them and, if necessary, by involvement of an arbitrator. A similar procedure was employed in coding the subject matter of items from the Canadian parliamentary question periods. Question period items were coded by one individual with those codes being checked by a senior research assistant.

For the analyses that follow, we collapsed the coding of content categories into five macro categories of relevance to Arctic policy components. This enables statistical comparisons across categories and settings that are not possible using the major content categories. The macro categories and their major issue areas are: (1) Human Services and Law – Civil Rights, Health, Employment and Labor Issues, Education, Law and Crime and Family Issues, Social and Welfare Issues, Community Housing and Development, and all non-appropriations Government Operations; (2) Public Lands and Agriculture – Agriculture, Public Lands and Water Management; (3) Environment; (4) Development – Energy, Transportation, Banking and Finance and Domestic Commerce, Macroeconomics, and Space, Science, Technology, and Communications; and (5) External Affairs – Defense, Foreign Trade, Foreign Aid and International Relations.

Policy centrality. The degree to which a given policy component targets a particular region or population is central to thinking about regional policies. As discussed above, we get at this with our notion of policy centrality. We conceptualize this as the degree to which a given policy component addresses the Arctic region or populations. Our measure of centrality is based on a coding of the percentage of a statute that contained Arctic policy aspects. We employed a four-point scale related to the percentage of the policy that is devoted to Arctic considerations:[4]

- *Key feature*: Arctic considerations are a key feature of the policy (50 to 100 per cent), or the search term is in the title;
- *Important feature*: Arctic considerations are important aspects of the policy (25 to 50 per cent);
- *Intermediate feature*: Arctic considerations have an intermediate standing for the policy (5 to 25 per cent);
- *Limited feature*: Arctic considerations have a limited standing for the policy (less than 5 per cent).

This coding scheme provides an assessment of the degree of targeting for a statute to Arctic issues. Each statute was coded for centrality by two research assistants. Differences in coding were resolved by discussion between them and, if necessary, by involvement of an arbitrator.

Our theorizing about policy targets also leads us to think about the extent to which indigenous populations are targets of Arctic-related policy components. For this, we developed a separate coding of whether the Arctic-related provisions of a given statute specifically addressed indigenous populations. This includes provisions that relate to native groups as defined by our listing of key groups in the statute search as well as provisions that relate to native groups as a whole.

Findings

Our discussion of the findings considers the patterns of Arctic policy agglomeration and the hypothesized differences between targeting of policy components in Canada and the United States. A key limitation of the data is the limited number of statutes being considered, especially for the Canadian data. This limits the power of statistical comparisons and the ability to disaggregate data. However, it is important to note that we are working with all of the data for the relevant periods. As such, statistical comparisons convey the variability between the respective data sets rather than provide tests of inferences from samples to populations.

Arctic Policy Agglomeration

Arctic policies in both Canada and the United States are clearly comprised of attention to a diversity of issues. Arctic policy components in each setting span the five macro categories of issues that we consider. No single component comprises more than 40 per cent of the total issue space. The largest category of attention is consideration of human services, which comprise some 39 per cent of all items in each setting. Attention to issues concerning public lands and agriculture constitute a fairly distant second area of attention (25 per cent of laws in Canada and 20 per cent in the United States). This is closely followed by consideration of economic development (19 per cent and 18 per cent respectively) and of environmental issues (14 per cent in each setting). Attention to external affairs is a lesser category for statutory attention in each setting (3 per cent in Canada and 9 per cent in the United States).

This distribution of Arctic policy components is illustrative of our notion of regional policy agglomeration. The diversity of Arctic policy is further suggested by the fact that none of the policy components dominate. The rankings of attention to the macro policy topics in each setting are identical. In other research (May *et al.* 2005), we examine the variation in attention to different policy components and the factors that affect that attention. The key point for this discussion is that Arctic policies in each setting are better characterized with respect to their policy components than in terms of over-arching policies.

Policy Targeting

We also consider the extent to which the components of Arctic policy specifically address Arctic regions and Arctic populations. Policy targeting concerns the degree to which a given region or population within that region are subjects of regional policies. The difference between a policy focused upon providing healthcare services to the Inuit alone and a policy providing healthcare to all Native Americans, including the Inuit, demonstrates differences in targeting. The former addresses the unique health needs of Arctic populations, while the latter is less specific in addressing such needs. The former is more target-focused, while the latter is more component-focused.

Targeting of place. Regional policy agglomeration can lead to a dissipation of a place-based focus, thereby weakening policy impact. This occurs when the component policies are not adequately targeted to the particular region or place of interest. To assess this for our data, we address the centrality of Arctic policy

Figure 1. Policy targeting of the Arctic region

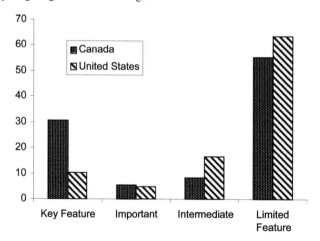

Note: Each policy component was coded for the centrality of Arctic provisions, based on 36 statutes in Canada and 126 in the United States. Each statute only has one code.
Source: Compiled by authors from coding of statutes for each setting.

components in each setting. Given the way our measure of centrality is constructed, more central policy components have greater targeting with respect to the Canadian Arctic or US Arctic region. Figure 1 shows the distributions of scores for policy centrality.

The limited foci on the Arctic is evidenced by the finding that only 31 per cent of the policy components in Canada and 10 per cent of those in the United States treat Arctic regions as key features. In keeping with our broader theorizing about regional policy agglomeration, these findings evidence policy components that address more than just the Arctic. For over 50 per cent of the statutes that we examined in each setting, Arctic areas were more likely to be mentioned in passing rather than highlighted as a central policy feature.

We hypothesized that Canadian policies target the Arctic region to a greater degree than United States' policies (H1). This hypothesis can be assessed by comparing mean scores of policy centrality for relevant statutes in each setting according to the centrality scale of 1 (limited feature) to 4 (key feature). As hypothesized, there is greater targeting of Arctic regions for the Canadian statutes than for the American statutes. The mean score for policy centrality is 2.11 in Canada and 1.57 in the United States (t-test = 2.21, $p = .03$).[5] The attention to the Arctic in Canada is also evident by considering the Arctic policy focus of relevant parliamentary question periods. The mean policy centrality for the question periods of 3.52 is even higher than the corresponding mean value of 2.11 for statutes in Canada (t-test = 6.14, $p < .01$). The higher mean score for question periods reflects the greater precision of topics that are addressed in that forum.

The variation in centrality scores across policy components for Canada as compared to the United States reinforces these findings. This provides an understanding of targeting for particular issue areas and provides a better understanding of the importance of different policy components than simply considering the frequency of attention to each. Issues concerning public lands had the highest centrality scores in each setting with comparable mean scores of 2.44 in Canada and 2.12 in the United States. The greatest differences in targeting between the two settings are for development and environmental policies with Canadian policies having average centrality scores for each of these components that are more than 40 per cent greater than those of corresponding US policies.[6] Although human service issues are the most frequent topic of consideration in both settings, they have lower centrality scores than the centrality of public lands, environmental issues or development.[7] We attribute this to the greater difficulty of targeting indigenous populations for those services, a topic to which we now turn.

Targeting of populations. Regional policies can also target specific groups within the relevant region. We hypothesized that the targeting of indigenous groups would be stronger in Canada than in the United States (H2). Consideration of the frequency of attention to indigenous populations provides results that are seemingly contrary to this hypothesis. In particular, there is greater frequency of attention to indigenous populations in the Arctic provisions for the United States than in those for Canada. Fifty-three per cent of Arctic-related statutes in the United States explicitly address indigenous populations whereas only 28 per cent of the statutes in Canada address indigenous populations. Not surprisingly, the attention to indigenous groups in each

Figure 2. Policy targeting of indigenous groups

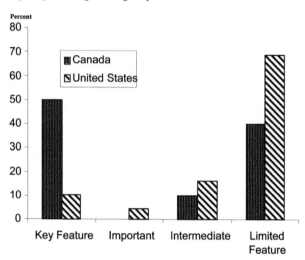

Note: Each policy component that referenced indigenous groups was coded for the centrality of Arctic provisions, based on 10 statutes in Canada and 67 in the United States. Each statute only has one code.
Source: Compiled by authors from coding of statutes for each setting.

setting is concentrated in policy components addressing human services and public lands.

However, more frequent mention of indigenous groups as part of Arctic policy components in the United States does not translate into greater policy focus on indigenous groups. As shown in Figure 2, the degree of attention in the United States to indigenous groups is limited. Only 10 per cent of the statutes in the United States that address indigenous populations focus on the Arctic as a key feature. The corresponding figure for the Canadian Arctic policy components is 50 per cent. These findings suggest that simply considering the frequency with which indigenous groups are mentioned in statutes is not a meaningful measure of the degree of targeting of these populations.

The strength of the policy targeting for indigenous groups can be more directly assessed with our measure of policy centrality. The relevant comparison is between the respective Arctic centrality scores for those policy components that explicitly address indigenous groups (shown in Figure 2). The mean Arctic policy centrality score for statutes concerning indigenous groups in Canada is 2.60 while the corresponding mean score for United States is 1.57 (t-test = 2.10, p = .06).[8] This finding of a higher score in Canada than the United States is consistent with our hypothesis (H2).

The centrality scores also tell us something about the relative difficulty of targeting indigenous groups as part of Arctic policies. The higher mean centrality score in Canada for policy components that target indigenous groups (2.60) in comparison to the mean score for those components that do not (1.92) reflects the concentration of groups in the Canadian Arctic and suggests the relative ease of targeting policies that address these groups (t-test = 1.34, p = .10 one-tailed). This is also evident when considering attention to indigenous populations during question periods in the Canadian Parliament. Nearly one-third of the Arctic-related question periods addressed issues related to indigenous populations. Arctic considerations were a key feature for 65 per cent of these.

In contrast, the difficulty of targeting indigenous groups as part of Arctic policy in the United States is evidenced by our finding of similar mean centrality scores for Arctic policy components in the United States that do and do not target indigenous groups (t-test = .05, p = .96). The broader geographical distribution of native populations in Alaska with large numbers living outside of the Arctic region makes it difficult to target indigenous populations as part of US Arctic policies. Either the group itself can be targeted, as is commonly done, or the Arctic region is targeted, not both.

Conclusions

We have considered Arctic policy in Canada and the United States as an example of what we label as regional policy agglomeration. We show that the domestic aspects of Arctic policies in these settings are comprised of a diversity of policy components with limited policy targeting for the Arctic region or populations. As a consequence, Arctic policy in each setting is more aptly considered a label for a collection of actions oriented toward the Arctic. In related analyses (May *et al.* 2005), we attribute these patterns to the differing issue politics of the various components of Arctic policy. The lack of a clear constituency and the lack of a stable policy subsystem for the Arctic create a policy environment for which the politics of particular issues dominates policy making for the Arctic.

The regional policy agglomeration for Arctic policy is evidenced by our finding of an Arctic policy space in Canada and the United States that is comprised of an array of largely discrete, non-overlapping policy components. No policy components dominate with the more central considerations in both settings concerning public lands, development, and the environment. The sense of an Arctic policy in each setting is further undermined by our finding of a lack of an Arctic focus for the component policies whether that focus is defined with respect to place or indigenous populations.

We find differences between the targeting of Arctic policy components when comparing Arctic policy in Canada and the United States. Policies addressing the Canadian Arctic have greater centrality with respect to both place and indigenous populations than do corresponding policies for the US Arctic. We attribute these differences to the historic dependence of the Canadian Northern Territories on Ottawa and the stronger political empowerment at the national level of Canadian First Nations' groups.

The broader contribution of this research concerns regional policies and the difficulties of fashioning regional strategies. We argue that regional policy making concerning urban areas, rural areas and specific regions such as the Arctic is more likely to entail an agglomeration of disparate policy components rather than a focused regional policy effort. Regional issues sort out in diverse ways for which there is rarely an over-arching constituency for an overall regional policy. In discussing why there is no coherent rural policy, James Bonnen (1992: 198) writes: "Due to the diversity of rural society there is no closely related or coherent bundle of issues to which most rural people respond and around which they might be organized". Instead, there are diverse constituencies for each of the policy components of the regional policy that often tug in different directions.

These dynamics may be heightened in the United States where the politics of particularistic issues and interests dominate. But, even in the United States regional policies need not be piecemeal. The experience with Appalachian policy in the United States provides a rare counter-example of regional policy for which the policy components more or less work together. As discussed by Bradshaw (1992), the Appalachian efforts entailed mobilizing a grass-roots constituency for the regional policy, institutionalization of the policy through creation of the Appalachian Regional Commission, and a consistent policy objective of regional development. These steps provide a policy glue that binds consistent policy objectives, a political basis of support for the overall policy and not just the separate components, and an institutional mechanism for sustaining the overarching regional policy.

The broadest contribution of this research is the introduction of concepts for thinking about the characterization of components of public policies and their relationships. Further research about the interplay of ideas, issues, and interests across policy components is needed for examining the coherence of regional and other targeted policies.

Acknowledgements

We thank Courtney Munson for invaluable research assistance and Josh Sapotichne and anonymous reviewers for helpful comments. Funding for this research was provided to the University of Washington by the National Science Foundation under grant no. OPP-0219543 under a project co-directed by Bryan D. Jones and Peter J. May. The findings of this research are not necessarily endorsed by the National Science Foundation or the University of Washington.

Notes

1. This discussion is based on a review of the issues raised in congressional hearings, conducted in 1982, prior to passage of the Arctic Research and Policy Act of 1984.
2. The Canadian Polar Commission Act of 1991 defines "polar regions" in relation to Canada as including all areas north of 60 degrees north latitude and all areas north of the southern limit of the discontinuous permafrost zone.
3. To assess whether this difference biased our findings, we compared mean policy centrality scores for the US data prior to 1996 with US data that are limited to the period of the Canadian statutes, 1996–2002. We failed to detect a difference in the mean centrality scores for these two sets of data (t-test = -1.10, $p = 0.27$). This suggests that the different periods are comparable with respect to the key variable of interest in this study.
4. The percentage of the statute devoted to Arctic considerations was estimated by coders, rather than calculated by counting lines or words. Any such count would have been problematic because of differences in the construction of statutes.
5. Another way to measure this difference is to compare the respective distribution of centrality scores that are shown in Figure 1. These distributions also differ (Chi square = 9.78, p = .02).

6. The mean centrality scores and one-tailed t-test for scores when comparing Canada and the United States respectively for environmental policies are 2.40 and 1.44 (t-test = 1.78, p = .05) and for development policies are 2.29 and 1.30 (t-test = 1.58, p = .08).
7. The mean centrality scores and one-tailed t-test for centrality scores when comparing Canada and the United States respectively for human services policies are 1.79 and 1.45 (t-test = .95, p = .18).
8. Another way to measure this difference is to compare the respective distribution of centrality scores that are shown in Figure 2. These distributions also differ (Chi square = 10.51, p = .02).

References

Abel, Kerry and Coates, Ken S., 2001, Introduction: the north and the nation, in: K. Abel and K. S. Coates (Eds) *Northern Visions, New Perspectives on the North in Canadian History* (Peterborough, Ontario: Broadview Press), pp. 7–21.

Baumgartner, Frank and Jones, Bryan D., 1993, *Agendas and Instability in American Politics* (Chicago: University of Chicago Press).

Baumgartner, Frank, Jones, Bryan D., and Wilkerson, John D., 2002, Studying policy dynamics, in: Frank R. Baumgartner and Bryan D. Jones (Eds) *Policy Dynamics* (Chicago: University of Chicago Press), pp. 29–46.

Bonnen, James T., 1992, Why is there no coherent U.S. rural policy? *Policy Studies Journal*, 20, 190–201.

Bradshaw, Michael, 1992, *The Appalachian Regional Commission: Twenty-Five Years of Governmental Policy* (Lexington, KY: University of Kentucky Press).

Browne, William P., 2001. *The Failure of National Rural Policy, Institutions and Interests* (Washington: Georgetown University Press).

Haycox, Stephen, 2001, Alaska and the Canadian North: Comparing conceptual frameworks, in: K. Abel and K. S. Coates (Eds) *Northern Visions, New Perspectives on the North in Canadian History* (Peterborough, Ontario: Broadview Press), pp. 141–157.

Huntington, Henry P., 2001, *Arctic Flora and Fauna: Status and Conservation* (Helsinki: Edita).

May, Peter J., Jones, Bryan D., Beem, Betsi E., Neff-Sharum, Emily A. and Poague, Melissa K., 2005, Policy coherence and component-driven policymaking: Arctic policy in Canada and the United States, *Policy Studies Journal*, 33, 37–63.

Myers, Heather, 2001, Changing environment, changing times: Environmental issues and political action in the Canadian North, *Environment*, 43, 34–44.

Ongtooguk, Paul, 1998, *The Annotated ANCSA* (Anchorage: University of Alaska, Anchorage Institute for Social and Economic Research).

Radin, Beryl and Boase, J. P., 2000, Federalism, political structure, and public policy in the United States and Canada, *Journal of Comparative Policy Analysis*, 2, 65–89.

Schneider, Anne Larason and Ingram, Helen, 1993, The social construction of target populations: Implications for politics and policy, *American Political Science Review*, 87, 334–347.

Smith, Eric Alden and McCarter, Joan (Eds), 1997, *Contested Arctic: Indigenous Peoples, Industrial States, and the Circumpolar Environment* (Seattle: University of Washington Press).

Soroka, Stuart A., 2002, *Agenda-Setting Dynamics in Canada* (Vancouver: UBC Press).

Appendix A. Methodological Appendix

Selection of Arctic-related Statutes

Search terms for Canadian Arctic include: Dene or Inuvialiut or Inuit or Inui or Sahtu or Gwich'in or Polar or Arctic or Permafrost or MacKenzie or Yukon or Yellowknife or Northwest Territories or Nunavut or Iqaluit or Inuvik or Kitikmeot or Fort Smith or Keewatin or Baffin or Beaufort Sea or Foxe Basin or Hudson Strait or Parry Channel or Great Bear Lake or Great Slave Lake or Aulavik or Auyuittuq or Tuktut Nogiat or Sirmlik or Ivvavik or Buntut or Nahanni or Nunavik or Ungava or Makivik or Smith Island or Gray Strait or Deception Bay or Northern Quebec.

Search terms for the US Arctic include: Arctic or Polar or Aleut or Aleutian or Kuskokwim or North Slope or Bering Sea or Yukon or Seward Peninsula or Kotzebue or Noatak or Eskimo or Pribilof Islands or Nome or Alaska. Other terms were used in the search that did not yield any statutes.

Inter-Coder Reliability

Table A1 presents findings about inter-coder reliability for the coding of policy centrality for the Canadian and US statutes. Separate coding was undertaken by two different coders for the rating of the Canadian statutes, the US statutes with specific Arctic search terms, and the US statutes for which search terms were identified by examining statutes concerning Alaska. Initial rounds of coding were undertaken without discussion of the codes between raters. The final round reflects the final codes that were established after differences between raters were discussed and, if necessary, arbitrated by a third party. The number of cases reported in the reliability measures for centrality coding is higher than the number of statutes we analyzed since these data reflect the coding of all Arctic-related statutes identified by our search terms.

Table A1. Inter-rater reliability for coding of statutes

Centrality coding	Canada	US Arctic	US Alaska
Initial round			
Agreement (%)	81.8	72.2	78.6
Gamma	0.92	0.89	0.93
Tau-B	0.82	0.78	0.78
Final round			
Agreement (%)	100	100	98.8
Gamma	1.00	1.00	0.99
Tau-B	1.00	1.00	0.97
Number of cases	44	44	148

Note: Two additional US statutes were added to our data after these calculations were made. As a consequence, the number of cases reported here does not match those reported in the text.

Index

Note: **Bold** page numbers refer to tables; *italic* page numbers refer to figures and page numbers followed by "n" denote endnotes.

Abel, Kerry 477
abortion: absence of policy reform in Chile 132–133; bold reform in Mexico City 134–135; health and social context of 128–129; legal framework of 127–128; limited reform in Colombia 133–134; social construction of abortion debate and role of different groups 129–131
abstract feminism 203
Act of Congress 347
Adachi, Yukio 3
Adams, C. T. 14
adaptational responses: measuring **309**, 309–311, **310**; and pressures 309–312; regional aid 309–312
Adenauer, Konrad 165
administration: transnational 14–15, 17, 21
Agencia Española de Cooperación Internacional para el Desarrollo (AECI) 245
agency relocation programs 430; cabinet performance 431–433, **432**, *433*; comparison of 430–431; entrepreneurial politics 432; interest group politics 432; Nordic countries 430–431
Agenda 21 391, 396
agglomeration 475; Arctic policy 481–482; regional policy and Arctic policy 477–478
air quality: and India 368; and PRC 367
Aisbitt, S. 213
Alaska Native Claims Settlement Act 477, 478
Alesina, A. 53, 54n4
Allen, Judith 465, 467
Allison, M. 94
Andrews, Kaliopa 462
Anessi-Pessina, E. 218
Angola: Angolan Ministry of Fisheries 325; fisheries regulations **331–332**; MCS systems 325; overfishing in 324–325; total allowed catch (TAC) 325; and UN Code of Conduct for Responsible Fishing 325

Angolan Ministry of Fisheries 325
Antonovsky, Aaron 80, 83–84
Anttonen, Anneli 162
Aquatic Biological Resources Act 325
Archer, S. 213
Arctic policy: agglomeration 481–482; in Canada 473–485; overview 473–474; policy centrality 480–481; policy components 480; policy targeting 482; and regional policies 474; and regional policy agglomeration 477–478; statutes 479–481; in the United States 473–485; *see also* Arctic region
Arctic Policy Research Act 475
Arctic region: and Canada 476; defining 475–476; targeting of place 482–483; targeting of populations 483–485, *484*; and United States 475–476; *see also* Arctic policy
Arctic Research and Policy Act 476
Argentina 132; abortion laws in 128; anti-abortion activism in 132; fertility rates in 137; higher education system organization 346; legislation on higher education of 343, 349n4; maturity and size of private higher education in **342**; private education institutions autonomy 344; private institution of higher education in 344
Argentine Supreme Court 138n4
Armstrong, K. 68–69
Article 29 Working Party 356–361, 363
Article 30 Working Party 356
artisanal fisheries: Mozambique 326; Tanzania 329
Asia: competitive business climate 373–374; and good governance 368–373; hazardous environmental conditions 367; inclusive asset-based policies in 235–238; increased reliance on markets 373–374; infrastructure investment and development 374–376; Korea 235–236; modes of governance in 381–389; Singapore 236–237; Taiwan 237–238; urban growth

management in 367–377; urban poverty 368; *see also specific countries*
Asian Barometer Survey (ABS) 92, 96, 103
Asian Development Bank (ADB) 368, 370, 372, 374–375
Asia Pacific Disaster Report 2010 412; *progress without cooperation* 412, 424–425
asset-based policy: asset building as social policy 231; evaluation in Korea 238–240; evaluation in Singapore 238–240; evaluation in Taiwan 238–240; inclusive asset-based policies in Asia 235–238; limitations of 233–235; overview 230–231; theory and progress of inclusive 232–233
Association Abbé Pierre 85
ATD-Quart Monde 85
Australian Accounting Standard Board (AASB) 1049 213
Austria 54n1, 315; concentration ratios **224**; expected adaptational pressures in **308**, 309; father-friendliness in **159**; paternal time in 151, **152**; relativized adjustments to non-financial resources for **221**
authoritarianism 21
autonomy: in Bolivia 345; definition 344; and legal directives 348; of private education institutions 344; of public education institutions 344–345

Bachelet, Michelle 133
"backward mapping" research technique 303
Baehler, K. J. 5
Baker, S. 381
Balaguer Coll, T. 214
Ball, Michael 464
Baltic Countries 177–190; background information about crisis in 181–183; crisis experience by civil servants 183–188; evaluation of crisis-time fiscal policy actions 185–186; learning from crisis regarding fiscal policy 186–188; perceptions of finance ministry officials about causes of crisis and prevention 184–185; policy learning by civil servants 183–188
Bangalore Citizen Report Card (CRC) 370
Bangkok Metropolitan Administration 376
Baumgartner, Frank 474, 480
Bayesian learning 62
Beach Management Units (BMUs) 329
Belgium 32, 215–216, 308–311, 315; concentration ratios **224**; relativized adjustments to non-financial resources for **221**
Benito, B. 217
Bennett, C. J. 178
Bertozzi, F. 68
birth control 131, 138
birth control pills 138n1

Bismarckian healthcare systems 282; governance in 283–285; healthcare regulation in 283–285; self-regulating 284; *see also* social health insurance (SHI)
Blair, Tony 232
Blossfeld, Hans-Peter 451
Boase, A. 7
Boase, J. P. 478
Bolivia 132; autonomy in 345; Educational Reform Law 346; maturity and size of private higher education in **342**; universities accreditation 347
Bonoli, G. 68
bonus-based performance system 278
Borras, S. 67, 71n1
"bottom-up learning" 60, 62–63, 67, 69–70
Bouckaert, G. 217
Bouget, Denis 166
Bourdieu, Pierre 168
Boushey, G. 7
Brans, M. 17
Brazil: building issue networks 132–135; Constitution of 1988 346; exploiting political opportunities 132–135; health and social context of abortion 128–129; higher education system organization 346; legal framework of abortion 127–128; legislation on higher education of 343; maturity and size of private higher education in **342**; National Programme on Human Rights 131; overview 125–127; private education institutions autonomy 344; social construction of abortion debate and role of different groups 129–131; students in private sector 342; transforming attitudes and re-aligning reform efforts in 135–137
Brennan, G. 37
Bretton Woods institutions 15
Brexit 19
bribe-based corruption 111
British Council 245
broad Economic Policy Guidelines (BEPG) 61, 66
brokerage roles **415**
brokered exchange 414
brokers: role in building emergency management systems 413–415; types of brokerage role **415**
Browne, William P. 474
Brundtland Report 394
Bruning, G. 144
Brunsson, N. 68
Brusca, I. 212, 214, 217, 218
Buchanan, J. 37
Buchs, M. 68
budgetary instrumentalism 37
budget consolidation: determinants of 39–43; overview 33–35
Bulgaria 18; concentration ratios **224**, 225; politicization of the senior civil service in **275**;

public personnel policies in 268; relativized adjustments to non-financial resources for **221**
bureaucracies: domestic 62; independent professional 108–120; international 15; Latin American 109
Burt, R. S. 413–414, 426
Business Environment Council Limited (BEC) 391

Caiden, G. 92
Caiden, N. 376–377
Calderon, Felipe 252
camarillas 247
Cambodia 374
Canache, D. 94
Canada 19; and Arctic 476; Arctic policy in 473–485
Canadian Polar Commission Act 476, 486n2
Capano, G. 7
capitalism 64
career management 279; personnel policies 273–275
Caritas Verband 168
Castles, F. G. 208
Catholic Church 130, 132
Catholicism 137
Catholics for the Right to Decide 136
Cavalli, Alessandro 465
Central and Eastern European Personal Data Protection Commissioners 357, 358
Central and East European (CEE) countries: development of public personnel policies in 268–272; governments of 268; healthcare governance in 282–297; politicization of senior civil service in **275**; position-based public service systems 274; public service legislation adoption in 270; public services challenges of 272; recruitment and selection in 273–275; responsibility for management of the public service 273; training and development 275–276
centralized recruitment procedures 274–275
Central Sickness Fund 288
Chamberlayne, Prue 174
Checkel, J. 63, 323
Chen Shui-bian 98, 394
childcare fee 197
Child Development Accounts (CDAs) 233, 236; children in 240; in Korea 235–236, **239**, 240; savings in 237; in Singapore 237, **239**; single-parent families and 239; in Taiwan **239**; in the US 234
children enrollment rates, in public pre-school facilities **198**
Child Trust Fund, UK 232
Chile 130; absence of policy reform in 132–133; legislation on higher education of 343; maturity and size of private higher education in **342**; Organic Law of Education 347; private education institutions autonomy 344; students in private sector 342
China 411–426; and air quality 367; Business Council for Sustainable Development 397; collaborative emergency response systems 413–415; open door policy 388; public ownership 388; and public service supply 374; relations with Korea 424
China Enterprise Confederation (CEC) 397
China's Agenda 21: Shanghai's Plan of Action 396
Chinese Communist Party (CCP) 387–389
Christiaens, J. 214
Chu, Y.-H. 387
Citizen Satisfaction Index System (CSIS) 373
civil servants: crisis experience and 183–188; policy learning by 183–188
Civil Service Law (CSL-2003) 248–251, 255–258; article 34 of 259, 261; article 37 of 254–255; and "career-based" system 254; design of 251; MBPP introduced by 246, 249; reforms 252; transitional article 3 253; and Vicente Fox 249; *see also* Servicio Profesional de Carrera
Civil Service Reform Plan 19
Civil Service Unit 248
classic civil service system 245
Clean Air Initiative for Asian Cities 373
cluster model 423
Coates, Ken S. 477
Code of Conduct for Responsible Fisheries 323
Code of Regulations (CR-2007) 258–260
Code of Regulations (the CR-2004) *see* "Reglamento" of 2004
COFOG (classification of functions of government) data 45, 53
cognitive convergence 68
Cohen, J. 369
collaborative emergency response systems: China 413–415; Japan 413–415; Korea 413–415; strategic use of brokers in building 413–415
collective bargaining: and Czech Republic HIFs 288; and Estonian Health Insurance Fund (EHIF) 289; and Poland public healthcare services 291; and Slovakia healthcare services 293; and Slovenia healthcare services 294
Colombia 127; limited reform in 133–134; quality of civil services in **115**; reported corruption in **114**
Committee on Fisheries (COFI) 323
communism 18, 206; economic legacy of 201
comparative housing: comparative study 450–452; criticism of 450–451; European Quality of Life Survey (EQLS) 452; housing conditions 452–455, **453–454**; *see also* households

comparative public administration (CPA) 13; overview 13–14; policy advisory systems 18–19; policy transfer 17–18; public sector reform as policy field 15–16; state and international development policy 16–17; transnational administration 14–15

comparative public policy (CPP) 13; analysis 304; overview 13–14; policy advisory systems 18–19; policy transfer 17–18; public sector reform as policy field 15–16; state and international development policy 16–17; transnational administration 14–15

competitive business climate 373–374

"Comprehensive Community Rebuilding" program 395–396

Computer-aided Sustainability Evaluation Tool (CASET) 390, 403n5

concrete feminism 203–206

Condor Lopez, V. 214

Congressional Information Service (CIS) 479

consolidations: determines performance within group of consolidators 47–52; strategies for sustainable 43–47

Constitution of Mexico 344

Construction 21 392

Control of Corruption (CC), World Bank 93

convergence 63

Cordes, U. 212

corporatism 53

corporatist-governed systems: and Bismarckian healthcare systems 284; and CEEC healthcare systems 294, 295–296; and Hungary HIF 290

corruption: bribe-based 111; citizens, perceptions of 94–96; developing indicators/indices of 92–93; experience-based measures of 92; experts, perceptions of 94–96; measuring 92–96; overview 90–92; perception-based measures of 92–93; perceptions in East and Southeast Asia 96–103; subjective measures of 92

Corruption Perception Index (CPI), (TI) 91

Costa Rica: autonomy to public education institutions 345; Constitution 345; maturity and size of private higher education in **342**; National Council of Rectors 346; students in private sector 342

Council of Cultural Development 395

Craig, R. 213

crisis experience and policy learning by civil servants 183–188

Crouch, Colin 161

cyclically-adjusted balance ratios (CAB) 33–34

cyclically-adjusted primary balances (CAPB) 33–34

Cyprus: concentration ratios **224**; relativized adjustments to non-financial resources for **221**

Cytotec 129

Czech Republic: concentration ratios **224**; health insurance funds in 287–288; Health Services Working Group 287; politicization of the senior civil service in **275**; public service vacancies in 274; relativized adjustments to non-financial resources for **221**; social health insurance in 283, 287–288

Daly, Mary 162
Danish data privacy authority 361
Danish Healthy City network 80
data privacy: European regulation 354; and information sharing 358; and regional implementation co-operation 357–361; and transgovernmental coordination 354, 356–357
daycare, and post-communist regimes 197–199
decentralization: importance of 369; in Philippines 372
deLeon, Peter 3
democracy 21; in Brazil 131, 138; representative 130; South America's transition to 130
democratic experimentalism 59
democratization backwards 387
Denmark 19, 313; adaptational pressures 310; changes in the dual carer regime 167; concentration ratios **224**; "Health Market" event 79; public health policies 79–81; and regional aid 307–308; relativized adjustments to non-financial resources for **221**
Department of the Interior and Local Government (DILG) 372
devolution of responsibilities 369
DG Competition 304–305, 315–316
discretionary fiscal policy 33
Dolowitz, D. 17
domestic bureaucracies 62
Dominican Republic 127
Donchev, D. 95
Douglas, Roger 54
dual system, housing tenure models 457
Dunleavy, P. 217

Earth Summit 389, 391
East Asia: perceptions of corruption in 96–103; sustainability practices in 381
"East European housing model" (EEHM) 457, 460–461, 464
"eclectic methodological approach" 464–465
Economic and Monetary Union (EMU) 43, 55n14
economic legacy of the communist past 201
EDP Notification Tables 212
Educational Reform Law 346
egalitarianism 146
Eigen, P. 109
Elmore, Richard 303
El Salvador 127, 137

Elvander, Nils 440
emergency contraception 125, 133, 138n1, 139
emergency management systems: brokers' role in 413–415; Northeast Asia 411–426; social capital 414; social network analysis 417–423, 426; structural embeddedness in 414; Tohoku, Japan triple disasters (2011) 415–417
emergency/sick child leave 149
Environmental Impact Assessment Ordinance 390
Environmental Impact Assessments (EIAs) 392
Environmental Protection Agency (EPA) 394
Esping-Andersen, Gøsta 146, 151, 161, 451, 464, 467
Estonia 183, 270; concentration ratios **224**; personnel development 276; personnel policies handling in 272; politicization of the senior civil service in **275**; public sector salary systems 277–278; relativized adjustments to non-financial resources for **221**; social health insurance in 283, 288–289
Estonian Health Insurance Fund (EHIF) 288–289
Estonian Medical Association (EAL) 289
Estonian Tax and Customs Board 289
EU-15 302, 304–306; familialist housing systems 468; housing tenure models 457; mass high-rise construction 462; and mortgage credit 464; population ceiling 305–306; social housing sectors 460
Europe: changing family policies in 165–167; cities, coping with work and childcare in four 167–172; data privacy regulation 354; housing conditions 452–455, **453–454**; housing tenure models 457; social policy rhetoric points towards strong support for families 167; trangovernmental co-ordination 355–357
"European Administrative Space" 271
European Anti-Poverty Network 67
European Coal and Steel Community (ECSC) 301
European Commission 33, 144, 188, 271, 303, 304–305, 356, 362; and Europeanization 312–316; and German regional policy relations 305; and population ceiling 313; regional aid mapping 306–309
European Communities Statistics Office (EUROSTAT) 212
European Community Household Panel survey (ECHP) 143, 149–150, 157n13, 157n15
European Court of Justice 62
European Data Privacy directive 353, 356
European Data Protection Supervisor 356
European Employment Strategy (EES) 61
European Industrial Relations Observatory 285
Europeanization 7, 302, 316–317; comparative public policy analysis 304; empirical research on 303–304; and European Commission 312–316; governance mechanisms and their limitations 64–65; learning at the top, from the top, and bottom-up 67–70; learning in public policy 61–64; measuring 312–316; measuring policy change **313**; OMC instruments and learning 65–67; open co-ordination 60–61; overview 58–60; of personnel policies 270–271; of public policy 302
European Monetary Union 38
European Parental Leave Directive 144, 149
European Parliament 67, 213
European Privacy Directive 362; Article 28(3) of 362
European Public Sector Accounting Standards (EPSAS) 213
European Quality of Life Survey (EQLS) 452
European System of National and Regional Accounts 1995 211
European Union (EU) 8, 75, 451; accumulated adjustment and positioning of countries 223–226; adjustments in personnel policies after joining 271–272; and CEE countries 279; classification of member states of 217; and data privacy legislation 353–354; empirical study of differences between budgetary and national accounting in 214–217; evolution of adjustments between 1995 and 2009 220–221; global assessment 218–219; governmental accounting diversity in 211–227; housing systems post-1990 *469*; housing systems prior to 1990 *468*; impact on national public policies 301; incidence of adjustments by country 221–222; information on stability and fiscal balance of MSs' public finances 214–216; methodology of empirical analysis 216–217; non-financial budgetary balance and net borrowing/lending 218–226; objectives of empirical analysis 216–217; regional aid control 304–306; regional aid guidelines 302; regional aid mapping 306–309; space analysis 221–222; Structural Funds programmes 305–307, 313, 315–316; temporal analysis 220–221
Evangeliche Kirsche 168
"evidence-based policymaking" 6
Executive Branch 345
Executive Decree 308 343

familialist housing strategies 465–467
families: European social policy rhetoric points towards strong support for 167; policies in Europe 165–167
family leave 143, 149; gender equality in policy of 157n21; paid 194, **195–196**
father-friendliness indices 151, **151**
father-friendly legislation **154**; data and methods 146–150; degree of awareness 149–150;

emergency/sick child leave 149; individual or family right 147–148; level of paid parental leave 148; literature review 144–145; overview 142–143; parental leave 147–148; part-*vs.* full-time parental leave 148; paternity leave provision 148–149; theory 145–146; universality of parental leave 148
federalism 37, 50, 52–53, 55n13, 347
federalism–unitarism score 50
Federal Trade Authority 357
feminism 200; abstract 203; concrete 203–206
Fernandez, R. M. 414
Ferrera, M. 68
Finan, F. 110
Finland: concentration ratios **224**; cross-national comparison 430; national policy performance 444–445; relativized adjustments to non-financial resources for **221**; relocation case history 1961–1976/77 438–439; relocation programs in 429–430
Fiscal Compact 187–190
fiscal decentralization 37, 55n13
fiscal policy 177–190, 178; background information about crisis in Baltic Countries 181–183; crisis experience and civil servants 183–188; discretionary 33; empirical study 181–188; overview 177–179; policy learning by civil servants 183–188; theoretical discussion 179–181
fiscal rule strength index (FRSI) 50
Fontes, A. 213
forward mapping research technique 303
Fox, Vicente 109, 245, 248
France 19; changes in family-oriented regime 166; concentration ratios **224**; public health policies 81–83; relativized adjustments to non-financial resources for **221**
Franchise 21 392
Freeman, Gary 8
Freeman, R. 283, 284
Friedrich, D. 68
Frisina, L. 283
Fukushima Daiichi Nuclear Power Plant 416
Fukuyama, F. 20
full-time parental leave 148

Galland, Olivier 465
Gandía Cabedo, J. L. 213
Garcia Benau, M. A. 213
Garreau, Brigitte 163
Garrido, P. 213
Gauthier, Ann 162
Geist, C. 146
gender contract 200
gender equality 130, 144, 146, 157n21, 194, 197, 200; under communist rule 200; feminism and 200–201, 203; percentage supporting *205*;

six-point index of 157n21; in Sweden 194; in Western Germany 194
Germany 285, 315; adaptational pressures 310; changes in male breadwinner model 166; concentration ratios **224**; and Europeanization 312; and population ceiling 313; and regional aid 307–308; relativized adjustments to non-financial resources for **221**
G&F Brokerage 420–421, 422
Giaimo, S. 283
Global Corruption Barometer (GCB), TI 94
good governance: accessible information 370–372; and Asia 368–373; assignment of responsibilities 368–370; performance management 372–373
Gornick, Janet 8, 162
Gould, R. V. 414
governance: good *see* good governance; healthcare *see* healthcare governance; modes in Asia 381–389; synthesized framework for understanding **382**
Governance and the Law (World Bank) 16
governance mechanisms: limitations of 64–65
governmental accounting diversity: differences between budgetary and national accounting in EU countries 214–217; in European Union 211–227; literature review 212–214; non-financial budgetary balance and net borrowing/lending 218–226; overview 211–212
Greece: concentration ratios **224**; relativized adjustments to non-financial resources for **221**
Green-Pedersen, C. 6
Green Plan 391
Groenewegen, P. P. 296
Guichard, S. 46
Guy, Peters B. 3

Haas, Ernst B. 301
Hacker, B. 296
Hallerberg, M. 50, 55n16
Han, C.-K. 234–235
Hansard 479, 480
Hantrais, Linda 162
Havelková, H. 202–203
Hawken, A. 93–94, 104n1
Haycox, Stephen 475
Heady, F. 14
healthcare governance: analytical framework and data 285–286; Central and East European (CEE) countries 282–297; and financing 283–284
Healthcare Surveillance Authority 293
Health For All by the Year 2000 program 80
health insurance funds (HIFs) 285; in Czech Republic 287–288; described 286; in Hungary 289–290; in Slovakia 292–293; in Slovenia 293–294

"Health Market" event 79–80
Healthy Cities movement 79
Heclo, H. 14, 178
Heidenheimer, A. J. 14
Hemerijck, A. 62
Heron 8
Hersoug, B. 333
"hierarchical learning" 60, 62, 67
higher education: Latin America 338–349; private–public differentiation in 339; system organization 346–347
historical institutional (HI) approach 431
HIV/AIDS 131
Holland: concentration ratios **224**; relativized adjustments to non-financial resources for **221**
"honeymoon" effect 45
Hong Kong 371, 381, 383, 401; as British colony 384; executive-led government 383–385; and mode of governance 383–385; per capita GDP 401; as Special Administrative Region (SAR) 384; and sustainable development 389–391
Hong Kong 2030: Planning Vision and Strategy 391
Hood, C. 180–181, 217
households: familialist housing strategies 465–467; formation patterns 465; and housing conditions 464–467, **466**
Housing and Social Theory (Kemeny) 450
housing conditions: Europe 452–455, **453–454**; and households 464–467; and market 462–464; mortgage debt *463*; and public expenditure *456*; and state intervention 455–462
housing tenure: dual system 457; Europe 457; in European countries (1990, 2000) *458*; housing outcomes by *459*; models 457; unitary system 457
Howlett, M. 18–19, 178
Hungary: Chamber of Pharmacists 290; concentration ratios **224**; health insurance funds in 289–290; Medical Chamber 290; performance management 276; personnel policies handling in 272; political appointments 274; politicization of the senior civil service in **275**; relativized adjustments to non-financial resources for **221**; social health insurance in 283, 289–290; systematic career management 274
Huntington, S. P. 20
Hurricane Katrina 425
Hyderabad (India) Metropolitan Water Supply and Sewerage Board 371
Hyogo Framework for Action (UNISDR) 412

Ibero-American Data Protection Network 357
ideological legacy and reform 200–201
Improving the Quality of Policy Advice 19

inclusive asset-based policies: in Asia 235–238; child development accounts (CDAs) 236; defined 230; institutional saving theory 232; key features of 233; in Korea 235, 238–240; progress 232; Seoul family development accounts 236; in Singapore 236–237, 238–240; in Taiwan 237–240; theory and progress of 232–233
independent professional bureaucracies 108–120
India: and air quality 368; and good governance 370
Industry 21 (I21) 392
information and communication technology (ICT) 370–371
information provision 355
information sharing: and data privacy 358; regional implementation co-operation 358; and transgovernmental co-ordination 358
innovation centers 67
"innovation enterprises" 67
Innovation for Environmental Sustainability Fund 392–393
Institute of Higher Education for Latin America and the Caribbean (IESALC) 342
institutional legacy 201–202
institutional saving theory 232
institutional theory: described 322; and overfishing issue 322
institution building 268–270
Inter-American Commission on Human Rights 130
Inter-American Development Bank 245
interest group politics 432
"international bureaucracy" 15
International Complaints Handling Workshop 358
International Conference of Data Protection Commissioners 356
International Crime Victimization Survey (ICVS) 94
international development policy: state and 16–17
International Journal of Public Administration 21
International Library of Policy Analysis 19
International Monetary Fund (IMF) 15, 33, 38, 50, 54n4, 179, 181, 183–186, 190
international organizations (IOs) 15
International Planned Parenthood Federation (IPPF) 130
International Plan of Action to Prevent, Deter and Eliminate Illegal, Unreported and Unregulated Fishing (IPOA-IUU) 323
International Public Sector Accounting Standards (IPSAS) 212–213
International Public Sector Accounting Standards Board (IPSASB) 212–213
International Research Society for Public Management 14

International Union for Conservation of Nature (IUCN) 328
International Women's Health Coalition 130
IPSASB Conceptual Framework for General Purpose Financial Reporting (GPFRs) 212
Ireland: concentration ratios **224**; relativized adjustments to non-financial resources for **221**
Islam 21
Italy: concentration ratios **224**; relativized adjustments to non-financial resources for **221**
IUU fishing: Angola 324–325; Mozambique 325–326; Namibia 327; South Africa 328–329; Tanzania 329–330; *see also* overfishing

Jacobsson, K. 67, 71n1
James Bay and Northern Quebec Agreement 478
Japan 411–426; broadband use in 371; collaborative emergency response systems 413–415
Japan disasters (2011) 415–417; brokering organizations **421**; descriptive statistics of **418**; network map of *419*
Japan Red Cross 418
Jasaitis, Edwardas 275
Jesús, M. A. 213
Jesus Christ 131
joint enforcement 354–356; Article 29 Working Party 363; and data privacy 359–361
Joint Statement on Disaster Management 412
Joint Supervisory Authority (JSA): for Customs 357; for Europol 357; for Schengen Information System 357, 361
Jones, Bryan D. 474, 480
Jones, R. 212
Jorge, S. 213
Jospin, Lionel 166
Journal of Comparative Policy Analysis (JCPA) 3–8
Journal of Public Administration Theory and Research 14
Jugendhilfe 164

Karran, T. 37
Kaufmann, D. 95
Kemeny, Jim 450–451, 457
Keohane, R. 355
Keuning, S. 212
Keynesian ideas 185–186
KidSave account program 234
Kingdon, J. 432
Kingdon, J. W. 139
"King's Dilemma" 20
Klitgaard, R. 110
Knack, S. 95
Knill, C. 68
Ko, K. 94
Kok, Wim 54, 59, 70

Kok Report 59
Korea 411–426; broadband use 371; child development accounts (CDAs) 236; collaborative emergency response systems 413–415; inclusive asset-based policies in 235, 238–240; inclusive asset-building policies in **239**; natural disasters management 412; relations with China 424; Seoul family development accounts 236
Korea Federation of Child Welfare 236
Korea–Japan–China Trilateral Summit 412
Kozlowski, Edward 461, 470
Kraay, A. 95
Kurz, Karin 451
Kyodo News 416

labor market policies: post-communist regimes 199–200
Laguna, M. I. D. 110
La Misère du Monde (Bourdieu) 168
Lande, E. 212
Latin America 349n4; administrative tradition of 246; comparing changes in civil service law and implementation in 108–120; higher education 338–349; merit based personnel policies in 244–262; Mexico as second largest country in 245; private higher education in countries of **342**
Latin American bureaucracies 109
Latin American Public Opinion Project (LAPOP) 109
Latvia 183, 271; concentration ratios **224**; pay-for-performance 278; performance management 276; politicization of the senior civil service in **275**; relativized adjustments to non-financial resources for **221**
law: as constitutive environment for organizations 339; definition of private and public sector 340; and private higher education 343, 348–349; and public higher education 343, 348–349; and public policies 338–339
Law 15, 661 343
"lean management" 18
learning: by arguing and persuasion 59; bottom-up 60, 62–63, 67, 69–70; hierarchical 60, 62, 67; by monitoring 59; in public policy 61–64; social 60–61, 70; by socialization 59; at the top, from the top, and bottom-up 67–70
legitimacy-driven rationality 68
Leibfried, Stephan 173
Lenschow, A. 68
Levy, D. C. 339
Lewis, Jane 162
Lijphart, A. 50
Lima, Fontes 213
Lindblom, C. E. 13
Lipponen, Paavo 54

INDEX

Lipset, S. M. 430
Lisbon European Council 59
Lisbon strategy for competitiveness 59–60, 64–65, 67
Lithuania 183; centralized recruitment procedures 275; concentration ratios **224**; pay-for-performance 278; performance management 276; personnel development 276; politicization of the senior civil service in **275**; relativized adjustments to non-financial resources for **221**
Lithuanian Law 275
Local Development Watch (DevWatch) 373
local government units (LGUs) 369–370, 372–373
local policy convergence: case study and method 77–78; integration of policy transfer within local public health policies 78–83; mapping circulation of policy transfer through actors' backgrounds 83–86; overview 74–75; reception of policy transfer 75–77
Local Productivity and Performance Measurement System (LPPMS) 372
local public health policies: integration of policy transfer within 78–83
Lowi, T. J. 7, 432
Lucking, Richard 269
Lüder, K. 212, 214
Luedtke, A. 7
Lula da Silva, Luiz Inácio 131, 136
Luxembourg: concentration ratios **224**; relativized adjustments to non-financial resources for **221**
Lynn, Laurence E. 3

Maastricht Treaty 211
Malta: concentration ratios **224**; relativized adjustments to non-financial resources for **221**
Manow, P. 283
Manpower 21 392
Marchais, Pierrick 163
Marine Living Resources Act 328
market, and housing conditions 462–464
Marmor, T. R. 283
Marree, J. 296
Marsden, P. 414
Marsh, David 17
martial law 387
Martin, Paul 54
Master Plan for the Conservation of Nature in Singapore 393
maternity leave 148, 171–172, 194–196, 205
May, Peter 69
McCarter, Joan 475
McDonald, P. 208
McRae, Duncan 3
Medical Congress 137

merit based personnel policies (MBPP): dependency relationships and co-ordination 256–258; design and implementation problems in Mexico 245, 246; external challenges for implementation of 251–252; in Latin America 244–262; recruitment and career management 273–275; time and resources 252–254; understanding, agreement and policy objectives 254–266
Merrill, Sally 470
Mexican administrative tradition 246–248, 255
Mexico 19; administrative reforms 245; administrative tradition of 246; Law for the coordination of higher education 347; legislation on higher education of 343; maturity and size of private higher education in **342**; MBPP implementation challenges in 245, 246; Servicio Profesional de Carrera in 245
Mexico City: bold reform in 134–135; changing the discourse and terms of debate 136–137
Microsoft 359
Mierau, J. O. 47
"misery index" 51
misoprostol 129
modern personnel policies 268–270
monitoring, control, and surveillance (MCS) systems 321; Angola 325; definition 322–323; installation by SADC countries 321; Mozambique 326; Namibia 327; South Africa 328; Tanzania 329–330
Montesinos Julve, V. 212, 214, 217, 218
Moran, M. 284
Mosher, J. 66, 68
Movement Toward Socialism party 132
Mozambique: artisanal fisheries 326; fisheries regulations **331–332**; license limitation for fishing 326; Marine Fisheries Regulation 326; MCS systems 326; and overfishing 325–326
Mulas-Granados, Carlos 38
Munck, G. 94, 104n1
Mutual Information System on Social Protection database 285

Namibia: fisheries regulations **331–332**; and IUU fishing 327; and MCS systems 327; and total allowed catch (TAC) 327
National Action Party 135
National Council for Sustainable Development (NCSD) 394
National Economic and Social Development Plan 376
National Health Fund (NHF) 290–291
National Health Insurance Fund Administration (NHIFA) 289
National Lawyer's Association 137

national policy performance: Finland 444–445; Norway 442–444; Sweden 440–442
National Preparatory Process (NPP) 392
National Pro-Choice Alliance, Mexico City 134
National Programme on Human Rights, Brazil 131
National Science and Technology Plan 2000 392
National Taiwan University 92
natural resource management 330; and overfishing 322–324
Nature Society (Singapore) (NSS) 393
Netherlands 311, 314
.NET Passport 359
New Ambitions for Our Country – A New Welfare Contract 165
New Public Management (NPM) 13, 16, 269; and Norway 437; and performance management 276–277
New Zealand 19, 47, 54n1, 249
Nicaragua 111, 113–116, 127, 130, 137
Nobes, C. 217
non-governmental organizations 78, 93, 95, 134
non-negligible cognitive convergence 68
Nordic countries: relocation programs in 429–430; *see also specific countries*
Nordic School of Health Promotion 84
Nordic School of Public Health in Sweden 84
Norman, Victor 437–438, 443, 444
Northcote-Trevelyan reforms 245
Northeast Asia: considerations to building collaborative systems in 425–426; emergency management systems 411–426; international collaboration in disaster management 412
Norway: cross-national comparison 430; national policy performance 442–444; relocation case history 1961–2007 435–438; relocation programs in 429–430
NUTS II 305–306
Nye, J. 355

Oates, W. E. 37
Obinger, Herbert 173
OECD Countries (1980–2005): budget consolidation, determinants of 39–43; budget consolidations 33–35; determining consolidation performance within group of consolidators 47–52; hypotheses 35–38; methods of analysis 38–39; overview 31–32; strategies for sustainable consolidations 43–47
Offe, Claus 161
Ooi, G.-L. 391
open co-ordination 60–61
Open Method of Coordination (OMC) 59; benchmarking and 66; instruments and learning 65–67; participation and 66–67
Opus Dei 130
Organic Law 343
Organization for Economic Co-operation and Development (OECD) 15, 160, 248, 268, 363
Organization of Urban Re-s (OURS) 395
Ortega, Daniel 130
Ottawa Charter for Health Promotion 78
overfishing: in Angola 324–325; and institutional theory 322; and Mozambique 325–326; and natural resource management 322–324; in Southern Africa 321–333; *see also* IUU fishing

Pachuashvili, P. 339
paid family leave **195–196**; post-communist regimes 194–197
paid parental leave 148
Palier, Bruno 166
parental leave: individual or family right 147–148; level of paid 148; paid 148; part- *vs.* full-time 148; universality of 148
"parties-do-matter" hypothesis 36
part-time parental leave 148
paternal time 143; across Western Europe 152, **152**; levels of substantial **154**
paternity leave provision 148–149
Paulsen, O. 333
pay-for-performance system 278
Pendleton Act 245
People's Action Party (PAP) 386
People's Republic of China (PRC) *see* China
performance management: in Central and East European (CEE) countries 276–277; and New Public Management (NPM) 276–277
persistence-driven rationality 68
personnel development 276; Estonia 276; Lithuania 276
personnel policies 279; "Europeanization" of 270–271; key areas of 272–278; modern 268–270; performance management 276–277; public *see* public personnel policies; recruitment and career management 273–275; rewards 277–278; training and development 275–276
Persson, Göran 54
Peru: civil service laws and practice in 115, **115**; IDAs 232; reported corruption in **114**; transforming attitudes and re-aligning reform efforts in 135–137
Peterson, S. 369
Philippines 371; decentralization in 372; money lending systems 374
Pina, V. 214, 217
Pinker, Robert 161
Pinochet, Augusto 133, 138
Plantenga, J. 144
Poland: centralized recruitment procedures 275; concentration ratios **224**; National Health Fund (NHF) 290–291; political appointments 274; politicization of senior civil service in **275**; relativized adjustments to non-financial

resources for **221**; social health insurance in 283, 290–291; systematic career management 274
Policy Advice Initiative 19
policy advisory systems 18–19
"policy ambassadors" 18
policy entrepreneurs 432
policy entrepreneurship: Finland 445; Norway 443; Sweden 441
policy learning, defined 178
policy targeting: and Arctic policy 482; Arctic region 474–475, *482*
policy transfer 17–18; integration within local public health policies 78–83; mapping circulation through actors' backgrounds 83–86; reception of 75–77
political democratization 386–387
political feedbacks, of transgovernmental coordination 361–363
politicization: of public service 274; of senior civil service in CEE countries **275**
politics: entrepreneurial 432; interest group 432; post-decisional 301–302
Polity Index of Democracy 113
Pollitt, C. 217
Pope Benedict XVI 131
population ceiling 305–306, 313
Population Council 130
population coverage, and regional aid 307
Portugal: concentration ratios **224**; relativized adjustments to non-financial resources for **221**
position-based public service systems 274
post-communist Central Europe: economic legacy of the communist past 201; "exit" and failure of post-communist family policies 202–206; ideological legacy and reform 200–201; institutional legacy 201–202; re-familization of family policies 194–200; "wrong" kind of exit 206–208
post-communist family policies: abstract feminism 203; concrete feminism 203–206; daycare 197–199; "exit" and the failure of 202–206; ideological climate 200; inability to organize 200–201; labor market policies 199–200; paid family leave 194–197; re-familization of 194–200; "wrong" kind of exit 206–208
"post-decisional politics" 301–302
Prabhakar, R. 234
PRD (Party of the Democratic Revolution) 134
private higher education: and law 343, 348–349; in selected countries of Latin America **342**; students in 342; *see also* higher education
private sectors: autonomy of 344; of higher education 339; *vs.* public sectors of higher education 339
"process tracing" techniques 303
Productivity Action 21 (ProAct21) 392

Professional Career Service (PCS) 251–255, 257, 261
professional competency 274
Promsex (Center for the Promotion and Defense of the Sexual and Reproductive Rights) 136
Protocol on the Excessive Deficit Procedure (EDP) 211
Provisional Legislative Council 403n3
public administration 13
Public Administration Review 13
Public Affairs Centre (PAC) 370
public health policies: Denmark 79–81; France 81–83; integration of policy transfer within local 78–83
public higher education: and law 343, 348–349; students in 342; *see also* higher education
public personnel policies 245; development in CEE countries 268–272; overview 267–268; personal policies key areas 272–278; professional competency 274
public policies 13; European Union impact on national 301; and law 338–339; learning in 61–64
public sectors: of higher education 339; *vs.* private sectors of higher education 339; reform, as policy field 15–16
public servants 279; and personnel reforms 279
public service: co-ordination and management in CEE countries **273**; legislation in selected CEE countries **270**; politicization of 274
Puchala, Donald J. 301–302

Quaglia, L. 68
"quasi-spoils system" 247–248
Quicklaw America 479

Radaelli, C. M. 304
Radin, Beryl 3, 7, 478
Radio Frequency Identification (RFID) technology 359
Ragin, C. C. 4
Ramesh, M. 18
Ramírez, G. I. 110, 120
Rapetti, Danielle 164
Razafindrakoto, M. 94
recruitment, and personnel policies 273–275
Red Cross agencies 418
re-familization of family policies 194–200
regional aid: adaptational responses 309–312; control and European Union (EU) 304–306; guidelines 302; mapping 306–309; and population coverage 307
regional implementation co-operation: and data privacy 357–361; information sharing 358; joint enforcement 359–361; standards harmonization 358–359
regional policies 474; and policy targeting 474–475

"Reglamento" of 2004 246, 249, 253
relocation programs: agency 430; in Nordic countries 429–430
Republic of Korea 371, 374
"research zone" 20, *20*
Review of Policy Expenditure and Advice 19
rewards: in CEE countries 277–278; personnel policies 277–278
"RHNet" system 253
Rico, A. 284
Roberts, Andrew 460
Rockman, B. A. 439
Romania: concentration ratios **224**; politicization of the senior civil service in **275**; relativized adjustments to non-financial resources for **221**
Rose, R. 387
Rose, Richard 17, 37
Rothgang, H. 284
Rothwell, D. W. 234
Roubaud, F. 94
Rousseff, Dilma 132

Sabatier, Paul 323
Sacchi, S. 68
Sainsbury, D. 194
Samajdar, A. 94
Sandinista Nicaragua 130
Saving for Education, Entrepreneurship, and Downpayment (SEED) initiative 232
Schmidt, M. G. 35
Schreiner, M. 232, 235
Secretaria de la Funcion Publica (Ministry of Public Administration, MPA) 246; CR-2007 258–259; roles of 256–257
Sen, Amartya 233
Sendi, Richard 462
Seoul family development accounts 236, **239**
Seoul Welfare Foundation 236
Serra, José 132
Servicio Profesional de Carrera: establishment of 244, 249; in Mexico 245; as position-based system 254; *see also* Civil Service Law (CSL-2003)
Severe Acute Respiratory Syndrome (SARS) epidemic 412
Shanghai (China): Chinese Communist Party (CCP) 387–389; per capita GDP 401; resource management 396–397; and sustainable development 396–397; urban governance 387–389
Sheingate, A. D. 7, 8
Sherraden, Michael 231, 232
Shin, D. C. 387
Shinhan Bank 236
Siedentopf, Heinrich 302
Sillince, John 462

Sinawatra, Thaksin 99
Singapore 371; domestic industries in 385; ecological footprint 404n10; economic policy 385; "green and clean" environment 397; inclusive asset-based policies in 236–237, 238–240; inclusive asset-building policies in **239**; and mode of governance 385–386; National Preparatory Process (NPP) 392; and People's Action Party 386; per capita GDP 401; small and medium-sized enterprises (SMEs) 385; and sustainable development 391–393
Singapore 21 Report 392
Singapore Green Plan (SGP) 2012 392
Singapore Green Plan 2012 (SGP2012) 392
Sipila, Jorma 162
Skinner, Christine 173
Slovakia: bonus-based performance system 278; centralized recruitment procedures 275; concentration ratios **224**; Healthcare Surveillance Authority 293; health insurance funds in 292–293; performance management 277; political appointments 274; politicization of senior civil service in **275**; relativized adjustments to non-financial resources for **221**; social health insurance in 283, 292–293; 2002–2006 reforms in healthcare 292
Slovenia: concentration ratios **224**; healthcare personnel 294; health insurance funds in 293–294; Medical Chamber 294; performance management 277; politicization of the senior civil service in **275**; relativized adjustments to non-financial resources for **221**; social health insurance in 283, 293–294; systematic career management 274
small and medium-sized enterprises (SMEs) 385
SME 21 392
Smith, Eric Alden 475
social capital 414, 424–425
social determinants of health (SDOH) 75, 77–87
Sociale tendenser (Social Trends) 167
social health insurance (SHI) 282; in Czech Republic 283, 287–288; empirical evidence 286–284; in Estonia 283, 288–289; in Hungary 283, 289–290; and medical professionals 288; in Poland 283, 290–291; political attractiveness 286–287; in Slovakia 283, 292–293; in Slovenia 283, 293–294
social housing sectors 460
social justice 125, 129–130, 134–137
social learning 60–61, 70
social network analysis (SNA) 417–423, 426
social policy, and asset building 231
"social rights" 53
Soroka, Stuart A. 479
South Africa: fisheries regulations **331–332**; IUU fishing in 328–329; Marine Living Resources

Act 328; MCS measures 328; total allowed catch (TAC) 328
South America: building issue networks and exploiting political opportunities 132–135; case of Brazil 131–132; health and social context of abortion 128–129; key indicators of abortion in **128**; legal framework of abortion 127–128; overview 125–127; re-aligning reform efforts in Brazil and Peru 135–137; social construction of abortion debate and role of groups 129–131; transforming attitudes in Brazil and Peru 135–137
Southeast Asia: perceptions of corruption in 96–103
Southern Africa: overfishing in 321–333; *see also specific countries*
Southern African Development Community (SADC) 333; installation of MCS systems 321; MCS of fisheries in coastal countries of 324–330; Protocol on Fisheries 322, 323
Spain: concentration ratios **224**; relativized adjustments to non-financial resources for **221**
SPAM 357
Stability and Growth Pact (SGP) agreements 211
standards harmonization 355; and data privacy 358–359; regional implementation co-operation 358–359
state: and international development policy 16–17; intervention, and housing conditions 455–462
statutes: Arctic policy 479–481; defined 479; selection of 479–480
Steccolini, I. 218
Straeng, Gunnar 434, 441, 443
Strauch, R. 45
street-level bribery 108–120
Strogatz, S. H. 413
Structural Funds programmes 305–307, 313, 315–316
sustainable consolidations 43–47
sustainable development 380–381, **398–400**; in East Asian global cities 389–402; and Hong Kong 389–391; and Shanghai 396–397; and Singapore 391–393; synthesized framework for understanding **382**; and Taipei 393–396
Sustainable Development Council 391
Sustainable Development for the 21st Century Study (SUSDEV 21) 390
Sweden 32, 145; Active Location Policy 435; concentration ratios **224**; cross-national comparison 430; national policy performance 440–442; relativized adjustments to non-financial resources for **221**; relocation case history 1957–1980/81 433–435, **434**; relocation programs in 429–430
Switzerland 18, 54n1, 215, 362
systematic career management 274

Taipei 240, 371, 383, 397, 401; innovative community actions 393–396; per capita GDP 402; planned market 386–387; political democratization 386–387; and sustainable development 393–396
Taipei Family Development Accounts (TFDA) 238
Taiwan: inclusive asset-based policies in 238–240; inclusive asset-building policies in **239**
Taiwan Business Council for Sustainable Development (BCSD) 396
Tang, C.-P. 387
Tanzania: artisanal fisheries 329; Beach Management Units (BMUs) 329; Fisheries Act 329; fisheries regulations **331–332**; IUU fishing 329–330; MCS measures 329–330; Village Environment Committees 329
"technocratic" goals 277
Technopreneurship 21 392
Temporão, José 136
Thailand 376, 425
Thatcher, Margaret 54, 297
Third Review of Progress of the 1989 White Paper: Pollution in Hong Kong – A Time to Act (PELB) 389–390
3P Partnership Fund 393
Tokyo Electric Power Company (TEPCO) 421–422
Tongeren, D. 212
Torres, L. 213, 214, 217
Tosics, Ivan 460–461
total allowed catch (TAC): and Angola 325; and Namibia 327; South Africa 328
"TrabajaEn" system 253
Trade 21 392
training and development: Central and East European (CEE) countries 275–276; personnel policies 275–276
transgovernmental coalitions: described 355–356; *vs.* transgovernmental coordination 355–356
transgovernmental coordination 355–357; and data privacy 354, 356–357; information provision 355; overview 355; political feedbacks of 361–363; standards harmonization 355; *vs.* transgovernmental coalitions 355–356
transnational administration 14–15, 17, 21
Transparency International (TI): Corruption Perception Index (CPI) 91; Global Corruption Barometer (GCB) 94
"treadmill" development 381
Triesman, D. 111
Trubek, David 62, 66
Tsuei Ma Ma Housing and Community Service Association (TMM) 395
Tuohy, C. 284

Ujhelyi, G. 95
UNESCO 342
unitary system, housing tenure models 457
United Kingdom (UK): changes in the liberal regime 165; concentration ratios **224**; Northcote-Trevelyan reforms 245; and population ceiling 313; regional aid and adaptational pressures 310; relativized adjustments to non-financial resources for **221**
United Nations Convention against Corruption (UNCAC) 92, 108
United Nations Food and Agriculture Organization (FAO) 321; definition of MCS 321–322
United Nations Office for the Coordination of Humanitarian Assistance (OCHA) 412, 423
United States: and Arctic 476; Arctic policy in 473–485; Federal Trade Authority 357; Pendleton Act 245
United States Environmental Protection Agency (USEPA) 401
universalism 146
universality of parental leave 148
unsafe abortion 129
urban governance: Chinese Communist Party (CCP) 387–389; Shanghai 387–389
urban growth: challenges 377; infrastructure investment and development 374–376; management in Asia 367–377
urban poverty, and Asia 368
Uruguay 343; maturity and size of private higher education in **342**; public sector of higher education 347, 350n9
US Agency for International Development (USAID) 245, 372
US Army 420, 422–423, 426n4
Uslaner, E. 110

Vanderbilt University 109, 111
Van de Walle, S. 17
Van Nispen, Frans 3
Vela Bargues, J. M. 212
Velvet Revolution 288
Verheijen, Tony 274–275
Viet Nam 373, 374, 376
Village Environment Committees 329
"Vision for Hong Kong" study group 391
Visser, J. 62, 68–69, 297
von Hagen, Jürgen 45, 55n16

Wallace, W. 302
Washington Consensus 16, 181
Watts, D. J. 413
Weaver, R. K. 439
Weber, Mark 13, 245
Wehner, J. 50
Weimer, David 3
Wendt, C. 284
Western Europe 296; Bismarckian healthcare systems in 283, 284, 294; paternal time across 152, **152**; SHI systems in 285; *see also* Europe
Whitehead, L. 381
WHO European Observatory 285
Wildavsky, A. 37, 376–377
Wilkerson, John D. 480
Wilson, J. Q. 432
Wilson, Woodrow 13
Windebank, Jan 162
Wolf, A. 5
Women's Link Worldwide 133
work and family life: changing family policies in Europe 165–167; coping with work and childcare in four European Cities 167–172; in Doulon in Nantes, France 169–170; in Heworth in York, UK 168–169; in Svogerslev in Roskilde, Denmark 171–172; in Wallstadt in Mannheim, Germany 170–171
Workers' Party (PT) 131
Working Party Strategy Document 360
World Bank 15, 93, 245, 268; Control of Corruption (CC) 93; Worldwide Governance Indicators (WGI) project 93
World Business Council for Sustainable Development 397
World Health Organization (WHO) 75, 377n1; *Health For All by the Year 2000* program 80; *Health for All* program 84; Healthy Cities movement 79
World Values Survey (WVS) 94
Worldwide Governance Indicators (WGI) project 93
Wright, Deil 7
Wu, X. 18

Zedillo, Ernesto 248
Zeitlin, J. 64, 71n1
Zhang, T. 389
Ziller, Jacques 302